# FROMMER'S
# DOLLARWISE GUIDE TO THE SOUTHEAST AND NEW ORLEANS

**by Susan Poole**

**1988–1989 Edition**

Published by Prentice Hall Press
A Division of Simon & Schuster, Inc.
Gulf + Western Building
One Gulf + Western Plaza
New York, NY 10023

ISBN 0–13–217670–X

Manufactured in the United States of America

# CONTENTS

# MAPS

*To my mother and father,*
*who gave me my southern heritage.*

**INFLATION ALERT:** In researching this book we have made every effort to obtain up-to-the-minute prices, but even the most conscientious researcher cannot keep up with fluctuations in the rate of inflation. As we go to press, we believe we have obtained the most reliable data possible. Nonetheless, in the lifetime of this edition—particularly in its second year (1989)—the wise traveler will add 15% to 20% to the prices quoted throughout these pages.

**A DISCLAIMER:** Although every effort was made to ensure the accuracy of the prices and travel information appearing in this book, it should be kept in mind that prices do fluctuate in the course of time, and that information does change under the impact of the varied and volatile factors that affect the travel industry.

Readers should also note that the establishments described under Readers' Selections or Suggestions have not in many cases been inspected by the author, and that the opinions expressed there are those of the individual reader(s) only. They do not in any way represent the opinions of the publisher or author of this guide.

*Chapter I*

# INTRODUCING THE SOUTHEAST AND NEW ORLEANS

**1. About This Book
2. How to Save Money on All Your
Travels—The $25-a-Day Travel Club
3. Getting There
4. Getting Around**

ASK ALMOST ANYBODY about to set out on a visit south of the Mason-Dixon Line what they expect to find and you'll get an amazingly muddled reply. Margaret Mitchell's *Gone with the Wind* antebellum South; William Faulkner's Mississippi Deep South; Tennessee Williams's aging New Orleans southern belles or would-be belles; Atlanta's shiny, cosmopolitan image of the "new South"; tales of notorious speedtraps for out-of-state cars—all come together in a confused preconception of the region.

My own expectations were somewhat different. I was born and raised in the Southeast, and my travels to research this book were almost in the nature of a return pilgrimage. Having lived "up North" for some years now, I headed for the southern states that line this country's eastern coast with a little apprehension and the awareness that I would be seeing them from a new perspective. Periodic trips back home to visit relatives were different. This time I would be looking at *my* part of the country with the eyes of an "outsider." I would try to see it from the viewpoint of someone who hadn't grown up with tales of colonial heroes who lived and fought and argued over constitutional phrases right in the neighborhood—to see with fresh vision the sandy beaches and unspoiled, almost wild, Outer Banks of North Carolina, the softer beauty of South Carolina's Hilton Head, and Georgia's Golden Isles. The Blue Ridge Mountains and Atlanta's intriguing mix of old and new must be seen as if for the first time. It would be my task to wander through the orderly, historic streets of Alexandria, Williamsburg, Savannah, and Charleston to find their unique charm all over again. St. Augustine's ancient streets and buildings, southern Florida's frenetic sightseeing attractions, the low-key abandon of Key West, and that state's Gulf Coast would have to be looked at as if I hadn't seen them before. New Orleans's

French Quarter, which I have loved all my life, would have to be approached as a stranger.

To my delight, I found that being a "tourist" in my home region is fun—the very things that made growing up there rather special were those that added zest and flavor to this odyssey. Expectations? They hadn't been high enough. Preconceptions? They were confirmed and refuted in varying degrees as I went from place to place, meeting people and places that hadn't changed in years and others that were completely different from my memories. As a visitor, I came away with the firm conviction that the Southeast is one of the most interesting and enjoyable sections of this country for the tourist. And above all, I came back with a renewed appreciation for its people.

Meeting people is, in my book, one of the primary joys of travel. Certainly that is true in the Southeast. There is an unfailing courtesy and native friendliness that marks everyone you meet. I was not, of course, totally unprepared for that, having been taught from childhood that rudeness is an unforgivable sin (my grandmother once told me that a lady could tell anyone to "go to hell" if she did it politely!). But courtesy to the tourist seems to extend far beyond mere politeness to a real concern for comfort and convenience. Hospitality, that much-advertised attribute of Southerners, extends to today's paying guests as much as it ever did to house guests. Pride, another much-portrayed southern characteristic, extends to the South as a whole, one's native state, one's own part of that state, and especially to a hometown, all of which Southerners are eager to share with visitors. "I'll be proud to show you around" comes naturally to Southerners. They are equally proud of history, of which there is plenty, and "progress," evident everywhere you turn. They'll point with regional pride to a relic of the Civil War (which most now consider valiantly fought and fortunately lost), then direct your attention to a new industry or cultural center that makes it plain the South has a future as well as a past.

The Old South? The New South? They're both here in these five states, and New Orleans is its own special blend of the two. Whatever your preconceptions, come with an open mind, come prepared to relax and enjoy, and come secure in the knowledge that nowhere will you be more welcomed or go away more satisfied.

## 1. About This Book

These five southeastern states—Virginia, North and South Carolina, Georgia, and Florida—have a total area of some 243,830 square miles. That's a lot of ground to cover, and if you head south with no definite idea of what you want most to see and do, where to stay and eat, you can waste time, money, and temper getting around. It is to help in making your plans before you start out that this book has been written.

The hotels, restaurants, sightseeing attractions, and nightspots you'll read about have been carefully checked out, not within any specified maximum or minimum in price, but with the notion that you should get the *most* for your money whether you go luxury, moderate, or budget class. Because, however, most of today's travelers are in the medium-income group, you will find the emphasis throughout the book on prices that are neither in the highest nor lowest range. My own experience has taught me that there are times when price has little to do with quality: a "luxury" restaurant may serve mediocre, or even poor food, and a budget establishment can be so loaded with charm that it would be a good buy at *any* price. The evaluations in this book were made with an eye on cost, of course (an expensive hotel or restaurant may, indeed, give you your money's worth but be well above the reach of most of us), but primarily with an eye on quality, and if you find a rave about an inexpensive place to stay or eat, it's because I found it exceptional as well as not costly. My judgments are, admittedly, entirely personal, and if the charm of a small hotel or restaurant means less to you than the sometimes colorless conveniences of large chains, the choice is yours to make (my choice is for the former). I hope that with these necessarily brief descriptions of what is available all along the way you'll be able to make that choice knowledgeably.

**A WORD ABOUT PRICES QUOTED:** Inflation, even with its occasional fluctuations, has become a part of the American scene. Thus the prices shown here are *only those in effect at the time of writing.* Nowhere did I run into an establishment that promised to keep its prices stabilized or to give readers of this book any sort of price guarantee. Even if there is a variation in price by the time you reach a particular destination, however, the price *range* is likely to be the same—a medium-range hotel today will probably still be medium-priced for the area even with a hike in charges, although "medium" may be somewhat higher than at the time of this writing. In this sense, this is a *guide,* as the name says, to finding low-, medium-, and top-priced facilities.

**HOTELS IN THE SOUTHEAST:** Most of the medium-priced hotel and motel chains have branches in the states written about in this book. Some of the luxury chains, such as Hilton and Hyatt, are also represented in larger cities. In *all* of these, you will find air conditioning, color TV, and two double beds (unless noted otherwise in a description). Holiday Inns, Howard Johnson's, and other like chains tend to be pretty standard, and if a particular member is outstanding or differs in any respect, I've noted that for you. The higher-priced, luxury hotels will have additional features in rooms, such as separate dressing rooms, extra washbasins, etc.

The prices quoted throughout this book are for double-occupancy *rooms,* not per person. A money-saving technique when more than two people travel together is room-sharing. Instead of paying for two double rooms, three or more people may rent one double room and pay a small extra fee for each additional *person,* which usually runs under $10 per night, much less than the cost of an extra room. If as many as five or six share a room, which will normally have two double beds, most motels will install rollaway cots for a small extra charge. Families, of course, often get a real price break when motels permit children under a certain age to occupy the same room as their parents at no additional charge. The age limit varies from 6 all the way up to 18, and unless you really can't stand having the kids underfoot at night, it will pay to look for these "family plan" establishments.

One further note about hotel accommodations: regardless of when you plan to travel—even if *you* consider it "off-season"—it's foolhardy to go without reservations. If your itinerary is not set and you cannot book for the entire trip before leaving home, it pays to call ahead just as soon as you know your next stopping point. Americans are on the road in increasing numbers and there is *always* the possibility of being stranded without a room. Many motel chains have toll-free telephone numbers and some will teletype ahead for you if you'll be staying in another chain member in the next city.

### A Dependable Budget Motel Chain

Travelers with families, as well as those who prefer to spend their hard-earned dollars for things other than a place to sleep, are always on the lookout for budget-priced accommodations. If there's a **Motel 6** on their destination horizon, however, their search will be a short one, for this dependable economy/limited-service motel chain maintains unusually high standards despite a price range of $17 to $26. The more than 400 motels in some 39 states have swimming pools, and guests can have color TV for a modest additional charge. Rooms are an adequate size and comfortably, though not luxuriously, furnished—the motto here is "Don't pay for what you don't choose to use," a philosophy that has great appeal to those of us who must keep a close watch on the budget. For a free copy of the current Motel 6 nationwide directory, write Motel 6, 51 Hitchcock Way, Santa Barbara, CA 93130.

### Bed-and-Breakfast

Even though bed-and-breakfast accommodations are becoming more and more popular across the country, it is sometimes difficult to know just how to go about finding one at your destination. There are, of course, several guidebooks now in bookshops, but not all are appropriate for all regions of the country. You can eliminate a lot of bookshop browsing by sending a stamped, self-addressed envelope to the **B&B Bookshelf**, Dept. SMC, American Bed & Breakfast Association, P.O. Box 23294, Washington, DC 20026, for a directory of the guidebooks now available.

### A Dependable Luxury Chain

Actually, this heading is a bit misleading for the elegant **Guest Quarters Hotels.** Luxury, they certainly are, yet prices are in many instances on a par with or lower than luxury hotels that offer only a room. At each Guest Quarters location, what you'll get for those prices is: a designer-furnished living room with dining area, completely equipped kitchen, one or two bedrooms, spacious closets and bath, and all the services of a fine hotel. All those in the areas covered by this book have outdoor swimming pools, and each has a guest library, a notary public, and secretarial services for business travelers. Those completely equipped kitchens include coffee and tea for your first day (complimentary), and there's a grocery shopping service if you decide to make full use of the facilities. Not only is this an ideal way for families to take a break from the constant eat-out routine, but for executives, it offers an opportunity to entertain important clients (catering can be arranged through the excellent restaurants at each hotel). Extras that are available include 24-hour full-menu suite service at many locations, membership privileges at sports clubs, courtesy transportation to airports or inter-city destinations, a self-service guest laundry, and babysitting services. In the Southeast, you'll find Guest Quarters in Alexandria, Virginia; Greensboro and Charlotte, North Carolina; Atlanta, Georgia; and Tampa, Florida. Rates range from $95 for a one-bedroom suite to $180 for two bedrooms (rates vary from location to location, with some two-bedrooms as low as $110). I'll list addresses and rates for those along the way, but for a complete listing of Guest Quarters in other locations, write: Guest Quarters, 2101 L St. NW, Washington, DC 20037 (tel. 202/861-6610, or toll free 800/424-2900).

**A WORD ABOUT NIGHTLIFE:** Nightlife in the Southeast, except for larger cities like Atlanta, Miami, and (of course!) New Orleans, tends to be concentrated in hotel lounges or to center around home entertaining. Where there are outstanding nightspots, you'll find them listed; otherwise, a friendly conversation or two with people who live in the locality will point you to the best current after-dark action.

**. . . AND SHOPPING:** Not being an avid shopper myself, I tend to overlook what may well be one of your primary interests. In the larger cities, I'll list major shopping centers for you, but all along the way, keep your eyes open for small, local shops—there are outstanding bargains to be found in small towns, where a little window-shopping during a lunch break may turn up a treasure. Look especially for locally made crafts, which will let you take a little of the regional charm home in your suitcase. In areas where such craft shops have been long established, I will tell you about them, but because they are sometimes transitory in nature and might have moved on while this book is still in print, a great many true artisans are no doubt omitted from these pages.

**AN INVITATION TO READERS:** Like all Dollarwise Guides, the *Dollarwise Guide to the Southeast and New Orleans* is my best effort to clue you in on how to get the most for your money. If, as a dollarwise traveler, you find I've missed an establishment that you find to be a particularly good value (or even one that's just fun and other readers ought to know about), I'd like to hear about it, and I invite you to write so it may be included in the next edition of this book. If, on the other hand, by the time you get to a particular destination you find a restaurant or hotel is *not* up to my description (chefs *do* change and hotels *do* deteriorate!), please write me about that, as well—the last thing I want in this book is misleading or untimely information. Any additional travel tips you may come up with (off days to visit attractions when they're less crowded, etc.) will also be appreciated. And, oh, yes, if you find this guide to be especially helpful, do drop me a line about *that.* Send whatever you have to say to me at Prentice Hall Press, One Gulf + Western Plaza, New York, NY 10023.

## 2. How to Save Money on All Your Travels—the $25-a-Day Travel Club

In this book we'll be looking at how to get your money's worth in the Southeast and New Orleans, but there is a "device" for saving money and determining value on *all* your trips. It's the popular, international $25-a-Day Travel Club, now in its 25th successful year of operation. The Club was formed at the urging of numerous readers of the $$$-a-Day and Dollarwise Guides, who felt that such an organization could provide continuing travel information and a sense of community to value-minded travelers in all parts of the world. And so it does!

In keeping with the budget concept, the annual membership fee is low and is immediately exceeded by the value of your benefits. Upon receipt of $18 (U.S. residents), or $20 U.S. by check drawn on a U.S. bank or via international postal money order in U.S. funds (Canadian, Mexican, and other foreign residents) to cover one year's membership, we will send all new members the following items.

### (1) *Any two* of the following books

Please designate in your letter which two you wish to receive:

*Frommer's $-A-Day Guides*
   Europe on $25 a Day
   Australia on $25 a Day
   Eastern Europe on $25 a Day
   England on $35 a Day
   Greece including Istanbul and Turkey's Aegean Coast on $25 a Day
   Hawaii on $50 a Day
   India on $15 & $25 a Day
   Ireland on $30 a Day
   Israel on $30 & $35 a Day
   Mexico on $20 a Day (plus Belize and Guatemala)

New York on $45 a Day
New Zealand on $25 a Day
Scandinavia on $50 a Day
Scotland and Wales on $35 a Day
South America on $30 a Day
Spain and Morocco (plus the Canary Is.) on $40 a Day
Turkey on $25 a Day
Washington, D.C., on $40 a Day

*Frommer's Dollarwise Guides*
Dollarwise Guide to Austria and Hungary
Dollarwise Guide to Belgium, Holland, & Luxembourg
Dollarwise Guide to Bermuda and The Bahamas
Dollarwise Guide to Canada
Dollarwise Guide to the Caribbean
Dollarwise Guide to Egypt
Dollarwise Guide to England and Scotland
Dollarwise Guide to France
Dollarwise Guide to Germany
Dollarwise Guide to Italy
Dollarwise Guide to Japan and Hong Kong
Dollarwise Guide to Portugal, Madeira, and the Azores
Dollarwise Guide to the South Pacific
Dollarwise Guide to Switzerland and Liechtenstein
Dollarwise Guide to Alaska
Dollarwise Guide to California and Las Vegas
Dollarwise Guide to Florida
Dollarwise Guide to the Mid-Atlantic States
Dollarwise Guide to New England
Dollarwise Guide to New York State
Dollarwise Guide to the Northwest
Dollarwise Guide to Skiing USA—East
Dollarwise Guide to Skiing USA—West
Dollarwise Guide to the Southeast and New Orleans
Dollarwise Guide to the Southwest
Dollarwise Guide to Texas
(Dollarwise Guides discuss accommodations and facilities in all price ranges, with emphasis on the medium-priced.)

*Frommer's Touring Guides*
Egypt
Florence
London
Paris
Venice
(These new, color illustrated guides include walking tours, cultural and historic sites, and other vital travel information.)

**A Shopper's Guide to Best Buys in England, Scotland, and Wales**
(Describes in detail hundreds of places to shop—department stores, factory outlets, street markets, and craft centers—for great quality British bargains.)

**A Shopper's Guide to the Caribbean**
(Two experienced Caribbean hands guide you through this shopper's paradise,

offering witty insights and helpful tips on the wares and emporia of more than 25 islands.)

**Bed & Breakfast—North America**
(This guide contains a directory of over 150 organizations that offer bed & breakfast referrals and reservations throughout North America. The scenic attractions and major schools and universities near the homes of each are also listed.)

**Dollarwise Guide to Cruises**
(This complete guide covers all the basics of cruising—ports of call, costs, fly-cruise package bargains, cabin selection booking, embarkation and debarkation and describes in detail over 60 or so ships cruising the waters of Alaska, the Caribbean, Mexico, Hawaii, Panama, Canada, and the United States.)

**Honeymoon Guide**
(A special guide for that most romantic trip of your life, with full details on planning and choosing the destination that will be just right in the U.S. [California, New England, Hawaii, Florida, New York, South Carolina, etc.], Canada, Mexico, and the Caribbean.)

**Dollarwise Guide to Skiing Europe**
(Describes top ski resorts in Austria, France, Italy, and Switzerland. Illustrated with maps of each resort area plus full-color trail maps.)

**Fast 'n' Easy Phrase Book**
(French, German, Spanish, and Italian—all in one convenient, easy-to-use phrase guide.)

**How to Beat the High Cost of Travel**
(This practical guide details how to save money on absolutely all travel items—accommodations, transportation, dining, sightseeing, shopping, taxes, and more. Includes special budget information for seniors, students, singles, and families.)

**Marilyn Wood's Wonderful Weekends**
(This very selective guide covers the best mini-vacation destinations within a 175-mile radius of New York City. It describes special country inns and other accommodations, restaurants, picnic spots, sights, and activities—all the information needed for a two- or three-day stay.)

**Motorist's Phrase Book**
(A practical phrase book in French, German, and Spanish designed specifically for the English-speaking motorist touring abroad.)

**Swap and Go—Home Exchanging Made Easy**
(Two veteran home exchangers explain in detail all the money-saving benefits of a home exchange, and then describe precisely how to do it. Also includes information on home rentals and many tips on low-cost travel.)

**The Candy Apple: New York for Kids**
(A spirited guide to the wonders of the Big Apple by a savvy New York grandmother with a kid's-eye view to fun. Indispensable for visitors and residents alike.)

**Travel Diary and Record Book**
(A 96-page diary for personal travel notes plus a section for such vital data as passport and traveler's check numbers, itinerary, postcard list, special people and places to visit, and a reference section with temperature and conversion charts, and world maps with distance zones.)

**Where to Stay USA**
(By the Council on International Educational Exchange, this extraordinary guide is the first to list accommodations in all 50 states that cost anywhere from $3 to $30 per night.)

### (2) A one-year subscription to *The Wonderful World of Budget Travel*

This quarterly eight-page tabloid newspaper keeps you up to date on fast-breaking developments in low-cost travel in all parts of the world bringing you the latest money-saving information—the kind of information you'd have to pay $25 a year to obtain elsewhere. This consumer-conscious publication also features columns of special interest to readers: **Hospitality Exchange** (members all over the world who are willing to provide hospitality to other members as they pass through their home cities—); **Share-a-Trip** (offers and requests from members for travel companions who can share costs and help avoid the burdensome single supplement); and **Readers Ask . . . Readers Reply** (travel questions from members to which other members reply with authentic firsthand information).

### (3) A copy of *Arthur Frommer's Guide to New York*

This is a pocket-size guide to hotels, restaurants, nightspots, and sightseeing attractions in all price ranges throughout the New York area.

### (4) Your personal membership card

Membership entitles you to purchase through the Club all Arthur Frommer publications for a third to a half off their regular retail prices during the term of your membership.

So why not join this hardy band of international budgeteers and participate in its exchange of travel information and hospitality? Simply send your name and address, together with your annual membership fee of $18 (U.S. residents) or $20 U.S. (Canadian, Mexican, and other foreign residents), by check drawn on a U.S. bank or via international postal money order in U.S. funds to: $25-A-Day Travel Club, Inc., Frommer Books, Gulf + Western Building, One Gulf + Western Plaza, New York, NY 10023. And please remember to specify which *two* of the books in section (1) above you wish to receive in your initial package of members' benefits. Or, if you prefer, use the last page of this book, simply checking off the two books you select and enclosing $18 or $20 in U.S. currency.

---

Once you are a member, there is no obligation to buy additional books. No books will be mailed to you without your specific order.

---

## 3. Getting There

Many factors will determine how you get to the Southeast—budget, first of all; the amount of time you'll have for the trip; and just *where* you're headed in the Southeast. If your time is limited and you're coming from a long way off, say, the West Coast, it would make sense to fly across country, then either rent a car or travel by public ground transportation. If your home is on the East Coast, you may be no more than a day or two of driving from your destination—or a train or bus ride of short duration. You'll find pertinent information about the public conveyances that reach each state in the introductory chapters for each. I'll let you in on some of my personal preferences (none of them based on solicitations or special considerations); however, remember that airlines, railroads, and bus companies *all offer frequent special fares, with substantial discounts and of limited duration,* that can save you considerable money. The fares shown are for regular, economy-class travel, but you should be *sure* to check on current details, schedules, and rates for all public carriers before figuring your costs. Remember, too, that public transportation can often turn out to be cheaper than driving, as well as letting you travel with the freedom to enjoy the scenery instead of constant map reading.

**BY AIR:** Flying is, of course, the fastest way to get where you're going. Figuring all costs, it may be no more expensive than some others, even cheaper than still others. And the smart traveler will consider buying such standard, always-in-effect, money-saving tickets as excursion plans and the limited-time promotional fares seen so often these days. These usually entail such inconveniences as traveling on certain days of the week, staying a specified length of time, or other limiting conditions. However, it is possible to travel much less expensively just by planning your trip to meet those conditions.

The sample fares for air travel to major points in the five southeastern states and New Orleans that are shown here are for economy-class, round-trip tickets *at the time of writing* (subject to almost certain change):

| To | From New York | From Chicago | From Los Angeles |
|---|---|---|---|
| Alexandria, Va. (Washington, D.C.) | $195 | $237 | $750 |
| Raleigh, N.C. | 220 | 307 | 797 |
| Charleston, S.C. | 227 | 315 | 827 |
| Atlanta, Ga. | 197 | 350 | 853 |
| Miami, Fla. | 325 | 415 | 965 |
| New Orleans, La. | 279 | 267 | 738 |

A rather special airline has come on the Southeast scene that warrants mention. While at present it serves only three destinations, its future looks bright and its services are unique. Also, **Air Atlanta** has connecting arrangements with Pan Am, allowing you to combine the routes of the two lines. What makes it special? For one thing, it offers express check-in, with ticketing right at the gate. For another, there's roll-on valet service for hanging garment bags (they're last on, first off, which cuts down considerably on aisle congestion). Then, in both Atlanta and Miami, gate lounges have a club-like atmosphere that includes complimentary telephones conveniently placed at chairside tables and complimentary refreshments, as well as wall displays of very good paintings. In Atlanta, a GateExpress shuttle service carries passengers directly from the terminal to the gate. Although it was founded with the business traveler in mind, these thoughtful extras reduce the usual airport hassles for all of us. Its on-time record is impressive, and rates are competitive. At present, it reaches Memphis, New York (both La Guardia and Kennedy Airports), and Miami, and I strongly suggest that you book at least one flight if you travel between any of these points.

**Delta** and **Eastern** also blanket the Southeast with frequent flights, and attractive fly-drive packages are available to many resort areas such as Miami, St. Petersburg, and Walt Disney World in Florida, and larger cities like New Orleans and Atlanta. You can save as much as 25% on air fare, have the convenience of a rental car (which will be waiting for you at the airport), and hotel arrangements are usually quite satisfactory, allowing enough flexibility in schedule and itinerary to permit comfortable travel. The airlines or your travel agent will have details and be able to make reservations.

In short, depending on your needs, the times you must fly, etc., you will find a sort of airline supermarket that will require some astute shopping on your part.

**BY TRAIN:** Amtrak serves the Southeast well. Of all modes of public transportation, rail represents the most economical use of fuel (Amtrak yields twice as many passenger miles per gallon as the next most economical, bus, and astonishingly higher percentages when compared to automobile and plane), and many travelers find it a transportation method which becomes positively addictive. I am, personally, so enamored of the "romance of the rails" that not even the convenience of my own automobile sways me when a journey of any distance looms.

Amtrak has also come up with rail/car packages to many destinations that will provide a rental car to be picked up and returned to train depots, thus combining the best features of both.

In addition, there's a good variety of package-tour programs for major southern cities. In 1987 the "Antebellum Era," six-day tour of Charleston and Savannah, included hotel, breakfasts, historic tours, and transportation between the two cities for a per-person, double-occupancy price of $265 plus train fare. Jamestown, Williamsburg, New Orleans, and several Florida destinations had similar bargains. For information on current offerings, consult your local Amtrak Tour Desk or call toll free 800/USA-RAIL (that's 800/872-7245) and request the "Amtrak Travel Planner."

On the whole, Amtrak has very good coverage along the eastern seaboard, rather spotty when you get away from the coast. My personal love of train travel is based both on economy and the fact that a train, unlike a plane or automobile travel along our superhighways, not only gives you a good look at the countryside, but some interesting backyards as well. In addition, today's trains are a pleasure to ride, with much more leg room than there used to be, wider seats, bar and restaurant (or snackbar) cars, and slumber coaches, roomettes, or compartments for longer trips. Diner-car meals suffered a bit during cost cutbacks but have now come almost up to the high standards they've always met in the past.

Booking train travel is now much more convenient than it once was, when Amtrak stations were the only ticket dispensers. Not only do more than 10,000 travel agents now issue tickets, but you can also call a computerized service (tel. toll free 800/USA-RAIL) for train, hotel, and rental-car reservations.

As economical as regular coach fares are on Amtrak, there are frequent special excursion rates that save as much as 35% to 40%. Also, there are periodic unlimited-travel passes available for specified time limits. In 1987 there were three Special All Aboard America fares that divided the country into three regions: Eastern, Central and Western. For round-trip travel within one region by coach, the fare was $118; within two contiguous regions, $158; and over the entire Amtrak system, $198. There was no advance-purchase requirement, the fare was good for up to 45 days, and the only restriction was no stopovers en route to or from the final destination. The regular All Aboard America fares, which allow one stopover in each direction, were $159, $239, and $299. As we go to press, there are no plans to terminate or increase these bargain fares. The alert train traveler will keep abreast of Amtrak's latest offerings and try to schedule trips to take advantage of them. Incidentally, the popular U.S.A. Rail-Pass is sold only outside the U.S. to residents of other countries—foreign visitors will also find available less expensive regional unlimited-travel passes, such as the Southern Region pass which is good for two weeks. Those, too, must be bought before coming to the U.S. Amtrak's Auto Train service from Lorton, Virginia, to Sandford, Florida, is another good buy (see Chapter XIV for details).

The sample rail fares shown below to major points in the Southeast are, with only one exception, Special All Aboard America round-trip coach costs at the time of writing.

| To | From New York | From Chicago | From Los Angeles |
|---|---|---|---|
| Alexandria, Va. | $ 63 | $118 | $198 |
| Raleigh, N.C. | 116 | 118 | 198 |
| Charleston, S.C. | 118 | 118 | 198 |
| Atlanta | 118 | 118 | 198 |
| Miami (via Chicago) | 118 | 118 | 198 |
| New Orleans | 118 | 118 | 158 |

In addition to excellent package deals available through its Tour Desk service, Amtrak can arrange discount car rentals at almost all destinations.

**BY BUS:** Those two cover-the-country giants, **Greyhound** and **Trailways,** will get you to the Southeast from almost any starting point. Furthermore, although their standard fares are the cheapest way to travel, they both offer even greater bargains. In 1987 both companies introduced "Go Anywhere" fares of $59 one way, $100 round trip, to cover travel between any two points within the country. At the time of writing, there are no plans to discontinue these amazingly low fares, so unless you are traveling a very short distance when the regular one-way fare falls below $59, you can count on a $100 ceiling.

**BY CAR:** Although there was a time that automobile travel to the Southeast could be hazardous if you wandered down the eastern coast via U.S. 1, there are now Interstate highways leading into the region from every direction, connecting with well-planned, beautifully maintained state and federal roadways within the several states with roadside rest areas at frequent intervals. Welcome Centers are at many state borders, providing special assistance to motorists as well as tons of tourist information. From a purely "easy to get around" point of view, driving is the most convenient way to come, particularly if you don't plan to stay in one of the metropolitan centers once you get there.

### A Word About Car Rentals

You'll find all major car-rental companies throughout the Southeast. However, my own experience with most of them leads to this personal recommendation. You'll find **Thrifty Car Rentals** throughout the Southeast, and best of all, you'll find rates that are usually far below those of the major firms, primarily because of their very realistic policy of not paying for high airport rental space, but offering instead an airport pickup service (the same is true of your hotel or motel if you wish). Most locations can furnish a wide range of car sizes (all the way up to a nine-passenger station wagon), and there are real money-saving specials offered from time to time at all locations. Thrifty also features cars for non-smokers and special rates for luxury cars. I'll list the locations in each state introductory chapter, but for a Thrifty world-wide directory and rate schedule, write Thrifty Rent-A-Car System, Inc., P.O. Box 35250, Tulsa, OK 74153-0250 (tel. 800/367-2277).

**BY YACHT:** No, this section is *not* devoted to yacht owners—it's meant to tell you about a delightful way to get to and around the Southeast as a quasi-private guest aboard a luxurious yacht. The Intracoastal Waterway, which runs all along the Atlantic seaboard from Norfolk, Virginia, to Fort Lauderdale, is the pathway for two deluxe yachts operated by **Clipper Cruise Line,** 7711 Bonhomme Ave., St. Louis, MO 63105 (tel. toll free 800/325-0010). The *Newport Clipper* and the *Nantucket Clipper* carry just 100 passengers each in accommodations that are likely to meet your fondest fantasies of sailing with the very rich. Decks are hand-laid of teakwood; public rooms all are circled by glass to give panoramic views; staterooms are beautifully done up and have wide picture windows; and crew members do indeed treat each passenger as an invited guest. Meals are served in one seating, with a cuisine featuring the freshest ingredients (many bought the same day) prepared to perfection. Low-key, high-caliber entertainment is provided in the evenings for those passengers who stay aboard rather than search out onshore events, and while there's plenty to keep you occupied (library, card games, etc.), there's never any pressure to join in group activities as is so often the case on more structured, large-ship cruises. Shore excursions are easy-going, with docking many times in marinas close to the center of land attractions. All in all, if you can't own a yacht of your own, this is the next best thing and will pamper you within an inch of your life!

Itineraries in the Southeast include a seven-day Colonial South cruise that drops anchor in Savannah, St. Simons Island, Beaufort, Charleston, and Hilton Head, as well as a Florida Waterways route (see Chapter XIV). There's also a Chesapeake Bay itinerary that includes Baltimore, Annapolis, St. Michaels, Yorktown (for Williamsburg excursions), St. Marys City, and Washington, D.C. (Outside our territory, but an intriguing possibility, is the seven-day Virgin Islands cruise to St. Thomas, Tortola, Norman Island, Virgin Gorda, Jost Van Dyke, and St. John—just thought I'd let you know about it.) Of course, the ultimate yachting experience would be the 29-day Great American Odyssey cruise that travels from Boston to Fort Lauderdale. Prices for all seven-day cruises in 1987 range from $1,495 to $1,895, double occupancy (slightly higher for singles). For full particulars, schedules, and booking, contact Clipper Cruise Line at the address above, or see your travel agent.

**READER'S TRANSPORTATION TIP:** "In planning and executing a trip to several places on the East Coast, all by air, we found that in many locations renting a car for the days we were there was no more expensive for the four of us than simple transit back and forth to the airport would have been. In other locations, such as Washington, D.C., only because we had lived there did we know that the sensible choice was to avoid Dulles and Baltimore/Friendship airports, fly into National, and get ourselves into the city via the Metro for a few cents each. It pays to gather information on the relative convenience and cost of traveling via public transportation between tourist attractions in a particular location" (M. Aldrich, Minneapolis, Minn.).

# 4. Getting Around

**BY AIR:** There are several local airlines that fly within the region, and Delta, Eastern, Piedmont, and Southern have rather frequent air service to major points. I'll supply names of the most prominent local airlines as we go along.

**BY TRAIN:** Introductory chapters for each state have Amtrak stops listed, but it would pay to investigate thoroughly schedules between interstate points. Connections are not always easy to plan and time can be lost between trains. The railroads offer very good access to the Southeast, not so good movement around it.

**BY BUS:** Greyhound, Trailways, and the local bus lines listed in each introductory chapter make it easy to get around and between states, and in most cases equipment is modern and quite comfortable.

**BY CAR:** As I said, highways in every southeastern state are in good shape, and it is seldom, if ever, that you'll run into a badly paved roadway. The famed speedtraps that visitors once feared in Georgia and South Carolina have been virtually eliminated, although most state patrolmen keep a close eye on motorists to see that the speed limit is not exceeded on state highways. There are frequent roadside picnic tables, some with outdoor grills, along both state and federal roads in this region, and picnicking can be a delightful way to save money, as well as a welcome break to enjoy the outdoors while you lunch or have a light supper. I have always found, too, that it's much easier when traveling by car to pack a small "hot pot" and cups for late-night or early-morning coffee. In fact, my family very often cuts down on eating costs by breakfasting in our room on sweet rolls or doughnuts bought the night before and served with instant coffee or hot chocolate, courtesy of the hot pot. Possible, of course, when you're traveling by other means, but most convenient when you can simply tuck a small box of eating supplies in the car.

# Chapter II

# INTRODUCTION TO VIRGINIA

### 1. By Way of Background
### 2. Traveling to Virginia
### 3. Traveling Within Virginia

THE COMMONWEALTH OF VIRGINIA, sometimes called "The Gateway to the South," is very much a part of my own growing up. I finished high school there, married and began my family on its coast, and somewhere along the line absorbed a love for its rich history that seems to imbue every native and is quick to hook most visitors. Virginia rightly claims "More America to the Mile" than any other part of the country (although New England states just might quarrel with that claim), and only the most complete dullard could travel the state and come away without a very real sense of this nation's beginnings.

## 1. By Way of Background

**VIRGINIA PAST AND PRESENT:** The Old Dominion, and this country, had its start in the London Company's small expeditionary force that settled at Jamestown on May 13, 1607. It was to become the first permanent English settlement, but for those first few years it almost didn't make it. Ill-suited to deal with the primitive conditions in which they found themselves, those first colonists fell prey to dysentery, plague, fire, hunger that amounted to near starvation in 1609, and much internal bickering. Things picked up in 1610 when new settlers and fresh supplies arrived from England. Then, when John Rolfe (who married the Indian princess Pocahontas) managed to convince enough farmers of the wisdom of growing tobacco as a "cash crop" and the first harvest was exported in 1614, they were off and running toward a sound economy. Two things happened in 1619 that would cast long shadows into the future: a representative legislative assembly was convened, and a Dutch man-of-war arrived carrying the first black indentured servants, the forerunner of a slave traffic that would later tear the nation apart.

Thus from its base of tobacco farming that spawned huge plantations along broad rivers and bays, an early democratic governing forum, and the use of slave labor, Virginia was a natural theater for the drama of history in which she would play a leading role. Bacon's Rebellion in 1676 was the first overt expression of dissatisfaction with British rule; it set the stage for events in the next century that sprang from the words and actions of Virginians such as Patrick

Henry, Thomas Jefferson, George Washington, George Mason, James Madison, and John Marshall, and led eventually to full independence for all the American colonies. And from Virginians the new nation got its Constitution, Bill of Rights, and four of its first five presidents (Virginians held the presidency for 32 of our first 36 years!).

From the end of the Revolution until 1861 when it seceded from the Union, Virginia expanded its productive farms and busy ports until it became the richest state in the South. With the war against slavery that erupted in 1861, she became the very heart and soul of the Confederacy, with Richmond serving as its capital almost to the bitter end in 1865. In fact, the first major battle of that long, bloody struggle was fought in the state at Manassas, and the final act was played out at Appomattox.

After digging itself out from the debris of the postwar Reconstruction years, Virginia set out once more on a course of industrial growth. Today you'll find it a harmonious blend of agriculture (tobacco, wheat, apples, corn, and hay), industry (not the least of which is tourism), and shipping. And following the philosophy that people who do not know their past can have no future, Virginia posts more than 1,500 historical markers throughout the state to remind you of its important role in history.

You'll also find that there's much more than simple history to entertain the visitor. The east coast has some of the most popular beach resorts in the East and is a virtual sportsman's paradise, with excellent fishing, surf-riding, hunting, tennis, and golf. To the west are the Shenandoah Valley and the Blue Ridge Mountains, with horseback riding, hunting, and camping, as well as such natural wonders as Natural Bridge and the Luray Caverns.

**VISITOR INFORMATION:** For general information about Virginia, write: **Virginia State Travel Service,** 202 N. 9th St., Suite 500, Richmond, VA 23219 (tel. 804/786-4484). If you're interested in golf, ask for "Golf in Virginia," their complete list of courses; in fishing, "Fresh Water Fishing in Virginia," a list of freshwater streams, lakes, and rivers, and "Salt Water Sport Fishing in Virginia," a guide to the annual saltwater sport-fishing tournament; in sightseeing with a historical bent, "Civil War Battlefield Parks," a guide to Civil War attractions, and "Historic Homes of Virginia," listing nearly 100 historic plantations, estates, and homes in the Old Dominion. Travelers with limited time or who wish to stick to the eastern part of the state should request the excellent "Historic Chesapeake Bay Circle Tour." A brochure on "Virginia Annual Events" may be obtained from the Travel Development Dept., **Virginia State Chamber of Commerce,** 611 E. Franklin St., Richmond, VA 23219. Outdoorsmen will want to write the **Virginia Commission of Game and Inland Fisheries,** P.O. Box 11104, Richmond, VA 23220, for Virginia hunting and fishing information, or call the Game Commission at 804/257-1000. New Yorkers will find a **Travel Service** office at 11 Rockefeller Plaza (tel. 212/245-3080).

**VIRGINIA TELEPHONE AREA CODES:** Alexandria, 804; Williamsburg, 804; Virginia Beach, 804; Charlottesville, 804; Roanoke, 703.

**HOTEL ACCOMMODATIONS:** Virginia has a generous supply of hotels, motels, campgrounds, and a few guesthouses in some locations. As for prices, they cover everything from super-deluxe to budget. The accommodations you'll find listed in this book have been selected purely on the basis of a personal inspection and evaluation, and the prices, it must be said again, are those in effect *at the time of writing*—and in these uncertain days of rising costs, are very much subject to change.

As a rule, reservations will be less tight in fall, winter, and early spring, since Virginia draws its largest crowds during the summer months. The one exception is the Blue Ridge section, where thousands throng the parkway in October and early November for a last look at fall foliage.

**CAMPING:** You'll find some campgrounds listed for each Virginia location, but two very helpful publications are available if you're planning to come via camp or trailer. Write for "Virginia State Parks General Information" brochure, and the "Cabin/Campsite Information and Reservation Form," from the Virginia Division of Parks and Recreation, 1201 Washington Bldg., Capitol Square, Richmond, VA 23219; and "Camping in Virginia" from the Virginia State Travel Service, 202 N. 9th St., Suite 500, Richmond, VA 23219.

**VIRGINIA RESTAURANTS:** One thing you can always do—and always do well—in Virginia is eat. From the strictly southern cured (or "Virginia") ham, fried chicken, and black-eyed peas to seafood you can count on to be deliciously fresh, you'll be fed well in restaurants that rival New York or San Francisco establishments, colonial taverns that have been serving food for centuries, plenty of medium-priced modern restaurants staffed by chefs steeped in regional cooking, or sometimes—if you're lucky—in very small, plain restaurants of the old-time, small-town-café home-cooking tradition. A reassuring thing to know is that compared to big-city prices, those in most restaurants in Virginia are modest.

As for alcoholic beverages, if you're 20 or older you can buy beer in state stores and licensed restaurants and food stores, but you'll have to wait for 21 to be served wine or mixed drinks. The licensing of restaurants and lounges to serve alcohol by the drink is on a local-option basis; you may run into a "dry" locality, but don't get upset—in most you can buy mixers and bring your own.

**CLIMATE:** As you can see, temperatures in Virginia are pretty much in the moderate range, falling slightly lower in fall and winter in Alexandria in the northern part of the state and Roanoke in the west than along the coast.

|  | *High* | *Low* |
|---|---|---|
| Alexandria | 87 | 29 |
| Norfolk | 88 | 32 |
| Roanoke | 88 | 29 |

## 2. Traveling to Virginia

**BY AIR:** American, Delta, Eastern, Pan Am, Northwest, TWA, USAir, United, and other domestic and international carriers fly into Washington National Airport and Dulles International, both of which are in Virginia and close to Alexandria. Piedmont serves Washington National Airport and also goes to Norfolk, Newport News, Charlottesville, Danville, Lynchburg, Roanoke, and Richmond.

**BY TRAIN:** Amtrak has stops in Alexandria, Fredericksburg, Richmond, Manassas, Charlottesville, Williamsburg, Newport News, Petersburg, Lynchburg and Danville. Bear in mind that Amtrak excursion and special discount fares are considerably lower than regular coach fares. Also, your nearest Amtrak Tour Desk can furnish details on such bargains as "Williamsburg Close Up" and "Jamestown, Williamsburg and Monticello" package tours.

**BY BUS:** Greyhound and Trailways will take you to almost any destination in the Old Dominion. As with Amtrak, check specials in effect when you plan your trip.

**BY CAR:** Several Interstate highways cross Virginia: I-64 runs east and west; I-77, north and south in the southwestern corner of the state; I-81, north and south the entire length of the western part of the state; I-95, north and south in the eastern part of the state. **Virginia Information Stations,** in attractive, colonial-style buildings, are located within a mile or two of major entry points.

## 3. Traveling Within Virginia

**BY AIR:** Within the state, United, TWA, and USAir have service between Washington's two airports (both in Virginia) and Norfolk. American has service between Washington's two airports and Richmond. Piedmont has frequent service to Charlottesville, Danville, Lynchburg, Newport News, Norfolk, Richmond, and Roanoke.

**BY TRAIN:** You *can* travel around the state via Amtrak, although be forwarned that it takes some doing, with a good deal of planning for connections between major and spur lines, and it will almost certainly involve considerable waits. Nevertheless, Amtrak has stops at Alexandria, Fredericksburg, Richmond, Williamsburg, Newport News, and Petersburg (with a bus connection to Norfolk and Virginia Beach) in the east. In other parts of the state, it's possible to go by train to Culpeper, Charlottesville, Monroe, Lynchburg, Danville, Staunton, Clifton Forge, Quantico, Ashland, and Lee Hall.

**BY BUS:** Greyhound and Trailways will take you almost anywhere.

**BY CAR:** Virginia has more than 54,000 miles of paved roads, so driving is a pleasure. My best advice is not to leave home without the official state highway map, issued free by the Virginia Department of Transportation, 1221 E. Broad St., Richmond, VA 23219. A letter will bring it to you, and besides road information, it's loaded with sightseeing information. It's also available at Welcome Centers at all major entry points.

All major car-rental firms have offices in key cities, and there are Thrifty offices in Alexandria, Bristol, Fredericksburg, Newport News, Norfolk, Richmond, Roanoke, and Springfield.

# Chapter III

# ALONG THE VIRGINIA COAST

**1. Alexandria
2. Williamsburg
3. Richmond
4. Tidewater Virginia and the Eastern Shore**

FOR SHEER DENSITY of tourist attractions and excursions into Virginia's history, its east coast takes top honors. It was here, after all, that the earliest arrivals set up shop at sites which provided port access for those all-important ships that linked them to England and which would later serve as jumping-off points for the push westward.

## 1. Alexandria

Alexandria is one of Virginia's 40 independent cities; that is, it's not a part of any county, but a separate entity. A sister city to Georgetown, just across the Potomac River, it was literally put on the map by George Washington, who helped lay out the streets and drew its first map as a 17-year-old surveyor's apprentice in the 1750s. As a matter of fact, our first president had many close ties to the town: he drilled his first troops in Market Square in 1754, held a pew at Christ Episcopal Church, and in later years quite often came up to Alexandria to transact business as well as to find diversion in its busy social life. A little later, Robert E. Lee spent much of his childhood and prepared for West Point in Alexandria.

**GETTING THERE:** If you're driving, Alexandria can be reached on I-95 from the north and west, I-495 from the south, U.S. 1 from north or south, and Va. 7 from the west. Washington National Airport is just ten minutes north on the George Washington Memorial Parkway, and Dulles International is 30 minutes to the northwest. Both the Greyhound bus terminal and the Southern Railroad train station are just minutes from the historic area of Old Town.

**A FIRST STOP:** A fantastic restoration and preservation of more than a thousand 18th- and 19th-century buildings in **Old Town** makes it easy for today's visitor to see how this historic port city went about its business in those far-off days.

It is even easier if that visitor heads for the historic Ramsay House that dates from 1724 and now houses the **Alexandria Tourist Council** at 221 King St. (tel. 703/549-0205). Their services far exceed those of many agencies of this kind; here are just some of the ways in which they'll make your stop in their town most interesting: they will show you a 13-minute color film; give you a free brochure for a self-guided walking tour; make hotel and restaurant reservations; provide foreign-language guides if you give them enough notice (their brochure is also available in more than 18 languages); arm you with more than 40 area attraction brochures, as well as lists of art galleries, specialty shops, antique shops, restaurants, hotels, and special events; and will even pass out free parking passes for out-of-town cars in the metered parking zones! And if you should need anything beyond all this, the friendly, efficient staff will almost certainly be able to help you out.

**WHERE TO STAY:** Guest Quarters–Alexandria, 100 S. Reynolds St., Alexandria, VA 22304 (tel. 703/370-9600, or toll free 800/424-2900), gives you the luxury of one- or two-bedroom suites in a peaceful setting combined with convenience to historic Old Town, shopping, corporate centers and downtown Washington (which is just about ten minutes away). You'll find their usual high standards of decor and service, and the lovely Quarters Court restaurant. Rates are $114 double in a one-bedroom suite and $136 for two bedrooms. There are also some studio apartments at $106 double. Each additional person pays $15, children under 13 stay free, and there are special weekend rates.

For convenience as well as comfort, there is no better place to stay than the **Old Town Holiday Inn**, 480 King St., Alexandria, VA 22314 (tel. 703/549-6080). The Robert E. Lee home is just a half mile away, Mount Vernon an easy eight-mile drive, and Washington's National Airport just three miles (they furnish free transportation to and from). And all of Old Town is just outside the door. The inn's brick exterior even looks like part of the restoration, and that illusion is reinforced when you walk into its lobby furnished with period reproductions. The Independence Restaurant has the same colonial decor and specializes in American dishes, with roast beef high on the list, as is fresh seafood. The Tavern, just down the hall from the restaurant, is all low lights, dark wood, and pewter, and there's entertainment most of the year. An indoor pool provides year-round swimming. Rooms are spacious and comfortable, and far from budget priced ($108 to $127 double; children under 19 stay free in the room with their parents), but as a close-at-hand refuge after a day of foot-weary touristing, it can't be beat. Weekend package plans offer attractive savings.

On the north side of town, the **Ramada Hotel–Old Town,** 901 N. Fairfax St., Alexandria, VA 22314 (tel. 703/683-6000), is an attractive high-rise with a pool, restaurant, and entertainment in the lounge. Rooms are a comfortable size and attractively decorated in bright colors. If you're arriving or departing at nearby airports, there's free shuttle service. Rates are in the upper brackets (doubles from $92 to $102), but children under 18 stay free in the room with their parents, and there are lower weekend rates available.

The **Old Colony Inn,** North Washington at 1st Street, Alexandria, VA 22314 (tel. 703/548-6300), is a complex of 11 brick buildings laid out in the style of a colonial estate. Located on the George Washington Memorial Parkway (which is Washington Street when it passes through Alexandria), the Old Colony is only five minutes away from Washington's National Airport (with free airport and Metro shuttle service every half hour) and especially convenient to Washington sightseeing. The desk clerk here is happy to arrange Gray Line tours, which begin and end at the motel. All 223 rooms are attractively decorated, some with canopied double beds, and most are furnished in a modified colonial decor. There's a pool, screened from traffic by a serpentine brick wall and landscaping. Also, a restaurant is on the premises as well as a cocktail lounge and free HBO in every room, and there are excellent dining facilities within walking distance. At this member of the Best Western chain, small pets are accepted, children under 16 stay free when sharing a room with their parents, and weekend rates are available. Doubles are in the $80 to $98 range, and kitchenette units, double occupancy, are $100.

The **Days Inn Alexandria**, 110 S. Bragg St., Alexandria, VA 22312 (tel. 703/354-4950), is just one block off the I-395/Duke Street intersection, with the top-quality accommodations typical of this chain. There's a pool, playground, and restaurant, and bring your pets along if you like (there's a small additional fee). This location is a good one if you plan much Washington sightseeing, since the Metro bus is just one block away. Rates are seasonal, with doubles running $52. Children under 18 pay $1.

## Guesthouses

Alexandria has a very good bed-and-breakfast program, with accommodations available in over 30 guesthouses in Old Town and surrounding areas. Contact E. J. Mansmann, 819 Prince St., Alexandria, VA 22314 (tel. 703/683-2159). Rates range from $61 to $90 for doubles, and there's a two-day minimum stay.

## Camping

If you're traveling the camper route, where you stay will depend on which direction you come from or are headed. Closest camping toward the west and the Blue Ridge Mountains is the **Greenville Farm Family Campground** at 14004 Shelter Lane in Haymarket (tel. 703/754-7944, or 754-8877 if no answer), about 40 miles away on Va. 234, eight miles northwest of I-66. Most of the 150 sites have water and electric hookups; there's a recreation building, pool, laundry, store, and LP gas service. Rates are $12 to $15, depending on full or no hook-ups.

From Williamsburg, the **Yogi Bear's Jellystone Park Camp,** 3071 Jefferson Davis Hwy., Stafford, VA 22554 (tel. 703/659-3447), is about 25 miles south of the Washington Beltway (or 20 miles south of Alexandria) off I-95 at Exit 48 (Aquia Interchange). Follow the signs about half a mile to the park. There are 121 sites for full hookups and tents, and a store, pool, laundry, mini-golf, and LP gas. Rates are $16.

**WHERE TO EAT:** Alexandria is filled with places to eat, most of them offering above-average fare, and part of the fun will be discovering your own favorites. I strongly recommend that you pick up the *Restaurant Guide* put out by the Tourist Council—it gives a very good rundown on the town's restaurants.

**Two Nineteen,** at 219 King St. (tel. 703/549-1141), is *the* place to go if you're seeking a Créole "fix." Many of its fresh products are flown in daily from New Orleans, and the menu artfully blends French and Louisiana Créole cookeries. The atmosphere is sumptuous: in a converted 1890 home, three formal dining rooms are bedecked with antique furnishings, marble fireplace mantels, crystal chandeliers, and Victorian paintings. There's nightly entertainment in the Basin Street Lounge. Lunch costs $5 to $11, and dinners are in the $10 to $20 range. Two Nineteen is open from 11:30 a.m. to 10:30 p.m. Monday through Thursday, to 11 p.m. on Friday and Saturday, and from 5 to 10:30 p.m. on Sunday. There's also a Sunday brunch from 11 a.m. to 4 p.m., and its costs range from $6 to $20. You can start with milk punch or a Ramos gin fizz, then feast on eggs Benedict, Hussarde, or Sardou, Louisiana-style catfish, jambalaya, and shrimp

Créole—close your eyes and you'll almost swear you were "way down yonder in New Orleans."

At **La Bergerie,** 218 N. Lee St. (tel. 703/683-1007), chef Jean Campagne presents an unusual mélange of French-Basque dishes, along with more traditional French specialties. There's a pleasant, welcoming atmosphere in this restored Victorian-era warehouse, and it's currently an "in" spot, voted Alexandria's favorite for several years by the *Alexandria Port Packet.* Only fresh seafood is served, and the menu changes to reflect current availability. All this does not come inexpensively: semi à la carte lunches range from $7 to $14; dinners, $12 to $25. If the youngsters have sophisticated palates, a children's menu is offered. There's a dress code, and reservations are requested.

**East Wind,** 809 King St. (tel. 703/836-1515), has been called the eastern seaboard's best Vietnamese restaurant. Specialties are subtly different from the varied Chinese cuisines, and perhaps more akin to Thai cookery. If you're not familiar, opt for char-broiled shrimps or scallops, or better yet, ask the advice of the patient, friendly staff. Vietnamese paintings adorn this charming small room, where lunches range from $7 to $10, and dinners run $11 to $15. It's open from 11:30 a.m. to 2:30 p.m. and 6 to 10 p.m. Monday through Thursday, to 10:30 p.m. on Friday and Saturday. It's locally popular, so best make reservations.

A sense of history permeates the very walls of **Gadsby's Tavern,** 138 N. Royal St. (tel. 703/548-1288), a long-ago stagecoach inn favored by George Washington. Costumed waiters serve lunch and dinner in this National Historic Landmark, and there's nightly colonial entertainment. Weather permitting, you can also dine in the charming open courtyard. Don't miss the Sally Lunn bread, and the proprietors vow that the duckling preparation and other colonial-era specialties were especially favored by Mr. Washington. Lunch is a moderate $5 to $6, and dinner will range from $10 to $18; a children's menu is available. It's open from 11:30 a.m. to 3 p.m. and 5:30 to 10 p.m. daily, and closes major holidays. It's a good idea to make reservations, since virtually every visitor seems to try to dine here at least once.

For inexpensive dining, don't miss **Chesapeake Bagel Bakery,** 601 King St. (tel. 703/684-3777), voted number one by the *Washington Post* for its nine bagel varieties freshly baked daily; **Bread and Chocolate,** 611 King St. (tel. 703/548-0992), a handsome café featuring fresh salads and sandwiches, homemade cakes and pastries, and cappuccino; and **Sam's Delicatessen,** 118 King St. (tel. 703/836-2200), where you can select from a wide variety of hot or cold sandwiches which you can carry out or eat under the skylights of the Small Mall.

**HISTORIC SITES:** When you stop by **Ramsay House,** 221 King St., to pick up those helpful brochures from the visitors center, take time to look around the historic old clapboard house and its garden. It was built about 1724 in Dumfries, Virginia, but was moved here in 1749. For a time it was the home of William Ramsay and his family. Ramsay was a hard-working Scotsman and a successful tradesman. George Washington walked in Ramsay's funeral procession in 1785. Before its restoration, the house was used as a tavern, grocery store, rooming house, and even a cigar factory. Of particular interest is the garden through which you enter the visitors center. It's an authentic 18th-century garden, with boxwood, cherry, laurel, a paper mulberry tree, tulips, and plantain lilies, all lovingly tended by the Hunting Creek Garden Club of Alexandria and the city of Alexandria. Hours are 9 a.m. to 5 p.m. daily except Thanksgiving, Christmas, and New Year's Days.

The **Carlyle House,** at 121 N. Fairfax St., was built in 1751–1753 as the home of John Carlyle, a Scottish emigrant and merchant who served as one of

Alexandria's first trustees. It was here that Gen. Edward Braddock and five co-lonial governors met and suggested that colonists be taxed to pay for Braddock's Duquesne expedition against the French. Furnishings in the restored house and kitchen date from the mid-18th century to the late 1780s. In a second-floor bed-room, the original construction of plaster, fireplace openings, and floor beams have been exposed. Open Tuesday through Saturday from 10 a.m. to 5 p.m., on Sunday from noon to 5 p.m.; closed Thanksgiving, Christmas, and New Year's Days. There's a $2 fee for adults, $1.50 for senior citizens, $1 for children 6 to 17, and special group rates are available.

The **Old Presbyterian Meeting House** at 321 S. Fairfax St. is a historic church still quite active in community programs. This is where George Washing-ton's funeral service was held when his own Christ Church was unreachable be-cause of bad weather and road conditions. The old churchyard contains the grave of the Unknown Soldier of the American Revolution, whose burial re-cords list him simply as "Old Revolutionary Soldier from Kentucky." The Meeting House is open without charge 9 a.m. to 4 p.m. on weekdays. Sunday services are at 11 a.m.

America's second-oldest apothecary shop, the **Stabler-Leadbeater Apothe-cary Shop,** 107 S. Fairfax St., was founded in 1792 and run by five generations of the same family until it closed in 1933. Today it's a museum (with medicines, mortars and pestles, and all sorts of medical equipment) of an early-day drug-store and an antique shop as well. It's open Monday through Saturday from 10 a.m. to 4 p.m. At the time of writing, there's no charge but voluntary contribu-tions are most welcome.

The **Robert E. Lee boyhood home,** 607 Oronoco St. (tel. 548-8454), was lived in by the great general intermittently from 1812 to 1825, and he went to school next door. There are some who say it's haunted—piano music has been heard by imaginative visitors, as well as the sound of a small boy running accom-panied by the barking of a dog. "'Tain't so," says the curator, so bring your imagination if you want to people the house with ghosts. Hours are 10 a.m. to 4 p.m. Monday through Saturday, noon to 4 p.m. on Sunday. Admission is $2 for adults, $1.50 for senior citizens, $1 for students 6 to 17. Closed December 15 to February 1. The stately house has recently been named to the National Register of Historic Places.

**Gadsby's Tavern,** at 134 N. Royal St., is where George Washington used to twirl his Martha around on the second-floor dance floor, as well as gather with cronies on quieter afternoons and nights. You can eat in the former stagecoach inn if you've a mind to (see "Where to Eat"). Even if you don't go for a meal, plan to visit the museum located in the gaming and assembly rooms of the City Tavern, and bedrooms and ballroom of the City Hotel, added in 1792. It's open Tuesday through Saturday from 10 a.m. to 5 p.m. and on Sunday from 1 to 5 p.m. (last tour at 4:15 p.m.). Admission is $2 for adults, $1 for children 6 to 17.

**Gentry Row** (200 block of Prince Street) and **Captain's Row** (100 block of Prince) are blocks of 18th- and 19th-century homes lining the cobblestone street. They're privately owned now, as when they were built for sea captains of the sailing ships that regularly sailed from the port city.

## OTHER HISTORIC SITES NEARBY: Mount Vernon (c/o Mount Vernon La-dies' Association; tel. 703/780-2000), George Washington's home from 1754 until he died in 1799, is nine miles south of Alexandria on the George Washing-ton Memorial Parkway, and nobody in his or her right mind would want to miss it. If our first president has always seemed cool and aloof, he'll become a living presence as you walk through this home he loved above all and where he spent his happiest years. Stand on the wide, two-story, columned porch and you'll see

the same peaceful view, with the long, green lawn sweeping down to the river. And inside, those responsible for restoration of the mansion have been careful to preserve the sense of "home" that warmed Washington's heart. Although only 500 of the 8,000 acres that made up the estate in its prime are still intact (outlying farms were willed by the president and his wife to various descendants), they have been maintained just as he planned them, with a small group of service buildings close by the mansion. You can visit about a dozen of these "dependencies" for a vivid picture of plantation life. And both George and Martha lie at rest in the tomb "at the foot of the vineyard enclosure," as he directed. Don't plan to hurry around Mount Vernon—allow yourself well over an hour to absorb this lovely memorial to our first president. It's open every day of the year, and it's usually jammed during the summer months, particularly on weekends and holidays. But go, even if you have to join the throngs during those times. Hours are 9 a.m. to 5 p.m., except for November through February when the gates close at 4 p.m. Admission is $4 for adults, $3.50 for those 62 and over, $2 for children 6 to 11; and there's a free Open House held the third Monday in February to celebrate Washington's birthday.

The **Mount Vernon Inn**, located at the gate entrance to the Mount Vernon estate, serves moderate-priced lunches (from $4) and dinners (from $12) in a colonial atmosphere. There's also a gift shop and snackbar.

Three miles west of Mount Vernon is **Woodlawn Plantation** (tel. 703/557-7880), the home built on property that Washington gave Nelly Custis (Martha's granddaughter) and her husband. Visiting hours are 9:30 a.m. to 4:30 p.m. every day except major holidays. Admission is $3 for adults, $2.50 for senior citizens, and $1.50 for students.

Still farther south of Alexandria (19 miles on the G. W. Parkway and U.S. 1) is **Gunston Hall** (tel. 703/550-9220), one of the most elegant of the historic houses in this area. Built between 1755 and 1758, the brick house was the residence of George Mason, who was often called the "Pen of the Revolution" for his work on the Fairfax Resolves, the first constitution of Virginia, and the Virginia Declaration of Rights (which formed the basis of the Federal Bill of Rights). He was one of the most active framers of the Constitution 200 years ago. Its formal interior is noted for its Palladian style and Chinese Chippendale woodwork. The gardens, built around a boxwood allee planted by George Mason, are a delight. It's open from 9:30 a.m. to 5 p.m. daily except Christmas; admission is $3 for adults, $2.50 for those over 60, $1 for students age 6 to 15.

The entire town of **Fredericksburg** (49 miles south of Alexandria on I-95 or U.S. 1) could qualify as a historic site, for since 1728 it has been witness to events momentous in the birth and development of the United States. James Monroe, Lafayette, and John Paul Jones all lived or visited here, and the **Rising Sun Tavern** was the scene of fiery political rallies before the Revolution. George Washington grew to manhood here, and it was here he chopped down that famous cherry tree. This is also the site of a major Civil War battle. An afternoon's stroll through the town with its many restored homes and public buildings (pick up self-guided walking tour information and the "Get a Taste of American History" brochure at the **Fredericksburg Visitor Center** at 706 Caroline St.; tel. 703/373-1776) will leave you feeling you should climb into a carriage or onto a horse to end it rather than into a 20th-century automobile! Aside from museums and historic buildings, you'll find craft shops, antique shops, and colonial-style restaurants to sustain that other-century atmosphere.

Not all history lies south of Alexandria, however. About 20 miles to the west, near the intersection of U.S. 29 and Va. 234, the **Manassas National Battlefield** was the scene of two major Civil War battles, both won by southern troops. There's an informative Visitors Center on the battlefield, and picnic facilities if you want to make a day of it. For full details on the battles and the park, write the National Park Service, Manassas National Battlefield Park, P.O. Box 1830, Manassas, VA 22110.

**WOLF TRAP FARM PARK:** Just 20 minutes away from Alexandria, the first national park dedicated to the performing arts, Wolf Trap Farm Park, has exciting ballet, opera, modern dance, jazz, symphony, and popular music concerts in its **Filene Center** from early June through the first part of September. Performances are in a Douglas fir amphitheater, and seats run $8 to $30 for evening shows. But a real bargain—and a delight in nice weather—are the lawn tickets which cost around $8. Bring a picnic if you like (a lot of Washingtonians and northern Virginians do and make it a lawn-party-type evening), or dine at the Meadows Restaurant on the grounds. To find out about current schedules, and program information, call 703/255-1900. Wolf Trap is at Vienna, just off I-495 (Capital Beltway at exit 10, then 2½ miles west on Va. 7). There's also an intimate year-round theater, The Barns of Wolf Trap, which presents drama, films, and music from jazz to opera. For current schedules, write 1624 Trap Rd., Vienna, VA 22180 (tel. 703/938-2404).

## 2. Williamsburg

Restoration of historic homes, public buildings, and even villages is not unique in the United States. Up and down the eastern seaboard and westward all the way to California, the history of the country has been preserved in buildings where much of it happened. But Colonial Williamsburg *is* unique—there's nothing quite like it anywhere else. It's almost as if, when you walk down Duke of Gloucester Street, the doors of the Raleigh Tavern may swing open at any moment and Patrick Henry emerge deep in heated discussion with Thomas Jefferson, so true to its original character has this town been restored. And though the faces under bonnets or above 18th-century shirts bear the stamp of today, the clothes, and even the manners, are those of the past. To visit Williamsburg is not to "do" it in the tourist sense, but to become surrounded by and immersed in a way of life that nurtured men who molded, and still mold by their works that have endured over the years, the future of this country.

Men in knee breeches and women in long-skirted, white-collared dresses walk the streets on their way to and from enterprises that engaged Williamsburg citizens back in 1699, when Virginia's capital was moved from Jamestown (the first settlement) up to the inland Middle Plantation, which was given the new name in honor of the reigning British monarch. Just as the town bustled then with the commerce of bootmaker, printer, wigmaker, and blacksmith, it is populated now with costumed artisans carrying on these same crafts. And even the crowds of visitors are fitting, for in the old days, when the courts were in session or the Assembly met, inns, taverns, and rooming houses swelled with outsiders.

After Williamsburg became the political and social center of the colony (it already had the 1693-chartered College of William and Mary, second in age only to Harvard University), the royal governor and Assembly laid out an orderly plan for its development on either side of mile-long Duke of Gloucester Street. A capitol building was erected at the east end of the street, and midway between it and the college, a magnificent Governor's Palace went up in a setting of formal gardens. Thomas Jefferson came in 1760 to study at the college and later met many of the men who would join him to put the growing spirit of independence into words that would pull together a nation from fragmented, widely separated groups of colonists: George Washington, Patrick Henry, Richard

Bland, and others. Patrick Henry led the fight against England's infamous Stamp Act Resolves. And in May of 1776 the Virginia Convention sent a resolution from Williamsburg to the Continental Congress that resulted in the Philadelphia declaration that the colonies were "absolved from all allegiance to the British Crown." George Mason's Virginia Declaration of Rights, which became the foundation of our constitutional Bill of Rights, was adopted here in June of the same year.

It was a vigorous, stimulating, sometimes rowdy town during those years, and remained so until the capital was moved again in 1780, this time to Richmond, still farther inland where it would be closer to the center of population and safer from attack by the British. After that, things settled down and Williamsburg's days of glory seemed ended forever, a feeling that intensified when federal troops occupied the area for over two years during the Civil War.

It wasn't until 1926, when the Rev. W. A. R. Goodwin, rector of Bruton Parish Church, infected John D. Rockefeller, Jr., with his own enthusiasm for restoring the colonial capital, that wheels were set in motion to give the American people this authentic, carefully researched and restored link with their past. Rockefeller hovered over the project right up to his death in 1960, pouring vast sums of money into the restoration of some 88 still-standing buildings and the faithful reconstruction of hundreds of other structures on their original foundations. And today the nonprofit Colonial Williamsburg Foundation, free from any affiliation with other organizations or governmental agencies, watches over the 173 acres, 276 costumed historical interpreters and craftspeople, 63 or more gardeners, and 3,460 other employees, meeting the $130 million annual operating costs through tourist income, investment returns from the permanent endowment left by Rockefeller, and donations.

What all this meticulous care and expenditure of money means to you and me is the opportunity to wander through this 18th-century "city" and literally feel the heartbeat of our nation when it was new in candlelight concerts at the Governor's Palace, fife and drum corps parades on Market Square Green, and in tavern meals that recall those long-ago menus.

**GETTING THERE:** Williamsburg can be reached by U.S. 60 and I-64 from the west, I-95 from the north and south. Greyhound and Trailways both have bus service, and Amtrak provides train service from Boston, New York, Philadelphia, Baltimore, and Washington, as well as excellent package tours. Newport News's Patrick Henry International Airport is only a 20-minute drive, and the Norfolk International Airport is a 50-minute drive.

**WHERE TO STAY:** Back in its colonial youth, Williamsburg boasted more than 30 inns, taverns, and "ordinaries" to accommodate the men of affairs who rode in from plantations, some several days away by horseback, to attend sessions of the legislature. It has been, from the first, a center of hospitality, and in that respect things haven't changed a bit in the last 200 years. The only difference is, of course, in size—today every road leading into Williamsburg is lined with motels; inside the city limits are scores more, offering a total of about 8,000 rooms; there are some 30 privately owned guesthouses; and those who carry their accommodations with them in the increasingly popular campers will find over a dozen campgrounds within easy driving distance. Whatever your budget, there's a suitable place to stay in Williamsburg.

In spite of this, I would again caution *don't come without a reservation.* Williamsburg's "season" is a long one—mid-March to early November—and visitors from all over the world throng its streets. An excellent way to be sure you will have a place to lay your head is to write for the directory of accommodations, attractions, camping, and dining facilities published by the Williamsburg–Williamsburg Area Tourism and Conference Bureau, P.O. Box GB, Williamsburg, VA 23187 (tel. 804/253-0192), under the title "Visitor's Guide to Virginia's Historic Triangle—Jamestown, Williamsburg and Yorktown." The Williamsburg Hotel and Motel Association (tel. toll free 800/446-9244, 800/582-8977 in Virginia) can also furnish current reservation information. And Colonial Williamsburg has a toll-free number for information and reservations for lodgings, dining, and group tours: 800/HISTORY. Or you may write Reservations Manager, Colonial Williamsburg, P.O. Box B, Williamsburg, VA 23187.

### The Best

If money is no object and you lean toward quiet elegance, there's just one place to stay, the **Williamsburg Inn,** Francis Street, Williamsburg, VA 23185 (tel. toll free 800/HISTORY). Owned and operated by the Colonial Williamsburg Foundation, the sprawling, whitewashed brick inn, located just one block from the restored area, will surround you with the graciousness of the famous 19th-century spa hotels; and its English Regency decor is a sure antidote to any 20th-century tensions you may have brought along. From the moment you step into the lobby, with a fireplace at each end and French doors across the entire rear wall, you'll begin to experience the relaxation that is the inn's keynote. Walk through those French doors and you're on a brick veranda that overlooks swimming pools, croquet grounds, tennis courts, lawn bowling greens, a putting green, a driving range, and two golf courses. Follow a courteous bellboy to your room and you'll find it spacious, modern in every convenience, furnished in the same Regency style as the public rooms. You might well fancy yourself a pampered guest at a Virginia country estate! Or maybe you'll feel like one of the kings and queens who've stayed here (Queen Elizabeth II and Prince Philip are on the royal heads-of-state guest list). U.S. Presidents Harry S. Truman and Dwight Eisenhower and foreign presidents also have enjoyed the inn's hospitality. Winston Churchill came to dinner, then reluctantly—audibly so—traveled on to Richmond.

If you stay in the main building, you'll find that rates for double occupancy start at $115, with a bed-sitting room costing $175 and a suite at $250. The most luxurious of the inn's rooms are in the newer (1972) Providence Hall, set in a wooded area just east of the main building. There's a private balcony or patio for each room, and each has a superb view. Double-occupancy tariff starts at $150, with suites ranging from $240 up.

There are several package plans at special rates: inquire about the Williamsburg Tavern Plan, Leisure Season, Colonial Weekends, and Tennis or Golf Plans.

Rates at the **Williamsburg Lodge,** a short distance away on South England Street, and only a little less elegant (the decor is modern, not Regency), are a more modest $87 to $150.

### Very Special

For a truly unique vacation experience, reserve at one of the **Colonial Houses** operated by the Williamsburg Inn, Francis Street, Williamsburg, VA 23185 (tel. toll free 800/HISTORY). There are 28 of them, ranging in size from a tiny cottage tucked away in a garden to a 16-room tavern. They're all in the Historic Area, furnished in period manner, and carry with them full guest privileges at the inn, at rates beginning at $110 for a room and $137 and up for a suite or complete house. For full details and reservations, call the toll-free number.

## Motels

The **Holiday Inn 1776 Resort,** Va. 60 Bypass Road, Williamsburg, VA 23185 (tel. 804/220-1776, or toll free 800/238-8000), has over 200 rooms in a beautiful, 42-acre woodland setting. Both the architecture and decor of all rooms reflect a colonial atmosphere, and some suites have ornamental fire-places. There's an Olympic-size pool, a par-three golf course, and four all-weather tennis courts. You can dine by candlelight in their restaurant and have drinks in the colonial taproom. Rates for doubles run from $50 off-season (November to March) to $95 in high season (April to October).

The **Gov. Spottswood,** 1508 Richmond Rd., Williamsburg, VA 23185 (tel. 804/229-6444, or toll free 800/368-1244, 800/572-4567 in Virginia), has 17 kitchen units and in-room coffee in the remainder of its 58 rooms. Rates are a moderate $44 to $90, and there's a pool and playground on the wooded premises, a coffeeshop and restaurant just across the street. It's one mile from the Historic Area.

The **Motor House** is operated by Colonial Williamsburg Hotel Properties, Inc. (tel. toll free 800/HISTORY), and is located at the Visitor Center. This sprawling, casual-contemporary complex is ideal for families. Doubles cost $75 and up; corner studios are $90 and up.

The **Cascades** is operated by Colonial Williamsburg Hotel Properties, Inc. (tel. toll free 800/HISTORY), and is located behind the Motor House at the Visitor Center. These rustic two-story buildings are located in a wooded area and offer mini-suites, all in a contemporary design. Doubles cost $88 and up. There are picture-window views from every room and facilities for swimming, horseshoe pitching, table tennis, badminton, a nine-hole putting green, an 18-hole miniature-golf course, a playground, and shuffleboard are available, as well as guest privileges at the Golden Horseshoe Club which has two golf courses. Two restaurants serve the Cascades and Motor House: The Cascades, specializing in Chesapeake Bay delicacies, and a cafeteria grill for quick service.

A welcome new addition to the Williamsburg scene is the spiffy 210-room **Days Inn East,** 90 Old York Rd. (P.O. Drawer GQ), Williamsburg, VA 23187 (tel. 804/253-6444). Newest of three area Days Inns, it nestles in a quiet, woodsy setting on Va. 199, across from Water Country USA. Youngsters under 12 dine free with adult guests in the casual, candlelit dining room, which showcases old Williamsburg and southern delicacies. And their parents can enjoy live weekend entertainment, late-night Friday to Sunday dancing. Doubles range from $49 to $57 June through September and drop considerably after that. Add $3 for each child under 18; those under 1 stay free.

In the super-budget category, the three-story, 169-room **Motel 6,** 3030 Richmond Rd., Williamsburg, VA 23185 (tel. 804/565-2710), is popular with travelers seeking clean, comfortable "no-frills" lodging. This doesn't mean austerity by a long shot: there's a swimming pool, and a color TV (for a nominal nightly charge). A nearby restaurant is open from 7 a.m. to 11 p.m. Doubles range from $25 to $29. For children 3 to 11, there's a $1-per-child cost, and lodging is free for those under 3. Cribs are also free. Each additional person over 11 may stay for $2 nightly. This fast-growing national chain consistently keeps its rates down and offers a great buy for the travel dollar. From I-64, eastbound or westbound, take Va. 646 south (Lightfoot exit) to U.S. 60 east (about two miles).

## Campgrounds

Located 4½ miles west of Williamsburg on U.S. 60, **Williamsburg Campsites,** 6967 Richmond, Williamsburg, VA 23185 (tel. 804/564-3101), has 300 sites and there's no charge for water or electric hookups. The swimming pool is also free and there are hot showers, toilets, a laundromat, grocery, and disposal station; $11.50 minimum for up to four people. Additional persons, $1.50 each; $2 extra for sewer. Rates are subject to change. Open year round and just across the road from Williamsburg Pottery (Exit 53 off I-64).

The **Jamestown Beach Campsite**, on Va. 31 South (P.O. Box CB), Williamsburg, VA 23185 (tel. 804/229-7609 or 229-3300), is set on 200 lovely acres along the James River, just 3½ miles from Williamsburg on Va. 31 south. There are 600 sites, plus amusement equipment, swimming in the pool or river, modern rest rooms, showers, miniature golf, groceries, and ice. Rates are $10 and up for up to four people, $1.50 for each additional; trailer hookups are extra.

Four miles west of Williamsburg on Va. 646 between U.S. 60 and I-64, the **Best Holiday Trav-L-Park Fair Oaks**, Rte. 9, Box 294A, Williamsburg, VA 23185 (tel. 804/565-2101), has 327 camping sites in a very attractive open shaded site. There are 160 sewer hookups, and amenities include a grocery store, firewood, laundry, tiled hot showers, a pump station, and metered LP gas. There's a pool, wading pool, fishing pond, recreation hall, playgrounds, four sheltered pavilions, nature and bike trails, and a mini-golf course. Clubs and caravans are welcome. The site is near the popular Williamsburg Pottery outlet shops (show $50 or $100 in pottery sales receipts for camping fee discounts at certain seasons). Rates are $9 to $11 nightly for a group of four; extra persons pay $1. Reservations are strongly recommended at this popular, well-maintained site, which remains open all year.

**WHERE TO EAT:** "This is the place to come if you really like good food," a Williamsburg native told me—and he's right. Good eating has been a tradition here since the early days, and you can find almost any cuisine your appetite fancies, in settings as varied as a colonial tavern and a New York deli.

### True Elegance

The **Williamsburg Inn** (tel. toll free 800/HISTORY) ranks first again, with its handsome **Regency Room** highlighted by bronze and crystal chandeliers, hand-painted Chinese wall paintings, tranquil green walls, and curved windows. There's dancing, and gentlemen are, of course, required to wear a jacket and tie at dinner. Breakfast in this elegant setting can be a simple repast for about $7, or you can go all the way with a champagne breakfast for two for $30. And somehow, a champagne breakfast seems appropriate! Lunch consists of sandwiches, salads, fresh fish or meat and vegetable plates ($8 and up).

But it's at dinner that the Regency Room outdoes itself—both cuisine and wine list are internationally respected. You might start with bouquet of shrimp suprême or Virginia ham on Boston lettuce with condiments, move on to lobster bisque Chantilly, then select from a dazzling array of seafoods—perhaps the croustade of lobster au whisky—or French lamb chops with minted pears from the grill. The salads are true creations, and rolls and breads are all fresh baked and of the melt-in-your-mouth variety. Desserts (if you're still hanging in there) include an extraordinary list of homemade pies, cakes, pastries, and such exotic ice creams (also homemade and *very* rich) as black walnut and rum (made with the real thing, of course). Entrees will run $19 to $26 on the à la carte menu. All in all, it's a rare epicurean experience. Reservations required.

The **Bay Room** at the **Williamsburg Lodge** (tel. toll free 800/HISTORY) also serves breakfast, lunch, and dinner, and features fresh seafood. On Friday and Saturday evenings its renowned Chesapeake Bay Feast draws hosts of regulars, as well it should. The overflowing buffet has a full array of appetizers—seafood soups and chowders, clams on the half shell, steamed shrimp, etc.—and there are as many seafood main dishes as the imagination can conjure up, plus sugar-cured Virginia ham and prime ribs of beef, with side dishes like spoon bread and European-blend vegetables. Each trip to the buffet will doubtless bring on an agony of indecision, and my advice is to keep your helpings small and try to sample some of each. The cost is $16 for adults, $10 for children, and beverages and desserts are extra (there's a very complete list of both alcoholic and nonalcoholic drinks, and try to save room for one of the yummy desserts.) The Feast is served from 6 to 9:15 p.m. Call for reservations.

The Hunt Breakfast Buffet at the **Cascades Restaurant,** Information Center Drive, is as sumptuous as the Chesapeake Bay Feast, only here it's early-morning fare. As one Williamsburg devotee advised, "You really should starve the day before so you can appreciate it fully!" Served Monday through Saturday from 7:30 to 10 a.m., the buffet is a modern-day version of the old plantation breakfast, with eggs, sausage, bacon, ham, fried chicken, grits, scalloped oysters, muffins, etc. Again there's no limit to the times you can visit the table, and the $6 ($5 for children) charge includes beverage. They also have an equally good Sunday brunch from 8:30 a.m. to 2:30 p.m. at $8.50 for adults, $6 for children.

## The Taverns

Part of the fun of a Williamsburg visit is eating in one of the three restored taverns that specialize in 18th-century food served by waiters in knee breeches and gaiters. You can eat in the garden at two, and have dinner by candlelight at all three. Prices are surprisingly moderate. Dinner reservations are required and can be made at all three taverns by calling 229-2141.

**Josiah Chowning's Tavern,** adjacent to Market Square (tel. 229-2141), serves lunch and dinner in the garden when weather permits. The Brunswick stew that is traditional here is $4.50 at lunch, $10.25 at dinner. Welsh rabbit ($5) is also a specialty, but prime ribs, ham, and barbecued pork ribs are all very, very good. Breads and desserts come from the same bake shop that serves the inn (true of all three taverns). But the best part of your meal at Chowning's might well be after it's over, when the "Gambols" begin at 9 p.m. You can sit back, order up a clay pipe exactly as Patrick Henry or Thomas Jefferson did, and enjoy the "diversions"—balladeers and games (backgammon, if you like). In fact, even if you dine elsewhere, you can amble over for the Gambols, only don't amble late—seating is on a strictly first-come, first-served basis. Lunch is from 11:30 a.m. to 3:30 p.m. The three dinner sittings are at 5, 6:45, and 8:30 p.m.

**Christiana Campbell's Tavern,** Waller Street (tel. 229-2141), was one of George Washington's favorites. Brunch (from 10 a.m. to 2:30 p.m.) includes such plantation fare as pecan waffles, country sausage, specialty omelets, and chicken dishes, costing from $5.25 to $7.50. Ale, beer, lemonade, cider, and iced tea are served, and dinner (with strolling musicians) is 5:30 to 9:30 p.m. Spoon bread, muffins, and homemade fig ice cream add just the right exclamation point.

**READER'S TAVERN SELECTION: "Christiana Campbell's Tavern** gives out their recipe for sweet potato muffins—in fact, they're already printed and readily available. We found 9 o'clock Sunday morning the loveliest time to visit areas of restored Williamsburg, before the crowds and while waiting to have that nice brunch at Christiana's" (G. Salassi, Baton Rouge, La.).

At the **King's Arms Tavern,** on Duke of Gloucester Street across from the Raleigh Tavern (tel. 229-2141), your costumed waiter will likely be a college student—it's a tradition that dates from the beginning of the restoration. Lunch (it might be Yorkshire meat pie or Virginia ham) is from 11:30 a.m. to 2:30 p.m.

Dinner hours are 5:30 to 9:30 p.m. The evening menu includes Cornish game hen, filet mignon stuffed with oysters, and colonial game pie (venison, duck, and rabbit), with prices ranging from $12 to $16.

## Other Choices

The **Old Chickahominy House,** 1211 Jamestown Rd. (tel. 229-4689), used to be in an old house on the river of that name, but the new location has every bit as much charm as the original. Dale and Maxine Henderson serve breakfast and lunch from 8:30 a.m. to 3 p.m. in a country setting of 18th-century antiques, many of which you can buy and take home if you've a mind. Besides the things for sale in the dining room, there's a large adjoining shop full of unusual items. Service is family style at large tables which seat from six to ten people (I found it a neat way to meet interesting people) and reservations are not necessary. You can breakfast simply on Miss Melinda's pancakes or fill up on the grits, hot biscuits, and coffee or tea. My own lunch favorite is Miss Melinda's special, which starts with a fruit salad, followed by a cup of Brunswick stew, smoked Virginia ham on hot biscuits, homemade pie (try the buttermilk pie for something different), and a beverage. They'll sell you Brunswick stew to take home or smoked Virginia ham, cured bacon and sausage, and water-ground cornmeal. Prices are moderate to cheap. It's hard to say whether the charm of this place or the food comes out on top!

**Beethoven's Inn,** 467 Merrimac Trail, in Williamsburg's Be-Lo Center on Va. 143 (tel. 229-7069), is that New York deli I mentioned, and during its short life it has attained a place in the hearts of locals that's just short of beloved. About six years ago Jim Wesson decided he'd had it with the business world in Washington, D.C., and moved his family here for a pressure-free lifestyle. True to his "quality of life" philosophy, Jim will tell you, "this is the most personality-oriented place you'll run into." He serves the deli food he loves himself, plays only his favorite classical records (most of them works of the great Ludwig, naturally), and even has a modest library of books for sale, but only those by authors of his personal choice. In the pleasant, red-carpeted dining room whose walls are hung with signed photos of performing artists and writers on one side and oil portraits of you-know-who, Mark Twain, Edgar Allan Poe, and the like on the other, you're likely to see students, college faculty, and local residents all munching happily on thick sandwiches of pastrami, liverwurst, and knockwurst with sauerkraut, or smiling over the superb onion soup that's a house specialty. There is even New York cream cheesecake that rivals my Manhattan favorite. And like its "up nawth" counterparts, it has a take-out service. Reservations aren't necessary—come any time from 11 a.m. to 8 p.m., until 9 p.m. on Friday and Saturday. Prices are in the $3 to $10 range.

A longtime favorite with both townspeople and William and Mary faculty members is the **Green Leafe Café,** 765 Scotland St. (tel. 220-3405). The rustic oak interior is an indoor garden (true to its name), accented by stained-glass windows from old Richmond homes that have yielded to the wrecker's ball. The cuisine is continental, ranging from veal parmesan to sausage lasagne to vegetarian dishes, and there are daily specials. Prices are in the $5 to $10 range. Hours are 4 to 9 p.m. daily. There's a late-night menu after 9 p.m.

Executive chef and co-owner Marcel Desaulniers has garnered wide acclaim as one of the up-and-coming new breed of American chefs for the fine contemporary cuisine of the **Trellis Café, Restaurant and Grill,** on Duke of Gloucester Street (tel. 804/229-8610), in Merchants Square just outside the Historic District. Personable, award-winning Marcel, who grew up in a French-Canadian family in Woonsocket, Rhode Island, insists that all ingredients be fresh and "impeccable." His seasonal menus change four times a year to take advantage of the freshest ingredients the region has to offer: local catfish, sea scallops, Virginia ham and peanuts, duck. And from what he modestly calls a "simple" cooking style emerge such wonders as grilled sea trout filet with tomatoes and cactus leaves on jalapeño chili rice; sautéed shad roe with lump backfin crabmeat, cucumbers, leeks, and scallion butter; sautéed venison with white trumpet mushrooms, Barlette onions, and chive butter on chive and roasted-garlic fettuccine; freshly shucked oysters and Shiitake mushrooms served in warm brioche. Simple? Simply wonderful! Surprisingly, dinner entrees range from $11 to $16. It's possible to have a salad, entree, and one of the most expensive desserts and stay under $20 per person. The average lunch—which runs to quiche, burgers, grilled chicken, and nutty-tuna sandwiches—costs about $7. "We're talking basic food at lunch," chef Marcel explains. But it's basic with superbly imaginative touches.

The Trellis has five rooms, each with a distinctive personality: the Café Bar, awash with Mexican and Italian tiles; the elegant Garden Room, with a lavish Venetian glass chandelier and mirrors; the Grill Room, with handmade oak tables and an open-hearth Texas mesquite grill; the Vault Room, which gives the impression of dining inside a wine barrel; and the airy Trellis Room, with its ceiling, booths, and floors of century-old pine from a Gimbels department store in Philadelphia. Sit wherever most pleases your fancy, but don't miss this one!

## Budget Eating

For a good, inexpensive meal or snack, head for the **Marketplace** in the Campus Center of the College of William and Mary. It's a popular "gourmetisserie" of food bars selling pizza, burgers, hot dogs, submarine sandwiches, ice cream, and the like.

**WHAT TO SEE:** The **Colonial Williamsburg Visitor Center,** Colonial Parkway and Va. 132 (tel. 229-1000)—just follow the signs posted all over town—is the place to start. A 35-minute color film, titled *Williamsburg—The Story of a Patriot,* is shown continuously until 6 p.m. each day, and do take time to see it. This is the best possible introduction and shouldn't be missed.

Three types of admission tickets are available for Colonial Williamsburg attractions. The popular **Patriot's Pass,** good for one year from date of purchase, provides unlimited admission to all exhibition buildings, the historical film, Carter's Grove Plantation, Governor's Palace, Public Hospital of 1773, DeWitt Wallace Gallery, the one-hour guided Patriot's Tour, Abby Aldrich Rockefeller Folk Art Center, and Bassett Hall (Williamsburg home of the Rockefellers). It costs $24.50 for adults, $12.25 for ages 6 to 12.

The **Royal Governor's Pass,** good for up to four consecutive days, provides admission to all exhibits in the Historic Area, including the Governor's Palace, DeWitt Wallace Gallery, and Patriot's Tour. Cost is $19.50 for adults, $9.75 for ages 6 to 12.

The **Basic Admission Ticket** admits you to up to 12 exhibition buildings in the Historic Area, plus reduced admission to the Governor's Palace, DeWitt Wallace Gallery, Carter's Grove, Folk Art Center, Bassett Hall, and the Patriot's Tour. It costs $14.50 for adults, $7.25 for ages 6 to 12. Major credit cards may be used to purchase all passes and tours.

All exhibition buildings are open from 9 a.m. to 5 p.m. in summer and 9:30 a.m. to 4:30 p.m. in winter. Some shops have evening hours during July and August.

For more complete information on points of interest before you come, contact Amanda Drew, Colonial Williamsburg Foundation, P.O. Box C, Williamsburg, VA 23187, or phone the Visitors Center (tel. 804/229-1000).

The foundation operates a special bus which circles the Historic Area, and your admission ticket allows you to catch it at any of the designated stops and ride as far as you like.

In fact, going the full circle is a good way to begin, after which you can get off at the first of the nine stops, spend as much time as you like, then reboard to ride to the next one. There are also horse-drawn carriages and wagon rides. Occasionally there are oxcart rides too. For the children, ask about the Once Upon a Town Tours (for ages 4 to 6), Time Trippers (for ages 7 to 10), and the Young Apprentice Tours (for ages 11 to 14).

Here are not-to-be-missed highlights:

The **Raleigh Tavern** was the scene of heated political debates, rollicking nighttime gaiety, and grand balls (in the Apollo Room).

The **Capitol** is one of the reconstructed buildings, but is faithful in detail to the original modified Renaissance style. This is where so much pre-Revolution political activity took place.

The **Governor's Palace** was home to seven royal governors and both Patrick Henry and Thomas Jefferson when they served as governor of the new state. What you see is a reconstruction of the original, which was destroyed by fire in 1781; Jefferson's detailed floor plan of 1779 was followed to ensure accuracy in the reconstruction.

The craft shops scattered throughout the Historic Area are functioning work museums, where costumed artisans use hand tools and colonial-vintage methods. There's an apothecary, basketmaker, miller, weaver, musical instrument maker, harnessmaker, and a long list of others.

Largest Williamsburg reconstruction in 51 years, the **Public Hospital** of 1773, which was opened in 1985, was the first American institution devoted to treating mental illness.

The **DeWitt Wallace Decorative Arts Gallery,** also added in 1985, was made possible in large measure by a gift of the founders of *The Reader's Digest,* as was the Public Hospital. Designed by renowned architect Kevin Roche, it displays over 8,000 priceless antiques and is one of the world's greatest collections of decorative arts.

The **Abby Aldrich Rockefeller Folk Art Center,** just outside the restored area, houses fascinating traditional arts ranging from paintings, drawings, and furniture to pottery, weathervanes, and toys.

And don't leave out the beautiful old walled campus of the **College of William and Mary**—look especially for the **Christopher Wren Building,** oldest academic building in America (1695) still in use.

Colonial Williamsburg is open year round, but if you can get there during the quiet months of January and February you'll not only avoid the crowds, you'll have the benefit of many reduced rates and special programs.

**SIGHTS AND SITES NEARBY:** Jamestown and Jamestown Festival Park (write: Superintendent, Colonial National Historical Park, P.O. Box 210, Yorktown, VA 23690; tel. 804/898-3400) are six miles away by way of the Colonial Parkway. Admission to the island is $5 per car, and the entrance gate is open from 8:30 a.m. to 4:30 p.m. Jamestown was the first permanent English settlement in America (May 1607), capital of the Virginia colony from 1607 to 1699, and the place where Capt. John Smith became acquainted with the young Pocahontas through her father, Powhatan. Stop at the visitor center for a film, tour information, and exhibits, before setting out to see the old Church Tower (1639) and other historic sites in the old village. The Festival Park is a year-round exhibit that includes replicas of the *Susan Constant* (you can go on board and poke around), the *Godspeed,* and the *Discovery,* the three tiny sailing ships in which

Jamestown's colonists crossed the Atlantic. The latter two are 1984 seaworthy replacements of earlier vessels. There's also a replica of the 1607 Jamestown fort and an Indian lodge. Slated for completion by early 1989 is a $2.8-million museum expansion devoted to the native Indians and early settlers. At that time the park will be renamed Jamestown Settlement. Open from 9 a.m. to 5 p.m. every day. Admission is $5 for adults, $2.50 for ages 6 to 12.

When Cornwallis surrendered at **Yorktown** in 1781, the fight for American independence was finally over. The free National Park Service visitors center (open 8:30 a.m. to 6 p.m. in the summer months; closes at 5:30 p.m. Labor Day through March) has guided bus and walking tours of the battlefield daily, as well as a film and a lot of interesting exhibits. The Yorktown Victory Center puts on an absolutely smashing Sound and Light show to dramatize the military goings-on here, for which there is a small charge.

Just for fun, visit Europe on this side of the Atlantic at **Busch Gardens, The Old Country,** P.O. Drawer FC, Williamsburg, VA 23187 (tel. 804/253-3350), located just three miles east of Williamsburg. It's a 360-acre family entertainment amusement park that re-creates 17th-century villages of England, France, Italy, and Germany, and throws in shows, a celebrity concert series, restaurants, and rides like the famous Loch Ness Monster. Billed as the tallest, fastest, fiercest roller coaster in the world, the Loch Ness Monster has double interlocking loops and a 114-foot drop where speed reaches 70 mph. New shows are presented each year. (In 1986 *Journey into Music,* a Broadway-style musical revue, and *The Enchanted Laboratory,* a computer-animated show featuring magnificent special effects and audio-animatronic characters were introduced.) Open weekends from April 4 to May 15 and September 12 to November 1, and daily from May 16 to September 7. One-day tickets (age 3 and up) are $16, two days cost $19, and there's a reduced rate after 5 p.m.

**Carter's Grove,** a 1755 restored plantation house that has been called "the most beautiful house in America," overlooks the James River just six miles to the southeast on U.S. 60. It's open daily March through November; $6.50 for adults, $3 for children to 12.

The **James River** between Williamsburg and Richmond might well be called "plantation row," since both Va. 5 and 10, on its north and south sides, are dotted with restored homes, many of which you can visit for a small fee. Highway markers are posted all along the way, giving directions for turning off the main road to reach them. Two of the more interesting ones are Shirley Plantation and Berkeley Plantation.

## 3. Richmond

The state capital since 1780, Richmond is 49 miles northwest of Williamsburg on I-64, and is well worth a day—or several more. It's rich in history—in 1865, for instance, after four years of almost constant attack by federal troops, it was evacuated and burned by its own citizens!

**THE SIGHTS:** The **Visitors Center** at 1700 Robin Hood Rd., Exit 14 at the intersection of I-95 and I-64 (tel. 804/358-5511), will point you in the direction of the historic and cultural attractions, shopping areas, and hotels (reservations may be made at the Visitors Center).

The following are sightseeing highlights: The **Capitol Building** (designed by Thomas Jefferson in 1785) at Capitol Square; the **Edgar Allan Poe Museum,** 1914 E. Main St. (he lived in Richmond for many years); the **Museum of the Confederacy,** 12th and Clay (it was Jefferson Davis's Confederate White House); **Hollywood Cemetery,** 412 S. Cherry St. at Albemarle Street (final resting place of Jefferson Davis, James Monroe, and other historic figures, as well as some 18,000 Confederate soldiers); the **Virginia Museum of Fine Arts;** and the **Science Museum of Virginia,** with its unique Planetarium-Space Theater.

If you're in the market for entertainment, be sure to check what's doing at the **Carpenter Center,** 525 E. Grace St. (tel. 804/782-3900), where performances range from Broadway shows to Shakespearean plays to jazz concerts to dance programs. The beautifully restored 1928 theater is well worth a stop even if you don't take in a performance.

Richmond is one of the few cities in this country whose Convention and Visitors Bureau offers **guided tours,** and this is one of the best ways to see the city, especially if time is limited. Foreign-language guides and tours of nearby destinations such as Williamsburg can be arranged with advance notice. For detailed information before you come, contact the Richmond Convention and Visitors Bureau, 300 E. Main St., Richmond, VA 23219 (tel. 804/782-2777).

### Especially for Families

If you're traveling with youngsters, they'll probably insist that you veer off the historical-cultural circuit one day and head for **Kings Dominion,** Doswell, VA 23047 (tel. 804/876-5000). You'll be glad you did, for there's fun for everybody at this sprightly 800-acre family-entertainment complex just 20 miles north of Richmond via I-95. In seven theme areas, you can enjoy over 100 rides, more than a dozen live-entertainment shows, dozens of shops, a Wild Animal Safari, and encounters with the Smurfs, Fred Flintstone, and Yogi Bear and his pals. Dominating the site is the Kings Dominion "landmark," a 330-foot Eiffel Tower replica. Thrill seekers can board such challenging rides as the Berserker, a big Viking ship that offers swooping 360°-loop rides, and Shockwave, the East Coast's first standup roller coaster. Brand new is the splashy Kids-Family water attraction area. The park is open daily June through Labor Day, selected weekends in spring and fall. Inquire locally for hours and rates, which vary with the season.

**WHERE TO STAY:** One of the South's most heralded "new" hotels is the magnificently restored 1895 **Jefferson Sheraton Hotel,** a National Historic Landmark at Franklin and Adams Streets, Richmond, VA 23220 (tel. 804/788-8000, or toll free 800/325-3535). Upon entering the massive, fanciful white brick structure, you're greeted in the soaring Palm Court Lobby Rotunda by the famed Edward Valentine statue of the hotel's "patron saint," Thomas Jefferson; it stands under a luminous stained-glass skylight. Just off the Rotunda is Richmond's new favorite rendezvous spot, T.J.'s restaurant and bar. In the Jefferson's specialty restaurant, Le Maire, guests dine in seven intimate formal rooms, one a library with the hotel's original leather-bound book collection. Fare is primarily continental, with a few regional touches. Another historic touch—the restaurant is named for the third president's French maître d'hôtel, who introduced cooking with wine to the fledgling nation. And if you're fond of french fries, you can thank Mr. Jefferson, who reputedly became captivated with them in France and brought the preparation back home with him. The hotel's 274 spacious rooms and suites are pleasingly decorated in mulberry, dusty rose, and mint green, and beautifully appointed with period reproduction furnishings. Doubles range from $99 to $109, and attractively priced weekend packages are available.

The **Hyatt Richmond at Brookfield,** 6624 W. Broad St., Richmond, VA 23230 (tel. 804/285-1234, or toll free 800/228-9000), has a very attractive suburban location in a west-end park just off I-64. There's a resort-like setting, indoor/outdoor pools, lighted tennis courts, a sauna, jogging course, and playground. All rooms have free HBO/CNN/ESPN cable, and parking is also complimentary. Lightfoot's offers live entertainment and dancing, and Hugo's is the elegant main dining room. Rates, double occupancy, range from $99 to $113, $123 on the Regency Club concierge floor. On weekends, rates can drop to $65 a night, single or double occupancy.

The always-reliable Days Inn chain has four locations in the area, including the **Richmond Days Inn,** W. Broad Street at 2100 Dickens Rd., Richmond, VA 28230 (tel. 804/282-3300, or toll free 800/325-2525). It's a handsome seven-story 185-room brick structure with some extra-large rooms, a gift shop, and a pool. Health center privileges are offered, and there's a restaurant nearby. Nonsmoking rooms are available, and some rooms are equipped for wheelchair travelers. Double rates range from $40 to $48; add $5 for each additional adult, $1 for each child under 18. Also ask about special features for business travelers.

If you're as fond of guesthouses as I am, you'll be delighted to know about the **Carrington Row Inn,** in the historic Church Hill district, 2309 W. Broad St., Richmond, VA 23223 (tel. 804/343-7005). In adjoining 1818 rowhouses, four guest rooms, two with private bath or fireplace, are lovingly furnished in period decor with four-poster twin, full, or queen-size mahogany beds. If privacy is your preference, request the upper level, which has its own sitting room adjacent to two guest rooms. Guests are welcomed with a glass of sherry before a fireplace which lends a welcome glow to nippy evenings. Continental breakfast is served each morning. Doubles with shared bath are in the $60 range, and with private bath about $75. One night's deposit is required to hold a reservation.

The owners, Dr. and Mrs. Abbott, also operate the equally engaging **Catlin-Abbott House,** another Federal structure, at 2304 E. Broad St. (tel. 804/780-3746).

**READER'S ACCOMMODATION SUGGESTION:** "For travelers who want to stay over in Richmond, meet someone local, and enjoy a home atmosphere, I can heartily recommend the guesthouse reservation service of **Lyn Benson,** who can book you into a private home, guest cottages, or apartments in Richmond. She has a variety of accommodations and neighborhoods and is very nice about trying to find just what you're looking for, and almost all her listings include a full breakfast. Rates are comparable to or lower than motels. Her address is Lyn M. Benson, Bensonhouse of Richmond, P.O. Box 15131, Richmond, VA 23227 (tel. 804/648-7560)" (S. Caliri, Wayne, N.J.).

# WHERE TO EAT: One of the Southeast's fastest-growing cities, Richmond offers an almost baffling choice of excellent dining rooms. For a good rundown, pick up the latest "Dining & Shopping Guide" from the Convention and Visitors Bureau, 300 E. Main St.

The **Tobacco Company Restaurant,** 12th and Cary Streets (tel. 804/782-9555), one of the city's abidingly popular dining spots, is ensconced in an 1870s tobacco warehouse in historic waterfront Shockhoe Slip. It's an amalgam of period furnishings, stained-glass windows, vintage signs, and an old brass elevator, guarded by a stern-faced carved wooden Indian. The first level, in an "old Richmond" atmosphere, encompasses an action-packed cocktail area with live entertainment; if you're in a quieter mood, head for the more sedate Victorian Lounge. The second- and third-floor dining rooms overlook a large airy atrium filled with suspended plants and a massive chandelier. Service is deft and friendly, and food choices include such delightful specialties as applewood-smoked chicken with rice pilaf, chutney-baked apple, and green peppercorn sauce ($12), and Coho salmon, broiled and served with avocado-lime butter, or poached and served with red pepper butter ($11). Chef Otto Bernet offers a to-die-for dessert buffet of luscious pastries, cakes, tortes, seasonal fruits, and cheeses for $4. Salads, fruit plates, sandwiches, burgers, omelets, and stir-fry specialties highlight a moderately priced luncheon menu. To commemorate downtown's continuous building projects, there's a Construction Lunch Buffet for $3.50 from 11:30 a.m. to 2:30 p.m. Monday through Friday. And chef Otto is right in there again, with such wicked excesses as trifle and Mary Martin's Cheese Pie, both steals at $2. Dinner hours are 5:30 to 10:30 p.m. Sunday to Friday, to midnight on Saturday. There's a hugely popular Sunday brunch from 10:30 a.m. to 2 p.m.

If you have a sense of history or if you just like good food in pleasant surroundings, make time for lunch or dinner at **Traveller's,** 707 E. Franklin St. (tel. 804/644-3976). It's located where the famed Confederate general's horse was stabled, and you'll enter through the basement of Lee's Richmond home, now a cocktail lounge. The rather limited menu runs to steaks, beef, and fresh seafoods. It's just a very relaxing place, and costs are moderate to somewhat expensive. Lunch is served from 11:30 a.m. to 2:30 p.m. Monday through Friday, and dinner is from 6 to 10 p.m. Monday through Saturday. Reservations are a good idea.

Since way back in 1903 residents have been flocking to Richmond's oldest continuously operating restaurant, the **Chesterfield Tea Room,** 900 W. Franklin St. (tel. 804/359-0474)—and with good reason! It's one of those wonderfully welcoming spots where you feel as if time has been reversed, or at least stopped in its tracks. Traditional southern fare is offered, along with newer "Williamsburg style" selections of seafood, veal, chicken, and beef. Saturday night is a favorite with romantics—the room is candlelit and classical music is gently played. Lunch is served from 11 a.m. to 2 p.m., and dinner from 4 to 8 p.m. Monday through Friday; that magical Saturday dinner is on from 5 to 9 p.m.; and a full-course dinner is offered from 11 a.m. to 3 p.m. Prices are in the modest $6 to $12 range. Reservations are suggested.

Richmond also boasts one of the South's most acclaimed rib houses, the cozy neighborhood **Commercial Café** at 111 N. Robinson St. (tel. 804/355-8206). Co-owners Ken Scott and Skip Doane (he's also the chef) jealously guard the recipe for their tangy, fruit-based sauce—and estimate that they sell over 40 tons of ribs a year. At dinner, serious eaters can order the pig-out plate for $14, a feast for $11.75, dinner for $9.75, or a "taster" for $7.50. There's a good choice of chicken, barbecue, ribs, and combination platters, along with barbecue and country Virginia ham sandwiches. Prices drop somewhat at lunch. So popular is the Commercial's fare that the owners recently added other locations in the trendy new 6th Street Marketplace.

**AN EXCURSION TO PETERSBURG:** Due south on I-95 at exit 3 is Petersburg, yet another Virginia town involved in the early history of this country. It's worth a visit to see the beautiful Victorian **Centre Hill Mansion,** 400 E. Washington St. (parking at Tabb and Adams Streets), and **Old Blandford Church,** 321 S. Crater Rd., with its 15 Tiffany glass windows. You can wander through the **Siege Museum,** 15 W. Bank St., which depicts the ten-month siege of the city during the Civil War; the **National Battlefield Park,** off Va. 36; the **U.S. Army Quartermaster Museum,** at nearby Fort Lee on Va. 36; the old **Farmers Bank;** and the rather eccentric early 1800s **Trapezium House,** 244 N. Market St., with its interior completely devoid of right angles. Admission costs to Centre Hill, Old Blandford Church, and the Siege Museum are $1 for adults, 50¢ for children ages 6 to 12, for each visit. Trapezium House admission is 50¢ for adults, 35¢ for children ages 6 to 12. Hours at all these attractions are 9 a.m. to 5 p.m. Monday through Saturday, 12:30 to 5 p.m. on Sunday, and they're closed only on Christmas and New Year's Days.

You can write ahead for maps and brochures to the **Petersburg Information Services,** P.O. Box 2107 (FP), Petersburg, VA 23804 (tel. 804/733-2400), or drop by the **Visitors Center** at the Farmers Bank, 19 Bollingbrook St. (tel. 804/733-2402).

# 4. Tidewater Virginia and the Eastern Shore

To Virginians, the term "Tidewater" means that whole area around the mouth of the great Chesapeake Bay, which stretches all the way up to Delaware. It encompasses Norfolk, an important port and U.S. naval base; Portsmouth, with its huge shipyard; Hampton and historic old Fort Monroe; Newport News, home of the world's largest shipbuilding company; and Virginia Beach, one of the most popular beach resorts in the Southeast. The 14-mile-long stretch where the Elizabeth, York, James, and Nansemond Rivers come together into the bay is known as Hampton Roads and is one of the best natural harbors in the world.

The Eastern Shore, across the bay from Tidewater (accessible only by ferry until the 17.6-mile-long Chesapeake Bay Bridge-Tunnel opened in 1964 to connect Cape Charles with Norfolk), has superb surf fishing, with charter boats going out in fleets for the albacore, channel bass, white marlin, bluefish, and other fish that populate waters offshore around uninhabited barrier islands. Pre-Revolution towns, wild ponies near Chincoteague, fishing villages, large strawberry farms, and some of the best oysters and clams to be found on the coast combine to make it a fascinating area to visit.

**Virginia Beach** makes an ideal base from which to explore both these interesting areas and has the added benefit of an ocean dip at the beginning or end of any sightseeing foray, even in the fall (you can swim comfortably until late September or early October). Driving is also easier from the beach, away from Norfolk's traffic congestion, and all points of interest can be reached on easy day trips. In case you prefer **Norfolk,** however, I've also included several lodging and dining suggestions in this fine old city.

**GETTING THERE:** Two excellent highways (U.S. 58 and U.S. 60) plus the Virginia Beach Expressway (Va. 44) lead to the beach from Norfolk. Piedmont and United fly into Norfolk from New York, and Amtrak reaches Newport News from Boston, New York, Philadelphia, and Washington. Both Greyhound and Trailways serve most of the Tidewater area.

**WHERE TO STAY IN VIRGINIA BEACH:** New luxury hotels, older ones that wear their age with dignity and comfort, full-size apartments, efficiencies, hospitable guesthouses—directly on the beach or a little bit away from it at lower prices—you'll find them all at Virginia Beach. For a complete list, including rates, write the **Virginia Beach Visitors Bureau,** P.O. Box 200, Virginia Beach, VA 23458 (tel. 804/446-8038), for their free accommodations directory.

## The Best

"The hotel that made Virginia Beach famous." That's how **The Cavalier** bills itself. But these days, it's the new Cavalier, Oceanfront at 42nd Street (P.O. Box 885), Virginia Beach, VA 23451 (tel. toll free 800/446-8199, 800/582-8324 in Virginia). In the days of my Virginia youth, it was the "old" Cavalier, a majestic structure situated across the highway from the ocean on a rise that put it literally head and shoulders above everything else at the beach. The dashing, swashbuckling Cavalier dominated the landscape and the social scene, drawing patrons in the upper brackets from the entire eastern seaboard. Over the years, however, its "swash" "buckled" somewhat and, while not exactly shabby, the grand old building relinquished its prestige to the new building across the road,

an 11-story high-rise with 270 superbly appointed rooms, each with an ocean view and private balcony.

But now the more-than-50-year-old hotel on the hill has been restored to its former elegance. For those who value graciousness above an oceanfront location, this is a "must." When booking, be *sure* to specify that it's the older hotel you want. The spaciousness of guest rooms was accomplished by knocking out the walls to double their size, leaving all bath and closet facilities intact—that means *two* full baths and closets in each. Closets are cedar lined, baths have retained their huge porcelain fixtures from the old days, and many beds are of the king-size variety. Smaller rooms for single occupancy are cozy, not tiny, and just as beautifully decorated with period furniture as the larger ones. Some are interesting, irregular shapes, following the contours of the building. Full dining service is available in the basement Hunt Room with its mammoth fireplace. The 20-acre wooded property has tennis courts and shuffleboard, and the oceanfront isn't all *that* far away. Golf privileges are available at nearby courses. Rates for doubles begin at $83.

Of course, if you come to the beach to *be* at the beach, the new Cavalier is for you. This is elegance in the modern style, and I found the staff as friendly and gracious as you might expect in the older establishment. Most rooms have two double beds (some king-size) and children under 12 stay free in the same room with their parents. There's platform tennis, deck shuffleboard, volleyball, archery, a game room, and a children's playground. The list of "extras" is impressive: baby cribs at no charge, irons and ironing boards, a copying service for businessmen, valet and laundry service, airport limousine, and special arrangements for fishing, golf, and water sports. They'll even plan a birthday or anniversary celebration. The Cavalier Lounge is just off the main lobby. The Sand Dollar Restaurant, also off the lobby, serves all three meals and cocktails, with outdoor dining in season at The Breeze overlooking the pool and beach. Orion's Roof (Top of the Cavalier) is one of Virginia Beach's "special" places for dining and dancing (see "Where to Eat"). Rates are seasonal: for double occupancy May 15 through September 15 the charge is $88, ocean-view, $124 oceanfront; lower other months.

## Also Good

The **Hilton Inn,** 8th Street and Oceanfront, Virginia Beach, VA 23458 (tel. 804/428-8935), is a sleek six-story semicircular structure wrapped around a sunstruck oceanfront terrace. There are heated outdoor and indoor pools, as well as a kiddie pool, sauna, whirlpool, and weight room. All 124 rooms have pleasing ocean views. There's a poolside cocktail/snack bar and seasonal entertainment in the lively Laverne's Lounge. The hotel dining room offers breakfast, lunch, and dinner; evening meals range from $8 to $20. All rooms of this impeccably maintained mini-resort are attractively decorated and spacious family rooms are available. In season (May 23 to August 31), double rates range from $99 to $124; they drop considerably off-season. There's no charge for children 12 and under in their parents' room.

The **Avamere,** 26th Street and Oceanfront, Virginia Beach, VA 23451 (tel. 804/428-2112), has been operated by Clarence Smith's family for nearly half a century, and he maintains the same atmosphere of easy informality that has made it a favorite on the beach. There are connecting rooms for families, an exceptionally fine dining room, and oceanfront verandas. Rates from mid-June through Labor Day begin at $104 for modified American plan (includes breakfast and dinner), lower May 15 to mid-June and the rest of September.

The **Dunes Motor Inn,** Oceanfront at 10th Street (P.O. Box 467), Virginia Beach, VA 23451 (tel. 804/428-7731), is a six-story motel that also offers kitchen units. There's a pool and a wading pool for the small fry. For a small fee, they'll provide a crib for children in the same room with their parents. The on-premises restaurant is open for all three meals and for room service. Rates for doubles start at $82 from June to August, lower other months. Closed mid-October through late March.

Although not right on the beach, the **EconoLodge,** 5819 Northhampton Blvd., Virginia Beach, VA 23455 (tel. 804/464-9306), has nicely done-up, good-size rooms with balconies, and there's no charge for cribs. The restaurant is open from 7 a.m. to 11 p.m. Doubles begin at $46 during high season, but prices drop other months. Kitchen units are available for $50 and up. Children under 12 stay free in their parents' room, and there are special senior citizen rates. Open year round.

### A Guesthouse

Conveniently located in the heart of Virginia Beach, just one block from the ocean, **Angie's Guest Cottage,** 302 24th St., Virginia Beach, VA 23451 (tel. 804/428-4690), has six nice bedrooms (one with private bath—the others convenient to two central baths) and two apartments. All have air conditioning, and some rooms have small refrigerators. There's a sundeck, barbecue pit, and picnic tables. All in all, this is a friendly family-type place to stay, just across the street from the Greyhound bus station, and you won't believe the low rates—$36 to $50 per night (including continental breakfast) from Memorial Day to Labor Day, $22 to $40 (without breakfast) at other times. Backpackers and bikers will find dormitory bunks for only $10 in season, $7 off-season, for AYH members ($13 and $10 respectively for nonmembers). Open April 1 to October 15.

### Campgrounds

The closest campground to the Virginia Beach oceanfront is **Holiday Trav-L-Park,** 1½ miles south of Rudee Inlet Bridge at 1075 Gen. Booth Blvd., Virginia Beach, VA 23452 (tel. 804/425-0249). It has 1000 sites, full hookups, a recreation building, store, pools, laundry, and LP gas. Prices are $14 to $20 for two people, $2 for each additional.

Also very near the beach (less than five minutes), the **Virginia Beach KOA,** 1240 Gen. Booth Blvd., Virginia Beach, VA 23451 (tel. 804/428-1444), has 750 sites, full hookups, three swimming pools, playgrounds, mini-golf, a store, and dump stations. They also furnish free bus service to the beach. Prices run $14 to $25.

**WHERE TO EAT IN VIRGINIA BEACH:** Virginia Beach has restaurants of all persuasions. Space will permit only a very subjective listing, but write the Virginia Beach Visitors Bureau, P.O. Box 200, Virginia Beach, VA 23458 (tel. 804/446-8038), for their *Restaurant Guide* (free), a full roster of pancake houses, coffeeshops, and restaurants serving Chinese, American, French, Greek, Mexican, Italian, Jewish, and, not surprisingly, seafood cuisines.

### Fancy and Very Special

**Orion's Roof,** at the new Cavalier, 42nd Street and Oceanfront (tel. 804/425-8555), is *the* place for a splendiferous evening of gourmet dining and dancing. The rooftop setting, with glass walls that look out on breathtaking ocean and city views, is enhanced by the elegant decor in soft tones of beige and brown. Entering via mosaic-tiled stepping stones over reflecting pools with splashing fountains, you may choose to sit a while in the pleasant, dimly lit lounge and just enjoy the view. It's a nice prelude to candlelight dining in the large dining room, where an orchestra plays for dancing on one side of the room. Most important, both the menu selections and the preparation of the food live up to the surroundings. Seafood dishes are a treat. I liked the scampi Savoy, butterfly shrimp in a special wine sauce served over seasoned rice; others in my party raved about the crabmeat and shrimp Norfolk. Beef dishes range from chateaubriand for two to beef brochette. Salads are fresh and crisp, there's a very good wine list, and rolls came to the table piping hot on a covered plate. It all adds up to a marvelous evening of good food in sophisticated surroundings—not always easy to come by at a beach resort. Hours are 6 p.m. to 1 a.m., and dinner from the à la carte menu can run from $15 to $40.

### Not So Fancy, But Very Good

Down at the very end of Virginia Beach, at Rudee Inlet, **The Lighthouse** (tel. 804/428-9851) began many years ago in a small wooden building with one dining room that held about 20 people, plus a screened-in porch overlooking the water. Shrimp, crab, and frosted mugs of beer about covered the menu. It's a different story today, however. Robert Herman, who has owned the place for more than 20 years, used to love visiting it with his wife, saw its potential, and never seems to be quite finished with improvements, additions, and innovations such as an outside patio, upstairs rooms overlooking the water, and a very nice lounge. Decor is, of course, nautical, but that doesn't begin to describe the interior. Divided into eight separate rooms to prevent a "barny" feeling in the large building, it has grown from that tiny wooden shack to such proportions that they can, and often do, feed 600 at once! There's an almost whimsical touch in the way standing brass ship compasses, mounted blue marlin and other fish (most are caught by Robert or members of the staff), a free-standing aquarium, ship lanterns, etc., are scattered around the place. One of the newer rooms, The Deck, has a heavenly view through bowed skylights. Every table has a sea view. It's simply impossible to summarize the long menu, much less to pick a personal favorite. But to list a few: deluxe lump crabmeat or shrimp sautéed in parsley butter (with soup, salad, baked potato, and coffee or tea); whole fresh flounder broiled or fried, or stuffed with crabmeat (both with all the accompaniments listed above); and a whopping fried seafood platter (fresh flounder, scallops, oysters, shrimp, crab cake, and fried clams). Lunch can run from $4 to $8; dinner, from $10 to $23. There's also a full range of sandwiches, beef, salads, and even hot pastrami. Locals have loved this place from its screened-porch days. Open from 10 a.m. to 11 p.m., or "whenever the last customer is through eating."

The **Three Ships Inn,** 3800 Shore Dr. (tel. 804/460-0055), resembles a weathered old inn, with an early English decor and candlelit tables. There's gourmet eating here, with such delicacies as chicken Kiev, quail, roast duckling, frogs' legs, Maine lobster, and fresh rainbow trout stuffed with backfin crabmeat, all at prices of $11 to $30. Flounder and sea trout are caught fresh daily in their own nets. Open for dinner from 6 to 11 p.m. daily

**WHERE TO STAY IN NORFOLK:** The **Omni International Hotel,** 777 Waterside Dr., Norfolk, VA 23510 (tel. 804/622-6664, or toll free 800/228-2121), was the first hotel in this fast-growing luxury system. It's so impeccably maintained that it might just have opened its doors. There are two fine dining rooms, the Riverwalk Café and the Esplanade (see "Where to Eat in Norfolk"). The Lobby Bar with its wide sweep of window wall overlooks the always-bustling harbor, and there's evening piano or trio entertainment here. Rooms are furnished in a warm, contemporary motif, with soft muted tones of rose, gray, beige, and blue predominating. There's valet parking (for a fee), a pool, and a jogging track. The Omni has some accommodations for wheelchair travelers, along with the special check-in and checkout, concierge services, and other touches this system provides. It's located adjacent to the Waterside Festival Marketplace and within walking distance of the Scope Convention Center. Double rates range from $81 to $91 for rooms facing the city, $101 to $111 for those with views of the harbor; on the top two concierge floors, they are $131 and $141 respectively.

The **Hotel Madison,** Granby and Freemason Streets, Norfolk, VA 23510 (tel. 804/622-6682, or toll free 800/522-0976, 800/552-6353 in Virginia), is a beautifully restored old hotel that reflects an era of bygone elegance. With its rich dark woods, crystal chandelier, hand-woven carpet, and baby grand piano, the lobby resembles that of an intimate small European hostelry. The Embassy Lounge features a raw bar and daily happy hour, and there's dining in the light and airy atmosphere of Dolley's or the sophisticated surroundings of the Embassy Restaurant. All 135 spacious guest rooms and suites are handsomely furnished and decorated in tones of gold, beige, cream, and burnt orange. Mornings, complimentary fresh brewed coffee, orange juice, pastries, and the daily paper are delivered to your room. There's concierge service, valet parking, and express check-in/out, and a free trolley takes guests to the Waterside and harbor. Doubles range from $75 to $85, and suites are $105.

The excellent Econo Lodge budget system has six motels in Norfolk. An especially pleasant location is the **Norfolk Ocean View,** 1111 E. Ocean View Ave., Norfolk, VA 23503 (tel. 804/480-1111, or toll free 800/446-6900); take I-64 through the Hampton Roads Tunnel to Ocean View and exit 60. The lodge is across from the beach, and a fishing pier and charter fishing are nearby, as is a popular seafood restaurant. All rooms have refrigerators and free cable color TVs with HBO, and there's free morning coffee. Doubles range from $46.50 to $48.50, and there's a $4 charge for each extra person, (also a $4 charge for a rollaway). Pets are welcome, with a deposit fee.

There's an attractive 160-room **Days Inn** at 5701 Chambers St. (U.S. 13 and I-264), Norfolk, VA 23502 (tel. 804/461-0100, or toll free 800/325-2525). It's just a ten-minute drive to downtown and the Waterside. Some rooms are equipped for wheelchair travelers, and there's a pool, free cable color TV, and the 24-hour Day Break Restaurant. Summer rates are $58 double, and they drop considerably in winter. Also, a "Simple Super Saver" rate of $35 (for one to four people) is available if you book 29 days in advance, and that's hard to top!

**WHERE TO EAT IN NORFOLK:** This burgeoning city offers a variety of dining experiences, from basic good down-home cookery to fine fresh seafood, continental, and nationality restaurants. Write the **Norfolk Visitors Bureau,** 236 E. Plume St., Norfolk, VA 23510 (tel. 804/441-5266, or toll free 800/368-3097 outside Virginia), for its "Norfolk-by-the-Sea Dining Guide."

The **Esplanade,** in the Omni International Hotel, 777 Waterside Dr. (tel. 804/623-0333), is a perfect choice if you're celebrating something special or just want to treat yourself to a memorable evening. In this exquisite small dining room overlooking the hotel's larger dining room, comfortable wing chairs surround intimate tables for two or four. Service is impeccable in this quiet enclave where you have a sense of absolute privacy. A recent memorable dinner included such choices as papillote of sea trout baked in parchment with shrimp and crab ($18), veal Lafayette with sautéed sea scallops ($22), and fresh breast of chicken stuffed and roasted with backfin crab and tarragon ($18). The presentation was artful, with carrots honey glazed with tomatoes, red cabbage, and sautéed green beans beautifully arranged as accompaniments on a separate plate. There's a memorable lobster bisque en croûte ($4), and appetizers are such imaginative delights as galatoire of salmon and sole or oysters with Smithfield ham (both $5). Mr. Lynnwood B. Craig, the personable maître d'hôtel, welcomes diners as if they were guests in a private home. The Esplanade is open from 6 to 11 p.m. Monday through Saturday. Reservations, and coat and tie for men, are requested.

A Norfolk institution, the **Ship's Cabin,** 4110 E. Ocean View Ave. (tel. 804/583-4659), is a large airy series of rooms decorated with Tiffany-style lamps and hanging baskets. It always seems crowded, but you'll never be rushed and service is especially pleasant. This is a wonderful spot to sample crab Norfolk ($14.50) or other such luscious entrees as shrimp Stella Oceanis topped with tomato, spices, and feta and parmesan cheeses ($16), and angel-hair pasta and backfin crabmeat with sun-dried tomatoes ($15). Mesquite grilling adds a delicious flavor to halibut, salmon, and swordfish, as well as steaks. It's open from 6 to 10 p.m. daily; closed major holidays (call for seasonal hours). There's an excellent choice of Virginia and California wines.

**Il Porto of Norfolk,** 333 Waterside Dr. (tel. 804/627-4400), is an ideal place in which to relax and view the passing Waterside scene as you enjoy your favorite pizza or pasta dish. It has a colorful, lively European taverna ambience, and just smells so great as you enter that you realize I'm talking honest-to-goodness hearty Italian cooking here. Lunch prices range from $5 to $7; dinners, from $7 to $11. It's open continuously from 11:15 a.m. to 2 a.m. (dinners not served after midnight), and there's live ragtime piano entertainment from 8:30 p.m. to 1:30 a.m. daily.

The **Grate Steak,** 1170 N. Military Hwy. (tel. 804/461-5501), offers a change of pace from all those fine seafood establishments. You can select your choice midwestern corn-fed steak and cook it to your own taste over live charcoal. It's open from 7 a.m. to 10 p.m. daily. Lunches range from $5 to $10, and dinners average $10 to $16. There's live piano entertainment at night.

**Café 21,** at 21st Street and Colley Avenue (tel. 804/625-4218), near the Ghent restoration area, is one of those great local spots that makes you feel as if you've made a real discovery. It's small, and everybody seems to know everybody else. Fare ranges from salads, sandwiches, and pizza to chicken, pasta, and other Italian dishes. It's moderately priced and serves both lunch and dinner. Call for hours, which may change seasonally.

Near Cafe 21, in the same shopping center, is **Courtney's** (tel. 804/625-0911). It's also locally popular for its California-style bar, fried veggies, and sesame chicken appetizers. There's a good sandwich selection too.

**NIGHTLIFE:** Both at Virginia Beach and nearby Norfolk, nightlife is found mostly in restaurants and motel or hotel lounges. Prime examples are **Orion's Roof** at the top of the New Cavalier, 42nd and Oceanfront (tel. 804/425-8555), **Shipmates,** in the Ramada Inn, Atlantic Avenue at 7th Street (tel. 804/425-5151), and **Alexander's,** in the Omni International Hotel, 777 Waterfront Dr. at St. Paul's Boulevard (tel. 804/622-6664). The **Tidewater Dinner Theater,** 6270 Northhampton Blvd. (tel. 804/461-2933), is in the Quality Inn; reservations are necessary and shows change frequently.

**THINGS TO SEE AND DO:** When I was growing up in Norfolk, all of Tidewater and the Eastern Shore seemed like one big playground to me. The beaches came first, of course; my father liked to fish, both surf casting and deep sea; there were the amusement parks at Virginia Beach and Ocean View; I played tennis on the courts at City Park; and there was always the excitement of living in a navy town, where new friends passed in and out of our lives regularly. It wasn't until my teen years that I began to appreciate the deeper, more meaningful attractions that lay around my hometown. History is all around, of course, but now there's space technology and industrial developments to add a new dimension to the area, and artistic and cultural events are housed in sparkling new edifices. The only way to get a handle on the widespread panorama of things to see and do is to break them up into localities:

## At Virginia Beach

The beach itself, complete with boardwalk, amusement park, fishing piers, bowling, tennis, miniature golf, waterskiing, and surf-riding, makes this the complete resort, especially when you add the seafood that's out of this world (in my case, I can't get enough of those Lynnhaven oysters, whether they're on the half shell, fried, or in a creamy stew). And I've always fantasized about the *Norwegian Lady* statue that stands at the very center of town on the oceanfront, a memorial to a sea captain's wife who was rescued by townspeople when his ship broke up during a storm. The **Information Center** is located at 19th Street and Pacific Avenue (tel. 804/425-7511, or toll free 800/446-8038) and will furnish specifics about restaurants, amusements, etc.

For sightseeing, there's the **Old Cape Henry Lighthouse** in the Fort Story Military Reservation, a little north of Virginia Beach on the shore drive. It was the first government-built lighthouse in the U.S. (1791). And close by is the plain **First Landing Cross** which marks the landing spot of the colonists who settled at Jamestown in 1607.

The **Adam Thoroughgood House,** thought to be over 300 years old and restored to its original design, is at 1636 Parrish Rd., eight miles northeast via Va. 166 and U.S. 13 on Lynnhaven Bay. It's a lovely old brick cottage-type house with a high-pitched roof, surrounded by ancient trees and boxwood. It's open Tuesday through Saturday from 10 a.m. to 5 p.m. and on Sunday from noon to 5 p.m. April 1 through December; Tuesday through Saturday from noon to 5 p.m. January 1 to March 31. Admission is $2 for adults, $1 for children 6 to 12; under 6, free.

**Lynnhaven House,** another 17th-century house, eight miles north off U.S. 225 on Wishart Road, is one of the nation's best-preserved 18th-century middle-class dwellings. Open Tuesday through Sunday from noon to 4 p.m. April through October; admission is $2 for adults, $1 for senior citizens, students, and children under 12; under 6, free.

The **Virginia Beach Maritime Historical Museum,** 24th Street and Oceanfront (tel. 804/422-1587), in the recently restored 1903 Seatack Lifesaving Station, has an excellent collection of nautical artifacts, scrimshaw, and ship models. Its well-stocked gift shop includes nautical brass and works by local artists. It's open from 10 a.m. to 9 p.m., Monday to Saturday and noon to 5 p.m. on Sunday, Memorial Day to October; closed Monday the rest of the year. Admission is $1.50 for adults, $1 for seniors and military, 50¢ for children ages 6 to 18.

At the splendid new "hands-on" **Virginia Marine Science Museum,** 717 General Booth Blvd. (tel. 804/425-FISH), you can explore the depths of the Atlantic Ocean, walk under waves of the Chesapeake Bay, see the life of a salt marsh firsthand, and visit a coastal plains "river," which is a 10,000 gallon aquarium brimming with local finny species. One of the South's finest new maritime exhibits, it's not to be missed! Open from 9 a.m. to 5 p.m. Monday through Sunday, September through May, call for extended summer hours. Admission is $3 for adults, $2.50 for seniors, and $2 for children.

**Wildwater Rapids Water Park,** 1049 General Booth Blvd. (tel. 804/425-1080), offers splashy great times for all the family on ten acres of flumes, slides, rapids, pools, and wave ponds. It's open from 10 a.m. to 10 p.m. Sunday through Saturday, Memorial Day through Labor Day, and weekends in May, weather permitting. Admission costs vary considerably, depending on the season, so it's advisable to phone for current rates.

## Norfolk

Norfolk is first, last, and always a seaport; from its earliest days (which is pretty early—the site was purchased for 10,000 pounds of tobacco in 1682), ships have come and gone in one of the best natural harbors in the world. Commercial ships still make up a great deal of water traffic, but in addition, the town, together with Portsmouth, is the site of one of the oldest U.S. Navy facilities in the country. The Naval Station and Naval Air Station, combined with Portsmouth's Naval Shipyard, comprise one of the largest naval facilities of any nation in the world, and the city's streets are filled at any given time with naval uniforms, both U.S. and foreign. It has been, in its time, a rough, rather rowdy liberty town for sailors (I remember seeing signs on lawns warning "Sailors and Dogs Keep Off the Grass"), but when World War II brought respectability to servicemen, all that changed and there's little left of the seamier sections that used to be the only place enlisted men found a welcome.

Downtown Norfolk has undergone quite a change in recent years with the transformation of the historic **Granby Street** main shopping area into a beautiful mall lined with trees and shrubs, fountains, and benches for resting weary feet. There are some very good shops within the mall, and sometimes there's street music and other entertainment. The **Scope complex,** a huge domed structure supported by 24 sculptured concrete buttresses, houses concerts, Broadway plays, and the Norfolk Symphony Orchestra. The **Waterside complex** is a delightful setting for more than 120 shops and restaurants and features street performers.

All in all, it's quite a different town from the one I knew, but it has a lot to see and do, and it's well worth a day or two of exploration. Look for blue and gold signs pointing the way to historic sites.

Before setting out, however, by all means stop by the downtown **Norfolk Visitors Bureau,** at 236 E. Plume St., Norfolk, VA 23510 (tel. 804/441-5266 or toll free 800/368-3097 outside Virginia). Or, even better, write before you come. They do a terrific job of supplying details on the entire Tidewater area.

One of my favorite spots is the lovely **Norfolk Botanical Gardens,** which I knew in my youth as the Azalea Gardens. These botanical gardens are eight miles east of the city, adjacent to the airport, on Azalea Garden Road near the junction of I-64 and Military Hwy. Don't miss the 4,000-plant, award-winning Rose Garden or the 300-flowering-tree Arboretum. A special feature is the Fragrance Garden for the blind, and there are narrated boat rides and train tours ($2 each, or $3 for a combination ticket) from mid-March to October.

There's a 1½-hour narrated cruise of the Norfolk–Portsmouth harbor aboard the *Carrie B,* replica of a 19th-century Mississippi riverboat. It leaves from Waterside behind Phillip's Seafood Restaurant, and fare is $8 for adults (one child under 12 is free with each paying adult; additional children, $4). From Portsmouth, you can tour Hampton Roads by boat, leaving from the foot of North Street at Portside in Historic Olde Towne for the same fares. Write **Harbor Tours,** End of Bay Street, Portsmouth, VA 23704 (tel. 804/393-4735).

You can tour by bus the gigantic **U.S. Naval Station** and the **U.S. Naval Air Station,** Hampton and Admiral Taussig Boulevards, and even go aboard one or more naval vessels on Saturday and Sunday from 1 to 4:30 p.m. Tours leave from Waterside and the Naval Base Tour and Information Center at 9809 Hampton Blvd. in Norfolk, and you should call (tel. 804/441-5266, or toll free 800/368-3097) for exact times, since they change according to the time of year.

There's a $4 charge for adults ($2 for ages 6 to 13; under 6, free) for the naval base tour. Ship visits are free.

You can hop aboard the **Norfolk Trolley Tour** mid-April through November for an hour-long narrated orientation jaunt through the historic downtown district. At various stops, you can get off, explore, and catch a later trolley. Cost is $1.50 for adults, 75¢ for children under 12, seniors, and handicapped. Phone the Norfolk Visitors Bureau, (tel. 804/441-5266, or toll free 800/368-3097 outside Virginia) for a schedule, which varies with the season.

The **Moses Myers Home** (1792) is at 323 E. Freemason St. (at Bank Street) and is a beautiful old Georgian home filled with over 60% of the original furnishings. From April through December, hours are 10 a.m. to 5 p.m. (noon to 5 p.m. on Sunday) every day except Monday. The rest of the year, it opens at noon. Cost is $2 for adults, $1 for ages 6 through 18; under 6 and military with ID, free.

A combination ticket with the Willoughby-Baylor Home and Adam Thoroughgood Home (in Virginia Beach) costs $3 for two houses, $4 for all three. The houses are administered by the Chrysler Museum.

The **Willoughby-Baylor Home** at 601 E. Freemason St. is a splendid 18th-century Georgian-Federal town house on a 1636 land grant. It showcases fine period furnishings, and its formal gardens are outstanding. Hours and costs are identical with the Moses Myers Home (see above).

The **Hermitage Foundation Museum,** 7637 N. Shore Rd., near the intersection of Hampton Boulevard (Va. 337) and Little Creek Road (Va. 165) is an elegant and unusually furnished riverside mansion housing an outstanding collection of Oriental and Western art. Built in 1908 by textilist William Sloane, this Tudor-style structure is highlighted by ivories, jade, and Chinese tomb figures from the T'ang Dynasty. It's open from 10 a.m. to 5 p.m. Monday through Saturday and 1 to 5 p.m. on Sunday. Admission is $3 for adults, $1 for ages 6 to 18; under 6 and military with ID, free.

In a restored old courthouse, the **General Douglas MacArthur Memorial,** City Hall Avenue and Bank Street, known as MacArthur Square (tel. 804/441-2965), holds the general's tomb and memorabilia of his life and military career. There's an interesting film biography. It's free and open from 10 a.m. to 5 p.m. Monday through Saturday, from 11 a.m. on Sunday.

The **Chrysler Museum,** Olney Road at Mowbray Arch, has been acclaimed as "one of the 20 top museums in the country" by the *Wall Street Journal.* Art from nearly every important culture, civilization, and historical period of the last 5,000 years is included in the collection. The museum also houses a 10,000-piece glass collection, considered one of the foremost worldwide; the only museum photography gallery in the state; and a fine collection of Worcester porcelain. Family programs, films, lectures, and concerts are offered in the museum theater on a regular basis. Admission: free. Hours: 10 a.m. to 4 p.m. Tuesday through Friday, 1 to 5 p.m. on Sunday. Call 804/622-1211 for further information. A $10-million-plus expansion project, slated for completion in early 1989, will almost double the museum's display area, adding nearly 30,000 stored items to its galleries.

## Newport News

During World Wars I and II, Newport News's docks were the jumping-off point for men and supplies headed into battle; they also served as a huge repair shop for naval vessels that had been damaged. Then, as now, it was dominated by the **Newport News Shipbuilding Company,** the world's largest, which has constructed some of our most famous ships—the *United States,* the *Enterprise,* and the *Kennedy* among them. The proud **Victory Arch,** at 25th Street and West

Avenue, stands as a memorial to American men and women who have served in all the wars of our history. Like Norfolk, Newport News directs you to points of interest with distinctive blue-and-gold markers. Incidentally, the "News" in its name was of the arrival back in the early 1600s of one Capt. Christopher Newport with supplies and settlers from England to join the tiny Jamestown colony. For all kinds of sightseeing assistance, contact: **Newport News Department of Recreation, Parks and Public Relations,** City Hall, Newport News, VA 23607 (tel. 804/838-4182 or 838-4184).

**Mariners Museum** (tel. 804/595-0368), three miles off I-64, exit 62A, has a marvelous collection of seafaring items and ship models in an 880-acre park with a fishing lake and picnic facilities. The museum is open from 9 a.m. to 5 p.m. Monday through Saturday (from noon on Sunday). It costs $3 for adults, $1.50 for ages 6 to 16; under 6, free.

At the **Virginia Living Museum,** 524 J. Clyde Morris Blvd. (tel. 804/595-1900), you can stroll a lakeside boardwalk to view carefully maintained wildlife exhibits in an eight-acre outdoor "living habitat." Indoor living displays include marine life, nocturnal animals, and microscopic life. There's also a planetarium and observatory. Open from 9 a.m. to 5 p.m. Monday through Saturday (and 7 to 9 p.m. on Thursday), and 1 to 5 p.m. on Sunday. Adult admission is $4 for the museum, $2 for the planetarium, $5 for a combination ticket; for children under 12, admission is $2 for the museum, $1.50 for the planetarium, $2.50 for a combination ticket (under 4, admission is free).

**Fort Eustis** is located on **Mulberry Island** at the northwest end of the city and is headquarters of the U.S. Transportation Center. Both the fort and the **Army Transportation Museum** (which traces the development of transportation from the wheel to the flying saucer) are free, and the museum or the Public Affairs Office can give you directions for a self-guided auto tour of the grounds.

## Hampton

Your first order of business in Hampton (or even before you come) should be to go by (or write) the **Hampton Visitors Center,** Settlers Landing and Eaton Street (via I-64, on the downtown waterfront), Hampton, VA 23669 (tel. 804/727-6108).

You can tour **Fort Monroe,** three miles southeast of Hampton (it's clearly marked from almost any point in town), free, and it makes for a fascinating day for the whole family. The first battle between the *Monitor* and the *Merrimac* was fought just off the fort in Hampton Roads on March 9, 1862, ending in a draw between the first two ironclads. The fort was held by Union troops throughout the Civil War—Abraham Lincoln plotted strategy against Norfolk here in May of 1862—and Jefferson Davis was imprisoned here following the downfall of the Confederacy. Ironically, Robert E. Lee, as a young engineer in the U.S. Army, helped with the construction of Fort Monroe, but was never able to effect its capture when he commanded Confederate forces. The **Casement Museum** (free) depicts these and many other stories in a panoramic painting, and there are all sorts of intriguing documents, pictures, and models on display. Kids will love the fact that the old fort was encircled by a moat.

The famous **Hampton University** (formerly known as the Hampton Institute), at the east end of Queen Street (exit off I-64), was established in 1868 by the Freedman's Bureau to teach former slaves how to read and write. Today it specializes in science, the liberal arts, business, teaching, nursing, architecture, and graduate studies. Don't miss the **museum** (free) in the Academy Building—it has an outstanding collection of Indian and African artifacts.

Also free are the film and special exhibits at the **NASA Langley Research Center,** three miles north on Va. 134 (tel. 804/865-2855), where you can see moon rockets, space suits, and an Apollo command module. Open Monday through Saturday from 8:30 a.m. to 4:30 p.m., from noon on Sunday. Closed on major holidays. If you're space-minded, go by the **Air Power Museum,** 413 W. Mercury Blvd., and see their impressive display of jet aircraft, rockets, missiles, and satellites.

**THE EASTERN SHORE:** The old Cape Charles ferry used to take almost three hours to cross Chesapeake Bay. Today you can "Follow the Gulls" (a neat blue-and-white sign with a white silhouetted seagull that points you to the 17.6-mile-long Chesapeake Bay Bridge-Tunnel from almost anywhere in the Tidewater area) and make the crossing in 23 minutes! And the trip is unforgettable—miles and miles of causeway, one rather high bridge, and two mile-long tunnels. This remarkable engineering feat was completed in 1964 and takes you from Norfolk to **Cape Charles.** Cross another causeway and bridge, and you'll reach **Assateague Island National Seashore,** one of the newest of our national parks. U.S. 13 runs through the long peninsula that has come to be known as **Delmarva** because it holds tiny portions of Delaware, Maryland, and Virginia. The toll is $9 each way, including passengers.

As an aside, let me point out that when you spend your day—and it will take a whole one—on the Eastern Shore, there's a very good restaurant at **America House** at the Cape Charles end of the bridge-tunnel which serves all three meals at reasonable prices. However, you're likely to find interesting places to eat also at **Chincoteague** (the town, not the island) or perhaps in other villages along the shore. I personally couldn't eat anything but the oysters, clams, and crabs that are such a specialty out here, and there are several small seafood restaurants scattered around. But America House is a sure thing, so keep it in mind. If you're an island person or just plain intrigued by this coastal country, you may want to plan more than just one day, in which case see "Where to Stay," below.

If you want to fish on the Eastern Shore, the pier at Cape Charles can furnish bait and tackle. You don't need a license, and there's no limit on the catch. For charter-boat fishing, go on to **Wachapreague** or Chincoteague and look for the charter signs.

Now, back to that National Seashore—it's Va. 175 (from U.S. 13) that will lead you the ten miles to **Chincoteague Island** and on to Assateague. There are two very special times of year to arrive on the islands: the first Wednesday in May is set aside for the **Eastern Shore Annual Seafood Festival,** which has gained such popularity since it began in 1969 that reservations start coming in as soon as tickets go on sale in October for the next year's festival. If you're early enough, you can (ticket in hand) wander from booth to booth sampling a seaside feast. But you *must* have that ticket, and be warned: they sometimes sell out the very first day they're offered! For ticket information, contact the Chamber of Commerce, P.O. Box 258, Chincoteague, VA 23336 (tel. 804/336-6161). Then, on the last Wednesday and Thursday in July, comes the "penning" of wild Chincoteague ponies, and it's really something! The shaggy little ponies, larger than a Shetland but smaller than a horse, are descendants of horses that swam ashore from a Spanish galleon that perished in these waters, so the legend goes. Through the centuries their growth became stunted from a steady diet of marsh grass. All year they roam wild on Assateague Island, but at the end of July Chincoteague citizens turn into cowboys, herd them into the water for the swim across the channel, and sell the foals for prices that range from $75 to $300 (all proceeds go to the volunteer fire department), then drive the mares and stallions back to Assateague for another year of breeding. It's a fun time to be here, with carnival amusements and general hilarity prevailing.

Other lively annual happenings include the well-known Columbus Day weekend Oyster Festival, and a juried Easter Decoy and Art Festival, which draws about 100 top exhibitors from throughout the East.

Those are highlights of the year on the Eastern Shore. But no matter when you come, there's much to fill your days. Across the bridge from Chincoteague, the island of **Assateague** was cut off from the longer extension of barrier islands (which runs from Massachusetts to Florida and includes many in South Carolina and Georgia—which we'll get to later in this book) by a storm in 1933. It's about 37 miles long, and its width varies from one-third of a mile to a little over a mile. Its gently shelving sand beach is just spectacular, and swimming is not perilous because the undertow here is very light. Virginia and Maryland share ownership of Assateague, and you can enter via bridges at either end. The State Park Information Center and Campground Registration Office is located at the north end, and there's a Visitors Center just over the bridge from Chincoteague. If you begin your trip from the north, plan to go over to Assateague from near Ocean City, Md. And you should know that because some 22 miles of roadless beach and marsh lie between the two entrances, you won't be able to drive from one end to the other, but must return to the mainland to reach the other end (about a 1½-hour drive). Assateague State Park and Assateague Island National Seashore are at the northern end, Chincoteague National Wildlife Refuge at the southern.

Up at **North Assateague,** you'll find camping sites (see "Where to Stay," below), bathhouses (in summer), bait and tackle shops, limited food service, and picnic tables. Also in summer, there are lifeguards stationed on those marvelous beaches. One of the two herds of wild ponies roams freely over this part of the island, and they are a thrilling sight running in groups or feeding quietly. Remember, these are *wild* animals—keep a respectable distance (they just may bite or kick if crowded), and *don't try to feed them.*

From Chincoteague, a paved road leads three miles through the **National Wildlife Refuge** before it reaches the beach. What you're likely to see along the way depends on the time of year: snow geese, Canada geese, and tundra swans regularly winter here, and there are always the shorebirds, some of which are seldom found anywhere else but along this stretch of coast. And, of course, there's that other herd of wild ponies (the ones that make the swim to Chincoteague each year).

At both ends of Assateague there is excellent fishing, clamming, and crabbing in addition to swimming. Canoe launch areas and camping are permitted on the Maryland portion (the northern end) of Assateague. The Chincoteague National Wildlife Refuge located on the southern end (the Virginia portion) prohibits the landing of a boat anywhere other than at Fishing Point at the very southern tip of the island. Each year, over 305 species of birds visit the refuge, and nature trails that wind through loblolly pines and freshwater marshes provide excellent opportunities to observe bird life, as well as many different mammals, reptiles, and amphibians.

Wildlife-oriented auditorium programs and walks are presented daily during the summer and on weekends during the spring and fall. Island Cruises, a concession operation of the Fish and Wildlife Service, conducts cruises and land safaris at various times during the year. For specific information on tours or programs, write Refuge Manager, Chincoteague National Wildlife Refuge, P.O. Box 62, Chincoteague, VA 23336 (tel. 804/336-6122).

This is old, old country, and if its history interests you, stop at **Accomac** to see the debtor's prison (there's another one at **Eastville**). Incidentally, the Eastville Courthouse, built in 1730, houses court records which date, unbroken, back to 1632!

## Where to Stay

There are motel facilities on the Delmarva Peninsula and in Chincoteague, campsites on both ends of Assateague. But my first recommendation may, at first blush, not belong in a guide to the Southeast. I'm putting it in for two reasons: first of all, many readers will be coming to the Eastern Shore from points north; and second, I've found the inn and its owners so completely charming that I think you should know about them.

The **Mainstay Inn,** 635 Columbia Ave., Cape May, NJ 08204 (tel. 609/884-8690), is convenient to the Cape May–Lewes, Delaware ferry, one of the most enjoyable ways to reach the Eastern Shore (fare is $12.50 per car and driver, $3 for each passenger over age 6), and a delightful place to begin or end a visit there. A lovely old Victorian mansion built in 1872, the Mainstay was once a "gaming parlor" known as Jackson's Clubhouse, where a sweet little old lady was stationed in a rocking chair on the veranda as a lookout for the law. Since then, it has been a rooming house and a local museum. But Tom and Sue Carroll, an enthusiastic couple in their early 40s, have given it a new, and one hopes a lasting, identity by refurbishing 12 rooms with Victorian and the warmth of patchwork quilts, braided rugs, and potted plants everywhere. The furnishings are impressive, with the ten-foot gilt mirror in the parlor a decided focal point. Most of the rooms have private bath; some share two "down the hall" facilities. In the guesthouse tradition, Tom and Sue serve a marvelous breakfast (included in the rates) and afternoon tea. Sue is usually the chef and sets a breakfast table that rates raves—strawberry crêpes, cheese soufflé, and fried apples are just some of the items that may appear. I don't really know if I am drawn most to this lovingly restored house or to the Carrolls, but I *do* know that there isn't a better travel buy anywhere in the neighborhood. Rates run from $60 to $95, and that includes both breakfast and afternoon tea. They do ask that you not bring pets, but they'll provide beach tags for the city beaches if you bring your own beach towels.

In Chincoteague, the **Channel Bass Inn,** 100 Church St., Chincoteague, VA 23336 (tel. 804/336-6148), is another hostelry loaded with charm and spiced by the enthusiasm of its owners. Jim and Kathleen Hanretta bought the rambling old house back in 1972, leaving careers as a classical and flamenco guitarist (Jim) and schoolteacher (Kathy) to devote themselves to converting the former boarding house into a first-class inn. The 11 rooms (eight with private bath) have all been done over (some with antique furnishings), and the Hanrettas have developed a restaurant that utilizes the best of all that fresh seafood on the island to turn out gourmet dinners that smack of both French and Spanish cuisine. Breakfasts are also available, by appointment. Doubles range from $125 to $250. Weekly rates are available, and all are lower January through March. Just one thing: Don't bring the children under 10, and leave Fido home.

Also in Chincoteague, **The Refuge,** one block west of Assateague Bridge, (P.O. Box 378), Chincoteague, VA 23336 (tel. 804/336-5511), is a two-story, 68-room building that overlooks the wildlife refuge and has rental bicycles as well as picnic tables with hibachis, a pool, whirlpool, sauna, and exercise room. Doubles here start at $55 in season, lower the rest of the year.

For budget accommodations in Chincoteague, you can't do better than the **Lighthouse Motel,** 224 N. Main St., Chincoteague, VA 23336 (tel. 804/336-5091). They have both rooms and efficiency apartments, and there's free coffee in rooms, a pool, cookout area, heated spas, and outdoor games. No pets. Doubles run $30 to $42, and efficiencies run $34 to $45 in season, as low as $20 and $25 in winter.

**America House Motor Inn,** P.O. Box 472, Cape Charles, VA 23310 (tel.

804/331-1776), is located on U.S. 13 not far from the Eastern Shore side of the Chesapeake Bay Bridge-Tunnel. Situated on 40 acres, with ten of them a private sandy beach, America House has spacious rooms that are modern in furnishings, but colonial in atmosphere due to prints, wall hangings, and other decorative touches that recall the Revolution. There's a high observation tower from which to get the lay of the land, and recreational facilities include sailboats, swimming pool, indoor shuffleboard, putting green, golf driving range, picnic areas, children's playground, and a game room with Ping-Pong and a pool table. Their restaurant, also in colonial decor, serves outstanding meals at very reasonable prices. Doubles here run $52 to $56, and studios are $54 to $56 in season (summer); all rates drop a bit off-season.

## Camping

On the northern end of **Assateague** there's a modern campground with hot showers, flush toilets, and 311 spaces for campers (no electric or water hookups) which are open most of the year. Space is usually allocated on a first-come, first-served basis, although some sites in summer may be reserved for a full week by contacting the Superintendent, Assateague State Park, Rte. 2, Box 293, Berlin, MD 21811 (tel. 301/641-2120).

Immediately south of the state park, the National Park Service operates smaller, primitive campgrounds (portable toilets and cold water only) year round. These family campgrounds and three backcountry, hike-in sites are always available on a first-come, first-served basis. Four bayside canoe-in sites are also available. Contact: Superintendent, Assateague Island National Seashore, Rte. 2, Box 294, Berlin, MD 21811 (tel. 301/641-1441).

# Chapter IV

# THE BLUE RIDGE MOUNTAINS

### 1. The Skyline Drive (Virginia)
### 2. The Blue Ridge Parkway (Virginia and North Carolina)

THERE'S SOMETHING ABOUT MOUNTAINS! "Majestic" is overworked, but it applies. A sense of timelessness—of patience and endurance. And there's just no better antidote to today's impatient rush toward tomorrow than the nearly 600-mile drive along the ridgecrest of the Blue Ridge Mountains that stretches down the western extremities of Virginia and North Carolina.

Beginning at Front Royal, Virginia, the Skyline Drive leads southward through 105 miles of the Shenandoah National Park to meet the Blue Ridge Parkway at Rockfish Gap, between Charlottesville and Waynesboro. The parkway then goes on for some 470 miles south, still along the crests of ancient mountains, until it reaches the Great Smoky Mountains National Park near the North Carolina–Tennessee border.

It's a drive of incredible beauty, with stunning mountain views and that increasingly rare commodity, a look at nature's face where "civilization" has been smart enough to protect it. All sorts of wild animals live here—bobcats, foxes, white-tailed deer, and black bear, to name a few. Streams are clear and forests of birch, poplar, beech, hickory, and oak (some more than 300 years old) are undisturbed. To come in late spring is to see green creeping up the peaks as trees leaf out. In summer, wildflowers blossom to make a carpet of colorful blooms. Fall brings vivid reds and yellows and oranges to give a flame-like hue to every mountainside. And the miracle is that although men and women have made their homes here since that first push westward, it is *nature* that endures. In fact, even the broad, well-paved highway, the carefully planned overlooks, the lodges and cabins and restaurants seem only to enhance what was here to begin with. The rigors of wilderness travel have been eliminated to leave only a natural, unspoiled area that can be traveled in comfort. For most of the year, that is. Fog is a problem at times, and some of the higher sections are closed during icy or snowy weather. It's best to plan this drive between mid-May and mid-November, when conditions are almost consistently good.

You *could,* of course, drive straight down the entire length of this gorgeous roadway. But if you did, you'd miss a wealth of sightseeing. All along the way there are not-to-be-missed historic sites and caverns and bridges that have been sculpted by the centuries just a few miles off the Drive and Parkway on either side. If time is a problem—it's a *long* drive and there are a lot of side trips—it's best to take one section at a time and come back later for the others. Personally, I prefer seeing it in small chunks (if those enormous vistas could be called "small"). So let's look at it that way.

## 1. The Skyline Drive (Virginia)

I find **Charlottesville,** at the southern end of the Drive, a perfect base. It's a full day's trip up to Front Royal and back, but accommodations are more plentiful and it's so central to sightseeing that I can leave the suitcase unpacked for a few days. An appealing alternative is to begin your journey about 15 miles north of Front Royal on I-81 in the little town of Middletown for no other reason than to stay at a very special inn dating back to Revolutionary days. Also, if you plan far enough in advance, the lodges at Big Meadow and Skyland are lovely—read on.

**WHERE TO STAY:** Both these lodges are almost at the center of the Drive and both are closed during the winter months. For full details on these and all other accommodations along the Drive, write: ARA Virginia Sky-Line Co., Inc., P.O. Box 727, Luray, VA 22835 (tel. 703/999-2266).

**Skyland Lodge,** P.O. Box 727, Luray, VA 22835 (tel. 703/999-2266), is open from early April until mid-November. It's ten miles south of the Thornton Gap entrance from Va. 211. This is the highest point on the Drive, and the glass-enclosed lobby takes full advantage of the spectacular view, with a fireplace to add just the right note of coziness on cool nights. There are rooms in the main lodge, as well as in separate cottages, and all are comfortable and attractive. Some suites have their own fireplaces. This is a great place for children: a playground, recreation room, lawn games, horses available (with trail maps) for hour-long, half- or full-day rides, and a planned children's program. The café serves all three meals and there's entertainment in the bar every night except Sunday. Doubles run $55 and up, with suites for two to six people beginning at $72. Children under 7 stay free in the same room with their parents. Pets are welcome, but must be kept on a leash.

**Big Meadows Lodge,** P.O. Box 727, Luray, VA 22835 (tel. 703/743-5108), 19 miles south of the Thornton Gap entrance, is smaller than Skyland and is open from March through December. Besides the main lodge, there's an annex and cottages. Rooms are quite nice and many have fireplaces. For children there's a playground and planned activities, a recreation room, and both horses and bicycles are available. All meals are served in the café (no room service) and the bar has entertainment every night except Wednesday. The leash rule applies to pets here too. Rates are $31 to $52 for double lodge rooms, $47 to $52 for motel rooms, $43 to $86 for cabins, $69 to $115 for suites that will sleep up to six (children under 16, free).

### Campsites

Campers will find tent and trailer sites at **Matthews Arm, Big Meadow, Lewis Mountain,** and **Loft Mountain,** but none has hookups. The rate is $7 per day and there's a 14-day limit. Write Superintendent, Shenandoah National Park, Rte. 4, Box 292, Luray, VA 22835 (tel. 703/999-2266), for full details.

### In Middletown, Va.

The **Wayside Inn Since 1797,** 7783 Main St., Middletown, VA 22645 (tel. 703/869-1797), began life in 1797 as Wilkinson's Tavern, offering bed and board to weary travelers in the Virginia wilderness. With the advent of the Shenandoah Valley Turnpike some 20 years later, it became a relay station for stagecoach drivers, as well as a welcome stop for their passengers. During the Civil War, Yankees and Rebels both frequented the place, and one of the war's fiercest battles was fought at nearby Cedar Creek. Today's motorcar travelers find the same warm hospitality, comfortable rooms, and outstanding food as did those earlier moveabouts. Rooms are decorated in a mixture of styles: heirlooms from England, lovingly brought over by early settlers; locally made "Early American" furniture; relics of the Victorian era; and touches of Oriental bric-a-brac brought home by wandering sea captains. There are canopied beds in some rooms, and even fireplaces in a few. Each room has its own personality, and when booking, you might specify if you'd prefer colonial, Chinese, Empire, or Victorian decor (no promise you'll get it, but the friendly owners do all they can to please, so it's worth a try). There are no elevators, so be prepared for stairs. There are seven dining rooms (I can't resist the Slave Quarters, with its crackling fire, high-back chairs, and bare wooden tables) and the Coachyard cocktail lounge, a throwback to the English pub tradition. As for the food, it's famed all through the valley—country-cured ham, peanut soup, pan-fried chicken, hot breads, and even chicken gumbo. And if sitting on the veranda in one of the white rocking chairs is a little too tame for your tastes, you can walk just a few yards to the Wayside Theater, where professional actors perform from June to September. The Wayside has become one of the most famous hostelries in Virginia, and in my book that's a reputation well earned. Doubles range from $70 to $100; suites are $90 to $125. A crib is $10. No pets.

### In Charlottesville, Va.

Call 804/293-6789 for a free local reservation service.

The **Boar's Head Inn**, P.O. Box 5185, Charlottesville, VA 22903 (tel. 804/296-2181), is one mile west of Va. 250-W Bypass and is one of the finest resort inns in the Commonwealth. An inn has stood here since 1763 when Terrell's Ordinary greeted travelers, and the present building dates its west wing from 1834. Decor is, as you'd expect, colonial, with a liberal supply of antiques in the attractive public areas. Rooms are beautifully decorated, some with lovely views of the mountains or the lake with its ducks and swans. There are facilities for tennis, squash, paddle tennis, and swimming (in season), plus exceptional health facilities. The tavern features live entertainment, and the dining room is considered one of the best places to eat in these parts (see "Where to Eat"). Doubles start at $88 and suites (some with fireplaces) at $125, and if you want to stay in this exceptionally beautiful place, you'd best reserve at least a month ahead. Children under 12 stay free with their parents, but there's a $3 charge for pets.

If you're interested in going the full luxury route, the sumptuous **Omni International Hotel** (formerly a Radisson) at 235 W. Main St., Charlottesville, VA 22901 (tel. 804/971-5500, or toll free 800/228-2121), is heartily recommended. In a historic redevelopment area in the heart of downtown, the seven-story bronze-and-glass contemporary structure is something of a surprising contrast to its surroundings. But it's tastefully done, and the 65-foot atrium lobby lounge is a real attention-getter. There's an elegantly appointed multilevel dining room with colonial touches, where dinners range from $10 to $22. A cocktail lounge, also bilevel, offers nightly entertainment, and there's an indoor/outdoor pool and complete health-fitness center. All in all, this 209-room charmer offers the amenities you can expect from this top-scale system, including special check-in and checkout and concierge services. Double rates for all this opulence will cost $92 a night.

Most of the large, convenient rooms at **Howard Johnson's**, 1309 W. Main St., Charlottesville, VA 22903 (tel. 804/296-8121), have balconies and attractive, modern decor. Directly across from the University of Virginia, the motel has indoor parking, an indoor pool, and a restaurant. Doubles run $52 to $62, and the only time advance reservations are necessary is at graduation time at the university (June).

The **Best Western Cavalier Inn,** P.O. Box 5647, Charlottesville, VA 22905 (tel. 804/296-8111), is also across from the university and has a pool, a 24-hour pancake house, and a family restaurant. They can also furnish a list of babysitters. Doubles here start at $57, but go up during special university events. Special vacation package rates are available.

Rooms at the budget-priced **Econolodge,** 2014 Holiday Dr., Charlottesville, VA 22901 (tel. 804/295-3185), are clean and comfortable and the inn offers free morning coffee and doughnuts. It's close to the university and a large shopping center. Advance reservations are advisable during June, July, and August. A double room here costs $37 to $45. Children under 12 stay free.

**READER'S GUESTHOUSE SUGGESTION:** "For lovely bed and breakfast accommodations in the Charlottesville area, contact the **Guesthouse Bed & Breakfast, Inc.,** people at P.O. Box 5737, Charlottesville, VA 22905 (tel. 804/979-7264). They do a very good job of booking you into just the type of place you want to stay, and there's always continental breakfast included in the rates, which we found on a par with local motels" (C. Harris, Arlington, Va.).

**WHERE TO EAT:** On the Skyline Drive itself, you'll find good food at moderate prices at both the lodges listed in the previous section. In addition, you'll be able to eat reasonably well at **Panorama,** or if a picnic seems like a good idea (it is!), you can pick up light lunches and groceries at **Elkwallow, Big Meadow,** and **Loft Mountain Waysides.**

### In Charlottesville, Va.

The Old Mill Room at the **Boar's Head Inn,** one mile west of Va. 250-W Bypass (tel. 804/296-2181), is in an 1834 gristmill now incorporated into the inn's west wing, and this is colonial-style dining at its best. Waitresses in colonial dress add to the early-days atmosphere in the candlelit room with its yellow-pine beams, fireplace, and antique furnishings. Escalope of veal Oscar is a favorite with patrons (appetizers, salads, and desserts extra). Dinner prices range from $12 to $20, and reservations are absolutely necessary. Lunch runs $5.50 to $9 and breakfast costs $3.50 to $6. Sunday brunch is $12.50. Hours are 7:30 to 10:30 a.m., noon to 2 p.m., and 6 to 9:30 p.m.—and best reserve. On the premises you'll also find a wine shop and country store.

The **Ivy Inn,** 2244 Old Ivy Rd., one mile from the University of Virginia, just off Va. 250 Bus. (tel. 804/977-1222), is in a 19th-century brick house. It, too, has fireplaces, and there's pleasant background music for candlelight dining. Featured dishes are veal, chicken, seafood, and steaks, and prices are in the $10 to $15 range. Dinner begins at 5 p.m., and reservations are a good idea. Closed Sunday.

Janice Amiss is now the owner-operator of the longtime favorite **Martha's Café,** just across from the university at 11 Elliewood Ave. (tel. 804/971-7530). This pleasant, homey restaurant attracts an appealing local clientele, many of them students, with its homemade dishes and friendly service. Quiches, muffins, and salads are excellent, and vegetables are always fresh. Lunch and dinner prices are surprisingly moderate (about $4 to $5 for lunch, $6 to $9 for dinner). It's a small, inviting restaurant with only 45 seats and reservations are not accepted, so you may have a bit of a wait (the outdoor patio adds 24 seats in summer); but for a light lunch or dinner, this is the place to go.

**The Garrett,** 102 14th St. NW (tel. 804/295-6060), is "on the corner," and is a favorite spot for the university and professional community. It's rustic, yet not without elegance, with a six-foot TV screen for major sports events. Specialties, all at moderate prices, vary daily. There's an above-average bar offering seasonal concoctions of their own which add to the general sparkle of the place. Sunday brunch is a local tradition (served from 10:30 a.m. to 2:30 p.m.). The Garrett is open from 11 a.m. to 4 p.m. for lunch Monday through Friday, and daily from 4 to 10:30 p.m. for dinner, with a late-night menu until closing. They also accept VISA and MasterCard.

**Le Snail,** 320 W. Main St. (tel. 804/295-4456), in a restored turn-of-the-century house in downtown Charlottesville is a refreshing change of scene from the area's prevailing colonial ambience. There's a main candlelit dining room and several smaller ones; the comfortable, rather eclectic decor might best be described as homey French provincial. Cuisine is highlighted by such impeccably continental specialties as la truite du chef, a luscious boned trout with assorted herbs and spices, wrapped in pastry and baked, and les crevettes Jafferen, shrimp in creamy orange sauce with rice. My favorite appetizer is special snails of the house in a delicate puff pastry. There's a dress code, only fitting in such a top-scale establishment. A la carte entrees, which include vegetables of the day, run from about $10 to $18. There's a $15 table d'hôte dinner Monday through Thursday. Le Snail is open Monday through Saturday from 6 to 10 p.m.; it closes December 25 to mid-January and the first three weeks of August. Reservations are urged!

For a moderate-priced lunch, there's historic old **Michie Tavern** (see "Things to See"), with a café that serves from 11:15 a.m. to 3 p.m.

**THINGS TO SEE:** If you're based at **Charlottesville,** plan at least one day to explore the historic sites and homes in this beautiful mountain town.

Make your first stop the **Thomas Jefferson Visitors Bureau** on Va. 20 South (tel. 804/293-6789) for free brochures, maps, and self-directed automobile and walking tours of the Charlottesville area. It's open from 9 a.m. to 5 p.m. Monday through Friday; closed major holidays. There's also a free local reservations service.

You can't miss the **University of Virginia** at the west end of Main Street, and certainly you *shouldn't* miss the experience of rambling around its campus for an hour or two. There are also free historical tours of the grounds and main points of interest that leave from the Rotunda Monday through Friday during the school term (call 804/924-1019 for times). Thomas Jefferson founded the school and drew plans for its grounds as well as many of its early buildings. Set in broad lawns with huge old trees and sweeping vistas, the handsome red-brick buildings with their white trim have an impressive, simple dignity. A classic example of Jefferson's architectural genius is the Rotunda, focal point of the oldest part of the campus, and the one-brick-thick serpentine wall and the columned porticoes that front student living quarters. Hostesses at the Rotunda will arrange student-guided tours on weekdays during the school year. The university opened its doors in 1825 with a student body of 68 and eight faculty members. Three of the first five U.S. presidents (Jefferson, Madison, and Monroe) served on its first board of trustees! Smaller today than many American universities, it has an annual enrollment of about 16,000—out of which it awards more graduate degrees than any other institution of higher learning in Virginia.

## Monticello and Vicinity

Jefferson's beloved home, **Monticello** (pronounced "Mont-i-*chell*-o") is on a mountaintop three miles southeast of Charlottesville on Va. 53 (tel. 804/295-

8181). He designed and built the house, using materials made right on the spot, from bricks right down to nails, on land that had come to his father in a land grant. Begun in 1769, it wasn't completed until 1809, although he lived in it from 1772. Jefferson died here on July 4, 1826, exactly 50 years after the signing of the Declaration of Independence, and his tomb is in the family cemetery. Restoration continues throughout the house, which contains many original furnishings. The gardens are extensive and include the newly replanted orchard. Open from 8 a.m. to 5 p.m. March to October, from 9 a.m. to 4:30 p.m. the remainder of the year. Admission is $5 for adults, $1 for children 6 to 11.

A recently added exhibit, "Thomas Jefferson & Monticello," in the **Visitors Center** on Va. 20 South offers fascinating glimpses into Mr. Jefferson's life and times via multimedia displays, artifacts, and family memorabilia. It's open from 9 a.m. to 5 p.m. daily except major holidays, and admission is free.

Just 2½ miles southeast of Monticello (off Va. 53 on County Road 795) is where the fifth U.S. president, James Monroe, lived at **Ash Lawn** ("Highland"), a modest country house on a 535-acre estate. Thomas Jefferson selected the house site and planted orchards for his neighbor. Now restored by the College of William and Mary, Ash Lawn offers tours of the house with its late-18th- and early-19th-century furnishings, including Monroe's furniture, periodic home-craft demonstrations, kitchen gardens, and truly magnificent boxwood hedges. There are peacocks among the boxwood, a Piccirilli statue of Monroe, quiet picnic spots, and great views of the Blue Ridge foothills. Special events include summer festivals of music and drama, and Christmas celebrations. Open daily from 9 a.m. to 6 p.m. March through October, from 10 a.m. to 5 p.m. November through February (closed Thanksgiving, Christmas, and New Year's Days). Admission is $4 for adults, $3.50 for seniors, $1 for ages 6 to 11, with special rates for groups of 15 or more.

Located high on a mountainside near Monticello, on Va. 53, historic **Michie Tavern** (tel. 804/977-1234) is one of the oldest homesteads remaining in the state. A Scotsman, John Michie, purchased the land from Patrick Henry's father in 1746 and built his home on what was a popular stagecoach route. In 1784 the commodious dwelling became a tavern and inn. Until 1910 Michie's descendants owned the property, but in 1927 the inn was dismantled and moved by horse and wagon and truck to its present site near Jefferson's Monticello. After a painstaking reconstruction, it opened in 1928 as a museum. Inside you'll find such handcrafted wooden household gadgets as a cheese press, apple peeler, potato cutter, etc., and a folding "Murphy bed" in an upstairs closet. The ballroom, keeping hall, ladies' and gentlemen's parlors, bedroom, and tap bar hold colonial and Revolutionary furniture and artifacts. Outbuildings include a log kitchen, "necessary," dairy, well house, and smoke house, as well as the Meadow Run grist mill that dates from about 1797. A colonial-style buffet is served daily in the "Ordinary," a 200-year-old slave house, from 11:30 a.m. to 3 p.m. The museum is open daily from 9 a.m. to 5 p.m., and admission is $3.50 for adults, $1.50 for children 6 to 12 (under 6, free).

## On and Near the Skyline Drive

There's a $2 charge per car to enter the Drive (for detailed information and pamphlets, contact: Superintendent, Shenandoah National Park, Luray, VA 22835; tel. 703/999-2266), and an *enforced* 35-mph speed limit (you won't want to speed through, anyway). The southernmost entrance at Rockfish Gap is 20 miles west of Charlottesville on U.S. 250. Other entries are at Swift Run Gap, between Stanardsville and Elkton on U.S. 33; Thornton Gap, on U.S. 211 between Luray and Sperryville; and at Front Royal (U.S. 340), its northernmost end.

At Big Meadows (Mile 51), the **Harry F. Byrd, Sr., Visitor Center** features a movie exploring man's relationship to the mountains and a historical and cultural museum. It's open every day, but only part-time during January and February. From April to November the **Dickey Ridge Visitor Center** near Front Royal is also open daily. **Shenandoah National Park headquarters** is five miles east of Luray on U.S. 211, and they'll send informative pamphlets if you write: Superintendent, Shenandoah National Park, Rte. 4, Box 292, Luray, VA 22835.

There are free **picnic grounds** with fireplaces, water, tables, and rest rooms at Dickey Ridge, Elkwallow, Pinnacles, Big Meadows, Lewis Mountain, South River, and Loft Mountain.

You can **trout fish** in some of the park streams from April to October 15, but you'll need a five-day state license (get them at park concession units).

If you bring Fido along, be *sure* to keep him on a leash—this is one regulation that's rigidly enforced.

You'll need at least one day—another if you plan to take in all the attractions just off the Drive—to drive to Front Royal and back. The views are breathtaking all along the way—across the Shenandoah Valley on your left lie the Massanutten Mountains, and beyond, the Alleghenies. There are parking overlooks at the most spectacular ones, and I defy you to drive right on by without making at least one stop! When you reach the north entrance to **Skyland,** you'll be at the highest point on the Drive, 3,680 feet above sea level. And not far from Thornton Gap, you'll pass through a 700-foot tunnel at **Mary's Rock.**

At Thornton Gap, you can turn west on U.S. 211 for a ten-minute drive to the **Luray Caverns** (tel. 703/743-6551). Its gigantic underground rooms—there's one that measures 300 feet wide, 500 feet long, and 140 feet high—are connected by natural corridors, and one features stereophonic music produced on an organ that uses reverberating stalactites instead of pipes! Be sure to bring that camera, for the lighting system makes color photos possible, and the staggering array of stalactites and stalagmites will arouse the photographer in you. About every 20 minutes or so, hour-long guided tours leave from the entrance of this majestic U.S. natural landmark, beginning at 9 a.m. The last tour leaves at 7 p.m. June 15 through Labor Day, at 6 p.m. March 15 to June 14 and after Labor Day to November 14, and at 4 p.m. Monday through Friday and at 5 p.m. on Saturday and Sunday the rest of the year. Adults pay $8 to explore this underworld magical kingdom, children 7 through 13 pay $4, and those under 7 are admitted free with their parents. Cost also includes admission to the **Car and Carriage Caravan,** a fascinating collection of antique cars, coaches, and costumes dating from 1625. There's no charge for the 45-minute (June through August) **carillon concerts** played every Tuesday, Thursday, Saturday, and Sunday by a world-famous carillonneur at the Luray Singing Tower, whose largest bell weighs 7,640 pounds and the smallest, 12½. Concerts are given weekends only, March through May and September through October.

Back on the Drive, ride on up to **Front Royal** (which got its name, incidentally, from the order of an out-of-patience drill sergeant to ill-trained local militia to "front to the royal oak," meaning the "royal" tree of England, when they had trouble following his regulation military command). The excellent **Thunderbird Museum and Archeological Park** (tel. 703/635-7337) is six miles south on U.S. 340, then half a mile west (you'll see the entrance signs), and here, for a fee of $2.50 (children 8 to 12, $1.75), you can watch archeologists at work during summer months. The museum displays some of their finds and explains exhibits, which show that early man was living here thousands of years before the Roman Empire. It also features an outdoor replica of an early Indian house.

The **Skyline Caverns,** P.O. Box 193, Front Royal, VA 22630 (tel. 703/635-4545), just one mile south of Front Royal on U.S. 340, have beautiful calcite formations known as "anthodites," which look like flowers, and whose estimated growth is only one inch every 7,000 years. The caverns are well lighted, there's a 37-foot waterfall, and you'll enjoy their Sound and Light show. Topside, a miniature train chugs around the wooded grounds ($1), and there are picnic grounds. Admission to the caverns is $6 (ages 7 to 13, $3), and they're open from 8:30 a.m. to 6:30 p.m. or 9 a.m. to 5:30 p.m., depending on the time of year. This is the nearest major caverns to the Skyline Drive.

On the return trip to Charlottesville, leave the Skyline Drive and take I-81 south to **Staunton** (forget about how it's spelled, pronounce it "Stanton"), one of the oldest cities west of the Blue Ridge Mountains. President Woodrow Wilson was born here, and his birthplace, a three-story Greek Revival mansion (tel. 703/885-0897) has been restored to its 1850s appearance when the Wilsons lived there. A film, exhibits, formal garden, and guided tour complete the visit. The house, at 24 N. Coalter St., is open every day from 9 a.m. to 5 p.m. (closed on Sunday December through February). Cost to enter is $3 for adults, $1 for children 6 to 12.

One of nature's greatest curiosities is at picturesque **Mount Solon,** 11 miles north of Staunton on U.S. 11, then west on Va. 646 to Va. 747. "Natural Chimneys" are seven huge limestone columns, rising to a height of 120 feet, which have been carved out of solid rock by the Shenandoah River over millions of years. From some vantage points they do indeed look like chimneys, but my fancy turns to the turrets and towers of a medieval castle. And I'm certainly not alone in that fancy, for back in 1821 people hereabouts started an annual jousting tournament in which "knights" with long lances attempt to spear a small, suspended ring while on horseback. Each knight gets three "tilts" and the winner is king of the tournament. If you're in these parts on the third Saturday in August, it's a fun day.

## 2. The Blue Ridge Parkway (Virginia and North Carolina)

From Waynesboro south, the Blue Ridge Parkway (write for maps and detailed information to: Superintendent, Blue Ridge Parkway, 700 Northwestern Plaza, Asheville, NC 28801; tel. 704/259-0779) takes up where the Skyline Drive leaves off, winding and twisting along the mountain crests right on through most of western North Carolina. You'll drive at elevations ranging from 649 to 6,053 feet above sea level. There's no toll on the Parkway, and there are rather frequent exits to nearby towns.

There are nine visitor centers; nine campgrounds (open May through October only, except for limited winter camping at Otter Creek, Roanoke Mountain, Price Park, and Linville Falls) with drinking water and comfort stations, but no shower or utility hookups (on a first-come, first-served basis—no reservations); restaurants and gas stations; and three lodges plus one location featuring rustic cabins for overnight accommodations (reservations are recommended). At many overlooks you'll see a squirrel-rifle-and-powder-horn symbol and the word "trail," which means that there are marked walking trails through the woods. Some take only 10 or 20 minutes and provide a delightful, leg-stretching break from the confines of the car. Others are longer and steeper and may take an hour or more if you go the entire way.

There are a few simple rules laid down by the National Park Service, which administers the Parkway: no commercial vehicles are permitted; no swimming in lakes and ponds; no hunting; pets must be kept on leash; and above all else, *no fire except in campground or picnic area fireplaces.* A good rule of your own to follow is to keep your gas tank half filled at all times—it's no place to be stranded! The higher sections of the Parkway, west of Asheville, are usually closed from mid-November to mid-April because of the danger of ice and snow, and should dangerous conditions exist at any other time of the year, sections affected are quickly closed to traffic. Oh, yes, the speed limit is 45 miles an hour —and they're quite serious about that.

Although Roanoke is just 120 miles south of Waynesboro, it probably should be your first overnight stop in order to spend at least one day at nearby Lexington and the Natural Bridge. From Roanoke to Asheville, North Carolina (the next city of any size), is too long to attempt in one day unless you're in a rush. And if you're in a rush, stay off the Parkway—first of all, there's that 45-mph speed limit; and second, if you don't have time to amble and drink in the beauty through which you're passing, wait and come back when you do. By breaking the drive at Boone, North Carolina (about ten miles off the Parkway), you'll have time to sightsee along the way and perhaps catch a performance of the outdoor drama *Horn in the West*. The final two legs of the trip—from Boone to Asheville and from there to Fontana Village—are easily accomplished in a day's drive.

## FROM CHARLOTTESVILLE TO ROANOKE, VA.: There are two lodges on the

Parkway in Virginia. **Peaks of Otter** (for details and rates, which vary, write Virginia Peaks of Otter Co., P.O. Box 489, Bedford, VA 24523; tel. 703/586-1081), some 86 miles from the northern end of the Parkway; and **Rocky Knob Cabins** (write National Park Concessions, Inc., Meadows of Dan, VA 24120), closer to the North Carolina border and south of Roanoke.

### A Very Special Detour

For a taste of that celebrated antebellum life, leave the Parkway at its intersection with I-64 and drive west to Covington, then north on U.S. 220, a total distance of about 60 miles, to the grand old resort hotel, **The Homestead**, at Hot Springs (U.S. 220, Hot Springs, VA 24445; tel. 703/839-5500). This classic, magnificent château holds over 600 rooms, and the tone is set from the minute you enter the 70-yard-long Great Hall, with its 16 Corinthian columns, 18 chandeliers, and two log-burning fireplaces. There are lobbies galore, many lounges, and two shopping areas, all on a very grand scale, indeed. And in keeping with its grand manner, the Homestead enforces a moderate dress code that rules out blue jeans and T-shirts (not that you'd *want* to wear them in such elegant surroundings). As for the rooms, there are spacious suites with parlors and big screened porches with magnificent mountain views, and penthouse duplexes in the South Wing, whose bedroom balconies are reached by spiral staircases (I *told* you this was a very special place). And there's a variety of recreational activities that is just simply outstanding: mineral baths or saunas, which were the original attractions; 16,000 acres of mountain forests and streams and meadows; horseback riding, hiking, fringed-surrey rides; an indoor and two outdoor pools; tennis courts (20); and three superb golf courses. Dining here is an experience. Both the cuisine and the service are legendary, and both more than live up to the elegance of the place. And that service doesn't flag even if you opt for room service in a room so beautifully furnished you just can't leave it. All in all, if a splurge is on your agenda or if posh is your natural style of travel, the Homestead is sure to fill the bill: it's been doing that since 1892. What you pay for such pampering is $125 to $165 (add $75 to $110 for those parlor suites) for doubles. There are some golf and tennis package plans—but don't expect huge reductions; it isn't that kind of place.

### Where to Stay in Roanoke

Roanoke was just a tiny village (population about 500) until it became a railroad center in the 1880s. One of the remnants of the prosperous times that followed is the **Roanoke Hotel,** 19 N. Jefferson St. (P.O. Box 12508), Roanoke, VA 24026 (tel. 703/343-6992), two blocks north off U.S. 220, U.S. 11, and I-581 (look for the "Downtown" exit). The large old "railroad hotel" is in the style of an English inn, albeit an elegant one. And both accommodations and service live up to that elegance. You'll really get the feeling of an era now passed when you settle into the groove of being a much-catered-to guest. There are three dining rooms (you can eat from 7 a.m. to 11 p.m.), bars, a heated indoor pool with poolside food service, babysitting service, and golf privileges at nearby courses. Doubles run $75 to $100; suites, $120 to $185.

There's a **Holiday Inn,** Orange Avenue at Williamson Road, Roanoke, VA 24012 (tel. 703/342-8961), in downtown Roanoke, with renovated large rooms and modern furnishings. Prices in the dining room (open for breakfast, lunch, and dinner) are moderate. Double-occupancy rooms are $60 to $64.

The **Days Inn Roanoke–Civic Center,** 535 Orange Ave. (P.O. Box 12325), Roanoke, VA 24024 (tel. 703/342-4551, or toll free 800/325-2525), at I-581 and U.S. 460, is conveniently located in the heart of downtown. Its 260 rooms offer the clean, comfortable, and spacious accommodations for which this system is noted. There's a pool and two lighted tennis courts, free HBO, and local phone calls are also free. Dining room costs are moderate, ranging from $4 to $7 for dinner. Doubles go for $32 to $36; add $4 for each additional adult, $2 for each child 2 to 18. If Fido comes along, he is charged $4.

## Where to Eat Along the Parkway

Restaurants, cafés, and picnic grounds are all in abundant supply at fairly convenient locations. If you decide on a picnic, however, stock up either before you go or at the first supply store you see—they aren't that plentiful once you're on the Parkway.

## Where to Eat in Roanoke

The **Hotel Roanoke's Regency Room** (tel. 703/343-6992) is far and away the best place to eat in this area. It's an elegant atmosphere (jacket and tie required at dinner), with entertainment and dancing. And there's delightful terrace dining when weather permits. Specialties include spoon bread (they do their own baking, so all breads are delicious), tournedos béarnaise, and steak Diane, and the tab will come to somewhere between $12 and $23 on the semi à la carte menu. Less formal meals are served in their Ad Lib lounge/restaurant.

For less expensive meals, try the dining rooms at the motels listed in the "Where to Stay" section.

**THINGS TO SEE AND DO:** Before setting off down the Parkway, there's a side trip you may want to take for half a day or so, especially if you were a fan of TV's Walton family. Some 30 miles south of Charlottesville, just off Va. 6 on a secondary road (800), the little town of Schuyler is where Earl Hamner grew up and the setting for "The Waltons" series. Aside from the absolutely gorgeous Blue Ridge Mountains scenery, you'll see the "Walton Home" and "Mr. Godsey's store" (Jim Bob's son may be behind the counter to sell you postcards or a snack). Or you can walk around the mill, now a soapstone factory. Don't expect guided tours or admission fees—just an easy, informal atmosphere and conversation with very friendly natives.

Now, back to the Parkway. About five miles from its northern end you'll come to **Humpback Rocks** and a reconstructed mountain farm. There's also a hiking trail a little farther along that leads three-quarters of a mile to the rocks. At **Yankee Horse,** look for an oldtime logging railroad spur, or take a short walk through the woods to see **Wigwam Falls.**

## Lexington

Take the U.S. 60 exit west from I-81 to Lexington, home and burial place of two famous Confederate generals, Robert E. Lee and "Stonewall" Jackson. The **Lexington Visitor Center,** 107 E. Washington St. (tel. 703/463-3777), will provide self-guided walking tours of historic sites, a short slide show, exhibits, and travel directions in Virginia. It's open from 9 a.m. to 5 p.m. daily except Thanksgiving, Christmas, and New Year's Days; open to 5:30 p.m. June through August.

Robert E. Lee came to Lexington following the Civil War to assume the presidency of the college which is today Washington and Lee University. The Lee family crypt, the famed Edward Valentine statue of General Lee, the Washington-Custis-Lee portrait collection, and General Lee's office, preserved as he left it, are located within the Lee Chapel on the university campus. The chapel is open mid-April to mid-October, Monday through Saturday from 9 a.m. to 5 p.m. (to 4 p.m. the rest of the year), and on Sunday from 2 to 5 p.m. except for major holidays.

Jackson's residence, the **Stonewall Jackson House,** 8 E. Washington St. (tel. 703/463-2552), was the only home he ever owned, and has been faithfully restored to tell the story of the man who was a professor at VMI prior to the Civil War. The house has been restored to its appearance when he and his second wife lived there from 1859 to 1861. It's open year round, Monday through Saturday from 9 a.m. to 4:30 p.m. and on Sunday from 1 to 4:30 p.m. There's an admission charge of $4 for adults, $2 for children. Closed Easter, Thanksgiving, Christmas, New Year's Day, and Sunday during January and February.

The **Virginia Military Institute,** on U.S. 11 has been sending graduates to war since the Mexican War of 1846. During the school year (September to May) you can see the colorful Guard Mount every day at 12:30 p.m. in nice weather and the dress parade on Friday at 4:15 p.m. The VMI Museum (tel. 703/463-6232) one of the finest college museums in the nation, with displays on the history of this unique institution, is free and open daily. During school sessions, guided tours by cadets are available. Gen. George C. Marshall's personal, military, and diplomatic papers and Nobel Peace Prize are housed in the Marshall Research Foundation's Library at the west end of the Parade Grounds, and there's an electric map that traces World War II developments. It's free and open Monday through Friday from 9 a.m. to 4:30 p.m., on Saturday from 9 a.m. to noon and 2 to 5 p.m.; and on Sunday from 2 to 5 p.m.

**Lexington Carriage Company tours** (tel. 703/463-9500) offer a delightful way to explore this charming city. Horse-drawn carriages ply the main streets, passing the colleges, historic structures, and restored 1860s Lexington. Stops are made at each historic site. Tours last about 40 minutes and leave from the Lexington Visitors Center from 9 a.m. to 5 p.m. Monday through Saturday April 1 through January 1. Cost is $5 per person, $20 to rent the entire carriage.

## Natural Bridge

South of Lexington on U.S. 11 you'll find one of the Seven Natural Wonders of the World, **Natural Bridge.** The 215-foot-high arch was an object of worship by Indians, and when Thomas Jefferson bought it for "20 shillings of good and lawful money" from King George III of England, he built a small cabin for visitors and hired a caretaker. His guests included such colonial greats as George Washington (who carved his initials in the limestone), Patrick Henry, James Monroe, and John Marshall. You reach the bridge by natural steps that wind down to Cedar Creek, past arborvitae trees estimated to be ten centuries old, or via the free shuttlebus. It's open daily year round from 7 a.m. until dusk. The *Drama of Creation,* a depiction of the world's beginning in special music, narration, and lighting, is presented after dark each night. There's a $4 charge for adults for either the day or night drama visit ($2 for ages 6 to 15); special combination tickets for both visits are $5 for adults, $2.50 for ages 6 to 15. Also on premises are a **Wax Museum and Caverns,** with special combination rates for all attractions.

The **Natural Bridge Hotel, Motor Lodge, and Inn** (tel. 703/291-2121, or toll free 800/336-5727, 800/533-1410 in Virginia), a full-service dining room, cafeteria, and snackbar adjoin.

You can rejoin the Parkway from Natural Bridge and follow it on to Roanoke.

### In and Around Roanoke

First thing on your agenda should be a visit to the **Roanoke Valley Convention and Visitors Bureau,** 14 W. Kirk Ave., Roanoke, VA 24011 (tel. 703/342-6025), for all sorts of helpful literature and information on current events. One block away, check out the bustling City Market.

Across the Walnut Avenue Bridge, off Va. 220, the **Mill Mountain city park** has a marvelous panoramic view of the city and its surroundings. There's also a children's zoo and a miniature train. Even if you don't visit the park, you'll be aware of it, for every night a 100-foot-high electric star is visible for miles around.

Drop by the 100-year-old downtown **Market Square,** longtime showcase for the fresh vegetables, fruits, and flowers of Shenandoah Valley farmers. Rescued after a period of rather sleazy decline, it has taken on new life as centerpiece of an exciting urban resurgence. Facing the square, the historic **City Market Building** has been transformed into a delightful festival marketplace, with oldtime gas lights and brick sidewalks lined with a bevy of smart shops, taverns, and restaurants. And, yes, farmers still come in from the country to hawk their fresh produce. Also facing the square is the impressive **Center in the Square,** which houses five cultural organizations under one roof and boasts both a theater and state-of-the-art planetarium.

At the **Virginia Museum of Transportation,** 303 Norfolk Ave. (tel. 703/342-5670), you can see steam, diesel, and electric locomotives amid one of the Southeast's most comprehensive collections of transportation artifacts. Other exhibits in this renovated former 1917 Norfolk and Western Railway freight depot range from horse-drawn carriages to space rockets. The museum is open from 10 a.m. to 5 p.m. Monday through Saturday and from noon to 5 p.m. on Sunday. Admission is $2 for adults, $1.60 for seniors, and $1 for children 3 to 12. Group rates are available.

The **Mill Mountain Theatre,** at Center in the Square, performs nightly, with Saturday and Sunday matinees, from December through August. Call 703/342-5740 for information about performance and reservations.

Check on current concerts and performances at the **Roanoke Civic Center,** 710 Williamson Rd. NE, Roanoke, VA 24016 (tel. 703/981-1201).

**Booker T. Washington's birthplace** is 20 miles southeast of Roanoke. Drive south on Va. 116 to Burnt Chimney, then take Va. 122 north (follow the signs). A Visitor Center has a 14-minute audio-visual biography of the black leader's life and accomplishments, as well as other exhibits, and there's a short, self-guiding trail walk past replicas of farm buildings that were on this tobacco farm where he was born as a slave in 1856. The farm is now worked much as it was when he lived here, and you'll see crops and animals similar to those he knew as a boy. The Visitor Center is open with no charge from 8:30 a.m. to 5 p.m. daily except for major holidays. For advance information, write: Booker T. Washington National Monument, Rte. 1, Box 195, Hardy, VA 24101 (tel. 703/721-2094).

If you're in Roanoke around July 4th, do take in part of the **Roanoke Valley Horse Show** at the nearby Salem Civic Center. It's one of the best in the country, and a fun way to celebrate the holiday.

**FROM ROANOKE TO BOONE:** Although it's only a 175-mile drive from Roanoke to Boone, you won't want to rush along this scenic route, and a stop at Boone is just about right to give you a full, unhurried day getting there.

## Where to Stay in Boone

One of the most exclusive resort lodges in this part of the country is near Boone, and if "deluxe" is your travel style, it will be a mountain visit par excellence if you reserve at **Hound Ears Lodge,** P.O. Box 188, Blowing Rock, NC 28605 (tel. 704/963-4321), which gets its unusual name from a nearby rock formation. It's five miles southwest of Boone on N.C. 105, then three-quarters of a mile south on Country Road 1568 (follow the signs). The setting is gorgeous, the rooms and suites are the ultimate in luxury, and this complete resort, surrounded by beautifully landscaped grounds, has a pool and facilities for golf, tennis, fishing, and skiing (in winter months, of course). Prices are steep—a whopping $220 per day for doubles, modified American plan.

**Holiday Inn,** 710 Blowing Rock Rd., Boone, NC 28607 (tel. 704/264-2451, or toll-free 800/465-4329), has a heated pool, health-exercise club, and running track, as well as a restaurant which serves moderately priced meals. Double-occupancy rooms are typical of this chain and range from $67 to $70.

## Where to Eat in Boone

Head straight for the **Dan'l Boone Inn,** 105 Hardin St. (tel. 704/264-8657), for family-style breakfasts, lunches, or dinners that are really something special —and at prices that won't hurt. Everything is home-cooked, and the fare is definitely southern: country ham and biscuits, fried chicken, and the like. Prices run from $5.50 for a family-style breakfast to $7.75 for dinner. Children's plates average $2.50.

The **Holiday Inn,** 710 Blowing Rock Rd. (tel. 704/264-2451), has an exceptionally nice dining room that specializes in steaks and other beef dishes at moderate prices ($7 to $10 for complete dinners). Like most of this chain's dining rooms, it serves all three meals, with hours from 6:30 a.m. to 10 p.m.

## Things to See and Do

Between Roanoke and the North Carolina border, be sure to stop at **Mabry Mill.** There's a lovely cluster of log cabins, farm buildings, a blacksmith shop, a church, and a water-powered gristmill straight out of pioneer days. The restaurant makes a good lunch stopover too.

If you're theater-minded, there's a detour off the Parkway onto I-81 that you really should take. In the town of **Abingdon,** something happened back in 1932 that has profoundly influenced the American theater ever since. A young enthusiastic actor, Robert Porterfield, figured out that hungry professional actors all over the country would be happy during those Depression years to exchange their talents for a place to work and food to eat. At the same time, he believed the theater-hungry mountain people (who had food aplenty) would welcome a chance to swap it for live productions. He was right, and the Barter Theatre he established has been a rousing success since those first days when playwrights like Austin Strong, Noel Coward, Thornton Wilder, Robert Sherwood, and Maxwell Anderson accepted hams and other country produce in payment for scripts, and one day's door receipts showed up on the little company's table the next day.

Since 1946 the Barter has been the **State Theatre of Virginia,** supported in part by legislative funds, and admissions nowadays are in the form of coin of the realm (I don't really know what would happen if you showed up with a ham, but they *do* invite you to call for barter procedure!). Many of our theatrical leading lights have had their early training here, among them: Hume Cronyn, Patricia Neal, Fritz Weaver, Ernest Borgnine, and Gregory Peck. Across the street, the Barter Playhouse has now become a full-fledged member of Actor's Equity and presents established works. The regular season runs from April to October, and people come from several hundred miles around (tourists often make this a primary stop). To find out about schedules and tickets, write the State Theatre of Virginia, Abingdon, VA 24210 (tel. 703/628-3991, or toll free 800/368-3240, 800/572-2081 in Virginia).

## For an Overnight Stay in Abingdon

It is not inconceivable that the Barter Playhouse or the State Theatre will entice you to stay overnight for a performance. If that happens, run—don't walk—over to the **Martha Washington Inn,** 150 W. Main St., Abingdon, VA 24210 (tel. 703/628-3161). Housed in what was built in 1830 as a private residence and then served nearly 100 years as a college, the inn was completely renovated in 1985, yet still retains the feeling of graciousness and hospitality native to those long-gone days. Lobbies and sitting rooms are furnished with antique grandfather clocks and glistening chandeliers. An elegant colonial staircase sweeps down into the wide central hall. Upstairs, many rooms have four-poster beds (some with canopies) and fireplaces, and all are beautifully and comfortably furnished. Whether you stay here or not, plan on at least one meal in the dining room, which features country ham and other southern specialties. Doubles are $72, and children under 12 stay free. Studios range from $90 to $110, and suites are $130 to $360.

## Sights In and Around Boone

There's so much to see and do here that it might be a good idea to make this a two- or three-day stop, especially during the summer months. Be sure to check with the **Boone Chamber of Commerce,** 701 Blowing Rock Rd., Boone, NC 28607 (tel. 704/264-2225, or toll free 800/438-7500 in the eastern U.S., 800/222-7515 in North Carolina).

The **Boone–Banner Elk–Blowing Rock** area, sometimes called "The High Country," has been a summer resort retreat for Southerners since the 1800s. But in recent years, skiers have been attracted to the high slopes during winter months as well. There are now excellent skiing facilities and a wealth of winter accommodations, restaurants, and entertainment spots at **Ski Beech Ski Resort,** P.O. Box 1118, Banner Elk, NC 28604 (tel. 704/387-2011). While I've never been attracted to the sport myself and cannot judge the quality of the snow (there are snowmakers to help out Mother Nature), runs, etc., friends who head for the hills every winter weekend tell me this is the best skiing in the South and among the best in the country. Day-long lift rates, subject to change, are in the $22 range, and increase to $27 on weekends and holidays. Rentals are $11 to $13 per day. The top-flight professional ski-school staff offers class lessons at $12 per person or a book of five lessons for $45; private lessons are $25 per person. There's also a children's ski program, at $45 daily per child, and nonskiing tykes can stay and play in the Land of Oz Nursery for $3 an hour or $20 per day.

Boone itself (named for Daniel, of course—he had a cabin here in the 1760s) draws hunters and fishermen to the abundantly stocked streams and forests. For the sportsman and non-sports-minded summer visitors alike, there's a beautifully produced outdoor drama, Kermit Hunter's *Horn in the West,* staged in the **Daniel Boone Theatre,** P.O. Box 295, Boone, NC 28607 (tel. 704/264-2120 or 264-9089), every night except Monday from late June through August. It tells a vivid story of pioneer efforts to win the friendship of native Cherokee Indians. Performances begin at 8:30 p.m. and admission is $7 to $8 (age 13 and under, half price).

Located adjacent to *Horn in the West* is the **Hickory Ridge Homestead Museum** (tel. 704/264-2120), an 18th-century living-history museum in a re-created log cabin. It's open from 6 to 8:30 p.m. Tuesday through Sunday during late June through mid-August performance season. Traditional craftspeople demonstrate their skills, and there's a homestead store. An apple festival is held on the grounds in late October, and Christmas events lighten mid-December.

In the immediate vicinity, don't miss **Blowing Rock,** two miles southeast of the town of the same name on U.S. 321 (tel. 704/295-7111), where you can stand on The Rock, as it's affectionately called, throw a handkerchief or some other light object off the edge, and have it sent right back up to you by strong updraft winds. And when you're not playing that rather fascinating game, the observation tower, gazebos, and gardens offer really splendid views of the **John's River Gorge** and nearby Blue Ridge peaks. The observation tower is open every day from 8:30 a.m. to 6 p.m. in April and May, from 8 a.m. to 8 p.m. June through August, and from 8 a.m. to 6 p.m. in September, October, and November (as long as weather permits). Adults pay $3; ages 6 to 11, $1; group rates are $2 for adults, 75¢ for children 6 to 11 in groups of 15 or more. Another natural phenomenon at Blowing Rock is **Mystery Hill,** where balls roll and water runs uphill. The **pioneer museum** is interesting and you'll get a kick out of the mock grave marked simply "He Wuz a Revenoor"—a pile of dirt with boots sticking out one end!

Don't think the **Tweetsie Railroad** (tel. 704/264-9061), halfway between Boone and Blowing Rock, is for the kiddies only; the whole family will enjoy this old narrow-gauge train (I love every toot of the sweet-toned whistle) as it winds through the mountains, suffering mock attacks by "Indians" and "outlaws." Mountain music and other entertainment waits at **Tweetside Palace** and the Junction and Mining Company are straight out of a history book. The train makes daily runs from 9 a.m. to 6 p.m. from late May to mid-October. Fare is $9 for adults and $7 for ages 4 to 12.

**Grandfather Mountain** (one mile off the Parkway on U.S. 221 near Linville) is the highest peak in the Blue Ridge. You can see as far as 100 miles from the **Mile High Swinging Bridge,** and the **Environmental Habitat** is home to Mildred the Bear and her black bear friends. In spacious separate sections you can also view native deer, cougars, and bald and golden eagles (which have been injured and cannot live in the wild on their own). This is the place where kilt-clad Scots gather (from Scotland as well as all parts of North America) early in July for the **Annual Highland Games and Gathering of the Clans.** Exciting bagpipe music, dancing, wrestling, and tossing the cabar (a telephone-pole-like shaft) contests—as well as the colorful mix of people bent on two days of fun—make it a spectacle not to be missed.

**FROM BOONE TO ASHEVILLE, N.C.:** A worthwhile detour from the Parkway at this point is **Burnsville,** where a delightful town square is surrounded by vintage buildings. From Burnsville you can return to the Parkway and stop at Little Switzerland for lunch or overnight at **Big Lynn Lodge,** Rte. 226A, P.O. Box 459, Little Switzerland, NC 28749 (tel. 704/765-4257), with doubles from $56 to $75 in summer, or at **The Chalet,** off the Blue Ridge Pkwy., mile post 334,

P.O. Box 399, Little Switzerland, NC 28749 (tel. 704/765-4089), where high-season doubles range from $35 to $70.

## Where to Stay in Asheville

Mountain vacationing can be rustic and at the same time luxurious. If you don't believe that, reserve at Asheville's **Grove Park Inn and Country Club,** 290 Macon Ave., Asheville, NC 28804 (tel. 704/252-2711, or toll free 800/438-5800), a favorite of southern gentry since 1913; host over the years to such notables as F. Scott Fitzgerald, F.D.R., Woodrow Wilson, Thomas Edison, and Henry Ford; and listed in the National Register of Historic Places.

Built on the side of Sunset Mountain at an elevation of 3,100 feet, the rambling main building is constructed of huge native boulders and its "great hall" lobby is flanked on each end by 14-foot fireplaces. The comfortably padded chairs and sofas create a feeling of coziness despite the 120-foot-long dimensions of the room. On crisp evenings (even in summer nighttime temperatures are often in the 50s and 60s), when fires are lit, a sort of magic takes over as special events are held here, transforming travelers from strangers into warm friends.

With an extensive renovation and expansion project completed in 1984, the resort is open on a year-round basis. It now includes 389 guest rooms, five restaurants, four lounges, a shopping arcade, seven tennis courts, both indoor and outdoor swimming pools, a sports center, and an 18-hole championship golf course.

Notable among the fine restaurants are the famed Sunset Terrace, an outdoor veranda overlooking the Blue Ridge Mountains and serving lunch and dinner with dancing in season; the Dynasty Restaurant and Lounge, featuring international cuisine and dancing; the Fox & Hounds, for continental dining in an English country setting; and the Carolina Café for light meals and continuous service.

Various package plans are offered for sports enthusiasts or for couples with something special to celebrate (perhaps a honeymoon, as was the case with my own parents). Room rates begin at $93 double until mid-April, $115 to $130 thereafter. If you prefer, there's a higher rate that covers all meals.

Deluxe accommodations are also on tap at the **Great Smokies Hilton,** 1 Hilton Dr., Asheville, NC 28806 (tel. 704/254-3211). In addition to the high-quality guest rooms (some with wet bars) that are typical of Hilton hotels, there are also a heated pool and sauna, tennis courts, and an 18-hole golf course. Rates from April through October are in the $65 to $80 range for singles, $75 to $95 for doubles, with family package rates available. Other months, rates are somewhat lower.

At the **Haywood Park Hotel,** 1 Battery Park Ave., Asheville, NC 28801 (tel. 704/252-2522), it's suites only in a sophisticated setting in the heart of downtown Asheville. Suites are a nice blend of luxury (such as marble baths, oversize tubs, Jacuzzis, mini-bars, and fridges in some) and practicality (computer hookups in all). Brenna's Restaurant and Lounge provides both casual and more formal dining. Rates begin at $80 single for a studio and run $100 to $125 double for one-bedroom superior suites.

If the budget calls for moderate rather than deluxe, head for Lloyd and Leone Kirk's **Forest Manor Motor Lodge,** U.S. 25 South, Asheville, NC 28803 (tel. 704/274-3531), 3½ miles from the city center. In a scenic, wooded setting, the bungalow-style rooms are pine paneled and attractively furnished, and each has an inviting front porch entrance bordered by well-tended flower beds. And the Kirks so pride themselves on cleanliness that if you find any evidence of dirt, there's no charge! The sounds of song birds and gentle breezes sighing through pine trees predominate over highway noises, which are reduced to a faint hum by the set-back location. It's a relaxed, very friendly place to stay, open year round. Rates are $58 to $88 double, April through October; $40 to $58 the rest of the year. There are kitchenettes available for a minimum of one week and rollaway beds or cribs are furnished at a small additional charge.

Asheville has a **Days Inn,** I-40 and U.S. 70 East, P.O. Box 9708, Asheville, NC 28815 (tel. 704/298-5140), situated on a hillside with mountain views that are especially spectacular, especially when autumn foliage begins to turn. There's a pool, kiddie playground, restaurant, gift shop, and laundry service. Only five miles from Biltmore House  Seasonal rates range from $27 to $40 for singles, $32 to $45 for doubles.

## Bed and Breakfast in Asheville

A stay at **Cedar Crest,** 674 Biltmore Ave., Asheville, NC 28803 (tel. 704/252-1389), is a lovely trip back to the Victorian era. Built in 1894, this grand mansion is a fantasy of leaded glass, ornately carved fireplaces, antique furnishings, and a massive oak staircase. Owners Barbara and Jack McEwan have indulged their romantic and whimsical imaginations in furnishing the 11 guest rooms—all have period antiques and the decor in each is unique, with a canopied ceiling in one, marvelous carved walnut bed in another, brass bedsteads, and even a "rope" bed with a feather mattress. All have private or semiprivate baths. Evening coffee and chocolate are served in the parlor, and a continental breakfast is included in the rates, which begin at $45 for singles and $58 for doubles with shared bath, and rise to $57 and $65 for semiprivate bath or $67 and $75 for private bath. Cedar Crest does not accept children under 12 or pets, and smoking is permitted only in designated areas.

**Reed House,** 119 Dodge St., Asheville, NC 28803 (tel. 704/274-1604), is another delightful old mansion that welcomes guests. Mrs. Marge Turcot presides over the 1892 house on a hill overlooking Biltmore Village. The five guest rooms come complete with working fireplaces and rocking chairs, and the complimentary continental breakfast features homemade, low-sodium muffins and rolls with homemade jam—a real southern treat! Rates at this friendly place begin at $45. Open from May 1 to November 1.

## A Nearby Mountain Retreat

About 45 miles south of Asheville, the **Greystone Inn,** P.O. Box 6, Lake Toxaway, NC 28747 (tel. 704/966-4700, or toll free 800/824-5766), is just the sort of getaway spot for which your heart and soul begin to yearn as the richness of Mother Nature's gifts to the scenic wonderland of the Blue Ridge Mountains unfolds around you. Set on a wooded peninsula on Lake Toxaway, this 1915 mansion has been restored to welcome guests with 15 rooms that feature an engaging mix of antique furnishings and modern comforts (there are even Jacuzzi baths in all but one!). Each has its own unique character, and many have working fireplaces. The stone fireplace is also a focal point in the gracious oak-paneled living room; the library is a beautifully appointed oasis that promises hours of reading pleasure; and the terrace is the perfect setting for before-dinner drinks. For dedicated do-nothings, there are wicker rocking chairs on the glassed-in sun porch overlooking the lake. For those of a more active nature, there are tennis courts, fishing, waterskiing, swimming, sailboating, and golf at the adjacent Lake Toxaway Country Club (membership is included in the inn rates). Meals in the Hearthsides dining room feature gourmet entrees such as veal française Scandi and rainbow mountain trout amandine. In addition to main-house guest rooms, there are six lovely cottages (two or three bedrooms) that come with full kitchens. Rates (which include a sumptuous country breakfast, midafternoon tea or coffee and cakes, and dinner) are in the $95 to $135 range, plus a 15% service charge and state and local taxes. The Greystone Inn is just off N.C. 64 between Brevard and Cashiers.

## Camping from Boone to Asheville

There are three campgrounds operated by the National Park Service on the Blue Ridge Parkway between Boone and Asheville. None has showers, and other facilities are limited, varying from one location to another. Rates are $6 per site and availability is on a first-come, first-served basis. For full details, you can contact each at these addresses:

**Open year round:** Linville Falls Campground, Rte. 1, Box 798, Spruce Pine, NC 28777 (tel. 704/765-7818); Julian Price Memorial Campground, Blowing Rock, NC 28605 (tel. 704/295-9031).

**Open May through October:** Blue Ridge Parkway, National Park Service, Doughton Park Campground, Rte. 1, Box 50, Laurel Springs, NC 28644 (tel. 919/372-8877).

## Where to Eat in Asheville

Some of the best eating in Asheville is to be found at the **Grove Park Inn,** 290 Macon Ave. (tel. 704/252-2711). Even if you stay elsewhere, you really should plan at least one meal at this great old hostelry. Sunday brunch in the **Plantation Room** is an Asheville tradition, with a sumptuous Southern breakfast buffet table laden with so many plantation "extras" (fried chicken, grilled trout, etc.) that any thought of sticking to a diet will evaporate at the mere sight. Priced at $15, it is extremely popular with locals, so reserve as early as possible. If an elegant, gourmet meal is what you're after, reserve at the Inn's **Dynasty Restaurant,** where polished, professional service complements such specialties as Veal Cordon Bleu and Peking Duck. It's open for dinner only (7 to 10 p.m.), prices are $30 and under, and there's dancing. For more casual meals, there's the lovely **Sunset Terrace** looking out to the mountains, with light lunches (salads, sandwiches, quiches, burgers, etc.) for under $10 and a very good dinner menu featuring sautéed scampi, fresh mountain trout, and the like for $22 and under, and in summer months, there's dancing. In the **Carolina Cafe,** either lunch or dinner will run no more than $10 for a simpler menu of salads, burgers, etc.

**Brenna's Restaurant and Lounge,** 1 Battery Park Ave. (tel. 704/252-2612), is an attractive, pleasant restaurant that serves excellent meals in a casual front room, as well as in the slightly more formal cozy back dining room. A specialty here is grilled salmon in red-pepper butter, but no matter what you order, you can be sure it's prepared from fresh ingredients, obtained locally whenever possible. Lunch will run from a moderate $3 to $5; dinner is in the $10 to $18 range. Hours are 7 to 10 a.m. for breakfast and 11 a.m. to 2 p.m. for lunch, Monday through Friday; 6 to 10 p.m. for dinner Tuesday through Saturday. Reservations are advisable (but not always necessary) at this popular restaurant.

In Biltmore Village, the charming **Depot Restaurant,** 30 Lodge St. (tel. 704/274-4826), is housed in the 1896 railway station. It's a relaxed place, with a large menu that includes chicken, seafood, pork, veal, and beef dishes. Most folks hereabout, however, come for the prime ribs (which are offered at the remarkable price of $7 in a six-course special on weekends!). Prices average around $4 at lunch, $10 at dinner. Hours are 11:30 a.m. to 10 p.m. Monday through Thursday, until 11 p.m. on Friday and Saturday, and to 7:30 p.m. on Sunday.

Also in Biltmore Village, the **Corner House Café,** 6 Boston Way (tel. 704/274-3086), is a delightful restaurant/bakery/deli. Casual diners love the glassed-in front porch, and there's more formal dining in bright inside rooms. In addition to moderately priced, delicious meals featuring seafood, poultry, beef, pork, and a vegetarian menu, there's a wide selection of salads and sandwiches, as well as fresh-baked croissants, assorted breads, muffins, etc., from their bakery. They'll also provide boxed picnic lunches and cheese-and-wine baskets to go. Hours are 8 a.m. to 6 p.m. Monday through Saturday.

If it's *real* southern mountain food you're after, you'll find yourself going back again and again to **Bill Stanley's Barbeque and Blue Grass,** 20 S. Spruce St. (tel. 704/253-4871). The large dining room has the look of an authentic "mountain rustic" decor, and the friendly staff brings a real "down-home" ambience right along with some of the most mouthwatering barbecue (beef, pork, and chicken) you're likely to encounter in the entire state. Piled-high dinner plates come with that scrumptious barbecue or smoked chicken, catfish, sliced ham, or sliced turkey, all at prices under $10! Side orders include such southern favorites as corn on the cob and potato salad, and it goes without saying that hush puppies are highlights of any meal. At lunch there's a large selection of sandwiches priced under $3.50, with side orders of coleslaw, corn on the cob, potato salad, french fries, etc., and a good choice of bottled beers. There's also a nice salad bar for under $3, and a marvelous "all you can eat" buffet for $7.50 at lunch. Hours are 11 a.m. to midnight Monday through Thursday, to 1 a.m. on Friday, and 6 p.m. to 1 a.m. on Saturday. One word of caution: If you come along after 8 p.m., be prepared to shake a leg or two to some of the best foot-stomping mountain music in the South (see "Things to See and Do," below) that has been known to entice even the most timid of diners out onto the floor.

## Things to See and Do in the Asheville Area

For detailed information on Asheville's many attractions (including the Blue Ridge Parkway), write or visit: **Asheville Area Chamber of Commerce,** 151 Haywood St. (P.O. Box 1011), Asheville, NC 28802 (tel. 704/258-3858).

Since 1797, Asheville has grown from a tiny mountain trading village at the confluence of the French Broad and Swannanoa Rivers into a year-round resort, gaining along the way architectural gems from several eras and cultural features that make it such an interesting place to visit. In recent years there's been a vigorous movement afoot to preserve and restore those remnants of the city's colorful past, and a concise "Asheville Heritage Tour" brochure, available from the Asheville Chamber of Commerce, will guide you through such points as the historic downtown district, **Biltmore Village** (a cluster of some 24 English-village cottages built in conjunction with Biltmore Estate and now housing interesting boutiques, craft shops, and restaurants), the **Chestnut Hill** historic district, with its more than 200 turn-of-the-century residences, and a number of outlying points of interest. In the downtown area, keep an eye out for marvelous art deco buildings now being restored, the **Lexington Park** area that is attracting artists and artisans whose studios and workshops are tucked away down a little alleyway, and **Pack Place,** which is being developed as a center for all sorts of cultural activities.

Incidentally, you shouldn't make the mistake of dismissing Biltmore Village as just one more shopping complex—the buildings are of interest in themselves, and browsing is a sightseeing adventure as you stop by such shops as the **Early Music Shop,** 3 Biltmore Plaza, that trades in oldtime instruments such as dulcimers and Celtic harps. At **Fireside Antiques,** 32 All Souls Crescent, owners Robert Griffin and Ronald Clemmer present a fine collection of European, Oriental, and American antiques and unique gift items, and stand ready at a drop of a question to wax enthusiastic about the preservation of Asheville's unique heritage. Booklovers will want to drop in at the **Book Mart,** 7 Biltmore Plaza, for a look at their old and rare books. Other shops are equally interesting, and there's good eating handy when stomach and feet call for a halt.

I've fantasized as long as I can remember about the life of the really rich and what it would be like to have unlimited money. Well, while my chances of ever knowing that lifestyle firsthand are nil (not *practically* nil, all-the-way nil), the fantasies get a shot in the arm every time I go to see the overwhelmingly magnificent **Biltmore Estate,** One North Pack Square, Asheville, NC 28801 (tel. 704/255-1700), on U.S. 25, two blocks north off I-40. The French Renaissance château built by George W. Vanderbilt has 250 rooms! And talk about the "grand manner"—it fills every nook and cranny of this house and its gardens. There just isn't an ordinary spot in the place, not even the kitchen. Vanderbilt, a man who lived out *my* fantasies, gathered furnishings and art treasures from all over the world for this palace (for instance, Napoleon's chess set and table from St. Helena are here) and then went further to plant one of the most lavish formal gardens you'll ever see. There are more than 200 varieties of azaleas alone, plus thousands of other plants and shrubs. Admission to the house and gardens is $15 for adults, $12 for children 12 to 17 (under 12 free with their parents). You should allow a minimum of two hours for the self-guided tour. If you plan to make a day of it, there's a charming restaurant in a renovated barn, as well as an interesting winery.

There's no charge to visit a pet project of Mrs. Vanderbilt's, the **Biltmore Homespun Shops,** two miles north of town on Macon Street via Charlotte Street, on the grounds of the Grove Park Inn (tel. 704/253-7651). Mrs. Vanderbilt wanted to preserve the ancient wool-manufacturing skills of the mountains and help the weavers turn those skills into a paying industry, so she set up the cluster of old-world-style buildings, found local orders for the beautiful handwoven fabrics, and eventually a mail-order business evolved which still thrives. You can visit the buildings, now covered with ivy to add to their charm, and see the whole wool-making process, from dyeing and carding to spinning to weaving on homemade oak looms to the final washing and sun-drying. There's an **Antique Automobile Museum,** also free, which holds cars dating back to 1905.

**Thomas Wolfe** grew up in Asheville and immortalized the town and its citizens (much to their dismay) in his *Look Homeward, Angel.* The boarding house, "Dixieland," that figures so prominently in the book, is at 48 Spruce St., and is maintained as a literary shrine, with hours that vary seasonally (call 704/253-8304 for details). Adults pay $1; children through high school, 50¢. Both Wolfe and William Sydney Porter (O. Henry) are buried in **Riverside Cemetery** (entrance on Birch Street off Pearson Drive).

Some five miles east of Asheville at Milepost 382 on the Blue Ridge Parkway, the **Folk Art Center,** P.O. Box 9545, Asheville, NC 28815 (tel. 704/298-7928), is operated by the Southern Highland Handicraft Guild. The large stone-and-wood building houses work by local mountain craftspeople, many of whom are on hand to talk about their work. If at all possible, plan your visit to include performances by the Folktellers, who are in residence from mid-July to mid-August for Thursday-through-Saturday tall-tale sessions and from mid- to late-October for Sunday shows. These talented young women, Barbara Freeman and Connie Regan-Blake, are among this country's best mountain storytellers, and their "Mountain Sweet-Talk" is a treat not to be missed. Call ahead for exact schedules.

A few miles from Asheville on N.C. 70, you'll find **Black Mountain,** a small mountain community that seems suspended in time. Stop by the Old Depot, which has been turned into a center for the work of local craftspeople and where you'll often hear the sweet music of oldtime dulcimers played by local musicians who also sing traditional ballads of these hills. If you should be in the area the first weekend in December, don't miss the heart-lifting lighting of a Christmas tree that floats on the small lake just back of the Depot—it's a lovely gathering of mountain people who begin the holiday season with this touching event.

**Chimney Rock Park** is 25 miles southeast of Asheville on U.S. 74 at N.C. 64 and N.C. 9. The huge granite monolith rises to a height of 315 feet, and you can reach its top by a stairway, a trail, or (as in my own case) by an elevator. There's an observation lounge open every day from mid-March through November (weather permitting), and the charge is $7 for adults, $4 for children 6 to 15. Trails lead to Needle's Eye, Moonshiner's Cave, and Devil's Head (on the way to Hickory Nut Falls, twice the height of Niagara). Food service is available, as are picnic facilities. For full details and a free vacation brochure and map, contact: Chimney Rock Co., P.O. Box 39, Chimney Rock, NC 28720 (tel. 704/625-9611).

Stately **Mount Mitchell** is in the **state park** that bears its name some 33 miles northeast on the Parkway, then five miles north on N.C. 128. There are a museum, a tower, and an observation lodge at Mount Mitchell; camping and picnicking facilities are available in the park.

About 30 miles southeast of Asheville on U.S. 25 is the little town of **Flat Rock,** home to the **North Carolina State Theater's Flat Rock Playhouse,** which stages performances from late June through August. It is better known, however, as the last home of two-time Pulitzer Prize–winning writer/poet/historian Carl Sandburg, who lived at **Connemara Farm** (on Little River Road, just west of U.S. 25) for some 22 years, longer than he'd ever lived in one place before. His home and the farm are preserved just as they were in his lifetime—the typewriter still sitting on an orange crate in his top-floor hideaway and his guitar propped against a chair in the living room—and there's no charge to visit and stroll around the grounds.

There are things to do in Asheville other than sightsee, however. For instance, if you land here the first week of August, don't miss the **Annual Mountain Dance and Folk Festival** held at the **Asheville Civic Center** on Haywood Street. It begins at sundown and goes on until the last fiddler, banjo picker, ballad singer, dulcimer player, and clog dancer has called it quits and there's nobody interested in one more square-dancing set. This is the oldest such festival in the country, everybody is invited, and you're encouraged to join in even if you don't know a "do-si-do" from a "swing-your-partner."

If you miss the festival, every Saturday night from early July through August (except for the first weekend in August) there's something called a **Shindig-on-the-Green** at the **City County Plaza,** where you'll find many of those same mountain musicians and dancers having an old-fashioned wingding. It's free, lots of fun, and again, you're invited to join in the fun. If sitting on the ground isn't your thing, take along a blanket or chair.

On a more personal level, lovers of mountain "hoedown" sessions should head for **Bill Stanley's,** 20 S. Spruce St. (tel. 704/253-4871), any night but Sunday, where local clog dancers often go through their spirited paces to the music of honest-to-goodness mountain musicians, and patrons are lured to join the ranks of square dancers even when they've never before even *seen* a set danced. Residents from miles around congregate here for the kind of traditional free-spirited fun that is a hallmark of the Blue Ridge Mountains. It's a good idea to phone ahead to find out just when the music begins. This is definitely a "don't miss"! (It's also a mecca for barbecue lovers—see "Where to Eat," above.)

And in **Brevard,** 27 miles southwest of Asheville, there's a **Music Festival** held throughout the summer months (late June through mid-August) at the **Brevard Music Center,** during which you can hear nationally and internationally famous artists perform in symphony, chamber music, band, recitals, choral works, musical comedy, and opera every night. Tickets run $4 to $10, $2 to $5 for those under 16, and you can write P.O. Box 592, Brevard, NC 28712, or call 704/884-2019, for schedules and reservations.

**FROM ASHEVILLE TO FONTANA DAM:** The Blue Ridge Parkway comes to an end at **Cherokee,** the largest organized Indian reservation in the East (see below). Just west of the reservation, on N.C. 28, is **Fontana Village,** Fontana Dam, NC 28733 (tel. 704/498-2238), a mountain resort that makes a perfect ending for your Parkway trip. Built near a 30-mile-long lake formed by the construction of Fontana Dam, the resort has a 94-room inn, a 30-room lodge, and 257 cottages with one to three bedrooms. Sports-minded people will be in their element here, with stocked trout ponds, tennis courts, riding horses, and miniature golf (plus a par-three course) right at hand. In addition, there are all sorts of crafts workshops with a charge for materials only and square dances from June through August. It really has something for almost anyone who loves the outdoors and an oldtime atmosphere. During the summer (June 1 through October 31), rates begin at $55 in the inn, $45 for a one-bedroom cottage (which will accommodate up to three if you use the living-room studio couch as a bed). The rest of the year, rates drop considerably, making it one of the best fall vacation spots I know of.

As for dining facilities, if you don't cook your own meals in the fully equipped cottage kitchens, there is a cafeteria and the Pioneer Dining Room, where the whole family can eat reasonably.

### Things to See and Do

A little south of Asheville on the Parkway, a turn east at Wagon Road Gap will take you down a steep, winding road to the first **forestry school** in the U.S. There's an interesting museum for visitors. Along the way, you go past **Sliding Rock,** where children often delight in sliding down the glass-slick surface, and **Looking Glass Falls.**

Nearer the end of the Parkway, at Maggie Valley on U.S. 19, the **Ghost Town in the Sky,** P.O. Box 790, Maggie Valley, NC 28715 (tel. 704/926-0256), entertainment center is great fun. Separate western, mining, and mountaineer towns have been re-created on different levels of the mountaintop and there's something going on in each one all the time. Shows are staged in the saloons, there are street gunfights, and all sorts of western and mountaineer types wander about. You reach the park, 3,364 feet up, by means of twin inclined railways or a chair lift. Kids will enjoy the rides. It's open from 9 a.m. to 6 p.m. daily from early May to early November (weather permitting). Admission is $10 per person (under 5, free).

From the middle of December until snow disappears in the spring, there's very good skiing at the **Cataloochee Ski Area** at Maggie Valley. For full information, write Rte. 1, Box 502, Maggie Valley, NC 28751 (tel. 704/926-0285). A base lodge serves three hearty meals daily in ski season.

Nearby **Cataloochee Ranch,** one of the South's few working guest ranches, offers lodging in private cabins, the main ranch house, and elegant new Silverbell Lodge. The bountiful home-cooking is something special, and there's horseback riding, tennis, hiking, and acres of glorious Great Smoky Mountains scenery to enjoy. Rates vary, depending on season and accommodations. Write Mrs. Alice Aumen, Cataloochee Ranch, Rte. 1, Box 500, Maggie Valley, NC 28751 (tel. 704/926-1401).

As mentioned, the Blue Ridge Parkway comes to an end at Cherokee, right at the entrance to the **Cherokee Indian Reservation,** where Indian life has moved into the 20th century with all kinds of modern inventions and conveniences, but has held on to age-old traditions. You can see competitions in archery and blowguns, for example, or watch a game of Indian stickball, one of the roughest games anywhere. If you're there at the right time, you'll also see dances that have been handed down from generation to generation. The some

8,000 Cherokee who live on the reservation are descendants of a proud tribe, many of whom hid out in the Great Smokies in 1838 to escape that blot on American history, the removal of all eastern tribes to the West. A government Indian agent, one William H. Thomas (part Indian himself), bought part of the land that is now reservation and gave it to the Cherokee who'd managed to stay, and later a total of 50,000 acres was handed over to the tribe by the U.S. government.

A powerful drama, *Unto These Hills,* now tells the moving story of those tragic days when so many Indians traveled the "Trail of Tears." It is presented at the outdoor **Mountainside Theater,** off U.S. 441 (P.O. Box 398, Cherokee, NC 28719; tel. 704/497-2111), from mid-June through late August at 8:45 p.m., Monday through Saturday—and many of the actors are portraying their own ancestors. Tickets are $6.50 to $8.50.

The **Museum of the Cherokee Indian,** on U.S. 441 at Drama Road (tel. 704/497-3481), tells the story of the Cherokee through exhibits of such items as spear points several centuries old and multimedia theater shows. It's open daily except major holidays year round for $3 (children 6 to 12, $1.50). Rates are lower from January through May.

But to really see Indian life among the Cherokee 250 years ago, you have to visit **Oconaluftee Indian Village,** off U.S. 441 (Cherokee, NC 28719; tel. 704/497-2111). It's an authentic Cherokee community whose residents wear the tribal dress (most wear conventional clothes in the town of Cherokee and throughout the reservation) and practice the same crafts as their ancestors. You'll see dart guns being made or a log canoe being shaped by fire, and beautiful beadwork taking shape under skilled fingers. And the seven-sided Council House conjures up images of the leaders of seven tribes gathered to thrash out problems or to worship their gods together. It's a kind of living museum of a way of life and a period of our country's history that is all too often distorted by fiction writers and Hollywood scenarios. You can visit the village any day from mid-May through late October for $5.50, $3.50 for children 6 to 12.

Youngsters will find Christmas alive and well even in the summer at **Santa's Land Park and Zoo,** 2½ miles east of Cherokee on U.S. 19. Santa and his helpers are busy getting ready for December 25 in a charming Christmas village, and there's a zoo with (what else?) reindeer and other domestic and exotic animals. And just for fun, there are some amusement rides. It's open for visitors from early May through October; and adults pay $8 (children 2 through 12, $7).

## A Side Trip for Rubies

Gem-quality blood-red rubies are found in only two places in the world—the Magok Valley in Burma and the **Cowee Valley** north of Franklin, N.C. While these ruby and sapphire mines are played out for commercial purposes, rockhounds are still finding many thousands of dollars in gem-quality stones every year. For an admission charge of about $5 a day (8 a.m. to 5 p.m. seven days a week, April through October) and about 25¢ a gallon, you can sort through the gem-bearing gravel—and keep anything you find. Two of the most reliable are the **Holbrook Ruby Mine** (tel. 704/524-3540), one of the original mines in the area, and the **Shuler Ruby Mine** (tel. 704/524-3551), both of which have only native stones and provide assistance to novice gem-seekers. Then stop in at **Ruth and Bud's Cowee Gem Shop** (tel. 704/369-8233), where Bud Schmidt, a former hobbyist rockhound himself, will examine your finds and offer expert faceting and mounting services. If you want to stay for more than a day, bunk in at **Miner's Rest** (within walking distance of the mines), where Ruth and Bud Schmidt provide three completely furnished efficiency apartments, each fully heated and air-conditioned, at $30 a day for three and $35 for four people (weekly and monthly rates available). For reservations, call 704/369-8233 (days) or 704/524-3902 (evenings), or write to Miner's Rest, 206 Ruby Mine Rd., Franklin, NC 28734.

To get to the mining area, take U.S. 23 from Asheville or U.S. 441 from Cherokee to Franklin, then N.C. 28 north for about six miles. After passing the Cowee Baptist Church, turn right onto Ruby Mine Road and drive about four more miles.

*Chapter V*

# INTRODUCTION TO NORTH CAROLINA

### 1. By Way of Background
### 2. Traveling to North Carolina
### 3. Traveling Within North Carolina

"WE FELT SO SORRY FOR HER," the lady from California told me, "that we came all the way across the country to cheer her up." She was speaking of her daughter, a brand-new lieutenant in the air force who had joined up primarily for the travel benefits. "North Carolina was not exactly what she had in mind," my new-found friend related. The whole family had been disappointed when news came of her assignment to Pope Field, close by Fort Bragg in the center of the state. "But since we've been here, it's a different story," the mother went on with a beaming face, "this state has *everything!* It's been a whole new experience for us, and well worth the trip just to get to know it."

This reaction by first-time visitors to the state that bills itself as the "Variety Vacationland" is not unusual. Although Southerners have long known and enjoyed North Carolina's resorts, "Yankees," Midwesterners, and those from the Far West have for the most part tended to think of it merely as a place to pass through on the way to points farther south. Yet within its borders lie tourist and vacation attractions numerous enough and varied enough to offer an appeal to almost any traveler, regardless of his or her special interests.

## 1. By Way of Background

**FROM SIR WALTER RALEIGH TO THE WRIGHT BROTHERS:** There's history aplenty, for it was here, on tiny Roanoke Island, that Sir Walter Raleigh's colony of 150 English settlers was "lost" in 1587, a full 20 years before Englishmen arrived farther north in Virginia's Jamestown. What happened to them (including Virginia Dare, the first child born of English parents in the New World) remains a mystery, since the only clue—if that's what it is—to their fate was the word "Croatan" (the name of a tribe of friendly Indians) carved on a tree.

Along the coast are stately old plantation homes, some with formal gardens still lovingly tended and open to visitors, which housed the planters who came and stayed to plow prosperity from the rich soil. And farther inland, at Winston-Salem, an entire village—Old Salem—has been restored to depict the lifestyle of Moravians who arrived in 1753 and created a community that has lived through the centuries.

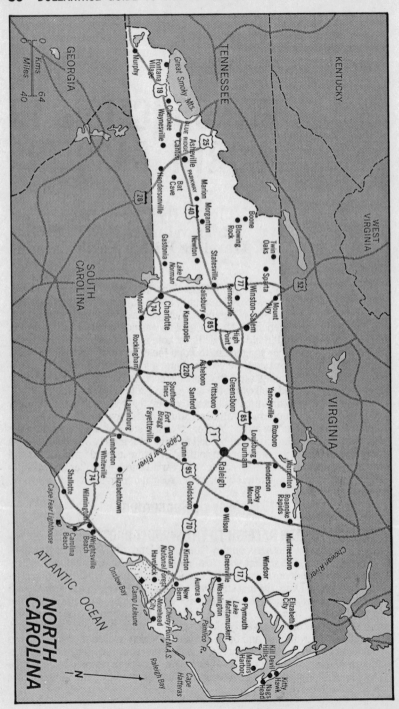

To the west in the mountains (the Blue Ridge, Great Smokies, Nantahalas, and others that form the southern Appalachians), history lives in the form of the Cherokee reservation—teeming with residents whose ancestors were here eons before a white face appeared—and towns like Boone (named for you-know-who) and Banner Elk (see Chapter IV for details on all these) that speak of the persevering frontiersmen whose restless western wanderings cleared the way for those who followed to settle down, bringing "civilization" with them.

In more recent times, man literally took off into the Age of Flight right here in North Carolina when Wilbur and Orville Wright made the first powered flight in 1903 at Kitty Hawk.

**WITH A VIEW TO THE PRESENT:** But if history isn't your thing, the Old North State has an ample supply of other attractions in its grab bag.

Its beaches, from Nags Head to Ocean Isle, are a delight, with broad stretches of white sand, waving sea oats, waves big enough to challenge the most skillful surfer, and seaside resorts located on outer banks, peninsulas, or off-shore islands that face sounds and rivers as well as the Atlantic. Fishing, boating, waterskiing, sand-skiing, and even hang-gliding from gigantic dunes are all part of the fun up and down the coastline. (And if you're a "sea nut," enamored of its mystery and many moods, you'll *love* the tales of Blackbeard, that fierce pirate who sailed these waters and met his end here, and looking for relics of the more than 2,000 shipwrecks claimed by the "Graveyard of the Atlantic.")

Tennis and golf lovers will find a home in the state too. Indeed, which of us doesn't equate the very word "golf" with Pinehurst? And no one would deny that the sport is at its best there, but neither should the fact be overlooked that the whole state has excellent courses and courts from one end to the other.

Equestrians will find some of the country's finest horses in North Carolina, along with miles and miles of riding trails. You'll see horses on the beaches, on sandy paths shaded by softly sighing long-leaf pines, and following ancient Indian routes through mountain passes.

And the mountains beckon hikers, climbers, skiers (the snow kind), and campers, then throw in Fontana, where square dancing and other oldtime recreations still hold sway (again, see Chapter IV).

Naturalists and others who'd rather bed down in a tent than the fanciest resort hotel will find an embarrassment of riches in the Great Smoky Mountains National Park, as well as two national seashores, four national forests, 36 state parks and recreation areas, 60 public and more than 300 privately owned campgrounds in the state.

**THREE STATES IN ONE:** As you may have gathered from the foregoing, North Carolina's geographical makeup divides into three distinct regions: the Coastal Plain, the Piedmont Plateau, and the Mountains. You can take your pick or sample all three: either way you're almost certain to be surprised by the sheer number of things to see and do.

**AND THEN THERE ARE THE PEOPLE:** One of your biggest surprises may well be the people who live here—"Tar Heels" they like to call themselves. (It is said that Gen. Robert E. Lee originated the name when North Carolina troops stuck so tenaciously in the front lines of battle during the Civil War.)

While all three regions have produced certain "personality" characteristics in the natives, there are some traits that all North Carolinians share, and they are a definite bonus to anyone visiting the state. Along with the courtesy and friendliness found among most southern people, those in North Carolina possess an engaging lack of pretense—you'll find few "phonies" here—and a delightful sense of humor. Basic good manners make them helpful at the drop of a question, and a sort of native sophistication may surprise you with the quality of the help. A resourcefulness and determination of high degree has, down through the years, been responsible for North Carolina's position as one of the most progressive southern states in industry, education, and agriculture; and even in remote areas you'll find the latest methods being employed by knowledgeable, well-informed citizens. Whether it's a fisherman at Ocracoke, a businessman in Raleigh, or a craftsman in the mountains at Brevard who winds up being a special friend during your visit (and you're bound to find one), the friendship is sure to be a lively, enjoyable, and lasting one.

**TO SUM UP:** North Carolina, then, does have a little bit of everything—something for everyone—and, as my friend from California said, it's well worth the trip.

**NORTH CAROLINA TELEPHONE AREA CODES:** Raleigh, 919; Winston-Salem, 919; Nags Head, 919; Wilmington (Wrightsville Beach), 919; Asheville, 704; Charlotte, 704.

**VISITOR INFORMATION:** For a packet of specific information brochures and bulletins before coming to North Carolina, contact: **North Carolina Travel and Tourism Division**, 430 N. Salisbury St., Raleigh, NC 27611 (tel. 919/733-4171, or toll free 800/VISIT-NC). Whether it's sightseeing, golf, fishing, or almost any other facet of travel you're interested in, you're likely to receive very complete, thorough answers to your questions.

**NORTH CAROLINA HOTELS:** You can find just about any-priced hotel accommodation in North Carolina, from the expensive Hyatt House in Winston-Salem to the budget Days Inn chain detailed in the introduction to this book. Aside from price, there is also a wide choice of *type* of accommodation: there are country inns, mountain lodges, tourist homes, and motels and hotels with a distinctive regional flavor.

### A Word of Warning

Just because *you* may not have thought of North Carolina as a prime tourist area, don't be deceived into believing that you can come without reserving ahead. 'Taint so, and I can attest to that fact on the basis of my own experience when I arrived "out of season" at the coast, only to find that the nearest room to be had was 40 miles inland because of the Annual Mullet Fishing Tournament! So, no matter when you plan to travel in the state, do yourself a favor and be sure your accommodations will be waiting.

**DINING OUT IN NORTH CAROLINA:** North Carolina's food is just as varied as its vacation attractions. And restaurants range all the way from fancy establishments that would rival the best in New York in decor to plain, road-house-looking cafés such as the one I found at Carteret. At either end of the spectrum, you're likely to find well-prepared, tasty North Carolina specialties—barbecued pork (the spicy, minced-up kind that's unique to this state—in particular, look for the Parker's chain, which serves some of the best barbecue on earth at very moderate prices), country ham, fresh seafood served with hush puppies (cornmeal batter-fried in deep fat), and always, grits served with breakfast (don't knock them until you've tried them served with globs of melting butter). I've tried to point out my own personal finds, but in this state especially, you stand a very good chance of running into a "special" place if you ask about local favorites.

You must be 21 to order anything stronger than beer or wine, which can be bought at age 19.

**NORTH CAROLINA CLIMATE:** North Carolina's climate is generally moderate, as can be seen from the following yearly highs and lows for various locations in the state:

|                | High | Low |
|----------------|------|-----|
| Cape Hatteras  | 84   | 40  |
| Raleigh        | 88   | 31  |
| Winston-Salem  | 88   | 32  |
| Asheville      | 85   | 30  |

## 2. Traveling to North Carolina

The best way for *you* to get to North Carolina depends, of course, on where you start, how much you can spend on transportation, and just how much time you have. These are the options that will let you find the mode of travel that best fits your circumstances.

**BY AIR:** Eastern, United, Delta, American, and USAir have direct flights into Raleigh/Durham, Charlotte, and Greensboro/High Point/Winston-Salem from major cities in the U.S. Piedmont, which flies direct to Asheville, is an airline I especially like for its pleasant, efficient service, and it has the largest number of North Carolina destinations from out of state, though not all are direct: Raleigh, Wilmington, Jacksonville, New Bern, Kinston, Fayetteville, Greensboro, Winston-Salem, Hickory, Charlotte, and Asheville. Inquire about their "Hopscotch" discount fares, some of which connect with other airlines.

**BY TRAIN:** North Carolina is on Amtrak's New York/Miami and Tampa runs, with stops in Raleigh, Hamlet, Southern Pines, Rocky Mount, Wilson, Selma, and Fayetteville. The New York/Washington/New Orleans *Southern Crescent* stops in Greensboro, High Point, Salisbury, Charlotte and Gastonia. Be sure to check for excursion fares or seasonal specials.

**BY BUS:** Greyhound and Trailways have good direct service to major cities in North Carolina from out of state, with connections to almost any destination within the state.

**BY CAR:** From Virginia and South Carolina, you can enter North Carolina on either I-95 or I-85, and I-27 and I-77 also lead in from South Carolina. The main Tennessee entry is I-40. All major border points have attractive, helpful Welcome Centers, some with cookout facilities and playground equipment in a park-like setting.

## 3. Traveling Within North Carolina

**BY AIR:** Piedmont, as noted above, has a number of in-state destinations, with connecting flights possible between most. Wheeler has limited flights within the state.

**BY BUS:** There are few places you can't reach by either Greyhound or Trailways.

**BY CAR:** Driving is a pleasure on North Carolina's 76,000 miles of toll-free, well-maintained highways. Most Interstate and U.S. highways and some state roads have periodic rest areas with picnic tables and outdoor cooking facilities. For a map that is one of the easiest to use I've come across, as well as a fount of tourist information on the state, write to Travel and Tourism NC, Dept. of Commerce, 430 N. Salisbury St., Raleigh, NC 27611, for the **Official Highway Map and Guide to Points of Interest.**

*Special Note:* North Carolina law is quite specific that *all* traffic must come to a standstill when a school bus is stopped on a highway, and this is stringently enforced. So if you see a bright-yellow school bus stopped—whether or not you see children getting on or off—save yourself a stiff fine and stop, and that applies whether you're meeting it or following behind.

You will find Thrifty Rental Car locations in Charlotte, Greensboro, and Raleigh.

**BY FERRY:** I'd go out of my way just to travel on one of this state's most enjoyable transportation facilities, the system of toll-free auto-ferries that ply the sounds and rivers of the coastal area. You can cross Currituck Sound from Currituck to Knotts Island, Hatteras Inlet, Pamlico River at Bayview, and Neuse River at Minnesott Beach. All schedules are printed on that wonderfully complete Official North Carolina Highway Map. For an up-to-date printed ferry schedule before you leave home, write: Director, Ferry Division, Room 116, Maritime Bldg., 113 Arendell St., Morehead City, NC 28557 (tel. 919/726-6446 or 726-6413).

# Chapter VI

# NORTH CAROLINA'S COASTAL PLAIN

### 1. Nags Head and the Outer Banks
### 2. Morehead City and Atlantic Beach
### 3. Wilmington and Wrightsville Beach

THE BEACHES ALONG NORTH CAROLINA'S Atlantic coastline are, to say the least, unusual. Most of them, in fact, lie technically offshore on the long string of narrow islands that make up the Outer Banks. And what beaches they are! The strand is wide, dunes are breathtakingly high, and interspersed with resort centers that have slowly developed over nearly 200 years are long stretches of natural beach where you can walk and swim and surfcast far from the madding crowd. But to begin at the beginning:

## 1. Nags Head and the Outer Banks

In 1899, when Nathaniel Gould emigrated from Cape Cod to Roanoke Island, he advised arriving guests at his newly opened Hotel Roanoke to take "any one of the Merchant and Miners Transportation Company's or the Old Dominion Steamship Company's boats, both lines stopping at Norfolk, Virginia, which connects with trains of the Norfolk & Southern Railroad to Elizabeth City, which connects with Steamer to Roanoke Island. In coming from the south, take Steamer from New Bern, N.C. Carriages will be in waiting at the steamboat wharf on the arrival of every boat, taking guests direct to the Hotel."

It's a much simpler matter today to reach the Outer Banks, thanks to a superb network of highways, bridges, and toll-free ferries. U.S. 158 eliminates the need for steamships from the north, and U.S. 64 provides easy access to visitors from the south.

**NAGS HEAD:** This largest resort in the Outer Banks area is ideal as a place to headquarter during your visit. Its odd name, according to local legend, comes from the practice of canny land pirates who in the old days would hang lanterns from the necks of ponies, parade them along the dunes at night, and lure unsuspecting ships onto shoals where they were grounded and their cargoes promptly stripped by the waiting robbers. Another theory holds that it was named for the

VIRGINIA

Knotts Is.

Great Dismal Swamp

Currituck Sound

Duck

Elizabeth City

Wright Bros. Mem.

Kill Devil Hills

Jockey's Ridge S.P.

Pasquotank R.

Perquimans R.

Nags Head

Ft. Raleigh

Roanoke Is.

Wanchese

Historic Edenton

Chowan R.

Albermarle Sound

Manns Harbor

Lost Colony

Pea Is.

Batchelor Bay

Columbia

Cresswell

Pettigrew S.P.

Lake Phelps

Elizabethan Garden

Rodanthe

Waves

Salvo

Fairfield

Lake Mattamuskeet

Engelhard

Avon

Belhaven

New Holland

Swanquarter

Pamlico Sound

Cape Hatteras Nat'l Seashore

Hatteras

Washington

Bath

Pamlico R.

Aurora

Ocracoke

Ocracoke Is.

Bayboro

Portsmouth Is.

Cedar Is.

Raleigh Bay

New Bern

Oriental

Minnesott Beach

Neuse R.

Croatan Nat'l Forest

Core Sound

Cape Lookout Nat'l Seashore

Havelock

Beaufort

Morehead City

Harkers Is.

Ft. Macon S.P.

Cape Lookout Lighthouse

Jacksonville

T. Roosevelt Natural Area S.P.

Camp Lejeune Marine Corps Base

Hammocks Beach S.P.

N

Surf City

Topsail Beach

Onslow Bay

Hampstead

Airlie Gardens

Wilmington

Wrightsville Beach

U.S.S. N.C. Battleship Mem.

Seabreeze

kms 20

Orton Plantation

Carolina Beach S.P.

miles 15

Kure

Southport

Ft. Fisher

Long Beach

Smith Is.

**NORTH CAROLINA COAST**

Cape Fear

highest point of Scilly Island, the last sight English colonists had of their homeland.

However it got its name, Nags Head has been one of the most popular beach resorts in North Carolina for over a century. The town itself is a collection of the usual beach houses, motels, and a few modern luxury hotels, and it has one of the finest beaches to be found in the state. **Jockey's Ridge,** highest sand dune on the East Coast, is located here also. Its 138-foot-high smooth, sandy slopes are popular with the sand-skiing and hang-gliding crowd, and since it is now a state park, it's open to all. And at **Kill Devil Hills** (named for a particularly potent rum once shipped from here), the Wright Brothers made that historic first flight back in 1903.

**Roanoke Island** is where Sir Walter Raleigh's colony of more than 100 men, women, and children settled when they landed here in 1587 in what was to be England's first permanent foothold in the New World. Virginia Dare, granddaughter of the little band's governor, John White, was born that year, the first child of English parents to be born in America. When White sailed back to England on the ships that had brought the settlers, it was his intention to secure additional provisions and perhaps more colonists, then return within the year. Instead, he found England so threatened by the Spanish Armada that Queen Elizabeth I refused to allow any large ships to leave. It wasn't until 1590 that White was able to get back to Roanoke, and what he found there was a mystery —one that remains to this day. The rude houses he had helped build were all dismantled and the entire area enclosed by a high palisade he later described as "very fort-like." At the entrance of the enclosure, crude letters spelled out the word "CROATAN" on a post from which the bark had been peeled.

Since their prearranged distress signal, a cross, was not there and no evidence suggested violence, his conclusion was that those he'd left on Roanoke Island must have joined the friendly Croatan Indian tribe. An unhappy chain of circumstances, however, forced him to set sail for England before a search could be made. Despite all sorts of theories about their fate, no link was ever established between the "lost" colonists and the Indians, nor was there ever any clue unearthed to reveal exactly what did happen. It would be 1607, at Jamestown, Virginia, before England could claim that permanently established settlement.

The **Fort Raleigh National Historic Site** was named in 1941, and its visitor center tells the story in exhibits and film. Paul Green's symphonic drama *The Lost Colony* brings it to life in the amphitheater that has been constructed at the edge of Roanoke Sound.

From **Whalebone Junction** at South Nags Head, the **Cape Hatteras National Seashore** stretches 70 miles down the Outer Banks barrier islands. The drive along N.C. 12 takes you through a wildlife refuge, pleasant little villages, long stretches of dunes with designated parking areas and ramps leading over to sand beaches that can only be called gorgeous, and on to **Buxton** and the **Cape Hatteras Lighthouse,** tallest on the American coast. It has stood since 1870 as a beacon for ships passing through these treacherous waters that have earned the title "Graveyard of the Atlantic," claiming more than 1,500 victims of foul weather, strong rip currents, and shifting shoals. This is where the iron-clad Union gunboat *Monitor* went down in a storm in December of 1862.

At the little village of **Hatteras,** a free auto-ferry makes the 40-minute crossing to **Ocracoke Island,** where more than 5,000 acres, including 16 miles of beach, are preserved by the National Park Service for recreation. It's also where the pirate Edward Teach (Blackbeard) met his end. From the southern end of the island, a toll auto-ferry takes you on a 2¼-hour voyage across **Pamlico Sound** to **Cedar Island.**

With no stops, it's about a 4½-hour drive—but by rights, it's an all-day trip or several half-day trips from a Nags Head base. Otherwise, you'll miss those beaches for swimming, fishing, or just walking along the sand, the breathtaking view from the top of Cape Hatteras Lighthouse. Most of all, you'd miss the chance to stop for lunch or a respite or to shop, all of which are perfect excuses to get to know the marvelous people who call this necklace of sand "home." They're hardy "Bankers" who've lived with winds and storms and high seas, and who can—and will, to friendly souls—recount tales of heroism at sea, the ghostly light that bobs over Teach's Hole, and wild ponies that have roamed Ocracoke Island for at least 400 years, all in the soft accent that some say harks back to Devon, home of shipwrecked sailors who came ashore here and stayed to become ancestors of those you'll meet today. If you miss the *people* of the Outer Banks, you'll miss the character of these islands. Take the day!

**WHERE TO STAY:** The choice of beach accommodations is wide, but one thing should be borne in mind: while the beaches are lined with cottage rentals, many of them are spoken for on a year-to-year basis, and it is absolutely essential to make your reservations well in advance. I'll list a few in the hotel-motel category, but if you'd like to settle down for a week or more, your best bet is to write the **Outer Banks Chamber of Commerce,** P.O. Box 1757, Kill Devil Hills, NC 27948 (tel. 919/441-1584), which can put you in touch with cottage and apartment owners.

The **Armada** is at the south end of Nags Head where U.S. 158 and U.S. 64 meet, Milepost 17 (P.O. Box 307), Nags Head, NC 27959 (tel. 919/441-6315, or toll free 800/334-3302, 800/233-5922 in North Carolina). Children 12 and under stay here *free,* and rates for double occupancy, oceanside, start at $95 Memorial Day through Labor Day, with much lower rates other seasons. Bayside rooms are a better buy at considerably lower rates. All rooms in the seven-story hotel are attractively decorated in a modern manner and oceanfronts have private balconies. The oceanside restaurant is especially pleasant, with above-average food. Henry's Pub, also on the ocean, features top entertainment and dancing during the summer months. They'll pack you a box lunch for day trips, or you can stay put on their private beach or the two oceanside pools. There's a playground for children, tennis courts for their parents, and access to two PGA-approved golf courses.

At the other end of the beach—in price as well as distance—is the **Quality Inn John Yancey,** P.O. Box 422, Kill Devil Hills, NC 27948 (tel. 919/441-7727, or toll free 800/228-5151). Considerably fewer frills, but the moderate price range is a joy, as are the efficiencies, which come completely equipped, right down to the coffee pot. There's no charge for children under 12 if they share a room with their parents, and the double-occupancy rates for a room (oceanfront) are from $80 in season all the way down to $40 off-season. Efficiencies cost $75 and up, depending on the time of year. Their Pancake House, serving good food at very reasonable prices, which you can eat in or take out, is just across the highway. A swimming pool provides swimming for those too fainthearted to brave the surf. Management here is especially friendly and helpful, and the rooms are cheerful.

The **Quality Inn Sea Ranch,** P.O. Box 325, Kill Devil Hills, NC 27948 (tel. 919/441-7126), at Milepost 7, has a posh oceanfront tower, with glass-enclosed balconies and rooms decorated with real flair. Each has two double beds or one king-size bed, and there are 12 efficiencies (with mini-kitchens—not really meant for cooking full dinners). New oceanfront luxury apartments have two bedrooms, two baths (one with full Jacuzzi), full kitchens, and glass-enclosed balconies. In the main building, you can choose rooms which come with one double and one single bed, or with sitting room area, and two double beds; all rooms have a mini-refrigerator. There's a quality boutique, a Nautilus health spa, an enclosed pool with a sliding-glass roof, and an indoor tennis club. Golf is just minutes away on two 18-hole championship courses. The window-walled Top of the Dune dining room serves all three meals (dinner is by candlelight), and there's dancing and entertainment in the cocktail lounge. Doubles start at $95 from mid-June to early September and drop by stages to around $40 from late November through mid-March.

At Milepost 11, the **Beacon Motor Lodge,** 2617 S. Virginia Dare Trail (P.O. Box 729), Nags Head, NC 27959 (tel. 919/441-5501), is a low, rambling complex offering rooms, efficiencies, and apartments. There are two swimming pools, and tennis and golf privileges at nearby facilities. Rooms are comfortably furnished and decorated in welcoming beiges and browns. All rooms have just been completely renovated, and all have room phones and refrigerators. There's a children's playground and coin-operated laundry. There's no restaurant on the premises of this oceanfront family motel, but there is one opposite and several more nearby. Doubles start at $55 from late May to early September, and drop during other months. Apartments are in the $500- to $525-per-week range in season, with daily maid service and linens furnished. Open late March through late October.

**WHERE TO EAT:** Dining out is no problem anywhere along North Carolina's coast, and Nags Head has plenty of small, good seafood restaurants. I'm listing only four, recognizing that the day's activities influence beach eating more strongly perhaps than in other locations.

**The Seafare,** at Milepost 5.2, U.S. 158 Bypass, in Seagate North Shopping Center (tel. 919/441-5554), is the worthy successor to the original restaurant in Old Nags Head, which, alas, burned some years ago. The same owner-management assures that you'll still find the fine cuisine, atmosphere, and service that has led local residents to patronize it since 1960, when descendants of Nathaniel Gould (the one who gave such explicit steamship instructions to his hotel guests) opened the Seafare after years of operating hotels whose dining rooms had become noted all up and down the coast. Although it's not quite as large as the original, it's a very attractive, spacious, tastefully decorated place with nautical touches, and the famous Seafare smörgåsbord is still being served —a truly groaning board heaped with fresh seafoods, roast beef, fresh salads and vegetables. The menu for table service is surprisingly extensive, featuring everything from several combination platters to a surf and turf plate of beef tenderloin (eight ounces) and a six-ounce rock lobster tail to a chateaubriand for two. Dinner, on the semi à la carte menu, can run from $9 to $22. There are also nightly dinner specials for a low, low $9! But it's the food, not the price, that's the attraction here—it's *all* good!

The Seafare doesn't take reservations, and dress is casual. Incidentally, don't bother asking for the recipe of their famous she-crab soup—that's the one recipe they won't give out. The selection of fine wines and international beers is outstanding. It's open seven days a week from 11:30 a.m. to 10 p.m. Call for seasonal hours.

**Owens' Restaurant,** Milepost 17, on the Beach Road in Nags Head (tel. 919/441-7309), is one of those great local favorites that just keeps getting better with the years. Just across from Owens' Motel, it has been owned by the same family for over 40 years. There's a welcoming family atmosphere you sense the moment you step inside this homey spot decorated with nautical relics and artifacts from the Outer Banks' "olden days." Fresh seafood is the specialty, and dinners range from $11 to $23. There's a child's menu as well, and if the kids prefer burgers and fries to broiled flounder, they can have them. You can enjoy nightly entertainment and your favorite libation in the Station Keepers Lounge. The restaurant is open from 5 to 10 p.m. mid-March to December 1; closed Thanksgiving Day.

A little farther south, next door to the Sea Oatel near the junction of U.S. 158 and U.S. 64, is another longtime Nags Head favorite, the **Dareolina Cove Restaurant** (tel. 919/441-7477). There are three dining rooms, but the one I especially like has wide windows opening to the Atlantic. It's a pleasant place during the day and downright romantic at night. Open from 7 a.m. to 2 p.m. and 5 to 10 p.m. in the summer, to 9 p.m. the rest of the year, the Dareolina serves all three meals and will fix box lunches for picnics or fishing trips. The menu is a long one and prices are moderate. As you might expect, fresh seafood is featured, along with prime steaks and home-baked pies and breads. My personal choice is the Nags Head crab (served on avocado halves). Dinner prices are in the $8 to $23 range. Like the Seafare, no reservations are required (at either place, you'll wait no more than 15 to 20 minutes). There's live entertainment on Friday and Saturday nights.

Dinner at **A Restaurant by George,** Milepost 11, Nags Head (tel. 919/441-4821), is a real treat. In an elegant East Indian setting, gourmet dishes are brought to the table by attentive, well-trained waiters. Prices are surprisingly moderate in light of both food and service, ranging from $9 to $20 (there's a children's menu with lower prices). Open all year, from 5:30 to 9:30 p.m. mid-September through May, 5:30 to 10 p.m. June to mid-September. Live jazz is featured in the lounge three to five nights weekly. Exotic drinks are a specialty and the lounge is open from 5:30 p.m. to 1 a.m.

There's a very good restaurant over at Wanchese (that's the south end of Roanoke Island), serving the freshest seafood, steaks, and chicken at moderate prices, and overlooking the harbor. **Fisherman's Wharf** (tel. 919/473-5205) also has a connected retail seafood market. Hours here are 11 a.m. to 3 p.m. for lunch, 5 to 9 p.m. for dinner, and it's closed Sunday.

## At Hatteras

The **Channel Bass,** on N.C. 12 at Hatteras (tel. 919/986-2250), has a clam chowder that will have you calling for seconds. In fact, all their seafood is fresh and cooked to perfection. The menu is semi à la carte, and dinner can run as low as $8 or as high as $9. It's closed from December 1 through March 28, and open 5 to 10 p.m. the rest of the year (to 9 p.m. on Sunday).

## At Ocracoke

The **Island Inn,** on Ocracoke Island, Hwy. 12 (tel. 919/928-4351), has been a part of the island since 1901 when it was built as an Odd Fellow's Lodge and housed the first public school on its ground floor. Over the years it has been moved across the street, served as a private home, been converted to a small inn, played host to naval officers during World War II as their Officers' Club, had wings added to accommodate more travelers, and wound up under the capable management of one native and another confirmed island lover. Larry Williams (he's the native) and his partner, Foy Shaw, have refurbished the rooms with plain but comfortable furnishings, added a heated swimming pool, and opened a restaurant that's earned an enviable reputation all along the Outer Banks. During the summer, it serves all three meals at moderate prices, breakfast 7 to 11 a.m., lunch 11 a.m. to 2 p.m., and dinner 5 to 9 p.m. Breakfast runs from $1.75 to $3.50 (and it's an islander's breakfast—hearty); lunch (including salads, sandwiches, and a couple of hot seafood platters), from $2.25 to $7.75;

and dinner—where almost anything that comes from the sea is served up, with sauteed crabmeat, clam chowder, and an enormous seafood platter sharing honors—from $7.50 to $16. This is fishhouse eating as it should be, and if you find a soul response to the little fishing village, you can stay over here for $35 to $75, double occupancy, depending on the season.

**THINGS TO SEE AND DO:** The Nags Head area has more than its share of things to keep you occupied when not on the beach, and the Outer Banks hold their own special appeal. For sightseeing particulars, contact the **Outer Banks Chamber of Commerce,** P.O. Box 1757, Kill Devil Hills, NC 27948 (tel. 919/441-1584).

### In and Near Nags Head

A little to the north, on U.S. 158 Bypass, at **Kill Devil Hills,** the **Wright Brothers National Memorial** is open to the public at no charge. Both the hangar and Orville and Wilbur's living quarters have been restored, and the visitor center holds a replica of that first airplane, as well as exhibits that tell the story of the two brothers who came here on vacations from their Dayton, Ohio, bicycle business to turn their dream into reality. It's an inspiration to see where they worked while you listen to the drone of modern airliners as they fly over this place where it all began.

From Whalebone Junction, U.S. 64–264 leads to **Roanoke Island** and the village of **Manteo.** Four miles west, you'll reach **Fort Raleigh National Historic Site,** where the old fort has been excavated and reconstructed just as it stood in 1585. The **visitor center** (tel. 919/473-5772) is a fascinating first stop, and they'll arrange guided tours by appointment. It's open 8 a.m. to 8 p.m. from mid-June to September 1, closing at 4:30 p.m. the rest of the year.

It is here, where it all happened, that Paul Green's moving drama, *The Lost Colony,* is presented in the **Waterside Theater,** Monday through Saturday at 8:30 p.m. from mid-June to late August. It's been running since 1937 (this country's first outdoor drama), and leaves you with a very real sense of what life was like for that courageous little band. The **Elizabethan Gardens** nearby, as well as the Tudor style of auxiliary buildings, remind all of us that this was the first connection between Elizabethan England and what was to become the United States of America. All seats for the outdoor drama are reserved (P.O. Box 40, Manteo, NC 27954; tel. 919/473-2127) and cost $9 for adults, $4 for those under 12. There's a $2.50 charge to enter the gardens (tel. 919/473-3234), and children under 12 go in for free.

Also when you're in Manteo, don't miss one of North Carolina's newest state historic sites, **Elizabeth II** (tel. 919/473-1144), moored across from the nicely renovated waterfront. This 69-foot-long three-masted bark was built with private funds for the nation's 400th Anniversary Commemoration. The proud beauty, a composite design of 16th-century ships, was presented to the state on July 13, 1984. Before boarding her, you'll first enter the visitor center, where exhibits describe exploration and shipboard life during those tenuous years. "A Roanoke Voyage" realistically depicts life aboard such a ship from the perspective of its voyagers. During the summer, living-history interpreters portray roles of colonists and mariners. The site is open daily from 10 a.m. to 6 p.m. April through October, and Tuesday through Sunday from 10 a.m. to 4 p.m. November through March; closed major holidays. Admission is $3 for adults, $2.50 for seniors, and $1.50 for ages 6 to 12.

About an hour and a half away from Nags Head (take U.S. 64, turn right at

N.C. 37, then left when you reach N.C. 32), a later phase of this country's history is preserved at **Edenton,** a lovely old town whose streets are lined with homes built by the planters and merchants who settled along the Albemarle Sound. The women of Edenton held their own Tea Party in 1774, the first recorded instance of American women taking a purely political action. Stop by the **Barker House Visitor Center** (tel. 919/482-3663) on North Broad Street (signs are posted throughout the town) to view a free 20-minute slide show. Here you can also purchase a historic district map for a nominal fee. The visitor center is open from 10 a.m. to 4:30 p.m. Monday through Saturday and from 2 to 5 p.m. on Sunday; closed major holidays. Guided tours of four historic buildings—the 1767 Chowan County Courthouse, 1725 Cupola House, 1776 James Iredell State Historic Site, and restored St. Paul's Episcopal Church—are conducted from 10 a.m. to 2:30 p.m. Monday through Saturday, and at 2:30 p.m. Sunday. The package tour is $3 for adults, $1.50 for ages 6 to 18; admission to individual buildings is $1.50 for adults, 75¢ for ages 6 to 18.

## Along the Outer Banks

The **Outer Banks Chamber of Commerce,** P.O. Box 1757, Kill Devil Hills, NC 27948 (tel. 919/441-1584), will send information about outdoor activities and the "Cape Hatteras Visible Shipwrecks" booklet that tells you where to look for the remains of wrecked ships along the beaches (they appear and disappear with shifting tides and sands).

Turn left off N.C. 12 about eight miles south of U.S. 158 to reach **Coquina Beach,** where there are bath shelters, lifeguards (from mid-June to Labor Day), picnic shelters, and beach walks guided by National Park Service naturalists.

Farther south, across **Oregon Inlet** (there's a bridge), the **Pea Island Wildlife Refuge** attracts birdwatchers from all over the country to see the snow geese which winter here and wading shore and upland birds in the summer months. There's a parking area and overlook.

All along N.C. 12, you'll see places to pull off and park to reach the beaches, which are hidden from view by huge protective sand dunes. A word of warning: *Don't* try to park anywhere else—the sands are very soft and it's easy to get stuck!

There are also **campgrounds** at various spots, but you should know in advance that they're flat, sandy areas with no shade and that you'll need tent stakes longer than you'd normally use. And no hookups are provided. Sites are on a first-come, first-served basis, and the maximum stay is 14 days from May 25 through September 10. Fees are $8 nightly for up to six people at all sites.

For private campgrounds in the area, which do have hookups, call the Outer Banks Chamber of Commerce at 919/441-1584 and they'll supply full information.

Whether you're camping or just stopping at the beaches where there are no lifeguards, you should always keep in mind that tides and currents along the Outer Banks are *very* strong and ocean swimming can be dangerous at times.

When you get to **Buxton,** turn left off N.C. 12 to see the **Cape Hatteras Lighthouse.** Its rotating duplex beacon has a 1,000-watt lamp in each side, and the 250,000 candlepower is visible 20 miles.

The little village of **Hatteras** exists now, as it has from the 1700s, as a fishing center, and there are large commercial and sport fleets that operate from its docks and marinas. In the spring and fall the boats bring in catches of sea trout, king and Spanish mackerel, bluefish, red drum, and striped bass, and in summer most of the action is offshore, where blue marlin and other billfish are in plentiful supply. Even if you're not fishing yourself, it's fun to watch the boats come in between 4 and 6 p.m. And if you'd rather be one of those coming in than a bystander, the **Outer Banks Chamber of Commerce,** P.O. Box 1757, Kill Devil Hills, NC 27948 (tel. 919/441-1584), can supply a list of charter boats available and fishing information.

From Hatteras, a free auto-ferry crosses the inlet to **Ocracoke** in 40 minutes. Especially during the summer peak tourist season, however, be prepared to wait in line to board the ferry.

Ocracoke has shown up on maps as far back as the late 1500s, when Sir Walter Raleigh's Roanoke Island party made a landfall here. It is rumored to have been Blackbeard's sailing headquarters and it was definitely his downfall. That wily pirate—who would braid pieces of hemp dipped in tallow into his long black beard and set them afire as he sailed into battle against merchant ships—made his peace with the Crown in 1712, receiving a full pardon from the king. Then, pretending to settle down to a peaceful life in the little town of Bath, he worked hand in glove with Gov. Charles Eden and Tobias Knight, the secretary of the colony, to go right on preying on ships from the Caribbean to the Virginia Capes. That fearsome head ended up, however, in 1718 adorning the prow of a sloop commanded by Lt. Richard Maynard, of the British Royal Navy, after he had engaged the pirate in a bloody duel in Ocracoke Inlet and captured his ship and crew. Maynard then sailed back to Virginia displaying his trophy to let ships along the coast know that the sea lanes were safe once more. Tales persist to this day of treasure stashed away or buried along the coast of North Carolina, but none has ever been found, and it's far more likely that Blackbeard sold his spoils quickly and squandered the proceeds.

When Ocracoke Island was isolated from the mainland and few visitors came by boat, as many as a thousand wild ponies roamed its dunes. Where they came from is uncertain, whether from shipwrecks, early Spanish explorers, or from original English settlers. At any rate, as more and more people traveled to and from the island, more and more ponies were rounded up, shipped to the mainland, and sold. The remnants of the herd—about a dozen—now live on a range seven miles north of Ocracoke village, where the National Park Service looks after them.

In a quiet little corner of Ocracoke Island, there's a bit of England, the **British Graveyard** that holds four British navy seamen whose bodies washed ashore when H.M.S. *Bedfordshire* was torpedoed offshore by a German submarine in 1942. It's leased by the British government, but lovingly tended by townspeople.

Ocracoke village has seen some changes since World War II, when the U.S. Navy dredged out Silver Lake harbor (still called "Cockle Creek" by many natives) and built a base here. They also brought the first public telephones and paved roads. In spite of the invasion of 20th-century mainland improvements, Ocracoke is essentially what it has always been—a fishing village whose manners and speech reflect 17th-century ancestors. It is by far the most picturesque spot on the Outer Banks.

To reach North Carolina's more southerly beaches, there's a ferry from Ocracoke to **Cedar Island.** Not only is there a toll; you have to make a reservation for the 2¼-hour trip! If you're leaving from Ocracoke, you must call within 30 days of departure (tel. 919/928-3841) and reserve space on one of the scheduled sailings; coming from Cedar Island, call 919/225-3551. The fare is $10 per car and occupants, $2 for bicycle and rider, and $1 for pedestrians. It's a wonderful, semi-ocean voyage on boats with names like *Pamlico, Silver Lake,* and *Sea Level,* manned by natives of the region whose creed is friendliness. For a complete list of ferries, schedules, and fares, write: Ferry Division, Dept. of Transportation, 113 Arundell St., Morehead City, NC 28857 (tel. 919/726-6446).

## 2. Morehead City and Atlantic Beach

From the Cedar Island ferry landing—where, incidentally, the **Pirate's Chest Restaurant** at the Driftwood Motel serves very good food at moderate prices, if you hit at eating time—it's almost a two-hour drive south to Morehead City and Atlantic Beach. Not that the distance is that long, it's just that the two-lane highway winds and curves through historic old fishing towns like Atlantic and Sealevel, under huge old water oaks hung with Spanish moss, emerging at intervals for long, straight patches of marshy savannahs of sea grass: it altogether discourages hurrying along.

Atlantic Beach is the oldest of the resorts on a 24-mile stretch of **Bogue Banks**, and most North Carolinians use the name Atlantic Beach to include the newer vacation centers of Pine Knoll Shores, Indian Beach, Emerald Isle, and Salter Path. The long, thin island began to develop back in 1927 when the first bridge was built across Bogue Sound to Morehead City, and it is now one of the state's most popular coastal areas, with fishing festivals and tournaments in the early spring and late fall making it virtually a year-round resort.

Morehead City, which has been an important port for oceangoing vessels since 1857, is the world's largest tobacco export terminal. Just across the sound, **Beaufort** (pronounced "*Bo*-fort") is a quaint old seaport that seems frozen in time, with narrow streets lined by white frame houses built when the town was young (it goes all the way back to 1709) in a distinctive, almost West Indian, style. It was once, believe it or not, a whaling center.

Less than 50 miles inland, **New Bern** was the provincial capital for several years. Swiss colonists gave it its name, perhaps in a fit of homesickness. When William Tyron was royal governor, he built a splendid "palace" here, considered at the time the "most beautiful building in the New World." Both the palace and the gardens around it have been restored to their former splendor.

But overshadowing everything else, the ocean is the focal point in the area. There is an almost complete preoccupation with fishing and water sports, with historic sites sort of thrown in as a bonus for the tourist, who will have come, the natives have no doubt, to enjoy the sea.

**WHERE TO STAY:** There are excellent motels spread up and down Bogue Banks, and like the natives, I'll use "Atlantic Beach" as a catch-all name.

The **Islander Motor Inn** at Emerald Isle (P.O. Box 1035), Swansboro, NC 28584 (tel. 919/354-3464, or toll free 800/354-3464 in North Carolina), has 80 rooms directly on the ocean and has become one of the most popular motels on the island. Its swimming pool sits right at the edge of a broad sand beach, and there's a sundeck with comfortable lounging chairs. The rooms, some with kitchenettes, are easily accessible to pool, beach, and restaurant. The manager will help arrange charter fishing or golf at the Star Hill Golf and Country Club. There's a lounge with entertainment and dancing on weekends. The restaurant here has gained a well-earned reputation as one of the better places to eat in eastern North Carolina (see "Where to Eat"). From April 1 through Labor Day, doubles start at $65, dropping after Labor Day.

At Atlantic Beach proper, and also directly on the ocean, the **Oceanana Resort Motel**, P.O. Box 250, Atlantic Beach, NC 28512 (tel. 919/726-4111), completely won me over as the perfect family vacation "home." There are so many extras here that it's hard to know where to start listing them. For starters, there's a free fishing pier for guests. Then, to make it easy for fishermen to turn the day's catch into the evening meal, there's a huge bin out by the pool that holds charcoal, grills, firestarter, and even ketchup and mustard (not for fish—they're for the hot dog/hamburger crowd). And there's never a charge for any of them. Picnic tables are right there also to make outdoor eating a pleasure. For the small fry, there's a playground with an attractive assortment of play equipment (like the pirate's lookout tower, swinging bridge, and pioneer wagon). For all ages, the semiweekly watermelon party out by the pool is a festive occasion, and you just have to see the free tropical breakfast spread under an open poolside pavilion to believe it—more than 15 fresh fruits! It's served every morning from 8 to 10 a.m. The coffeeshop is open from 5 a.m. to midnight, and there's a grill for fast-order foods out by the fishing pier. And the Man-Chun House just across the highway (it serves the best Chinese food this side of New York, as well as a wide selection of American dishes). Every room has a refrigerator, some have stoves. And those portable grills may be brought to the lawn area in front of your room (but not on upper-floor decks) to cook dinner right at your front door. Doubles range from $52 to $57, and kitchen units from $73 to $145 from May 20 to Labor Day, then drop.

A. B. Cooper, the owner-manager, tells me that reservations are necessary at least a month in advance—people keep coming back each year and the place stays pretty well booked. And that's been going on so long, over 40 years, that he keeps a "growing scale" posted to measure the height of children who come each year. It really is a super vacation spot, even if the only "family" you bring along is yourself.

Facing 1,000 feet of broad ocean beach on Salter Path Road, the **John Yancey Motor Hotel**, P.O. Box 790, Atlantic Beach, NC 28512 (tel. 919/726-5188, or toll free 800/533-3700, 800/682-3700 in North Carolina), has more than 95 rooms, a games room, free coffee and doughnuts, a pool, and nearby golf and tennis privileges. I find this chain's rooms much more spacious than most, and the rates modest. Doubles during the peak season are $57 to $75. From Labor Day to April 15, they drop considerably, and there's always a 10% discount for senior citizens. Youngsters 12 and under stay free in their parents' room.

For a very comprehensive listing of motels, restaurants, and attractions, write the **Carteret County Chamber of Commerce**, P.O. Box 1198, Morehead City, NC 28557 (tel. 919/726-6831), and ask for their free "Crystal Coast" vacation guide.

## Campgrounds

The **Salter Path Campground** on Salter Path Road (P.O. Box 721), Morehead City, NC 28557 (tel. 919/247-3525), overlooks the ocean on one side, Bogue Sound on the other. There are full hookups, a boat ramp, bathhouses, and a playground. Rates are $12 and up. For reservations, send a deposit.

Also on Salter Path Road, the **Arrowhead** Rte. 1, Box 792, Morehead City, NC 28557 (tel. 919/247-3838), has showers, a store, pier fishing, a playground, drive-through waterfront sites, and golf nearby. Rates begin at $12.

**WHERE TO EAT:** The restaurant at the **Islander Motor Inn**, at Emerald Isle in Swansboro (tel. 919/354-3464), has become a favorite of both local North Carolinians and those who summer at Atlantic Beach. There's continuous service from 7 a.m. to 10 p.m. Seafood is a specialty, but there are such oldtime southern favorites as country fried chicken, ham steak, and pork chops with applesauce, all at moderate prices. You can buy their homemade chicken and rice or vegetable soup by the quart to take out.

In Morehead City, Mrs. Russell Willis's family has been serving the public since 1952 at **Mrs. Willis Restaurant** on N.C. 70A (tel. 919/726-3741). There's seafood, as you'd expect in this fishing center, but in addition, you'll find pit barbecue and choice charcoal steaks on the semi à la carte menu, at prices that start at $4 and go up to $15. It's a cozy place, with a fireplace, background music, and very friendly service. You'll need to bring your own liquor; mixers are available. Open from 11:30 a.m. to 10 p.m.

Less than 20 miles south of Morehead there are two eating places worth looking up. The **T & W Oyster Bar and Restaurant,** N.C. 58 (tel. 919/393-8838), looks like a country roadhouse from the outside, but inside, the sloping, beamed ceiling and two large dining rooms, each with a fireplace, have a simplicity bordering on sophistication. Seafood is featured, reservations aren't necessary, and dress is casual. Prices for a regular dinner are $6 to $7, and seafood combination plates run $7 to $8 depending on the assortment you wish to order. The oyster bar is very popular here, with a half dozen on the half shell costing only $2.50 (a fact that made me cringe when I remembered New York prices). And they sell steamed oysters and clams by the half *peck* ($5). It isn't too hard to find. Just take N.C. 24 south from Morehead City, turn right on N.C. 58, and T & W is about five miles down the road. It opens at 5 p.m. and closes around 10 p.m. Monday through Saturday; on Sunday it's open after church to 10 p.m.

**THINGS TO SEE AND DO:** Beach activities, naturally, are the top attraction along the coast. And fishing is especially good here—the Gulf Stream brings in blue marlin, tarpon, and other prizes in addition to inshore fish. There are some 80 miles of surf in this area and 400 miles of protected waterways. If you're a boatowner, there's an excellent marina on **Harkers Island,** Calico Jack's Marina (tel. 919/728-3575). And if you don't have your own boat, there's a ferry that leaves from Harkers Island Fishing Center (tel. 919/728-3907) for Cape Lookout (a 35-minute trip) between April and December for a day of surf fishing or beachcombing (for details, write: Superintendent, Cape Lookout National Seashore, P.O. Box 690, Beaufort, NC 28516). The fee is modest, and once at the cape, you can use the jitney service that roams up and down the sands between Cape Point and the lighthouse to move fishermen from one spot to another. Bring a picnic, insect repellent, and your own water supply. I love the "getaway-from-it-all" island atmosphere, and it's perfect for anyone who likes sailboats, lots of sun, and miles and miles of sand beach. Incidentally, the unique diamond-patterned lighthouse has stood here since 1859.

When you begin to feel a bit waterlogged, plenty of sightseeing is within easy reach. For instance, down at the very tip of **Bogue Island** (you're on it if you stay at Atlantic Beach) sits old **Fort Macon,** a Civil War landmark now restored and open to the public at no charge. The jetties (designed by Robert E. Lee), moats, gun emplacements, and dungeons make up terrific exploring territory. The museum is quite good, though small, and the public beach has bathhouses, a snackbar, and lifeguards.

A trip to **Beaufort** is—that overworked phrase—really a "trip back in time." North Carolina's third-oldest town, it dates back to 1713 and still reflects its early history. There are two 200-year-old houses and more than a hundred that are over 100 years old along the narrow streets. The old graveyard (still called the "Burying Ground") positions its occupants facing east so they will be facing the rising sun on "Judgment Morn"; and it holds the remains of a British officer who wanted to be buried with his boots on, so was lowered into the grave in a standing-up position. The earliest markers that are still legible are dated 1756, and the headquarters of the **Beaufort Historical Association** in the 1825 Josiah Bell House, 138 Turner St. (tel. 919/728-5225), will furnish a map of the cemetery. The last weekend in June, Beaufort holds an **Old Homes Tour** and a reenactment of the Pirate Invasion of 1747. Any time, you can stop by the Historical Association headquarters for self-guiding tour maps of the **Beaufort Restoration Area,** which includes the 1767 Joseph Bell House, 1796 Carteret County Courthouse, 1829 county jail, 1859 apothecary shop, and 1778 Samuel

Leffers House, home of the region's first schoolmaster. The 1830 Rustell House functions as an art gallery from June through Labor Day. Charming costumed hostesses guide visitors through the restored area of the state's third-oldest town, which is open from 9:30 a.m. to 4:30 p.m. Monday through Saturday. Admission is $3 for adults, $1.25 for ages 8 to 12.

And don't miss the fine new state-owned **North Carolina Maritime Museum** at 315 Front St. (tel. 919/728-7317). It has splendid natural and maritime history exhibits, ship models, and shell collections, and offers intriguing field trips, lectures, and programs for all ages. The Wooden Boat Show is held here annually in early June, and on the third Thursday in August it's the site of one of the South's zaniest events, the Strange Seafood Festival. It's your golden opportunity to chow down on marinated octopus, squid, stingray casserole, and other deep-sea delicacies. Admission is $5, and it's so popular you must reserve in advance! Museum admission is free, and it's open from 9 a.m. to 5 p.m. Monday through Friday, from 10 a.m. to 5 p.m. on Saturday and from 2 to 5 p.m. on Sunday; closed major holidays.

**New Bern,** a little inland on U.S. Bus. 70 and U.S. 17, was once the capital of North Carolina when it was a royal colony. The 48-room **Tryon Palace,** 613 Pollock St. (tel. 638-1560 or 638-5109), built as both the capitol and residence for the royal governor, has been authentically restored and beautifully furnished. It's easy to see, walking through the elegant rooms, why this mansion was once called the most beautiful in America. It was built in 1767–1770; then the main building burned in 1798. After that it lay in ruins until the restoration in 1952–1959. The handsome grounds and gardens surrounding Tryon Palace are designed in 18th-century style. Two other exhibition landmarks in the 13-acre Tryon Palace complex are the **John Wright Stanly House** (1780), a sophisticated late-Georgian-style mansion, with town-house gardens, and the **Stevenson House** (1805), built by a sea captain and noted for its rare Federal antiques. Costumed hostesses guide tours Monday through Saturday from 9:30 a.m. to 4 p.m., from 1:30 to 4 p.m. on Sunday. Closed Thanksgiving Day, December 24 to 26, and New Year's Day. General Admission (good for all tours, the landmarks, and the gardens) is $9 for adults, $4 for children through high school; for the palace and gardens only, it's $6 for adults, $2 for children. On the grounds, craftsfolk demonstrate 18th-century home arts. Historical dramas supplement the regular hostess interpretation during the summer months. Special events, including candlelight tours of the complex, are held at Christmas and other seasons.

The **New Bern Firemen's Museum,** 420 Broad St. (tel. 919/637-3105), is 2½ blocks from the Tryon Palace Restoration and Gardens Complex. Firefighting equipment dating back to the early 19th century, memorabilia from the mother city of Bern, Switzerland, and Civil War artifacts make this a memorable, small museum. Admission is 75¢ for adults, 25¢ for children. Open Tuesday through Saturday from 9:30 a.m. to noon and 1 to 5 p.m., on Sunday from 1 to 5 p.m.

Historic **Christ Episcopal Church, First Presbyterian Church,** and **National Cemetery** are among the many sites that may be visited in old New Bern. There are over 180 18th- and 19th-century structures in New Bern listed on the National Register of Historic Places. For full details and self-guided walking tours, contact the **Craven County Visitor Information Center,** 211 Broad St. (P.O. Drawer C), New Bern, NC 25860 (tel. 919/637-3111 or 637-9400).

## 3. Wilmington and Wrightsville Beach

Down near the southern end of North Carolina's coast is Wilmington, a city that has figured prominently in the state's history since 1732. Known first as New Carthage, then New Liverpool, New Town, and Newton, in 1739 it was given its present name in honor of the Earl of Wilmington. Technically it isn't even on the coast—it's inland a bit at the junction of the Cape Fear River's northeast and northwest branches. And given the treacherous shoals that guarded the mouth of the Cape Fear when explorers first arrived in 1524, it's a wonder upriver Wilmington ever developed into an important port. But its protected riverfront site gave access to a valuable waterway for the movement of goods to and from Europe during colonial days, and since then the town has grown steadily as a commercial shipping center.

The first English settlers, from the Massachusetts Bay Colony, actually landed on the west bank of the river in 1662, and they were followed shortly by another group from Barbados. But they suffered mightily from Indian conflicts and from virtual abandonment by England. Pirates roamed the river freely and there wasn't much of a settlement until Brunswick Town was founded about 16 miles south of Wilmington in 1725 and a fort built to guard the passageway up Cape Fear. Soon surrounded by large, thriving plantations (some of them still intact today), Brunswick prospered until the British tried to destroy it by fire in 1776. It never really recovered, and it ceased to exist as a town about 1830, becoming a part of the landholdings of Orton Plantation until it was named a State Historic Site in this century.

Wilmington, too, played a part in the Revolution. In 1765, eight years before the Boston Tea Party, patriots here refused to allow the unloading of stamps to implement the infamous Stamp Act and forced the resignation of the stamp master. But in 1780 the city fell to Lord Cornwallis and he headquartered in a house (still standing) all that winter before leaving for Yorktown and ultimate defeat.

This was one of the principal ports of the Confederacy during the Civil War, and many blockade runners, who eluded both northern ships that patrolled the coastline and the Cape Fear shoals to bring in supplies to the South, found a home berth here. So important was Wilmington that Fort Fisher, on the eastern shore of the river, sustained one of the heaviest bombardments of the war, falling just 90 days before the Confederacy met defeat.

During both World Wars, Wilmington was a major port for the export of naval stores. Today the river is busier than ever with industrial shipping, and the town has become an important rail center as well.

The city holds on to its history in the visible remnants that are lovingly restored and maintained. All those exciting events from the past seem very close to the present when you walk through the old residential section of town (now an official "Historic Area"), around the grounds of Orton Plantation, among the excavated foundations of Brunswick Town houses, or examine blockade runner relics at Fort Fisher. And just a hop, skip, and a jump away over on the coast, Wrightsville Beach (a family-oriented resort for generations) is the perfect place from which to explore the whole region—in between swimming, beachcombing, fishing, sailing, or just plain loafing, that is.

**WHERE TO STAY:** The **New Hanover County Convention and Visitors Bureau,** P.O. Box 266, Wilmington, NC 28402 (tel. 919/762-2900, or toll free 800/222-4757 in the eastern U.S., 800/922-7117 in North Carolina), will do more than just send you their "Accommodations Guide." If you're in the market for an apartment or cottage for a week or more (a dollar-saving method of vacationing that's hard to beat), and will write them far enough in advance describing just what you have in mind, they'll circulate your requirements in a bulletin that goes to owners and managers in the area who will then contact you directly.

If you want to stay in Wilmington rather than at Wrightsville Beach, the **Hilton Inn,** 301 N. Water St., Wilmington, NC 28401 (tel. 919/763-9881), has superior rooms with doubles ranging from $75 to $90. Two good, less expensive motels are the **Days Inn,** U.S. 17 and U.S. 74, 5040 Market St., Wilmington, NC 28405 (tel. 919/799-6300, or toll free 800/325-2525), where doubles range from $33 to $45; and the **Heart of Wilmington Motel,** 311 N. 3rd St. (P.O. Box 195), Wilmington, NC 28401 (tel. 919/763-0121), with doubles from $38 to $51.

At the **Sheraton Wrightsville Beach Hotel** (formerly the Holiday Inn), 1706 N. Lumina Ave., Wrightsville Beach, NC 28480 (tel. 919/256-2231, or toll free 800/325-3535), all rooms have an ocean view, all have balconies or patios, and all are attractively furnished. Those that actually face the ocean are especially nice, with glass sliding doors opening directly to the beach on the first floor and individual balconies on upper levels. A large, oceanside pool has shade areas and a refreshment bar, and there's a wading pool for young children. The lounge offers dancing and seasonal entertainment. Dinners in the charming dining room are good and moderately priced in the $9 to $15 range. Guests enjoy golf privileges at a nearby private course, and would-be sailors will find sailboat rentals available. The hotel will also arrange golf package weekends and charter-boat fishing trips. In fact, I found the staff here exceptionally friendly and helpful in all respects during my stay. Seasonal rates for doubles are $75 to $99 June through August, lower other months.

About a mile down the beach, the seven-story **Blockade Runner Resort Hotel & Conference Center,** P.O. Box 555, Wrightsville Beach, NC 28480 (tel. 919/256-2251), has luxury rooms, heated oceanside pool, nightly entertainment, a playground for children, and sailboats for rent. The bright, cheerful dining room serves continental cuisine at moderate prices. Double rooms are $90 and up mid-May to mid-September, lower the rest of the year.

The **Waterway Motor Lodge,** P.O. Box 545, Wrightsville Beach, NC 28480 (tel. 919/256-3771), as its name implies, is on the Intracoastal Waterway rather than the ocean. It's right at the bridge, about three-quarters of a mile from the beach. There's a pool, a playground, and a babysitter list. A moderately priced restaurant is three short blocks away, and the motel furnishes free morning coffee. Rates are $52 to $55 for doubles during peak season, somewhat lower during fall and winter.

## Campgrounds

The **Camelot Campground** (formerly the Wilmington Safari Campground), 7415 Market St., Wilmington, NC 28405 (tel. 919/686-7705), sits on 43 wooded acres on U.S. 17. New owners, the St. John family, are dedicated to family camping. There's a pool, recreation room, playground, laundry, grocery store, and propane gas. Rates start at $10.50.

**WHERE TO EAT:** As is true of so many coastal towns, Wilmington's best dining spots are at the beaches or on its fringes, and you'll find more seafood spots (most of them excellent) than you'll have time to sample.

In-town exceptions are topped by **Stemmerman's,** 138 S. Front St. (tel. 919/763-0248), a charmingly converted 1855 grocery store. There are such unexpected features as stained-glass windows, chandeliers, and a river view. Best of all, seafood is fresh and intriguingly prepared (try the broiled flounder with shrimp and oyster sauce). Lunch is mostly soups, salads, and sandwiches, with a price range of $4 to $8, and dinner prices run $8 to $17.

If your palate calls for something other than seafood, the **Riverview Restaurant,** 226 S. Front St. (tel. 919/763-5767), serves lamb, veal, pasta, and a nice array of other French and continental menu items for $8 to $20 at dinner. It's open evenings Monday through Saturday.

The popular **Pilot House Restaurant,** 2 Ann St. in Chandler's Wharf (tel.

919/343-0200), is lively at lunchtime when shoppers, downtown workers, and tourists surge in for crab quiche or Carolina seafood chowder. Dinner specialties range from fresh local seafoods to veal, beef, and fowl entrees, all prepared with deft special touches. Save room for the Caribbean fudge pie! Lunch ranges from $2.75 to $6.50, and dinner is in the $9 to $16 bracket. It's open from 11 a.m. to 3:30 p.m. and 5:30 to 10 p.m. Monday through Saturday.

For distinctively "down east" North Carolina barbecue, make a bee-line for **Skinner & Daniels,** 5214 Market St. (tel. 919/799-1790). Its heaping plates of barbecued pork, chicken, beef, short ribs, or Brunswick stew will satisfy the strongest "Q" craving at amazingly modest cost. It's open from 10 a.m. to 9 p.m. Monday through Saturday, and you can place take-out orders until 9 p.m.

**Annabelle's** (formerly Tuesday's), 4106 Oleander Dr. (tel. 919/791-4955), was the first in what has become a chain of unusual, fun places to eat (see the Winston-Salem listing, Piedmont section, for another), started a few years ago by Buddy Gerald when he expanded a very successful string of pizza parlors into restaurants with full meals in settings that are showcases for his collection of antiques. When you see a stagecoach in front, for example, you'll know you're at Annabelle's. And the inside is chock-full of such items as the old trolley car that used to run from Wilmington to Wrightsville Beach and, as is true in most of the restaurants, an old jail. My first reaction when I saw the Winston-Salem location was that the food probably wouldn't measure up in a place that puts so much emphasis on decor. Well, I was wrong! Everything from hamburgers to steaks is delicious, and each place has a salad bar that includes every ingredient you can imagine, and then some. Prices are moderate ($4 to $13) and the menu is extremely varied.

The **King Neptune** is right in the center of Wrightsville Beach at 11 N. Lumina St. (tel. 919/256-2525), and is a very informal, very nautical place with two large dining rooms and a gift shop to one side. Fishnets, shells, reproductions of old pendulum clocks (which can be bought in the gift shop), and a mural of King Neptune riding a sea horse adorn the paneled walls. The menu announces that "It's fun to eat at the King Neptune," and indeed it is, for sometimes it seems that about half the permanent residents and almost all the tourists in town congregate here. The atmosphere is lively and the food is superb. You can probably guess what gets star billing, but there is also a good selection of beef and even a long list of pizza choices. Lunch prices can run anywhere from $3.50 (for a small pizza) to $15 (for a choice T-bone steak). Most dinner entrees on the à la carte menu are in the $6.50 to $18 range. Service is continuous from 11:30 a.m. to 11:30 p.m., and they don't accept reservations (except for large parties in the private room).

Right at the Wilmington edge of the Wrightsville Beach–Wilmington drawbridge (on your left if you're coming from the beach), is the **Bridge Tender,** Airlie Road on the Sound (tel. 919/256-4519). I found it the best possible way: someone told me about it! "It's reasonable," she told me, "yet has an elegant feeling, and it's relaxing to watch the boats go past and the bridge when it's raised." I found the Bridge Tender all of that, and in addition the food was just superb. Manager David Nye told me that Jim Wright, the young owner, purposely keeps the menu limited in order to serve top-quality meats and seafoods cooked by expert chefs. And it *is* limited in the number of items, but certainly not in imaginative preparation. There's an excellent Polynesian chicken, tender filets of chicken breast marinated in a special teriyaki sauce and broiled just right, and tender Alaskan King crab legs served on long-grain and wild rice with drawn butter. Prices run $11 to $22 at dinner, $4.75 to $7 at lunch. And there's a very good salad bar (you serve yourself there with every dinner or lunch entree). The walnut layer cake brought back fond memories of those my grandmother used to make; it's a very southern dessert and I've rarely run into it in northern climes. They're open seven days a week for lunch (11:30 a.m. to 2 p.m.) and dinner (5:30 to 11 p.m.). It's a good idea to reserve for dinner or the locally popular Sunday buffet.

Everybody in the area knows and loves **The Raw Bar,** at 13 E. Salisbury St. at the beach, right where U.S. 74 meets the ocean. This highly informal and very often crowded restaurant serves oysters and clams, both on the half shell and steamed, as well as delicious seafood platters, either broiled or fired. Prices range from downright inexpensive to moderate. This "drop-in" place is open from 5 to 10 p.m.

Sooner or later you're bound to hear the name **Calabash** in connection with food. Well, that's a town about 35 miles south of Wilmington (almost to the South Carolina border, in fact) on U.S. 17 that's so small it wasn't even shown on state maps for years. What literally put it on the map is the cluster of about 20 seafood restaurants that vie with each other to serve the biggest and best platter of seafood at the lowest price. The 150 residents of this small village use family recipes handed down from generation to generation and last year they served 1½ *million* people some 668,000 pounds of flounder and 378,000 pounds of shrimp, to say nothing of tons and tons of oysters, scallops, and other fish. That's an impressive record, and although I found the Wrightsville Beach area more than adequate when it comes to food, a Calabash trip is an experience. Recommendations for specific restaurants? I wouldn't even try! And you won't need them—according to locals, you can't miss, no matter which one you choose.

**THINGS TO SEE AND DO:** To get a delightful overview of the historic Wilmington waterfront, hop aboard the *Capt. J. N. Maffitt* **riverboat** (tel. 919/343-1776), which departs from the foot of Ann Street at Chandler's Wharf for a five-mile loop of the Cape Fear River. It skirts the busy harbor, passes the Cotton Exchange renovation, the new Waterfront Park, the U.S. Coast Guard icebreaker *Northwind,* and stops at the dock for passengers who wish to disembark to tour the battleship U.S.S. *North Carolina.* The half-hour trips leave daily at 11 a.m. and 3 p.m. January through August, and at 3 p.m. in May and September. Cost is $2.50 for adults, $1.25 for ages 1 to 12.

Before you begin any sort of sightseeing tour, I strongly suggest that you stop by the **New Hanover County Convention and Visitors Bureau** (tel. 919/762-2900, or toll free 800/222-4757 in the eastern U.S., 800/922-7117 in North Carolina) to pick up their free brochures on the many attractions of Cape Fear County. This super-efficient staff was slated to move into new quarters after this revised volume went to press. So phone them to find their location, or write for information in advance to P.O. Box 266, Wilmington, NC 28402. There's a self-guided walking tour of historic Wilmington in great detail, giving background information on everything you'll want to see, including the **Cotton Exchange.** That's an in-town shopping center of malls, arcades, and courtyards in the old cotton exchange with its two-foot-thick brick walls and hurricane rods. The small shops and restaurants are a delight, and the wroughtiron lanterns and benches add to the charm of their setting. It's right on the riverfront, just across from the Hilton Inn, and there's an ample parking deck adjacent.

Another "must" is **Chandler's Wharf,** also on the riverfront, at the southern end. It encompasses a fine nautical museum with a two-masted schooner, the 147-foot-long *Harry W. Adams,* and four other vessels, along with spiffy specialty shops in renovated and restored buildings. Across the street, two warehouses are home to more shops, galleries, and restaurants. Wooden sidewalks, white picket fences, and cobblestone alleyways lend the shopping-museum complex a distinctive 19th-century ambience.

If you'd rather have a guide for that walking tour, they're available at **Thalian Hall** from Historic Wilmington Tours, 3rd and Princess Streets (tel. 919/763-9328). Tickets are $6 for adults, $1 for students; children under 6 are free. Those prices cover an audio-visual orientation and admission to all buildings, as well as your guide.

In the **Historic Wilmington** old residential area, bounded roughly by Nun, Princess, Front, and 4th Streets, the **Burgwin-Wright House,** 224 Market St. (tel. 919/762-0570), was built in 1771 and used by Lord Cornwallis as his headquarters in 1781. It's a perfect, beautifully restored example of a colonial gentleman's town house. You can tour the interior Tuesday through Saturday from 10 a.m. to 5 p.m. Adults pay $2.50; children, $1.

Also at 3rd and Market is **St. James Episcopal Church,** a beautiful building erected in 1839 to replace the 1751 church which had been used by the British as a stable during the Revolution. The Spanish painting *Ecce Homo* which hangs inside was taken from a captured pirate ship in 1748 and has been estimated to be between 400 and 600 years old.

The **New Hanover County Museum,** 814 Market St. (tel. 919/763-0852), showcases the lower Cape Fear region's social and natural history. Especially fascinating are the Civil War artifacts and dioramas from the former Blockade Runner Museum. Followers of fashion will appreciate the fine collection of 19th- and 20th-century costumes. It's free and open from 9 a.m. to 5 p.m. Tuesday through Saturday, and from 2 to 5 p.m. Sunday.

These are only highlights—just walking the old tree-shaded streets is an exercise in imagination.

Outside Wilmington, take U.S. 76 toward the beach and watch for **Airlie Gardens.** Once the plantation home of a wealthy rice planter, Airlie is surrounded by huge lawns, serene lakes, and natural, wooded gardens that hold just about every kind of azalea in existence. Admission is $5 per adult, $2 for children, and the gardens are open during the daylight hours from early March until late fall. The blooms are at their height in the early spring, but even when they've faded, this is a lovely spot that will set you dreaming of Old South life.

**Poplar Grove Plantation,** a restored Greek Revival manor house and estate dating from 1850, is nine miles northeast of town on U.S. 17 (tel. 919/686-9518). Outbuildings include a smokehouse and slave quarters, and there's a country store and tea room. "Living History" tours are conducted (adults pay $2.75; under 12, $2) daily: from 9 a.m. to 5 p.m. Monday through Saturday, and from noon to 6 p.m. on Sunday, except for the month of January, when it's closed. Outbuildings, gardens, farmyard, farm animals, picnic tables, craft artists-in-residence, and a country store are all covered by the admission charge. Group hayrides are available at just 25¢ per person, and there are special outdoor events in the fall and spring. Moderately priced meals are served from 11 a.m. to 3 p.m. weekdays and noon to 5 p.m. on Sunday in the Plantation Tea Room.

**Greenfield Gardens,** just off U.S. 421 South, is Wilmington's largest municipal park justly famous for its scenic millpond, a sunken garden of native North Carolina flowers, and the Venus fly trap, which is native to no other place in the world except this state. In the spring and summer, camellias, azaleas, and roses bloom in profusion, and the five-mile drive around Greenfield Lake is beautiful any time of the year.

Follow U.S. 421 South from the park and you'll reach the remains of **Fort Fisher** (tel. 919/458-5538). One of the Confederacy's largest, most technically advanced forts, it protected Blockade Runners bringing in vital goods to the port of Wilmington. After withstanding two of the heaviest naval bombardments of the Civil War, the fort finally fell to Union forces in the conflict's largest land-sea battle. The visitor center displays artifact exhibits of that era, and an audio-visual program is given. Costumed tour guides welcome visitors, and seasonal living-history events are depicted. The fort and visitor center are open from 9 a.m. to 5 p.m. Monday through Saturday and from 1 to 5 p.m. on Sunday; closed Monday in winter. Admission is free.

Not far from Fort Fisher, a toll ($3 for car and passengers) ferry makes the half-hour crossing of the Cape Fear River and deposits you at the quaint little village of Southport. Turning north on N.C. 87, then left at N.C. 133, you'll reach **Brunswick Town State Historic Site.** The excavated home foundations have been left as archeological exhibits, but there are displays that re-create colonial life here, and the walls of St. Phillip's Anglican Church are still partially standing. The visitor center is open from 9 a.m. to 5 p.m. Monday through Saturday and from 1 to 5 p.m. on Sunday April through October; the rest of the year it's open from 10 a.m. to 4 p.m. Tuesday through Saturday and from 1 to 4 p.m. on Sunday. Admission is free. For information, write Rte. 1, Box 55, Winnabow, NC 28479 (tel. 919/371-6613).

**Orton Plantation,** between Southport and Wilmington on N.C. 133 (tel. 919/371-6851), is a private residence and the mansion is not open to the public. But the magnificent gardens, bordered by long avenues of live oaks and planted with camellias, azaleas, and thousands of other ornamental plants, can be seen March through November (8 a.m. to 5 p.m.) for an admission of $5 ($2 for children 6 to 12). The formal and informal gardens are in a lovely setting overlooking old rice fields and the Cape Fear River.

Back at Wilmington, you'll see signs on U.S. 74 (it's also U.S. 17 and U.S. 76 at this point) leading to the **U.S.S. North Carolina Battleship Memorial** (tel. 919/762-1829). The ship, which was commissioned in 1941, is permanently berthed here as a memorial to the state's World War II dead. You can tour most of the ship, and the museum presents a pictorial history of the *North Carolina*'s Pacific campaigns. It's open daily from 8 a.m. to sunset, and costs $4 for adults, $2 for children 6 to 11. From early June through Labor Day, there's a 70-minute Sound and Light show, *The Immortal Showboat,* at 9 p.m. every night, at a cost $3 for adults, $1.50 for children. A recently opened visitors center has a large gift shop and snackbar, as well as an auditorium where a ten-minute orientation film is shown.

North Carolina's first battle of the Revolution took place 20 miles northwest of Wilmington (via U.S. 421 and N.C. 210) at **Moores Creek.** The site is now a National Battlefield, as well it might be, since the victory of local patriots squelched a Tory scheme to invade and seize all the southern colonies. The earthworks and bridge have been reconstructed, and there's a visitor center and museum.

# Chapter VII

# PIEDMONT NORTH CAROLINA

### 1. Raleigh, Durham, Chapel Hill
### 2. Winston-Salem
### 3. Pinehurst
### 4. Charlotte

PERHAPS NOWHERE IN THE SOUTH do the old and the new come together quite so dramatically as in that section of North Carolina that lies between the coastal plains and the mountains. The Piedmont, as this region is called, holds mementos of American history that predate the Revolution (it was in 1771 that some 2,000 farmers of Alamance County organized to protest British taxation and were savagely subdued by a royal governor at the Battle of Alamance near Burlington) as well as the first nuclear reactor building in the country devoted exclusively to the peaceful use of the atom (on the North Carolina State University campus in Raleigh).

The contrast is especially marked in cities such as Winston-Salem, where the mammoth tobacco industry is represented by R. J. Reynolds Tobacco Company, manufacturers of several major cigarette brands and pipe blends, and the Joseph Schlitz Brewing Company produces over four million barrels of beer each year in one of the largest such plants under a single roof; while in another part of town the streets and buildings of Old Salem are perfectly restored to reflect the life of Moravians who planned the community in 1766.

The land itself is as varied in this region as the industry, agriculture, and recreation that utilize it. From the red clay hills around Raleigh and Greensboro, to the flat fields of tobacco, peanuts, and vegetables in the midlands, to the rolling sand dunes alive with long-leaf pines and peach orchards in the Sandhills farther south, there is a pleasant, ever-changing character to the landscape. Some of my most cherished childhood memories were formed against the background of wind softly sighing through those pines, and the white blossoms of dogwood growing wild in wooded stretches along the highways always reminded me of snowdrifts sprinkled among other just-greening trees in early spring. Azaleas, camellias, and a host of summer-blooming flowers add to the visual beauty of this part of the state.

Higher forms of education are also an important part of the Piedmont character, where the "Research Triangle" you'll run across so often in conversation and directions refers to Duke University in Durham, the University of North Carolina in Chapel Hill, and North Carolina State in Raleigh. Wake Forest University, founded in 1834 in the town of that name near Raleigh and relocated to the western edge of Winston-Salem in the 1950s, is another leading educational institution. And literally scores of small private colleges and junior colleges are located throughout the region.

For the visitor, the Piedmont has sophisticated entertainment in its cities, the simplicity of rustic, outdoor life in fishing camps along the Catawba, Cape Fear, and Neuse Rivers, the excitement of intramural collegiate sports competitions, and the challenge of some of the world's greatest championship golf courses. Throw in sightseeing trips that will delight any history buff, and you have in this one 21,000-square-mile region much of the "variety" of that "Variety Vacationland" slogan.

# 1. Raleigh, Durham, Chapel Hill

**RALEIGH:** State government has been the principal business conducted in Raleigh since 1792, when it became the state's capital. A five-acre square that holds the State Capitol is the focal point for a cluster of state office buildings in the heart of the city. From it radiate wide boulevards and lovely residential streets shaded by trees that frame some of the older homes. Downtown Raleigh has been transformed by a $2-million mall, where trees and fountains and statuary create a park-like shopping oasis from the Capitol to the Civic Center. No fewer than six college campuses dot the city streets with wide lawns and impressive brick buildings. The oldest, St. Mary's College, was founded in 1842, and the "youngest," North Carolina State University, in 1887. New suburbs and gigantic shopping centers dominate the outskirts, but they somehow escape the "little boxes" image of so much suburban construction, with nicely designed homes blending into a landscape that retains much of its original wooded character.

Raleigh has, of course, witnessed much of the state's history: it was the setting for fiery legislative debate just prior to the Civil War that led at last to North Carolina's secession from the Union in 1861 (the last southern state to pull out); it endured Union occupation by General Sherman in 1865; and it saw the west wing of its imposing Grecian Doric capitol building turned into a rowdy barroom by "carpetbagger" and "scalawag" legislators during Reconstruction days, its steps permanently nicked from whiskey barrels rolling in and out of the building. It was the stage on which Gov. Charles Aycock launched his campaign for education revival in the early 1900s, and from its state buildings has come strong support for industrial development that makes North Carolina one of the most progressive of the southern states.

All of this, plus the abundance of good accommodations, makes Raleigh the ideal base from which to explore the Triangle area—which is what we'll do here. Both Chapel Hill and Durham are within easy reach for day trips, and after a day of sightseeing, the capital city becomes an entertainment center for anything from smart, supperclub shows and dancing to Broadway theater to cultural events.

## Where to Stay

If you're going first class or feel the need to splurge for a night or two and want a truly "southern" ambience, your best bet is the Quality Inn **Plantation Inn**, 6401 North Blvd. (P.O. Box 11333), Raleigh, NC 27604 (tel. 919/876-1411, or toll free 800/992-9662, 800/521-1932 in North Carolina), located in a restful, pine-wooded setting on U.S. 1 North, some five miles out of town. The main building, a colonial, white-columned structure, evokes visions of the Old South. And that legendary southern hospitality is embodied in a coffee bar which dispenses free cups 24 hours a day in the gracious lobby (sporting portraits of Robert E. Lee and Stonewall Jackson), which opens onto a terrazzo terrace overlooking the lake and wooded lawn. Rates for the large, handsomely furnished rooms begin at $65 for a double; and the tastefully appointed restaurant serves everything from a hamburger to a superb buffet at lunch or dinner featuring roast prime ribs of beef au jus at $15. Other dinner entrees range from $8 to $17. There's live organ music during dinner hours, and the Carriage Club Lounge on the lake level of the main building is a pleasant before- or after-dinner retreat. This is a favorite of international business travelers, and you may well encounter an Arab executive in native dress or a Japanese technician and his family quartered here while looking for a permanent home. Because it is so popular, it's advisable to reserve rooms at least three weeks in advance.

More centrally located, and a great local favorite, is the **Velvet Cloak Inn,** 1505 Hillsborough St., Raleigh, NC 27605 (tel. 919/828-0333), within a few blocks of both downtown and the North Carolina State University campus. A pseudo–New Orleans motif is carried out with wrought-iron balconies and in the room decor. There is an indoor swimming pool, and the Charter Room Restaurant and Baron's Supper Club are both on the premises. Rates here range from $78 to $103 for doubles.

The **Holiday Inn North,** on U.S. 1 North, 2815 North Blvd., Raleigh, NC 27604 (tel. 919/872-7666, or toll free 800/465-4329), is an exceptionally nice member of this chain, having just added a new tower, renovated all older guest rooms, built a Holidome that encloses an indoor pool, Jacuzzi, mini-golf, and assorted games, all surrounded by an abundance of plants and trees and fountains. The new Syd's Holidome Restaurant serves all three meals, and there's dancing in Syd's Lounge every night except Sunday. Doubles here start at $75 for standard rooms, $77 in the Holidome; king-size doubles start at $78.

At the Raleigh-Durham Airport (2½ miles west of U.S. 70), the **Best Western Triangle Inn/Airport** P.O. Box 10951, Raleigh, NC 27605 (tel. 919/787-8121, or toll free 800/528-1234), has well-decorated rooms in a moderate price range. Beds here are extra-long, and a special feature is a wheelchair ramp for the disabled. There's a pool, and a 24-hour café is just a block away. Doubles start at $55.

The **Econo Lodge/West,** 5110 Holly Ridge Dr., Raleigh, NC 27611 (tel. 919/782-3201), is right next door to the Oak Park Shopping Center. Rooms are especially nice for the budget price with Touch Tone telephones, HBO, color TV, and while there's no restaurant on the premises, there are an even dozen within a half mile. Doubles run from $33.

## Where to Eat

For dinner in an elegant setting (French provincial furnishings, gold-framed mirrors, candlelight, and fresh flowers on each table), do reserve at the three-star **Scotch Bonnets Restaurant** in the Marriott Hotel, 4500 Marriott Dr. (tel. 919/781-7000). The menu is continental, with emphasis on fresh seafood dishes such as stir-fried shrimp, scallops, or salmon poached or sautéed to perfection and served with a béarnaise sauce. For meat-eaters, there are steak, veal, and chicken offerings, as well, and each night there's a Chef's Special of the Day. Prices range from $14 to $22. To top off your dinner with an elegance that matches its setting, however, you really should order one of their luscious flambéed desserts (bananas Foster or pineapples in a peppered fruit sauce, at about $8) and finish with one of the exotic coffees, prepared at your table from a tray of condiments such as chocolate bits, brown sugar, lemon rind, cinnamon sticks, etc. Hours are 5:30 to 10 p.m.

For the younger crowd (of any age), it's **Darryl's 1849 Restaurant,** N.C. 70 West (tel. 919/782-1849), **Darryl's 1906 Restaurant and Tavern** at 1906 Hillsborough St. (tel. 919/833-1906), or **Darryl's 1840 Restaurant** at 4309 Old Wake Forest Rd. (tel. 919/872-1840). All are rustic in atmosphere and feature first-rate Italian dinners, a wide variety of sandwiches, beef and pork ribs, steak, seafood, and pizza. Beer comes by the mug or pitcher, cocktails are served, and prices are moderate. This is a popular chain, with branches in Durham, Greensboro, Greenville, Charlotte, and Winston-Salem.

About 12½ miles northwest on U.S. 70 West, you'll find the **Angus Barn** (tel. 919/787-3505), one of the best places for charcoal-broiled steak or choice ribs of beef in these parts. There's also an excellent selection of fresh seafoods. The setting is rustic (it's a restored 19th-century barn), but you'll not feel like one of the "overalls" set here. Fireplaces add a grace note and the food is superior. Semi à la carte prices range from $12 to $25, with beer, wine, and cocktails available. It's open from 5 to 11 p.m. every day (closes at 10 p.m. on Sunday) and is well worth the drive. Better reserve.

*Special Note:* I've eaten barbecued pork in a lot of places, but nowhere on earth does it taste quite like that of Piedmont North Carolina. Slow-cooked in an open pit over hickory chips and basted all the while with a highly seasoned sauce, then finely chopped (no slabs of pork slathered with sauce, such as you get in New York, for instance), it is truly a food fit for kings. But you really have to know your cook, even in North Carolina, and almost every locality has a favorite. In Rocky Mount, it's **Bob Melton's;** in Wilson, it's **Parkers,** etc. Well, the word in Raleigh is that **Cooper's Barbecue,** 109 E. Davie St., is *the* place. My best advice is GO! Even if you're a fan of that Texas stuff, you'll leave Cooper's a convert. Prices are reasonable and portions are generous. One final word: Don't expect anything elegant by way of decor—part of the mystique of North Carolina barbecue is that it's always served in plain surroundings, with lots of hushpuppies and coleslaw. And that's what you'll find here.

For good food at truly budget prices, look for the **K & W Cafeteria** in the North Hills Shopping Center on Six Forks Road, about five miles out the U.S. 1/64 Bypass (tel. 919/782-0353), where lunch will run about $4 to $5, and dinner no more than $6.50. Hours are 10:45 a.m. to 8:30 p.m. Tuesday through Friday, and 11 a.m. to 8 p.m. Saturday through Monday.

## Nightlife

There's nighttime entertainment and dancing at the **Brownstone Hotel** (formerly the Hilton Inn), 1707 Hillsborough St. (tel. 919/828-0811), every night except Sunday. Dancing every night except Sunday, also, at the **Holiday Inn North,** 2815 North Blvd. (tel. 919/872-7666). And the **Velvet Cloak Inn,** 1505 Hillsborough St. (tel. 919/828-0333), has both entertainment and dancing except Sunday. Check local newspapers for the current disco scene, which tends to change too frequently to report in this book.

The **Raleigh Little Theatre,** one of the best community playhouses in the country, presents Broadway productions (check local newspapers for current shows and prices), and during fall and winter months the **North Carolina Symphony** is heard at **Memorial Auditorium.** Nationally and internationally known concert artists also appear at the Auditorium during the season, and while most seats are sold on a subscription basis, it's sometimes possible to obtain single tickets.

## Things to See and Do

For sightseeing brochures, maps, etc., on Raleigh, write or go by the **Raleigh Chamber of Commerce,** 800 S. Salisbury St. (P.O. Box 2978), Raleigh, NC 27602 (tel. 919/833-3005).

Besides sightseeing, which I'll get to in a minute, there are several recreational possibilities in the Triangle area. **William B. Umstead State Park,** halfway between Raleigh and Durham on U.S. 70 (Rte. 8, Box 130, Raleigh, NC 27612), has camping (on a first-come, first-served basis) and picnicking facilities (for details call 919/787-3033). You can fish or just enjoy boating at the municipally owned and operated **Lake Wheeler,** five miles southwest of Raleigh on Rhamkatte Road, from 10 a.m. until sundown every day except Monday for a modest fee (phone 919/772-1173 for details).

Now, for the best possible tour of the capital city, your first stop should be the **Capital Area Visitor Center.** It's in a 1918 mansion called the **Andrews-London House** at 301 N. Blount St. (tel. 919/733-3456). It's open from 8 a.m. to 5 p.m. Monday through Friday, 9 a.m. to 5 p.m. on Saturday, and 1 to 5 p.m. on Sunday. They'll start you off with an orientation film, arm you with brochures and loads of background information, and coordinate walking or driving tours of the area. For further information, write the **North Carolina Department of Cultural Resources,** Raleigh, NC 27611.

The **State Capitol** (tel. 919/733-4994), a stately Greek Revival structure (constructed 1833–1840), has been named a National Historic Landmark and is currently being refurnished to its 1840–1865 appearance. All state business was conducted here until 1888. The building now contains the offices of the governor and secretary of state as well as restored legislative chambers. Beneath the awe-inspiring 97½-foot copper dome there's a duplicate of Antonio Canova's marble statue of George Washington, dressed as a Roman general. The Capitol, on Union (Capitol) Square, is open from 8 a.m. to 5 p.m. Monday through Saturday (from 9 a.m. Friday), and 1 to 5 p.m. on Sunday, is free, and takes about 30 to 45 minutes to tour.

Across from the Capitol, on Bicentennial Plaza, the **North Carolina State Museum of Natural Sciences** is so full of fascinating displays of the state's gems, Indian artifacts, animals, and plants that you'll need at least an hour to explore its contents. There's even a bird hall and live snake collection. One of my favorites here is the whale fossil found near the center of North Carolina, evidence of a long-ago coastline quite different from that of today. There's no charge here, and it's open from 9 a.m. to 5 p.m. Monday through Saturday and 1 to 5 p.m. on Sunday.

The **Legislative Building,** on Jones Street between Wilmington and Salisbury Streets, is a striking contemporary building designed by Edward Durrell Stone, the same architect who drew plans for the Kennedy Center for the Performing Arts in Washington, D.C. Allow about 45 minutes to go through it, longer if you happen to hit there when the legislature is in session (that's every other year, unless it's called into special session), since you'll be able to watch the proceedings. It's free and open from 8 a.m. to 5 p.m. Monday through Friday, 9 a.m. to 5 p.m. on Saturday, and 1 to 5 p.m. on Sunday.

Be sure and save a half hour or so to see the **Governor's Mansion** at 200 N. Blount St. You'll have to make an appointment through the visitor center, but the grand old Victorian home shouldn't be missed. It's built of North Carolina brick and wood, and although it was begun in 1883, the first occupant didn't move in until 1891. There's no charge for a look around. Tours are offered only at certain times: Tuesday and Friday morning and afternoon, March through May; Tuesday and Friday mornings only, September through November.

At 109 E. Jones St., the state's history is pictured in relics of colonial, Revolutionary, and Civil War eras at the **North Carolina Museum of History,** which is also free to visitors. It closes on Monday, and is open 9 a.m. to 5 p.m. Tuesday through Saturday and 1 to 6 p.m. on Sunday, and you'll want to plan about an hour and a half here.

The **North Carolina Museum of Art,** 2110 Blue Ridge Blvd., houses an important collection of European paintings. There are American, 20th-century, ancient, African, Oceanic, and New World collections. A variety of special exhibitions and programs is offered. Hours are 10 a.m. to 5 p.m. Tuesday through Saturday (to 9 p.m. on Friday) and noon to 5 p.m. on Sunday, and there's no admission charge.

One of North Carolina's three native sons who became president, Andrew Johnson, was born in a small cabin about a block from the capitol building. The 17th president's birthplace has been moved to **Mordecai Place** and is open to visitors.

And speaking of Mordecai Place, be sure to see the restored 1785 **Mordecai House,** at 1 Mimosa St. off Wake Forest Road (tel. 919/834-4844). Five generations of one of North Carolina's oldest families lived here (until 1964, in fact), and the original furnishings give it a "lived in" look. There's no admission charge, although donations are accepted. A guide will show you around from 10 a.m. to 2 p.m. Tuesday through Thursday and 1 to 4 p.m. on Saturday and Sunday. Closed January and February, and Tuesday in September.

**Christ Episcopal Church,** at 120 E. Edenton St., is a lovely Gothic Revival building which dates back to the 1840s. When Sherman's troops left town after occupying Raleigh and the state capitol building during the 1860s, they had so stripped the town that it was said the weathercock on this church's steeple was the only chicken left in town.

By contrast to all that history, the "age of the atom" is very much a part of the Raleigh scene, and you can visit the first college-owned reactor in the country on the North Carolina State University campus. Emphasis here is on *peaceful* utilization of atom-splitting. The university is on Hillsborough Street, and you can't miss it. Once on campus, ask for directions to the nuclear reactor building.

One final note about Raleigh: If you can get there in mid-October, you're in luck, for the **North Carolina State Fair** is a real oldtime event that draws crowds from all over and is fun from one end of the fairgrounds to the other (they're located one mile west of town on Blue Ridge Boulevard and I-40). For exact dates the year you plan to come, contact: North Carolina State Fair, 1025 Blue Ridge Blvd., Raleigh, NC 27607 (tel. 919/733-2145).

**RESEARCH TRIANGLE PARK:** By the time you leave Raleigh for Durham or Chapel Hill, you'll have seen highway signs pointing to the Research Triangle Park, which is located on 5,200 acres in the center of a rough triangle formed by the three cities. While it doesn't qualify as a true "sightseeing" destination, it's worthwhile to turn off the highway and drive around, for this is one of the most unique research centers in the country. Some of our brightest scientific minds work here in an atmosphere that carries the "think tank" concept a step further to application of research principles to industry, environment, and government.

Over 50 institutions (including the Environmental Protection Agency, General Electric, DuPont, the National Institute for Environmental Health Sciences, the Burroughs-Wellcome Foundation, and I.B.M. Corporation) represent a constantly increasing multi-million-dollar investment in projects underway, completed, or projected. The payroll (to more than 25,000 staffers) exceeds $700 million annually.

To reach the park, turn off the East-West Expressway from Raleigh to Durham onto N.C. 54—actually, you don't have to bother with highway numbers, the markers are that numerous and prominent.

**DURHAM:** A real-life "American dream" success story was played out in Durham back in the late 1880s, when Washington Duke walked 137 miles back to his farm after being mustered out of the Confederate forces at the end of the Civil War and took up life again as a tobacco farmer. That first year, he started grinding and packaging the crop to sell in small packets. Then, in 1880, Duke decided there was a future in the novelty "cigarettes" and set to work with his three sons to manufacture them on a small scale. By 1890 business had grown so that they formed the American Tobacco Company, and a legendary American manufacturing empire was underway. Durham, which was a small village when Duke came home from war, blossomed into an industrial city, taking its commercial life from the "golden weed." And it still does. From September until the end of December, tobacco warehouses ring with the chants of auctioneers moving from one batch of the cured tobacco to the next, followed by buyers who indicate their bids with nods or hand signals (remember that "Sold American" commercial back in the heyday of radio?). And there's a constant traffic all year of bright leaf tobacco coming into the city and cigarettes and pipe tobacco leaving it.

Even Duke University, the cultural heart of Durham, owes its life's breath to tobacco, for it was little noticed as Trinity College until national and international prominence came with a Duke family endowment of $40 million in 1924. Along with a change in name, the university gained a new West Campus, complete with massive Gothic structures of native stone, flagstone walks, and box hedges that would do justice to Oxford or Cambridge. Its Medical Center has become one of the most highly respected in the world.

## Where to Eat in Durham

You'll find **Claire's,** 2701 Chapel Hill Rd. (tel. 919/493-5721), in a lovely 1909 house that has been renovated to accommodate five dining rooms, with outdoor dining during warm months. There's a nice selection of appetizers (try the escargots or oysters imperial). The cuisine, which is primarily continental, features fresh seafood, beef tenderloin, prime rib, veal, lamb, and duckling preparations. For such quality, prices are moderate: $9.50 to $15.50. Claire's is open for dinner only, nightly from 5 to 10:30 p.m. There's a large and varied wine list, and the comfortable Claire's Lounge serves beer and cocktails.

## Things to See and Do in Durham

Stop by the **Greater Durham Chamber of Commerce,** 201 N. Roxboro St., Northwestern Bank Bldg., Durham, NC 27701 (tel. 919/682-2133), for detailed sightseeing information.

**Washington Duke's homestead,** where it all began, has been named a State Historic Site and National Historical Landmark, and you can visit the home, the original factory building, and farm. There's a visitor center and it's open at no charge from 9 a.m. to 5 p.m. Monday through Saturday and 1 to 5 p.m. on Sunday April through October; from November through March it's open from 10 a.m. to 4 p.m. Tuesday through Saturday and from 1 to 4 p.m. on Sunday. It's located on (what else!) Duke Homestead Road, half a mile north of I-85 and the Guess Road exit. While there, take time to go through the *Tobacco Museum,* which traces the history of tobacco from Indian days to the present. A color film, *Carolina Bright,* is shown on a daily basis as an orientation to the site.

The East and West Campuses of **Duke University** cover more than 1,000 acres on the west side of the city, and it's a good idea to keep the car handy to drive from one "walking tour" to another. The **East Campus,** which was the old Trinity College, features Georgian architecture, and its red-brick and limestone buildings border a half-mile-long grassy mall. There's an excellent **Museum of Art** on this campus, just off West Main Street, that's free (open 9 a.m. to 5 p.m. Tuesday through Friday, 10 a.m. to 1 p.m. on Saturday, and 2 to 5 p.m. on Sunday) and holds marvelous collections of classical art, and pre-Columbian, African, medieval, European, American, and Oriental art, and coins.

It's the **West Campus** (a short drive away on winding, wooded Campus Drive), however, that really steals the university show. Its Gothic-style buildings and beautifully landscaped grounds are nothing short of breathtaking. And the showplace of this showplace is **Duke Chapel,** which brings back memories of England's Canterbury Cathedral. James B. Duke felt strongly that religion should play a prominent part in university life, and the splendor of this chapel assures a religious emphasis at Duke. The bell tower of the majestic cruciform chapel rises 210 feet and houses a 50-bell carillon that rings out at the end of each work day and on Sunday. There's a half-million-dollar Flentrop organ with more than 5,000 pipes (said to be one of the finest in the western hemisphere) in a special oak gallery, its case 40 feet high. Renowned organists perform at the console in public recitals on the first Sunday of each month.

It's impossible to describe the sheer beauty of the chapel's interior: 77 stained-glass windows light the long nave with soft shades of reds, blues, greens, and yellows, and highlight an ornate screen and carved oak choir stalls. Visiting hours are 8:30 a.m. to 5 p.m. daily, and there are interdenominational services every Sunday at 11 a.m.

The university's **Botany Department Greenhouses** (some 13 rooms of plants, both native and rare) are open to the public from 10 a.m. to 4:30 p.m. every day of the week and hold the most diverse collection of plants in the Carolinas.

The West Campus is also the setting of Duke's **Medical Center,** which has gained worldwide fame for its extensive treatment facilities and varied research programs.

To find out more about Duke, call the Special Events Office, 403 Union Tower (tel. 919/684-3710). They'll be glad to arrange special guided tours, and one I especially recommend is of the **Sarah P. Duke Memorial Gardens,** a 55-acre garden on the West Campus that draws more than 100,000 visitors each year. This beauty spot lies in a valley bordered by a pine forest and features a lily pond, stone terraces, and a wisteria-draped pergola, with seasonal plantings that provide an ever-changing color scheme. It's open every day from 8 a.m. to 5 p.m. and is a good place to end a day of campus sightseeing.

Durham's **Museum of Life and Science,** 433 Murray Ave., is especially planned for children, but no matter what your age, I'll wager you'll be intrigued by the life-size models of dinosaurs on a "pathway through the past," and the NASA spacecraft that highlights a large diorama of the Apollo 15 lunar landing site complete with a sample of moon rock. And surely no youngster of any age could resist the exciting "hands-on" exhibits in the Science Arcade. The 78 acres also hold a wildlife sanctuary, barnyard, and mile-long narrow-gauge railroad. Monday through Saturday hours are 10 a.m. to 5 p.m. and 1 to 5 p.m. on Sunday. From Memorial Day through Labor Day the museum is open one hour later each day. Adults pay $3; for ages 4 to 12 and senior citizens it's $2, and for children 3 and under it's free.

**CHAPEL HILL:** The third point of the Triangle area is Chapel Hill, a small city that has managed to hold on to its "village" atmosphere in spite of a university that annually enrolls over 22,000 students. Chapel Hill *is* the University of North Carolina, and it has been universally loved by graduates since 1795, when it was the first state university in the country. The 2,000-acre campus holds 125 buildings, ranging from Old East, the oldest state university building in the country (its cornerstone was laid in 1793), to Morehead Planetarium, which was an astronaut-training center in the early days of manned space flights. And its history is as varied as its buildings. When the Civil War erupted, the student body was second only to Yale's in size—until the fighting started and most of the undergraduates and faculty left for battlefields. Reconstruction finished its destruction and it closed down from 1868 to 1875. Since its reopening, however, it has consistently been a leader in American education and a center of liberal intellectualism (rather surprising, since North Carolina is a generally conservative state). So strong is the attachment and affection of those connected with the university that more than once it and Chapel Hill have been described as "the southern part of heaven."

Chapel Hill's appearance may be village-like but its spirit is lively. Those ivy-covered brick buildings have nurtured such mavericks of the literary world as Thomas Wolfe and Paul Green (who wrote the first outdoor drama produced in the country). And the quiet, tree-lined streets lined with homes set in flower-bordered lawns have been "home" to some of the most innovative intellectuals America has produced.

### Where to Eat in Chapel Hill

**Restaurant La Residence,** 220 W. Rosemary St. (tel. 919/967-2506), is in a 50-year-old residence surrounded by gardens. Each of the small dining rooms has its own decor, and the menu changes daily in order to utilize the freshest available ingredients (they get fresh mountain trout weekly, and if that's your weakness, call to see which day they expect it). The menu, while limited, is composed of exquisite—and delicious—creations which the chef boasts is "the most innovative food in the Triangle area." You might, for instance, order the chicken stuffed (under the skin) with spinach; or from July through September, North Carolina duck with blackberry sauce. As for desserts, don't pass up their homemade ice creams and sorbets, unless, that is, you yield to the temptation of white-chocolate charlotte with raspberry sauce, or the cappuccino cheesecake. Dinner hours are 6 to 9:30 p.m., and it's best to reserve. As you might expect, there's an exceptionally fine (but limited) wine list. Prices for the table d'hôte dinner will run anywhere from $12 to $25.

Elegance in the modern vein best describes dining at **Rubens,** in the Hotel Europa, Europa Drive (tel. 919/968-4900). In a setting of off-white, grays, pinks, beiges, and tan, the atmosphere is one of lighthearted luxury, with a distinctly French accent. An unusual feature of the hotel is its stained-glass elevator! Tea is served in the lounge/lobby every day from 3 to 6 p.m. and features the delicious homemade pastries for which they are locally famous. At lunch, there are light luncheon selections at moderate prices, as well as more substantial fare such as veal, beef, or seafood, most prepared in the French style. The dinner menu is quite extensive, with many specialties. Prices are in the $10 to $25 range at dinner, lower for lunch, and if you just want a touch of elegance, drop in for breakfast, which will run $4 to $8. Hours are 6:30 a.m. to 11 a.m., 11:30 a.m. to 2:30 p.m., and 5:30 to 10:30 p.m. There's a Sunday brunch from 11 a.m. to 2:30 p.m.

The decor is Victorian at the **Pyewacket Restaurant,** in The Courtyard, 431 W. Franklin St. (tel. 919/929-0297). The cozy lounge has comfortable couches and is dimly lit; there are two high-ceilinged rooms done in red and brown, and the greenhouse dining room is windowed all around, filled with plants (no smokers allowed in this area). There's a nice selection of pasta, soups, sandwiches, omelets, salads, and desserts at lunch with prices that run from $3 to $6, and at dinner seafood, vegetarian, and continental entrees are featured at prices of $5.50 to $12. A wide variety of coffees features espresso made in their own espresso machine. Hours are 11:30 a.m. to 2:30 p.m. and 5:30 to 9:30 p.m. Monday through Thursday, to 10 p.m. on Friday and Saturday, and 5:30 to 9:30 p.m. on Sunday.

Behind the rather quirky façade of **Crook's Corner,** 610 W. Franklin St. (tel. 919/929-7643), lurks one of the South's most superb new restaurants. Young co-owner/chef Bill Neal, formerly chef-manager of Restaurant La Residence, has zoomed to prominence as one of the nation's most up-and-coming chefs. No less a luminary than Craig Claiborne has proclaimed him a "genius of the stove." The restaurant showcases many of the recipes Neal features in his widely acclaimed *Bill Neal's Southern Cooking* (University of North Carolina Press). The menu varies with the season and may include such delights as shrimp and grits or sea scallops sautéed with mushrooms, scallions, sweet red peppers, and new potatoes in a lemon juice–garlic sauce. Side dishes are such down-home delicacies with subtle touches as fresh collard greens or Hoppin' John, black-eyed peas, and rice with scallions, tomato, and cheddar (both $2). Entrees range from $7 to $16.

The quirky façade? The roof is adorned with pigs, alligators, rabbits, squirrels, and other critters produced from scrap lumber by an area primitive artist. Inside, the walls are decorated with whimsical art deco–style sculptures of deep-sea denizens. Seating capacity is limited to 70, and there's seating for about 50 more outside in nice weather. Crook's doesn't take reservations, so you may have to wait—but it's worth it. It's open from 5 p.m. to midnight Sunday through Thursday, to 1 a.m. on Friday and Saturday.

For something a little different, try the **Mariakakis Restaurant and Bakery** (tel. 919/942-1453), on U.S. 15-501 Bypass, across from the Holiday Inn. The menu includes Greek and Italian food, homemade thick-crust pizza, and deli sandwiches. Beer and wine are served, and a gourmet shop and a bakery are on the premises. Prices are moderate, and hours are 9 a.m. to 9 p.m. Monday to Saturday.

## Things to See and Do in Chapel Hill

To best arm yourself for sightseeing, contact the **Chapel Hill Carrboro Chamber of Commerce,** 104 S. Estes Dr. (P.O. Box 2897), Chapel Hill, NC 27514 (tel. 919/967-7075).

Your best introduction to the university community is a free, one-hour campus tour that leaves from Morehead Planetarium (the west entrance) on East Franklin Street at 2:15 p.m. daily March through November (other times by appointment).

With the tour or on your own, look for the **Old Well,** once the only source of drinking water for Chapel Hill. It stands in the center of the campus on Cameron Avenue, in a small, temple-like enclosure with a dome supported by classic columns. Just east of it is **Old East,** begun in 1793 and the country's oldest state university building. Across the way stands the "newcomer," **Old West,** built in 1824. **South Main Building** is nearby, a structure that was begun in 1798 and not finished until 1814—students lived inside the empty shell in rude huts during that time. And look for the **Coker Arboretum** at Cameron Avenue and Raleigh Street, where five acres are planted in a wide variety of temperate-zone plants. As you walk the campus you'll hear popular tunes coming from the 167-foot **Morehead-Patterson Bell Tower,** whose Italian Renaissance campanile rings throughout the day. And just back of the bell tower is **Kenan Stadium,** in a wooded natural bowl setting, with a 44,000-seat capacity.

And of course you won't want to miss **Morehead Planetarium.** It was a 1947 gift of John Motley Morehead and houses the first Carl Zeiss instrument located on a U.S. college campus (there are only 12 in the whole country) in a 68-foot domed theater. The "star" of its permanent scientific exhibits is a large orrery showing the simultaneous action of planets revolving around the suns, moons revolving around planets, and planets rotating on their axes. There are main feature shows at 8 p.m. Monday through Sunday, and also at 1, 3, and 8 p.m. on Saturday and Sunday. A children's show is given at 11 a.m. on Saturday. Admission is $3 for adults, $2.50 for students and senior citizens, and $2 for children under 12. A 35-mm wide-angle film is presented at 7 p.m. Saturday through Thursday, and at 2, 4, and 7 p.m. on Saturday and Sunday. *Sky Rambles* is a 7 p.m. Friday feature. Admission to these shows is $2 for all ages, or $1.50 with admission to the main feature.

Try to catch a PlayMakers Repertory Company production at the **Play-Makers Theatre** (tel. 919/962-1121), a Greek Revival structure whose Corinthian columns are adorned with corn and wheat designs instead of the traditional acanthus leaves. You could see classical or contemporary drama, as well as new works—they're professional in both areas and sometimes perform in the modern Paul Green Theatre.

Off campus, the **North Carolina Botanical Garden,** on Laurel Hill Road and U.S. 15-501 Bypass (tel. 919/967-2246), is open from 8 a.m. to 5 p.m. weekdays, and its three miles of easily followed nature trails are lined with native plants of this region. It's free, and a botanical education with herb gardens, and carnivorous plants and native plants in habitat settings.

## 2. Winston-Salem

Before 1913 the twin communities of Winston and Salem coexisted in perfect harmony, and their incorporation that year into a single city has proved a happy, productive union. Winston, founded in 1849, contributed an industry-based economy, while Salem added the crafts, educational emphasis, and sense of order that its Moravian settlers brought from Pennsylvania in 1766.

Actually, Salem (the name comes from the Hebrew word *shalom*, meaning peace) was the last of three settlements by Moravian clergy and laymen who came to the Piedmont looking for townsites in the early 1750s—the little towns of Bethabara and Bethania came first. But Salem proved to be the main establishment, and the hard-working newcomers laid out a pleasant community with their traditional Single Brothers and Single Sisters houses as focal points for unmarried members of the congregation. Once married, the couples often set up shop right in their own homes. They were hardy, devout, Germanic people who had fled persecution in Europe and brought to the New World their artisans' skills, a deep love of music and education, and absolute rejection of violence in any form.

As "progress" began to encroach on the boundaries of the beautiful, orderly old congregational town, an organized effort was begun in 1949 to restore those homes and shops that were in a state of deterioration and to reconstruct others that had disappeared. Today there are more than 30 buildings restored with meticulous attention to authenticity and still others in the process of renovation. Devout the Moravians were, glum they were not; and the bright, cheerful reds and blues and soft greens and yellows in the restored interiors (exteriors as well) are duplicates of the colors with which they surrounded themselves in those early days. They also loved good food, and that too has been lovingly preserved in Old Salem: today's tourist can sit down to lunch or dinner in the Tavern Dining Room (see below) in an authentic colonial Moravian setting. Most entrees are contemporary American/continental, but you can select such specialties as Moravian chicken pie or ragoût of beef, and one dessert is a wonderful Moravian gingerbread topped with homemade lemon ice cream.

Flowing around the center island of Old Salem, the vigorous new city goes about its business of commerce and industry in a manner that somehow escapes the environmental blight that marks other manufacturing centers. Maybe that's due in part to the fact that it is not too large (latest population figures are 132,000), or maybe it's because it's citizens have retained a sense of aesthetic values handed down from those early arrivals. At any rate, although this is the home base for such giants as one of the South's largest banks, (Wachovia National), and Piedmont Airlines, there is a genteel air about the place that almost convinces you progress doesn't *have* to be abrasive.

For the traveler, there are points of interest outside Winston-Salem itself, making Winston-Salem a perfect base for day trips to Greensboro, High Point, and the pottery center at Seagrove which dates back 200 years.

**WHERE TO STAY:** It's not in town, but the **Tanglewood Park, Lodge and Manor House,** Clemmons, NC 27012 (tel. 919/766-0591), is an experience not to be missed. It's about 12 miles west of Winston-Salem, just off I-40 (the exit is marked). Once upon a time, Indians roamed this lush, wooded section of the Yadkin River Valley. When the Moravians arrived in 1753 and settled the Wachovia tract, one square mile of land was deeded by Lord Linville to the Ellis family, who leased it briefly for "five shillings lawful money of Great Britain in hand and a yearly rent of one peppercorn payment at the Feast of Saint Michael, the archangel." In 1757 the Johnson family acquired it and held on to it until 1921, when William N. Reynolds, the tobacco tycoon, decided it was just the place to build his country home. Never a man to do things on a small scale, "Mr. Will" kept adding acres of contiguous land until the total stood at 1,100. The lovely old Johnson homeplace, built in 1859, sprouted wings on either side and became a true manor house. The Reynoldses named the estate Tanglewood.

Well, five shillings and a peppercorn won't get you far at Tanglewood these days, but the Manor House *can* be your country home, if only for a day—since 1951, Tanglewood (officially, it's the William and Kate B. Reynolds Memorial Park) has been open to the public, operated as a department of county government. For remarkably reasonable rates, you can sleep in a spacious master bedroom complete with fireplace and canopied double beds, dine in an elegant colonial-style dining room (there are five, one with a mammoth stone fireplace) on gourmet fare, roam the well-kept terraces and lawns, and play the country squire to your heart's content. The cost of this plush living runs $44 to $65.

There are only 11 bedrooms in the Manor House, so there's no mob scene to detract you from your fantasy of "lord of the manor," and the nearby Motor Lodge has just 18 units and an apartment, with rates from $44 to $57. If your idea of country living runs along more rustic lines, there are five vacation cottages in a secluded woodland area overlooking Mallard Lake. The two- and three-bedroom cottages, completely furnished and with fully equipped kitchens, rent for $275 to $300 per week for five or fewer people. More rugged types can reserve one of the 100 family campground sites in one corner of the vast estate. Most have electric and water hookups, all have picnic tables and campfire space, and there are two large bathhouses and a dumping station: $11 a day for those with hookups ($70 per week) and $9 without.

If you think "country" equates with "boredom," 'taint so, at least not here. At Tanglewood, you can play tennis on one of nine courts, swim in a large pool, go paddleboating or canoeing or trail riding. And, of course, there's golf, on an excellent course right on the grounds. There's even steeplechase racing the third Saturday of every April, the last meet of the year on the Carolina circuit; but don't expect to stay at Tanglewood then—all rooms and cottages are held for racing participants. As for other times of the year, better reserve three or four weeks ahead, because the place is a year-round favorite with regulars.

## In Winston-Salem

Right in the heart of town at 300 W. 5th St., Winston-Salem, NC 27102, is the **Hyatt Winston-Salem** (tel. 919/725-1234, or toll free 800/228-9000). Recently renovated to the tune of over $4 million, it's a winner for travelers going the deluxe route. The nine-story open lobby has the look of an indoor park, and its glass-bubble elevators overlook reflecting pools, fountains, hanging gardens, and a 30-foot waterfall that splashes into the second-story-level swimming pool. For all its modern luxury, the place can lay claim to a southern heritage, since for more than half a century this was the site of the Robert E. Lee Hotel, and a portrait of the general hangs in the lobby, on loan from the local chapter of the United Daughters of the Confederacy (who even imported Robert E. Lee IV for their presentation ceremonies). The Salem Tavern, which hosted George Washington in 1791, is preserved in spirit in the elegant, newly redecorated Smithfield's on Fifth, with a warm, comfortable atmosphere. The sophisticated and varied menu features some imaginative entrees for the fitness-conscious diner. Luncheons are in the $4 to $8 range, and dinners are about $10 to $20. A testament to the restaurant's excellence is its popularity with the local gentry. The adjoining lounge is a great place to relax and unwind, with live entertainment and dancing. The Greenhouse Restaurant, overlooking the lobby, offers everything from a hearty country breakfast to sandwiches to steaks, and is open from 7 a.m. until 11 p.m.

As for the rooms, each of the 305 has either a balcony view of the lobby or an outside view of the city, but if you're ready for some very special pampering, ask for a room on the ninth-floor Regency Club level. You begin the day there in a graciously appointed drawing room with a continental breakfast buffet and end it with sherry and cheese. Rates on this level are $120 and include the services of a concierge, who will do everything from making travel, rental car, or dinner reservations to finding a babysitter. The *Wall Street Journal* and other out-of-town newspapers appear at your door every morning—just state your preference. Less elegant rooms (although all are first class) run $90 to $110. Except during special events, some rates drop considerably on Friday and Saturday nights.

In a more moderate price category, the **Holiday Inn North**, 3050 N. Cherry-Marshall Expressway, Winston-Salem, NC 27105 (tel. 919/723-2911, or toll free 800/465-4329), is a good bet. Just across from the center of all major sports events in this area (you guessed it—the Coliseum), it also affords easy access to most sightseeing spots. For example, Old Salem is a straight shot through the city center on the expressway (clearly marked) and R.J. Reynolds World and Reynolda House and Gardens are close by. Rooms are large and decor is modern (doubles are $52 and up) and local telephone calls are free, as is transportation to and from the airport. There's piano music in the Open Forum Dining Room on Sunday, where southern fried chicken has brought travelers and local residents back for more over the years. Pets are welcomed here if they stay in the kennel.

*Special Note:* A recent joyful discovery is the **Brookstown Inn**, 200 Brookstown Ave., Winston-Salem, NC 27101 (tel. 919/725-1120). In part of an old 1837 cotton mill that wove and dyed material for Confederate uniforms, this absolute jewel of a 40-room (plus 12 suites) inn offers spacious accommodations with two double beds, a chest of drawers, armoire (hiding a remote-control TV), love seat, desk, chairs, tables, and a live palm tree. The suites have a separate sitting room and hot tub. Silk flowers, quilts, baskets, and wooden decoys adorn the parlor areas, decorated in lovely Wedgwood blue, burgundy, gold, and olive, and accented by old brick and exposed wooden beams. Double rates begin at

$75, and you're welcomed with complimentary afternoon wine and cheese, and a continental breakfast highlighted by luscious Moravian lovefeast buns. The inn, on the National Register of Historic Places, is conveniently near the Old Salem restoration. Another area of the mill, its former boiler, is site of one of the popular Darryl's Restaurants.

## In Nearby Greensboro

There's an elegant **Guest Quarters** at 5929 W. Friendly Ave., Greensboro, NC 27410 (tel. 919/292-9821), with one- and two-bedroom suites and all the exceptional service features of this fine chain (see Chapter I). This location has tennis courts and jogging trails, as well as a lovely swimming pool with deck area. Convenient to the airport and the city's corporate centers, Guest Quarters rates here are $92 double for the one-bedroom suites and $100 double for two bedrooms.

The 11-story **Sheraton Greensboro,** 3 Southern Life Center, Greensboro, NC 27401 (tel. 919/379-8000, or toll free 800/325-3535), right in the heart of downtown, was built around the historic 1926 Greensboro Central Fire Station (which has been renovated to house the elegant Central Station Restaurant). Guest rooms are all beautifully decorated, with mirrored closet doors, built-in headboards, and brass reading lamps. The most striking feature in many are their lovely bay windows. Doubles range from $88 to $98. Continental dishes in the Central Station Restaurant run from $13 to $22, with hours of 4 to 11 p.m. The more moderately priced Café is open from 6:30 a.m. to 10:30 p.m.

**WHERE TO EAT:** Far and away the most atmospheric place to eat is the **Old Salem Tavern,** 736 S. Main St. in Old Salem (tel. 919/748-8585). Here, as everywhere else in the restored village, authenticity is the keynote. The dining rooms were built in 1816 as an annex to the 1784 Tavern next door, and the simply furnished rooms and colonial-costumed waiters and waitresses provide an appropriate, early-18th-century ambience for your lunch (11:30 a.m. to 2 p.m.) or après-sightseeing dinner (5:30 to 9 p.m. every day but Sunday when hours are noon to 4 p.m.). During summer months you can eat in the outdoor arbor, which, like the indoor rooms, is candlelit at night. Always available are such favorites as Tavern chicken pie (at lunch), and rack of lamb and roast duckling (dinner only). The pumpkin and raisin muffins are a specialty. Reservations are preferred at dinner and for luncheon parties of five or more. Lunch runs $5 to $10; dinner, $9 to $16.

You can have a meal behind bars at **Annabelle's** (formerly Tuesday's 1865 Eating Establishment), in the sprawling Hanes Mall just off I-40 (look for the Silas Creek Parkway exit (tel. 919/768-2132)—after which you're free to leave. Nostalgia is the theme, and good food at reasonable prices in a fun atmosphere is the name of the game at this new-old restaurant. The rustic old barn doors open to stained glass, carved woodwork, gaslights, ceiling fans, and a collection of memorabilia that is a delight. As for the authentic old jail, complete with massive barred doors, it has been moved intact to the balcony; and if that doesn't suit your fancy, you can choose to sit beneath the painted hobby horses that prance across the ceiling or in sight of the early-vintage Shell gas pump and advertising sign for Clabber Girl Baking Powder. Every item is a genuine antique, many salvaged from old homes and junkyards in North Carolina and Virginia. (For the story of how this all came about, see the writeup of Annabelle's in the Wilmington section of Chapter VI.)

As for the food, it's both good and, as mentioned, affordable. The self-service salad wagon is an especially good buy—it's the most extensive selection

I've encountered in a long time, with all the usual fare, plus such unexpected treats as herring, apple rings, and a large variety of fresh fruits. You go for refills as many times as your appetite dictates. Deviled mushrooms are a personal lunchtime favorite, but heartier meals like the ranch hand rib-eye loin, wrangler's sirloin (that's New York strip steak), or stuffed flounder come with salad from the salad wagon, a choice of baked or french-fried potatoes, or corn on the cob, and homemade bread at moderate prices. The large antique bar serves beer and wines (quite a good selection). If you've ever longed for "the good old days," turn off I-40 and find Annabelle's. It's large and reservations are not necessary.

*Special Note:* At 801 Waughton St. is one of those treasures travelers dream about—an inexpensive place to eat with food that's *really* good! At the **Biscuit House** (tel. 919/788-8861), Charles Munday serves a menu that's limited but southern to the core, at prices you won't believe. For less than $2 you can buy two pieces of fried chicken and a large, light, yummy buttered biscuit (as one who grew up with the world's best biscuit-cooking mother, I know my biscuits and can speak with authority!). You can have a full dinner with two pieces, and if you're really a chicken lover, the four-piece dinner. Mr. Munday also serves biscuits with ham, sausage, and steak for under $3. The chicken is as good as the biscuits, and that says it all—and there's a new addition to the menu, a chicken filet. For just pennies, a bowl of delicious, home-cooked pinto beans accents any of the above. Don't miss this one, even if money is no object.

For other good eating spots, try the **Hyatt House** and **Holiday Inn** eateries.

**THINGS TO DO AND SEE:** For detailed sightseeing information, contact the **Greater Winston-Salem Chamber of Commerce**, P.O. Box 1408, Winston-Salem, NC 27102 (tel. 919/725-2361).

Near the very center of the city (just off U.S. 52 on Old Salem Road), **Old Salem** has *got* to be the place you head for first in Winston-Salem. The Visitor Center, on Old Salem Road, will start you off with exhibits that trace the Moravians' journey from Europe to America and finally to North Carolina. And they'll sell you combination tickets to the restored buildings that are open Monday through Saturday from 9:30 a.m. to 4:30 p.m. and 1:30 to 4:30 p.m. on Sunday at $10 for adults, $5 for students. Of course, if you want to include the **Museum of Early Southern Decoration**, the price goes up—$12.50 and $6.25. Individual admission to each building is $1 to $3. Costumed hosts and hostesses will show you around, and you'll also see craftsmen in Moravian dress practicing the trades of the original settlement.

And speaking of crafts, when Moravian boys reached the age of 14, they moved into the **Single Brothers House,** the first, half-timbered section of which was built in 1769 and the newer, brick wing in 1786, where they began an apprenticeship to a master artisan for seven years. Academic studies went on as they learned to be gunsmiths, tailors, potters, shoemakers, or whatever. Adolescent girls, too, left home to live in the **Single Sisters House,** diagonally across the town square, and learn the domestic arts they would need when marrying time arrived. Single girls *still* live in this building—it's a dormitory for Salem College—although their present-day education differs considerably.

Be sure to go into the **Tavern.** The one you see was built in 1784 to replace an earlier one which burned, and once inside you'll understand why travelers often came out of their way to stop here and enjoy its hospitality. George Washington spent two nights here in 1791 and commented in his diary on the industriousness of the Moravians. The dining room, sleeping rooms, barns, and grounds are not much different now from when he stopped by, and those cooking utensils you see in the stone-floored kitchen with its twin fireplaces are the real thing.

The **Wachovia Museum** (this whole area was named Wachovia by the original settlers after a district in Saxony that had offered refuge to the sect) was once the boys' school. There are tape recordings of music being played on the old musical instruments you see displayed here and a host of other historical items. You can also visit the **Market-Firehouse** and the **Winkler Bakery.** Bread and cookies are still baked in the big wood-burning ovens at the bakery. Many of the homes have distinctive signs hanging outside to identify the shops inside, and one of my favorites is the tobacco shop of Matthew Miksch, a sunny-yellow weather-boarded log cottage with a miniature man hanging at the door clutching tobacco leaves and a snuff box.

Like the Historic District of Williamsburg, Virginia, Old Salem still functions as a living community, and many of the homes you see restored on the outside are private residences, as modern inside as a contemporary ranch-style. And the young people you see walking the old streets with such familiarity are no doubt students at Salem College, living a 20th-century campus life in an 18th-century setting.

On the square, the **Home Moravian Church,** which dates from 1800, is the center of the denomination in the South. Visitors are always welcomed to the services, and hundreds show up for the Easter Sunrise Service (held continuously in Old Salem for over 200 years), the Christmas Lovefeasts (on December 24), and the New Year's Eve Watch Night Service. One block north of the square, the graveyard named "God's Acre" is a visual reminder that death is the great equalizer, since the more than 4,000 graves are marked with almost identical stones—prince and pauper are shown the same respect.

Three miles northwest of Winston-Salem, near Cherry Marshall and University Hwys. (just follow the signs), is historic **Bethabara Park,** site of the first Moravian settlement in North Carolina. There are two restored 18th-century buildings, an early 19th-century Brewer's House, and the excavated foundations of the town of Bethabara, begun in 1753, along with a rebuilt fort in its original trench. The guided tour is free (9:30 a.m. to 4:30 p.m. Monday through Friday, 1:30 to 4:30 p.m. on Saturday, Sunday, and holidays) and there are nature trails and picnic grounds. Open April to mid-December.

A prominent citizen of Winston lived at **Reynolda House** (just off Reynolda Road near Wake Forest University): R. J. Reynolds, the tobacco tycoon, built the mansion, which now holds an excellent collection of furnishings and American art, as well as a 1905–1950 ladies' costume display. The gardens are especially lovely in late March or early April, when they're abloom with Japanese cherry trees. The house is open Tuesday through Saturday from 9:30 a.m. to 4:30 p.m. and on Sunday from 1:30 p.m. and costs $4 for adults, $3 for senior citizens, and $2 for students and children. The gardens are free and open every day from 7:30 a.m. to 5 p.m.

No matter where you choose to stay in Winston-Salem, include **Tanglewood** in your sightseeing (see "Where to Stay," above). The beautiful recreation area is ten miles southwest of town on U.S. 158, and the exit is marked.

Both the **Stroh Brewery,** 5½ miles south on U.S. 52 (tel. 919/788-6710, ext. 252), and the **R. J. Reynolds Tobacco Company,** off Cherry Street on 33rd Street (tel. 919/773-2000), will show you through their plants.

O. Henry's hometown, Greensboro, is less than 30 miles away. Of course, the short story writer was known as William Sidney Porter in these parts, and you can see an exhibit illustrating his life and work at the **Greensboro Historical Museum,** 130 Summit Ave. (tel. 919/373-2043). Greensboro was also the birthplace of Dolley Madison. This museum houses a fine collection from her life as the only native-born North Carolina first lady. Other exhibits include early modes of transportation, furnishings, pottery, textiles, and military artifacts. There is no admission charge. Hours are 10 a.m. to 5 p.m. Tuesday through Saturday and 2 to 5 p.m. on Sunday.

Six miles northwest of Greensboro on U.S. 220, a 220-acre park—**Guilford Courthouse National Military Park,** P.O. Box 9806, Greensboro, NC 27429 (tel. 919/288-1776)—marks one of the closing battles of the Revolution, the Battle of Guilford Courthouse on March 15, 1781. Gen. Nathanael Greene (Greensboro was named for him) led a group of inexperienced troops against Lord Cornwallis, and although he was defeated, he inflicted severe losses on the British. Cornwallis hotfooted it out of this part of the country and headed for Yorktown, Virginia, where he surrendered his depleted forces just seven months later, on October 19. The Visitor Center is open from 8:30 a.m. to 5 p.m. daily, and has films, brochures, and displays about the historic battle. There are also wayside exhibits along the two-mile, self-guided auto-tour road that leads to some of the many monuments. No charge.

Six miles southwest of nearby Burlington, on N.C. 62, is where those upstart farmers marched against Royal Governor Tryon in 1771 to protest British taxes. Ill-trained and poorly equipped, they were soundly defeated—the battle lasted only two hours—but the stouthearted "Regulators" were among the first southern colonists to demonstrate their objection to royal rule. The **Almance Battleground State Historic Site** has a Visitor Center (with audio-visual presentations) that's open Monday through Saturday from 9 a.m. to 5 p.m. and on Sunday from 1 to 5 p.m., April through October; Tuesday through Saturday from 10 a.m. to 4 p.m. and on Sunday from 1 to 4 p.m., November through March. Admission is free.

Just south of Greensboro, **High Point** is one of the leading furniture-manufacturing centers in the U.S. High Point (which got its name because it was the highest point along the 1853 North Carolina and Midland Railroad from Salem to Fayetteville) has a very good museum at 1805 E. Lexington Ave. (at McGuinn Avenue), with displays of Indian artifacts and Quaker history exhibits. Right next door there's a restored 1786 Flemish bond-pattern-brick stagecoach stop, the **John Haley House,** a Quaker home with a still-functioning blacksmith shop.

Just about halfway between Greensboro and Charlotte, a little off I-85 (near historic Salisbury), the little town of Spencer is a mecca for dyed-in-the-wool railway buffs who come here to wander through the **Spencer Shops,** 411 S. Salisbury Ave. (tel. 704/636-2889), which were established in 1896 as a major repair facility for the Southern Railway. Opened as a museum in 1983, the Master Mechanics Building is the focal point in the 57-acre site. Indeed, visitors are free to wander at will among the growing collection of transportation memorabilia (with emphasis, of course, on trains) and let their imagination people the railyards with those hard-working, hard-living railroad men who once (in the 1930s) built a locomotive in one day. It's a friendly, informal place, where the project director, Michael Wells, or any member of his staff is likely to jump in with anecdotes about the shops' history at your first show of enthusiasm. It's free, and hours are 9 a.m. to 5 p.m. Monday through Saturday, from 1 p.m. on Sunday April through October; and from 10 a.m. to 4 p.m. Tuesday through Saturday, from 1 to 4 p.m. on Sunday, November through March. Hours are subject to change. Rail rides have recently been added and a large museum shop offers unusual railroad items ranging from 15¢ maps to *Orient Express* crystal. *Note:* Just across the street, stop in at **Krider's restaurant** (tel. 704/633-5219), where Evelyn Krider loves to recall the days when railroading was the hub of activity in Spencer—she also serves up *very* good home-cooked meals at unbelievably low prices.

# 3. Pinehurst

The Sandhills' porous, sandy soil is a reminder that in prehistoric times Atlantic Ocean waves rolled over the land. It also provides an ideal drainage situation that is a big factor in the area's "Golf Capital, U.S.A." standing, for no matter what the rainfall, no puddles accumulate on the rolling green golf courses (there are 27 within a 15-mile radius). And with temperatures that range between 78° and 44°, the games go on year round.

But golf hasn't always been king here. In fact, when Boston philanthropist James Walker Tufts bought up 5,000 acres of land in 1895 at $1 per, his main thought was to build the little resort village of Pinehurst as a retreat from harsher climes for wealthy Northerners. Recreation for guests back then consisted mainly of croquet on the grassy lawns, outdoor concerts, hayrides, or just quiet walks through the pines. The story goes that his attention first turned to golf, which had only recently arrived in the U.S. from Great Britain, when one of his dairy employees complained that guests were "hitting the cows with a little white ball." By 1900 Tufts had enlisted Donald Ross (whose skill had been gained at Scotland's St. Andrews) to come to Pinehurst and introduce golf. In time (he remained in the Sandhills the rest of his life) Ross designed courses here that drew some of the most distinguished golfers in the world: Ben Hogan, Walter Travis, Bobby Jones, Walter Hagen, Patty Berg, Sam Snead, Arnold Palmer, Gary Player, Jack Nicklaus—and that's only a partial list!

For years, golf on the superb courses, beginning and ending at the Pinehurst Country Club's clubhouse, was by invitation only, and the list of invitees was so exclusive that Walter Hagen is reported to have said (after finally receiving the treasured summons) on returning from his first game, "The place is so exclusive that, hell, the Duke of Windsor would have trouble getting in!" Today, however, although the golf world's top players no doubt consider Pinehurst their own turf, you don't have to wait for an invitation, nor do you have to be a millionaire to play. Prices are certainly high enough at the Pinehurst Hotel, but they're not exorbitant by comparison with other luxury hotels around the country. And there is a profusion of other hotels and motels, something in almost any price range; and, expert or duffer, guests can always play the courses.

In 1973 the first World Open Championship was played in Pinehurst, replaced in 1977 by the Colgate–Hall of Fame Classic. In September of 1974 President Gerald Ford presided at the opening of the World Golf Hall of Fame, overlooking Ross's famous Number Two Course (one of the top ten in the country), with all the living inductees there for the ceremonies.

Through all the hullabaloo over celebrity golf matches, Pinehurst has retained its New England village air, built by Frederick Law Olmstead (the architect-landscaper who also planned New York's Central Park), with a Village Green and shaded residential streets, many paved only by a carpet of pine needles. It hasn't changed, but continues to carry out the Tufts concept of a retreat here in the Sandhills. Year-round greenery is provided by pines (some with needles 15 inches long), stately magnolias, and hollies. Moderate temperatures account for color through all seasons—camellias, azaleas, wisteria, peach trees, dogwoods, and summer-blooming yard flowers. And the village is a private business, owned and operated by the Club Corporation of America. Shops, restaurants, hotels, and other business enterprises make it a complete, self-sufficient community, yet none intrude in an abrasive way, all adhering to the original style and preserving a leisurely graciousness that's as refreshing to the spirit as to the eye.

For those whose idea of a good time is *not* chasing around after that elusive little white ball (you can count me in that esteemed company), there are plenty of other things to do. There's a tennis club, any number of excellent courts, over 200 miles of riding trails and stables with good mounts for hire, boating on a 200-acre lake, trap and skeet ranges, archery, over 9,000 acres of woods to explore via meandering pathways, and shopping in the little boutiques that is out of this world.

Pinehurst's sister town (it's a *real* town, not corporation owned), **Southern Pines,** is a delight too. The short drive on Midland Road (N.C. 2), a double-lane highway divided by a strip of pines and bordered by lovely homes and lavish gardens, goes right past **Midland Crafters.** You'll see it on your right, and take my word for it, stop. The rambling white building is a virtual gallery of American crafts, ranging from beanbags to paintings to furniture, to candles, to pottery, to glassware, to . . . well, almost any handcraft you can think of.

Stop, too, at the Sand Hills Area **Chamber of Commerce,** at 125 S.E. Broad St., on the corner of Pennsylvania Avenue (tel. 919/692-3926)—it's right in the middle of town, you can't miss it—to pick up information on the area and meet the friendly, helpful staff. And park your car—this is as pretty a walking town as you'll find anywhere. It will take you longer than you imagine just to wander up and down the five or six blocks of Broad Street, Pennsylvania Avenue, and Bennett Street.

Like those in Pinehurst, shops here are small, charming, and filled with interesting, often exquisite items. Outstanding among the offbeat shops is **Something Special,** on Pennsylvania Avenue (tel. 919/692-9602). Inside are collectors' dolls and dollhouses, miniature grandfather clocks that keep time, all kinds of materials to make your own dollhouse, and items so unique (like the miniature dentures I saw there) that people come here from all over the Southeast to have a look.

The handsome Georgian house on East Connecticut Avenue, once the Campbell family residence, is a **cultural and visitor center,** with a small golf museum and an equestrian room filled with trophies, racing silks, and prints of hunts and races. That's not surprising, since there are so many fine horse farms in the Sandhills. Steeplechasers trained here show up regularly at tracks in New York, Florida, Kentucky, and Maryland. Trotters and pacers are also trained around here, and Del Cameron, one of only two living three-time winners of the Hambletonian, has kept a winter training stable in this area for more than 30 years.

All this will give you some idea of what to expect when you come to this part of North Carolina's Piedmont, but I strongly recommend that you write ahead for detailed information on Pinehurst (Pinehurst Hotel and Country Club, Pinehurst, NC 28374) and the entire Sandhills (**Sandhills Area Chamber of Commerce,** P.O. Box 458, Southern Pines, NC 28387; tel. 919/692-3926).

**WHERE TO STAY:** Although the **Pinehurst Hotel and Country Club,** P.O. Box 4000, Pinehurst, NC 28374 (tel. 919/295-6811, or toll free 800/334-9560, 800/672-4644 in North Carolina), is still *the* place to stay in Pinehurst, as it has been from the beginning, though there are several other hotels in the village that offer luxury on a smaller scale and graciousness on the same level at somewhat more moderate prices. And, of course, Southern Pines is close by, with numerous motels catering to Pinehurst visitors.

About that grand old Pinehurst Hotel: Now owned by Club Corporation of America, it proudly rears its head with all the splendid aristocracy of the past enhanced by the most modern improvements (for example, in the old days the only air conditioning came from open windows or fans). The white, four-story,

300-room building, with wings on each side sporting broad, columned porches lined with comfortable rocking chairs, was called the Carolina for years, and you'll still hear residents refer to it by that name. Whatever you call it, when you drive up to the columned portico and walk through its huge lobby furnished with a pleasing mixture of antique and contemporary fittings, you'll know this is a place where the art of gracious living is still practiced. Public rooms and guest rooms have undergone extensive renovation, and while bright, cheerful colors predominate in the spacious accommodations, there's an air of subdued elegance that newer establishments never seem quite able to achieve. And besides the main building, there are over 160 one-, and two-, and three-bedroom condominiums.

The tennis complex, with some 28 courts (18 are clay), is presided over by a highly professional staff. Clinics and individual instruction are available to all guests.

For equestrians, saddle horses are available, and there are miles of riding trails, supervised and unsupervised riding, instructions, and, if you bring your own mount, boarding. The stables also offer carriage rides, a particularly charming way to see the village. Archery is available, and there are nine trap and skeet fields (two of which are lighted).

But, of course, the major attraction is those seven 18-hole golf courses, especially the world-famous Number Two. Five begin and end at the clubhouse (and that, alone, is worth the trip, even if you're the world's worst duffer—it's everything a clubhouse should be and more, with the same elegant air and attention to service as the hotel). Greens fees for all except Number Two are $25; Number Two's fees are higher.

To all this add bicycles, a huge L-shaped pool and deck area, a game room, health spa, and fishing, boating, and swimming at Lake Pinehurst (200 acres worth), and you have a resort with facilities second to none. As for food and sophisticated dinner-dancing and entertainment, the hotel draws a large crowd of North Carolinians who sometimes travel quite a distance, as well as guests who seldom venture elsewhere for nighttime activities.

There are three seasons in Pinehurst: March to June and September to November are high season; June to September, midseason; and December to March, off-season. During high season, rates are $96 *per person* double occupancy, modified American plan, in the hotel. In the condominiums, it's $81 *per person,* European plan. They are considerably lower the rest of the year. There are a number of attractive golf and tennis package plans offered by the hotel.

Another resort with extensive facilities is the **Mid Pines Resort,** a Quality Royale, on Midland Road, Southern Pines, NC 28387 (tel. 919/692-2114). It's a graceful, colonial-style building with wings stretching out on either side of the main entrance. That main entrance leads to a lobby rotunda that is strikingly beautiful, with twin white staircases. There are 63 rooms in the three-story hotel, and all are decorated with style. And if cottage living suits you best, there are several on the premises, some with fireplaces, accommodating up to 17. There's an 18-hole golf course, a putting green, a landscaped pool (set off by a charming split-rail fence), four tennis courts which are lighted at night, and a recreation room. Both the lovely formal dining room and the more informal Terrace (overlooking the fairways of the championship golf course) serve excellent meals—I especially liked the buffet lunch on the Terrace—at moderate to expensive prices. Double-room rates (full American plan) run $160 to $180 in season, lower other months, and cottages are $198.

The **Pine Crest Inn,** right in the heart of the Village on Dogwood Road, Pinehurst, NC 28374 (tel. 919/295-6121), was described by an English visitor as having "all the flavor and courtesies of our countryside inns," but for me it's the southern counterpart of New York's Algonquin Hotel—the same informal, semi-elegance and friendly, makes-you-feel-at-home feeling, the same small, intimate sort of place that draws people back year after year. In fact, Bob Barrett (proprietor since 1961) tells me that some 80% of his guests are returnees. And small wonder, for the two-story, white-columned building radiates warmth from the moment you enter the lobby with its comfortable armchairs, fireplace, and informal dining room and bar to one side; and guest rooms reflect the same inviting "stay a while" atmosphere. Meals in the three dining rooms (with fireplaces and pretty wallpaper) are of such quality that they draw people from Raleigh and Charlotte as well as the immediate vicinity (see "Dining in and Around Pinehurst," below). Golf privileges, it goes without saying, are extended to guests here, and Mr. Barrett will even arrange starting times. Tennis and horseback riding can be arranged at nearby facilities. Modified American plan (breakfast and dinner) rates *per person,* double occupancy, run $50 to $75, depending on the season. Golf and "all sports" packages are available.

The **Sheraton Inn,** on U.S. 1 at Morgantown Road (P.O. Box 1467), Southern Pines, NC 28387 (tel. 919/692-8585), has oversize beds in its cheerful, modern rooms. Two lounges provide entertainment and dancing, and there are tennis courts and a jogging trail. And, of course, golf privileges. Doubles here range from $45 to $52 in season, lower other months.

## Campgrounds

The **Heritage Country Camping Resort,** N.C. 3, Whispering Pines, NC 28327 (tel. 919/949-3433), is one of the most peaceful, relaxing sites you can imagine. With a spring-fed, 14-acre lake (for swimming, pedal boats, fishing), a playground, Ping-Pong, a large recreation hall overlooking the lake, a putting green, nature trails, and horseback riding, there's no lack of things to do, but it's the beautiful wooded setting that gives this place special appeal, and it's still only minutes to fine shops and elegant restaurants. There are 50 sites (22 with full hookups), flush toilets, hot showers, sewage disposal, laundry, ice, picnic tables, and firewood. Rates start at $13.

**DINING IN AND AROUND PINEHURST:** Almost all the inns, hotels, and motels in the Pinehurst area have very good dining rooms. Noteworthy are the **Pine Needles** dining room, as well as those at **Whispering Pines** and **Foxfire,** which overlooks lakes and golf courses. For good measure, I'm listing a small, very good luncheon spot in Southern Pines, a delightful midday stop when you're browsing through the shops that line Broad Street.

The **Carolina Room** at the Pinehurst Hotel (tel. 919/295-6811) is a formal dining room that serves dinner from 6:30 to 10 p.m. in candlelit elegance. The menu is extensive and a five-course meal will average $20. Needless to say, the service is impeccable. During the season, there's top-flight entertainment and dinner-dancing.

Although small, the **Pine Crest Inn** (tel. 919/295-6121) has made such a name for itself in the food field that reservations are made from towns all over the state. Their prime beef, homemade pastries, and insistence on the freshest of vegetables are the reasons for that reputation. And as good as the food is, I'm firmly convinced people come back, too, for the warm hospitality that pervades this place. There's dancing in Mr. B's Lounge. Dinner prices range from $9 to $18 complete, and you really must reserve ahead here.

About that lunch spot in Southern Pines: it's called the **Quarter,** 130 S.W. Broad St. (tel. 919/692-2221), and is open for lunch only. Almost all of the first floor of this gift and women's sportswear shop has been converted into a very special sort of tea room. The ladderback chairs, paisley-print cloths, and bamboo accents in furniture and accessories create a light, airy feeling that is complemented by a light menu of soups, salads, sandwiches, and pastries, all homemade. The chicken gumbo is a treat, and tomato aspic here has a tangy flavor that I found unique. Lunch hours are noon to 3 p.m., and an average tab is about $4 to $5.

**THINGS TO SEE AND DO:** For advance sightseeing information, you can contact **Resorts of Pinehurst, Inc.,** Pinehurst Hotel and Country Club, P.O. Box 4000, Pinehurst, NC 28374 (tel. 919/295-6811), and/or the Sand Hills Area **Chamber of Commerce,** Southern Pines, NC 28387 (tel. 919/692-3926).

Golf, golf, and more golf—that's really why most people come to Pinehurst. And if there's a hotel or motel that doesn't arrange play for its guests, I didn't find it. Most can also set you up for tennis, cycling, or boat rentals on one of the many lakes around.

Horseback riders can arrange for mounts by calling the **Pinehurst Stables** (tel. 919/295-6811), where expert instruction is available for novices; Mrs. Harold Sadler at **The Heritage** (tel. 919/949-3433); or the **Full Cry Farm** (tel. 919/692-2838), which specializes in instruction.

Aside from recreation facilities, the Pinehurst area also offers the **World Golf Hall of Fame,** and even nongolfers will be impressed by the white-columned porticoes and sparkling fountains of the Entrance Pavilion, which overlooks Pinehurst Country Club's Number Two course and the new Number Seven course. The Entrance Pavilion is centered by a pool and another fountain and leads to the main lobby of the museum. Even before you enter the lobby, you'll see a ten-foot statue of Bobby Jones through the glass doors. The north and south wings of the museum tell the story of the development of golf and people associated with it like Henry VIII's first wife, Katherine, who loved it as much as Scotland's three Kings James (II, III, and IV) hated it. And hundreds of golf items from the past are displayed (there are balls used from 1750 to 1850 made of tanned animal hides stuffed with leather). The Ryder Cup Room, Old Clubmakers Shop, and new Walter Hagen exhibit offer other fascinating insights into the grand old game.

The theater is the only one in the world devoted exclusively to golf, and it features films of major tournaments as well as instructional pictures. Behind the museum is the actual Hall of Fame with bronzes of the inductees, a shrine completely surrounded by water, approached by a covered walkway. It is open from 9 a.m. to 5 p.m. daily from mid-March through November, and admission is $3 for adults, $2 for ages 10 to 18, and free for those under 10.

On the Fort Bragg–Aberdeen Road, 1½ miles southeast of Southern Pines, you'll come to **Weymouth Woods–Sandhills Nature Preserve,** a beautiful nature spot with foot and bridle paths and some 600 acres of pine-covered "sandridges." There's also a natural history museum, free, that's open Monday through Saturday from 9 a.m. to 6 p.m., on Sunday from noon to 5 p.m.

In autumn an annual tournament, the PGA/World Golf Hall of Fame Pro-Am Tournament, is held here as part of Pinehurst's **Grand Week of Golf,** with net proceeds from the $250,000 tournament going to the nonprofit World Golf Hall of Fame Foundation. For full details, write: P.O. Box 1908, Pinehurst, NC 28374 (tel. 919/295-6651).

The **Mid-South Horse Show Association** holds schooling shows every Sunday afternoon from January to April; in early March there's the **Moore County Hounds Hunter Trials** at Scotts Corner, Southern Pines, with reserved parking spaces overlooking the course for spectators; and the **Stoneybrook Steeplechase Races** are held on a Saturday in early April on a farm near Southern Pines where race horses are bred and trained the rest of the year by Michael G. Walsh, owner, an Irishman from County Cork. The Sandhills Area Chamber of Commerce, P.O. Box 458, Southern Pines, NC 28387, can furnish exact dates and full details on all these events, as well as others throughout the year.

About halfway between Southern Pines and Pinehurst, on Midland Road, you'll find one of those craft shops mentioned in Chapter I. It's the **Midland Crafters** (tel. 919/295-6156), run by Vesta and Bob Stern. Inside, you'll find all sorts of North American craft items—pottery, woodwork, jewelry, etc.—as well as paintings and a million other things that will tempt you to part with your money. Not all are locally made, but all are good quality, and there's a good price spread so you can "pick up that little something" or perhaps discover a lasting treasure. Note to the ladies: Right next door is **Papillon** (tel. 919/295-1182), a marvelous shop filled with fine sportswear, formal wear, and accessories.

About an hour's drive to the northwest is the little town of **Seagrove** (it's on U.S. 220), which has been turning out pottery for over 200 years. The red and gray clays of this section of the Piedmont were first used by settlers from Staffordshire, England, and the very first items they produced were jugs for transporting whisky. The art is practiced today just as it was then: clays are ground and mixed by machines turned by mules, simple designs are fashioned on kick wheels, and glazing is still done in wood-burning kilns. Many of the potters work in or behind their homes, with only a small sign outside to identify their trade, so if you have difficulty finding them, stop and ask—everybody does, so don't be shy. There are some sales rooms in the town, but the real fun is seeing the pottery actually being made. And while you're asking, inquire about Jugtown, a group of rustic, log-hewn buildings in a grove of pines where potters demonstrate their art with pride Monday through Saturday. On Sunday there's no one there, only a sign that proclaims " 'Tis the Sabbath."

A little north of Seagrove (still on U.S. 220), you'll come to **Asheboro,** where you should turn on to U.S. 64, going southeast, to reach the **North Carolina Zoological Park** (Rte. 4, Box 83, Asheboro, NC 27203; tel. 919/879-5606). On 300 of 1,371 acres, 700 exotic African animals live in barless natural habitats. In the still-developing park, one of the Southeast's finest new zoos, gorillas and 200 rare animals such as meerkats inhabit the African Pavilion, while lions, elephants, and chimpanzees roam the 40-acre African Plains. The R. J. Reynolds Forest Aviary is home to 150 colorful birds which fly freely amid lush tropical trees and plants. There's a tram ride, picnic area, restaurants, and gift shops. The park is open Monday through Friday from 9 a.m. to 6 p.m., on Saturday, Sunday, and holidays from 10 a.m. to 6 p.m., April through October 15; from October 16 through March, hours are from 9 a.m. to 5 p.m. daily. Admission is $3 for adults, $1 for ages 2 to 15 and senior citizens.

## 4. Charlotte

The largest city in the Piedmont—in both North and South Carolina, as a matter of fact—is Charlotte. It was named for King George III's wife, Queen Charlotte, but evidently its residents didn't take their royal affiliation too seriously, for when Lord Cornwallis occupied the town briefly in 1780, he was so annoyed by patriot activities that he called the town a "hornet's nest," a name that stuck and now proudly adorns the city seal. He should have known what to expect, because more than a year before the Declaration of Independence was signed in Philadelphia, the Mecklenburg document declaring independence from Britain was signed in Charlotte—on May 20, 1775 to be exact. Present-day citizens will tell you that Thomas Jefferson used *their* declaration as a model for the one he wrote. Charlotte was prominent in national history again in 1865, when Jefferson Davis convened his last full cabinet meeting here that year.

After the Confederacy fell and the local boys came home from war, the city set out on a course that would free it of dependence on slave labor and that would eventually lead it to a position of industrial leadership in the South. The Catawba River furnished a rich supply of water power for industrialization, and development of manufacturing plants and textile mills was rather rapid. There are now more than 600 textile plants within a 100-mile radius.

Charlotte is also the center of a region that was for years the major gold producer for the United States. In fact, a branch of the U.S. mint was located here from 1837 to 1913, although it was inoperative from 1861 to 1867 because of the Civil War. This exquisite original 1835 William Strickland structure is now the Mint Museum, and with its $7.5-million expansion, houses one of the Southeast's major art collections.

In the last decade or so, Charlotte has sprouted skyscrapers at an amazing rate, and one of the most interesting punctuation points of its skyline is the 40-story, trapezoidal steel-and-glass tower of the North Carolina National Bank Plaza. Throughout the 1980s a new tall building has been started before its predecessor was finished. When it's completed by the early 1990s, a 50-story NCNB Charter Properties office tower will be the tallest structure between Philadelphia and Atlanta.

Suburban areas too have mushroomed, with landscaped housing developments and enormous shopping malls springing up in every direction. This is one of the Southeast's most graphic examples of the "new" South building squarely on the foundation of that fabled Old South.

**WHERE TO STAY:** The **Radisson Plaza Hotel,** 2 NCNB Plaza, Charlotte, NC 28280 (tel. 704/377-0400, or toll free 800/228-9822), is of trapezoidal shape to blend harmoniously with the North Carolina National Bank Plaza of which it is a part. It's connected by a covered walkway above the street to Charlotte's new Convention Center. The 381 rooms are the ultimate in comfort and contemporary design. There's concierge service, a pool, a health club, and free covered parking. The hotel has a bright, airy coffeeshop and an elegant upscale restaurant, Reflections, where semi à la carte dinners range from $11 to $20. One of the city's most popular Sunday brunches is held here from 11:30 a.m. to 2 p.m., and it's in the $12 to $15 range. Doubles begin at $104; on the Plaza Club concierge floor it's $113. This is one of the most convenient locations in town, at the corner of Trade and Tryon Streets.

It's a pleasure just to check in at the sleek new downtown **Marriott-City Center,** 100 W. Trade St., Charlotte, NC 28202 (tel. 704/333-9000, or toll free 800/228-9290 except in North Carolina). The enthusiastic young front desk staff is especially helpful and friendly without being overbouncy. And the rooms, tastefully decorated with period reproduction furnishings and fabrics, exude a warmly welcoming ambience. There's a coin laundry, heated pool, and health club, along with valet parking (for a fee). There are two excellent dining rooms, Sweetbay (entrees range from about $8 to $13), named for the area showcasing a fabulous dessert buffet, and the somewhat pricier Chardonnay, where entrees are about $12 to $22. The room is impeccably decorated in tones of rose and gray, and highlighted with fine oil portraits, landscapes, and Oriental porcelains. A pianist plays softly in the foyer, and the fresh seafood entrees are especially good. Doubles are $99, $114 on the concierge floor, and corporate rates and senior citizen discounts are available.

There's an all-suite **Guest Quarters** at 6300 Morrison Blvd., Charlotte, NC 28211 (tel. 704/364-2400, or toll free 800/424-2900), with a price range of $115, double occupancy, for a one-bedroom suite and $160 (one to four people) for two bedrooms. Highly recommended.

The dependable **Days Inn** people have three motels in Charlotte, and I especially like the one at 122 W. Woodlawn Rd., Charlotte, NC 28210 (tel. 704/527-1620), which is convenient to the airport and Carowinds. I've never yet run across a Days Inn with disappointing accommodations, and this was no exception. Rooms are always adequate in size, comfortable, and the decor pleasing. This one has a pool, a restaurant, and one unit especially fitted for the handicapped. Doubles are $40 to $50.

The popular **Econo Lodge** system, with national headquarters in Charlotte, has five locations in the city. Its conveniently located Charlotte Airport facility, I-85 and Little Rock Road (P.O. Box 668203), Charlotte, NC 28266 (tel. 704/394-0172, or toll free 800/446-6900), is just four miles from downtown and offers free airport limousine service. There's a pool, restaurant, free cribs, and color satellite TV. Doubles are $36, and it's $4 each for additional guests sharing. Senior citizen and family discounts are offered.

**Motel 6,** 3433 Mulberry Church Rd., Charlotte, NC 28208 (tel. 704/394-0899), has a very convenient location if you're driving in via I-85. Either north or southbound, take exit 33 (Billy Graham Parkway–Mulberry Church Road) south one block, turn left across the divided parkway onto Mulberry Church Road; then turn left and it's one block to the motel. From I-77, exit onto Billy Graham Parkway and go north to Mulberry Church Road. This is one of the best buys in the area. Rates are $27 double; each additional person over 12 stays for $2, children 3 to 11 stay for $1 each, and it's free for those under 3. This is a very well-maintained, clean, and comfortable new inn. It has a pool, and you can have color TV for a modest extra charge. Restaurants are nearby.

**WHERE TO EAT:** For broiled live lobster, steak, or prime ribs, you probably can't do better in the Charlotte area than the **Epicurean,** 1324 East Blvd. (tel. 704/377-4529), which has been in business more than a quarter of a century. This is a chef-owned establishment, which probably accounts for the excellence of its food and its popularity locally. It boasts one of the city's most extensive wine lists, and not surprisingly, there is a dress code. The semi à la carte prices range from $12 to $19, but there are children's plates for about $7. It's advisable to call ahead to reserve for dinner, which is served from 6 to 10 p.m. Closed Sunday and the first two weeks in July.

**La Tache,** an award-winning dining room in the Registry Inn Motor Hotel, 321 W. Woodlawn Rd. at I-77 (tel. 704/525-4441), is one of Charlotte's prettiest —and priciest—places to eat. A series of airy, mirror-lined rooms open onto each other in a Valentine-like setting enhanced by soft pink tablecloths topped with vases of pink and white flowers. Luminous Oriental vases are reflected in the mirrors. Dinner appetizers include smoked sliced Canadian salmon with horseradish-dill sauce ($7), and there's an astounding soup—essence of wild duck with quail eggs, covered with puff pastry ($4). Among the entrees are steak Diane with mushrooms and cream, prepared tableside ($20), and sautéed veal and lobster with cognac, finished with cream ($25). As I said, it's pricey, but worthy of your attention for a special occasion. The adjoining lounge with its dramatic light-spattered black ceiling is a locally popular piano bar where you can enjoy complimentary hors d'oeuvres weekdays from 5 to 8 p.m. At lunch you'll find sandwiches in the $5.25 to $6 range or can create your own omelet for $6. There's a weekday buffet for $8. La Tache is open from 6:30 to 11 a.m., 11:30 a.m. to 2 p.m., and 6 to 11 p.m. daily.

**Eli's on East,** 311 East Blvd. (tel. 704/375-0756), is one of those delightful "in" places favored by locals. It's in a charming 1908 Victorian frame house, where author Carson McCullers lived briefly in the 1930s. 'Tis said she did her research while sipping sherry from a Thermos in the local library. There's a basic American menu with continental touches, featuring beef, veal, flounder, and salmon, along with such lighter luncheon fare as salads, quiches, and burgers. One house specialty is an uncommonly delicious Indian mulligatawny soup. Save room for fried ice cream or peanut butter pie with fudge sauce! Eli's is open from 11:30 a.m. to 2 p.m. and 5:30 to 10 p.m. Tuesday through Thursday, to 11 p.m. on Friday and Saturday. Also, on Saturday and Sunday brunch is served from 10:30 a.m. to 3 p.m. Lunch is in the $5 to $8 range, and a semi à la carte dinner costs $11 to $17. Reservations are suggested.

For a special late-night treat, **Jonathan's Uptown,** 330 N. Tryon St. (tel. 704/332-3663), is a popular late-night rendezvous spot for upwardly mobile young Charlotteans who drop in for live jazz and fresh American cuisine after a Spirit Square performance. It's a sophisticated "big city" room with a dramatic black-and-white decor, where service is deft and friendly at the same time. The menu is anything but basic, highlighted by such entrees as broiled halibut topped with orange-pecan butter and boneless chicken breast sautéed in white wine and cream, topped with crabmeat, artichoke hearts, and parmesan. The carrot and chocolate-raspberry cakes melt in your mouth. Jonathan's boasts a climate-controlled wine cellar with 22,000-bottle capacity. Evenings there's a pianist, and occasionally one of the servers goes on stage to sing along. Lunch ranges from $5 to $8, and dinner from $11 to $17. Dress may be casual, but this definitely doesn't mean jeans, tennis shoes, or cutoffs. If you're staying in the uptown Radisson or Marriott, it's a short couple-of-blocks' stroll to Jonathan's, which is open from 11:30 a.m. to 2:30 p.m. Monday through Friday, from 6 to 10:30 p.m. Monday through Saturday, and from 6 to 9:30 p.m. on Sunday. The Jazz Lounge (admission $5) is open from 9 p.m. to 1 a.m. Monday through Saturday. A limited menu is also served in the bar adjoining the dining room from 4:30 to 11:30 p.m. Monday through Saturday.

Whenever I visit friends in Charlotte, we always seem to wind up in their favorite neighborhood Chinese restaurant, the **Golden Palace,** 6437 Albemarle Rd., in Loehmann Plaza (tel. 704/568-3216 or 568-3217). It's about a half mile past the popular Eastland Mall shopping center, and it has become my favorite too for its wonderful range of Chinese dishes at moderate cost. It's hard to top the special dinner, which for $6.50 will bring you a choice of wonton or eggdrop soup, eggroll or paper chicken, one of 15 entrees—including sweet-and-sour shrimp (marvelous huge prawns), beef with bean sprouts, or almond fried chicken—fortune or almond cookies, and a pot of tea, of course. A house specialty is sizzling Wor Bar—chunks of lobster, shrimp, chicken, roast pork, and fresh Chinese veggies, served sizzling tableside over crispy rice patties, for just $8. And although the owner-chefs come from southern China (the Canton area), that doesn't stop them from being expert in preparation of such spicy Szechuan delicacies as shredded beef with hot chili ($6.50) or kung-po chicken ding, with diced bamboo shoots, chilis, water chestnuts, peanuts, celery, mushrooms, and scallions ($6.25). Service is continuous from 11:30 a.m. to 10 p.m. Monday through Friday, from 5 to 11 p.m. on Saturday, and from noon to 10 p.m. on Sunday. From 11:30 a.m. to 2:30 p.m. Monday through Friday, there are special luncheon plates or platters from $2.25 to $4. You can come in as casually dressed as you please, settle down cozily in one of two dining rooms adorned with Chinese scroll paintings, and prepare for a culinary treat.

The Charlotte area is notable for its "fish camps"—homey, informal, family-style restaurants which serve gargantuan portions of fresh seafood at moderate cost. The **Fish Farm,** 1200 Sam Newell Rd. in nearby Matthews (tel. 704/847-8578), is not as laid-back and rustic as some of the riverside "camps," but since 1975 this locally popular restaurant has had a wide following for its fresh broiled or fried seafoods. All-you-can-eat specials include Carolina flounder ($6), steamed-in-the-shell shrimp ($10), Calabash-style shrimp ($7), and catfish ($7). The Fish Farm is open from 4:30 to 9:30 p.m. Tuesday through Thursday, to 10 p.m. on Friday and Saturday, and to 9:30 p.m. on Sunday. To reach it from Charlotte, drive east on East Independence Boulevard, turn right on Sam Newell Road, and drive about half a mile.

**Arthur's,** in three Ivey's department stores—Uptown, 127 N. Tryon St. (tel. 704/333-4867); Eastland Mall, 5501 Central Ave. (tel. 704/588-0210); and Southpark Mall, 4400 Sharon Rd. (tel. 704/366-6456)—offers freshly made sandwiches, hoagies, quiches, soups, and salads in a comfortable café atmosphere. Each includes a wine shop. They're open from 10 a.m. to 8:30 p.m. Monday through Saturday, and from 12:30 to 5 p.m. on Sunday. You can have a very good repast for under $5.

You'll find one of the reliable **Morrison's Cafeterias** at 5633 Central Ave., in the Eastland Mall (tel. 704/568-7136). You can have breakfast for about $2, and there are daily Monday through Saturday $3 daily specials (Monday, it's baked, chopped steak with rice or potato; Tuesday, one-quarter broiled or fried chicken with vegetable and potato; other equally good stick-to-your-ribs specials are offered each day). Sunday dinner, served all day, is turkey and dressing, salad, vegetable, bread, and dessert, for $5. Morrison's is open daily, including major holidays, from 11 a.m. until 8:30 p.m.

**THINGS TO DO AND SEE:** For sightseeing in detail, contact: **Charlotte Convention & Visitors Bureau,** 229 N. Church St., Charlotte, NC 28202 (tel. 704/ 334-2282, or toll free 800/231-4636 outside North Carolina).

The **Mint Museum of Art,** 2730 Randolph Rd. (tel. 704/337-2000), with the recently added Dalton wing, displays fine European and American survey collections, the internationally recognized Delhom Collection of porcelain and pottery, pre-Columbian art, contemporary American prints, African objects, vast costume and antique maps collections, and gold coins originally minted at the facility. It's open from 10 a.m. to 10 p.m. on Tuesday, to 5 p.m. Wednesday through Saturday, and from 1 to 6 p.m. on Sunday. Admission is $2 for adults, $1 for students and senior citizens, free for ages 12 and under; it's also free from 5 to 10 p.m. on Tuesday.

If you're in Charlotte during April and May, drive north on N.C. 49 to the **University of North Carolina at Charlotte** campus to see their rhododendron garden—spectacular! And if you're on campus at either 7:30 a.m. or 5:15 p.m., you'll get in on the carillon concerts (on Sunday, it's 3:30 p.m.).

Take the children to the **Charlotte Nature Museum and Planetarium** at 1658 Sterling Rd. (enter via East Boulevard)—exhibits are especially planned for developing an awareness and appreciation of nature through displays and programs designed especially for young children. There's also a planetarium, a puppet theater, and a nature trail. Admission to the museum is 75¢ (under 3, free with parents), and hours are 9 a.m. to 5 p.m. Monday through Saturday, 1 to 6 p.m. on Sunday. Planetarium shows are at 3 and 4 p.m. on Saturday and Sunday, and cost $1 for adults and 75¢ for students. Special children's shows at 1:30 and 2:30 p.m. on Saturday, and at 2:30 p.m. on Sunday, cost 75¢ for all ages.

Joining with the Nature Museum to form the combined Science Museums of Charlotte, Inc., is the **Discovery Place Science and Technology Center** at 301 N. Tryon St. in uptown Charlotte. Discovery Place takes you through eight major exhibit areas, including a tropical rain forest, an aquarium, and a life center, and stresses a "hands-on" approach to learning. There's a $3 admission for adults, $2 for students and senior citizens, and hours are 9 a.m. to 6 p.m. Monday through Saturday and 1 to 6 p.m. on Sunday.

The 11th president of the United States, James K. Polk, was born at **Pineville,** just 12 miles south of Charlotte on U.S. 521. His log cabin and the outbuildings have been reconstructed and there's a Visitor Center which shows an interesting film. It's free and open from 9 a.m. to 5 p.m. Monday through Saturday and from 1 to 5 p.m. on Sunday, April through October; from 10 a.m. to 4 p.m. Tuesday through Saturday and from 1 to 4 p.m. on Sunday, November through March.

The **Charlotte Motor Speedway,** 12 miles northeast of Charlotte on U.S. 29 (or just off I-85), is host in late May (Memorial Day Sunday) of each year to the **Coca-Cola 600 NASCAR Winston Cup Stock Car Race,** longest and richest such race in the U.S., which draws upward of 160,000 enthusiastic fans. If you're a devotee of the daredevil sport, you may want to plan your trip then or in early October, when the **Oakwood Homes 500 Winston Cup Stock Car Race** is run. You can get exact dates and full details of both events by writing Charlotte Motor Speedway, P.O. Box 600, Harrisburg, NC 28075 (tel. 704/455-2121).

If you're taking children along on your Charlotte trip, you undoubtedly already know about **Carowinds Theme Park,** I-77 at the North Carolina–South Carolina border (tel. 704/588-2600). But even without the kids, it's worth a day just for fun. The $40-million park straddles the North and South Carolina state line, and has nine theme areas reflecting facets of the two states' past and present. The rides are entertaining and inventive, especially the flume and mine train rides, although I must confess my romantic favorite is the sternwheeler that set me thinking of slower days. For the more adventurous, the Thunder Road and White Lightnin' roller coasters may beckon you. On the sightseeing side of things, look for a re-creation of the Old Charleston waterfront, Pirate Island, and enjoy fast-paced revues at Midway Music Hall and Troubador's Roost Theatre. In Blue Ridge Junction, you'll enjoy the shops and crafts (from the days of British rule) at Queen's Colony; and you can tap your toes to bluegrass music in Harmony Hall. One cautionary word: They won't let you bring pets in; however, there is a kennel for stashing them. Admission, which includes all rides and most entertainments, is $14.50 for ages 7 and over, $7.25 for ages 4 to 6 and over 60, and free for children 3 and under; and there's a $2 parking fee. The park is open every day except Friday from 10 a.m. to 8 p.m. from the second week in June through mid-August; weekends only in mid-March, April, May, September, and early October. It's closed from mid-October through March.

# Chapter VIII

# INTRODUCTION TO SOUTH CAROLINA

### 1. By Way of Background
### 2. Traveling to South Carolina
### 3. Traveling Within South Carolina

THERE ARE REALLY TWO South Carolinas, with differences between the coastal "low country" and the "up country" (including the rolling midlands) so distinct I sometimes feel there should be a state line between the two. South Carolinians, however, seem able to hold on to those divisions and at the same time take great pride in presenting a united front to the rest of the world.

## 1. By Way of Background

**1526 TO 1987:** It isn't only the topography of the state that makes for the distinctiveness of each section, although like most states along the Atlantic, South Carolina has its coastal plain, piedmont, and mountains. The differences really spring from a history of settlement and development that saw aristocratic rice and indigo planters build one lifestyle along the coast and German, Scottish-Irish, and Welsh immigrants gravitate farther inland to build another. The first attempts to settle along the coast were as early as 1526 and 1562, but nothing came of them. It wasn't until Charles II of England granted both the Carolinas to eight noblemen, the lords proprietors, that colonists arrived to stay. Charles Towne was established at Albemarle Point in 1670, then moved ten years later to the peninsula formed by the Ashley and Cooper Rivers.

That low, marshy country proved ideal for large rice and indigo plantations, and Charles Towne's harbor was perfect for shipping these crops around the world. Successful planters maintained huge homes on outlying farms, and most built sumptuous mansions in town as well. A life of formal ease and graciousness developed that has never entirely disappeared, even though the low country has seen great fortunes come and go with the changes of time.

Away from the coast, those hardy frontiersmen—who set up small farms, built up a brisk trade in pelts, and fought off Indians, often with no help from their British landlords—had little time or inclination for the social goings-on in Charles Towne. And a sore point was the issue of taxation—but with a local twist: in spite of the fact that everyone paid taxes, only the low country had any say in how things were run. And that remained the case until 1770, even though there had been popular representation in the colonial government as early as 1693. The rift between the two groups would be a long time healing, and even during the Revolution (although the first decisive American victory was won here at Fort Moultrie in June 1776), South Carolina suffered about equally from British troops and local loyalists, mostly from the low country.

When Charles Towne was finally occupied by the British in 1780, it was supposed to be the jumping-off point for a spearhead drive to join forces in the north which would crush Washington's troops. But thanks to the efforts of Continental troops under Gen. Nathanael Greene and South Carolina natives who followed "the Swamp Fox" (Frances Marion) and "the Game-cock" (Thomas Sumter) in a very effective sort of guerrilla warfare, the royal soldiers were more or less confined to Charles Towne (renamed Charleston in 1783). There are some historians who contend that the battles of Kings Mountain (in 1780) and Cowpens (1781) were *the* decisive encounters of the Revolution. When independence was finally achieved, South Carolina was the eighth state to ratify the Federal Constitution, in 1788.

By 1790 those cantankerous up-country citizens made such a fuss about the state's capital remaining in low-country Charleston, when four-fifths of the white population lived inland, that the state government was moved to neutral ground, centrally located Columbia. Not to be outdone, the low-country population (which controlled four-fifths of the *wealth*) continued to maintain state offices, and the Supreme Court actually met in both cities to hear appeals until 1865.

When tensions between the North and South reached the breaking point in 1860, fiery John C. Calhoun led the state legislature to pass an Ordinance of Secession in December that made South Carolina the first state to secede from the Union. And in *that* step, citizens seemed united. In fact their first military action was to take Fort Sumter from the federal troops garrisoned there, and they continued to hold it until 1865. Altogether, the state lost 22% of its population in the bitter Civil War; and General Sherman, in his "march to the sea," saw to it that just about the entire state was left in shambles.

If there's one thing *all* South Carolinians—low- or up-country—have in abundance, it's pride. And that pride suffered greatly, along with the economy, as carpetbaggers and scalawags moved in during Reconstruction. I always feel, when traveling in this state, that "Yankee" and "Rebel" distinctions are more alive here today than in any other single place in the South. That's not really surprising, however, when you remember that not until World War II did South Carolina begin to get back on its feet economically. Ironically, it was "Yankee" industry, moving to a location of enormous waterpowered energy and supply and a ready labor market, that led the state's booming industrialization. And just in the last 20 or 30 years the Civil War scars have faded more quickly than before.

As a place to visit, the state is a tourist's goldmine—more than 280 miles of seashore, with lovely white sand beaches shaded by palms, resort islands like Hilton Head that are a world apart, and Charleston's gracious Old South charm still intact. The area around Columbia reflects both the "New South" of vitality and some of the Old in the university campus which has served, with its great old oaks and early 1800s buildings, as the background for several movies about antebellum life. Sportsmen, drawn to coastal and inland fishing, also come here for the unusually long hunting season (Thanksgiving, more or less, to March 1) for such game as deer, wild turkey, quail, fox, and many more. Equestrians come for horse shows, polo, the Carolina Cup Steeplechase (in early April) and Colonial Cup Steeplechase (in mid-November) at Camden, and harness racing

and other horse events in Aiken (beginning about the middle of March). And the Darlington Raceway features the "Rebel 500" (in mid-April) and "Southern 500" (Labor Day) late-model stock-car races. History buffs, of course, can retrace all those colonial, Revolution, and Civil War events to their hearts' content.

## SOUTH CAROLINA TELEPHONE AREA CODE: The entire state is in the 803 area code zone.

## ABOUT SOUTH CAROLINA'S HOTELS: You'll find just about every imaginable type of accommodation in South Carolina, although there's not always a wide range of choice in a specific location. Coastal resorts offer everything from posh luxury hotels to modest, inexpensive motels. And Charleston has several small inns that offer southern hospitality of the Old South style which simply cannot be equaled. In between, almost every town and city has representatives of the major chains and independently owned modern motels which more than adequately meet the traveler's needs. As everywhere else, it pays to reserve ahead. If you should get here *without* a reservation, there are **Welcome Centers** at nine major entry points of entry whose hostesses operate a free reservation service. But that's risky, especially if you come during spring or summer—rooms can be scarce even as late as October along the coast.

An alternative to hotel/motel vacationing—and one that works particularly well for families, I think—is the rental of a cottage or apartment. South Carolina's resort areas have literally hundreds available on a weekly basis, and it's a fairly simple matter to engage one *if you plan far enough in advance.*

There are also cabin accommodations available all year in 13 of South Carolina's state parks. All are heated and air-conditioned and fully equipped, including cooking utensils, tableware, and linens. Rentals range from $25 to $78 per night, $90 to $468 per week, and the cabins accommodate anywhere from 4 to 12 people. Here again, however, advance planning is absolutely necessary for summer reservations. For full details on these cabins, how to file an application, rates, and accommodations at the 31 other state parks, write: **South Carolina State Parks,** 1205 Pendleton St., Columbia, SC 29201 (tel. 803/734-0156).

## AS FOR FOOD: South Carolina menus vary across the state in a reflection of its population mix. Low-country seafood ragoûts and Charleston's famous she-crab soup dominate coastal cooking, while country ham and grits served up with "red eye" gravy are prominent on inland tables. The best meals are undoubtedly served in private homes, for as in most southern states, cooking is an art lovingly transferred from one generation to another. But restaurants, too, seem to take particular pride in their kitchens, and I've had some exquisite meals in small, unpretentious establishments where the management would be embarrassed if you called their food "gourmet," but where that term nevertheless fits. And there are many fine restaurants that would no doubt be embarrassed if you *didn't* use "gourmet" in describing their cuisine—and most of it is. All in all, South Carolina is a good place to eat, with plenty of dining places handy for the traveler.

You'll be able to buy alcoholic beverages in many restaurants. Some are licensed to serve only beer and wine, but a great many serve those plus liquor (which is served in mini-bottles to be added to cocktail mixes). And if you think you'll want a drink on Sunday, stock up: there's no alcohol sold in the state on the Sabbath. The minimum drinking age is 18 for beer and wine, 21 for liquor.

## SOUTH CAROLINA CLIMATE: Although parts of South Carolina can be very

hot and steamy in summer, temperatures are never extreme, as is shown in the average highs and lows noted below.

|  | High | Low |
|---|---|---|
| Charleston | 88 | 44 |
| Columbia | 93 | 35 |

**VISITOR INFORMATION:** In order to do a good job with your homework before coming to South Carolina, write or call ahead for any specific information on sports (fishing, hunting, beaches, etc.) and sightseeing to: **South Carolina Dept. of Parks, Recreation & Tourism,** 1205 Pendleton St., Columbia, SC 29201 (tel. 803/253-6318).

## 2. Traveling to South Carolina

**BY AIR:** You can fly into Charleston's International Airport on Delta, Eastern, and Piedmont, and all also serve Columbia. Eastern and Piedmont reach the Greenville–Spartanburg region, and Piedmont goes to Florence, Hilton Head Island, and Myrtle Beach.

**BY TRAIN:** Amtrak has fairly good coverage of the state, with terminals at Charleston, Dillon, Florence, Kingstree, Yemassee, and Columbia. Also, as part of its "Southeast Sojourns" tour program, Amtrak has a six-day "Antebellum Era" package that offers hotel, breakfasts, and historic site tours in Charleston, S.C., and Savannah, Ga. Rates for these packages are a real bargain.

**BY BUS:** Trailways and Greyhound reach almost any destination in South Carolina.

**BY CAR:** The many-laned, divided I-95 superhighway enters South Carolina from the north near Dillon and runs straight through the state to Hardeeville on the Georgia border. From Georgia, U.S. 301 also crosses the entire state to North Carolina. The major east-west highway artery is I-26, from Charleston northwest through Columbia and on up to Hendersonville, North Carolina. Along the coast, U.S. 17 stretches from Georgia to North Carolina. In the western region, I-85 crosses from Georgia to North Carolina. The state does a beautiful job of furnishing travel information to motorists, and there are well-equipped, efficiently staffed **Visitor Welcome Centers** at the northern entrances on U.S. 17, I-95, I-85, and I-26, as well as the southern ends of I-85, I-20, and U.S. 301.

## 3. Traveling Within South Carolina

**BY AIR:** Delta, Piedmont, and Commuter airlines all have connecting flights to South Carolina airports, although schedules are sometimes awkward for connections.

**BY TRAIN:** Amtrak stops at Spartanburg, Greenville, Clemson, Cheraw, Camden, Columbia, Dillard, Florence, Kingstree, Charleston, and Yemassee.

**BY BUS:** Greyhound and Trailways operate intrastate routes to most South Carolina towns.

**BY CAR:** Those marvelous Interstate and U.S. highways listed in the above section give South Carolina a network of exceptionally good roadways. However, even when you leave the highways for the state-maintained byways, driving is easy on well-maintained roads. South Carolina used to be one of those notorious "speedtrap" states for visitors, and while the setups and rigged stoplights have been gone for a while now, it *does* pay to watch the speed limits: they still keep an eye on out-of-state drivers (and in-state as well, I suspect).

You will find **Thrifty Car Rentals** locations in Charleston, Columbia, Summerville, and Hilton Head Island, with their usual good service and rates.

# Chapter IX

# "LOW COUNTRY" SOUTH CAROLINA

### 1. The Grand Strand
### 2. Charleston
### 3. Hilton Head Island

ALL THE ROMANCE, BEAUTY, and graciousness of the Old South manage to survive in South Carolina's low country. Well, maybe it isn't all that evident visually along the Grand Strand up around Myrtle Beach, which looks pretty much like most other beach resort areas—although even this section exudes southern charm in its slow-paced vacation outlook and the warm hospitality of the locals. A little farther south, however, at Georgetown, then Charleston, and all the way to Beaufort at the bottom of the state's coastline, automobiles, and modern dress seem almost out of place when you drive through old, cobblestone streets under trees draped with the mysterious Spanish moss and past antebellum homes built in the early days of this country. Oh, they've been outfitted with all the conveniences of today, but I often think they could revert easily to their original state and keep occupants comfortable even in the face of an oil crisis that forced the return of wood-burning fireplaces and kerosene lamps or candles. As for the people who live in them, you'll find they possess for the most part an appreciation of up-to-date, sophisticated lifestyles (very few, if any, rednecks in *this* part of the South!), as well as an active memory of things as they once were—a happy mixture, indeed.

Physically, the low country is almost breathtakingly beautiful. Its broad, white-sand beaches are warmed by the Gulf Stream just a few miles offshore and fringed with palm trees and rolling dunes. Palms mingle with live oaks, dogwood, and pines all along the coast, and everywhere you'll see the silver-gray something called Spanish moss that drapes airily from tree branches, lending a dream-like softness to the landscape. I call it "something" because even scientists can't quite figure out what it is—it isn't *really* a moss, because that grows on the ground; it isn't a parasite, because it doesn't feed on sap from the trees; and it has no roots, seeming to extract nourishment somehow from the air. They call it an epiphyte (air plant), but as yet they aren't sure—even after exhaustive tests —just how it manages to keep alive and grow. My favorite quotation about Spanish moss is the answer given northern tourists by a South Carolina publication to all those questions about the lovely mystery: "Yes, it does grow on trees; no, it isn't a parasite; no, they *don't* take it in at night and put it out in the morning."

# THE GRAND STRAND

FLORENCE

LORIS

COOL SPRING

WILMINGTON

LONGS

LITTLE RIVER

CONWAY

CHERRY GROVE

OCEAN DRIVE SECTION

**NORTH MYRTLE BEACH**

CRESCENT BEACH SECTION

ATLANTIC BEACH

WINDY HILL SECTION

Intracoastal Waterway

**MYRTLE BEACH**

SOCASTEE

SURFSIDE BEACH

GARDEN CITY

YAUHANNAH

MURRELLS INLET

PLANTERSVILLE

LITCHFIELD BEACH

Waccamaw River

PAWLEYS ISLAND

**ATLANTIC OCEAN**

GEORGETOWN

CHARLESTON

Winyah Bay

*Map Courtesy of the Greater Myrtle Beach Chamber of Commerce*

Speaking of native plants: Whatever you do, don't pull the graceful sea oats that grow on sand-dune stretches along the beaches—it's against the law and an infraction carries a stiff fine. The hardy plant (it grows from Cape Charles, Virginia, to the Gulf Coast of Mexico and is officially named *Uniola paniculato*) not only acts as a natural anchor for the dunes, but also serves as a plentiful food supply for shore birds. Actually, it is also instrumental in the forming of new or higher dunes, since it catches and holds blowing sands. So look, enjoy their spare beauty, but don't touch.

As I've said, low-country South Carolina is full of memories, but it's also a place to *make* memories—whether of the recreation, sightseeing, or just plain relaxing genre. The subtropical climate, where spring arrives early and summer lingers until late October, permits golf, tennis, fishing (public piers, at Cherry Grove Beach, Tilghman Beach, Crescent Beach, Windy Hill, Myrtle Beach, Isle of Palms, and Folly Beach; and charter boats for deep-sea fishing), sightseeing in that grand old lady of the low country, Charleston, or sitting on an uncrowded beach (as I did once for an entire October week at Hilton Head). There are islands that don't even require a boat for a visit (South Carolina has provided marvelous double-laned causeways), like Pawleys, Seabrook, Edisto, and Hilton Island.

## 1. The Grand Strand

Myrtle Beach, with a permanent population of about 20,000 is at the center of the Grand Strand, a 55-mile string of beaches that includes Little River, Cherry Grove, Crescent Beach, Ocean Drive, Atlantic Beach, Surfside Beach, Garden City, Murrells Inlet, Litchfield Beach, and Pawleys Island. And besides the beaches, there are amusement parks, stock-car races, nightspots with top entertainment, an internationally known sculpture garden, some of the best seafood restaurants on the Atlantic coast, and all those golf courses. Named for all the myrtle trees in this area, Myrtle Beach itself is an ideal base for a Grand Strand vacation. Maybe I should say here that my personal feeling about this resort is that if you're looking for a wild, swinging kind of beach resort, this isn't it—there's plenty to do, of course, and it certainly isn't dull, but the whole tone is that of a *family* resort, with almost as much attention paid at the various hotels and motels to children's needs as to those of adults. Many provide activity programs and playgrounds with supervision, and nearly all have babysitter lists for parents who like a little nightlife. It's a nice sort of place and one that looks out for all members of the family.

**WHERE TO STAY:** The Grand Strand is literally lined with hotels, motels, condominiums, and cottages. The **Myrtle Beach Area Chamber of Commerce,** 1301 N. Kings Hwy. (P.O. Box 2115), Myrtle Beach, SC 29578 (tel. 803/626-7444, or toll free 800/722-3224), publishes two directories that will be a great help in making a selection and both are free. Because of its central location, Myrtle Beach itself is my personal choice—attractions north or south of it are within easy reach—and with only one exception (included because of its special character) all the listings that follow are either in Myrtle Beach or just a short distance north of the city limits. "In season" means June 15 through Labor Day, and rates quoted are for double occupancy. And once again I would remind you that the prices quoted are *as of the time of writing* and (like everything else in these inflationary times) subject to change.

### Deluxe

The Beachcomber, 1705 S. Ocean Blvd., Myrtle Beach, SC 29577 (tel. 803/448-4345), offers deluxe rooms (with refrigerators) and one- or two-bedroom, fully equipped efficiencies. Oceanfront units have private balconies, and connecting units are available. There are two pools (one for children), and there's a washerette on the premises. Both golf and tennis privileges are available at nearby facilities. Shopping and amusement centers, as well as restaurants, are close at hand. In-season rates for oceanfront rooms start at $76. After Labor Day, the same accommodations drop considerably. Open all year.

## Moderate

The **Jamaican,** 3006 N. Ocean Blvd., Myrtle Beach, SC 29577 (tel. 803/448-4321), is an inviting, five-story motel at the edge of Myrtle Beach's north-end residential section. Its rooms, efficiencies, and suites are bright and airy, each with a private balcony and ocean view, and I found the staff here exceptionally pleasant and helpful. The beach is less crowded here, and right next door is one of the area's top restaurants, the Sea Captain's House (see "Where to Eat," below). The boardwalk, Pavilion, and amusement area are 20 rather short blocks to the south—a very long stroll or a short drive away. There's an oceanfront pool (a kiddie pool is also on the ocean), and both golf and tennis facilities are close by. This is, in my opinion, one of the best motels on the beach in the moderate price range. In season, rooms begin at $59, efficiencies at $79, with varying lower rates the rest of the year. Weekly rates are available.

Not just a motel, but a complete resort, the **Sea Mist,** 1200 S. Ocean Blvd., Myrtle Beach, SC 29577 (tel. 803/502-1551, or toll free 800/732-6478), has ten pools (one is enclosed for year-round use), Jacuzzis, a tennis court, supervised children's programs, playgrounds, a recreation room, ice-cream parlor, gift cove, and guest privileges at 40 golf courses. The 666 units consist of large rooms, apartments, suites, and even a penthouse and villas. There are special package plans for honeymooners, tennis players, and golfers. The elegant dining room, softly lit by candles, has old-world charm, and the Prime Rib Room features entertainment most of the year, along with prime beef and fresh seafood. Rates during the season range from $50 to $90, but there's a special low rate between September and May (and don't forget that swimming is good here until late October).

For luxury rooms, efficiencies, and suites at moderate prices, the **St. John's Inn,** 6801 N. Ocean Blvd., Myrtle Beach, SC 29577 (tel. 803/449-5251, or toll free 800/845-0624), is one of the best. All rooms have balconies, the swimming pool is heated on cool days, and golf and tennis packages are available. There's a restaurant and coffeeshop. Rates are in the $70 to $125 range in season, lower other times. Open year round.

The **Dunes Village,** 5200 N. Ocean Blvd., Myrtle Beach, SC 29577 (tel. 803/449-5275, or toll free 800/845-4501), is another exceptionally nice motel in the moderate range, with a heated pool, a wading pool for the kiddies, tennis, shuffleboard, picnic tables, and grills. Most of the well-appointed rooms have an ocean view, and some are oceanfront. Doubles rent for $64 in season (kitchen apartments for $79 for two people; up to four people, $140), but prices drop in other months.

**Myrtle Shores,** 1902–1904 N. Ocean Blvd. (P.O. Box 335), Myrtle Beach, SC 29578 (tel. 803/448-1434), is an apartment motel in a pleasant oceanfront setting, and is very popular with families. It has a dozen spacious and attractive two-bedroom units and 26 efficiencies with refrigerators. Most units have private balconies, and all have free cable color TV. There's a heated pool, and golf and tennis privileges are available. Daily maid service is offered, and there are coin-operated washers and dryers. Rates range from $50 to $64 for doubles June through August, and can drop as low as $35 off-season. Ask, too, about special long-term winter rates.

The **Teakwood Motel,** 7201 N. Ocean Blvd., Myrtle Beach, SC 29577 (tel. 803/449-5653), is a most attractive and welcoming family inn across from the ocean. Walt and Karen Fisher, the owners-managers, are cordial, caring hosts who make guests feel right at home. The 25 rooms are attractively furnished, some in Polynesian decor; and 12 of them are efficiencies with refrigerators. There's a social lobby with free coffee, a heated pool, a playground, and a pleasant cookout area. Airport transportation is offered, along with golf privileges. From June through August, doubles are $49 to $55 and can drop to $30 off-season. Weekly rates are offered too. A reservation deposit is required.

### Budget

The **Ocean Front Motel,** 510 N. Ocean Blvd., Myrtle Beach, SC 29577 (tel. 803/626-9473), is a family-owned 30-unit establishment that caters to families. It's a pleasant place right on the ocean, just two blocks from the pavilion, and there are restaurants nearby. You can have your choice of single rooms, a two-bedroom unit, or an efficiency; all have refrigerators and free color TV. There are adult and kiddie pools, both heated, along with on-premises laundry facilities. You can also have daily maid service. Doubles for two people, one bed, begin at $42 from late May through August, and can drop to under $30 at other times. A reservation deposit is required.

### Campgrounds

There is a generous supply of campsites along the Grand Strand, many on the oceanfront. Rates drop considerably after Labor Day. Most will accept families only—no singles. The following is located about halfway between Myrtle Beach and North Myrtle Beach, and is on the ocean.

There are 760 sites at the **Apache Family Campground,** 9700 Kings Rd., Myrtle Beach, SC 29577 (tel. 803/449-7323). Here the amenities include a free swimming pool and recreation pavilion, water, electricity, shade shelters, modern bathhouses with hot water, sewer hookups, carpet golf, a laundromat, trading post, playground, public telephones, ice, beach umbrellas, floats for rent, and golf privileges. You can reserve here year round except for the week of July 4th. Rates are $11 to $20.

**READER'S BEACH ACCOMMODATIONS SUGGESTIONS:** "About 15 miles northeast of Myrtle Beach, halfway between there and Wilmington, N.C., we found beautiful oceanfront accommodations at the **Winds of Ocean Isle,** 310 E. First St., Ocean Isle Beach, NC 28459 (tel. 919/579-6275 or toll free 800/334-3581). They have motel units, studio efficiencies, suites, and villa units at rates we thought were very reasonable for this quiet, get-away-from-it-all bit of beach paradise. Daily rates aren't always available for all types of accommodations, but we can't imagine not wanting to spend a week" (S. Ramsauer, Orangeburg, S.C.).

**WHERE TO EAT:** You may be tempted to eat more than three meals a day just to sample the many restaurants along the Grand Strand. My own weakness for fresh seafood well prepared always produces a noticeable expansion of the waistline during my stay. And price should by no means be a measure of quality, for prices are unexpectedly moderate at even the best of the lot.

### Not to Be Missed

Treat yourself to at least one dinner at the **Rice Planter's,** 6707 Kings Hwy. North, which is another name for Hwy. 17 (tel. 803/449-3456). The present large, old-brick building replaces the original which burned in 1975, resulting in a loss of irreplaceable artifacts and antiques from rice plantations in the area. Not lost, however, was the charm of the place, which is as much alive in the new as it was in the old. The high-ceilinged main dining room, warmed by a fire in the brick hearth on cool nights, is overlooked by an open balcony reached by a graceful stairway and divided into alcoves for individual parties of six or eight. Exposed-brick walls, copper kettles at the fireplace, dark-stained woodwork and beams, old-fashioned ceiling fans and frosted glass chandeliers, red-checked tablecloths, and candlelight add up to a perfect setting for dining that can only be described as sumptuous. And the personable manager, David Gilbert, seems to be everywhere at once with a warm welcome and a watchful eye on the service, which matches the food in excellence. Seafood is featured, and a favorite is the Rice Planter's Dinner, which begins with shrimp or oyster cocktail, followed by clam chowder, fried shrimp, filet of fish, oysters, baked crabmeat, and deep-sea scallops. It comes with a crisp salad of greens, potato, coleslaw, tartar sauce, and home-baked bread. And—would you believe it?—the price is just $16. If you're not a seafood lover, try one of their low-country specialties: Carolina cured ham or southern fried chicken, both served with rice and gravy, salad, and that same good home-baked bread. It's open for dinner only, from 5 to 10 p.m., with prices ranging from $9.50 to $18.

Over on the beach, David Brittain presides over the **Sea Captain's House,** 3002 N. Ocean Blvd. (tel. 803/448-8082), in an old beach home. The restaurant has been family run since 1963 and is known and loved by a host of South Carolinians, as well as "outsider" regulars who vacation at Myrtle Beach year after year. There's a fireplace in the paneled inner dining room and its glow adds to the informal, friendly atmosphere on cool nights. A many-windowed porch room affords a superb ocean view. She-crab soup is on the menu; the seafood platter includes five different fish, served with slaw, potatoes, and hushpuppies; and there's a selection of flame-broiled steaks, lamb chops, and country ham steak at prices from $8 to $18. Lunch is served from 11:30 a.m. to 2:30 p.m., and dinner from 5 to 10 p.m. seven days a week (except for January, when it's closed).

**Tony's,** 1407 U.S. 17, across from Robber's Roost golf course (tel. 803/249-1314), offers a welcome respite when you seek a change from all that wonderful fresh seafood. The oldest Italian restaurant on the Grand Strand, it's about a 20-minute drive north from the heart of Myrtle Beach. It's a casual, cozy, welcoming place with such perfectly scrumptious specialties as fresh veal dishes and homemade pastas. There'll usually be fresh clams on the menu too. Children's plates are available, and the youngsters can even have a burger if they're not into Italian fare. The semi à la carte meals range from $7 to $18, and Tony's is open daily from 5 to 10 p.m. in peak season; it closes Sunday from September through May and December through January.

## Motel Dining Rooms

The **Safari Room** at the Breakers, Oceanfront at 21st Avenue (tel. 803/448-2474), serves such delicacies as flounder stuffed with crabmeat, sautéed shrimp, and beef tips with mushrooms, peppers, and onions with an extensive salad bar, vegetables, potato, and rolls or hushpuppies included for prices of $6 to $16. Its Friday night seafood buffet (all you can eat for $14) is so popular that reservations must be made ahead as early as Monday night!

At the **Ocean Dunes,** 74th Avenue North (tel. 803/449-7441), there's dancing and entertainment year round in the Brass Anchor lounge and restaurant. Particularly noteworthy is the seafood buffet on Tuesday and Friday, one of the best in the area ($15). Wednesday and Sunday, prime ribs (served buffet style, all you can eat) are featured at the same price. All prices are for complete dinners and include a trip to the very good salad bar. Dinner hours are 6 to 10 p.m., but the lounge is active from 4 p.m. to 1:30 a.m.

Right next door to the Ocean Dunes, and under the same management, the **Sand Dunes** (tel. 803/449-3313) also has dancing and live entertainment. The unique decor of the dining room and lounge carries out an aviation theme— very attractive—and both food and entertainment are tops. Breakfast, lunch, and dinner are served in the dining room; lounge hours are 4 p.m. to 1:30 a.m.

## Family Dining at Budget Prices

It is possible to eat quite well without spending a fortune at Myrtle Beach, and here's a quick rundown on just two of the budget restaurants in town.

There are two locations for **Western Sizzlin Steak House,** 2300 S. Kings Hwy. and 2900 N. Kings Hwy., and both serve steak and a variety of other dishes at extremely moderate prices. They're open from 11 a.m. to 11 p.m. seven days a week.

## North on the Strand

**Little River,** a fishing village on the Intracoastal Waterway at the northern tip of the Grand Strand, has several good restaurants that feature just-caught fish. The best known is **Captain Juel's Hurricane** (tel. 803/249-2211), which began back in 1945 as a tiny waterfront restaurant nestled in a grove of 300-year-old, moss-draped live oaks and has grown to become one of the largest seafood restaurants in the area. Pana Robertson and Helen Kaltsunis, the present owners, see to it, however, that the small-restaurant atmosphere is maintained. There are six separate rooms, each with an individual character (my favorite is the glass-enclosed porch where you can watch boats traveling past) and there's music most nights. Prices are moderate, the salad bar (each dinner includes as many trips as you wish) is really spectacular, and the seafood platter is a bargain.

## At Murrel's Inlet

Way back when, low-country families used to entertain and dine on the wide porches that ran between the main house and the summer kitchen out back. One of the finest restaurants along the Strand takes its name from that custom, and it's a "must" for good eating in a garden atmosphere that recreates the graciousness of the old days. **The Planters Back Porch,** 6707 U.S. 17 North (tel. 803/651-5263 or 651-5544), is in an old farmhouse built before the turn of the century, and photos hanging just inside the entrance show it as it used to be. The new interior is bright and cheerful, done in garden colors accented by lots of white—white chairs, white latticework partitions, etc. You can dine on enclosed porches that run down each side, but my favorite is the main room with its cathedral ceiling and fireplace at one end. The Spring House lounge is all done up in keeping with the rest of the house and features frozen cocktails that have become legendary. Since it's operated by the Rice Planter's people, I don't have to tell you that the food is superb (and similarly priced), but I *should* tell you about the Back Porch Inlet Dinner, a seafood feast that goes on and on. Hours here are 5 to 10 p.m. with a price range of $8 to $17.

**NIGHTLIFE:** Most of the nightlife along the Grand Strand is centered in hotel or motel lounges, some in leading restaurants. Music may vary from country and western to jazz to nostalgia to rock and roll to disco. Among the better places (where there's usually dancing as well as entertainment), are:

The **Brass Anchor** lounge in the Ocean Dunes, 74th Avenue North (tel. 803/449-7441)—see "Where to Eat," above—has top vocal groups and entertainers.

At the Sheraton, there's the lovely rooftop **Pinnacle Supper Club,** 7100 N. Ocean Blvd. (tel. 803/449-4411), that really shouldn't be missed by nightlifers.

The **Top of the Green Lounge** at The Breakers, Oceanfront at 21st Avenue North (tel. 803/448-2474), has dancing and entertainment from 5 p.m. until 2 a.m. Monday through Friday and 5 p.m. until midnight on Saturday.

And if you've a yen for the "oldies" in music, drop by the **Santa Maria,** 6900 N. Ocean Blvd., adjacent to the Caravelle Hotel.

**THINGS TO SEE AND DO:** There are **two publications** just filled with specific information on what, where, when, and how much along the Grand Strand, and either or both will be helpful in planning your vacation here. *Coast* is distributed free by most hotels and motels and is also on counters in many retail establishments and restaurants. The Myrtle Beach Area Chamber of Commerce puts out *See & Do,* and they'll send you a copy if you write them at P.O. Box 2115, Myrtle Beach, SC 29578 (tel. 803/626-7444, or toll free 800/722-3224), or drop by their 1301 N. Kings Hwy. office.

Of course, the big attraction is the **beach**—and sunbathing, swimming, boating, and all the other water sports rank first among things to do. **Fishing** is right up there with them, and whether you cast your line from the surf, a public pier, or a charter boat, you'll probably wind up with a pretty good catch. Surf fishing is permitted all along the beach, and there are fishing piers at Garden City, Surfside, Second Avenue, State Park, Windy Hill, Kits, Crescent Beach, Tilghman Beach, Cherry Grove, and Springmaid.

**Charter boats** (if you want to sound like a native, call them "head boats") are available at marinas up and down the Strand. In Little River, Vance Kinlaw helps operate daily half-day and longer day trips from Little River Inlet (tel. 803/249-1824). Capt. Everett Ayers operates half-day trips aboard the *New Inlet Princess* from Capt. Dick's Marina at Murrel's Inlet (tel. 803/651-3676); *The Flying Fisher* will take you out for six hours from the Anchor Marina at Murrells Inlet (tel. 803/651-0028); and Capt. Frank Juel's *Hurricane* is available for charter at Little River (tel. 803/249-3571). These are just a few, but they're typical, and even at the height of the season you'll be able to book a trip without much difficulty. Depending on the season, your catch may include croaker, bluefish, flounder, spot, pompano, black seabass, or whiting.

If you're not swimming or fishing, chances are you'll be out on the links swinging a club in one of the three dozen or so championship golf courses. Most, if not all, of the motels and hotels hold memberships in more than one club and will issue guest cards (which entitle you to reduced greens fees). Fees may run anywhere from $8 to $25, depending on the club and the time of the year. It really doesn't matter much which course you play—they're all well laid out and maintained. As for the time of year, the "season" is virtually year round, extending from February through November. Play is heaviest, however, from early February until late April. A golfer friend tells me that if you're planning to spend much time on the Grand Strand courses, you should practice your long shots from the sand; not being a devotee of the game, I'm not quite sure what that means, but it probably has something to do with the sandy roughs I hear mentioned in golfing conversations. At any rate, for what it's worth, I pass it along.

Your **tennis** racquet will get a workout if you bring it along, for there are more than 150 public and private courts in the Grand Strand area. A typical tennis facility is the **Dunes Golf and Beach Club** in the Dunes section of Myrtle Beach (tel. 803/449-5914), which has asphalt courts and charges $7 per person per hour for singles.

And when you get tired of all that sports activity, there's the **Pavilion and Amusement Park** on the ocean at Ninth Avenue North (open every day from late May through September; closed October until late March; open weekends only from then until May). It's a fairly large park and has more than 25 rides, a large arcade with games, souvenir shops, and fast foods, a grandstand act in front of the Pavilion, and dancing to two live bands in the "Magic Attic" every night except Sunday. It will be a sure hit for the kids, and there are few mamas and papas who don't rediscover a little kid inside themselves when they make the obligatory trip—in fact, I must confess that I've made a trip or two on my own without a kid in sight as my excuse!

Myrtle Beach is a good touring center when you tire of the beach, and if you'd rather leave the driving to someone else, **Leisure Time Unlimited** has an excellent schedule of historic tours, both north and south of the Grand Strand. They use a 15-passenger touring van, furnish lunch, and visit such places as Georgetown, Charleston, Orton Plantation, and Historic Wilmington (N.C.), and low-country, privately owned plantations. For current schedules, fees, and reservations, call them at 803/448-9483.

If you'd rather do it yourself, **Georgetown** is a short drive south on U.S. 17, but an incredibly long step back in time. The pre-Revolutionary houses, churches, and public buildings are best seen on a train tour that runs daily at 10 and 11 a.m. and 1, 2, and 3 p.m. with an excellent commentary. For reservations and fare information, contact the **Georgetown Chamber of Commerce,** 600 Front St. (tel. 803/546-8436). They will also set you out on self-guided tours armed with maps and brochures.

On your way to or from Georgetown, you'll pass the charming old fishing village of **Munnel's Inlet** (home of terrific seafood restaurants—see above) and **Pawleys Island,** which has been a resort for over 200 years and is a great place to shop for handcrafts, like the famous Pawleys Island rope hammock. In fact, look for the **Hammock Shop,** which is in a sort of village of handcraft shops called **Plantation Stores,** where you'll find wicker, pewter, miniature doll furniture, brass, china, and all sorts of goodies.

Halfway between Myrtle Beach and Georgetown on U.S. 17 (near Litchfield Beach) is a unique sculpture garden and wildlife park on the grounds of a colonial rice plantation. **Brookgreen Gardens** (tel. 803/237-4218) was begun in 1931 as a setting for representative American garden sculpture from mid-19th century to the present. Archer Milton and Anna Hyatt Huntington planned the garden walks in the shape of a butterfly with outspread wings, all leading back to the central space which was the site of the plantation house. On opposite sides of this space are the Small Sculpture Gallery and the original plantation kitchen. In the wildlife park, an outstanding feature is the Cypress Bird Sanctuary, a 90-foot-tall aviary housing species of wading birds within half an acre of cypress swamp. The gardens are open daily except Christmas from 9:30 a.m. to 4:45 p.m., and admission is $4 for adults, $1 for children 6 to 12, free to those under 6. Tape tours are available for $1.

**READER'S SIGHTSEEING SUGGESTION:** "We found golf on **Kiawah Island** (not far from Myrtle Beach) to be absolutely superb, and the place itself is an ecological wonderland. The peace and quiet and chance to see so much of nature left unspoiled were a real treat—this is one place man has managed to make room for his own pleasures without displacing the natural inhabitants" (T. Gleason, Bogota, N.J.).

# 2. Charleston

If the Old South still lives all through South Carolina's low country, it positively thrives in Charleston. And that's just as it should be, for all our romantic notions of antebellum days—stately homes, courtly manners, gracious hospitality, and, above all, gentle dignity—are facts of everyday life in the old city. Oh, it's kept pace with the times, all right—in fact, many "firsts" in its history mark it as a leader in changing trends. Just a few examples: The first indigo crop in the U.S. was grown here in 1690 and proved the basis, along with rice, for many a Charleston family fortune; America's first fire insurance company, "The Friendly Society for the Mutual Insurance of Houses Against Fire," was established in 1736 in Charleston (but was wiped out financially when a disastrous fire in 1740 burned down half the city); the first "weather man" in America, Dr. John Lening, began recording daily temperatures in 1738 to study the effect of weather on the human body; the first shipment of American cotton abroad (seven bags exported to England, at a value of about $873) was from Charleston in 1748; its Chamber of Commerce, organized in 1773, was the first in America; a British flag was pulled down in Charleston and replaced by the Stars and Stripes in 1775, the first time it happened in the colonies; the country's first "fireproof" building was constructed here in 1826, designed by Robert Mills (designer of the Washington Monument, among other landmarks); the first steam locomotive hauling passengers in America ran from Charleston to Hamberg, S.C., in 1831, as one newspaper reported, "on the wings of the wind, annihilating space and leaving all the world behind at the fantastic speed of 15 m.p.h."; the first shot in the "War for Southern Independence" was fired here in 1861; and more recently, Charleston was the first port in the world to approve the transport of atomic material. From this impressive *partial* list of leadership, you can see that this "grand old southern belle" has always been—and still is—quite a dame!

Her history clearly shows Charleston to have been a spirited lady right from the start. It all began when King Charles of England magnanimously gave eight of his royal friends a strip of land that included the area between the 29th and 36th parallels of latitude and westward to the Pacific (somehow overlooking the fact that France and Spain already claimed much of that land). Anyway, the lords proprietors sent out colonists who first settled at Albemarle Point, then moved to the peninsula as a location more easily defensible against surprise attack. By the mid-1770s Charleston (originally named Charles Towne) was an important seaport. As the mood for independence grew, Charlestonians threw out the last royal governor, built a palmetto-log and sand fort on Sullivan's Island (that was Fort Moultrie, and it stayed a working fort right on through World War II), repulsed a British fleet on June 28, 1776, then sent couriers to Philadelphia to tell of the victory just in time to convince the Continental Congress that it could be done. The British returned, however, in 1780 with a large land force and took the city, holding it (with the support of loyal Tories) until December of 1782, when it took more than 300 ships to move them out— soldiers, Tories, slaves, and tons of loot.

Then, in 1797, Charleston's spirit reared its head again when a native son, Charles Cotesworth Pinckney, then minister to the French Republic, spoke the supremely American words, "Millions for defense, but not one damned penny for tribute!"—and very nearly got us into war with France.

That first Ordinance of Secession, passed in Columbia in 1860, was actually signed here in Charleston when an epidemic caused the legislature to move, and that fateful shot from Fort Johnson against the Union-held Fort Sumter set the Civil War off and running. The city remained a Confederate stronghold until February of 1865, although it was attacked again and again during the war

During all those tumultuous years, Charleston was essentially a center of gentility and culture, of wealthy rice and indigo planters who pleasured themselves with imported luxuries, built magnificent town houses (to which they regularly repaired for the summer on May 10 of each year to escape back-country mosquitoes and malaria), supported the first theater in America, held glittering "socials," originated the "Planters Punch" drink, and ran the state government with an iron hand (in the classic silk glove, of course) until up-country people forced a new capital in 1790.

Many of those families still own and live in the homes their planter ancestors built, and they still take pride in beautiful, walled gardens, a cultured lifestyle, and a gracious welcome to visitors. Despite the ups and downs of family fortunes, Charlestonians manage to maintain a way of life that, in many respects, has little to do with wealth. I lived here a while during World War II, when there wasn't much socializing, yet the simplest encounter with Charleston natives—even in such ordinary activities as grocery shopping—seemed invested with a "social" air, as though I were a valued guest to be pleased. And I've met with that same treatment on each return trip. Now I've met those who feel a certain snobbishness in Charlestonians, and in truth, I think you'd have to live here a few hundred years to be considered an "insider"—but I'll settle for this kind of "outsider" (I prefer to think it's really "guest") acceptance anytime!

Walk along the palmetto-lined Battery or through narrow, crooked streets (some are called "alleys"—but they're not your usual ashcan alleys), or down Cabbage Row (which you will know as Catfish Row of *Porgy and Bess* fame), or drive out to the famous Middleton or Magnolia plantation gardens, and by all means get to know Charlestonians in restaurants or simply on the street, and you'll leave the city as much a "Charleston lover" as everyone else who visits here.

**WHERE TO STAY:** Charleston's hotels and motels are priced in direct ratio to their proximity to the 789-acre historic district, but if the tariffs close in are too high for your budget, it's really no great problem to drive in from "west of the Ashley," where rates are lower.

### Unique

This gracious old city boasts several charming small inns. One of my favorites, an elegant restoration of 18th-century Charleston, is the **Indigo Inn,** 1 Maiden Lane, Charleston, SC 29401 (tel. 803/577-5900, or toll free 800/845-7639). Located in the Historic District, it has 40 lovely rooms, all of which face the inner courtyard and are furnished with antiques and reproductions. There's a scrumptious buffet hunt breakfast served from a 1700s Sheraton sideboard every morning, and it's within easy walking distance of major sightseeing attractions. Doubles run about $85 to $95.

The **Elliott House Inn,** 78 Queen St., Charleston, SC 29401 (tel. 803/723-1855, or toll free 800/845-7638, 800/922-7638 in South Carolina), survived the Civil War, earthquakes, and hurricanes to become transformed into one of Charleston's most elegant small inns. Its 26 rooms are appointed with canopied beds, period furnishings, and Oriental rugs. Mornings begin with a sumptuous breakfast of Benedict cheesecake and ham croissants presented in your room on a silver service; each afternoon you'll find a complimentary bottle of imported wine in your room. There's afternoon tea in the landscaped courtyard, and after a complimentary bicycle ride, you'll surely want to relax in the heated courtyard Jacuzzi. Doubles range from $85 to $120, and the numerous seasonal packages and senior citizen discounts can bring that down considerably.

The **Lodge Alley Inn,** 195 E. Bay St., Charleston, SC 29401 (tel. 803/722-1611, or toll free 800/845-1004 outside South Carolina), offers 34 luxurious rooms, each with a fireplace; 37 one- and two-bedroom suites; and a two-bedroom penthouse. All are luxuriously decorated with Charleston period reproduction furnishings and Oriental carpets. You'll find your refrigerator stocked with refreshments, including a complimentary bottle of wine. The French Quarter, one of Charleston's most imaginative new dining rooms, features a grand rôtisserie where the chef prepares roast squab, saddle of lamb, and other house specialties. À la carte entrees are in the $13 to $25 range. And the Charleston Tea Party Lounge, with its ornate bar, is a favorite local watering spot. There's a valet parking lot. Doubles range from $98 to $120, and drop somewhat from mid-November to early February.

The elegant **Planters Inn,** Market at Meeting Street, Charleston, SC 29401 (tel. 803/722-2345, or toll free 800/845-7082 outside South Carolina), near the fine Old City Market, combines the warmth and graciousness of an intimate inn with the amenities of a truly grand hotel. Its 46 guest rooms are impeccably decorated with four-poster beds, and there has been a faithful use of Charleston fabrics and colors. Large travertine marble baths are complete with French milled soap and plush towels, and pamperings continue with nightly turndown service and Italian chocolates on the pillows. Its popular dining room, Eli's on the Market (formerly Silks), features fresh seafoods, California and Oriental cuisines, and there's a lavish Sunday brunch. À la carte entrees range from about $10 to $18. Doubles begin at $100 and drop December through February and from mid-June to mid-September.

The **Middleton Inn & Conference Center,** at Middleton Place, U.S. 61 (Ashley River Road), Charleston, SC 29407 (tel. 803/556-0500, or toll free 800/ 334-9098, 800/827-5650 in South Carolina), is one of Charleston's newest inns— and surely one of the most appealing you'll find anywhere! High on a secluded bluff, linked to the famed Middleton Gardens by a winding footpath, it is made up of a cluster of four separate, architecturally simple contemporary buildings which blend in with the colors and textures of the surrounding woodlands. The 55 spacious rooms (including eight parlor suites and a master suite) are decorated with understated elegance. Floor-to-ceiling windows with louvered wooden shutters open to views of the woods and river, and all rooms have a working fireplace with ironwork forged by the plantation's blacksmith. Large European-style bathrooms have hand-laid tile tubs and floors of gray Carrara marble. There's remote-control television in recessed wall niches, in-room movies are offered, and all rooms and suites have refrigerators. There are three restaurants on the premises, and guests have full access to the Middleton Place house, gardens, and stableyards. There's riding from Middleton Stables, miles of jogging trails and scenic walks, lighted tennis courts, and a heated swimming pool. Complimentary golfing and spa privileges are available. All in all, it's the perfect hideaway you owe yourself at least once! Doubles begin at $95 March through June and drop to $70 to $85 at other times. There are also discounts for senior citizens.

## A Touch of Luxury

The **Mills House Hotel,** 115 Meeting St., Charleston, SC 29401 (tel. 803/ 577-2400, or toll free 800/465-4329), was widely heralded as one of the city's finest reconstructions when it opened on the site of an earlier historic hostelry. With its painstaking attention to period decor and ambience amid the expected 20th-century amenities, it's a heartening example of how past and present can blend beautifully. All 214 spacious rooms and suites are beautifully furnished in period, and public areas are enhanced with antiques and Oriental porcelains. There's a pool, concierge service, and valet parking (for a fee), plus carriage rides are available to tour the historic district. Doubles range from $104 to $130 mid-March to mid-June and mid-September to mid-November. Children under 19 stay free in a room with their parents. Rates drop at other times of the year. The Mills House is a Holiday Inn affiliate and boasts one of Charleston's finest dining rooms (see "Dining in Charleston").

The **Omni Hotel at Charleston Place,** 130 Market St., Charleston, SC 29401 (tel. 803/722-4900, or toll free 800/228-2121), opened late in 1986, bringing Charleston its first world-class hostelry. Adjoining the Old Center Market, it so mirrors the ambience of its 18th- and 19th-century surroundings that it almost seems to have been there all along. The lobby welcomes you with a pristine expanse of Italian marble, and whitewashed Georgian pillars frame a stately double staircase. In 450 guest rooms and suites, period furnishings include poster beds, an armoire, and a ceiling fan, along with such modern conveniences as a wet bar. There's a complete health club with a pool, gymnasium, sauna, steambath, and Jacuzzi. There's dining in the Palmetto Café and the Shaftesbury Room, which features regional and historical recipes. Doubles range from $110 to $140, and the top two floors are Omni Clubs, with full concierge service, complimentary cocktails and continental breakfast, and upgraded guest-room decor. The hotel is part of the block-square, $78-million Charleston Place revitalization, which includes 40 upscale shops such as Gucci, Godiva, Laura Ashley, and Banana Republic.

### The Best of the Rest

The **Francis Marion–Radisson Hotel,** 387 King St., Charleston, SC 29403 (tel. 803/722-8831, or toll free 800/228-9828), is a landmark hotel whose loyal following will be delighted to know it has been beautifully renovated and restored. Its location in the historic district opposite Marion Square is delightful, and there's concierge service, along with complimentary evening cocktails and hors d'oeuvres at the piano bar and a morning paper delivered to your door. There's a coffeeshop and dining room where entrees are in the $5 to $13 range. Doubles range from $63 to $70 April through mid-June and mid-September through October, and drop considerably at other times. Teens under 16 stay free in their parents' room. Altogether this is a most cheery and welcoming "home away from home."

Not in the historic district, but only five minutes away, the red-and-white **Charleston Inn,** 35 Lockwood Blvd., Charleston, SC 29403 (tel. 803/723-7461), is on the banks of the Ashley River right at U.S. 17. The 116 units are well kept and attractive, there's a pool (the largest in Charleston) and children's playground, and Richard Lynch, the accommodating general manager, can arrange deep-sea fishing charters. Facilities include a lounge and an excellent restaurant. I especially liked the spacious lobby and the fact that special rates are provided prospective patients at the huge hospital across the way as well as families visiting patients there—which says something very nice about the management, I think. There are also discounts for AARP, NRTA, APA, and ACT members. Rates are under $50 for doubles, and children 12 and under are accommodated free in the same room with their parents.

Across the Ashley River Bridge on U.S. 17S at 1501 Savannah Hwy., Charleston, SC 29407 (tel. 803/766-1611), the 48-unit **Lord Ashley** is a well-run, pleasant place to stay. Golf privileges are extended and babysitters can be arranged. There is a pool, though no dining room (restaurants are not far away). Rates are in the $34 to $40 range.

The **Best Western King Charles Inn,** 237 Meeting St., Charleston, SC 29401 (tel. 803/723-7451, or toll free 800/528-1234), just one block from the historic district's market area, has bright, comfortable rooms, a pool, a restaurant that serves breakfast only, and a lounge. Doubles here range from $64 to $90, depending on season.

The circular, 13-story **Holiday Inn–Riverview,** U.S. 17 at Ashley River, Charleston, SC 29407 (tel. 803/556-7100, or toll free 800/465-4329), overlooks the river and the city on the opposite bank. It's just two miles from the center of town, not at all inconvenient. Rooms have balconies; there's a pool, a dining room that serves all meals, and a lounge that features entertainment and dancing. Two rooms have been fitted for the handicapped. Doubles begin at $53.

If Charleston's famous gardens are on your "must see" lists, the **Econo-Lodge,** 2237 Savannah Hwy., Charleston, SC 29407 (tel. 803/571-1880, or toll free 800/446-6900), offers budget prices combined with convenience. Both Magnolia and Middleton Gardens are close by, as is Charlestowne Landing. Several golf courses are also in the vicinity. As is true of all members of this chain, there is no pool and no restaurant (Perkins Pancake House is just down the road, however). Rooms are more than adequate, and the price of a double is only $38 to $40.

**La Quinta Motor Inn,** 2499 La Quinta Lane, North Charleston, SC 29405 (tel. 803/797-8181, or toll free 800/531-5900), is near the handsome new Charleston International Airport, and there's a direct line in the baggage claim area to call for free pickup service; if you're driving in off I-26, take exit 209. This fast-growing Texas-based system now has a number of moderately priced inns in the Southeast, and I have always found them clean, comfortable, well run, and a good buy. This one is no exception. Rooms are attractively furnished, the beds are extra-long, and there's free cable color TV along with free local phone calls. You can also request a nonsmoking room. There's a pool, and a Shoney's restaurant is next door; you can even call them for room service from 6 a.m. to 11 p.m. Double rate is $41, and a 20% senior citizen discount is available. Cribs are free, and children under 18 stay free in their parents' room. Fido is welcome too!

**Motel 6,** 2058 Savannah Hwy., Charleston, SC 29407 (tel. 803/571-0560), offers the clean, comfortable accommodations I have come to expect from this fast-growing system, and I applaud its efforts to keep rates economical, as some others continue to escalate. It has a pool, offers color TV for a modest charge, and there's a restaurant nearby. Rates are $27 double; each additional person over 12 stays for $2, children 3 to 11 stay for $1 each, and it's free for those under 3.

**READERS' GUESTHOUSE SELECTIONS:** "In Charleston, we made a special find. We stayed at the **Battery Carriage House,** 20 South Battery (tel. 803/723-9881, or toll free 800/845-7638, 800/922-7638 in South Carolina), a ten-room carriage house which had just been restored to a guesthouse (we were there the first month). The rooms were most attractive, the owners pleasant and helpful, and the service elegant (a butler served a continental breakfast on a silver tray). Also in Charleston, we had a delicious meal at the lovely **Mills Hyatt House Hotel**" (J. Prince, Pottstown, Penna.).

"Not enough recommendations can be given Charleston's **Sweet Grass Inn,** 23 Vendue Range, Charleston, SC 29401. It is superbly managed by a minister and his charming wife. What a find! Full southern breakfast is included, either in a quaint and tastefully decorated dining room, in your own room, or on the roof terrace with its views of the river and the city. The room, which was quite large, was beautifully furnished with antiques" (M. Ryan, New York, N.Y.). [*Author's Note:* Near the colorful waterfront, it's now part of the adjacent Vendue Inn, and both are indeed delightful places to stay. For reservations or information at both, phone 803/723-9980, or toll free 800/845-7900, 800/922-7900 in South Carolina.]

## Campgrounds

The **Charleston KOA** (write Ladson, SC 29456; tel. 803/797-1045) is about 15 miles northwest on U.S. 78, one mile west of its junction with I-26. There are shaded (and some open), level sites, a disposal station, laundry, store, propane gas, pool, recreation room, and playground. You'll need to send a deposit to hold your reservation. Rates are $16 and up.

**DINING IN CHARLESTON:** There's good eating everywhere you turn in

*Map Courtesy of the Charleston Trident Chamber of Commerce*

Charleston, so I've made the arbitrary decision to list a very personal selection of restaurants, most of them in the historic old market area—the character of the city is most reflected here, I think.

## In or Near the Market

Robert Dickson, owner, chef, and star attraction of **Robert's of Charleston,** 42 N. Market St. in the Rainbow Market (tel. 803/577-7565), asked me to explain to readers that because the elegant but small restaurant seats only 48, reservations for weekend evenings must be made two months or more in advance. Since the place has received rave reviews in popular publications, this young man has had to disappoint hundreds of travelers who simply don't understand the space limitations. Well, now that you're forewarned, I'll tell you what you're likely to miss unless you can plan to come during the week. Robert and his wife, Pam, are displaced Yankees now firmly entrenched in the South who serve a six-course, prix-fixe dinner, with one sitting at 8 p.m. every night except Sunday and Monday. The entree is confined to a single item each evening, and is always a masterpiece of perfection, as are the fish course, salad, duck course, fresh fruits, fresh vegetables, grilled tenderloin, and dessert. Robert introduces each course with song, either show music or opera, in a rich bass baritone, and dinner becomes an event. The cost is a whopping $55—and cheap at the price (includes dinner, wine, and gratuities). So call in advance for a reservation or a place on the waiting list, and keep your fingers crossed.

**Henry's,** 48-54 Market St., is a Charleston institution, having been in the same location and run by the same family since the 1930s. There are three dining rooms, one dominated by a carved mahogany bar. Prices run from $6 for a half dozen oysters to $12 for baked stuffed flounder à la Gherardi, beautifully seasoned and moistened with sherry. Some entrees are in the $15 range. You don't need reservations, just come in any time from 11 a.m. to 10 p.m. (Note: Henry's recently came under new ownership, so it's a good idea to inquire locally about any time changes. Phone 803/723-4363.

Just a few blocks away on the waterfront, the **Colony House,** 35 Prioleau St. (tel. 803/723-3424), occupies a historic old warehouse, but there's nothing in its present appearance that even remotely suggests that lowly past. "Elegant" is the only word for the sparkling white exterior with black shutters framing windows adorned inside with rich draperies. The Colony House features murals of Charleston's famous Cypress, Middleton, and Magnolia gardens, and offers seafood, beef, fowl and veal dishes; while the Wine Cellar (tel. 803/723-9463)— a charming room you really have to see to appreciate—offers luscious French delicacies like escalope de veau aux chanterelles on a $30- to $35-prix-fixe menu and is open for dinner only: 6:30 to 9:30 p.m. Monday through Saturday. The charming Sam Prioleau's Tavern serves creative drinks. Prices in the main dining rooms are also expensive by Charleston standards ($5 to $10 at lunch, $10 to $21 for à la carte dinners), but both food and atmosphere are memorable. There are also children's menus. Lunch is served here from 11:30 a.m. to 3 p.m. Monday through Saturday, dinner from 5:30 to 10:30 p.m. Monday through Saturday, to 9:30 p.m. on Sunday. Reservations are advisable, and there is an evening dress code.

The **Barbadoes Room,** in the Mills House Hotel, Queen and Meeting Streets (tel. 803/577-2400), is in an elegantly appointed formal setting overlooking a garden courtyard with a gently splashing fountain. Its notable low-country dinner specialties include shrimp Middleton, sautéed with garlic and Dijon mustard, flamed with white wine and blended with cream ($15), and snapper Dorchester, poached with white wine and mushrooms ($13). This is the perfect spot to sample sherry-dolloped she-crab soup, so named because the crab roe offers a unique flavor. And don't miss the famous Mills House mud pie, mocha ice cream in a chocolate-cookie crust, topped with fudge, whipped cream, and pecans! There's a varied luncheon menu of sandwiches, omelets, seafoods, and other entrees in the $4.75 to $6.50 range. The Sunday brunch buffet, from 11 a.m. to 3 p.m., is a Charleston institution. The Barbadoes (that's the original spelling of the island) Room is open for breakfast from 7 a.m. to 11 a.m. (to 10:30 a.m. on Sunday), from 11 a.m. to 3 p.m. for lunch, and from 5:30 to 10:30 p.m. for dinner. Reservations are required for brunch and dinner, and jackets are a must, as they should be in this elegant room, after 7 p.m.

**82 Queen,** at 82 Queen St. (tel. 803/723-7591), one of Charleston's most popular new restaurants, offers both outdoor and indoor dining in a handsomely restored 19th-century town house. Specialties include veal scallopine, softshell crabs, and shrimp-and-chicken Sonoma—local shrimp and julienned chicken breast, poached in white wine and topped with seedless white grapes, served over pasta. There's a wonderful cioppino suprême, lobster, mussels, shrimp, scallops, and oysters in a spicy Créole-style tomato stew. Entrees range from $13 to $17.75, and there's always a fresh catch of the day. Luncheons are in the $6 to $9 range, and are served daily from 11:30 a.m. to 2 p.m.; dinner is daily from 6 to 10 p.m. It's a good idea to make reservations.

The **East Bay Trading Company,** Queen and East Bay Streets (tel. 803/722-0722), keeps drawing me back both for its wonderful ambience and menu selections. In this former warehouse, antiques, artifacts, and lush greenery decorate three stunning levels which encompass a dramatic, skylight-topped atrium. Entrees range from Carolina quail and fresh seafoods to beef, lamb, and some continental preparations. Lunches range from $5 to $10, and dinners average $10 to $16. It's open from 11:30 a.m. to 10:30 p.m. Monday through Saturday, from 5:30 to 11 p.m. on Saturday, and from 1 to 9 p.m. on Sunday. Parties of six or more should call for reservations.

**Le Midi,** 337 King St. (tel. 803/577-5571), is one of the fine new French restaurants that are adding another dimension to the Charleston dining experience. Behind the unpretentious storefront façade of this locally popular café you'll discover superb French country cooking: boneless breast of chicken sautéed in champagne sauce with cream and mushrooms ($10.25), scalloped veal sautéed in a lemon-butter sauce ($12), lamb shanks cooked in white wine, tomatoes, and spices ($9.50), and the list goes on from there, tempting me even now to hop on the next plane for Charleston. Luncheon prices are even lower. Hours tend to vary with the season, so call in advance to check them.

**The Trawler,** four miles southeast on U.S. 17 at Shem Creek, in Mount Pleasant (tel. 803/884-2560), is an excellent choice to stop for a hearty seafood lunch or dinner if you're visiting the Patriots Point Naval-maritime museum. Local, freshly caught seafood, broiled or fried, is the order of the day, and there's a good salad bar. Specialties include fish stew, and shrimp à la Newberg. There's a pleasantly casual nautical ambience, and you'll need to make reservations only in the somewhat fancier Captain's Table Room, which is open only from 5 to 9 p.m. Dinners are $8 to $19, lunches somewhat less, and there's a children's menu. The Trawler is open from 5 to 10:30 p.m. Monday through Friday, noon to 10:30 p.m. on Saturday, and from noon to 9 p.m. on Sunday.

## The Best for the Budget

In an unpainted wooden house on stilts right at the edge of the Ashley River, next to the Municipal Marina, the **Variety Store** (tel. 803/723-6325) is a good place to feed an entire family on appetizing dishes without serious injury to the pocketbook. The restaurant occupies one side of a store that sells fishing supplies and souvenirs. You can enjoy okra soup (I'll bet you've never tasted it—do, it's delicious!) or chili, a variety of sandwiches, or fried fish dinners, all at budget prices. Breakfast is served anytime: two eggs, bacon or sausage, toast, and of course, grits, cost about $3. Picture windows frame the comings and goings of all sorts of boats—I even saw a Chinese junk sail past. Orders are placed at the counter and waitresses bring the food to comfortable booths. There's a relaxed atmosphere that I, for one, thoroughly enjoyed. Mike Altine, Jr., manager and son of the owner, tells me that the store has been serving locals and boatowners who put in to the adjacent dock for some 25 years. Hours are 6:30 a.m. to 3 p.m. and 5 to 10 p.m. Monday through Saturday, 7 a.m. to 3 p.m. and 5 to 9 p.m. on Sunday.

**THINGS TO SEE AND DO:** The Visitor Information Center at 85 Calhoun St. (across from the Gaillard Municipal Auditorium) should be your first destination. They have brochures, self-guided walking and driving tour maps, up-to-the minute information on cultural events, and a staff that exemplifies Charleston charm. You might want to write ahead, in fact, for their vacation guide (P.O. Box 975, Charleston, SC 29402; tel. 803/722-5225). The center stays open from 8:30 a.m. to 5:30 p.m. Monday through Friday, to 5 p.m. on Saturday and Sunday.

Located just behind the Information Center, the **Adventure Theatre** presents a multi-image look at Charleston called *The Charleston Adventure.* On a 40-foot-wide screen, color panoramas and an interesting narrative give you a 38-minute preview of what lies in store during your visit. Check with the Information Center for exact show times and admission charges (minimal).

A Charlestonian once told me that in 1860 "South Carolina seceded from the Union, Charleston seceded from South Carolina, and South of Broad Street seceded from Charleston." Well, I don't know about *that,* but I *do* know that "south of Broad Street" is the heart of Old Charleston and the place to walk or cycle back to another world.

I always head for the **Battery** (if you want to be official about it, the **White Point Gardens**) to get back into the feel of this city. It's right on the end of the peninsula, facing the Cooper River and the harbor. There's a lovely park, shaded by palmettos and live oaks and filled with walkways that pass old monuments, cannon, and other war relics, and that view of the harbor looks out to Fort Sumter. I like to walk along the sea wall on East Battery and Murray Boulevard (where a blue marlin or some such large ocean fish entertained me with acrobatics one afternoon for nearly an hour) and sink slowly into the history of Charleston. Turning your back to the water, you'll face a row of large, graceful houses that line South Battery, so that when you walk away from the park, it's as though you're going through a sort of gateway into the rest of the town.

Once off South Battery, almost every home is of historic or architectural interest, and I'd need an entire book to tell you about them all. But some you really shouldn't miss are: the **Edmondston-Alston House,** 21 East Battery, built in 1828 by a wealthy merchant and wharf owner and later bought by a Colonel Alston, whose son redid it in the Greek Revival style. Guided tours run from 10 a.m. to 5 p.m. Monday through Saturday, and 2 to 5 p.m. on Sunday and holidays and cost $3.50. You can purchase combination tickets that include this and the Russell House for $5. The **Nathaniel Russell House,** 51 Meeting St., was built before 1809 and has a lovely, unusual, free-flying staircase. Hours and prices are the same as above. The 1803 **Joseph Manigault House,** 350 Meeting St., is an Adams-style structure and also has a notable staircase. It's open every day from 10 a.m. to 5 p.m.; adults pay $3, and children 3 to 12, $1. There is a combination ticket ($5) that includes the **Heyward-Washington House,** 87 Church St., which was built in 1772, and was the home of a signer of the Declaration of Independence. Open every day from 10 a.m. to 4:30 p.m.; admission is $3 for adults, $1 for ages 6 to 18. Combination tickets available (see above). The **Thomas Elfe Workshop,** 54 Queen St., built prior to 1760 by Charleston's most famous cabinetmaker, is a charming small version of a Charleston "single house," and its collections of cabinetmaking tools and artifacts add to its appeal. An adjoining gift shop showcases 18th-century reproductions and accessories, low-country gift items. Tours are offered at 10 and 11 a.m., noon, and 2:30, 3:30, and 4:30 p.m. Monday through Friday, and at 10 and 11 a.m. and noon on Saturday. Admission is $3. The **Aiken-Rhett Mansion,** 48 Elizabeth St., home of Gov. William Aiken, displays some original furnishings, paint and wallpaper. It's under restoration by the Charleston Museum and is open from 10 a.m. to 5 p.m. Wednesday through Saturday and 1 to 5 p.m. Sunday. Guided tours are $3 for adults, $1 for juniors; combination tickets are offered with the Heyward-Washington and Joseph Manigault Houses.

And don't miss the **Dock Street Theatre,** at the corner of Church and Queen Streets. When it opened in 1736, it was the first building in the colonies planned just for theater. The first building burned, and in the early 1800s the Planters Hotel, a very popular local drinking spot, was built around its ruins (that's where "Planters Punch" came from, they say). The theater's back now (since 1936), remodeled and still doing business, with plays, ballet performances, concerts, and other events (it's the longtime home of the Footlight Players, Charleston's resident theater company, and opera and drama here are a part of the annual Spoleto Festival U.S.A. in May and June). The **Charleston Trident Chamber of Commerce,** 17 Lockwood Dr., Charleston, SC 29401, can give you a current "Schedule of Events," but even if nothing is going on at the moment, you can visit the theater Monday through Friday from noon to 6 p.m. There are guided tours on Saturday at a cost of $1 for adults, 50¢ for children. Call 723-5648 for hours.

Charleston has been a church town from the start, and there are several worth a visit: **St. Michael's Episcopal Church,** Meeting at Broad Streets, is the oldest in the city, dating back to 1761. Its eight bells (imported in 1764) are historic and well traveled: they were taken as a British prize of war in the Revolution and sent back to England, then burned during the Civil War, having to cross the Atlantic again for recasting. The chandelier, installed in 1803, has been lighted by candles, gas, and electricity. Washington worshipped here during his 1791 southern tour.

At 136 Church St., the present **French Huguenot Church** (1844–1845) is the fourth version on this site, the first being built in 1687. In the early days, so many of the congregation came downriver by boat that services were planned so they could arrive on the ebb tide and go home on the flood. It's the only French Huguenot church in the U.S. that still uses the French liturgy.

**Congregation Beth Elohim,** 90 Hassel St., is the oldest synagogue in continuous use in the U.S., and the second oldest in the country, dating from 1840. This is a replacement for the original, built in 1794, which burned in 1838, and its Greek Revival architecture is considered one of America's finest examples of that style.

The Mother Church of the Roman Catholic dioceses of South Carolina, North Carolina, and Georgia is **St. Mary's,** at 89 Hasell St. It's another replacement (in 1839) for an earlier church (1789) which burned in 1838.

Now, about **Catfish Row**—its real name is **Cabbage Row** (because of the vegetables that used to be sold on the sidewalk) and it's a row of connected buildings from 89 to 91 Church St. that surround a courtyard. DuBose Heyward changed its name in his novel *Porgy,* and when he and George Gershwin collaborated on the *Porgy and Bess* opera, its fame spread all over the world.

The **Old City Market,** at East Bay and Market Streets, still functions, its open stalls under brick sheds with tile roofs that stretch for roughly three blocks. All sorts of things are sold at the stalls, one of the most interesting being Sea Island vegetables brought in daily by owners of small outlying farms. On either side of the open sheds, old market buildings have been leased to small boutiques filled with marvelous linens, cookware, clothing, gifts, etc. Some of the best restaurants (and some of the oldest) are here also (see "Dining in Charleston," above). A few blocks away from the market, at the corner of Meeting and Broad Streets, look for the **"Flower Ladies"** who sell colorful bunches of blooms from the nearby islands.

The **Citadel,** Moultrie Street and Elmwood Avenue, was established in 1842 on the site of a fortress originally built as an arsenal to suppress any slave uprising (and as a refuge for whites if it came to that). In 1922, it moved to its present location. The campus of this military school, with its buildings of Moorish design, including crenelated battlements and sentry towers, is especially interesting when the college is in session; and the public is invited to a precision drill parade on the quadrangle at 3:45 p.m. every Friday. To book free guided tours, call 792-6846. There's also an interesting World War II photomural of Europe, with narration, among the Gen. Mark Clark archives (he was president of the college from 1954 to 1965) at the **Citadel Memorial Archives Museum** (free; open Monday through Friday from 2 to 5 p.m., on Saturday from 9 a.m., and on Sunday from 10 a.m.).

I sometimes get the feeling that the whole city is a museum, but then I remember its several outstanding museums of the "standard" sort. For instance, there's the **Charleston Museum,** founded in 1773, making it the oldest in the country. It's at 360 Meeting St., in a $6-million complex at the corner of Meeting and John Streets (tel. 803/722-2996). There are more than a million items in the museum's collection, including a full-scale replica of the famed Confederate submarine, *Hunley,* and those on display include early crafts of the area (look for the massive collection of Charleston silver), natural history relics, anthropological exhibits, and a children's Discovery Room. It's open from 9 a.m. to 5 p.m. Monday through Saturday, and 1 to 5 p.m. on Sunday. Admission is $3 for adults, $1.50 for children.

The **Old Slave Mart Museum,** 6 Chalmers St., in the National Register of Historic Places, is the oldest museum in the country (1938) devoted exclusively to the contributions of blacks to American culture. It is poetic justice, indeed, that this building, once used to auction slaves, now exhibits African arts and crafts as well as those of American blacks both before and after the days of slavery. Open Monday through Saturday from 10 a.m. to 4:30 p.m. Adults pay $2; children, 50¢.

Kids will love the **aircraft carrier** U.S.S. *Yorktown* at Patriot's Point (on the Mount Pleasant Side of the Cooper River Bridge), and I suspect all navy veterans will too. The World War II, Korea, and Vietnam exploits of "the Fighting Lady" are, as you'd expect, well documented, and in addition naval history is illustrated through models of ships, planes, and weapons. You can wander through the bridge, wheelhouse, flight and hangar decks, chapel, sick bay, and several other areas, and view the film, *The Fighting Lady,* depicting life aboard the carrier. The *Yorktown* is the nucleus of the world's largest naval and maritime museum. Also at Patriots Point, and welcoming visitors aboard, are the nuclear ship *Savannah,* the world's first nuclear-powered merchant ship; the World War II destroyer *Laffey;* the World War II submarine *Clamagore;* and the cutter *Comanche.* Patriot's Point is open from 9 a.m. to 6 p.m. daily April through October, to 5 p.m. November through March. Admission is $6.50 for adults, $6 for those over 62 and military personnel in uniform, and $4 for children ages 6 to 11. Adjoining is the fine 18-hole public Patriot's Point golf course. For information, telephone 803/884-2727.

**Charles Towne Landing**, on the site of that first 1670 settlement, is a 663-acre park on S.C. 171 at 1500 Old Town Rd., between U.S. 17 and I-126 (tel. 803/556-4450). An open-air, rather modernistic Interpretive Center has underground exhibits that show the colony's history, and there's a re-creation of a small village, a full-scale replica of a 17th-century trading ship, and a tram tour for 75¢ (or you can rent a bike for $1 an hour). Best of all, there's no flashy "theme park" atmosphere: what you see as you walk under huge old oaks, past freshwater lagoons, and through the Animal Forest (which has animals of the same species that lived here in 1670) is what those early settlers saw. The park is open every day, all year, from 9 a.m. to 5 p.m. Adults pay $3; children 6 to 14, $1; senior citizens, $1.50; free for the handicapped.

A lot of people come to Charleston just for the "gardens"—and they are lovely. Of course, there are gardens everywhere you look in the city, but when natives use the word, they're referring to Middleton Place, Magnolia Plantation, Cypress Gardens, Charles Towne Landing's 85-acre English Park Garden, and Boone Hall Plantation.

The formal **Gardens at Middleton Place** (14 miles northwest on S.C. 61) is America's oldest, laid out in 1741 and requiring ten years to complete its terraces, ornamental lakes, and plantings of camellias, azaleas, magnolias, and crêpes myrtles. Its creator, Henry Middleton, was the president of the first Continental Congress. The house was built in 1755 (all but the south flank was ransacked and burned by Union troops in 1865) and was restored in the 1870s as a family residence. It now holds period portraits, silver, and antiques. The whole estate is breathtakingly beautiful, but children will probably want to head straight for the stableyards, which are maintained as if for a working low-country plantation, with animals, artifacts, and craft exhibits. There's a cozy restaurant that serves plantation fare like okra gumbo, she-crab soup, plantation chicken, and ham biscuits. Lunch costs less than $7. Hours are 10 a.m. to 4 p.m. for the house (it's closed in late winter), 9 a.m. to 5 p.m. for the gardens and stableyard. Admission is $8 for adults, $4 for children 4 to 12 ($4 extra to tour the house), March through mid-June; slightly lower in other months.

Ten generations of the Drayton family have lived continuously at **Magnolia Plantation** (ten miles northwest of S.C. 61; tel. 803/571-1266) since the 1670s. They haven't had much luck keeping a roof over their heads: the first mansion burned just after the Revolution and its replacement was burned by Sherman. But you can't call *its* replacement "modern" (or even Victorian)—a simple, pre-Revolutionary house was barged down from Summerville and set on the basement foundations of its unfortunate predecessors. The magnificent gardens of camellias and azaleas, however, have been among the most beautiful in America down through the years. They reach their height of bloom in March and April, but the gardens are colorful year round. You can tour the house, the gardens (which include a herb garden, horticultural maze, topiary garden, and biblical garden), and a petting zoo; stroll down the Audubon swamp boardwalk; ride canoes through a 125-acre waterfowl refuge; or walk or cycle through wildlife trails. It's open daily from 8 a.m. to dusk, and costs $6 for adults, $5 for senior citizens, (over 65), $4 for teens, and $3 for ages 4 to 12 (under 4, free).

There are footpaths and boats to take you through flower-filled **Cypress Gardens**, 23 miles from Charleston on S.C. 52 (look for turnoff signs). The swamp garden was used as a freshwater reserve for Dean Hall, a huge Cooper River rice plantation, and was given to the city in 1963. Hours are 8 a.m. to 5 p.m. daily and admission is $5 for adults, $2 for children 6 to 16, and $4 for senior citizens. Boat rides are extra. Open year round.

**Boone Hall Plantation,** six miles north on U.S. 17 (tel. 803/884-4371), is approached by a famous "Avenue of Oaks," huge old moss-draped trees planted in 1743 by one Capt. Thomas Boone. The first floor of the beautiful plantation house is elegantly furnished and open to the public. Hours are 8:30 a.m. to 6:30 p.m. Monday through Saturday and 1 to 5 p.m. on Sunday, April through Labor Day; 9 a.m. to 5 p.m. Monday through Saturday and 1 to 4 p.m. on Sunday in other months. The guided tour is $4.25 for adults, $4 for seniors (over 60), and $1 for ages 6 to 12.

Nine miles from Charleston, on the Ashley River Road (S.C. 61; tel. 803/766-0180), **Drayton Hall** is one of the oldest surviving plantations. Built in 1738, it was owned by the Drayton family until 1974. Framed by majestic live oaks, the lovely old Georgian-Palladian house is now a property of the National Trust for Historic Preservation (and if you're a member of the Trust, you get in free with your membership card). It's open from 10 a.m. to 4 p.m. daily, with tours on the hour (last one at 3 p.m.). Rates are $6 for adults and $3 for school-age children. Closed Thanksgiving, Christmas, and New Year's Days.

## Tours

There are several very good tours of Charleston and the area, among them: the **Riverboat Rambler,** City Marina, Lockwood Boulevard (tel. 803/722-1691 or 723-5858), a 2¼-hour lecture tour, covering 85 points of interest within 30 miles ($7.50 for adults, $3.50 for ages 6 to 12); **Charleston Carriage Company,** 96 N. Market St. (tel. 803/577-0042), horse-drawn carriage tours (narrated) depart from "The Buggy Whip," 96 N. Market St., from 9 a.m. until dusk at $9 for adults, $4.50 ages 2 to 12 (call to reserve); **Palmetto Carriage Works, Ltd.,** 8 Guignard St. (tel. 803/723-8145), $9 for adults, $4 for ages 4 to 11; cassette walking or driving tours from **Charles Towne Tours,** P.O. Box 243, Charleston, SC 29402 (tel. 803/883-3320), available at the Mills Hyatt House gift shop, the Days Inn Downtown, and Quality Inn Downtown, which cost $8; **Gray Line Bus Tours** (leave from Information Center and all downtown hotels; tel. 803/722-4444), two-hour lecture tours.

Both **Fort Moultrie,** on Sullivan's Island, West Middle Street, ten miles east of the city (tel. 803/833-3123), and **Fort Sumter** (in the harbor) are open to visitors. There's no charge at Fort Moultrie, which is open from 9 a.m. to 6 p.m. in summer and 9 a.m. to 5 p.m. in winter, and there's a visitor center. To reach Fort Sumter, the U.S. Coast Guard supervises sightseeing yachts operated by **Fort Sumter Tours,** write to them at P.O. Box 59, Charleston, SC 29402 (located in the Municipal Marina at the foot of Calhoun Street on Lockwood Boulevard; tel. 803/722-1691). The 2½-hour tours are scheduled at hours that vary seasonally. Fare is $6.50, $3.50 for those under 12. Besides visiting the fort, on the swing around the harbor you'll see the **U.S. Coast Guard Base** (on the site of an old rice mill), **Fort Johnson** (the one that fired on Sumter to start "the war"), Fort Moultrie (from the water), the **Cooper River Bridges** (two of the largest in the world), and several other harbor sights, all the subject of an interesting commentary as you pass by.

One last "thing to do": In May of 1977 Charleston inaugurated an annual **Spoleto Festival U.S.A.,** a 17-day culture explosion that brought 600 performers and over 100 events (opera, theater, ballet, jazz, symphony, choral concerts, and art shows) directed by Gian Carlo Menotti, who orchestrates the Spoleto, Italy, festival each summer. The first festival was a rousing success, fun for everybody, and it gets better every year. Write Spoleto U.S.A., P.O. Box 704, Charleston, SC 29402 (tel. 803/722-2764), for future dates if you're interested.

# 3. Hilton Head Island

Colonization efforts and squabbling over ownership of Hilton Head—the largest sea island between New Jersey and Florida—went on among Spain, France, and England from the early 1600s until the mid-1700s. Native Indians, certain of their claim to the land, harassed them all. But by the end of the 18th century, things had quieted down enough for large plantations to flourish, and a leisurely island lifestyle evolved. Today's "plantations" (most resort areas define their boundaries by the term) hold on to that leisure—indeed, offer it to all comers—and modern "crops" come in the form of tourism instead of rice. Some 450,000 to 500,000 resort guests visit the island annually, and that's some "harvest" for a permanent population of about 7,500 (most of whom are engaged in attracting or servicing the visitors).

Although only 42 square miles in area (12 miles long and 5 miles at its widest), Hilton Head has a feeling of spaciousness, due to judicious planning from the start of its development in 1952. The only "city" (of sorts) is Harbour Town at Sea Pines Plantation. The broad beaches on its ocean side, beautiful sea marshes over on the sound, natural wooded areas of live and water oak, pine, bay, and palmetto trees have all been carefully preserved amid the commercial enterprise that has created over 2,000 hotel rooms (mostly oceanfront) and some 4,000 vacation villas, condominiums, and retirement homes. It's an environmental paradise that regularly attracts artists, writers, musicians (jazz, classical, and even rock), theater groups, and craftsmen.

Recreation, Hilton Head's economic base, goes on year round in a subtropical climate that ranges from the low 50s in winter to mid-80s in summer. There are 23 golf courses (18 are championship caliber—the Heritage Gold Classic and Women's International Professional are annual events), over 300 tennis courts (which are settings for the World Invitational Tennis Classic, Avon Futures Tennis Championship, and the Family Circle Cup), eight marinas that can dock yachts up to 100 feet long, a sailing club, all sorts of rental boats, charter fishing boats for hire (there's an annual billfishing tournament), miles and miles of beach (some up to 600 feet wide at low tide), rental bicycles and 25 miles of rambling bike paths, four riding stables (with boarding facilities for those who bring their own mounts), 15 shopping centers (with exquisite craft shops and elegant resort-apparel boutiques), some 100 restaurants that range from gourmet to fast food, and . . . well, you name it and it's probably here. Nightlife is found chiefly in hotel or shopping-center lounges, which can be quiet, intimate rendezvous spots or lively entertainment centers with sophisticated bands for dancing and top performers doing their thing.

**GETTING THERE:** Even though Hilton Head is an island, you get there over a bridge (about 40 miles east of I-95, 30 miles north of Savannah, Georgia). Piedmont flies directly to Hilton Head, and American, Piedmont, Delta, and Eastern Airlines all fly into Savannah, where there's limousine service. Of course, if you fly your own, you'll land directly at the island's airport, a 3,700-foot paved runway that can handle most nonjet private planes. For boatowners, getting there is simple, since it's directly on the Intracoastal Waterway. Amtrak, Greyhound, and Trailways take train and bus riders to Savannah.

Incidentally, the **Hilton Head Island Chamber of Commerce,** P.O. Box 5647, Hilton Head Island, SC 29938 (tel. 803/785-3673), is especially helpful in planning a visit, either before or after your arrival.

**WHERE TO STAY:** There is really no such thing as "budget" on Hilton Head Island. However, it *is* possible these days to spend time here for a *reasonable* cost. Of course, the older resort establishments (called plantations) are the very embodiment of luxury, with prices to match.

There is, however, a central reservation service which can book you into various rooms and villas almost anywhere on the island. Write or call: **Hilton Head Central Reservation Service,** P.O. Box 5312, Hilton Head Island, SC 29938 (tel. 803/785-9050, or toll free 800/845-7018).

Another suggestion is the rental of private homes, and for up-to-date availability, rates, and bookings, you can contact **Island Rentals and Real Estate, Inc.,** P.O. Box 5915, Hilton Head Island, SC 29938 (tel. 803/785-3813, or toll free 800/845-6134).

## The Luxury Level

**Sea Pines Plantation** (write Sea Pines Resort, Hilton Head Island, SC 29938; tel. 803/785-3333, or toll free 800/845-6131) was Hilton Head's first resort and has a faithful following who would not stay anywhere else. Spread over more than 5,000 acres, it has four miles of ocean beach, 14 miles of bike trails, three championship golf courses, 80 lighted tennis courts, an outstanding children's summer recreation program, and over a dozen restaurants and entertainment spots within its boundaries. You can eat, shop, or enjoy nightlife without being a Sea Pines guest, but there's a small fee to enter the grounds if you're not. Double rooms at the oceanfront Hilton Head Inn rent for $85 and up per night in season (late March to December), and there are over 700 rental villas, completely furnished, which rent for $115 to $250 per day and range from one to four bedrooms. Prices vary by season, location, view, and number of bedrooms. There are package plans for golf, tennis, families, and honeymooners, and the best way to get full details is to write for their free "Sea Pines Vacation Guide" and package brochure.

The **Hyatt Regency Hilton Head,** P.O. Box 6167, One Hyatt Cir., Hilton Head Island, SC 29938 (tel. 803/785-1234), is a 505-room deluxe oceanfront hotel with complete resort facilities. There are three restaurants, a pool bar, two lounges with entertainment, an outdoor pool and whirlpool, and health-club facilities complete with saunas, whirlpool, indoor pool, and exercise/weight room. In addition, there are three 18-hole golf courses, 25 tennis courts, and sailboats. In the summer months there's a good children's program available. Luxuriously appointed guest rooms all have private balconies, and rates range from $105 to $185.

## The "Reasonable" Level

The **Sea Crest Motel,** Avocet Street, north of Coligny Circle (P.O. Box 5818), Hilton Head Island, SC 29938 (tel. 803/785-2121), has 92 rooms, all of which overlook either pool or ocean. The exceptionally large and attractive rooms all have two double beds ($85 oceanfront, $75 poolside) and there are two-bedroom apartments ($720 and $660 weekly) and rooms with kitchenettes ($540 and $480 weekly) available. These are seasonal rates—March 1 to November 1—and they drop considerably at other times. Golf and tennis privileges can be arranged here. This is, I think, the prettiest of the reasonably priced motels, and it's the site of two fine restaurants. The gourmet dining room, the Captain's Table, is unquestionably one of the island's finest (see "Dining on the Island," below).

## Campgrounds

Those with recreational vehicles will find over 400 paved lots, full hookups, tennis courts, a pool, recreation area, and health club at the **Outdoor Resorts of**

**America.** For current rates and bookings, contact them at P.O. Box 5405, 19 Arrow Rd., Hilton Head Island, SC 29938 (tel. 803/785-7699).

**DINING ON THE ISLAND:** I counted some 75 eating spots on Hilton Head—and I may have missed a few. So, whatever else you have in mind, rest assured that a restaurant—and a good one—will never be far away during your stay. Needless to say, every one of the hotels offers food, and most of the dining rooms are pretty good. I am listing only one such here, and that only because it's superior to most others on the island; but mostly, I want to tell you about those places *other* than hotels where you'll find good food and/or atmosphere.

### The Oldest and the Best

There's no printed menu at the **Captain's Table,** in the Sea Crest Motel, Avocet Street on the ocean just north of Coligny Circle (tel. 803/785-4950), and dinner is by reservation only. Gourmet dinners are supervised by Franz Auer, an Austrian who came to Hilton Head by way of Paris, Montréal, and New York. His partner, Klaus Jackel, began life in Berlin, was maître d' at New York's Rainbow Room for a spell, and met Franz in Montréal. Sharing an entrance with the Treasure Cove Restaurant (see below), the Captain's Table is a romantic, candlelit room with a nautical decor (what else!) and serves only 50 at one sitting. The à la carte continental menu at the Captain's Table features beef, veal, seafood, or whatever else Franz has on for the evening. Ingredients are always the very best and the freshest, and preparation is absolutely perfection. This is dining at its very best in an atmosphere of intimate elegance. And, as is fitting, jackets and ties are required. Dinner is from 6:30 to 10 p.m. and entrees run $16 to $22—and remember, it's by reservation only (a day or two in advance, if possible, or you may be disappointed).

### Also Very Good

The **Treasure Cove,** also run by the above mentioned Klaus and Franz, is one of the prettiest restaurants around. The high, sloping ceiling has baskets of greenery hanging from exposed beams, and nautical artifacts are tastefully displayed around the room. "I'm Chris," my friendly and efficient waitress introduced herself, "and if you want anything, please let me know." Well, I never had to take her up on that, for my dinner companion and I were served every course at exactly the right time; it turned out to be a leisurely meal, without either a sense of hurry or those gaps that sometimes leave you wondering what comes next—or when. Our filet of flounder (the "Catch of the Day") was beautifully broiled, moist, and tender, and same-day fresh. Home-baked bread arrived hot and wrapped to keep it that way. There were other seafood selections on the menu, including a local-recipe low-country seafood ragoût (oysters, shrimp, and chicken in a white wine sauce) and several beef dishes, all served with fresh salad (we chose Franz's cheese dressing, which I would classify as "gourmet" in itself), parsley potatoes, and a delicately seasoned medley of peas, carrots, and cauliflower. Reservations are not necessary for breakfast (7 to 10 a.m.), lunch (noon to 2:30 p.m.), or dinner (6:30 to 10 p.m.), and dress is casual. Entrees begin at $8.

**Hudson's Seafood House on the Docks,** on the water between Intracoastal Waterway markers 13 and 14 (tel. 803/681-2772), was built as a seafood processing factory in 1912 and still processes fish, clams, and oysters for local distribution—so there's no need to mention freshness. Service is on a first-come, first-served basis, and if you're seated in the north dining room, you'll be eating in the original oyster factory. A few "drydock" courses show up on the menu (a 12-ounce rib-eye steak, for example), but I strongly recommend that you opt for seafood, such as stuffed prawns or blackened redfish. Everything is cooked to order and very, very good. Before and after dinner (6 to 10 p.m. daily; closed Wednesday September 1 to April 1), you're welcome to stroll on the docks past shrimp boats and enjoy the view of the mainland and nearby Parris Island. Sunsets here are always spectacular, and are accompanied by live entertainment.

Over at Harbor Town, a former artist's studio has been turned into a delightful restaurant and lounge that serves lunch from 11:30 a.m. to 3 p.m. and dinner from 6 to 10 p.m. Monday through Saturday. The glassed-in porch area at **CO's,** Area 4, Lighthouse Road, Harbour Town, Sea Pines Plantation (tel. 803/671-2779), is shaded by huge oaks and pines, and the decor is reminiscent of a New York pub. Quiches, crêpes, seafood, and beef specialties are excellent— as well as quite moderate in price. The staff here is one of the friendliest and most helpful anywhere, which helps account for CQ's popularity (you may have a short wait to be seated, but *do* stay).

The attractive, energetic young owners of CQ's, Dick Werth and Orrie Scarminach, also operate another restaurant located in Palmetto Dunes Resort. **Alexander's,** Area 2, Queen's Folly Road, Palmetto Dunes Resort (tel. 803/785-4999), features high ceilings, lots of glass, and is on a picturesque lagoon close to the Hyatt Hotel. Lunch is served from noon to 3 p.m., dinner from 6:30 to 10 p.m., Monday through Saturday (dinner only on Sunday).

**THINGS TO SEE AND DO:** Golf and tennis compete with beach activities for first place on the "what to do" list. Facilities for all three come with your hotel reservation. Greens fees will run $15 to $25. Court fees are in the $8- to $15-per-hour range. Instruction is available in both sports.

Sailing devotees can join a three-hour cruise aboard the 41-foot *Ocean House* (which carries up to six) by contacting the **Harbour Town Marine** (tel. 803/671-4534).

For **fishing** information and reservations, call Harbour Town Fishing Office (tel. 803/671-4534).

In Hilton Head Plantation, **Seabrook Farm Stables** (tel. 803/785-5415) can furnish horses and guides for beach and trail rides, Monday through Saturday.

Cyclists can rent bikes from **Sea Pines Bicycle Rentals** (tel. 803/671-5899).

Exploring South Carolina's low country off the island is fun, and **Travel Ventures** (tel. 803/785-5237) will arrange a four-hour tour of Historic Savannah, an eight-hour visit to Charleston and Middleton Gardens, or a four-hour tour of Beaufort, Parris Island (to visit the museum at the U.S. Marine Corps base there), and various rice, indigo, and cotton plantation sites, all in air-conditioned motorcoaches with knowledgeable guides.

An interesting do-it-yourself tour is a half-day drive to **Beaufort** (low-country pronunciation is *"Bew-*fort"), the picturesque old seaport just a few miles away on S.C. 170. "Quaint" is the only way to describe its narrow streets shaded by huge old live oaks and homes that have survived from the 1700s (the oldest was built in 1717 and is at Port Republic and New Streets). This was the second area in North America discovered by the Spanish (1520), the site of the first fort (1525) and of the first attempted settlement (1562), and several forts have been excavated which date from 1566 and 1577. The **Beaufort Chamber of Commerce** on Freedom Mall, 1006 Bay St. (P.O. Box 910), Beaufort, SC 29901 (tel. 803/524-3163), has self-guided tours and lots of other information about the historic town. And if your trip plans are for mid-October, write the **Historic Beaufort Foundation,** P.O. Box 11, Beaufort, SC 29901, for specific dates and detailed information on their two days of antebellum plantation houses and gardens tours.

**READERS' GUESTHOUSE AND RESTAURANT SUGGESTIONS—BEAUFORT:** "It's terrific to stay in a real antebellum home in Beaufort, like the **Bay Street Inn** at 601 Bay St., Beaufort, SC 29902 (tel. 803/524-7720). All five of their third-floor rooms have marvelous river views and a fireplace. Also, private baths. Breakfast can be either in your room or the garden, and they furnish bicycles for touring" (M. Lee, Savannah, Ga.). . . . "Two really fine restaurants are the **Anchorage,** on Bay Street in Beaufort, and the **White Hall Inn,** across the river from Beaufort" (P. Brown, New York, N.Y.).

# Chapter X

# SOUTH CAROLINA: THE MIDLANDS AND "UP COUNTRY"

### 1. Columbia
### 2. Around Columbia

THE "NEW SOUTH" IS REFLECTED all across this part of South Carolina. Industries such as textiles, chemicals, precision-tool making, and metalworks, making full use of the abundant waterpower, thrive happily alongside large dairy farms and others that produce tobacco, soybeans, peaches, wheat, and cotton as money crops, and still others with large stands of pine trees for an ever-growing paper industry. There's a vitality which springs no doubt from those early settlers who scorned the leisurely "low-country" pace from the start —yet there's certainly no lack of warmth and hospitality throughout the region. Traditional southern customs are very much alive and well, but they mingle without friction with those of the modern world.

## 1. Columbia

Columbia, unlike many of our older cities, has the orderly look of a planned community, with streets laid out in an almost unbroken checkerboard pattern, and broad boulevards giving it a particularly graceful beauty. All of that is not surprising, since it was in fact created back in 1786 as a compromise capital to satisfy both "low-" and "up"-country factions. It's just three miles from the exact geographical center of the state, and no point in South Carolina is more than two hours' drive from the capital city. Washington paid a visit to Columbia in 1791, just one year after the first General Assembly convened in the brand-new city.

It was here that things came to a head in the North/South dispute that eventually became the Civil War. The trouble that had been brewing for years erupted in a convention held in the First Baptist Church here which passed the first Ordinance of Secession in the southern states on December 17, 1860. (Because of a local smallpox epidemic, however, it was actually signed in Charleston.) The city itself was little touched by battle until General Sherman arrived with his Union troops on February 17, 1865, and virtually wiped out the town by fire: an 84-block area and some 1,386 buildings were left in ashes, although the new State House (still under construction), the university, and the home of the French consul on Main Street were spared.

Although recovery during Reconstruction was slow, the city that emerged from almost complete devastation is one of stately homes and public buildings, with government and education (there are seven colleges located here) playing leading roles in its economy, followed closely by a wide diversity of industry. Fort Jackson, a U.S. Army basic training post on the southeast edge of town, adds another element to the economic mix.

**WHERE TO STAY:** The **Radisson Hotel Columbia,** 937 Assembly St., Columbia, SC 29201 (tel. 803/799-8200, or toll free 800/228-9822), is a 14-story highrise, with some 240 rooms, located within walking distance of the State House, the University of South Carolina, the Coliseum, the Columbia Museum of Art, and downtown shopping, theaters, and restaurants. Spacious rooms are tastefully furnished in a traditional decor, and many have oversize beds. There's an Olympic-size pool, and Beau's Lounge, which features "no cover, no minimum" popular, beach, and dance music. Remington's Restaurant on the first floor is a great favorite of local business people and politicians and is open for breakfast and lunch from 7 a.m. to 2:30 p.m., for dinner from 6 to 11 p.m. (prices in the $12 to $20 range). Doubles start at $78.

Another centrally located, very popular hotel is the **Town House,** 1615 Gervais St., at Henderson Street, Columbia, SC 29201 (tel. 803/771-8711). Maybe it was that convenient location that led General Sherman to pick the site as his headquarters in February of 1865—but you won't find any evidence there today of that gentleman's brief encampment on the spot. The hotel is heavily patronized by government personnel, and local industrial firms often quarter important visitors here. Recent renovations have upgraded the lobby, Mimnaugh's café, bar, and restaurant, and the guest rooms, which are larger than most and decorated in contemporary fabrics and white pine furniture. There's an outdoor pool available almost year round in the warm climate. Also, the staff here is especially friendly and helpful. How much you pay for a double or king-bedded room depends on where your room is situated, although there's little difference in the quality among the rooms themselves. Rooms in the Tower Section (facing Gervais Street) start at $60, and rooms in the Courtyard Section begin at $55. There's no charge for children up to 18 in the same room with their parents.

In Cayce (that's really Columbia, and just a mile from the State Capitol), the **Tremont Motor Inn,** 111 Knox Abbott Dr., Cayce, SC 29033 (tel. 803/796-6240), is set back from the road in wooded, landscaped grounds. Not only is the staff at the Tremont extremely helpful and friendly, the list of extras is also impressive. To begin with, beds are oversize in the cheerfully decorated rooms. Then there are irons and ironing boards available, a swimming pool, coin laundry, valet service, room service (unusual in a motel), babysitting service, children's playground, and complimentary coffee in the lobby. There's a 24-hour restaurant and a lounge that's open until the wee hours. Rates for doubles range from $35 to $47.

At the Broad River Road exit on I-20, the **Quality Inn,** 1029 Briargate Circle, Columbia, SC 29210 (tel. 803/772-0270), is also out of the downtown area, a convenient location for getting to the lovely Riverbanks Park. Rooms are large (some have kitchens), there's a heated pool, they'll let you bring Fido along, and the office keeps an up-to-date babysitter list—all of which makes this a good family vacation headquarters. The dining room is open from 6:30 a.m. to 2 p.m. and 5 to 10 p.m., the bar from 5 p.m. to 1 a.m. They also arrange golf privileges at one of Columbia's private golf courses. Double rooms start at $45; those with kitchens cost an additional $5.

The **Holiday Inn–Northwest,** P.O. Box 258, West Columbia, SC 29169 (tel. 803/794-9440), is five miles from downtown at the intersection of U.S. 1 and I-26. Some of the attractive rooms have king-size beds, and all are large and comfortable. In addition to the pool, there's a children's playground and a kennel for pets. The dining room serves all meals and there's entertainment in the lounge every night except Sunday and Monday. Double rooms are in the $45 to $55 range and they can arrange family-plan rates.

Economy-minded travelers will find the **Days Inn,** 7128 Parklane Rd. (two blocks off I-20), Columbia, SC 29223 (tel. 803/736-0000), a comfortable, budget-priced place to stay, with a restaurant on the premises. Double rooms here cost a mere $36.

**WHERE TO EAT:** Le Petit Château, 4423 Devine St. (tel. 803/782-7231), on U.S. 76 at Fort Jackson Boulevard, is a lovely French restaurant serving such delicacies as roast duckling and veal in various guises. There's also a good wine list at reasonable prices. So popular is this place that you'd best reserve on Friday or Saturday, when locals are in attendance in large numbers. Dinner from the semi à la carte menu will run between $10 and $18, and hours are 6 to 10:30 p.m. Tuesday through Saturday; closed Sunday and Monday and most holidays.

**Hennessey's,** 1649 Main St. (tel. 803/799-8280), is an atmospheric restaurant set in an old hardware store that's been converted into one of Columbia's most interesting restaurants. Emphasis here is on seafood, and the Maryland crab cakes take top billing, in my opinion. They do their own baking, so save room for desserts, and for the lighter-minded diner, there's a good salad bar at lunch. Prices on the semi à la carte menu at lunch are in the $5 to $8 range, while dinner will average about $9 to $18. Hours are 11 a.m. to 3 p.m. and 6 to 10 p.m. Monday through Thursday, until 11 p.m. on Friday and Saturday.

Columbia has one of those homey, pleasant eateries serving good, plain food in an unpretentious setting at reasonable (correction: budget) prices that always delight me—they're usually known only to residents, and I always seem to find them almost by accident. The **Winner's Circle Restaurant,** 1111 Green St. (tel. 803/799-5242), has a loyal following among university students and faculty and the local white-collar crowd, none of whom seems to mind its grill-like, plastic-booth decor. My daughter (who lives in Columbia and loves this place) classifies the food as "pretty good southern to very good southern," and I have to go along with her. Turnip greens, cornbread, and black-eyed peas just don't show up on too many menus, and when they do, they all too often don't have that home-cooked flavor; here, they do! But that's not all they serve: there's a wide variety of sandwiches, ranging from $2 to $4; a nice selection of salads (including Greek), from $1.50 to $3; a supper special of half a fried chicken or an eight-ounce steak, with baked potato or french fries, tossed salad, and french bread for $5; and a buffet that features fried chicken, knockwurst, fish, roast beef, ham, and country-fried steak, two vegetables, bread, and beverage for an unbelievable $5! Breakfast, which is served from 7 to 10:45 a.m., costs about $2.50 (that's for two eggs, ham, bacon, or sausage, grits, toast and jelly, and coffee). On weekdays, lunch and dinner are served nonstop from 11 a.m. to 8 p.m., and on Sunday it's 11 a.m. to 3 p.m.

**THINGS TO SEE AND DO:** Before you do anything else in Columbia, go by the **Columbia Chamber of Commerce** at 1308 Laurel St., Columbia, SC 29202 (tel. 803/733-1110). They have an excellent Visitor Center there and can be invaluable in helping you plan sightseeing in the Greater Columbia area. The **Greater**

**Columbia Convention and Visitors Bureau,** 1527 Senate St., Columbia, SC 29201 (tel. 803/254-0479), can also furnish sightseeing information.

The **State House,** Main and Gervais Streets, was begun in 1855 and only half-finished when General Sherman bombarded Columbia in 1865. The west and south walls are marked with bronze stars where shells struck. In the fire that wiped out so much of the city, the State House escaped destruction, but the architect's plans were burned, with the result that the dome is not the one originally envisioned. Despite that, the building, with its Corinthian granite columns, is considered one of the most beautiful state capitols in the country. It is always interesting to visit—the landscaped grounds hold memorial tablets and monuments and inside are portraits and statues of South Carolina greats—but especially so when the legislature is in session from mid-January through May. The building is open every weekday from 9 a.m. to 5 p.m.

The **Governor's Mansion,** 800 Richland St. at Gadsden Street, was originally built as officers' quarters for Arsenal Academy. When Sherman swept through the town, this was the only building on the Academy grounds left standing. South Carolina governors have lived here since 1868. For a free, 30-minute guided tour (Tuesday through Thursday), call 803/758-3452 for an appointment.

There's no charge to visit the **Columbia Museum,** 1112 Bull St. (tel. 803/799-2810), except for the planetarium shows, which cost $1 for adults, 50¢ for students, military personnel, and children 6 through 11. There's an outstanding collection of Renaissance paintings and sculpture (including treasures from the Samuel H. Kress collection), as well as a host of South Carolina historical silver, pottery, and furniture. Each month, several temporary collections go on exhibit. Check to see if musical concerts or historical lectures are scheduled during your stay—some of them are quite good. Changing temporary shows, a nature garden, and physical science and aquatic displays are featured in the science section. Films on subject matter ranging from history to astronomy to art are shown Sunday at 3 p.m. The planetarium shows are at 3 p.m. on Saturday and Sunday.

The 218-acre **University of South Carolina campus** is bounded by Gregg, Pendleton, and Main Streets. The grounds are really lovely—so beautiful, in fact, that Hollywood has several times filmed antebellum story background shots on the Horseshoe, lined with buildings dating from the early 1800s (the university was founded in 1801) and filled with ancient oaks and magnolias. While you're there, it's worth half an hour or so to go by the **McKissick Museums** which are housed in the fine old McKissick Library Building, located at the head of the historic Horseshoe on the corner of Pendleton and Sumter Streets. Remodeled in 1976 to serve as a center for the university's museums, art gallery, and archives, the museums are open from 9 a.m. to 4 p.m. Monday through Friday, and during the school year on Sunday from 1 to 5 p.m. There is no admission charge.

You can buy a ticket for **Woodrow Wilson's boyhood home** at 1705 Hampton St., the restored 1820 **Hampton-Preston House** at 1615 Blanding St., or the **Robert Mills Historic House and Park** at 1616 Blanding St., at $3 for the Mills House, $2.50 for each of the other two (half price for students). Woodrow Wilson you know; Wade Hampton was a South Carolina hero from a family of state leaders; and Robert Mills served seven presidents as our first federal architect, designing such landmarks as the Washington Monument, the U.S. Treasury Building, and the Old Patent Office in Washington. All three houses are furnished with originals, and the Mills House has some outstanding mantels and chandeliers of the Regency period. They're open from 10 a.m. to 4 p.m. Tuesday through Saturday and 2 to 5 p.m. on Sunday; closed Thanksgiving, Christmas, and New Year's Days.

If you're a lover of church architecture, be sure to visit **Trinity Church,** 1100 Sumter St. between Senate and Gervaise Streets. It's an exquisite example of English Gothic, modeled after York Cathedral in England. It's open Monday through Friday from 9 a.m. to 4 p.m., on Saturday from 9 a.m. to noon.

Whatever else you plan to do in Columbia, save time to drive out to the **Riverbanks Zoological Gardens** at the intersection of Greystone Boulevard and I-126 (tel. 803/779-8717 or 779-8730). In a relatively small space, something of a miracle has been accomplished in establishing a refuge for many endangered species (such as the American bald eagle). The animals and birds (more than 700!) here are the healthiest, liveliest I've ever seen in a zoo—for instance, rather than simply standing around, two young elephants I saw were playing as naturally and delightfully as if they were in their native habitat. Penguins are kept happy in an environmental duplicate of the bacteria-free Antarctic ice shelf. Botanically significant trees and plants are labeled throughout the park. It's open seven days a week (except Christmas Day) from 9 a.m. to 5 p.m., with a $3.25 charge for adults, $1.25 for children 6 to 12 (under 6, free). The last tickets are sold one hour before closing.

I don't know if the back of a commercial building can really be called a "sightseeing" item, but there's one in Columbia that I found absolutely intriguing. The **Farm Credit Bank Building,** on Marion Street where it intersects with Hampton Street, has turned its parking lot into a sort of "event" by commissioning a local artist with the interesting name of Blue Sky to paint a 50- by 75-foot mural on the back of the bank building. Now, outdoor paintings aren't that unusual, but this one, to quote a local publication, could literally drive you "up a wall." Named *Tunnelvision,* it pictures a highway tunnel opening onto a mountain sunrise so realistically that it looks as if you could drive right into it! And, indeed, you *can* drive through the lot and up to the wall itself, which is even spookier if you park at the "tunnel's" entrance. If you're in this part of town, even at night (when it's floodlit), swing by and take a look—it's really something.

## 2. Around Columbia

Within an hour or two of Columbia, there are several places worth the drive. For example, on I-85 just across the border from North Carolina the **Kings Mountain National Military Park** marks the site of a Revolutionary battle that some historians label crucial to the eventual American victory. The southern Appalachians had been almost totally undisturbed by the war until 1780, when British Maj. Patrick Ferguson, who had threatened to "lay the country waste with fire and sword," set up camp here with a large Loyalist force. Well, local backwoodsmen recruited Whigs from Virginia and North Carolina to form a largely untrained, but very determined, army to throw the invaders out. The colonists were not only ill-trained, they were outnumbered, but they converged on Kings Mountain and simply kept on advancing on Ferguson's men—in spite of wave after wave of bayonet charges—until they took the summit. Ferguson himself was killed in the battle, and the Appalachians were once more under colonial control. You can see the battle re-created in a diorama at the Visitor Center, along with other relics. It's open every day of the year except Christmas, from 9 a.m. to 5 p.m., and it's free.

In the same general area (11 miles northwest of Gaffney at the junction of S.C. 11 and 110), another decisive colonial victory was won at **The Cowpens** in January of 1781. Gen. Nathanael Greene, who headed the American forces in the South, sent one Daniel Morgan to divert Cornwallis (who was still in South Carolina with a large British force) from his reorganization of colonial troops. When General Morgan threatened the British fort at Ninety-Six, Cornwallis dispatched a large number of infantry and dragoons to repulse the backwoods army, and the two forces met at The Cowpens (named for a nearby winter cattle enclosure). Morgan was brilliant in his use of guerrilla tactics, and when the British were at last defeated, they had suffered 110 men killed, 200 wounded, and another 550 captured—while Morgan lost 12 men and counted 60 wounded! This defeat of a corps of professional British Regulars was not only important militarily; it also spurred some patriots into action who had previously doubted an American victory and probably swung over a good many wavering loyalists.

If you take I-85 south from Gaffney through Spartanburg, you'll find a really superb example of a colonial plantation house—although it won't fit most people's image of that term: it's simply a large farmhouse typical of landowners' homes in this region, not the stately, columned sort found in the low country. **Walnut Grove Plantation** (tel. 803/576-6546) is 9½ miles south of I-85 on I-26, just one mile from its intersection with U.S. 221. It was built in 1765 on a land grant from King George III when this was the western frontier. The house itself is fascinating, with its authentic furnishings (I love the separate kitchen filled with early vintage gadgets), and the outbuildings include a barn which holds a Conestoga-type wagon. Walnut Grove is open April to October from 11 a.m. to 5 p.m. Tuesday through Saturday, and on Sunday from 2 to 5 p.m. all year; closed on major holidays. Adults pay $3 for a tour; students, $1.50.

Incidentally, while you're poking around this area, keep an eye out for **"fish camp"** signs—very often you'll run across terrific fish dinners (all you can eat for practically nothing!) in rustic cafés down unpaved side roads. If that whets your appetite, stop at a gas station or some other local establishment and ask—everybody has a favorite, and believe me, it's worth an exploratory detour to find the hospitable fish camp eateries, if you like that sort of thing. (I've also picked up some classic fish stories in these surroundings.)

The **Pendleton Historic District,** 15 miles north of Anderson off U.S. 76, has free self-guided tours and auto tape tours ($4) of some 45 historic homes and town buildings. Stop by the **Historical and Recreational Commission** at 125 E. Queen St. in Pendleton (tel. 803/646-3782) for tour information and to see their museum, research library, and arts and crafts shop.

West and south of Anderson via U.S. 29 or S.C. 24, the **Hartwell Dam** and lake has 962 miles of shoreline and all sorts of water-sports facilities (swimming, fishing, waterskiing, etc.), as well as free primitive campsites and developed campsites which rent (from the U.S. Army Corps of Engineers) on a first-come, first-served basis (tel. 404/376-4788).

Members of the "horsey set" can use Columbia as a base from which to run down to **Aiken** (south on U.S. 1) for all sorts of horse events from January through April. For instance, there are polo games at Whitney Field every Sunday afternoon (starting at 3:30 p.m.) during that period. And harness racing at Aiken Mile Track (Triple Crown harness races are held the last three weekends in May); steeplechase at Steeplechase Field; trials at Aiken Training Track; horse shows in mid-March; and . . . well, check the Columbia newspaper sports pages to see what's going on in Aiken.

To visit beautiful **Edisto Gardens,** drive southeast from Columbia to **Orangeburg.** The 110-acre city park located on U.S. 301, along the banks of the North Edisto River, is a wonderland of moss-draped oaks, camellias, and azaleas (which bloom from mid-March to mid-April), flowering crabapple, day lilies, dogwoods, and over 9,500 roses which bloom from the middle of April until early October. It's one of the loveliest truly "southern" gardens anywhere. There are also tennis courts and picnic areas, and it's free (open every day).

Incidentally, a little north of the Edisto Gardens entrance, on the right-hand side of U.S. 301, there's a marvelous restaurant you're likely to ride right by because of its rather misleading name. It's the **House of Pizza,** 910 Calhoun Dr. (U.S. 301), Orangeburg, SC 29115 (tel. 803/531-4000). Well, they *do* serve pizza, all right—16 versions, in fact—as well as sandwiches, burgers, and salads. But the real specialties in this superb eatery are the Greek dishes like moussaka, or biftekia, or the Greek-style stuffed peppers and tomatoes, or—my own weakness—the honey-sweet baklava. Their Greek salad is nothing short of spectacular. And there's beer and wine to accompany whatever you choose. Surprising to find this cuisine in a South Carolina setting, but it seems that the Dimopoulos brothers, after leaving Greece and living for several years in Massachusetts, tired of the climate in the North and simply headed south with their families. Orangeburg is where they settled, and their House of Pizza quickly became a favorite with locals as well as travelers. Prices are budget to moderate; the place has a bright, cheerful atmosphere, with Greek music playing softly in the background, and they have a take-out service if you should want to picnic in the gardens. Hours are 11 a.m. to 10:30 p.m. Monday to Thursday, 11 a.m. to 11:30 p.m. on Friday and Saturday, and 4 to 10:30 p.m. on Sunday. I strongly suggest that you stop, whether your tastes run to pizza or the Greek specialties.

# Chapter XI

# INTRODUCTION TO GEORGIA

### 1. By Way of Background
### 2. Traveling to Georgia
### 3. Traveling Within Georgia

GEORGIA IS NOT ONLY the largest state east of the Mississippi—it is also one of the most varied and complex. Its public image is all too often an antebellum one, full of Tara-like plantations, a slow-moving social life, and a warm southern climate that encourages drowsiness. Well, all of that is there, but from the beginning there has been an energetic bustle about Georgia's commerce that marked even those early planters and was the very basis of much interior settlement. Savannah, surrounded by cotton and rice plantations, was always an enterprising seaport, with its plantation owners as much involved in shipping and the course of trade as in overseeing their large land holdings. Atlanta began as a railroad terminal; and Columbus came into being because of the waterpower of the Chattahoochee and its nine-foot-deep channel (navigable all the way to the Gulf of Mexico) that provided easy access to the world's markets for industrial products. Unlike many other southern states, industry and agriculture, social graciousness, and business activity have not been sharply defined by either the state's geography or its citizens' interests—all those elements have been intertwined into a Georgia that very often comes as a surprise to a first-time visitor.

## 1. By Way of Background

**FROM HERNANDO DE SOTO TO JIMMY CARTER:** As is always the case, Georgia's present (and most probably her future) is explained by and built solidly on her past. That past reaches back to 1540 and Hernando de Soto's first European exploration of Creek and Cherokee lands along the coast. Spanish missions had settled in by 1566 (but not to stay, as it turned out), and by 1733 the English had arrived in the person of Gen. James Oglethorpe and his small band of settlers (whose personal motives for colonization were several degrees loftier than those of King George II, who was keeping a wary eye on the Spanish in Florida and along the Georgia coast). But it was not until a back-and-forth, four-year struggle called the War of Jenkins Ear (1739–1743) was settled by Oglethorpe's decisive victory at the Battle of Bloody Marsh that the future course of the colony could be determined. From 1745, when Oglethorpe and his trustees surrendered their charter to the king, until 1788, when Georgia became the fourth of the original 13 states, the region was a royal province.

As news of Georgia's wealth of natural resources spread, it drew new settlers from the north and from all over Europe; Germans, Scottish Highlanders, Swiss, Welsh, French, and Irish all arrived with varying dreams and aspirations, but perhaps most important, with a driving industriousness. They followed the rivers inland, explored and settled the rolling piedmont, and pushed on into the western mountains. As the Revolution approached, those from the north spread their burning zeal for freedom from the British and were in bitter conflict with the entrenched loyalists along the coast—until they managed to convince most of the 50,000 residents that the troubles of the northern colonies were the troubles of all colonies and Georgia unanimously joined in the fight for independence.

There was division and conflict among Georgians again just prior to the Civil War over the issue of slavery, a conflict that was finally settled when the state seceded from the Union in 1861 and joined the Confederacy. The war was a complete disaster for the state. Its manufacturing plants lay in ruins, plantations and small farms alike were burned over, and most of the young men were either killed or suffered lifelong wounds. It remained for the older leaders to rebuild a shattered economy, and they did it (with the help of youngsters not old enough to go off to war) in a surprisingly short span. What had been large plantations, useless without slave labor, became small, privately owned farms. Out of the ashes of Atlanta rose an even greater metropolis, still based on transportation (railroads then, airlines today); manufacturing plants sprouted all over the state; the textile industry became important as a means of converting one of the state's most important crops into finished products; Jimmy Carter went from peanut farming to the governor's chair, then on to the U.S. presidency; and all the native industriousness and emotional intensity Georgians had inherited from their forebearers led them to create present-day Georgia, a state that cherishes its past, but does not dwell on it, looking instead to the future.

The same diversity that characterizes Georgia in everything else extends to recreation and sightseeing. The beaches and creature comforts of the Golden Isles would probably claim first place on my own list of where to go and what to do. But that's most likely because Brunswick and Savannah, with history enough to fill any vacation, aren't that far away. And then, the big-city excitement of Atlanta has its own special lure. If you're looking for that antebellum Old South, Thomasville's plantation country is perfect (and the chamber of commerce there aids and abets any such quest with lots of maps and information). Outdoorsmen can fish and hunt, white-water enthusiasts will have no trouble finding canoe trails down the state's rushing rivers, golfers bump into excellent courses all over the state (or can simply gape at the world's finest players in the Masters Golf Tournament in April every year at Augusta), and—well, I just can't think of any vacation activity you *won't* find in Georgia. Which accounts, I suppose, for the fact that tourism is high among its principal industries, with close to $2 billion a year coming into the state in the form of tourist dollars.

**GEORGIA AREA CODES:** Savannah, 912; Brunswick and the Golden Isles, 912; Atlanta, 404; Columbus and Pine Mountain, 404.

**GEORGIA'S HOTELS:** These range from the beachfront luxury of the Cloisters on Sea Island to the skyscraper luxury of Atlanta's soaring Peachtree Plaza to a multitude of Holiday Inns and other moderately priced motels to one of the best budget-priced chains in the country, Days Inn, with headquarters in Atlanta

and a good distribution of locations around the state. As always, advance reservations will spare you a lot of grief.

**CAMPING IN GEORGIA:** There are 41 state parks in Georgia that welcome campers to sites that rent for $6 and up per night. Some 25 parks have vacation cottages that rent for $34 (one bedroom), $42 (two bedrooms), and $48 (three bedrooms) per night. In addition, Unicoi State Park rents lodge rooms for $35 single, $40 double. All rates are in-season, and drop other months. Reservations must be made at each park. For more information on these and other park facilities and programs, contact the **Georgia Department of Natural Resources,** Communications Office, 205 Butler St. SE, Suite 1258, Atlanta, GA 30334 (tel. toll free 800/5GA-PARK, 800/3GA-PARK in Georgia).

**GEORGIA'S RESTAURANTS:** Eating out in Georgia can mean having southern-style meals in a rustic setting; spicy, low-country cuisine in Savannah's elegant and historic restaurants; or sophisticated continental dishes in Atlanta's cosmopolitan dining rooms. As for price, except for a few "ultra-elegant" restaurants in Atlanta, even the costliest meals are in the lower register of "expensive." And all across the state, you'll find quite good food at surprisingly modest prices.

As for alcoholic beverages, you can buy them at retail package stores between 8 a.m. and 11:45 p.m. (except on Sunday, election days, Thanksgiving, and Christmas); and whether or not you'll be able to buy mixed drinks in lounges and restaurants depends on which county you're in—that's a local option, although beer and wines are available everywhere. Of course, you have to be 21 to indulge.

**GEORGIA CLIMATE:** The average high and low temperatures at coastal Savannah and central Atlanta show that "low-country" locations are somewhat warmer year round than those further inland.

|  | High | Low |
|---|---|---|
| Savannah | 91 | 40 |
| Atlanta | 88 | 36 |
| Columbus | 92 | 37 |

**VISITOR INFORMATION:** For advance reading and planning before you come to Georgia, contact the **Division of Tourism,** Georgia Department of Industry & Trade, P.O. Box 1776, Atlanta, GA 30301 (tel. 404/646-3590). Be sure to ask for information on specific interests such as fishing, golfing, beach resorts, etc., but inquire as well about the comprehensive booklet "Georgia, This Way to Fun," which gives details on all regions within the state. Also, at least until the end of February 1985 (and there are plans to extend it), there's a marvelous discount program in effect called "Nobody Treats You Better Than Georgia." The discount card will entitle travelers within the state to substantial discounts at a wide variety of sightseeing, shopping, accommodation, and restaurant spots, and there's a booklet which lists all participants. Ask them, as well, for a calendar of events—some pretty special things happen around the state during the year.

## 2. Traveling to Georgia

**BY AIR:** Home base for Delta Air Lines, and Eastern's largest hub, Atlanta's busy **Hartsfield International Airport** is the world's second busiest, with more than 41 million annual passengers. This is also home base for Air Atlanta (see Chapter I). From Atlanta, there are connecting flights into Augusta, Savannah, Albany, Brunswick, and (on commuter line) into several smaller cities around the state. Travel agents or any of the leading airlines can furnish specific information about possiblities through Atlanta's airport.

**BY TRAIN:** Amtrak has stops in Atlanta, Savannah, Jesup, Gainesville, and Toccoa. Amtrak frequently has real bargain fares in effect for limited periods, and you should always check for the most economical way to schedule your trip. As we go to press, attractive Amtrak tours are available to Atlanta and Savannah at bargain prices.

**BY BUS:** Both Greyhound and Trailways reach not only the major points in Georgia, but also go into almost any smaller town you might want to visit in the state. As with Amtrak, the bus lines run periodic special rates that are real money-savers, so check.

**BY CAR:** I can remember driving in Georgia over unpaved red-clay roads which turned into slippery obstacle courses that not infrequently slid you right into a roadside ditch. But that was a long time ago, and today the state's highways are a real pleasure to travel. Several Interstate highways crisscross the state, giving easy access to major points: from west to east, I-16 goes through Macon, Dublin, and Savannah; and I-20 reaches Atlanta, Decatur, Conyers, Madison, Thomson, and Augusta. From north to south, I-75 runs from Dalton to Calhoun, Marietta, Atlanta, Macon, Perry, Cordele, Tifton, Valdosta; I-85 reaches Lavonia, Atlanta, La Grange, and West Point; and I-95 goes to Savannah, Brunswick, and Kingsland. There are state-run **Welcome Centers** at all major points of entry, staffed with knowledgeable, helpful Georgians who can often give you local tips as to timesaving routes.

You will find **Thrifty Car Rental** offices in Atlanta, Augusta, Brunswick, and Savannah.

# 3. Traveling Within Georgia

**BY AIR:** Eastern and Commuter airlines both have connecting service within the state. (For other possibilities from Atlanta, see "Traveling to Georgia," above.)

**BY TRAIN:** Amtrak runs from Toccoa to Gainesville and Atlanta, as well as from Savannah to Jesup, and Georgia Railroad operates between Atlanta and Augusta.

**BY BUS:** Besides Trailways and Greyhound, Southeastern Motor Lines, Inc., operates to intrastate cities and smaller towns.

**BY CAR:** In addition to the Interstates that make it easy to get around the state, U.S. 84 crosses from the Alabama state line southeast to Macon and Valdosta and on south to Florida; and U.S. 441 runs from the North Carolina border south to Athens, Dublin, and the Florida state line. Thrifty Car Rental offices are in Atlanta, Augusta, Brunswick, Macon, and Savannah.

# Chapter XII

# GEORGIA'S COAST

## 1. Savannah
## 2. Brunswick and the Golden Isles
## 3. Cumberland Island

NO MORE THAN 150 miles long, Georgia's coastline is everything you'd imagine a semitropical, wildly romantic, richly historic stretch of waterfront to be. There are moss-draped live oaks and palmettos (some of the prettiest driving in the South is along Georgia's portion of U.S. 17), broad beaches, creeks and rivers, the remains of early-day plantations, offshore islands with resort accommodations that make you feel like an instant member of the "millionaires' club" that first developed them, that lady-like queen of Atlantic seaports, Savannah, and the newest National Seashore, still under development. Since 1540 (when Hernando de Soto became the first European to set foot on what would one day be Georgia), it has sheltered Indians, Spanish missionaries, British colonists, pirates, cotton growers and shippers, English troops, an infamous (to the southern way of thinking; "ruthless" to Northerners) Union general during the Civil War, wealthy Yankees seeking an unspoiled retreat—and most recently, a former president of the United States.

Spanish missions had gained a foothold on St. Simons and Jekyll Islands as early as 1566, but civilization came to stay on this part of the Atlantic coast with Gen. James Oglethorpe and a tiny band of settlers in 1733, who looked to the New World for a new beginning that would win respectability for former inmates of England's debtor prisons and Protestants (both groups held in the same contempt back home). The Revolution brought bitter conflict between prosperous, "status quo" Loyalists and those who sympathized with the cause of American independence, with Savannah changing hands with the tide of battle.

The Civil War brought almost complete devastation to the area, since Sherman ended his "march to the sea" here in Savannah (which, however, escaped almost unscathed). But a Yankee invasion of another sort has since blossomed into the prosperity of tourism, and today's visitor will find the coast a real delight, from Savannah all the way down to Brunswick and those offshore "golden isles."

## 1. Savannah

When Gen. James Oglethorpe landed at Yamacraw Bluff on February 12, 1733, with his 125 English settlers, his idealism went beyond a new future for those unfortunates he'd brought with him, and extended to a town plan that would assure spaciousness, beauty, and comfort for every resident of the colony. A sketch in Robert Castell's *Village of the Ancients* inspired him to lay out a settlement of houses, each with its own garden plot, town squares (there were 24 in the original plan), and an orderly mercantile section. Thus Savannah was America's very first "planned city," and it is still studied by modern urban planners.

The natural deep-water harbor very soon attracted Spanish, Portuguese, German, Scottish, and Irish immigrants, and as wharves sprang up along the bustling waterfront, a lively sea trade brought seafarers from all over the world —along with hordes of pirates who put into the port from time to time. The town never lost its atmosphere of gentility, but rowdyism was rampant along the docks and in seamen's inns and taverns.

When Savannah got word of the colonial victory at Lexington, there was jubilation, a "liberty pole," and a hastily formed patriot battalion, all of which led the royal governor to ship out for Nova Scotia. He came back, however, in December of 1778 and stayed until 1782, when "Mad Anthony" Wayne was finally successful in recapturing the city. There had been an unsuccessful attempt by American and French troops to take the city in the fall of 1779, with disastrous defeat for "our" side—some 800 men were lost, including the Polish hero, Count Casimir Pulaski. Savannah, which had been named the state capital following the 1776 Declaration of Independence, remained so until 1807, when proslavers managed to have it moved to Milledgeville.

The years between the Revolutionary and Civil Wars were a period of great prosperity for Savannah, and many of the Classic Revival, Regency, and Georgian colonial homes you'll see restored today were built at that time. It was the day of "King Cotton" and great tobacco farms. Cotton "factors" (brokers) kept track of huge fortunes along River Street on what came to be known as Factors' Row. And always, builders, merchants, and shippers kept to Oglethorpe's master plan for the city, preserving the parks and squares in the midst of all that commercial hubbub.

When secession rumblings reached fever pitch in 1861, Georgia's Governor Brown ordered state troops to seize Fort Pulaski, 15 miles east of Savannah, even though the state did not withdraw from the Union until 16 days later. So in a sense, the Civil War could be said to have begun here. And it certainly ended for Georgia in Savannah, when Sherman marched in more quietly than was his usual custom, since Confederate General Hardee had evacuated his troops to prevent the destruction Sherman had left in his wake all across the state. In spite of Reconstruction difficulties, Savannah's port was soon humming again, with cotton once more ruling the economy, closely followed by a developing lumber and resin trade based on its surrounding pine forests. Manufacturing began to take hold, and by the early 1900s there were infant industries that would grow to a total of 200 by the outbreak of World War II. Shipbuilding was a natural here and led the list during both World Wars.

Today the economy and much of city life still revolve around port activity. But for the visitor, it's Old Savannah, in a beautifully restored and maintained Historic Area, that draws the most attention. And for that we can thank seven Savannah ladies who literally snatched the first restoration from the wrecker's ball in 1954. They had watched mansion after mansion go down in the name of "progress" and managed to raise funds to buy the Isaiah Davenport house (which had deteriorated into a virtual slum) just hours before it was slated for demolition to make way for a funeral parlor's parking lot. What has grown from that first determined effort to preserve Savannah's history is an inspiration to other American cities, which seem headed more and more toward the facelessness of "no-character" glass and steel. They banded together as the Historic Savannah Foundation, then went to work buying up architecturally valuable buildings and (herein lies the sheer genius of their plan) reselling them to private owners *who would promise to restore them.* As a result of the foresight and dedication of those ladies and others who joined them, more than 800 of the 1,100 historic buildings of Old Savannah have been restored (they're even painted in the original colors of the town, after volunteers chipped away layers of paint to disclose the pinks and reds and blues and greens first used). The "living museum" they've created is now the largest urban National Historic Landmark District in the country—some 2½ square miles, including 20 one-acre squares that still survive from Oglethorpe's dream of a gracious city.

An entire book could be written about this charming and lively city—I'll do my best to tell you about it in our limited space.

**WHERE TO STAY:** There are several major motel chains represented in Savannah, all pretty standard for their chain. I am listing them here (because reservations are sometimes hard to come by in Savannah and you may not be able to book your first choice) after those local hostelries which provide a very special, regional atmosphere.

### In the Old South Tradition

Back in the 1920s, a group of Savannah's wealthiest citizens banded together to build an elegant and exclusive resort hotel of the country-club variety just outside the city on Wilmington Island. Their efforts and investment were such that today when you drive up to the **Sheraton Savannah Resort and Country Club,** 612 Wilmington Island Rd., Savannah, GA 31410 (tel. 912/897-1612), there's a sense of driving back in time to an era when such establishments were of a classic and enduring nature. Just across the Wilmington River Bridge, a short drive from town, the resort is set in more than 200 lush coastal acres, with the 18-hole, Donald Ross–designed championship golf course on the premises (this is the scene of the annual Michelob Georgia Open), as well as facilities for tennis, fishing, sailing, boating, jogging (along scenic trails), bicycling, and sunning on a man-made beach (there's an Olympic-size pool for swimming).

Accommodations here have always been posh, but a renovation program to the tune of some $4.1 million has seen every guest room in the beautiful main building, as well as the Country Club Villas, refurbished with fine period reproductions (and most have one king-size or two double beds). The splendid public rooms are graciously furnished, with the warm glow of carved wood reflecting in the shimmer of crystal chandeliers. Aunnie Belle's Café is an ideal place for casual breakfasting and lunching; the 19th Hole Lounge serves cocktails from 11 a.m. until 7 p.m. (after which H.P.'s Lounge takes over and adds entertainment until 1 a.m.); and H.P.'s Restaurant, which overlooks the water, serves some of the best seafood dishes around (as well as beef, chicken, and veal entrees), and throws in spectacular sunset views.

Double-room rates at this very special place range from $60 to $112, and the villas are $130 to $300. They offer many attractive golf packages, as well as a very good honeymoon special (and I, personally, cannot think of a better place in which to begin married life!).

### Deluxe in the Historic District

Located on the site of the historic DeSoto Hotel (gone many years now), the **DeSoto Hilton,** 15 E. Liberty St. (P.O. Box 8207), Savannah, GA 31412 (tel. 912/232-9000, or toll free 800/445-8667), is in the very heart of downtown Savannah, within easy walking distance of the riverfront, almost all major historical attractions, shopping, and some of the finest restaurants in town. There's a tour service located right in the lobby, as well as some airline reservation services. Rooms are definitely in the deluxe class, there's top-notch entertainment in the

SAVANNAH

Savannah River

N

RIVER STREET

RIVER STREET
Ships of the Sea Museum
FACTORS WALK
Cotton Exchange
Old Harbor Light
BAY ST.
City Hall
BAY ST.
Emmet Park

BRYAN ST.

Franklin Sq.
Ellis Sq.
CONGRESS ST.
Johnson Sq.
Reynolds Sq.
Warren Sq.
Washington Sq.

Christ Episcopal Church

BROUGHTON ST.

STATE ST.
Lutheran Church of the Ascension
Owens-Thomas House
Davenport House

WEST BROAD ST.
Liberty Sq.
Telfair Sq.
YORK ST.
Wright Sq.
Oglethorpe Sq.
Columbia Sq.
Greene Sq.
Old Courthouse

EAST BROAD ST.

BULL ST.

MONTGOMERY ST.
JEFFERSON ST.
BARNARD ST.
OGLETHORPE AVE.
LINCOLN ST.
HABERSHAM ST.
PRICE ST.
HULL ST.

HULL ST.
First Baptist Church
Orleans Sq.
Chippewa Sq.
MCDONOUGH ST.
Colonial Park Cemetery
Crawford Sq.
PERRY ST.

WHITAKER ST.
ABERCORN ST.

Civic Center

DRAYTON ST.
LIBERTY ST.

LIBERTY ST.

Green-Meldrim Mansion
HARRIS ST.

JEFFERSON ST.
TATNALL ST.
Pulaski Sq.
Madison Sq.
Lafayette Sq.
Troup Sq.
MACON ST.

St. John's Episc. Church
Colonial Dames House

BARNARD ST.
BULL ST.
JONES ST.
LINCOLN ST.
JONES ST.

TAYLOR ST.
TAYLOR ST.

WAYNE ST.
Chatham Sq.
Monterey Sq.
WAYNE ST.
Calhoun Sq.
Whitefield Sq.
GORDON ST.

Mikve Israel Synagogue
Wesley Mon. Meth. Church
GASTON ST.

GASTON ST.

HARTRIDGE ST.

HUNTINGDON ST.
HUNTINGDON ST.
HUNTINGDON ST.

LORCH ST.
Forsyth Park
HABERSHAM ST.
PRICE ST.
NICOLL ST.

HALL ST.
HALL ST.

GOODWIN ST.
ABERCORN ST.
EAST BROAD ST.

GWINNETT ST.
GWINNETT ST.

Red Lion Lounge, and the Pavilion Restaurant is excellent. An outdoor pool is on the premises, and the lounge offers entertainment nightly. Rates vary according to location within the hotel, and run from $70 up, with no charge for children staying in the same room with their parents.

Also in the Historic District and right on the riverfront is the spectacular **Hyatt Regency Savannah,** 2 W. Bay St., Savannah, GA 31401 (tel. 912/238-1234, or toll free 800/228-9000). Its style is strikingly contemporary, yet blends surprisingly well into Riverfront Plaza restorations. There's a seven-story, open-atrium lobby (complete with concierge to give personalized attention to guests) which features a cocktail lounge named, appropriately, The Landing; a delightful, casual Patrick's Porch restaurant which serves all three meals at moderate prices (from 6:30 a.m. to 11 p.m. Sunday to Thursday, to midnight on Friday and Saturday); the elegant Windows restaurant for lunch and dinner, overlooking the river and specializing in superb seafood dishes (11:30 a.m. to 2 p.m. and 6 to 11 p.m., with dinner prices in the $9 to $19 range) and Sunday brunch from 10:30 a.m. to 3 p.m.; and M.D.'s Lounge for cocktails and live entertainment. Guest rooms are lovely, definitely in the luxury class, and there's an indoor pool and sundeck. Doubles range from $99 up.

## Lovely, Historic Small Inns

If you want to experience Savannah graciousness firsthand, then by all means book into one of the small inns springing up in the Historic District, most in lovely old homes that have been brought up-to-date with the most modern conveniences, while retaining every bit of their original charm. One of my personal favorites is the **Ballastone Inn,** 14 E. Oglethorpe Ave., Savannah, GA 31401 (tel. 912/236-1484). It's right next door to the Juliette Gordon Low Girl Scout shrine, and convenient to everything in the Historic District. The 19 rooms are all superbly decorated with antiques or authentic reproductions, ceiling fans (air conditioning is also provided), and Scalamandré wallpapers, and each has a distinctive decorative theme. Many regulars have become attached to "their" particular room, and the friendly staff here do their best to cater to such personal tastes. Incidentally, if your tastes happen to run to low-ceilinged coziness rather than the more formal elegance of 14-foot ceilings, ask for one of the garden-level rooms, which are in the original servants' quarters and have a more rustic appearance, with brick walls, exposed beams, and more casual furnishings. Even more gracious than furnishings at the Ballastone is the pampering each guest receives—that friendly staff has seen to it that fresh fruit and flowers are in your room on arrival, that shoes left outside the door will be polished overnight, and that your bed is turned down, with a praline on your pillow and a brandy on the bedside table when it's time to retire. A continental breakfast is included in the rate, and you can have it in the privacy of your room or in the lovely little courtyard with other guests. A feature I especially enjoy is the inviting parlor, where there is always coffee or tea available, as well as almost any liquid refreshment you could wish for, from fresh fruit juice to a cocktail. It's especially pleasant to end the day here (by an open fire on cool evenings) in the company of other guests. Rates begin at $85 for most rooms, $150 for Master Rooms, which are especially large and have a separate dressing room and wet bar. Incidentally, it's a good idea to book well in advance.

Unlike the two inns above, the **Mulberry Inn,** 601 E. Bay St., Savannah, GA 31401 (tel. 912/238-1200), is located in what was a warehouse back in the 1860s. It then became the area's first Coca-Cola bottling factory, and when it began life as a small inn, in the fall of 1982, its size had been doubled with new construction designed to blend nicely with the original structure. The plain, cream-colored exterior, with its mulberry-striped awnings, gives little hint of the elegance inside. The Regency entranceway opens to a three-story open area, from which you can see the dining room (more about that later), the registration desk, and the gift shop. Some guest rooms open onto a covered walkway alongside that interior courtyard (which is landscaped with native shrubs and a fountain), and some suites overlook the river. All furnishings are either antiques or authentic reproductions from the Victorian, American Federal, and Regency periods, and Savannah colors of burgundy, aqua, and peach have been used throughout. So outstanding are the paintings, furnishings, and fabrics used in decorating the inn that the management has taken the unusual step of compiling a written guide for guests and visitors to use on a walking tour of the interior!

The dining room specializes in low-country fare, with fresh seafood, delicate sauces, and fresh fruits and vegetables. It's furnished with formal, Regency furniture and features a fireplace and a lovely custom-made china. An especially nice function is the formal afternoon tea served in this gracious room, although any meal is a special occasion here.

Rates for double rooms (which are all luxuriously furnished) begin at $95, and those riverfront suites (sitting room, bedroom, and service area with sink and refrigerator) begin at $125.

## Charming Guesthouse

For an even more personal touch of Savannah hospitality, let me suggest from my heart that you book for your stay by dialing 912/BEDROOM (that's 912/233-7666) between the hours of 9 a.m. and 9 p.m. any day of the week. This is a **reservation service** which can put you into private homes in the Historic District or nearby in either a bed-and-breakfast room or self-contained suite that will probably include a continental breakfast in its rate. In every case, you'll be hosted by a prime example of Savannah charm, and in many, you'll be surrounded by antique furnishings, brass beds and the like, fireplaces that actually work, and enough intimate knowledge of the city and what it holds for the visitor to make you want to double the length of your stay. Rates can range from $45 to $95, depending on what you want.

Mary Ann Smith is the charming hostess at the **Morel House,** 117 W. Perry St., Savannah, GA 31401 (tel. 912/234-4088). The four-story wooden home was built in 1818 and overlooks Orleans Square, right in the heart of the Historic District. Mary Ann reserves for overnight (or longer) guests a lovely groundfloor apartment with a working fireplace in the large living room, bedroom, bath, and kitchen with an eating area. Coffee, juice, and danish pastries are a part of the kitchen furnishings, and there's guest parking in the rear of the house. Rates are $60 for one bedroom, $90 for two, and you're asked to send a $25 deposit when booking. *Note:* Mary Ann, a native of Savannah, will also arrange special activities for groups (dinners or cocktails in private homes, etc.) that can greatly enhance any visit to the city.

Hugh and Roberta Lineberger are the genial hosts at the **Gastonian Inn,** 218 E. Gaston St., Savannah, GA 31401 (tel. 912/232-2869). Thirteen rooms in a pair of lovely town houses are graced with American and European antiques and art. The $85.50 average rate for a two-room suite includes a full breakfast, wine, and hot tub.

Facing Forsyth Park, the **Magnolia Place Inn,** 503 Whitaker St., Savannah, GA 31401 (tel. 912/236-7674, or toll free 800/238-7674 outside Georgia), also comes with canopied beds, and the luxury of in-room Jacuzzis for $75 to $135.

New in 1987, **River Street Place,** 115 E. River St., Savannah, GA 31401 (tel. 912/234-6400, or toll free 800/253-4229 outside Georgia), houses you in romantic luxury, right in the middle of the Riverfront Plaza action. Doubles run $65 to $120.

## Local Motels

Savannah, or rather Tybee Island, saw the beginning of that dependable budget motel chain, Days Inn, because its founder, the late Cecil B. Day, spent so many summers there in his younger days. Well, now there's a Days Inn that deserves special mention, and it's smack in the middle of the Historic District. When a new building was constructed here for the **Days Inn** at 201 W. Bay St., Savannah, GA 31401 (tel. 912/236-4440), in 1981, it was cited by the Historic Savannah Foundation "For their sensitive design of a new hotel within Savannah's historic Market District," and indeed you would be forgiven for taking the new structure for one of the area's original warehouses that had been lovingly restored. The 196 rooms are all up to the usual Days Inn high standards, and there's a 24-hour restaurant right on the premises, parking facilities, and a game room, as well as a tour service. Rates for doubles run $48 to $52. Adjacent to the new building is The Executive Center Suite Building, which would justify another award for its renovation of a building that really is a part of the city's history. Much care has been taken in creating some 57 suites (each with a kitchen complete right down to a dishwasher, living room, bedroom, and bath, and views of either the river, one block away, or the historic city center) not to violate the exterior, but to keep the four-story brick building's façade much as it was when it was a part of the active market district. Holding to its usual budget rate structure, Days Inn charges rates of $52 to $73 for these choice accommodations in a choice location.

## Chain Motels

**Holiday Inn Downtown,** 121 W. Boundary St., Savannah, GA 31402 (tel. 912/236-1355), has doubles for $45 and up in a Historic District location, with newly renovated rooms, two pools, and a good restaurant; **Howard Johnson's–Downtown,** near the Historic Area, 224 W. Boundary St., Savannah, GA 31401 (tel. 912/232-4371), charges $38 to $55; and another **Days Inn,** 114 Mall Blvd., Savannah, GA 31406 (tel. 912/352-4455), with doubles at $39.

## Campground

The **Safari Bellaire Woods Campground,** Ga. 204, 2½ miles west of I-95, 4½ miles west of U.S. 17—write Rte. 4, Box 451-B, Savannah, GA 31419 (tel. 912/748-4000)—is 12 miles from the Savannah Historic District on the banks of the Ogeechee River. There are full hookups, LP gas service, a store, self-service gas and diesel fuel, dump station, hot showers, laundry, swimming pool, and recreation hall. Boat and canoe rentals with a boat ramp are also available. Rates start at $12, and reservations are accepted with a $12 deposit.

**THAT GOOD SAVANNAH EATING:** Savannah cuisine is a happy combination of coastal and low-country cooking with a special dish of its own added to hearty okra and vegetable soups. If you're asked "One or two?" when soup comes to the tables in a steaming tureen, your host is inquiring how many little green hot peppers you want mashed in the plate before soup is poured. Your answer should depend, of course, on your personal taste, but even if you have a cast-iron stomach, don't fail to remove the pepper itself, for as one native puts it, "a touch of the pepper is purgatory undiluted!"

## A Savannah Institution

Remember the days of the boarding houses, when everybody sat together and food was served in big dishes placed in the center of the table? Well, **Mrs. Sema Wilkes** has been serving locals and travelers in just that manner since the 1940s, and for some of the region's best home-cooking, practice up that "boarding house reach" and head for 107 W. Jones St., between 11:30 a.m. and 3 p.m. any weekday. You won't find a sign ("it would look so commercial, not at all like home," according to Mrs. Wilkes), but what you're likely to find is a long line of people patiently waiting for a seat at one of the six tables in the basement dining room of an 1870 gray brick house with curving steps and cast-iron trim. If you take your place and wait it out (as Kate Smith, Richard Chamberlain, and scores of other celebrities have in the past), you'll be rewarded by a tasty, well-balanced lunch cooked to perfection with whatever fresh foods are available. Mrs. Wilkes believes in freshness and plans her daily menu around the seasons. She also believes in people getting enough to eat, and $6 buys all you can put down. Rest assured your food will be a true reflection of the cuisine Savannah residents have enjoyed for generations.

## The Best of the Rest

I heard about the **Boar's Head,** 1 N. Lincoln St. (tel. 912/232-3196), in Atlanta, New Orleans, and Miami, and truthfully, I was inclined to doubt that it could live up to all the accolades. Well, it can, and I can now be counted a loyal member of its widespread fan club. Situated on the waterfront (Lincoln Street is one of those that dead-ends into River Street) in a 200-year-old warehouse, the Boar's Head has a sophistication in atmosphere and service and an excellence in cuisine that would make it outstanding in any setting. First of all, there's that marvelous river view, and every table is placed to take advantage of it. Then, fresh flowers on every table, hanging baskets of greenery, and soft candlelight make for a cozy, intimate atmosphere that creates just the right mood for the professionalism that comes from the kitchen. Most of this is directly due to Heinz Lindeman, the owner-manager, but credit must also go to the staff he has assembled. From the handsome host to the waiter who began things by introducing himself, there was no snag in providing a memorable meal. The menu is continental and American, with superb seafood, veal, and steaks. My selection was a bouillabaisse that turned out to be perfect, but others in my party sampled dishes such as a seafood casserole au gratin and pepper steak. All were excellent, with prices of $10 to $15. It's open daily for lunch from 11:30 a.m. to 2:30 p.m. and dinner from 6 to 10:30 p.m. or later, and reservations are strongly suggested, since it's been a favorite with locals for years, as well as with tourists.

The **Pirates' House,** 20 E. Broad St. (tel. 912/233-5757), holds a restaurant, a rain-forest bar, gift shop, and museum. The 1754 inn was a rendezvous for pirates and rough-and-tumble sailors who put into the port of Savannah way back when. There are legends galore associated with the place, and Robert Louis Stevenson used it as part of the setting of *Treasure Island.* It's listed as an authentic house museum by the American Museum Society, and you'll want to set aside time to explore every one of the 23 fascinating dining rooms. There are seafood specialties, of course, like oysters Savannah or sherry-flavored shrimp and crabmeat Newburg, as well as chicken Cordon Bleu, duck à l'orange, and a variety of flaming entrees and some 36 desserts. If you come during summer months without a reservation, you're likely to have a wait. But that's not all that bad—if there isn't room at the bar, a cocktail waitress will come down the line and take your order (but do try for the rain-forest bar—it's entertaining and lively). And bring the children: the friendly staff here will give them special attention, and they'll each leave with a pirate's mask as a souvenir. The food here is very good, and more than that, it's a fun place to dine. Prices range from $8.75 to $16 at dinner, $4.75 to $10 at lunch. This winner of the National Restaurant Association's Great Menu Award is open seven days a week from 11:30 a.m. to 3 p.m. and 5 to 10 p.m.

Elizabeth and Michael Terry have added a real charmer to the Savannah restaurant scene with their **Elizabeth on 37th Restaurant and Dessert Café,** 105 E. 37th St. (tel. 912/236-5547). Michael, an attorney who turned his back on the legal profession, welcomes diners and serves as wine steward, while Elizabeth presides over the kitchen in a charming turn-of-the-century mansion. There's a full menu, specializing in fresh seafood from local waters. For non-seafood-lovers there are outstanding lamb, steak, veal, and chicken dishes, and Elizabeth even caters to vegetarian tastes with several entrees. There's an excellent wine list, and on Thursday all wines are sold by the glass. As you might guess from its name, desserts are something to write home about, so bear that in mind when perusing the entrees. Prices are in the $7 to $12 range at lunch and $14 to $25 at dinner (special children's plates are less) on the semi à la carte menu. Hours are 11:30 a.m. to 2:30 p.m. and 6 to 10:30 p.m. Tuesday through Saturday. Best reserve.

Decor at the **Shrimp Factory,** 313 River St. (tel. 912/236-4229), reflects the whimsical mind of Janie Harris, a lively lady who (with her husband, Frank) is determined to set a table truly representative of this region. In an 1826 cotton warehouse setting of exposed old brick, wooden plank walls, and a marvelous salad bar resting next to a minature shrimp boat, the Harrises serve the freshest seafoods from local waters (their Savannah shrimp Créole is without peer), salads that are real creations, and steak and chicken dishes for those who can pass up seafood. Prices at dinner range from $8 to $19 and include salad bar and after-dinner cordial. Now, while seafood may be a bit old hat along the coast, you aren't likely to find pine-bark stew many places other than the Shrimp Factory. It's a terrific seafood stew, served in a little iron pot with a bottle of sherry on the side, that's been simmered with a delicate herb seasoning and comes with french bread and a whipped cheese spread. You won't have to ask how it came by its peculiar name—the legend is printed right on the menu. At lunch, there's a soup, sandwich, and salad bar combination for just $4.50. Janie is almost always on hand. The large bar is a popular hangout for Savannahians both before and after dinner, and there's live music in the bar most nights. Hours are 11 a.m. to 10 p.m. Monday through Thursday, to 11 p.m. on Friday and Saturday, and 12 to 10 p.m. on Sunday. Oh, be sure to ask about their Chatham Artillery Punch, and if you dare, try one—delicious (also, potent).

The **Olde Pink House Restaurant and Planters' Tavern,** 23 Abercorn St. (tel. 912/232-4286), is another dining spot that will send you spinning back in time. Built in 1771, the old house has been a private residence, a bank, headquarters for one of Sherman's generals, and a tea room. Now restored and containing an antique shop as well as the restaurant, it's an ideal spot for lunch Monday through Saturday from 11:30 a.m. to 3:30 p.m. in a lovely colonial room or in front of the Planters' Tavern's large open fireplaces. Lunch prices run $5 to $7. Dinner is by candlelight and quite elegant (6 to 11 p.m. daily). Prices start at $15 to $25 for complete dinners which include such dishes as riverfront gumbo, black turtle bean soup, baby flounder stuffed with crab, Old Savannah trifle, and the like, all delicious!

The **Crystal Beer Parlor,** 301 W. Jones St. (tel. 912/232-1153), has been a favorite of just about everybody in Savannah since it opened its doors in the Depression days of 1933 and sold huge sandwiches for a dime. Prices may have gone up since then, but the affection for this plain, unpretentious place has diminished not one whit. So popular is it that my best advice is to try to go earlier or later than peak lunch or dinner hours (if you get there at noon, you'll be in for a lengthy wait). Inside, things haven't changed all that much since its opening— you can order draft beer in a frosted mug, and owner Conrad Thomson still serves up great fried oyster and shrimp salad sandwiches, crab stew and chili, but you really shouldn't miss the seafood gumbo, one of the best in the Southeast, in my personal opinion. Hours are 11 a.m. to 9 p.m., prices are in the modest range (no item on the menu runs over $6!), and there's ample parking in the lot off Jones Street. This is a "don't miss" for me.

There's been a **Frank Paris Seafood Restaurant** in Savannah since the present owner's father first opened his doors downtown in 1923. He moved out to the old Tybee Road in 1930, and when the new Thunderbolt Bridge was built, Frank Paris, Jr., simply moved the restaurant back to accommodate the wider highway. What you'll find these days on Ga. 80, a hair just past the Thunderbolt Bridge at 3521 Macceo Dr. (tel. 912/897-2155), is a relaxed, friendly atmosphere, attentive service, and seafood that's outstanding. Everything, from crab stew, shrimp Créole, Alaskan king crab legs, and crab au gratin to the special shore dinner and combination seafood platters, is prepared to perfection. And if seafood isn't your particular passion, there are Italian dishes like rigatoni, spaghetti, and spaghetti Genovesa, as well as steaks, hamburgers, and sandwiches. Prices are moderate, to say the least, in the $6.50 to $10 range for dinner, with a lunch buffet every day except Monday for just $5. Hours are 11 a.m. to 3 p.m. for lunch, 6 to 10:30 p.m. for dinner (to 11:30 p.m. on weekends).

The **Chart House,** 202 W. Bay St. (tel. 912/233-6686), is a snug and very nautical seafood restaurant overlooking Riverfront Plaza and the big ships on the Savannah River. Oysters, shrimp, crab, and other local catches are excellent, and the bar is a cozy meeting place. Dinners range from about $7 to $14. Hours are 5 to 10 p.m. Sunday through Thursday, to 11 p.m. on Friday and Saturday.

The **Exchange Tavern,** 201 E. River St. (tel. 912/234-9311), has a great selection of sandwiches, an interesting clock collection, and is open Monday through Saturday from 10:30 a.m. to 2 a.m., on Sunday from noon to 6 p.m. Beer and cocktails are served in this tavern that really *looks* like a tavern, and it proved to be one of my favorite "drop in" places, for food, atmosphere, and relaxation.

**READER'S DINING SUGGESTION:** "Even if you don't take in **Capt. Sam's** river cruises, you shouldn't miss the excellent food on his riverboat moored at 9 E. River Street (tel. 912/ 234-7248). The best barbecued ribs we found in the South, along with sandwiches and salads at lunch and complete dinners in the evening. There's even live music from time to time." (D. Jones, New York, N.Y.).

**A WORD ABOUT NIGHTLIFE:** As is true in so many southern cities, Savannah's nightlife is largely to be found in motel or hotel lounges or restaurants that offer dinner-dancing. But for my money, hotel lounges are hotel lounges the world over, and the nighttime Savannah *I* like best is in the taverns on the waterfront. **Spanky's Pizza Galley & Saloon,** 317 E. River St. (tel. 912/236-3009), is a fun place, where the food is both good and inexpensive. **Emma's,** 224 W. Bay St. (tel. 912/232-1223), near the Hyatt Regency, stars the wonderful Emma Kelly, a chanteuse and pianist who has delighted Savannah for many a year. If you request an old favorite, don't be surprised to find yourself at the piano singing it along with her. Open 6 p.m. to midnight Monday through Saturday. **Kevin Barry's,** 117 W. River St. (tel. 912/233-9626), is a typical Irish pub, open seven days a week from 11:30 a.m. to 3 a.m., with both food and music (the music is live Wednesday through Sunday). The **Night Flight,** 121 Congress St. (tel. 912/236-7309), has live entertainment (jazz, blues, folk, rock, or country music, depending on the current resident musician) nightly (very popular) from about 9:30 p.m. Monday through Saturday (closed Sunday). There's entertainment Monday through Saturday at the **Long Branch Saloon,** 215 E. River

St. (tel. 912/236-9350), along with soups, salads, and sandwiches. **Shucker's,** 225 W. River St. (tel. 912/236-1427), is always a lively place after dark. Nightspots come and go along the waterfront, but I'm sure you'll find your own favorites—just walk along River Street and join the other nightlifers who've discovered this strip of Old Savannah that invites tavern hopping.

More sedate dance music can be found out at the Savannah Resort's **H.P.'s Lounge** and in **Johnny Harris's** popular restaurant on Victory Drive.

**SHOPPING:** There's great shopping all along River Street and on Factors Walk. Don't miss **The Home Maiden,** 124 E. Upper Factors Walk (tel. 912/234-6895), where Bill and Faye Tompkins have local handcrafts. Bill will engrave any glassware you purchase (three initials or first name, free, and there's a large assortment of designs from which to choose). At **The Ship's Wheel,** 123 E. River St. (tel. 912/232-1624), you'll find almost anything you can imagine (and a few things you couldn't) in the nautical line. Ship's wheels, clocks, flags, brass items, lamps, and even hatchcover furniture. For clothing of a nautical nature, as well as intriguing giftware, try **Washed Ashore,** 101 River St. (tel. 912/234-6100). And inside the lobby of the Hyatt Regency, 2 W. Bay St. (tel. 912/235-5556), there's a nice selection of classic fashions at the **Carolina Closet.**

**SAVANNAH SIGHTS:** Savannah's **Visitor Center** (which also houses the Savannah Area Chamber of Commerce and the Convention and Visitors Bureau) *is* one of the city's sights. It's in the restored Central of Georgia Railroad passenger station dating from the late 1850s, part of a 35-acre railroad-yard complex that once bustled with train traffic. The mid-Victorian building is decorated with "Savannah colors" (the Factors red, Tabby white, and Geechee teal, among others, unearthed by all those determined, chisel-wielding citizens who chipped away at building exteriors until they revealed original 18th- and 19th-century paints), and the train shed out back houses the Great Savannah Exposition (see below). The extremely friendly and efficient staff can tell you anything you want to know about Georgia's "mother city," give you a free orientation slide show, help you join an organized tour (several originate here), or send you off on self-guided walking, driving, or bike (very popular) tours with excellent maps, cassette tapes, and brochures. From I-16, you reach the center by taking the "Downtown" exit and turning left at the first traffic light. The route is well marked, and there's plenty of free parking. The address is 301 W. Broad St., Savannah, GA 31499 (tel. 912/233-3067), and it's open from 8:30 a.m. to 5 p.m. Monday through Friday, from 9 a.m. to 5 p.m. on Saturday, Sunday, and holidays.

As a prelude to *any* sightseeing, walk out back of the Visitors Center and take in the **Great Savannah Exposition,** 303 W. Broad St., Savannah, GA 31499 (tel. 912/238-1778 or 238-1779). Housed in the restored train shed of the old Central of Georgia Railway station, the Exposition is a smashing introduction to this charming city, its history, and its present. There are two theaters, each of which uses film, computer-controlled figures, and stereophonic sound to present outstanding performances. In the Spirit of the South theater, you're witness to such historic milestones as Oglethorpe's meeting with the Yamacraw Indian chief Tomochichi, secret revolutionary meetings in Tondee's Tavern, the coming of the cotton gin, the sailing of the first steamship to cross the Atlantic (the S.S. *Savannah,* in 1819), and a host of other events that bring you right up to today's city. In the second theater, the Siege of Savannah during the Revolution is played out before your eyes in a way that will change forever the way in which you view this city. In addition to the theatrics, there's a museum-like exhibition hall displaying all manner of memorabilia from every era of Savannah's history, from the early Indians to the first colonists to the cotton industry to the city's varying architectural styles, ethnic groups, and commercial enterprises. There's food service aboard two beautifully restored train cars and at The Crossings Restaurant. Hours are 9 a.m. to 5 p.m. April through September, till 4 p.m. October through March; admission is $5.50 for adults, $2.75 for children 12 and under—money well spent!

Savannah's history comes full circle around Ellis and Franklin Squares. Back in 1954, the demolition of the century-old City Market outraged Savannahians and sparked the "restoration rebellion." Now, the unsightly garage has come down for an exciting **New City Market.** Opened in the spring of 1987, the four-block Market is a festive bazaar, à la Baltimore's Harborplace and New York's South Street Seaport, full of intriguing little eateries and nightspots, shops, sidewalk vendors, strolling entertainers, seafood, flower and produce stalls.

You will surely want to pick up a copy of *Sojourn in Savannah,* which was approved before it went to press by both the Savannah Area Chamber of Commerce and the Historic Savannah Foundation. It is such an interesting, informative guide to this city and the surrounding area that I think it may be underpriced at $4. It's on sale at the center, or you can order by sending $5 (including postage and handling) to *Sojourn in Savannah,* 708 E. 46th St., Savannah, GA 31405. It's a beautifully printed book and a lasting souvenir of your visit.

There's so much to see in Savannah that it's really hard to say where to start. Personally, I like a stroll along the **waterfront**—it's unlike any you'll find elsewhere. Like the rest of the city's restored and preserved historical district, the old buildings that line Factors Row are in actual use, not set aside as sterile museums. It's as lively a commercial center today as it was in its rowdier days, the only difference being that now there are charming boutiques, restaurants, and taverns in what used to be brokers' offices and warehouses. Strung along the river's edge alongside a high bluff, the brick buildings rise three (sometimes more) stories above River Street and date from the early 1800s. Each level has its own street—River Street, Lower Factors Walk, Upper Factors Walk—and there are bridgeways connecting each level to streets along the bluff. The entrance ramps, from Bay Street down to River Street, are paved with cobblestones that crossed the Atlantic as ballast in sailing ships. It's a fascinating, fun sort of place that (perhaps even more than those lovely homes that border Savannah's wide streets) gives you a feeling of the *continuing* history of this town. And if you happen to be there on the first Saturday of any month, you'll be swept up in a River Street festival, with live entertainment, street vendors, and sidewalk artists and craftsmen, that is something special.

Incidentally, that statue at the foot of the East Broad Street ramp of a young girl waving toward the harbor is in memory of Florence Martus, who (so they say) fell in love with a sailor, promised to greet every ship until he returned to marry her, and henceforth for 44 years waved a white cloth by day and a lantern by night to every ship entering the harbor past the Elba Island Light, where she lived with her brother who tended the light. She was greatly loved by seamen and was looked for eagerly, never missing a ship (she said she could "feel" one approaching) and assisting in at least one heroic rescue of sailors from a sinking ship. Sadly, her own sailor never returned for the wedding. Her story is the subject of a ballet, *The Legend of the Waving Girl,* choreographed by the Savannah Ballet's artistic director, Bojan Spassoff, presented for the first time in January of 1977.

Then there's **Bull Street,** stretching south from the river and marking the division between east and west on streets that cross it. It was named for Col. William Bull, an aide to General Oglethorpe, and it holds five of those lovely squares, coming at last to Forsyth Park. Revolutionary War hero Nathanael Greene is buried in **Johnson Square,** the first of the five, between Bay and Congress Streets. **Wright Square,** between York and State, holds a large memorial honoring Tomochichi, the Yamacraw Indian chief without whose friendship the Oglethorpe settlement might have perished. A bronze figure of Oglethorpe himself stands in **Chippewa Square** (between Perry and Hull); and **Madison Square** (between Harris and Charlton) and **Monterrey Square** (between Taylor and Gordon) each have monuments and statues commemorating people important to Savannah's history. The people of Savannah love their squares, and they are wonderfully relaxed "people-watching" stations.

The white, cast-iron fountain in **Forsyth Park** is one focal point for Savannah residents, who sit on its railing, feed pigeons, listen to strolling musicians, and generally take a break from the rigors of modern-day life. But aside from the squares and parks, just strolling the streets is an escape from today into yesterday. **Gordon Row,** for example, has town houses with graceful curving stair rails made from ornate ironwork, and the handsome brick homes on **Marshall Row** face a broad avenue with grass and trees down its center. Indeed, to my way of thinking, sightseeing in Savannah should either begin or end with a day of walking—along the waterfront, through the squares, and along the streets—in order to get an overall picture of what the city is all about.

## Old Savannah

To see where those seven determined ladies started the whole restoration thing, see the **Davenport House** at 324 E. State St. (on Columbia Square), built between 1815 and 1820 by master builder Isaiah Davenport. It's one of the truly great Federal-style houses in this country, and has lovely, delicate ironwork and a handsome elliptical stairway. The house is open Monday to Saturday from 10 a.m. to 4 p.m., on Sunday from 1:30 to 4:30 p.m. (it closes Thanksgiving, Christmas, and New Year's Days), and admission is $2.50 for adults, $1.25 for ages 10 and under.

The Gothic-style **Green-Meldrim Home,** 14 W. Macon St., is where General Sherman headquartered when his troops occupied Savannah in 1864. In fact, it was from this house that the general sent his famous (in Savannah, at least) telegram to President Lincoln offering him the city as a Christmas gift. The house now belongs to St. John's Church, which uses the former kitchen, servants' quarters, and stable as its rectory. The rest of the premises is open to visitors on Tuesday, Thursday, Friday, and Saturday from 10 a.m. to 4 p.m. (adults pay $2; students, $1; under 6, free).

Girl Scouts will be especially interested in **Juliette Gordon Low's birthplace** at 142 Bull and Oglethorpe Avenue (as will non–Girl Scouts). The founder of Girl Scouting lived in a Regency-style house that is maintained both as a memorial to her and as a National Program Center. The Victorian additions to the 1818 house were made in 1886, just before Juliette (called "Daisy" by her family) married William Mackay Low. It's open daily, except Wednesday, from 10 a.m. to 4 p.m., on Sunday from 11 a.m. to 4:30 p.m. (closed Sunday in January and December and major holidays). Admission is $2.50 for adults, $1.75 for students (Girl Scout leaders pay $2.25; Girl Scouts under 18, $1.50).

After her marriage, Juliette lived at what is now the **Andrew Low House** (built in 1848) at 329 Abercorn St., facing Lafayette Square, and it was here that she actually founded the Girl Scouts. She died here in 1927. The classic mid-19th-century house is of stucco over brick with elaborate ironwork outside, jalousied porches, carved woodwork, and crystal chandeliers. William

Makepeace Thackeray visited here twice (the desk at which he worked is in one bedroom), as did Robert E. Lee, in 1870, who was entertained at a gala reception in the double parlors. In 1928 the house was bought by the Georgia Colonial Dames as their headquarters, and the carriage house is now headquarters for the local Girl Scout council. Visiting hours are 10:30 a.m. to 4 p.m. every day (except Thursday and national holidays), with a donation of $2.50 for adults, $1.75 for ages 6 to 10.

The National Endowment for the Humanities underwrites an exhibition in the **William Scarbrough House,** 41 W. Broad St., of Savannah-made items, as well as some imports, dating from 1820 to 1860, a period of rapid growth for the town from a small center of some 7,500 to an important cotton port of more than 22,000. The house is now a National Historic Landmark, a museum, and headquarters for the Historic Savannah Foundation. It's open to the public Monday to Saturday from 10 a.m. to 4 p.m. (closed holidays and on Saturday in December and January) for a donation of $2 from adults, $1 from children.

## Museums

Tidal-river (that's what the Savannah River is) reptiles and amphibians can be seen at the **Savannah Science Museum,** 4405 Paulsen St., along with native plants and science, industry, and Indian exhibits, as well as the second-largest solar-energy unit in the state. There's a $1 charge (children, 50¢), and it's open Tuesday through Saturday from 10 a.m. to 5 p.m. and 2 to 5 p.m. on Sunday. There is also a planetarium lecture every Saturday and Sunday at 3 p.m. with a $1.50 admission. And a reptile and amphibian "hands on" lecture at 3 p.m. every Saturday.

## Tours

The river has always been a focal point for Savannah, and one of the best ways to see the city is from the water, aboard the *Cap'n Sam,* the *Harbor Queen,* or the *Waving Girl,* under the able hand of Capt. Sam Stevens. Cap'n Sam has been on the river for most of his lifetime and shares with his passengers a knowledge that comes from long (nearly 60 years) association with Savannah's growth. **Harbor tours** leave seven days a week at noon from a dock on River Street at the foot of Bull Street, behind City Hall. The two-hour narrated trip includes all historic and shipping sites along the harbor (about 20 miles). There's also a twilight cocktail cruise, as well as moonlight supper cruises. The two-hour harbor cruise costs $6.50 for adults, $3.50 for children under 12. Call 912/234-7248 for information and reservations.

Another delightful way to see Savannah (and save your feet) is by **horse-drawn carriage.** Authentic antique carriages, painstakingly restored, carry you over cobblestone streets as the coachman spins a tale of the town's history. The one-hour tours cover 15 of the 20 squares. Rates are $8.50 for adults, $4 for children. Reservations are required—contact Savannah Carriage Co., DeSoto Hilton Hotel, Liberty and Bull Streets (tel. 912/236-6756), to reserve and for departure times.

**Gray Line Savannah Landmark Tours, Inc.,** 215 W. Boundary St., and **Historic Savannah Foundations Tours** (tel. 912/233-3597) have narrated bus tours of museums, squares, parks, and homes. Reservations must be made for all tours, and most have starting points at the Visitor Center and pickup points at various hotels and motels.

There are tours on tape for self-guided driving, walking, or bike excursions available at costs ranging from $6 to $12 (including a tape player and maps) from **Tours on Tape,** 17 Price St. Telephone 912/234-9992 for information on locations where tapes may be rented.

In late March or early April, the **Homes and Gardens Tour** shows off more than 30 homes, gardens, and museums in four days of daylight and candlelight tours. For specific dates, hours, and charges, write Savannah Tour of Homes and Gardens, 18 Abercorn St., Savannah, GA 31401 (tel. 912/233-7703).

## Outside the City

About 2½ miles from downtown Savannah via U.S. 80, there's a fort with a nine-foot-deep tidal moat around its brick walls. It's **Fort Jackson,** which was built by the U.S. Corps of Engineers between 1809 and 1879 at a strategic point on the Savannah River. This is the fort that Georgia troops occupied before the outbreak of the Civil War and held until Sherman arrived in 1864. Its arched rooms (designed to support the weight of heavy cannon mounted above, which commanded the harbor entrance) hold 13 exhibit areas. During June, July, and August there are daily cannon-firing demonstrations, and a Saturday-evening military tattoo from 5 to 7 p.m. Hours are Tuesday through Sunday from 9 a.m. to 5 p.m. (weekends only in December, January, and February), and admission is $1.75 for adults, $1.25 for students, military personnel, and senior citizens; call 912/232-3945 if you need additional information.

**Fort McAllister** is ten miles east of U.S. 17 at Richmond Hill, on the banks of the Great Ogeechee River, and was a Confederate earthenwork fortification. There's a visitor center with historic exhibits, and there's a $1 fee for adults, 50¢ for children. Open Tuesday to Saturday from 9 a.m. to 5 p.m. and on Sunday from 2 to 5:30 p.m.

**Fort Pulaski,** a National Monument, is 15 miles east of Savannah off U.S. 80 on Cockspur and McQueens Islands at the very mouth of the Savannah River. It took 18 years to complete the massive, pentagonally shaped fort, with its casemate galleries and drawbridges crossing the moat. It was captured by Union troops in 1862 after a 30-hour bombardment, and you can still see shells from that battle embedded in the walls. There are exhibits on the fort's history in the visitor center, which is open every day except Christmas and New Year's Days from 8:30 a.m. to 5:30 p.m. (to 7 p.m. in summer), and admission is $1 per car. (For complete information, write: Superintendent, Fort Pulaski, P.O. Box 98, Savannah, GA 31328.)

There's a quiet little beach over on **Tybee Island,** a short drive from Savannah on U.S. 80. Oglethorpe built a lighthouse here in 1736, which was destroyed by a storm and replaced in 1773 by a structure you can visit and even climb. Pirates sought haven on Tybee Island, and it was a favorite place for duels between Savannah gentlemen—but today it's a relaxing memorial park playground, with a fishing pier, boat-launching ramp, marina, and a museum featuring historical dioramas, documents, relics, and artwork. For details, contact the Tybee Island Chamber of Commerce, P.O. Box 491, Tybee Island, GA 31328 (tel. 912/786-5444).

If you opt for a few days at this friendly, very casual beach settlement, the very first **Days Inn,** 1402 Butler Ave. (P.O. Box 696), Tybee Island, GA 31328 (tel. 912/786-4576), is still here—it was built in 1970, and is a plain, two-story building just off the oceanfront. Rates are seasonal, with doubles running from $40 to $50. Directly behind it, on the waterfront, the pleasant Veranda Restaurant serves everything from snacks to full meals (home-cooked and delicious) at very moderate prices.

## Some Very Special Events

On the third Sunday of June every year, shrimp boats in and around Savannah gather at Thunderbolt (just over the bridge) for the annual **Blessing of the Fleet.** But if you'd like to see this traditional ceremony and the colorful religious pageant that accompanies it, by all means plan to get there at least three days in advance. There are all sorts of gala activities before the big day itself, and the dances, street fairs, art exhibits, and a general air of celebration create a sort of carnival atmosphere.

They say in New York that "there's a little of Irish in every New Yorker on St. Paddy's Day." Well, in Savannah the same thing goes—their **St. Patrick's Day Parade** on March 17 is second in size only to New York's, and everybody gets into the act, even the Savannah River, which they tell me is dyed green for the day (can't really vouch for *that,* but I can tell you it's a great time to be in the city).

No matter what your ethnic background, you'll fit right in at the annual **Night in Old Savannah,** which celebrates all this country's cultural groups. Blocks are set aside for what amounts to a massive street fair. For three enchanted days there's ethnic food and entertainment in historic Johnson Square. The date is usually in late April, and for specific dates and details, write or call Night in Old Savannah, P.O. Box 14147, Savannah, GA 31416 (tel. 912/355-2422).

Christmas in Savannah is a time of warm sociability, and if you plan to be there during that season, be sure to book for the **Christmas Tour of Homes** sponsored by the Downtown Neighborhood Association. Seven homes are shown on one day of the weekend event, with another seven the next, and there's a candlelight tour included in your ticket. Carriage rides, complete with hand-bell ringers and carolers, are a part of the experience too. For dates, prices, and reservations, contact: Savannah Hospitality Association, P.O. Box 9841, Savannah, GA 31412 (tel. 912/964-1421).

## 2. Brunswick and the Golden Isles

Brunswick is just 81 miles south of Savannah (I-95 is quicker; U.S. 17 more beautiful, although a little longer in mileage). A stopover at Midway, some 30 miles south of Savannah, is worthwhile if only to see the **Midway Church,** which dates back to 1792 (an earlier one burned—this is the "new" church), with its large slave gallery, high pulpit, and colonial-era headstones in the tiny graveyard.

The Colonial Council of the Royal Province of Georgia laid out Brunswick's streets back in 1771, making it another of early Georgia's planned cities. It has always been an important port, with a natural harbor that can handle oceangoing ships. Over the years it has also developed into quite a manufacturing and food-processing center (principally seafood), but there are still several vestiges of its colonial past. It is also a very pretty town, with palms, flowering shrubs, and moss-draped live oaks all over the place. And watching the large fleet of shrimp boats (Brunswick calls itself "Shrimp Capital of the World") put in on a sunny afternoon is a favorite pastime for both locals and visitors.

In addition, Brunswick is the gateway to Georgia's "Golden Isles" (a local appellation), the three best known of that string of lush, semitropical islands that runs the length of the state's coastline. **Sea Island** and **St. Simons** are just across the Torras Causeway (which passes over the famous "Marshes of Glynn" immortalized by poet Sidney Lanier, who came from these parts), and **Jekyll Island** is south of town across the Lanier Bridge, then south on Ga. 50 (don't bother looking for highway numbers, though—large signs point the way). Together, they form one of the loveliest resort areas along the entire Atlantic coast.

The islands haven't always been dedicated to fun in the sun, however. The Spanish had missions on them as early as 1566, and there were peaceful Creek Indians fishing, hunting, and farming here from 2500 B.C., say anthropologists who've studied the evidence. And St. Simons was the scene of the small but important "Battle of Bloody Marsh" in 1742 that probably determined once and for all that the southern part of the country would remain under British, not Spanish, domination. General Oglethorpe had built Fort Frederica on the west side of St. Simons and a smaller battery, Fort St. Simons, on the south end as a defense against the Spanish, who were entrenched in nearby Florida and had a greedy eye on the lands to their north. He didn't have nearly enough troops to repulse any serious Spanish attack, but after the British victory at Bloody Marsh, and some brilliant strategy that included parading the same seven horsemen up and down a faraway beach during one whole day of negotiations to give the illusion of a full complement of cavlary, the Spanish finally were convinced that his position was much stronger than it really was and withdrew from the territory for good.

After the Revolution, the islands were world famous for their Sea Island cotton, grown on huge plantations supported mainly by slave labor. So important was slavery to their economy, in fact, that the last slaver, the *Wanderer,* landed its cargo of Africans on Jekyll Island as late as 1858, with the world looking on: the importing of slaves was by that time illegal, and its crew was promptly arrested. After the Civil War, without their large labor force, the plantations languished and finally disappeared. There was a brief period of prosperity based on a lumber mill on St. Simons (from the 1870s to 1903), and the first daily postal service began in 1876.

It was in the late 1880s, however, that the Golden Isles got into the resort business, when a group of Yankee millionaires "discovered" Jekyll Island and decided it was the ideal retreat from shivery northern weather during January, February, and March. They bought the island for $125,000 and built "cottages" with anywhere from 15 to 25 rooms (remember, these were men with names like J.P. Morgan, P. Lorillard, Vanderbilt, Goodyear, etc.) and a Club House large enough to accommodate up to 100 members. From then until 1947, when second-generation members of the Jekyll Island Club found the island life less glamorous than other "jet set" resorts and sold Jekyll to the state of Georgia for $675,000, the "Millionaires' Village" was so exclusive that no uninvited guest *ever* set foot on the place and even invited guests were limited to visits of no more than two weeks if they stayed in the Club House. Many of those cottages are open to visitors today, and all the attractions that drew those men of wealth and their families are public property, with plenty of accommodations to take care of us "ordinary" folk. One of the not-so-ordinary people to look for relaxation on St. Simons is former President Jimmy Carter, who headed straight there following his election.

As for Sea Island, it was purchased back in 1927 by Howard Coffin (he already owned another "golden isle," Sapelo Island), who built a causeway from St. Simons to reach the five-mile-long barrier island, then set about developing what has become a world-famous resort, The Cloister, which opened in October 1928.

Incidentally, no matter how you approach Brunswick, I strongly recommend a trip to the **Brunswick–Golden Isles Welcome Center,** on I-95 southbound between Exits 8 and 9 (mail address: 4 Glynn Ave., Brunswick, GA 31520; tel. 912/264-0202). The attractive center rivals any state welcome center I've ever seen. The friendly staff can give you any kind of area information you want (and some you may not have even known you wanted); and if you should happen to land here without reservations (God forbid!), they have an electronic reservations board for more than 20 hotels and motels with up-to-the-minute vacancy data and can book a room for you right there. There's also a Welcome Center at 2000 Glynn Ave., Brunswick, GA 31520 (tel. 912/264-5337).

**WHERE TO STAY:** Where you stay will probably depend on how you plan to visit the islands. If this is only a way station for you, with just a quick look around, then your best bet is to stop at one of the motels clustered at the U.S. 341/I-95 interchange, where restaurants, service stations, stores, gift shops, and easy access to the islands causeway add up to real convenience. It's a different story, of course, if a few days' escape from the cares of civilization in an island setting is what you're after.

## Sea Island

Sea Island (northernmost of the Golden Isles) *means* the world-famous **Cloister Hotel,** Sea Island, GA 31561 (tel. toll free 800/841-3223, 800/342-6874 in Georgia). Operating on full American plan (which means three superb meals a day are included), the Cloister, a Spanish-Moorish-style complex roofed with red tile, has 264 rooms in the main building and its newer, adjacent low-rise hotel structures (separately sited, with garden-like surroundings), all complete with the ultimate in luxury, convenience, and comfort. Hotel guests and occupants of some 400 privately owned homes (often available for rental) enjoy the Sea Island Beach Club, with a diving pool, heated swimming pool, wading pool, sundecks for acquiring that island tan, luxurious dining rooms right at the ocean's edge, and the particularly charming Spanish Lounge, with three cloister windows, high wooden ceilings, wood-burning fireplaces, and oversize armchairs. Facilities also include golf (54 holes), tennis (18 all-weather courts), riding stables, skeet and trap shooting, fishing and boating docks, bicycles (the best way of all to get around, in my humble opinion), and lawn sports like croquet, shuffleboard, and chip and putt. There's dancing every night and special events feature plantation suppers, cookouts, musical happenings, and al fresco dinner-dances. This elegant place has been family owned since it opened in 1928, and with a staff ratio of three employees to every two guests, you'll begin to get that pampered feeling the minute you register. Rates change with the seasons and vary according to room type and location. From March 15 to May 31, doubles run $176 to $304, but drop drastically other months. And remember, *rates include all meals.* Golf, tennis, and honeymoon (and what a perfect honeymoon spot!) package plans are available.

## St. Simons

The **King and Prince Beach Hotel,** Arnold Road, St. Simons Island, GA 31522 (tel. 912/638-3631), is more an experience than just a hotel. The 95-room inn is directly on the ocean, and from the moment you step into the elegant and long verandas and patios, shaded by ancient oaks and lots and lots of palm trees, are an open invitation to sit and unwind. The food is legendary and includes a chicken with wine sauce and a "Mile High Pie" that's out of this world. When you're tired of sitting, there's a pool (and the beach, of course), tennis, golf, fishing, sailing, horseback riding, and bikes for exploring the island. Oceanfront doubles range from $60 to $115, with rates descending for ocean view, courtyard view (charming), and studio rooms. Three-bedroom villas run $115 to $220.

**Sea Palms Golf and Tennis Resort,** Frederica Road, St. Simons Island, GA 31522 (tel. 912/638-3351, or toll free 800/841-6268), covers some 800 acres that accommodate both permanent residents and vacationers. Thus holidayers become part of an entire community, rather than simply a resort development. There are fully furnished one-, two-, and three-bedroom villas overlooking the golf course and the Marshes of Glynn, as well as the newer, very posh Sea Marsh Villas. A championship golf course and the wooded, secluded Sea Palms

Racquet Club with 12 all-weather, lighted courts are highlights. Other amenities include pools, a playground, health center, sauna and whirlpool, and the delightful Oglethorpe's Restaurant. Rates for hotel rooms range from $70 to $196; villas are $120 to $214. Best buys, however, are the large range of tennis and golf plans, and off-season lower rates.

The less expensive **Sea Gate Inn**, 1014 Ocean Blvd., St. Simons Island, GA 31522 (tel. 912/638-8661), has 49 rooms. All are bright and colorful and some have kitchens, private patios, or balconies. There's free coffee for all, and although there is no dining room, restaurants are only three blocks away. Rates range from $40 to $85 for rooms, $90 to $130 for one- or two-bedroom condos.

**Queen's Court Motel**, 437 Kings Way, St. Simons Island, GA 31522 (tel. 912/638-8459), is a complex of two-story buildings surrounding a shaded, grassy lawn. Rooms come with one double bed or two single beds, and there are suites with two double beds and a large sitting room, as well as kitchenette units. Rates for doubles range from $35 to $55, depending on the type of accommodation. No pets allowed.

Private cottages are available for weekly or monthly rental on St. Simons, and you can get an illustrated brochure with rates and availability information from: **Parker-Kaufman Realtors**, 1699 Frederica Rd., St. Simons Island, GA 31522 (tel. 912/638-3368).

## Jekyll Island

The newest star on Jekyll Island is the **Jekyll Club Hotel**, 371 Riverview Dr., Jekyll Island, GA 31520 (tel. 912/635-2600, or toll free 800/822-1886, 800/843-5355 in Georgia). In the heyday of Jekyll's millionaires, the rambling, white-shingled Club was the center of social activities, and deluxe lodgings for privileged guests. In 1987 the Club reopened as a Radisson Hotels Resort, with 136 gorgeous guest rooms, pool, tennis, shopping, and access to the island's 63 holes of golf and ten miles of beaches. Doubles are $75 to $115; suites, $125 to $250.

The **Quality Inn Buccaneer**, 85 Beachview Dr., Jekyll Island, GA 31520 (tel. 912/635-2261, or toll free 800/228-5151), is a 214-room beach resort in a setting of lush foliage. Rooms all have a private balcony or terrace and border on the luxurious. For families, there are kitchenettes available and the children's playground comes in handy. Golfers and tennis buffs will find a home here, and there's a pool in addition to that gorgeous beach. The ocean-view restaurant features very good regional cooking. Rates April through Labor Day are $38 to $89 for double rooms, with lower rates the rest of the year.

**Villa-by-the-Sea**, 1175 N. Beachview Dr., Jekyll Island, GA 31520 (tel. 912/635-2521, or toll free 800/841-6262), has 160 villas for an oceanside home away from home. They furnish free island and airport transportation, and other amenities include daily maid service, laundromats, babysitting, and planned activities for adults and children. Golf, tennis, and pool or ocean swimming come along with the sumptuous apartments. An excellent restaurant specializes in fresh seafood, and there's a lounge with entertainment. Double-occupancy rates range from $70 to $120 in high season, lower other months.

**Jekyll Island Hilton Inn**, 975 N. Beachview Dr., Jekyll Island, GA 31520 (tel. 912/635-2531), on the northern end of Jekyll Island, is a cluster of townhouse accommodations and 264 spacious rooms. All are beautifully appointed and offer a wide selection of location and view. All town houses are fully equipped with kitchens. The restaurant features coastal seafood specialties, and there's a lounge that commands a spectacular view of the Atlantic Ocean. Rates: June 16 to September 15, $70 and up; lower other months. Very good golf packages are offered.

Jekyll Island cottage rental rates and availability can be obtained through **Parker-Kaufman Realtors**, Beachview Drive (P.O. Box 3126), Jekyll Island, GA 31520 (tel. 912/635-2512).

## Camping

Jekyll Island has a family campground with per-night or weekly rates. The **Cherokee Campground** (tel. 912/635-2592) charges $12 per night or $70.50 per week for sites with electric and/or sewer hookup, lower rates without. Facilities include bathhouses, automatic laundry equipment, pure tapwater, garbage pickup (as well as an emptying station for self-contained units), LP gas service, and bike rentals. Some tent sites are also available at lower rates.

**EATING ON THE ISLANDS:** Gourmet dining reigns supreme at most of the hotels listed for all three islands, but be sure to reserve for dinner at places like **The Cloister** (use the telephone numbers shown for the hotels, above). However, excellent dining at less expensive prices is also available on St. Simons.

**Blanche's Courtyard**, 440 Kings Way (tel. 912/638-8892), serves mostly seafood in a Victorian atmosphere, with lots of old brickwork, antiques, and a private patio. On Friday and Saturday, there's entertainment (dress is casual). Dinner hours are 5:30 to 10 p.m., and prices range from $9 to $16.

Altogether different is the rustic decor of the **Crab Trap**, 1209 Ocean Blvd. (tel. 912/638-3552). No fancy trappings, but the seafood is superb. Fresh local shrimp, oysters, and scallops come with coleslaw and hushpuppies, at prices that range from $6 to $12. Dinner is served Monday through Saturday from 5 to 10 p.m.

**Emmeline and Hessie**, 100 Marina Dr. (tel. 912/638-9084), was named after two ferries that once plied the waters between Brunswick and St. Simons, a fitting appellation for this unique restaurant overlooking the Intracoastal Waterway and St. Simons Bay. So well does it fit into its setting that raccoons come right up to the picture windows, begging to be fed. Inside, its ship decor is cozied up by plants and more plants. As you'd expect, seafood tops the menu here, with a live lobster tank, specialty shrimp dishes, and an excellent oyster bar. They do their own baking and dish up homemade soup and sauces. Hours are 11:30 a.m. to midnight daily except Sunday, and dinner prices are in the $9 to $18 range (with children's plates from $6).

A warm, rustic interior with lots of exposed beams greets you at **Frederica House**, 3611 Frederica Rd. (tel. 912/638-6789). It's right in the center of St. Simons, and serves regional seafood specialties, as well as beef dishes, at dinner only. Hours are 6 to 10 p.m., and reservations are definitely in order (casual dress is also in order).

At **Poor Stephen's**, on Frederica Road (tel. 912/638-7316), they serve burgers, chowder, salads, and *great* sandwiches from noon until ? (that usually means about 11 p.m., but they refuse to post a quitting time). There's a lounge, very popular with islanders, that stays open from noon until 2 a.m. Prices run from under a dollar to about $5, dress is casual, and this place is a real find.

On Jekyll Island, look for the small, rustic **café** at the end of the pier at the Marina, where fresh-caught seafood is sold at remarkably low prices.

**READER'S DINING SUGGESTION:** "A nice stop for us at St. Simons was **Dana's**, near the St. Simons pier—good chili and other snacks, very reasonable, in a woody, barn-like building" (M. Ryan, New York, N.Y.).

**ISLAND ACTIVITIES:** Well, there are the **beaches**—and they're absolutely gorgeous on all three islands. Sunning or splashing, you'll find the fine-sand strand and the gentle-surfed ocean ideal. There are beachfront bathhouses on Jekyll's east shore.

Golfers can pretend they're Jekyll Island millionaires and play the Ocean-side Nine holes those gentlemen patterned after the "olde" course at St. Andrews, Scotland. Or the three 18-hole **golf** courses on the island, **Oleander, Pine Lakes,** and **Indian Mound.** Fees are $9 a day for nine holes, $14.50 for unlimited, all-day play.

Also on Jekyll Island are eight outdoor **tennis** courts ($6 an hour) and one indoor ($8 an hour), **bicycle** rentals ($3 an hour, $6 for four hours, $10 for all day) and bike paths, pier **fishing** (at no charge), and charter boats for offshore and inlet fishing. No license is required for saltwater fishing; freshwater licenses cost $6 for five days and can be obtained at most hardware or sporting goods stores or at the **Howard Coffin Recreational Park** in Brunswick (freshwater fish around here include bream, red breast, crappie or white perch, shad, bass, and trout). Deep-sea fishing can be arranged by calling the **Troupe Creek Marina** (it's on Yacht Road, east of U.S. 17N) at 912/264-3862.

The **Aquarama,** on Beachview Drive and Parkway, is a modernistic structure with a circular ballroom for dancing and an Olympic-size outdoor swimming pool overlooking the ocean. Check when you get there about dancing times and charges.

You can visit the Jekyll Island Club Historical District and the **Millionaires' Village "cottages"** (translate "mansions") on a 1½-hour interpretive tour. The tour originates at the Museum Orientation Center on Stable Road (tel. 635-2762 or 635-2727). Highlights of the tour include a stained-glass window that Louis Comfort Tiffany personally installed in Faith Chapel in 1904 and several of the buildings themselves (all others may only be seen from the outside). Adults pay $6; students 6 to 18 years, $4; and children under 6, free.

Jekyll is also the site of Georgia's first **brewery** (on the northwest end of the island), started by General Oglethorpe, who evidently knew how to "put first things first" for his settlers. Very near the brewery stand the ruins of a home built in 1738 by William Horton, one of Oglethorpe's captains. It was constructed of "tabby," a mortar made of lime, sand, oyster shells, and water, and much used in coastal areas during colonial times.

St. Simons Island is real sightseeing territory. No sightseer worthy of the name would miss **Fort Frederica National Monument** on the northwest end of the island. About all that's left of the original construction is a small portion of the King's Magazine and the barracks tower, but archeological excavations have unearthed many foundations, and the visitor center has a film on the history of the fort and the town, which once had a population of 1,000. There's a donation box, with a possible $1.50 admission fee in the near future, and it's open every day from 8 a.m. to 5 p.m., later during the summer.

I guess my personal favorite on St. Simons is the **Museum of Coastal History,** in the restored lighthouse keeper's house next to the St. Simons Light at 600 Beachview Dr. There are six rooms of artifacts, books, letters, photos, and a Victorian parlor that sets my romantic mind dreaming. Hardy souls will want to climb the lighthouse's 129 steps for a spectacular view of the Golden Isles. There are changing exhibits, and the $1.50 admission for adults, $1 for ages 6 to 12, includes the museum and the lighthouse. Hours are 10 a.m. to 5 p.m. Tuesday through Saturday and 1:30 to 5 p.m. on Sunday, from Memorial Day to Labor Day; 1 to 4 p.m. Tuesday through Saturday and 1:30 to 4 p.m. on Sunday, in other months.

Then there's the **Coastal Center for the Arts,** on Demere Road near the airport, where local and "traveling" art and craft exhibits are displayed, and there are lectures, classes, and demonstrations. It is open from 11 a.m. to 5 p.m.

weekdays, September through May; 10 a.m. to 5 p.m. in June, July, and August.

Scattered from end to end of St. Simons are ruins of the plantation era: **Hampton Plantation** (where Aaron Burr spent a month after his duel with Alexander Hamilton), and **Cannon's Point** on the north; **West Point, Pines Bluff,** and **Hamilton Plantations** on the west along the Frederica River; **Harrington Hall** and **Mulberry Grove** in the interior; **Lawrence, St. Clair, Black Banks, The Village,** and **Kelvyn Grove** on the east; and **Retreat Plantation** on the south end. Ruins are about all you'll see today, but there's a restored chapel on the West Point Plantation (made of tabby, the mortar turned pink because of an unusual lichen; natives say it reflected blood on the hands of Dr. Thomas Hazzard, who killed a neighbor in a land dispute and built the chapel after being so ostracized by island society that he would not attend Christ Church), and tabby slave cabins which have been restored and put to use (one is an activity center of the Methodist-run Epworth-by-the-Sea; another is home of the Island Garden Club on Gascoigne Bluff).

**Christ Church,** 6329 Frederica Rd. at the north end of the island, was built first in 1820, on ground where John and Charles Wesley had preached under the oaks in 1736. It was virtually destroyed when Union troops camped here during the Civil War, burning pews for firewood and butchering cattle in the chapel. Then, in 1886, Anson Greene Phelps Dodge, Jr., restored it as a memorial to his first wife, who had died on their honeymoon. It's a serene, white wooden building nestled under huge old oaks and looks exactly as an island church should. The doors are open every day from 2 to 5 p.m. during Daylight Saving Time months, 1 to 4 p.m. other times, and there is, of course, no charge to go inside.

**NIGHTLIFE:** After dark, social life centers around motel lounges, like the Buccaneer's **Leeward Lounge** or the Wanderer's **Pirates Cove,** with more elegant entertainment at **The Cloister.** There's entertainment also at **Misty's Lounge** in the Hilton Inn. Check with the Information Center on Jekyll Island to see what's going on when you're there.

**EXCURSIONS FROM THE GOLDEN ISLES:** There are several day and half-day trips from the islands. **Brunswick,** for example, has some sights to see: the **James Oglethorpe Monument** (a statue of Georgia's founder) in Queens Square on the east side of Newcastle Street; the **Lover's Oak,** a giant, 900-year-old oak at Albany and Prince Streets; **Lanier's Oak** (honoring the poet), half a mile south of town on U.S. 17; and **Bay Street** (between Third and Gloucester), lined with seafood-processing plants, where you can watch the shrimp boats dock beginning about 3 p.m., a lively, interesting spectacle.

A longer trip is the one inland to Waycross to visit the **Okefenokee Swamp.** This is the largest freshwater swamp still preserved in the U.S., some 700 square miles, and it really presents a picture of nature in the raw. The best entrance is about eight miles south of Waycross on U.S. 1, U.S. 23, and Ga. 177, where there are cypress boardwalks out over the swamp, an observation tower, serpentarium, picnic area, and interpretive centers. The admission charge ($5 for adults, $3 for children under 12) includes a two-mile boat trip along waterways lined with thickly tangled growth and alive with snakes, alligators, and lovely white blossoms of water plants. The swamp is a fantastic "other world," but it may not be for you if you're squeamish when it comes to reptiles, spiders (they come in giant sizes), and the like. If you're squeamish but still interested, a better place to visit is the **Okefenokee Heritage Center,** two miles west of Waycross on U.S. 82 (tel. 912/285-4260). There are a restored 1912 steam locomotive and depot, an "operating" 1890 print shop, the restored 1840 Gen. Thomas Hilliard

House, and general exhibits on local history, the arts, sciences, and special studies. There's a small admission fee, and hours are 10 a.m. to 5 p.m. Tuesday through Saturday, and 2 to 4 p.m. on Sunday.

At that same site, there's no charge to visit the **Southern Forest World** (tel. 912/285-4056), a museum depicting the development and history of the forest industry in the South. The collection includes a logging train, tools, and other forestry-related artifacts, as well as a variety of audio-visuals to expound on the subject. Hours are the same as at the Heritage Center.

## 3. Cumberland Island

If the semisophistication and wide variety of things to do at the above islands are what you're looking for on Georgia's coast, you're not likely to want to come to Cumberland Island. If, on the other hand, total peace, unspoiled natural surroundings, and a sense of what these islands were like from the beginning of time until man started "developing" them, have special meaning for you, then Cumberland will draw you like a magnet! Nowhere else on the East Coast are those island qualities so perfectly preserved.

On this little bit of offshore land (just 16 miles long and 3 miles across at its widest point), man has been in residence since as long as 4,000 years ago, but rather than "develop" the resources here, he has lived in harmony with all manner of wildlife and spectacular tree and plant life, using only those necessary for survival and moving in rhythm with nature's patterns. True, timber was harvested here at one time to supply shipbuilders. True, also, cotton was once cultivated on the island as a commercial crop. But neither was undertaken on a destructive, industrial basis, and nothing was done to upset the balance struck by natural forces as they piled up sand and marshes to create this little bit of paradise that one writer describes as existing "somewhere between Atlantis, Bali Hai, and the Garden of Eden."

To step onto Cumberland Island is to step into a wilderness of maritime forest (with tunnel-like roads canopied by live oaks, cabbage palms, magnolia, holly, red cedar, and pine), salt marshes alive with waving grasses, sand dunes arranged by wind and tide into a double line of defense against destruction by those very forces, and gleaming sand beaches that measure a few hundred yards at low tide. It is to enter a breathtaking world of animal life, where alligators wallow in marshes, whitetailed deer bound through the trees or graze peacefully at dusk, wild pigs snuffle the undergrowth for food, armadillos move their armored-tank shapes about freely, wild turkeys roam unmolested, over 300 species of birds wheel overhead, and wild horses canter in herds or pick their way peacefully to watering holes.

It's enchanted, this island.

**WHERE TO STAY:** There's only one place *to* stay on Cumberland, and it's no less enchanted than the island itself. The only commercial building (if you can call it that), **Greyfield Inn** (Drawer B, Fernandina Beach, FL 32034; tel. 904/261-6408) is a three-story plantation mansion with a wide, inviting veranda set in a grove of live oaks. Built shortly after the turn of the century as a summer retreat by Thomas Carnegie (Andrew's brother and partner), Greyfield has remained family property ever since. Guests today are treated very much like family visitors in years past—the extensive and very valuable library is open for your perusal; furnishings are those the family has always used; the bar is an open one, operated on an honor system (you simply pour your own and note it on a pad); meals are served buffet style from a mahogany sideboard and you dine at the long family table, adorned with heirloom silver candlesticks; and you're at liberty to browse through old family photo albums, scrapbooks, and other memorabilia scattered about the large, paneled living room (if the weather is cool, there'll be a fire in the oversize fireplace). Soft chimes announce meals (dinnertime means "dress"—informal dresses and jackets, no shorts or jeans). And what meals! Seafood is likely to have been caught that very morning, and cooked to perfection. It's roast beef on Saturday night, and a fun-for-all oyster roast every Sunday night. Breakfasts are also sumptuous, and if beachcombing or exploring is what you have in mind for the day, the inn will pack a picnic lunch to carry along. As for the upstairs rooms, they vary in size from the large suite once used by the mother of Lucy Carnegie Ferguson (Thomas's granddaughter and the present owner) to less spacious ones. Bathrooms are shared and still hold the original, old-fashioned massive fittings.

In short, you will, as I said before, feel exactly like a family guest at Greyfield. Best of all, the friendly staff will *treat* you like family. The inn is staffed by Mrs. Ferguson's grandchildren. They're all on a first-name basis with guests and full of knowledge about Cumberland and how to enjoy it.

Rates at this unique inn, which include all three meals, are $90 to $95 per person daily (10% discount for children under 10). Since there are accommodations for only 18 guests, reservations must be made well in advance. A 50% deposit is required, and a 15% gratuity will be added to your bill, as well as a 5% tax.

### How to Get There

There's an airstrip near the inn, and air taxi arrangements can be made from Jacksonville or St. Simons Island (call the inn for details). But the best way to reach Greyfield is by its own ferry, the *Robert W. Ferguson*, which maintains a regular schedule to Fernandina Beach, Florida (a few miles east of I-95 on Ga. 40). Reservations are necessary on the *R.W.*, as it is affectionately known, and must be made through the inn. Round trip for passengers is $15. For cars, there's a $35 one-way fare. I strongly urge that you take your car or a bicycle, since there's no transportation on the island. If you don't wish to do so, however, you can leave your car with complete safety in the Fernandina Beach parking lot (across from the police station) until you return.

**THINGS TO SEE AND DO:** Don't look for a swimming pool, tennis courts, or a golf course—Cumberland's attractions are a different sort. The inn is just a short walk from those high sand dunes and a wild, undeveloped beach that had me looking for Long John Silver's longboat coming through the swells. Beachcombing, swimming, shelling, and fishing are high on the list of activities, but exploring the island and drinking in its long history offer stiff competition.

There are no signs left of the Indians who lived here some 4,000 years ago, unless you count the base of shells that underlies almost all roadways on the island. Nor can you find traces of Franciscan missionaries who came to convert the Indians during the 1500s. No ruins exist of the fort built at each end by Gen. James Oglethorpe in the 1700s as protection against Spanish invaders. The only thing that remains of Oglethorpe's hunting lodge is its name, Dungeness, a name that has clung to Gen. Nathanael Greene's post-Revolutionary mansion built of tabby (which burned to the ground after the Civil War) and its successor, a massive Carnegie mansion built on the same site.

What you *can* find as you poke around this fascinating place are: the ruins of Carnegie's Dungeness (which burned in 1959) and the still-standing recreation building which housed spacious guest rooms, an indoor swimming pool, squash court, gymnasium, and billiard room; the Greene-Miller (Phineas Miller was Mrs. Greene's second husband) cemetery that first held the remains of

Henry "Lighthorse Harry" Lee before they were removed to Virginia and still evokes ghosts of its inhabitants from Revolutionary times right through the Civil War era; Stafford plantation house and, down the lane a bit, "the chimneys," a melancholy ruin of post–Civil War drama (ask at the inn for the full story); Plum Orchard, a magnificent Carnegie mansion, fully furnished but unoccupied and now the property of the National Park Service; and most of all, the hushed solemnity of island roads, pathways, and fields being reclaimed by native plants and wildlife. In a very real sense, the past lives vividly in today's unchanged island environment.

**SPECIAL NOTE:** Since 1972, most of Cumberland Island has been a National Seashore administered by the National Park Service. Ferry service is available from St. Marys, Ga., by reservation (write: Superintendent, P.O. Box 806, St. Marys, GA 31558; tel. 912/882-4335). There are usually two trips in each direction daily from Memorial Day to Labor Day, weekdays only thereafter, but schedules and fares are subject to change.

Along with Cumberland, you can savor the wild beauty of Georgia's coast on **Little St. Simons Island.** Reached by boat from St. Simons, Little St. Simons, P.O. Box 1078, St. Simons Island, GA 31577 (tel. 912/638-7472), is a 10,000-acre privately owned sanctuary that offers you the uncrowded run of six miles of undeveloped beaches, fishing, swimming, horseback riding, and birdwatching for 200 species. Accommodations are rustic but comfortable lodges, some built before 1920, and newer ones opened in the past three years. Meals, served family style, feature locally caught seafoods and southern staples like fried chicken and barbecue. Singles are $145, and doubles run $225, including all meals and facilities.

# Chapter XIII

# CENTRAL AND WESTERN GEORGIA

## 1. Atlanta
## 2. Pine Mountain
## 3. Plains and Other Area Attractions

THIS INLAND SECTION of Georgia is the land of Scarlett O'Hara, Martin Luther King, Jr., Coca-Cola, peach orchards, pecan groves, and Jimmy Carter. It is also a land of giant textile mills, pulp and paper plants, and manufacturing centers for automobiles, metal, chemicals, and furniture that bear the definite stamp of the New South. Which is not to say that Georgia, which suffered mightily under the heel of General Sherman during the Civil War, does not retain and value its Old South heritage. It does, and there are symbols of it everywhere. But primarily this part of the state looks forward, not backward.

Atlanta, the state's capital since 1868, typifies the economic vigor of inland Georgia, having recovered from almost total destruction to become the leading manufacturing and commercial center in the entire South. Agriculture, which has always been important, is now practiced on a grand scale, with tobacco, watermelons, sugarcane, okra, and pimiento peppers following close behind peaches, pecans, and peanuts in importance. And the region is rich in commercial clays and limestone, marble, granite, bauxite, talc, and feldspar, all of which are mined profitably.

## 1. Atlanta

Georgia's capital is literally a railroad city. In fact, for a long time it had no name except "The Terminus," since it was the southern end of a Western and Atlantic Railroad spur linking the state with Tennessee and points west. A civil engineer who had surveyed the rail route is said to have predicted that it would "be a good location for one tavern, a blacksmith shop, a grocery store, and nothing else." That was back in 1837 (the first run on the line did not come until 1842), and the little settlement of dirt-floored shacks and wide-open bars kept its "work camp" atmosphere through two name changes (first to Marthasville, then Atlanta—a female form of the "Atlantic" in the railroad's name) and a municipal charter in 1847 that made it a legitimate town.

But as more and more rail lines met at the junction, life became more civilized and businessmen arrived to attend to the warehousing, distributing, and wholesaling of freight coming in by rail. When the Confederacy came into being, Atlanta was an important supply and arms center, a role for which it paid dearly when Gen. William T. Sherman fought a long, bitter battle to win the city for the Union, kept it under harsh military rule from September to November of 1864 (most civilians were evacuated during this period), then burned all but 400 of its 3,600 homes and destroyed its railroads before setting out on his "march to the sea."

Only four years later, however, Atlanta had recovered to the point that it could be named the state capital (partly because of its location and the accessibility through rebuilt railroads to all parts of the state). The collapse of a slavery-based plantation economy proved a boon to this trade-oriented city and its growth hasn't faltered since those Reconstruction recovery days. It has enlarged its rail transportation system, brought in six Interstate highways (the trucking industry is now an important part of the local scene), and acquired an airport second only to Chicago's O'Hare in traffic. Its standing in the business world is such that 450 of the "Fortune 500" national corporations have offices here, and many have moved their home offices to the city.

The effect on Atlantans of all this commerce with the outside world has been to breed a cosmopolitanism and sort of acquired sophistication that keeps them constantly working to bring culture (whether it be in the form of the classical arts or entertainment of the "popular" genre) to their city. Although it never has been one of those legendary "sleepy southern towns," Atlanta today almost wiggles visibly with cultural activity. There are concerts and cabarets, ballets and bar-lounges, art galleries and avant-garde "happenings"—and the influx of European-cuisine restaurants has made it harder and harder to find fried chicken, country ham, hot biscuits, and grits. Today's Atlantans will tell you that their town is the "New York of the South"—and then proceed to take you by the hand and prove it.

**GETTING AROUND ATLANTA:** I'd like to offer one vital bit of advice to Atlanta visitors—if a native offers to show you around, by all means go! Otherwise, park your car and take advantage of the city's excellent bus and rapid rail system. **MARTA,** Metropolitan Atlanta Rapid Transit System, has 140 bus routes, and a clean, modern rapid rail system. The East-West rapid rail line runs from suburban Decatur and Avondale on the east, through the Georgia State University/State Capitol area downtown, to the western suburbs, where you may make a bus connection for Six Flags Over Georgia theme park. By 1988 the North-South Line will extend from Hartsfield International Airport, through downtown to the Woodruff Arts Center and the Buckhead/Lenox Square area. The two lines converge at the Five Points Station downtown. Fare is 60¢ one way, 30¢ for senior citizens with cards purchased at the Five Points Station. All-day parking is available at many suburban stations for 60¢. Change machines are located inside the stations. Trains run every five to seven minutes from 5 a.m. to 1:30 a.m. seven days. Phone 404/522-4711 for schedules and information.

Atlanta's **taxis** are a major *caveat emptor.* Many are unclean, mechanically suspect, and manned by drivers not familiar with the city. Be sure your driver has a lock on your destination, and that the fare is settled, before setting off. The most reliable are **Yellow Cab** (tel. 404/521-0200) and **London Cab** (tel. 404/681-2280). The fixed rate between the airport and downtown hotels is $13.50. Taxis usually cannot be flagged down on the streets, as in New York, but must be called, or met at major hotels.

I can tell you from a long history of turning around and going back that

Atlanta is one of the hardest cities on the face of the earth to get around if you weren't born and raised in its street "system," which isn't a system at all, just a perplexing maze of streets (at least to a stranger) that seem to have no particular plan. I don't think I've ever been in the city behind a wheel without being lost at least once. On the other hand, the buses or the monorail go everywhere, taxis are plentiful (although you usually have to get them at a hotel stand or by telephoning; see above), and even if you get lost while driving, some helpful local will set you straight with a friendly smile.

Having said all that, for what it's worth here are a few tips about Atlanta's streets. In the center of the downtown area, Peachtree, Marietta, Decatur, Edgewood, and Whitehall Streets come together at **Five Points Intersection**; and all those NE, NW, SE, and SW addresses stem from this point. Peachtree runs north and south through the city, North Avenue and Ponce de Leon run east and west, and I-75 (Northwest and South Expressways) and I-85 (Northeast Expressway) circle downtown. I-20 (the East and West Expressways) runs through the city center. And don't be misled by "Expressway": at rush hours, they're as clogged as city streets, so plan accordingly. Another thing to remember is that "Peachtree" doesn't always mean Peachtree *Street* (which is the *real* main street in Atlanta): there are 26 "Peachtrees"—if it's followed by Drive, View, Circle, Avenue, or anything else, it isn't *the* Peachtree Street!

**ATLANTA CAR RENTALS:** If you arrive in Atlanta via public transportation, but feel the need for wheels during your stay, there is a firm you should know about to save considerably over rates at major rental firms. **Rent-a-Bug**, 1377 Virginia Ave., East Point (that's near the airport), Atlanta, GA 30344 (tel. 404/763-2313), no longer rents VWs. However, they do have Toyotas, Ford Escorts, and a few other makes, most of which are compacts. There are 200 free miles for daily rentals, 1,000 on a weekly basis. This friendly, family-owned business is also helpful with maps and general directions. You pay for gas, and you should give as much advance notice as possible, since it's extremely popular.

**WHERE TO STAY:** Two of Atlanta's splashiest hotels are in large complexes. The Peachtree Plaza is surrounded by a forest of shops, and the Omni International Hotel is neighbor to shops, movie theaters, discos, restaurants, and a three-block-long convention center. Both are in the heart of town, and both are terribly expensive. But luxury hotels are nothing new to Atlanta, and although I have tried throughout this book to stress moderately priced accommodations (and will do so here, as well), there are hotels which fall into the expensive category that simply cannot be omitted in any discussion of this city. More than that, Atlanta now has an exquisite old-world hotel in a downtown location that would top any traveler's list for pure charm.

### Old-World Elegance

While Atlanta has for years had a plentiful supply of glittering high-rise hotels that offer the ultimate in luxury, the **Ritz-Carlton, Atlanta,** 181 Peachtree St. NE, Atlanta, GA 30303 (tel. 404/659-0400, or toll free 800/241-3333), is the welcome addition of a small, personal-service hotel. Located right in the heart of the business district on the corner of Peachtree and Ellis Streets, the Ritz-Carlton is a 25-story, rose-marble structure whose interior projects an old-world graciousness and charm very rare in modern hotels. The sunken lobby features Oriental rugs, paneled walls, touches of bronze, and fine antique furnishings interspersed with comfortable seating. Up the dramatic stairway there's one of the most club-like, intimate lounges I've come across, beyond which is the elegant dining room called simply The Restaurant. Even the elevators exude elegance, with the same paneling and bronze as the lobby. Guest rooms are restful refuges of traditional furnishings, bay windows, an honor bar, fresh flowers, and marble bathrooms. If there's an "extra" they've omitted, *I* couldn't think of it! And both the 24th and 25th floors have been set apart as The Club, where guests enjoy a private lounge with complimentary refreshments and the services of a personal concierge. Personal service, however, is not limited to those floors: under the watchful eye of the personable head concierge, Ronald Beattie (a Scotsman with long years of service at Glen Eagles behind him), every guest has access to a bevy of friendly, efficient assistants who happily arrange for limousine airport pickup, business services, tickets to local events, personal shopping, and almost any whim your fancy can whip up. Lunch and dinners in The Restaurant are both gourmet quality and accompanied by sophisticated piano music; The Café, just off the lobby, serves lighter fare from 6:30 a.m. to midnight; and the small lobby lounge offers continental breakfasts, afternoon tea, and cocktails. This is truly a gem of a hotel in one of the city's most convenient locations. Double rates range from $140 to $195.

If an "uptown" Buckhead location suits your purposes better, there's the **Ritz-Carlton, Buckhead,** 3434 Peachtree Rd. NE, Atlanta, GA 30326 (tel. 404/237-2700, or toll free 800/241-3333). The three-year-old hotel completed an extensive rejuvenation in early 1987, and now is more splendid than ever. Public areas and dining rooms are rich with Italian marble, mahogany, crystal, and rare African woods. A museum's worth of 18th- and 19th-century English and French paintings and artworks further add to the luster of this magnificent hotel. With its dark-wood paneling, cheery fireplaces, and artworks, the new Ritz-Carlton Bar is reminiscent of Claridge's in London. The hotel is one of only two in Georgia, and 45 in the U.S., Canada, and Mexico, to receive AAA's Five Diamond Award. Doubles run $165 to $195.

## Expensive

The **Westin Peachtree Plaza,** 210 Peachtree St. NE, Atlanta, GA 30303 (tel. 404/659-1400, or toll free 800/228-3000), is that circular tower you'll notice soaring over Atlanta's skyline. It's 73 stories high, North America's tallest hotel, designed by Atlanta architect John Portman, who helped set the trend to atrium-lobby hotels with the Hyatt Regency a few years back. There's a Tivoli Gardens look to the newly renovated lobby, and glass elevators climb all the way to the top on the outside of the building. Rooms are plush, to say the least, with vibrant, modern furnishings. Needless to say, nothing has been overlooked in the way of guest facilities: there's a heated pool, several bars and restaurants, a health club and sauna, and a revolving rooftop bar and Sun Dial Restaurant (which also has a stationary level just in case you don't *want* to revolve). If big, innovative, and opulent is your thing, this is certainly the place to find it! Double rooms start at $124 and go up—and if you're really a big spender, you can get a two-floor "super-suite" for $1,000!

The **Omni International,** 1 CNN Center, Atlanta, GA 30335 (tel. 404/659-0000 or toll free 800/843-6664), anchors a modernistic megastructure that's now home of Ted Turner's Cable News Network. The marble lobby and tastefully luxurious guest rooms are very European. Doubles are in the $90 to $170 range. The hotel is across the street from the Georgia World's Congress Center and the Omni coliseum.

The **Hyatt Regency,** 265 Peachtree St. NE, Atlanta, GA 30303 (tel. 404/577-1234 or toll free 800/228-9000), was the first of Atlanta's "super hotels," and I confess to preferring it over many of the others. Its 23-story atrium lobby is somewhat more subdued, although it definitely is striking, with a gold and silver aluminum and stainless-steel sculpture that extends from the second level to the

12th, much greenery, and glass elevators that go all the way to the blue-domed, revolving restaurant and cocktail lounge. This hotel, with over 1,300 rooms and suites, has just completed a major renovation in preparation for its 20th anniversary. There's an outdoor pool, hot tub, several lounges, and four restaurants. Rates range from $100 to $375 for deluxe suites, with reduced $59 weekend rates and seasonal special rates.

The **Atlanta Hilton & Towers,** 255 Courtland St., at Harris Street, Atlanta, GA 30043 (tel. 404/659-2000, or toll free 800/445-8667), is downtown Atlanta's only resort hotel. Located just off I-75/85, in the heart of the business and entertainment district, the Hilton features lighted tennis courts, a jogging track, swimming pool, and a health club with an exercise room, whirlpool, and sauna. Seven restaurants and lounges include the four-star Nikolai's Roof, Café de la Paix, and Trader Vic's restaurants, a 24-hour coffeeshop, and Another World, the exotic nightclub atop the hotel. The International Shopping Mall houses gift and variety shops along with a hi-tech business support center. Double rooms run $119 to $159.

## All-Suites

There are two Guest Quarters locations in Atlanta, one slightly lower in rates than the other, both superbly equipped with all the deluxe features that distinguish this chain (see Chapter I). There is one addition in both hotels, however, that is definitely worth a mention—it's the wittily written "Best of Atlanta" guide furnished each guest, which details the top dining, entertainment, shopping, and "pertinent and impertinent" spots in the city. Compiled with a great deal of care, and even more personality, it provides good reading as well as useful information.

The **Guest Quarters–Perimeter Center,** 111 Perimeter Center West, Atlanta, GA 30346 (tel. 404/396-6800, or toll free 800/424-2900), is just off I-285, and furnishes courtesy transportation for nearby tennis and golf facilities. There are some 242 suites, surrounded by landscaped grounds, and the Perimeter Mall Shopping Center is just across the highway. Double-occupancy rates here are $120 to $146 for a one-bedroom suite, $180 to $186 for two bedrooms.

The garden-type **Guest Quarters–Roswell Road,** 7000 Roswell Rd., Atlanta, GA 30328 (tel. 404/394-6300, or toll free 800/424-2900), provides an Olympic-size pool, volleyball, and health-club privileges. Suites have private patios or balconies. Rates begin at $99 for one bedroom, $109 for two, and $120 for three —all for double occupancy. Single-occupancy rates are slightly lower.

## Moderate

With two exceptions most of the moderately priced motels in the Atlanta area are members of national chains.

The Marriott Corporation has located six of its moderately priced **Courtyard By Marriott Hotels** in the metro Atlanta suburbs. Rooms are spacious, attractively furnished, and offer guests the use of swimming pools, restaurants, and lounges at rates in the $60 double category. Area locations include: Atlanta Airport, 2050 Sullivan Rd., College Park, GA 30337 (tel. 404/997-2220); Northlake, 4083 Lavista Rd., at I-285, Tucker, GA 30329 (tel. 404/938-1200); Peachtree Corners, 3209 Holcomb Bridge Rd., Norcross, GA 30071 (tel. 404/446-3777); Peachtree-Dunwoody, 5601 Peachtree-Dunwoody Rd., Atlanta, GA 30346 (tel. 404/843-2300); Windy Hill Road, 2045 S. Park Pl., Smyrna, GA 30080 (tel. 404/955-3838); and Executive Park, 1236 Executive Park Dr., at I-85 North, Atlanta, GA 30329 (tel. 404/728-0708). Other locations are planned. For reservations nationwide phone toll free 800/321-2211.

In the downtown hotel and convention district, the spiffy new **Hotel Ibis,**

101 International Blvd., Atlanta, GA 30303 (tel. 404/524-5555), with doubles in the $50 to $60 range, has made a hit with budget travelers and people doing business at the nearby Atlanta Merchandise Mart and Apparel Mart. Rooms have a delightful French panache, there's a good restaurant and bar.

The **Comfort Inn of Atlanta,** 120 North Ave., at I-75/85, Atlanta, GA 30313 (tel. 404/441-6788, or toll free 800/228-5150), is a small, well-kept chain motor hotel, convenient to Georgia Tech, Coca-Cola headquarters, and downtown Atlanta. Doubles are about $50.

The **Quality Inn Habersham Hotel,** 330 Peachtree St. NE, Atlanta, GA 30308 (tel. collect 404/577-1980, or toll free 800/241-4288), is a small, well-run hotel in downtown Atlanta which wears a semi-European air. Complimentary fresh-squeezed juice and coffee are served in your room. There are executive-size rooms, king-size beds, and in some rooms a wet bar with refrigerator. Doubles start at $62, and there are family plans and weekend packages available.

There is little to distinguish the chains from one another except location, although facilities do vary slightly. Those listed here can be assumed to have the standard, motel-quality rooms and decor, and I've added some of the nicer locally owned hostelries.

The **Holiday Inn–Downtown,** 175 Piedmont Ave. NE, Atlanta, GA 30303 (tel. 404/659-2727, or toll free 800/HOLIDAY), is within walking distance of Peachtree Street, the Civic Center, and several shopping plazas. The 470 rooms, most with two double beds, are available at an average rate of $74, and children under 18 stay free with their parents. An outdoor swimming pool, dining room (open from 6 a.m. to 10 p.m.), and two lounges, one with live entertainment, offer a choice of relaxed or active atmosphere. It's very much the same out at the **Holiday Inn–Airport,** 1380 Virginia Ave., Atlanta, GA 30344 (tel. 404/762-8411, or toll free 800/HOLIDAY), which is about seven miles from the city center. There's free shuttle bus service to and from the airport, lighted tennis courts, sauna, pool, disco, and live entertainment in the lounges, and two restaurants. Doubles start at $65, and children under 18 stay free in the room with their parents.

The **Atlanta Central TraveLodge,** 311 Courtland St. NE, Atlanta, GA 30303 (tel. 404/659-4545, or toll free 800/255-3050), furnishes free coffee and pastries in all rooms (there's a 24-hour restaurant just half a block away), has a heated pool and queen-size beds in many rooms (and cable TV in all), and furnishes irons and ironing boards on request. Doubles start at $55, with lower weekend rates.

The **Lanier Plaza Hotel,** I-85 at Monroe Drive, 418 Armour Dr., Atlanta, GA 30324 (tel. 404/873-4661, or toll free 800/554-8444), has a pool, restaurant, and lounge with entertainment. Double rooms, which are very attractively decorated, are in the $65 to $75 range, with no charge for children under 17 in the same room with their parents.

**Stone Mountain Inn,** Jefferson Davis Rd., inside Stone Mountain Park, P.O. Box 775, Stone Mountain, GA 30086 (tel. 404/469-3311), is 16 miles east of the city, but there's public transportation on city buses from Stone Mountain Park, and it's a good location for avoiding city traffic. Rooms are especially comfortable and nicely decorated in 18th-century style. There's a heated pool (with a wading section for the kids and beverage service for the grownups). Rates are seasonal: $80 for double rooms from June 1 through Labor Day, a little lower other months.

Directly across from the Atlanta Merchandise Mart, and only four blocks from the World Congress Center, a mile from the State Capitol and a half mile from the Civic Center, the **Days Inn Downtown Atlanta,** Spring Street at Baker Street, Atlanta, GA 30303 (tel. 404/523-1144, or toll free 800/325-2525), offers doubles for $85 and there's a restaurant and a pool.

## Bed-and-Breakfast

B&Bs are available in Atlanta in grand style—host homes range from modest, middle-class houses to some of the city's finest residences. And they're located in the downtown area, suburban neighborhoods, and even in Stone Mountain. So if this is your favorite way to get to know an area, you're sure to find one convenient to your personal interests. As a bonus, you'll probably effect even greater savings as local hosts clue you in to shopping bargains, entertainment, etc. As far in advance as possible, contact **Bed & Breakfast Atlanta,** 1801 Piedmont Ave., Suite 208, Atlanta, GA 30324 (tel. 404/875-0525). They carefully screen all host homes and will place you as near as possible to the section of the city you prefer. Rates run $28 to $60, with some exceptional lodgings in the $48 to $100 range. And that includes a continental breakfast.

## Campgrounds

To the east of the city about 16 miles, the **Stone Mountain Campground** has 500 sites, full hookups, LP gas, showers, a laundry, supply store, restaurant, mini-golf, swimming, boating, and fishing. Rates begin at $9. To reach it, take I-285 to the Stone Mountain exit, then drive 7½ miles east on Ga. 78 to Stone Mountain Park and then follow the signs. For full details, write Stone Mountain Campground, P.O. Box 778, Stone Mountain, GA 30086 (tel. 404/498-5600).

## ATLANTA'S RESTAURANTS: It's a point of pride with Atlantans that their

town has more fine restaurants than any other major southern city (excluding, of course, New Orleans and Miami, each in a class by itself). Another point that should be made is that *real* southern cooking is surprisingly hard to come by in Atlanta's restaurants. What there is tends to be overdone, soggy, and far from the cuisine of southern homes (if you can wangle a dinner invitation "at home," you'll taste the real thing). There are two establishments that do a good job in this department, however, and because I've tried to emphasize regional cuisine throughout this book, these top my list of places to eat, even though neither is expensive or flashy—the important thing is that both are "southern."

## To "Eat Southern"

Atlanta's best southern restaurant isn't in Atlanta at all, but in nearby Smyrna. I remember fondly the delicious meals and entertaining evenings I had at **Aunt Fanny's Cabin,** 2155 Campbell Rd., Smyrna (tel. 404/436-5218), when my home was in this area—but it's more than nostalgia: Aunt Fanny's is always the same when I return. Be forewarned, however, that the restaurant, in a former slave cabin, has a decided "plantation days" atmosphere in both the cuisine and its presentation. There really was an "Aunt Fanny" Williams, and this was her home (and some of the employees have worked here over 30 years). It's over 130 years old and Aunt Fanny was in her 70s when she first began serving meals to the public in 1941. She bustled around the kitchen as long as she was able, then took to a rocking chair to personally greet guests. The fireplaces, the antique furniture, the old copper cookware hanging about, and the soft glow of candlelight in an essentially rustic setting all combine to re-create the world in which Aunt Fanny grew up (she died in 1949); and people from 59 countries have dined here over the years, including foreign ministers, cabinet members, state governors, senators, and countless entertainment personalities.

In all, it's a thoroughly delightful, very friendly place, and the food, too, is straight out of the Old South (in fact, many of the recipes were Aunt Fanny's). The menu is limited—fried chicken, Smithfield ham, charcoal-broiled steak, and fresh rainbow trout—and all entrees except fried chicken ($13) and steak ($17) are $13.50. Vegetables are fresh, with a true home-cooked flavor—their baked squash belongs in a culinary hall of fame, as far as I'm concerned! All dishes are served family style, coming to the table in large dishes: and if there's chicken, for instance, left on the platter at the end of a meal, brown bags appear for you to take the remains home. Both beer and wine are served, and there's a bar that serves mint juleps along with other cocktails. Aunt Fanny's is open from 11:30 a.m. to 2 p.m. (all lunches are $5, complete) and 6 to 10 p.m. Monday through Friday, to 10:30 p.m. on Saturday, and from 1 to 10 p.m. on Sunday, and it's worth the drive for the experience.

On the northern edge of the midtown section, **Mary Mac's Tea Room,** 224 Ponce de Leon (tel. 404/875-4337), has been operated for almost a quarter of a century by Mrs. Margaret Lupo, now assisted by two of her six offspring. She advertises "southern hospitality with damyankee efficiency." With some 2,000 people served daily, they *have* to be efficient, but that doesn't seem to diminish either the hospitality or the quality of food. Fried chicken and country ham are really good here, and they—like Aunt Fanny's—do an especially good job with fresh vegetables and hot breads. Mary Mac's is open from 11:15 a.m. to 4 p.m. for lunch, 5 to 8 p.m. for dinner, and prices are very moderate: most dinners (meat, three vegetables, bread, and beverage) run $6 to $9, with a 10% discount to college students who show an ID card. Look for **Mary Mac's To Go** at 5674 Roswell Rd. (tel. 404/252-4819).

## Expensive

The Dining Room of the **Ritz-Carlton Buckhead Hotel,** 3434 Peachtree Rd. NE (tel. 404/237-2700). Atlanta's most fashionable hotel boasts one of its loveliest dining rooms. Much-awarded chef Guenther Seeger creates nouvelle cuisine with celestial finesse and style in this beautiful, darkly romantic room, with its fresh flowers and English hunting portraits. Sauces, even Seeger's luscious-looking desserts, are so light you may sample several dishes and still leave feeling comfortably happy. Lunch is served Monday through Friday from 11:30 a.m. to 2:30 p.m., and dinner is Monday through Saturday from 6 to 10 p.m. A full dinner for two with wine will cost about $80 to $100.

**Hedgerose Heights Inn,** 490 E. Paces Ferry Rd., Buckhead (tel. 404/233-7673). Old-world grandeur, courtly service, and imaginative Swiss/French/German cuisine by owner Heinz Schwab make Hedgerose another memorable dining experience. Dinner is served from 6 to 10 p.m. Monday through Saturday, and a meal for two with wine runs about $80 to $100.

**LaGrotta Ristorante Italiano,** 2637 Peachtree Rd. NE (tel. 404/231-1368). Northern Italian pastas, seafood, veal, and chicken dishes are at their absolute finest in this lively subterranean dining room that crackles with self-confidence and good cheer. Dinner is served Tuesday through Saturday 6 to 10:30 p.m. Dinner for two with wine costs about $75 to $90.

**Ruth Chris Steak House,** 950 E. Paces Ferry Rd., Buckland (tel. 404/365-0660), with a stunning contemporary dining room, has taken Atlanta beef lovers by storm. Aged prime strips, filets, and rib eyes, served on sizzling hot platters, are the hallmark. The large menu also features seafood, excellent side dishes, a large wine list, and super desserts like blueberry cheesecake and New Orleans–style praline freezes. Hours are Monday through Friday from 11 a.m. to 11 p.m., and on Saturday and Sunday from 4 to 11 p.m. Dinner for two, with wine, will run about $70 to $80.

## Moderate

Two blocks south of Atlanta's famous Fox Theater, the **Pleasant Peasant,** 555 Peachtree St. (tel. 404/874-3223), is in what used to be a Victorian ice-cream parlor, which, although renovated, retains much of that old style. Live plants and antiques scattered about give it an almost intimate atmosphere. They don't accept reservations, and it's always crowded, but the service is consistently good. There is a daily special (might be veal paprikash, a specialty), and other menu items include scallops parisienne and pork piquant at prices ranging from $7.50 to $18.50. There is full bar service and a respectable wine list. Dinner hours are 5:30 p.m. to midnight every day except Friday and Saturday, when they serve until 1 a.m.

Those of us who find Greek food irresistible will want to return again and again to **Niko's Greek Restaurant,** 1789 Cheshire Bridge Rd. (tel. 404/872-1254). Nikos Letsos, his wife, Anna, and their three daughters run this marvelous place in northeast Atlanta, creating an atmosphere which is both relaxing and zestful at the same time, something that seems to come naturally to Greeks. Begin with specialties like the saganaki appetizer which is flamed at your table with accompanying shouts of "Opa" from waiters and other diners. And the Zorba Special—a combination plate of moussaka, pastitsio, and dolmades served with Greek beans and Greek salad—will bring you to your feet with "Opas" of your own. Then there are those luscious Greek desserts like baklava and rizogalo. All to the accompaniment of Greek music. Makes me hungry just remembering my last feast at this friendly and lively place! Prices are extremely moderate, in the $7 to $11 range, and there's a "Menu for Little Greeks." Hours are 11 a.m. to 11 p.m. Monday through Thursday, to 11:30 p.m. on Friday, from noon to 11:30 p.m. on Saturday, and 5 to 10:30 p.m. on Sunday.

In very short order, Indigo, a Coastal Grill, and its next-door sibling, Partners Morningside Café, have captured the imagination of Atlanta's trend-conscious diners. Both these wonderful little restaurants are owned by the husband-wife team of Dan Carson and Alix Kenagy, and are jammed to their 80-seat capacity even in midweek. Waiting's part of the experience. You'll meet lots of upbeat Atlantans at the bar areas, and around the sidewalk gliders and lawn chairs. **Indigo, a Coastal Grill,** 1397 N. Highland Ave. (tel. 404/876-0676), is like a campy Caribbean–Key West seafood café. There's a vintage fridge behind the bar, '50s couches in the small waiting area, stuffed fish and other oddities on the walls. There's nothing odd about the menu. Start with Bahamian conch fritters, roasted oysters or tangy lime soup, and move on to fresh salmon or sea bass and vegetables in a bamboo steamer, and wind up with sure-enough-authentic Key West key lime pie, and you'll join the list of regulars. **Partners Morningside Café,** 1399 N. Highland Ave. (tel. 404/875-0202), buzzes with conversation and contemporary art. Friendly young servers present enormous platters of freshly made pastas, seafood in light sauces, creative chicken dishes, salads, and terrific desserts. Meat lovers' favorites include blackened rib eye, and lamb Wyoming in a herb cream sauce. Both restaurants are open for dinner Tuesday through Saturday from 6 to 11 p.m. A full dinner for two with drinks or wine will be about $50.

Next door to Partners, but independently owned, **Café Rôtisserie,** 1409 N. Highland Ave. (tel. 404/874-1343), is another trendy hot spot. It's like an old-fashioned American diner, given a zingy mid-'80s twist. Specialties include the rôtisserie-roasted chicken, mammoth deli sandwiches, and multilayer desserts and pastries. It's open Monday through Thursday from 11 a.m. to 11 p.m., on

Friday and Saturday to midnight, and on Sunday from noon to 11 p.m. You can eat very well for $12 or less.

Two blocks south of this threesome, **Camille's,** 1186 N. Highland Ave. (tel. 404/872-7203), is straight out of Italian New York. The perpetually busy little place does a land-office business in such temptations as stuffed artichokes; linguine pie; mussels, clams, shrimp, and squid in rich red sauces; and chicken and pastas of all sorts. Save room for ricotta cheesecake and espresso. In warm weather, find places at the red-checkered picnic tables outside. Lunch and dinner are on from 11 a.m. to 11 p.m. daily. Dishes start at about $6, and go up to $13 for some specials. Camille's is three blocks north of the lively Virginia/ Highland corner.

Looking for a good steak at moderate prices? Head for one of the seven **Longhorn Steak Restaurant & Saloons** around town. There's one at 2151 Peachtree Rd. (tel. 404/351-6086), about halfway between downtown and Buckhead. They're open daily from 11:30 a.m. to 11 p.m. Two of you can dine very well, with drinks and side dishes, for $40 or less.

## Budget

"Budget" doesn't have to mean "fast-food" in Atlanta. Consider the following. At **Katz's Delicatessen,** 2205 Cheshire Bridge Rd. NE (tel. 404/321-7444), you'll find pastrami, corned beef, pastries, homemade soups, and home-baked bread from 8 a.m. to 10 p.m. every day except Friday and Saturday, when it's open until midnight (closed Tuesday), at prices of $2 to $6. Or **Aunt Charley's,** 3107 Peachtree Rd. NE (tel. 404/231-8503), where a satisfying meal of homemade soups, outstanding salads, entrees, and sandwiches will cost no more than $2 to $7 (open from 11:30 a.m. to 2 a.m. every day).

**The Colonnade,** 1879 Cheshire Bridge Rd. NE (tel. 404/874-5642), has been an Atlanta favorite for 30 years. Like a cheerful American restaurant of the 1950s, this friendly place serves delicious breakfasts, and moderately, even cheaply, priced steaks, chops, seafoods, southern fried chicken, and vegetables, every day. Breakfast is from 7 to 10 a.m.; lunch, 11 a.m. to 2:30 p.m.; and dinner, 5 to 9 p.m.

**Touch of India,** 970 Peachtree St. (tel. 404/876-7777), serves spicy Indian curries, tandooris, and breads to appreciative intown adventurers at very modest prices. Lunch is served Monday through Friday from 11:30 a.m. to 2:30 p.m.; dinner, daily from 5 to 11 p.m.

If you're a born shopper and plan to spend a lot of time in Atlanta's fabulous malls, eating won't break the budget. At Lenox Square Shopping Center, there are simply too many to name—just look around when your feet begin to hurt and you're sure to spot one. In the Cherokee Plaza Shopping Center, lunch of quiche (or other entree), salad, and pastry will cost no more than $6 at **Maison Robert,** 3867 Peachtree Rd. NE (tel. 404/237-3675), Tuesday through Saturday from 11:30 a.m. to 2:30 p.m.

There are 11 locations of the **Old Hickory House** around Atlanta, all serving barbecued pork, beef, chicken, and ribs at prices that range from budget to moderate. If southern barbecue is a weakness, keep an eye out for their sign— I've had better in the South, but the Hickory House brand is above average. All locations feature a rustic decor and prices that range from $3.50 to $6.50. Hours vary, but most are open from 11 a.m. to 10:30 p.m., some until 11 p.m.

Just a couple of blocks from the Georgia Tech campus (alongside I-75 and I-85 where North Avenue crosses over the highway) is an Atlanta institution— the **Varsity Drive-In.** Now maybe a drive-in doesn't qualify as a "restaurant," but for budget eating, you just can't beat the Varsity and some 16,000 people a day agree with me. The food is good, service (both carside and inside, where they have seats and stand-up eating counters) is excellent and very fast, and prices are definitely budget for the hot dog, hamburger, french fries fare. They're open 24 hours daily.

There are an even dozen **Morrison's Cafeterias** around town. Locations include 1025 Virginia Ave., near Hartsfield International Airport (tel. 404/761-8066); and Ansley Mall Shopping Center, Piedmont Avenue and Monroe Drive (tel. 404/872-8091). Open seven days, with continuous service from lunch through dinner.

## Virginia Highlands

In the past few years a lively, interesting resurrection has been taking place out at the intersection of Virginia and Highland Avenues, as an area which had become more or less run-down until its discovery by an energetic, youngish crowd. Now there has sprung up a cluster of restaurants and shops that are well worth a visit. Perhaps the most intriguing of these restaurants (and certainly the most expensive) is **Walter Mitty's,** 816 N. Highland Ave. NE (tel. 404/876-7115). It's in an elegantly restored building, and outstanding veal and seafood dishes are featured at prices of $9 to $20. There's terrific jazz in a downstairs room. Hours are 6 to 11 p.m. (to midnight on Friday and Saturday); jazz hours are 9 p.m. to 2 a.m. seven days a week. Less pricey, but equally good in the food department, is **Capo's Café,** 992 Virginia Ave. NE (tel. 404/876-6655). A small, homey (and very popular) place, it specializes in scallops, beef, chicken, and a fettuccine Alfredo that's out of this world. Prices are $5.25 to $8, and hours are 5:30 to 10:45 p.m. For your sweet tooth, **The Dessert Place,** 1000 Virginia Ave. NE (tel. 404/892-8912), has yummy pastries, cakes, cookies, and a long list of special coffees. Take them out, or have a seat in the garden-type back room. Closed Monday. Two other locations are 279 E. Paces Ferry Rd. (tel. 404/233-2331) and 180 Peachtree St. NE (in Macy's; tel. 404/221-7931).

## For Cheese Lovers

It's hard to know just *where* to list **Dante's Down the Hatch,** 3380 Peachtree *Road,* across the street from Lenox Square (tel. 404/266-1600). Because its menu is made up largely of cheese trays, cheese and beef fondues, and four complete fondue dinners, I'm not sure it qualifies as a restaurant. On the other hand, if you are a dedicated cheese lover, as I am, Dante's should top all other eating spots on your Atlanta list. Never mind the unique setting, service by people who know and care about cheeses, and superb entertainment (more about that in the nightlife section)—it's the *cheeses* under discussion here. As every cheeselover knows, ordering brie in a restaurant is chancey, to say the least. It has to be the most temperamental of them all, and I've nibbled at underripe, "green" brie, spooned up runny, overripe brie, and just walked away from brie impossible to eat for whatever mysterious reason. Not so at Dante's. The cheese board that arrived at my table held a brie worthy of a poetic hymn of praise, and I have it on good authority (Atlanta friends who are regulars, backed up by Jerry Margolus, longtime manager here) that this was no accident—when the unpredictable delicacy doesn't measure up, it comes off the menu. For my money, that speaks volumes for this place. Fondues are prepared with imported cheeses and loving care, and if you're in the mood for meat, the quality of beef is just as good as that brie. Restaurant, nightspot, or whatnot, Dante's Down the Hatch is a cheeselover's haven. It's open seven days a week from 1 p.m. to 2 a.m., and prices are in the $8 to $15 range. Reservations are a good idea.

**READER'S DINING SELECTION:** "We had the most outstanding meal on our trip at **Pano's and Paul's,** 1232 W. Paces Ferry Rd. (tel. 404/261-4739). It's not cheap but if you stay away from the wine and the coffee Diablo, I would guess a couple could dine sumptuously for under $40. This is a top-drawer place" (G. Reeves, Philadelphia, Pa.).

**ATLANTA NIGHTLIFE:** If there is one thing Atlanta is rich in, it's nightlife—of all kinds! There is dinner theater, symphony, ballet, nightclub, lounge music (country and western, jazz, and rock and roll), cabaret, and almost any other kind of nocturnal entertainment you could name. Most hotels and motels distribute free the publications *Where, Key—This Week in Atlanta,* or *After Hours,* all good guides for where to find what. And for a complete rundown on what's going on while you're there, pick up the Saturday edition of the *Atlanta Constitution* (the local morning newspaper) with its "Weekend" amusement section. Depending on the time of year, you'll see listed performances by the Atlanta Symphony Orchestra and Chamber Chorus, the Atlanta Ballet (the country's oldest regional company), the Southern Ballet of Atlanta, the Ruth Mitchell Dance Company, the Academy Theatre, Alliance Theatre, and scores of other concerts or other cultural events. And no matter when you come to town, you'll find entertainment at the following:

### Nightclubs, Cabarets, Lounges, Etc.

In the Robert W. Woodruff Arts Center, at Peachtree and 15th Streets, you'll find the **Alliance Theatre** (tel. 404/892-2414), which presents some 12 productions each season (September through May) by its resident troupe of performers on its two stages, plus the Atlanta Symphony Orchestra in a full season of orchestral and choral concerts.

My own longtime favorite after-dark has been **Dante's Down the Hatch,** across the street from Lenox Square (3380 Peachtree *Road;* tel. 404/266-1600), with entertainment, and those cheeses I carried on so about earlier. Let me tell you about that decor: Dante has created the illusion of a pirate ship tied up to an old Mediterranean wharf, and the result is an engaging spot that combines fun with sophistication. In the "wharf" section, there is folk singing during the week, classical and flamenco guitar on Sunday. The Paul Mitchell Trio is on hand in the "ship" section. Paul is a jazz pianist who ranks with the greats, and his sidemen match his brilliant artistry. As for the "crew," most have been aboard for a long time, and all really make you feel cared for. Then, of course, there are those cheeses, fondues, special drinks, and an excellent wine list. Add to this the fact that Dante himself is always on hand to see that you have a good time, and you have a truly outstanding place to spend an evening. It's so popular that reservations are really a "must," and there's an entertainment charge of $3 per person after 7 p.m. on the ship ($4 on Friday and Saturday).

Dante's Buckhead neighborhood is the liveliest entertainment zone in town. Much of the fun is conveniently clustered around the triangular junction of Peachtree, Roswell, East and West Paces Ferry Roads. **Blues Harbor,** 3179 Peachtree Rd. (tel. 404/261-6717), features a revolving lineup of Chicago-style blues and jazz artists. Across the way at 3166 Peachtree Rd. (tel. 404/231-8666), **Tom Foolery** is one of the city's best-loved little clubs. Once the show starts, the magic pranks and surprises fly nonstop. The Foolery is just around a literal corner from Olde England and Ireland. The **Churchill Arms Pub,** 3223 Cains Hill Pl. (tel. 404/233-5633), lures local anglophiles with Bass ale, darts, a sing-along piano, and big pictures of Charles and Di; across the street at 56 E. Andrews Dr. (tel. 404/262-2227), the **County Cork Pub** headlines Guinness stout, Harp ale, and balladeers from Dublin and Belfast.

Beneath County Cork, in the same courtyard-style complex, **56 East,** 56 E. Andrews Dr. (tel. 404/364-WINE), serves 150 wines by the glass and a trendy menu of salads, pastas, veal, and chicken dishes. **Popz,** 1923 Peachtree Rd. (tel.

404/352-3052), is another chic little spot, serving champagne by the glass, and a menu of your favorite caviars.

The affluent yuppie set currently favors the bar and outdoor patio of **Peachtree Café,** 268 E. Paces Ferry Rd. (tel. 404/233-4402). Also in vogue is **Rio Bravo Cantina,** a campy Tex-Mex eatery and bar with delicious fajitas and margaritas and live mariachi music at 3172 Roswell Rd. (tel. 404/262-7431). **Jerry Farber's Club,** 54 Pharr Rd. (tel. 404/237-5181) is an intimate bistro with top-notch jazz.

The **Punch Line,** 280 Hildebrand Dr. (tel. 404/252-5233), keeps 'em laughing with locally and nationally known comedians.

**Limelight,** 3330 Piedmont Rd. (tel. 404/231-3520), is Atlanta's best-known nightclub. The cavernous complex of bars and a vast disco floor are equipped with the latest hi-tech sound and light effects, and attract a gaudy crowd of locals and visiting firemen. It's about the best place in town to spot movie, TV, and sports celebrities.

Elsewhere around town, you'll find jazz at **Walter Mitty's Jazz Club,** 816 N. Highland Ave. NE (tel. 404/876-7115), where reservations are usually necessary; and big-band music à la the '30s and '40s at **Johnny's Hideaway,** 3771 Roswell Rd. NW (tel. 404/233-8026).

## ATLANTA SHOPPING: There's no doubt about it, Atlanta is undoubtedly the best shopping city in the Southeast, with regional shopping centers on or near every one of the metropolitan freeways. Downtown Atlanta is far from being a depressed shopping area drained off by these outlying malls, however, and there are two outstanding places to spend your money right at its heart.

**Macy's Department Store** (formerly Davison's), at 180 Peachtree St., at Ellis Street (tel. 404/221-7500), has received a major glamorization during the past couple of years, and is truly dazzling. Macy's Cellar is a fun place to browse for gourmet cookwares and fancy foods, and enjoy a pub-style lunch.

The **Peachtree Center Shopping Gallery,** two blocks north of Macy's, has also put on a chic new face. Numerous small shops and eateries are tucked into the three-level gallery, which connects via covered bridge with the Hyatt Regency and Marriott Marquis Hotels. There's also a MARTA rapid rail station.

**Buckhead,** a little north of the downtown area, has **Lenox Square,** with more than 130 stores in its enclosed mall, and **Phipps Plaza,** diagonally across the intersection, with branches of New York stores such as Saks Fifth Avenue, Lord & Taylor, and Tiffany.

## SPORTS: When I lived near Atlanta (almost two decades ago), the city was as sports-happy as it is today. The only difference is that then it was concerned primarily with collegiate events, and now (while college competitions *still* keep alumni glued to TV sets and the bookies busy) it has added professional teams that elicit the same sort of loyalty.

Depending on which season finds you in Atlanta, call the following numbers for sports information: **Braves** baseball, 404/522-7630; **Falcons** football, 404/588-1111; **Hawks** basketball, 404/681-3600; **International Raceway** (auto), 404/946-4411.

## SIGHTSEEING IN ATLANTA: Before you start out sightseeing, contact the **Atlanta Convention and Visitors Bureau,** Harris Tower, Suite 200, 233 Peachtree St. NE, Atlanta, GA 30343 (tel. 404/521-6633), or go by the Welcome Center at Peachtree Center Mall or Lenox Square Mall.

The **Carter Presidential Center,** at North Highland and Cleburne Avenues (tel. 404/331-3942), is Atlanta's newest major attraction and a "must-see" for every visitor. Two miles east of downtown, with the skyline as dramatic backdrop, the center's four contemporary circular buildings are set among 30 acres of trees, gardens, lakes, and waterfalls. Inside are thousands of documents, photos, gifts, and memorabilia of Jimmy Carter's White House years. The center is also a tribute to all who have held our nation's highest office. You may walk into a full-scale reproduction of the Oval Office. On a keyboard and video monitor, choose your response to a terrorist crisis, and watch as President Carter spells out the consequences. Photos follow Carter from his boyhood in Plains, through his navy career, state politics, and the presidency. Gifts range from splendid silver, ivory, and crystal from heads of state, to paintings and peanut carving from admirers around the world. *Presidents,* a 30-minute film, looks at the crises and triumphs that hallmarked past administrations. You may have a light lunch, with a view of the gardens, in the center's restaurant. It's open daily from 9 a.m. to 5 p.m. Adults pay $2.50 admission; under age 16, no charge.

If you come looking for Margaret Mitchell's *Gone with the Wind* antebellum Atlanta, you won't find it, thanks to General Sherman, who burned it all down in 1864. However, it's worth the time and effort to drive northwest of the city's business district (five miles or so out Peachtree Street) to Peachtree Battle Avenue, then left to Habersham Drive, Northside Drive, West Paces Ferry Road (that's the **Governor's Mansion** at no. 391, by the way, and it's open from 10 to 11:45 a.m. Tuesday through Thursday at no charge), to Tuxedo Road. It's in a residential area that can, despite its more recent vintage, rival any antebellum section, with dogwoods, azaleas, magnolias, and some of the most beautiful private residences you could find anywhere in the country. Not far from the Governor's Mansion, at 3101 Andrews Dr. NW, the Atlanta Historical Society maintains the **Swan House,** an opulent 1920s Palladian-style mansion, and the **Tullie Smith House** (same address), an 1840s southern farmhouse. They are open to the public with a combined admission of $4.50 for adults, $2 for children, from 9 a.m. to 5 p.m. Monday through Saturday, from noon to 5 p.m. on Sunday. Atlanta's history and its present affluence are perhaps epitomized in this section of town.

A short drive to the little community of **Roswell,** just north of Atlanta, will also take you back to pre–Civil War days. There are a number of homes of that vintage which have either been preserved through continuous residency or restored by enthusiastic and appreciative new owners. The childhood home of President Theodore Roosevelt's mother, Bulloch Hall, is in Roswell.

Right in the center of town, a four-block tract of Atlanta's history lies beneath newer city streets. Called **Underground Atlanta,** this was an empty catacomb that lay deserted and gathering dust for the better part of a century when railroad viaducts were built over its rococo buildings in post–Civil War days. Then a group of far-sighted and determined Atlanta businessmen decided to restore the crumbling area, and the result was an authentic, completely charming picture of Atlanta in the 1800s. Then, over the years, the historic "city beneath a city" became a little shabby, so much so that in 1977 a new renovation effort was mounted. For a time after that the Underground fairly sparkled with specialty shops, restaurants, and bars—even street entertainment. Then another decline set in and the Underground was closed, but it won't be for long. In conjunction with the Rouse Company, developers of New York's South Street Seaport, Baltimore's Harborplace, and Boston's Faneuil Hall Marketplace, the city is resurrecting Underground. The first of more than 200 shops, restaurants, and small museums are expected to open in spring 1988. Since this is literally the point at which Atlanta was born, with the planting of Zero Milepost in 1837, it's good to see it come to life again.

The **Martin Luther King National Historic District,** 449 Auburn Ave. (tel.

404/524-1956 or 331-3919), includes the major landmarks of the civil rights leader's life. His white marble tomb, with an eternal flame symbolizing his dream of a brotherhood of mankind, is the heart of the Freedom Hall Complex. You may also view a multimedia presentation on his life; tour Ebenezer Baptist Church, where he was pastor and from which he was buried; and walk one block east to the Victorian home where he was born on January 15, 1929. The two-square block area is included in the Martin Luther King, Jr., National Historic District. National Park Service rangers, headquartered across the street from Freedom Hall, lead half-hour walking tours of the neighborhood. The tomb and other outdoor areas may be visited without charge, but donations are requested at Ebenezer Church, the birthplace, and the film. Open daily.

Much of your Atlanta sightseeing will be concentrated in **Grant Park,** between Cherokee Avenue and Boulevard SE. There are miles and miles of walkways and roads through the park, some of them along the breastwork built for the city's defense in 1864. The **zoo** is here, and it's a good one, with a special children's zoo and a miniature railroad. Admission is $2.50 for adults, $1.25 for ages 4 to 11 (children 3 and under are free, but not admitted without an adult). You can also see in the park a restored Confederate battery, **Fort Walker** (no charge).

For a breathtaking view of the Battle of Atlanta, go by the neoclassical building that houses the **Cyclorama,** 800 Cherokee Ave. in Grant Park (tel. 404/624-1071), a 42-foot-high, 356-foot-circumference, 100-year-old painting with a three-dimensional foreground and special lighting, music, and sound effects. It's impressive, and when you see the monumental work, you'll know why Sherman made that famous "War is hell" remark! This is one of only three cycloramas in the U.S., and has recently been fully restored—it's an artistic and historical treasure not to be missed. There are 15 shows daily, from 9:30 a.m. to 4:30 p.m. Adults pay $3; senior citizens, $2.50; children 6 through 12, $1.50; and those under 6, free.

The **State Capitol,** built in 1884, is on Capitol Square, and the gold-topped dome stands 237 feet above the city. Besides a **Hall of Fame** (with busts of famous Georgians) and a **Hall of Flags** (with U.S., state, and Confederate battle flags), it houses the **Georgia State Museum,** which is free and open from 8 a.m. to 5:30 p.m. Monday through Friday. In the museum, you'll find collections of Georgia minerals and Indian artifacts, dioramas of famous places in the state, and fish and wildlife exhibits.

Remember the "Uncle Remus" stories? Well, Joel Chandler Harris, who created the lovable character and his stories, lived at 1050 Gordon St. SW. **Wren's Nest,** his home (named for wrens who nested in the mailbox), has the original furnishings and his books and photographs, and is open Monday through Saturday from 9:30 a.m. to 5 p.m. (on Sunday from 2 p.m.) at a charge of $2.50 for adults, $1.25 for teenagers, and 75¢ for ages 4 to 12.

In the Robert W. Woodruff Arts Center, 1280 Peachtree St. NE, the **High Museum of Art** (tel. 404/892-4444) houses impressive collections of Western art, African art, and first-rate traveling exhibitions. Hours are 10 a.m. to 5 p.m. Tuesday through Saturday (until 9 p.m. on Wednesday), from noon on Sunday, with a $3 admission charge.

About 12 miles west of downtown, just off I-20 West, the **Six Flags Over Georgia** theme park, 7561 Six Flags Rd., is one of the best in the country. There are more than 100 rides (including the giant "Great American Scream Machine" roller coaster), a multitude of shows, and several restaurants. The $16.50 admission charge covers all rides and shows. Ages 55 and over and children 42 inches tall and under pay $10. It's open late May through Labor Day from 10 a.m. to 10 p.m., seven days a week (until midnight on Friday and Saturday); weekends only other times (call 404/948-9290 for specific information, or write P.O. Box 43187, Atlanta, GA 30378). The park is dedicated to Georgia's history under the flags of England, France, Spain, the Confederacy, Georgia, and the U.S. Hours and prices are subject to change, so call to check.

Off U.S. 78/Stone Mountain Freeway, 16 miles east of downtown, **Stone Mountain Park** (tel. 404/498-5600) in Stone Mountain, is one of the Southeast's premier attractions. More than six million visitors, second only to Walt Disney World, flock to the 3,200-acre park each year to enjoy a wealth of attractions and recreation. Foremost, of course, is the world's largest granite monolith, which rises from a five-mile circumference to 825 feet. Carved on its sheer north flank is the world's largest sculpture, a 90- by 190-foot carving of Confederate heroes Robert E. Lee, Thomas "Stonewall" Jackson, and President Jefferson Davis. You can take a Swiss skylift to the top, or hike up an easy trail on the other side. Elsewhere in the park you can play golf, swim from a sand beach, visit an authentic antebellum plantation, an antique auto and music museum, and ride around the mountain's base on a steam locomotive. There's also an ice skating rink, biking, fishing, and campgrounds, all done in extremely good taste. One-time admission to the park is $4 per car, $15 for an annual permit. The six major attractions—skylift, auto/music museum, railroad, riverboat, plantation, wildlife trails—are each $2.50 for adults, $1.50 for children ages 4 to 11. Golf greens fees are $15 for 18 holes Tuesday through Friday, $17 on Saturday and Sunday. RV sites in the campground are $8.50 for partial hookups and $9.50 for full hookups. Tent sites are $8 per night. You can also stay at the Stone Mountain Inn (see "Where to Stay," above). The park is open daily year around: in summer from 10 a.m. to 9 p.m., in other seasons from 10 a.m. to 5:30 p.m.

## Tours

**Gray Line,** 3745 Zip Industrial Blvd. (tel. 404/767-0594), has a "Grand Circle" tour that can run from $14 to $19, depending on how "grand" you want your "circle" to be. They also have a *great* "Gone with the Wind" tour that lasts about 4½ hours and visits old plantations around Atlanta. Call for specific dates and times (it doesn't run every day).

**EXCURSIONS FROM ATLANTA:** Besides its own long list of attractions, Atlanta is a good jumping-off point for a multitude of sights and activities—both historical and modern, natural and man-made. I'll start with—

### Antebellum Georgia

If you looked for antebellum Georgia around Atlanta, you were in the right church but the wrong pew. The state's pre–Civil War moonlight-and-magnolias romance lives on, 60 to 100 miles east of Atlanta in charming towns with patriotic names like Washington, Madison, Monticello, Milledgeville, Eatonton, and a host of others.

**Madison,** off I-20 an hour's drive from Atlanta, is most people's favorite. Late in 1864, with Atlanta in flames behind them, Gen. William T. Sherman's Union juggernaut reached Madison's outskirts. Happily for us, they were met by former U.S. Sen. Joshua Hill, a secession opponent who'd known Sherman in Washington. Old ties prevailed, and the town was spared. Stop first at the **Madison-Morgan Cultural Center,** 434 S. Main St., which is U.S. 441 (tel. 404/342-4743). The red-brick schoolhouse, circa 1895, displays a delightful collection of vintage tools and furniture, Civil War artifacts and photos, and an early

1800s log house. Live programs range from Shakespeare and Gilbert & Sullivan, to gospel singing and clog dancing. It's open Monday through Friday from 10 a.m. to 4:30 p.m., on Saturday and Sunday from 2 to 5 p.m. Adults pay $2; students, $1 (free on Wednesday).

Pick up a self-guided walking tour map and other information at the center and walk past the majestic Greek Revival, Federal, Georgian, neoclassical, and Victorian homes lining Main Street, Academy Street, Old Post Road, and the pretty courthouse square. You'll also find plenty of places to purchase antiques and handcrafts. When you're famished, stop by **Ye Old Colonial Restaurant,** on the square (tel. 404/342-2211), a Victorian bank building where you can "cash in" on excellent southern cooking at very modest prices Monday through Saturday.

East of Madison, **Washington** has even more antebellum homes. Landmarks include the **Washington-Wilkes Historical Museum,** 308 E. Robert Toombs Ave. (tel. 404/678-2105), open Tuesday through Saturday from 10 a.m. to 5 p.m. Adults pay $1; children, 50¢. Also, check out the **home of Robert Toombs,** the Confederacy's flamboyant secretary of state, at 216 Robert Toombs Ave. (tel. 404/678-2226), open Tuesday through Saturday from 9 a.m. to 5 p.m., and on Sunday from 2 to 5:30 p.m. Admission is $1 for adults, 50¢ for children. Head for lunch at **Another Thyme,** a delightful spot on the courthouse square (tel. 404/678-1672).

Just 20 miles southeast of Washington, **Liberty Hall,** at sleepy little Crawfordville, was the home of Confederate Vice-President Alexander Hamilton Stephens. The adjoining **Confederate Museum,** (tel. 404/456-2221) has an extensive collection of Civil War memorabilia. It's open Tuesday through Saturday from 9 a.m. to 5 p.m., and on Sunday from 2 to 5:30 p.m. Adults are charged $1; children, 50¢. Don't leave Crawfordville without stopping by **Mrs. Bonner's Café** (tel. 404/456-2347), across from the red-brick courthouse. The delightful Mrs. "B" has served her legendary sweet tater pie and other southern favorites for more than 50 years. You may camp out, swim, and fish at **Alexander Stephens State Park,** near Liberty Hall (tel. 404/456-2602).

South of Madison on U.S. 441, Eatonton was the home of author Joel Chandler Harris. Look for the statue of Br'er Rabbit on the courthouse lawn. The **Uncle Remus Museum** has a wonderful collection of memorabilia about Br'er Rabbit, Br'er Fox, and Harris's other storybook critters. It's open Tuesday through Saturday from 9 a.m. to 5 p.m., on Sunday from 2 to 5:30 p.m. Adults pay $1; children, 50¢.

South of Eatonton, **Milledgeville** was Georgia's capital from 1803 to 1868. Like Madison, it was miraculously spared Sherman's wrath, and today is a treasure trove of antebellum architecture. Pick up a guided-tour map at the **Baldwin County Chamber of Commerce,** 130 S. Jefferson St., and walk back into history. The **Old Governors Mansion,** a pink-marble Palladian-style beauty at 120 S. Clark St. (tel. 912/453-4545), has been exquisitely restored and refurnished as the home of the president of Georgia College. You may tour the antique-rich public rooms Tuesday through Saturday from 9 a.m. to 5 p.m., and on Sunday from 2 to 5 p.m. Admission is $1 for adults, 50¢ for children. Fans of the late author Flannery O'Connor (*The Violent Bear It Away, A Good Man Is Hard to Find*) should see her memorial room in the library of **Georgia College.**

You can temper all this history with delicious relaxation at **Hard Labor Creek State Park** (tel. 404/557-2863), near Madison. *Golf* magazine rates the park's scenic 18-hole course as one of the finest public courses in America. You can also swim at a sand beach, fish for bass and catfish, and hike the 5,000 wooded acres. The park has 49 campsites with electricity, water, rest rooms, and showers for $7 a night; and 20 fully furnished cottages at $38 for two bedrooms, $44 for three bedrooms. For more information, call the number above or write: Superintendent, Hard Labor Creek State Park, Rutledge, GA 30663.

Hard Labor Creek is just one of scores of parks in Georgia's excellent system. From the mountains down to the coast, they're great places to break your trip for a day or so, or spend an entire vacation. For information contact, Georgia Natural Resources Department, Parks, Recreation & Historic Sites Division, 205 Butler St. SE, Atlanta, GA 30334 (tel. toll free 800/542-7275, 800/422-9275 in Georgia).

### Northeast Georgia Mountains

For a metropolitan area of 2½ million, Atlanta is amazingly close to nature. Within 70 to 120 miles, or about a 1½- to 2½-hour drive, city dwellers can hike through national forests and test their mettle on the rugged Appalachian Trail, scale Georgia's highest peak, fish trout streams, and canoe and swim in mountain lakes. They may come up for a day and browse Tyrolean shops in an "Alpine Village," and see the site of America's first gold rush. At dusk, they can return home, or stay over in a comfortable lodge, a country inn, or a fully furnished state-park cottage or campground.

About 70 miles north of Atlanta, the little town of **Dahlonega** is ideal as a one-day mini-adventure, or the start of a longer exploration. So the story goes, back in 1828 a trapper named Benjamin Parks stubbed his toe on a rock and uncovered a vein of gold that quickly sent prospectors streaming into the hills. Dahlonega is a Cherokee Indian word, meaning "precious yellow," and until the War Between the States, the precious substance flowed into a major U.S. Treasury mint. Although it's no longer a major industry, enough gold is still around to periodically releaf the dome of Georgia's State Capitol, and intrigue visitors who pan for it at **Crisson's Mine,** outside town (tel. 404/864-6363).

True to its heritage, Dahlonega's public square sports a rustic yesteryear look. Old galleried brick buildings and stores have been turned into shops purveying gold-panning equipment, gold jewelry, mountain handcrafts, antiques, ice cream, and fudge. In the center of the square, the red-brick **Gold Museum** chronicles the history of the gold rush and the many mines that flourished in these parts. A 28-minute film is especially worthwhile. Operated by the Georgia Parks Department, the museum is open Tuesday through Saturday from 9 a.m. to 5 p.m., and on Sunday from 2 to 5:30 p.m. Adults pay $1; ages 6 to 12, 50¢.

Dahlonega's second most famous landmark is just off the square. The **Smith House,** 202 S. Chestatee St. (tel. 404/864-3566), is renowned for its monumental family-style southern buffets that include fried chicken, ham, roast beef, barbecue, a dozen or more vegetables, relishes, cornbread, and biscuits, and dessert for $10.75 per person. Breakfast is served on Saturday and Sunday only, from 7 to 10 a.m. Lunch is offered Tuesday through Friday from 11 a.m. to 3 p.m., and dinner Tuesday through Sunday from 5 to 8 p.m.

A block away, the **Worley Homestead,** 410 W. Main St., Dahlonega, GA 30533 (tel. 404/864-7002), is one of the northern Georgia's most charming bed-and-breakfast inns. Seven guest rooms in the 1845-era home are furnished with antiques. Rates of $50 to $60 double include a whopping southern breakfast.

From Dahlonega, U.S. 19 winds scenically north into the mountains, toward one of the state's prettiest parks. At Neel's Gap, take a break at the **Mountain Crossing / Walasi-Yi Center.** The stone-and-log building is a legacy of the Depression-era Civilian Conservation Corps, and a landmark on the Appalachian Trail, which crosses here on its way to Maine. You can sip cider at the little snackbar, and purchase mountain crafts and guidebooks. Five miles farther north, about 20 miles from Dahlonega, **Vogel State Park,** Blairsville, GA 30512 (tel. 404/745-2628), invites you to hike around pretty Lake Trahlyta, fish for bass and bream, canoe, and in summer have a refreshing swim. Nestled in the vale of soft-green mountains, campsites have power and water hookups, hot showers, and laundries. Cottages are comfortably furnished, with wood-burning fireplaces. Lodging charges are standardized throughout the state park system: rates are $6 a night for tent and pop-up camping, $7 for RV hookups; cottages cost of $30 a night for a one-bedroom, $38 for a two-bedroom, and $44 for a three-bedroom, November 1 to March 31; and $34, $42, and $48 respectively, April 1 to October 31.

From Vogel, drive north five miles on U.S. 19 and head east on Ga. 180. At the junction of Ga. 180 and Ga. 348, either continue east to **Brasstown Bald Mountain,** or head south on Ga. 348 and drive across the spectacular Richard Russell Scenic Hwy. Or you can have your Bald and your scenic highway too. Drive on to **Brasstown,** and take the paved road to within 930 yards of the summit of Georgia's highest mountain (4,784 feet). At the parking area, you'll find picnic tables, vending machines, and scenic overlooks. The most panoramic views are from the very top, reached by hiking a woodland trail, or in summer by riding a minibus. The glass-enclosed visitors center on top has displays of mountain flora and fauna, and on clear days you can see across northern Georgia, into Tennessee and the Carolinas.

After exploring Brasstown, backtrack on Ga. 180, and head south on the **Richard Russell Scenic Hwy.** Along the two-lane road's 16-mile course, stop several times to gaze across mountains and valleys. The drive is especially awesome in fall, when hardwoods blaze with colors. At 3,500-foot Tesnatee Gap, the highway crosses the Appalachian Trail. Park by the roadside and take a ten-minute walk among the earnest backpackers. Follow Ga. 348 to its dead-end at Ga. 75-Alt. Turn left and drive 2.3 miles to a dead-end at Ga. 17/75. Go right three-tenths of a mile, then left on Ga. 356 and 1½ miles into Unicoi State Park.

**Unicoi State Park,** P.O. Box 256, Helen, GA 30545 (tel. 404/878-2824), is even more beautiful than Vogel. Around a pristine lake, in the midst of 1,000 acres of woodlands, the heart of the park is the Unicoi Lodge and Conference Center. Warm and wood-beamed, the lodge has an excellent cafeteria-style dining room, serving three meals a day at very modest prices. There's also a gift shop stocked with mountain arts and crafts. Furnished cottages and campsites are tucked into the wooded hillsides.

Anna Ruby Falls is the scenic masterpiece of a 1,600-acre **Chattahoochee National Forest** recreation area adjoining Unicoi. From a paved parking area, it's an easy and very beautiful half-mile walk through the woods, by a rushing white-water stream, to an observation platform at the base of 153- and 50-foot cascades.

From Unicoi, drive two miles south into **"Alpine Helen."** Once a quiet Appalachian village, Helen has been turned into a bit of Bavaria in the Georgia hills. Main Street buildings wear red roofs, flower boxes, balconies, and murals. You can shop for sweaters, porcelains, cuckoo clocks, and Christmas ornaments; enjoy wurst and beer to oom-pah music at an outdoor biergarten; and in September and October join the revelery of Oktoberfest. Numerous alpine-style hotels have comfortable accommodations and restaurants. More Appalachian than Alpine, **Betty's Country Store,** at the north end of town (tel. 404/878-2943), serves sandwiches and chili, and is a fun place to browse for mountain produce and cookbooks.

Five miles east of Helen on Ga. 255, the **Stovall House,** Rte. 1, Box 103-A, Sautee, GA 30571 (tel. 404/878-3355), is one of the prettiest country inns you'll ever happen onto. Under the stewardship of affable Ham and Kathy Schwartz, the 1837-era farmhouse has five lovely guest rooms, furnished with antiques and all the modern comforts. Amenities include a wide veranda for leisurely rocking, and a restaurant serving first-rate southern, American, and continental dishes at moderate prices. Rooms are $25 single, $50 double; children 12 and under stay free with their parents.

Another 20 miles farther east, the Lake Rabun Hotel is another mountain gem. The lake itself may remind you of *On Golden Pond.* Ringed by mountains and summer cottages, dotted with canoes and sailboats, it is tranquility personified. Built in 1922, the **Lake Rabun Hotel,** Lakemont, GA 30552 (tel. 404/782-4946), is a 16-room wood-and-stone time warp. Knotty-pine rooms are filled with handmade rhododendron furniture, vintage photos, and piles of parlor games. There's no TV or room phones. The hospitality of owners Dick and Barbara Gray is legendary. During the day, you may hike the surrounding woodlands, and fish and canoe on the lake, and look forward to rehashing your adventures with fellow guests around the fireplace. Rates are an amazingly low $32 double. The hotel is open from April 1 to October 31.

## 2. Pine Mountain

Over on Georgia's western edge, almost at the Alabama line, there's a resort that comes close to qualifying as a philanthropic enterprise and makes an ideal headquarters for exploring points west and south of Atlanta.

**Callaway Gardens,** on U.S. 27 at Pine Mountain, were begun back in the '30s, and—like Colonial Williamsburg—every cent of profit generated by the resort is plowed back into development. In other words, the Callaway family, which built this beautiful place, derives no private gain at all from its operation, with all monies administered by a nonprofit, state-chartered foundation.

The gardens themselves are a fantastically complete collection of native plants and flowers, to which experimental gardening adds an exotic note. Recreational facilities include swimming and boating, 63 holes of golf on courses that serve as the site of the PGA National Junior Championships and the PGA Club Professional Championships, 19 tennis courts, fishing, biking, horseback trail riding, quail hunting, and skeet and trap shooting. And all this on 2,500 acres of what used to be abandoned, worn-out farmland.

This lovely resort is the result of one man's dedicated efforts to restore the natural beauty of the region and create a restful, scenic recreational environment for Georgia residents. Cason Callaway, head of one of Georgia's most prosperous textile mills, once said, "What I'm trying to do here is hang the picture a little higher on the wall for the people of this region. Every child ought to see something beautiful before he's six years old. . . . All I've done is try to fix it so that anybody who came here would see something beautiful wherever he might look." So well did he succeed that people from all over the world visit Callaway Gardens each year.

By rebuilding the soil, nurturing the plant life already there and importing more, building a sand beach that is the largest man-made inland beach in the world, providing inn and cottage accommodations, and opening it all to people of modest means, Cason Callaway did indeed "hang his picture a little higher"; and by the time of his death in 1961 thousands were walking the nature trails and making full use of the facilities he'd provided in a breathtaking scenic setting. And it would have gladdened his heart to see the busloads of schoolchildren that roll into the gardens each academic year for free horticultural, botanical, and nature study educational programs sponsored by the foundation.

**WHERE TO STAY:** The best possible place to stay is at the gardens themselves. However, because of their popularity, reservations must be made as far in advance as possible—at least a month, longer if you can.

There are 350 rooms in the **Callaway Gardens Inn,** Pine Mountain, GA 31822 (tel. 404/663-2281, or toll free 800/282-8181), all spacious with a brightly colored, homey decor that seems just right for this setting. Two pools and a wading pool, nature programs, bicycles, fishing, and access to beach facilities are part of the package when you stay at Callaway Gardens. There are fees, however, for fishing, tennis, horseback riding, hunting, and skeet and trap (see "Things to See and Do," below). Rates are seasonal, with doubles ranging from $65 to $120.

In addition to the inn, there are the lovely Mountain Creek Villas, with fireplaces, screened porches or patios, and fully equipped with all cooking utensils and dishes, linens, televisions, and outdoor grills. The one-bedroom size will accommodate four adults, or a family of up to six (or eight if you squeeze a little). These are beautifully situated on wooded sites and make a great stopover on an extended trip or an ideal "home away from home" on a "stay put" vacation in this area. The same free family facilities apply to the cottages as at the inn. Cottages are available on a per-day basis anytime except the summer months, when they are reserved for families only, on a weekly basis. For cottage rates and reservations, you should write well in advance to Central Reservations, Dept. R, Callaway Gardens, Pine Mountain, GA 31822, or call 404/663-2281, or toll free 800/282-8181.

*Note:* Both the inn and the cottages have golf and tennis package deals, and both offer courtesy cars for transportation throughout the gardens.

### Other Choices in the Area

Very close to Callaway Gardens, the **White Columns Motel,** Pine Mountain, GA 31822 (tel. 404/663-2312), is within walking distance of two good, moderately priced restaurants and is in a comfortable, convenient location, with the beach entrance to Callaway Gardens just a hop, skip, and a jump away. Rates at the White Columns vary from $35 up, seasonally, and they accept pets.

And at the little town of Hamilton, just five miles away, the **Valley Inn,** Hwy. 27, Hamilton, GA 31811 (tel. 404/628-4454) is also a small, well-run motel with accommodations that are sort of "motel standard," plus a pool and restaurant. Rates (which include admission to the gardens) range from $45 to $55 over the course of the year.

**DINING AT THE GARDENS:** There are five places to eat in the gardens themselves, all very good, with quite moderate prices. The **Plantation Room,** in the inn itself, is tastefully decorated in a country-dining-room style, with flowered wallpaper, deep carpets, and comfortable oak chairs. There's an à la carte menu and children's plates (with baked ham, fried chicken, roast beef, and the like), but it really outdoes itself in the three buffets each day. For breakfast there's an array of bacon, sausage, ham (all homemade), eggs, french toast, their own speckled heart grits, fresh berries and fruits (according to season), the beverage of your choice, and almost anything you can imagine—really a feast, and one of the best meals of the day at the inn. The lunch buffet and the one at dinner not only offer the meats mentioned above, but sometimes throw in continental dishes like crêpes and quiche. And on Friday, the evening Captain's Galley seafood buffet can only be called sumptuous. As for vegetables, well, they're the freshest, especially during the summer, when they come to the table just one or two hours after being picked in Mr. Cason's Vegetable Garden—and I've always found the seasonings excellent, with the taste of "southern" but without the overcooking that so often goes with it. If you've never eaten corn just pulled from the stalk, for example, you'll find out here that it's quite different from the "store-bought" kind pulled days before.

For intimate, candlelit dinners, the **Georgia Room** provides just the right elegant setting, with a continental menu and soft piano music.

The English Tudor-style **Gardens Restaurant** also has a country air, and it overlooks Mountain Creek Lake and the Lake View Golf Course. No breakfast here, but lunch (from 11:30 a.m. to 2 p.m.) is sometimes a soup-and-salad buffet (salads are a real specialty in this room, with ingredients coming from the Vegetable Garden in the summer), and there's always a good variety of hot dishes. At dinner (6:30 to 9:30 p.m.), the star of the menu, I think, is the French onion soup—delicious! Entrees usually include baked ham, chicken in one form or another, and one or two other meats (veal, lamb, etc.).

**The Veranda** is the place for dinner in a setting of casual charm.

Up in the country store, the **Country Kitchen** has a cozy, old-fashioned atmosphere and serves breakfast and lunch only (hours are 8:30 a.m. to 5 p.m., and they'll fix breakfast any time of the day). The ham, bacon, and sausage are homemade and the speckled heart grits are a trademark of the gardens and the Country Kitchen. Also, don't miss trying the many varieties of muscadine sauces, jams, and jellies that you'll find on your table. These are grown and manufactured right in the gardens. The luncheon menu features generous salads, hamburgers (big, juicy, and good), and the prices are slightly higher than, say, Burger King (only to be expected, since "hamburger" here means much more than meat on a bun).

Golf and tennis pro shops both have snackshops, with hot dogs, hamburgers, soft drinks, etc., at budget prices.

**THINGS TO SEE AND DO:** Callaway Gardens—which includes floral and hiking trails, a greenhouse complex, Pioneer Log Cabin, the Ida Cason Callaway Memorial Chapel (a lovely native-fieldstone and log structure by a waterfall on a small lake), Mr. Cason's Vegetable Garden, and acres of picnic grounds—has an admission price of $4 for adults and $1 for children 6 to 11 (children under 6, free). Of course, if you're a guest at the inn or the cottages, there's no charge.

The best place to start any exploration of the gardens is the **Information Center,** where an eight-minute slide show lets you get your bearings as to what is here, as well as giving you the fascinating history of this place. Spring is especially lovely, with more than 600 varieties of azaleas, but it doesn't matter what season it is when you enter the five-acre **John A. Sibley Horticulture Center,** an innovative indoor-outdoor complex. The **Vegetable Garden** comprises 7½ acres planted with fruits and vegetables, and the 160-year-old **Pioneer Log Cabin,** with authentic furnishings, paints a vivid picture of early settler life. The nondenominational **Ida Cason Callaway Memorial Chapel** (named for Cason Callaway's mother) is simplicity itself, yet quite elegant, with stained-glass windows depicting the seasons at the gardens. Organ concerts are scheduled throughout the year, marriages take place within its walls with comparative frequency, and it's open for a moment of quiet meditation at all times.

One of my favorite spots in the garden is the **Country Store** (actually, it isn't in the gardens, but close by the entrance). In fact, for several years following my trek north, I ordered three-pound slabs of their marvelous country-cured bacon sent to me in New York each month, where my family pronounced it "real" bacon, as opposed to the thin-sliced, "chip" bacon available in supermarkets. The bacon and cured ham, preserves, grits, water-ground cornmeal, and hundreds of other items, both locally made and imported, keep me window-shopping long after I've met the upper limits of my shopping budget.

As for recreation, if you're a day visitor in the summer, the charge is $9 for adults, $4 for ages 6 to 11 (no charge for those under 6), for admission to the **Robin Lake Beach.** That one price entitles you to swim (the sand beach is a man-made creation that rivals the things nature does herself), play miniature golf, use paddleboats for the deep water, and ride a riverboat, train, or canoe; as well as enjoy a Water Ski Spectacular and a "Flying High Circus," performed by members of the Florida State University troupe. These facilities, like the gardens, are free to guests at the inn or cottages.

Golfers will find three 18-hole courses as well as one 9-hole executive (par 31) course, with two pro shops and fees that run as follows: $20 to $25 for daily greens fees, $22 for power cart for 18 holes. Tennis courts (including eight Rubico and nine all-weather) cost $12 and $10, respectively, per hour.

Fishing (with artificial lures only) is available at $12 per person for a half day (includes boat with electric trolling motor), $22 for two people, and $32 for three.

Hunters can go for quail on a large preserve that's open from October 1 to March 31 for $125 for a half day (which includes guides and dogs) if they have the required Georgia hunting license—and there's skeet and trap shooting every day at the hunting preserve for $3 per round, plus shells (no charge for guns). The ranges are lit for night shooting.

## 3. Plains and Other Area Attractions

This corner of Georgia has had special significance for two U.S. presidents. Franklin D. Roosevelt retreated to his "Little White House" at Warm Springs for spiritual and physical refreshment, and Jimmy Carter was born in Plains, a little town that often didn't even appear on state maps. Both are within easy sightseeing distance from Callaway Gardens, which I recommend as the overnight base. In addition, Columbus is just 30 miles away, with antebellum and Victorian homes, plus an opera house dating from the Civil War that was rescued from decay and destruction by city citizens. There's an infamous Civil War prison camp, Andersonville, just a day trip away, a restored 1850s village, Westville, and in between, driving is made a pleasure by scenery that varies from mountains to rolling plains, from wooded areas to prosperous farms.

**WARM SPRINGS:** Just 17 miles from Callaway Gardens (take Ga. 190 and follow the signs) is the simple white wooden house that was FDR's **"Little White House."** He had discovered Warm Springs as far back as 1924, shortly after he contracted polio, when he went there for the beneficial effect of swimming in the warm spring water; then in 1926 he bought the springs, hotel, and some cottages and began developing facilities to help paralytic patients from all over the country through the Georgia Warm Springs Foundation, which he founded. Later, when he became president, this was the retreat he loved most, and the house you visit today is much as he left it when he suffered a massive cerebral hemorrhage in 1945 and died while sitting for a portrait in the Warm Springs cottage. The unfinished portrait (by artist Elizabeth Shoumatoff), his wheelchair, Fala's dog chain, ship models, sea paintings, and gifts from citizens of which he was particularly fond are preserved as he last saw them.

Next door on the historic site, the **Franklin D. Roosevelt Museum** (tel. 404/655-3511) holds more memorabilia and shows a 12-minute movie depicting his life when in Warm Springs. The Little White House is open daily from 9 a.m. to 5 p.m. (closed Thanksgiving and Christmas Days), and admission fees of $3 for adults, $1.50 for ages 6 to 12, cover both.

**PLAINS:** Jimmy Carter, 39th president of the U.S., was born 80 miles southeast of the Gardens (U.S. 27 south to Columbus, then Ga. 280 east). You'll know Plains by the little green-and-white train depot, the water tower brightly painted with the stars and stripes. Despite the fame of its most outstanding citizens, there is still a small-town charm that clings to both the town and the people. The early 1900s buildings are much like they were before the Depression of the '30s forced their closing (most were used as warehouses until Jimmy Carter's campaign got under way and brought business back to town). Turner's Hardware and Walters Grocery Store are longtime establishments. The depot (built in 1888) now houses a visitors center and a gift and book shop, but its looks haven't changed a great deal. All in all, Plains can be proud of the common sense that has recognized the importance of preserving the surroundings from which a rural peanut grower went out and became president of the U.S.

Of course, you can almost stand in the middle of "downtown" and see the whole town, but for do-it-yourself walking or driving tours, go by the **Plains Visitor Center,** east of Plains on U.S. 280, where Sibyl McGlaun and her very friendly staff will furnish maps and brochures. If you'd like advance information, write them at P.O. Box 69, Plains, GA 31780. Two publications I particularly liked (and have had fun reading even after coming home) are "Plains, Carter Country U.S.A." and "Armchair Tour of Jimmy Carter Country," both of which I picked up at the depot.

The one-story, ranch-style brick house that is **the Carter home,** the home of our former Chief Executive, is on Woodland Drive, and there are Secret Service booths at both this entrance and the one on Paschal Street (you can get a pretty good look at it by walking or driving west on Church Street). Then there's the **Plains Methodist Church,** at the corner of Church and Thomas, where Jimmy asked Rosalynn for their first date. When he's in town, Jimmy teaches Sunday school at Maranatha Baptist Church. Visitors are invited—check the notice in the window of Hugh Carter's Antiques on Main Street. If you want to see an even *more* rural, now-historic site, take a 2½-mile drive out to **Archery,** where Jimmy Carter lived as a child when his father operated a country store. It's west of town on U.S. 280 (it's really *off* U.S. 280, but anybody in town can give you explicit directions).

In nearby **Americus,** on the grounds of Georgia Southwestern College, Wheatly and Glessner Streets (tel. 912/928-1273), the **James Earl Carter Library** holds a permanent display of memorabilia of the Carter family, with the focus on the former president and his first lady.

It's worth the trip to Americus to spend a blissful day and night at the **Merriwood Country Inn,** Rte. 6, Box 50, Americus, GA 31709 (tel. 912/924-4992). You know it's going to be special when you're met at the tree-shaded farmhouse by a welcoming committee of geese, goats, canines, and kittens. Owner JoAnn Davis will show you to a country-comfortable guest room, and invite you to relax in the spacious sitting room or fish in the nearby pond. She'll send you off in the morning with a bountiful southern breakfast. Rates are $25 to $45, including breakfast.

In downtown Americus, **The Cheeseboard,** 116 W. Lamar St. (tel. 912/928-3353), is a spiffy little café with a tempting selection of gourmet sandwiches, pastas, quiche, soups, salads, desserts, beer, and wine. Open Monday through Saturday for lunch and dinner.

The **Plains Bed and Breakfast,** P.O. Box 217, Plains, GA 31780 (tel. 912/824-7252), is the Victorian home where Jimmy Carter's parents spent their early married life. Now operated by affable Grace and Buck Jackson, the four guest rooms have private baths and breakfast for $50 to $55.

**ANDERSONVILLE:** Twenty miles northeast of Plains (U.S. 280 to Americus, then Ga. 49 north) is a National Historic Site that marks the most infamous of Confederate prison camps. Conditions at Andersonville were unspeakably horrible, with severe overcrowding (it was built to hold 10,000, but had at one time a prisoner population of over 32,000), polluted water (from a creek), and star-vation rations which led to nearly 15,000 deaths. The commander, Capt. Henry Wirtz, although powerless to prevent the fatalities and an absolute victim of cir-cumstances he had no way of controlling, was tried and hung after the Civil War on charges of having conspired to murder Union prisoners of war. Today you can visit a small museum, see slide shows on the camp's sad history, see the remains of wells and escape tunnels, and see Providence Springs, which legend says gushed up in answer to prayers of prisoners during the drought of 1864. The site is open daily, and there's no admission charge.

After visiting the historic site, browse the antique shops in the adjacent vil-lage of Andersonville. Stop by the **Visitors Center** in the old train depot and meet Peggy Sheppard, a gregarious transplanted New Yorker who spearheaded the village's rejuvenation. Also, see the fascinating Civil War artifacts at the **Little Drummer Boy Museum.**

The small town of **Montezuma,** 12 miles north of Andersonville, is the cen-ter of an 85-family Mennonite dairy-farming community. You may enjoy Penn-sylvania Dutch–style roast beef and shoo-fly pie, and first-class southern cooking, at **Yoder's Dietsch Haus** on Ga. 26, three miles east of Montezuma (tel. 912/472-2024). This clean-as-a-whistle cafeteria is open for breakfast, lunch, and dinner Monday through Saturday, and also has a too-tempting bread and pastry shop.

**WESTVILLE:** An intriguing day trip from Callaway Gardens is the 50-mile drive south on U.S. 27 to Lumpkin and the little village of Westville, a restored 1850s town with unpaved streets, 19th-century buildings and homes, and crafts-men who demonstrate such oldtime skills as syrup-making, cotton-ginning, and blacksmithing. It's open every day except major holidays from 10 a.m. to 5 p.m. during the week, 1 to 5 p.m. on Sunday; and admission is $3.50 for adults, $1.50 for students, no charge for preschoolers.

**COLUMBUS:** This was the last frontier town of the original 13 colonies, and its wide streets (99 to 164 feet), shaded by marvelous old trees in grass plots, still reveal much of the original city plan of 1828. Situated on the Chattahoochee River at the foot of a series of falls, Columbus early utilized its water supply to become an important manufacturing center, supplying swords, pistols, cannon, gunboats, and other articles of war to the Confederate Army during the Civil War (it fell to Union forces in April of 1865 in one of the last battles of the war). Today there's a lovely riverside walkway, the **Columbus Chattahoochee Prome-nade,** with gazebos and historical displays, stretching from the Columbus Iron Works Trade and Convention Center to Oglethorpe Bridge, which is open from 10 a.m. to 5 p.m. Tuesday through Friday and 1 to 5 p.m. on Saturday and Sun-day. The **Columbus Chamber of Commerce,** 901 Front Ave. (tel. 404/327-1566), and the **Georgia Welcome Center,** Victory Drive and Tenth Avenue (tel. 404/571-7455), can furnish detailed sightseeing information. **Heritage Tours** leave (from the Hilton Hotel) on Wednesday and Saturday at 10 a.m. for two-hour guided tours that visit the **Springer Opera House** (a restored 1871 theater in which Edwin Booth and other distinguished actors performed, and which was refurbished by Columbians to become a cultural center once again) and several other historic houses. The tour fee is $5 for adults, $2.50 for ages 6 through 12.

**Fort Benning** (tel. 404/545-2958) is five miles south of the city on U.S. 27, and there is an interesting **National Infantry Museum** reflecting the history of the footsoldier from Revolutionary days up to the present. It's free, and open weekdays except Monday from 10 a.m. to 4:30 p.m., from 12:30 p.m. on Satur-day and Sunday.

If you're staying overnight, the **Columbus Hilton,** 800 Front Ave., Columbus, GA 31901 (tel. 404/324-1800), adjoins the Iron Works Convention Center. One wing of the 178-room hotel was part of the brick and wood-beamed Empire Mills complex. Doubles are $60 to $80. In the historic district, the **DeLoffre House,** 812 Broadway, Columbus, GA 31901 (tel. 404/324-1144), is a cozy inn with four antique-filled guest rooms, fireplaces, and all the modern amenities. Doubles are $55 to $60.

*Chapter XIV*

# INTRODUCTION TO FLORIDA

1. By Way of Background
2. Traveling to Florida
3. Traveling Within Florida
4. Cruising Around Florida

FLORIDA. The word has a magic ring. To some 39 million visitors every year it means two weeks or more in the sun. To almost 10 million more it is home in a year-round tropical climate. To countless others it's the promised land of retirement at the end of a lifetime's work in less friendly climes. To those who till its soil, it is the source of over $4 *billion* in agricultural products every year. To commercial fishermen, it's a happy hunting ground for more than 195 million pounds of fish and shellfish annually. To entertainers it's what the Palace once was to vaudeville stars. To kids it's Walt Disney World. To golfers it's more than 400 courses, many of championship caliber. To the sportsman it's the dogs at Tampa–St. Pete, the horses at Hialeah, jai-alai, and deep-sea fishing almost anywhere off its 8,426-mile shoreline. To mapmakers it's that 447-mile-long peninsula at the eastern bottom of the U.S., little more than 150 miles wide at any point. To weathermen it is very often the warmest spot on the weather map. To the aerospace world it's the jumping-off point to the unknown. To historians it is the site of this country's first permanent European settlement. To the U.S. Navy it's Pensacola or Jacksonville. To the Seminole Indians it's the Everglades. To artists and writers it's Key West or Sarasota. In short, Florida is . . . well, it's *Florida!*

## 1. By Way of Background

**FROM THE FOUNTAIN OF YOUTH TO DISNEY WORLD:** There has always been a "promised land" aura about Florida, with riches of one sort or another the goal of even its earliest tourists. Ponce de León came in April of 1513, after hearing tales from Puerto Rican Indians of a land of much gold and a miraculous, health-restoring fountain of youth. He landed near what would become St. Augustine, named the disappointingly poor land "La Florida," then left after only six days. Later, Panfilo de Narvaez would land near Tampa Bay; Hernando de Soto would pass through in 1539 on his explorations which would end in death on the Mississippi; and the Spanish, under various leaders, would rule Florida until 1763, in spite of a brief, unsuccessful attempt by the French to es-

GULF OF MEXICO

*FLORIDA*

tablish a foothold in 1564. Spain traded it to the eager British in 1763 for repossession of Havana. By 1783 Spain had recaptured West Florida and the Bahamas, and the Treaty of Paris gave them back the rest of the state. In 1812 a group of Americans (70 Georgians and nine Floridians) raised a "patriot flag" and declared it an independent republic, and in 1819 the U.S. paid Spain $5 million and formally took title.

By then, Florida had seen the flags of Spain, France, Great Britain, the State of Muskogee (unfurled by one William Augustus Bowles, who got himself elected "Director General of the State of Muskogee" by a congress of Seminoles and Creeks in 1799 and claimed the state for almost four years), the patriots, and even Mexico (for three months in 1817) fly in its sunlit skies. Small wonder then that in 1845 when it was admitted to the Union its first state flag declared in bold letters "LET US ALONE"!

Well, although the slogan disappeared from the flag in short order, people pretty much did leave Florida alone until Henry Plant built his Atlantic Coast railroad system through central Florida to Tampa in 1881, joining the east and west coasts. Then Henry Flagler, a Standard Oil associate of the Rockefellers, began his Florida East Coast Line in 1883, and the two millionaires embarked on a luxury-hotel-resort-building battle that started an influx of tourists that has just kept growing ever since. It reached frenzy proportions in the 1920s when land values soared and more than $100 million was spent in Miami on new buildings in one year. Then came the crash in 1929, which really only slowed tourism down, and by the '40s the state was back on its feet. World War II brought prosperity in the form of military installations, and the '50s saw many ex-servicemen returning to the scene to vacation or to set up residence. Since then, prosperity hasn't even slowed down—and I expect instant execution would be the fate of any present-day Floridian who dared utter that old slogan "Let Us Alone."

When Plant and Flagler began their promotion of the state, they touted its warm winters, and for many years that's when the crowds came. However, soon after World War II people from all over the country began to capitalize on the lower summer rates and to pour in during the months the kids were out of school. Nowadays more people come in summer than in winter, and "the season" has less and less meaning. Of course, the wealthier still favor winter months—they stay longer and spend more money—and Miami and Palm Beach fairly reek of money from December through May. But when they depart, families not only take their place in the "off-season" half-priced luxury accommodations, they also flock to the Panhandle's Miracle Strip (where summer *is* the season), St. Augustine, the Tampa Bay area, and—all year, in fact—Walt Disney World.

Actually, that old dream of Florida riches isn't so farfetched if you think in vacation terms. The beaches, of course, are a sort of "white gold," with wide strands of white sand and differing Atlantic and Gulf of Mexico surfs. But in addition to that, there are 166 rivers, more than 30,000 lakes (ranging in size from tiny "mud holes" to the giant 700-square-mile Lake Okeechobee), and artesian springs that are crystal clear and inhabited by ersatz "mermaids" who perform for visitors. And the vegetation is lush—cool, green pines up around the Georgia border, palms and sea grape, bougainvillea and hibiscus in a riot of color, sawgrass and cypress from the mysterious Everglades all the way down the Keys.

Superimposed on all these gifts of Mother Nature are man's contributions, many of them with no purpose except to accommodate a tourism industry that annually amounts to about $9 billion in revenue. The hotels, motels, and restaurants—along with flashy amusement centers, high-rise concrete condominiums, and crowded freeways—have created a landscape of another sort. But in the end it's Mother Nature who dominates, and the Sunshine State has lost none of the lure it held back in Ponce de León's day.

**ADVANCE INFORMATION:** Tourism is Florida's chief business, and the state goes all out to be sure no tourist will lack information. There are **welcome centers** for motorists at most major entrances as well as visitor centers at several outstanding sightseeing attractions around the state. Travel agents are generally loaded with tourist brochures for those coming by plane or other nondriving transportation. A letter to the Florida **Division of Tourism,** Visitor Inquiry, 126 Van Buren St., Tallahassee, FL 32301 (tel. 904/487-1462), will bring a healthy packet of statewide information, and almost every city and town has a chamber of commerce eager to send you facts and figures on their area. If you're driving, it's a good idea to specifically request a copy of the official state road map and the handy booklet "Florida Driver Information." And if you ask, they'll send a "Schedule of Events," which is issued seasonally and covers the goings-on all over the state for the time you plan to go. A request to the Tallahassee address will bring you a copy of the latest "Florida Vacation Guide."

Boaters arriving via the Intracoastal Waterway will find an excellent Marine Welcome Station at Fernandina Beach at the Waterway's Florida entrance.

**FLORIDA TELEPHONE AREA CODES:** St. Augustine, 904; Miami, 305; St. Petersburg, 813.

**FLORIDA'S HOTELS:** Well, there are, as I said, hotels and motels *ad infinitum* throughout the state. There are those that represent the last word in luxury and those that compete for the budget dollar. Nearly *all* vary in price according to the time of year. For example, a Miami deluxe hotel may rent a room for $110 during winter months and the same room will cost $45 in the summer. Farther north, in St. Augustine, the reverse is true. Generally speaking, the best accommodation buys in southern Florida are in October and November, when warm weather is a contrast to colder northern states and the winter rates are not yet in effect (they usually go up about December 15). In the upper part of the state, you'll get reductions after Labor Day until spring. Many hotels, in all price brackets, offer special weekend, golf, or tennis package plans that are real money-savers.

**BED-AND-BREAKFAST:** In the last few years a network of bed-and-breakfast associations has sprung up throughout Florida—good news for those of us who enjoy the personal contact with locals these accommodations provide. Each association has a coordinator who will do his or her best to match your preferences and special interests with private homeowners in the area you want to visit. Just let them know if you'd like a waterfront home, one close to golf or tennis, one with a swimming pool, etc.

The following is a list of some of the leading B&B associations: **Bed & Breakfast of the Palm Beaches,** c/o Mrs. Eliza Hofmeister, 205 Circle West, Jupiter, FL 33458 (tel. 305/746-2545); **Suncoast Accommodations,** c/o Ms. Bobbi Seligman, 13700 Gulf Blvd., Madeira Beach, FL 33708 (tel. 813/393-7020); **Tropical Isles Bed & Breakfast,** c/o Ms. Ursula Mucci, P.O. Box 490382, Key Biscayne, FL 33149 (tel. 305/361-2937); **The Bed & Breakfast Company,** c/o Ms. Marcella Schaible, 1205 Mariposa Ave., No. 233, Miami, FL 33146 (tel. 305/661-3270); **Florida Lifestyles Bed & Breakfast,** c/o Mr. Jack Donovan, 445 SW 2nd St., No. 30, Pompano Beach, FL 33060 (tel. 305/781-0888); **Florida & England B&B Accommodations,** c/o Ms. Carol Hart, P.O. Box 12, Palm Harbor,

FL 33563 (tel. 813/784-5118); and **Bed 'n Breakfast Gulf Coast,** c/o Jim and Jane Clowe, P.O. Box 12561, Pensacola, FL 32573 (tel. 904/438-7968).

**FOR THE HANDICAPPED:** The **Florida Council of Handicapped Organizations** can furnish information on facilities for the handicapped at Florida accommodations, restaurants, and recreation sites. Contact: Barbara Bernhart, Pres., F.C.H.O., c/o Space Coast Association of the Physically Handicapped, Center for Independent Living, P.O. Box 2027, Satellite Beach, FL 32937 (tel. 305/777-2964).

**CAMPING IN FLORIDA:** It seems that every major commercial campground chain has camps in Florida—you'll see them all along the way. In addition, the state has 40 state parks with camping facilities; sites cost $6 to $8 plus tax (more in the Keys) per night (electricity is $2 per night), with a two-week limit for your stay at any one park. Half these may be reserved in advance by telephone. There are also vacation cabins available in parks. For a complete list of state parks, regulations, and telephone numbers to reserve, write: **Florida Department of Natural Resources,** Bureau of Education and Information, Room 616, 3900 Commonwealth Blvd., Tallahassee, FL 32303 (tel. 904/488-7326), and ask for *Florida State Parks Guide.*

**FLORIDA'S RESTAURANTS:** All those restaurants in Florida include lavishly decorated gourmet rooms with exorbitantly priced menus and dockside seafood bars where you can eat well for a pittance—and often they're right across the dock from each other. Except in the notoriously high-priced establishments (mostly in Palm Beach and Miami), I find prices more reasonable than expensive, at least as measured by those in other resort areas of the country. And there is very good eating in motel and hotel dining rooms, which usually are in the moderate range. Also, most of the major fast-food and budget-food chains have branches scattered all over the state, where prices and quality are pretty dependable.

Most restaurants of any size or reputation sell alcoholic beverages by the drink, and wine and beer show up on the most unexpected menus. You can buy your own at retail liquor stores (Sunday sales, however, are subject to local option). Legal drinking age is 21.

**READER'S RESTAURANT SUGGESTION:** "We found the **Red Lobster restaurant chain** in Florida to be a reliable source for good seafood at very reasonable prices, and they are located in almost every town in Florida" (A. Nunez, Lodi, N.J.).

**FLORIDA CLIMATE:** The Gulf Stream in the Atlantic and the tropical currents of the Gulf of Mexico keep the state warmer than most of the rest of the continental United States in winter and can make temperatures as high as 95° in the summer. However, in Miami, summer temperatures average between 80° and 85° and winter temperatures are generally in the mid-70s. The most *comfortable* time to visit southern Florida, if you can't come in winter, is late April through May, before really hot weather sets in and before summer showers, which are an almost daily occurrence (although they're quite brief), begin. In the upper part of the state, you can count on things being about ten degrees cooler in every season. Some representative averages around the state are:

|                    | High | Low |
|--------------------|------|-----|
| St. Augustine      | 89   | 47  |
| Miami              | 90   | 58 ⸲ |
| Tampa–St. Petersburg | 90 | 51  |

Humidity can be a problem, making temperatures feel much higher than they are, so if you're going in midsummer, take along cool, airy clothes. Insects, however, which were once such a nuisance in the tropical climate, have been reduced considerably due to an effective pest-control program in most sections of the state.

# 2. Traveling to Florida

**BY AIR:** Florida has five international airports—Miami, Fort Lauderdale, Jacksonville, Orlando, and Tampa/St. Petersburg—with every major airline (and some not so major) reaching the state from almost anywhere in the United States and major overseas departure points. There are nearly always special promotional fares being offered to Florida, so be *sure* to shop around.

### Package Deals
Many of the major airlines offer packages to Miami and Orlando (Walt Disney World) which can represent real savings. Your travel agent or local airline office can fill you in on current offerings and prices.

**BY TRAIN:** Amtrak has service to Florida from all across the country—direct routes down the eastern seaboard and from the Midwest, connecting schedules from the West Coast. For example, to come from Los Angeles to Miami, you would travel first to Chicago, then to Florida after a change of trains. Check Amtrak's excellent special rates, which change from time to time, but which are real dollar-stretchers. So be sure to check out current specials when planning your trip by train. There are also many attractive Amtrak package tours to Florida's most popular spots.

### Auto Train
Amtrak has revived its popular Auto Train service from Lorton, Virginia (near Washington, D.C.), to Sanford, Florida (near Orlando), with greatly improved equipment and several extras that make this an enjoyable way to get yourself and your car to Florida without a long, exhausting drive. All Auto Train tickets cover a buffet dinner with wine, continental breakfast, complimentary snacks served in the attractive lounge, and en route movies. There are high-level Vista-Dome cars that give superb views of the changing countryside, and the basic fare gives you a reclining, leg-rest coach seat. For even more comfort, you can opt for a bedroom that sleeps two (for an additional $225) or a roomette that sleeps one (at $110 extra). Auto Trains leave each point daily at 4:30 p.m., arriving at the other end at 8:30 a.m. the next day. Regular one-way fares are $130 for adults, $98 for ages 2 through 11, and $220 for autos. If you travel off-peak, however—March 1 to June 15 southbound—prices drop by 50%. A leisurely, hassle-free way to travel down the East Coast for a Florida holiday!

**BY BUS:** Both Greyhound and Trailways have rather direct express routes to major Florida cities from most points in the country. Both offer much lower excursion rates from time to time, and you should be sure to look into these carefully.

**BY CAR:** Both I-95 and I-75 are major arteries entering Florida from Georgia. I-95 runs all the way south to Miami and is by far the quickest way to get there. U.S. 1 also enters from the northeast and runs along Florida's east coast, but this is a frustrating, stoplight-infested way to go, and a better choice (albeit a little slower) is the scenic A1A, which hugs the shoreline, often affording beautiful sea vistas, and leisurely zigzags through coastal resort towns. I-75 goes through north-central Florida, then swings west to Tampa–St. Petersburg.

From Alabama, I-10 runs across northern Florida to Jacksonville; U.S. 98 follows the Panhandle coastline to U.S. 19, which goes down the Gulf Coast to Tampa–St. Petersburg and joins U.S. 41 (the Tamiami Trail), which in turn follows the west coast down to Naples, where it turns across the state, skirting the Everglades, to terminate in Miami.

Along three of Florida's major Interstates—I-75, I-95, and I-4—you'll find many of the highlight attractions of a vacation in the state. A free "Florida Travelers Discount Guide," featuring discount coupons for attractions, fuel, shopping, hotels, restaurants, and campgrounds along these routes is now available. It also contains an exit guide, maps, and mileage charts to help with your holiday planning. Contact: Florida Travelers Discount Guide, 618 S. Main St., Gainesville, FL 32601 (tel. 904/371-EXIT).

# 3. Traveling Within Florida

**BY AIR:** Within the state, Eastern, Pan Am, Delta, Southern, Commuter, Piedmont and PBA fly to numerous destinations.

**PBA** provides perhaps the most widespread service, flying regular schedules to some 13 airports: Jacksonville, Tallahassee, Tampa, Sarasota, Punta Gordo, Fort Myers, Naples, Marco Island, West Palm Beach, Miami, Ocean Reef (South Miami), Marathon, and Key West. This airline, America's oldest regional air service and one that confines its routes to New England and Florida, has a large fleet of planes of varying sizes, from the small Cessna 402 to the Douglas DC-3. I don't know about you, but the smaller planes have—for me—a particular fascination, and I fly them whenever possible. Somehow, I have a more intense experience of actually *flying* than in the larger, hotel-like planes. If you're squeamish about small planes, however, best inquire about the size of aircraft when you book on PBA. As for me, it's one of my favorite ways to get around Florida. For reservations and schedule information, call 813/774-3838, or toll free 800/282-3197 within Florida, 800/237-7640 from all other southeastern states.

**BY TRAIN:** Amtrak stops within the state are at: Jacksonville, Palm Beach, Delray Beach, Deerfield Beach, Fort Lauderdale, Hollywood, Miami, Orlando, Kissimmee, Lakeland, Winter Haven, Sebring, Tampa, Clearwater, St. Petersburg, Gainesville, Ocala, Wildwood, Palatka, Deland, Sanford, and Winter Park. Amtrak service also connects Miami Beach and Tampa, with a link to Walt Disney World.

**BY BUS:** Gulf Coast Motor Lines has intrastate service, and of course Greyhound and Trailways both have connecting service to most points within the state.

## Bus Tours

**Gray Lines** offers excellent one- and two-day tours from most major cities to sightseeing attractions such as Walt Disney World and Key West. And for those who truly want to "leave the driving" to someone else, **Tauck Tours** has an excellent seven-day Florida Triangle Tour departing from Tampa. Travel is on comfortable, air-conditioned motor coaches, with seating shifted twice each day. During the seven days, there is a total of 15 hours' riding time, with hotel accommodations and meals included in the tour price. Arrangements for both tours can be made through travel agents all over the country.

**BY CAR:** Florida is crisscrossed by an excellent network of highways. Major Interstates run through or close to the following towns:

**I-75,** traveling north to south, goes through Jennings, Jasper, Lake City, Gainesville, Ocala, Bushnell, Dade City, Tampa, and terminates at St. Petersburg.

**I-95,** on the east coast, runs north to south through Yulee, Jacksonville, St. Augustine and St. Augustine Beach, Marineland, Daytona Beach, Cocoa Beach, Melbourne, Vero Beach, Port St. Lucie, Fort Pierce, Stuart, Palm Beach and West Palm Beach, Lake Worth, Delray Beach, Boca Raton, Pompano Beach, Fort Lauderdale, Hollywood, Hallandale, Surfside, Hialeah, Miami and Miami Beach, and Coral Gables.

From west to east, **I-10** goes to Pensacola, Crestview, Tallahassee, Lake City, and Jacksonville.

In the center of the state, also west to east, **I-4** begins at St. Petersburg and runs through Tampa, Lakeland, Winter Haven, Haines City, Kissimmee (Walt Disney World), Lake Buena Vista, Winter Garden, Orlando, Winter Park, Sanford, Deland, and Daytona Beach.

While almost all car-rental rates in Florida are low, **Budget Rent-a-Car** offers something a bit special. At rates even lower than those charged by most companies for compact cars, Budget will give you a luxury Lincoln Town Car or Chrysler Fifth Avenue, Mustang or Dodge 600 convertible, all with unlimited mileage. Talk about driving around in style! It isn't often that "budget" equates with "luxury," but in this case they are the same. And if you're booked into one of their participating hotels or resorts, you may qualify for even lower discounted rates. For particulars and booking, call toll free 800/527-0700.

**Thrifty Rental Car** locations are scattered throughout the state, at Daytona Beach, Delray Beach, Fort Lauderdale, Fort Myers, Gainesville, Hollywood, Jacksonville, Miami, Ocala, Orlando, Panama City, Pensacola, Pompano Beach, Sarasota, St. Petersburg, Stuart, Tallahassee, Tampa, and West Palm Beach.

**BY BOAT:** There are 349 miles of the **Intracoastal Waterway** from Jacksonville to Miami, with many canals connecting it to the ocean. If you're planning to float to Florida, contact the Department of Natural Resources, 3900 Commonwealth Blvd., Tallahassee, FL 32303, for helpful boating information.

# 4. Cruising Around Florida

By using one of the most "dollarwise" methods I can think of, you can make your Florida holiday do double duty by combining a stay in the state with one of the excellent short cruises that operate out of the Port of Miami. You'll experience both the highlights of Florida and the excitement of exotic destinations in the Bahamas, as well as soul-soothing sea voyages. From personal experience, I can tell you that it's the biggest dollar-stretcher you're likely to find anywhere. Both the companies listed below offer real bargains in fly/sail/drive package tours that take much of the drudgery out of vacation planning without plugging you into a straitjacket itinerary.

**Eastern Cruise Lines,** 1220 Biscayne Blvd. (P.O. Box 010882), Miami, FL 33101 (tel. 305/373-7501), sends the lovely S.S. *Emerald Seas* on three-night cruises to Nassau and Freeport and four-night sailings that throw in a carefree day on their private uninhabited island, Little Stirrup Cay. The ship itself is a beauty, fresh from a $3-million renovation, with staterooms about a third larger than most cruise ships (for a confirmed shower-hater like me, the full bathtubs were a special surprise and treat). Some can easily accommodate as many as four, with the third person charged a lower rate and the fourth traveling free during certain seasons. There's entertainment, gambling, and shopping aboard ship as well as ashore, and the day at Little Stirrup Cay gives you a beach picnic plus your choice of no fewer than four beaches and a bevy of beach activities— or a relaxing day spent suspended in a hammock, if you prefer. The passenger list covers just about all age ranges, with shipboard activities for each, from a swinging disco for the younger set to sophisticated shows and dance music for those of a more sedate nature. The land portion of Eastern's package tours covers the Miami/Miami Beach area and/or Walt Disney World. Prices vary according to season and stateroom choice, and you can book only the cruise at a lower cost (1987 prices ranged from $350 to $800). Bookings may be made through travel agents or Eastern Cruise Lines.

**Carnival Cruise Lines,** Carnival Tours, 3915 Biscayne Blvd., Miami, FL 33137, bills its ships as "The Fun Ships." Cruises may be for three, four, or seven days, with at least one full day at sea on each and shipboard activities including such fun events as the Masquerade Ball and the tamer Bingo playoffs. Although Carnival cruises seem to attract a larger percentage of young passengers, there is really something for everyone included in the on-board program (for examples, a Grandmother's Bragging Party, movies, bridge games, gym, etc.). Gambling and shopping are available on all ships, as well. The S.S. *Carnivale* makes three- and four-day cruises with port calls in Nassau and Freeport; the S.S. *Festivale* sails for seven days and touches San Juan, Puerto Rico, and St. Thomas, as well as Nassau; the S.S. *Holiday* adds St. Maarten; and the S.S. *Mardi Gras* sails to Cozumél, Playa del Carmen, Grand Cayman, and Ocho Ríos. Land portions include a choice of the Miami Bay area, Orlando and Walt Disney World, Key West, Cable Beach (Nassau), and for passengers traveling to Miami from the West Coast, three nights in New Orleans. Amtrak offers rail/sail packages on Carnival Lines ships from ten cities on its New York/Miami *Silver Star* route. For schedules and reservations, see your travel agent.

For the ultimate in cruising along the Atlantic seaboard, there are two yacht-style cruise vessels that ply the Intracoastal Waterway. The *Newport Clipper* and the *Nantucket Clipper* are the closest many of us will ever come to sailing on a luxurious private yacht. The *Charleston Clipper* is due to join them in early 1988. From their hand-laid teakwood decks to glass-enclosed lounges and dining rooms to nicely appointed staterooms with picture windows, to a degree of personal attention and service impossible on larger cruise ships, they represent a unique travel experience for nonmillionaires. Carrying only about 100 passengers, each yacht provides the ambience of a private party made up of invited guests, and there is never the "enforced joy hour" attitude that pervades many a larger cruise ship. One-seating-only meals are a culinary delight, and a nice touch in the a.m. is the continental breakfast provided for sleep-ins who prefer to skip the earlier full breakfast. Dockings are many times in yacht basins not reachable by larger ships, and shore excursions provide leisurely sightseeing just steps away from the yacht. This kind of pampering is the stuff of fantasies, and I highly recommend indulging in at least one dream-come-true holiday in every lifetime! The seven-day Florida Waterways Itinerary puts in at Fort Lauderdale, Palm Beach, Cocoa Beach (for excursions to Walt Disney World), St. Augustine, St. Simons Island (Georgia), ending in Savannah, with 1987 fares ranging from $1,495 to $1,895 (double occupancy; singles pay slightly higher rates). Golfers can book a special package deal that includes the championship courses at Hilton Head Island, South Carolina. For other southeastern itineraries, see Chapter I. For additional information, schedules, and bookings, contact **Clipper Cruise Line,** 7711 Bonhomme Ave., St. Louis, MO 63105 (tel. toll free 800/325-0010), or your travel agent.

# Chapter XV

# FLORIDA: DOWN THE EAST COAST

### 1. St. Augustine
### 2. Daytona Beach
### 3. Walt Disney World and Epcot Center
### 4. Palm Beach
### 5. Boca Raton

FLORIDA'S EAST COAST from St. Augustine to Palm Beach is a varied, fascinating world unto itself. It encompasses this country's oldest city, St. Augustine, and the point from which we launched our nation into the Space Age, Cape Canaveral. It holds a fantasyland of the imagination, Disney World, and a fantasyland of untold wealth and its attendant lifestyle, Palm Beach. And by the time you get from one end of this world to another, even the "season" will have changed—around St. Augustine, the "season" is the summer; at Palm Beach, winter is the favored time of year.

## 1. St. Augustine

It would take a separate book to do justice to the rich history of the United States' oldest city. And dates like 1513 and 1565 make the "lost" colonists of North Carolina and the Massachusetts Pilgrims sound like Johnny-come-latelies. With such an early start, Spain might have changed the course of world history by extending her colonization and holding on to her New World territories, with the result that a lot more people might very well have surnames and accents reflecting Spanish rather than English and northern European culture. But she didn't, and most of our Spanish heritage today comes from the Caribbean, via a roundabout course from the homeland.

Ponce de León was the first Spaniard to land here, in 1513, vainly looking for eternal youth. He didn't find it, of course, but he did plant Spain's flag and claim possession. Pedro Menendez de Aviles arrived in 1565 to establish St. Augustine, the first permanent European settlement in the U.S. It was a strategic location, but also very vulnerable, and twice the city was sacked by pirates, once in the 16th century and again in the 17th. By the time the English started looking south at Spain's foothold on the continent, St. Augustine had been the seat of government for some 30 missions along the coast, as well as all other Spanish possessions in Florida and Georgia. As the English threat grew, the Spanish began construction of the Castillo de San Marcos in 1672, at a cost of some $30 million.

What the British couldn't win by battle, they took by treaty, and St. Augustine was ceded to them in 1763. It was an important point of refuge for loyalists during the Revolution, and the Castillo was used to imprison patriots who had chosen the "wrong" side from the British point of view.

In 1783 Florida went back to Spain, again by treaty, and the Spanish were lavish with land grants, moving hundreds of Americans into lands vacated by former British owners. The United States gained possession of the state in 1821, and St. Augustine was peaceful until the 1830s, when the Seminole Wars broke out and it once again played a military role (now the Castillo held Indian prisoners).

Of the American influences that have marked St. Augustine, that of Henry W. Flagler is probably the most important. In his zest to develop the whole state, he built two extravagant hotels to lure the North's wealthy to St. Augustine and made it the headquarters for his Florida East Coast Railroad.

Today you'll find traces of every phase of its history written across St. Augustine's face, and there has been a concerted effort in recent years to restore the old Spanish city for visitors. The heart of the restoration area is narrow, quaint St. George Street, which starts at the City Gate and runs to Plaza de la Constitucion, with more than 50 houses along the way, either on St. George Street or those that branch off it. And for beach-oriented vacationers, there are miles and miles of beach across the Bridge of Lions at St. Augustine Beach.

**WHERE TO STAY:** Whether you stay in the city itself, at Vilano Beach (A1A North), or St. Augustine Beach (A1A South) will depend largely on whether you're sightseeing or beach oriented. Their proximity makes any one convenient to the other. Because I, personally, love the history of the place, the city is my preference, but there are good choices in all three locations.

### In St. Augustine

The **Marion Motor Lodge,** 120 Avenida de Menendez, St. Augustine, FL 32084 (tel. 904/829-2261), is a sparkling-white motel, accented by wrought-iron balconies and hanging baskets of greenery, almost directly across from the Municipal Yacht Pier. A Marion has been on this site for 45 years, the present structure replacing a luxury hotel that was torn down a few years ago. Rooms are bright and colorful (they all face the bay), and there's a pool and sundeck. Two fine restaurants are within 200 feet of the motel, and it's an easy walk to the Historic Restoration Area. The friendly management will arrange all sorts of sightseeing tours and can fix you up with charter-boat fishing. Rates for double occupancy are $45 to $55.

Also close to the Historic Restoration Area, **Whetstone's Bay Front Inn,** 138 Avenida Menendez, St. Augustine, FL 32084 (tel. 904/824-1681), has large rooms, a swimming pool, and a beautiful view of Matanzas Bay. Architecture is Spanish, and the atmosphere relaxing. No restaurant, but several are within walking distance. Doubles run $35 to $50.

Across the Bridge of Lions from the heart of town, six blocks south on A1A, look for signs to the **Conch House Marina Resort,** 57 Comares Ave., St. Augustine, FL 32084 (tel. 904/829-8646, or toll free 800/874-0853). It's in a quiet, secluded, palm-shaded area right on the water. There's a fishing pier, boat slips, private patios, and a pool. There's also an attractive lounge over the water and restaurant featuring fresh seafood. Rooms are quite nice, varying from standard units to suites at $58 to $110.

The large (200 rooms) **Ponce de Leon,** Ponce de Leon Boulevard, U.S. 1 North, St. Augustine, FL 32084 (tel. 904/824-2821, or toll free 800/824-2821), is a short three miles north of the center of town on U.S. 1, and its spacious grounds hold a rather complete resort. In addition to the huge, cloverleaf pool, there's a championship 18-hole golf course, lighted tennis courts, a lovely restaurant, dancing, and entertainment. The rooms are all large, done up in bright, resort colors, and some have extra basins in the dressing area. Private patios and balconies abound. Doubles here are in the $60 to $70 range.

The **Kenwood Inn,** 38 Marine St., St. Augustine, FL 32084 (tel. 904/824-2116), is one of Florida's charming small inns. Located on the corner of Marine and Bridge Streets, just a half block from the water, it has 15 rooms with Victorian furnishings, all air-conditioned, and a continental breakfast comes with your room. There's a pool and tennis privileges at nearby facilities. Doubles are in the $40 to $65 range.

## St. Augustine Beach (Anastasia Isle—A1A South)

The **Sheraton Anastasia Inn,** A1A at Pope Road, St. Augustine, FL 32084 (tel. 904/471-2575, or toll free 800/325-3535), offers deluxe beach accommodations directly on the ocean at slightly more than moderate prices. There are kitchenettes among the 144 units, a pool, a restaurant, and a lounge with entertainment and dancing. In-season (summer) rates range from $40 to $75 for large rooms furnished in a modern decor; kitchen units run $55 to $85, and off-season rates are lower.

Budget prices that begin at $20 prevail at the **Sea Shore Motel,** A1A at 12th Street, St. Augustine Beach, FL 32084 (tel. 904/471-3101), which is also on the ocean side of the highway. Many units here have kitchenettes and all are exceptionally well furnished for the price. Restaurants, a grocery store, fishing pier, and laundry are nearby. Weekly rates are also available (location and time of year determine the rates, but all are budget).

## A Special Place Worth the Extra Drive

Admittedly, it's an hour-and-a-half drive from St. Augustine north to **Amelia Island Plantation,** Amelia Island, FL 32034 (tel. toll-free 800/874-6878, 800/342-6841 in Florida). That makes St. Augustine an easy day trip for sightseeing—this is, however, such a lovely spot that the drive is a small price to pay, and indeed you may never want to leave the island at all. The island itself is a historic one, named by Governor Oglethorpe for the daughter of King George II of England (there are those who will take an oath that the princess's spirit sometimes roams the island's beaches, but I can't vouch for that!). Accommodations come in the form of deluxe guest rooms at the inn or in vacation villas whose private owners make them available for rental. There are numerous fine dining rooms and restaurants, a full range of sports facilities, miles of good beaches, golf, tennis, paddleboats, sailing, etc. High-season rates for doubles are in the $133 to $161 range, and villas start at $159. A wide variety of vacation packages, however, lower those rates considerably—for example, in 1987 there were rates as low as $77 to $145 *per person* for one to five nights available under these plans during winter months. And of course all rates drop from May to November.

## Campgrounds

This is an especially good camping base, with Jacksonville to the north and A1A's long stretches of undeveloped beach south to Flagler Beach. There are eight commercial campgrounds in the area, and the St. Augustine Chamber of Commerce can furnish a complete list. The one I most liked was the **St. Augustine Ocean Resort** Rte. 5, A1A, Box 18P, St. Augustine, FL 32084 (tel. 904/471-3353), eight miles south on A1A in a quiet, clean oceanfront setting. The 240 sites have electric, cable TV, water, and sewer hookups, and there's a dumping station, laundry facilities, pool, tennis court, shuffleboard, game room, and adult lounge. Rates begin at $19 and VISA and MasterCard are accepted.

**WHERE TO EAT:** Good eating doesn't come high in St. Augustine. Most restaurants are quite moderate in price, and there are some very good places to dine.

"This is my trade—I love to cater to people," Claude Sinatsches, Swiss-trained chef at **Le Pavillon,** 45 San Marco Ave. (tel. 904/824-6202), will tell you, and cater to them he does. In fact, part of the pleasure in eating here comes from the warmth and graciousness of Claude, his wife, Gisele, and her brother, Fritz Dold. The German-Swiss family group has turned an 85-year-old St. Augustine home into an utterly charming European restaurant with specialties such as wienerschnitzel Viennese style, sauerbraten and spätzle, and red snapper in papillote, all accompanied by the special house salad, German home-fried potatoes, red cabbage, and hot rolls. If you happen to be a crêpe lover (which I confess to be), there's an amazing variety of fillings, and the crêpes themselves are perfection. The low $6 tab includes three crêpes, tossed greens or fresh fruit salad, and parmesan sticks. Whether you eat on the candlelit, screened-in front porch or in one of the inner rooms, best reserve ahead for dinner, when there's live entertainment and always a large contingent of local folks. Open for lunch from 11:30 a.m. to 2:30 p.m., for dinner from 5 to 10 p.m., at prices of $6 to $18.

You could go to the **Chimes Restaurant,** 12 Avenida Menendez (tel. 904/829-8141), just for the view—it overlooks Matanzas Bay and the Castillo de San Marcos—but it's reassuring to know that the food is *almost* as good as the view. James Kalivas, the owner-chef, makes all the pastries and puts out breakfast waffles that are as much a treat as the seafood and steaks he serves at lunch and dinner. The restaurant is open seven days a week from 7 a.m. to 9 p.m., and I found the prices very low for the high-quality meals. Breakfast is in the $2 to $3.75 range, lunch is $3 to $6, and dinner runs $6 to $15.

There's a little corner of France right where picturesque Charlotte Street and Artillery Lane come together in the heart of the restored area. The **Guy Denoel French Pastry Shop,** like its European counterparts, sells fresh-baked, melt-in-your-mouth pastries ($1 to $2 each) that you can take out or eat (with coffee if you like) at one of the small tables in this bistro-like setting. It's an ideal sit-down break in the day's sightseeing; and Guy and Christine Denoel, who've been at this location for more than 20 years, will send you away refreshed, with a definite "hang the calories" attitude. The pleasant shop is closed Tuesday, open 10 a.m. to 5 p.m. other days.

**NIGHTLIFE:** You'll find most after-dark activity centered in St. Augustine's hotel and motel cocktail lounges, some simply "bend an elbow" spots, others with live entertainment and dancing.

The **Sheraton Anastasia,** out on St. Augustine Beach (tel. 904/471-2575), has entertainment until 1 a.m. every night in the lounge (which opens at 4 p.m.). Casual, beach-type dress is in order.

On Ocean Trace Road at St. Augustine Beach, the Holiday Inn by the Sea has live entertainment and dancing in its **Ship Ahoy Lounge** until 1 a.m.

On Cuna Street (across from the Old Fort), the **White Lion Tavern** has an old English pub atmosphere, Ladies Night on Monday, and entertainment every night until 1 a.m.

**THINGS TO SEE AND DO:** Stop by the **Visitor Information Center** at 10 Castillo Dr., St. Augustine, FL 32084 (it's near the City Gate), to see a comprehen-

HISTORIC ST. AUGUSTINE

*Map Courtesy of The Explorer*

sive orientation film ($2 for adults, free for those under 16) that will make any subsequent sightseeing more meaningful. They can also furnish complete guided-tour information and brochures to help do-it-yourselfers.

In my opinion, there's no better way to sightsee St. Augustine's historic area than aboard the delightful motorized **tour trains**, 170 San Marco Dr. (tel. 904/829-6545). The open cars have rain curtains; the guides give a lively, informative spiel as you move from place to place; and your $6 ticket ($2.50 for ages 6 through 12) is good for the duration of your visit—you can stop off and spend as much time as you want at various destinations and, since the trains run on 15- to 20-minute schedules, there's no long wait to hop on the next one to move on. Besides, given the city's narrow streets, sometimes heavy traffic, parking problems, etc., it's *so* much easier! There are also delightful tours run by **Colee's Horse-Drawn Carriage Tours** (tel. 904/829-2818). Phone for exact times, prices, and pickup points.

---

**GUIDE TO THE NUMBERED REFERENCES ON THE "HISTORIC ST. AUGUSTINE" MAP:** 1.—Florida School for the Deaf & Blind; 2.—Fountain of Youth; 3.—Mission of Nombre de Dios; 4.—Authentic Old Jail; 5.—Old Sugar Mill; 6.—Ripley Museum; 7.—Visitors Information Center; 8.—Castillo de San Marcos; 9.—Old World Shop; 10.—The Old Drugstore and the Spanish Cemetery; 11.—Museum; 12.—Lighthouse Park & Fishing Pier; 13.—St. Augustine Alligator Farm; 14.—Cross & Sword Amphitheater; 15.—Marina and Sightseeing Boat Cruise; 16.—Potter's Wax Museum; 17.—Old Market; 18.—Government House; 19.—Flagler College; 20.—Trailways Bus Station; 21.—Greyhound Bus Station; 22.—Shrimp Boat Docks; 23.—U.S. Post Office; 24.—Zorayda Castle; 25.—Lightner Municipal Expo.; 26.—County Building; 27.—Spanish Hospital; 28.—Old Store Museum; 29.—Art Center; 30.—Historical Society Library; 31.—Oldest House; 32.—State Arsenal; 33.—Indian Museum; 34.—Llambias House; 35.—St. Francis Inn; 36.—City Gates; 37.—Ximenes-Fatio House; 38.—Old School House; 39.—San Augustin Antiguo Museum Houses.

---

The **Old City Gate,** not far from the Visitor Information Center, was once the only entrance to the town through the wall that surrounded it. A moat ran eastward from the San Sebastian River to the Castillo, and a drawbridge at this gate was raised each evening and lowered at daybreak. St. George Street, which begins here and runs south, was once known as "The Street that goes to the Land Gate." Close by, you'll see the **Old World Shop** (it's the main office of the sightseeing trains), which has complete tourist information, all sorts of souvenirs, and light snacks.

The **Oldest Wooden Schoolhouse,** 14 St. George St., was constructed sometime during the first Spanish period (1565–1763) and served both as a private home and a schoolhouse prior to "the war" (Civil, that is). It's open every day from 9 a.m. to 5 p.m. June through August, to 5 p.m. September through May; admission is $2 for adults, $1 for ages 6 through 11.

The **Castillo de San Marcos,** 1 Castillo Dr. (tel. 904/829-6506), is one of the most impressive things you'll see in St. Augustine. Begun in 1672 and finished in 1695 by the Spanish, it is the oldest masonry fortification in the U.S. (it replaced several earlier wooden ones which had rotted away). It's built of coquina, a shellrock formation quarried on Anastasia Island, and it withstood two major English sieges—in fact, it was never captured by an enemy. General Oglethorpe, from his Georgia base, once vowed to take the Castillo or leave his bones before its walls, but as it turned out, he did neither. Over the years it has seen 18th-century "modernizations," and has held "rebels" during the Revolution, Seminole leaders, both Confederate and Union troops during the Civil War, and American deserters during the Spanish-American War. Rangers are on duty for interpretive talks, and during the summer months weapon-firing demonstrations are presented on weekends. Admission costs $1 (children 15 and under are free when accompanied by an adult), and it's open from 8:30 a.m. to 5:15 p.m. from the last Sunday in October to the last Saturday in April, and 9 a.m. to 5:45 p.m. from the last Sunday in April to the last Saturday in October. The park is open daily except Christmas Day.

Across from the Castillo is the Restoration Area—**San Augustin Antiguo** on St. George Street. You pay a general admission $3 ($1.50 for students 6 to 18) which admits you to several houses inside that have individual fees. There are authentically furnished homes (some with life-size wax figures), craft demonstrations (a blacksmith, leatherworker, pottery, print shop, and Spanish bakery), and gardens. Guides in period dress demonstrate daily life activities in a 1740s Spanish garrison town.

That elaborate complex of buildings you see on King Street was once the most flamboyant resort hotel built by railroad tycoon Henry Flagler, the Ponce de Leon. It took three years to complete, 1885 to 1888, and became a mecca for wealthy Northerners at the turn of the century. It remained a hotel until 1967, when **Flagler College,** a four-year liberal arts school, moved in.

Across the street, the **Lightner Museum** was another Flagler hostelry, the Alcazar Hotel, built in 1888. It lasted as a hotel only until 1930, and remained vacant until 1947, when Otto C. Lightner, of Chicago, bought it, moved in his substantial personal collection of artworks, then donated it to the city. The museum's atmosphere is essentially that of the Gay '90s, with a "Victorian Village," Tiffany glass, and such, but it also holds such treasures as Napoleon's desk, doll collections, and a natural science wing with an Egyptian mummy. The building and gardens cover three city blocks, and St. Augustine's City Hall is on the grounds. The museum is open daily from 9 a.m. to 5 p.m. and costs $3 for adults, $1 for ages 12 through 18.

The **González-Alvanez Oldest House,** 14 St. Francis St., was built soon after St. Augustine was burned by the British in the siege of 1702, but the site has been used for a residence since the early 1600s. It is built of coquina, with tabby (a mixture of limestone, sand, and seashells) floors, and is furnished with authentic antiques. Both the house and the adjacent museum (the **Webb Memorial,** an interpretive museum of the city's history) are maintained by the St. Augustine Historic Society. Both are open from 9 a.m. to 5 p.m. every day and your $3 admission ($1.50 for ages 10 through 18) covers both, as well as a museum store, gardens, and picnic area.

That mythical **Fountain of Youth** (which I sometimes think we're still searching for in Florida) supposedly flows from the stone fountain at 155 Magnolia Ave. What the heck, you might as well take a drink! The park is a memorial to Juan Ponce de León and his landing in this area in 1513, and the grounds also hold a planetarium and space globe, as well as a museum and swan pool. It's open 9 a.m. to 5 p.m. every day and costs $3 for adults, $1.50 for children.

There's a real "castle" in St. Augustine, the **Zorayda Castle** at 83 King St. Built in 1883, it's a one-tenth scale replica of one wing of Spain's Alhambra, and inside you get a vivid picture of how the Moorish kings lived and entertained. We don't have many castles in this country, and this one is fun to visit—certainly the kids will love it! Hours are 9 a.m. to 5:30 p.m. and admission is $3 for adults, $1.50 for ages 6 through 12; under 6, free.

**Cross and Sword,** the official state play of Florida, an excellent outdoor musical drama, is performed nightly (except Sunday) by a cast of 70 singers, dancers, and actors from mid-June through late August in the St. Augustine Amphitheater (south of the city on A1A). It tells the story of the city's founding and early days, and tickets are $6 and $4 for reserved seats, $5 for general admission (under age 12, general admission is $3).

Also, if you happen to be in St. Augustine in mid-August, check with the Visitor Information Center for exact dates of the annual "**Days in Spain**," a three-day festival held in The Plaza. Sword fighting, parades, fireworks, nightly entertainment, and general merriment in the streets celebrate St. Augustine's founding, and the whole affair is climaxed by the cutting of a birthday cake.

## Special Day Trips

Fourteen miles south of St. Augustine on what is now A1A, the Matanzas Inlet has been the entrance to a waterway navigable all the way to St. Augustine, providing an open back door to that city. Therefore in 1569 the Spanish built successive wooden watchtowers to watch the inlet. In 1740 the Spanish felt the need to erect a strong masonry fort there to prevent enemy use of the Matanzas Inlet and River into St. Augustine, and to keep an alternative avenue of communication open if St. Augustine Inlet were to be blocked. In 1742 **Fort Matanzas** was completed, and became an integral part of the defenses of St. Augustine. The fort was occupied by both the Spanish and the British; however, in 1821, when the United States gained the Territory of Florida, its military use was ended.

Visitors are provided with passenger-ferry service from the visitor center area to Rattlesnake Island, the site of Fort Matanzas. The ferry operates from 9 a.m. to 4:30 p.m. seven days a week except Christmas Day. The ferry schedule may change so for correct and updated information, call 904/471-1006.

There is no admission charge at Fort Matanzas National Monument. Rangers are on duty to provide additional historical information. The park is open daily, except Christmas Day, from 8:30 a.m. to 5:30 p.m.

Still farther south on A1A, about 18 miles from the city, **Marineland of Florida** (tel. 904/471-1111) presents six daily programs that are a real delight. There are performing porpoises, penguins in Whitney Park, marine exhibits, and a truly unique, multidimensional film presentation in the Aquarius Theatre. The all-inclusive admission is $8 for adults, $4 for ages 3 through 11.

## 2. Daytona Beach

The beach at Daytona, a little over 23 miles long and some 500 feet wide at low tide, made it one of Florida's first popular resorts, back in the 1870s. It was the automobile, however, that brought it into its own. The hard-packed sand on the strand was a natural speedway, and records were being set here as early as 1903, when Alexander Winton hit the phenomenal speed of 68 miles per hour—the fastest in the world at that time. In subsequent years, Sir Malcolm Campbell and other auto-racing stars have come here to set faster and faster world records. Nowadays races are held at the Daytona International Speedway, about 2½ miles west of the beach on U.S. 92.

You can still drive along the water's edge, however, all the way from Ormond Beach to Ponce de León Inlet—but no racing. The speed limit is 10 miles per hour, and it's strictly enforced. If you're going for a beach drive, do it at low tide or when the tide is going out, and *never* drive into the water or in the soft areas, which are well marked. There's unlimited parking on the beach during daylight, but overnight parking and camping are illegal.

Besides all that marvelous beach and almost year-round swimming temperatures, Daytona Beach has an amusement area near the fishing pier with a sightseeing tower and sky ride, as well as numerous other games, shops, and food stands. A wide promenade runs through it right along the oceanfront, making strolling a real pleasure.

**WHERE TO STAY:** Like so many of Florida's resort areas, Daytona Beach is lined with high-rise hotels and motels. Almost every major chain is represented, and I suggest that you write the **Daytona Beach Chamber of Commerce,** P.O. Box 2775, Daytona Beach, FL 32015 (tel. 904/255-0981), for their free directory. A word of warning: Rates at most of the larger hotels and motels go up when racing events are scheduled, so be *sure* you get a confirmed quotation before you come. And note that among the range of prices quoted here, the higher prices apply to oceanfront locations, lower prices to rooms not directly facing the ocean, although almost all have an ocean view of some sort.

The **Ramada Inn Surfside,** 3125 S. Atlantic Ave., Daytona Beach, FL 32018 (tel. 904/788-1000, or toll free 800/322-1322), is a gleaming white, seven-story resort with nicely furnished and decorated rooms, all of which face the ocean. There are also some 80 efficiencies with large kitchens. There are two pools (one for the small fry), a game room, the Engine House Restaurant, and the Hook and Ladder Lounge (where there's dancing in the evenings). Seasonal room rates range from $40 to $96, efficiencies run $45 to $106, and there are weekly rates available. Children 17 and under stay free in the same room with their parents.

The **TraveLodge Daytona Oceanfront,** 3135 S. Atlantic Ave., Daytona Beach, FL 32018 (tel. 904/767-8533), is especially geared to families, with a choice of motel rooms, rooms with kitchenettes, or rooms with fully equipped kitchens. There's also a game room, kiddie pool, shuffleboard, and a playground for the younger generation. Parents will appreciate the convenience of a coin laundry. There's a restaurant, but no lounge (the Hook and Ladder Lounge at the Surfside is just next door). Rates range from $40 to $80 for motel rooms according to season; efficiencies from $45 to $85. Those under 17 stay free in the same room with their parents, and there are attractive weekly rates available.

All rooms at the **Pirate's Cove,** 3501 S. Atlantic Ave., Daytona Beach, FL 32019 (tel. 904/767-8749, or toll free 800/874-6996), are either oceanfront or have a good view of the ocean. There's a beachside pool, game room, laundry facilities, the Crow's Nest Restaurant, and the Gangplank Lounge (with nightly entertainment in season). Efficiencies have full electric kitchens. Seasonal rates run $40 to $70 for motel rooms, $45 to $80 for efficiencies, with no charge for those 17 and under, and good weekly rates.

The oceanfront **Daytona Sands Beach,** 2523 S. Atlantic Ave., Daytona Beach, FL 32018 (tel. 904/767-2551), comes close to being in the budget range, as prices go at Daytona Beach. Yet its rooms certainly don't have a "budget" look—they are bright and colorful, with modern decor, and some have private patios or balconies. There's the obligatory heated pool and ironing boards are standard equipment in the rooms (you can request an iron from the office). They also have free morning coffee; no dining room, but there's a restaurant across the highway. Doubles run $38 to $44 in season, and there are some kitchenettes, which cost $45 and up. *Note:* If you don't mind crossing the highway to get to the beach, the Daytona Sands has ten lower-priced rooms on that side.

**WHERE TO EAT:** A few blocks west of A1A, **Chez Bruchez,** 304 Seabreeze Blvd. (tel. 904/252-6656), serves a French-American menu in a charming French Provincial atmosphere—with background music that's a pleasure, not an intrusion. Easy to see why it has thrived for nearly 40 years! There are specialties like frogs' legs provençale, but I particularly liked the rich, creamy mousse au chocolat. Lunch hours are 11:30 a.m. to 2 p.m. ($6 to $9), dinner from 5 to 9 p.m. ($9.50 to $16), and reservations are definitely in order. Closed Sunday, and September and October.

In a Spanish setting, the **King's Cellar,** in the Best Western Americano, 1260 N. Atlantic Ave. (tel. 904/255-3014), purveys Italian dishes, along with seafood and prime ribs. The lovely atmosphere is enhanced by dinner music and dancing, and there's a bar. Prices, which are semi à la carte, are $5.50 and up (children's menu, $4), and dinner is served from 5 to 10 p.m.; closed Tuesday.

**Morrison's,** 200 N. Ridgewood (tel. 904/258-6396), has one of its good, inexpensive cafeterias here, and like most in this excellent chain, they do their own baking. It's standard cafeteria fare, of course, but consistently good (and I think their fried shrimp are super). Lunch will set you back about $5, dinner only a little more. Hours are 11 a.m. to 8:30 p.m., and they also have a take-out service.

**NIGHTLIFE:** Most of the after-dark activity is found in hotel and motel lounges, and while the "names" that play here aren't such big ones (not to be compared with Miami Beach, for example), there's often quite good entertainment around. It's a good place to lounge-hop until you find the entertainer who suits you best.

Musical events that range from light classical to pop take place in the bandshell at the north end of the promenade in the amusement area (in **Oceanfront Park**) almost every night in season. Concert times vary, and sometimes nonmusical acts appear. Whatever's going on, however, is free, and sitting under the stars with the ocean in the background is enjoyable.

The **Daytona Playhouse,** 100 Jessamine Blvd., presents light musical productions and plays year round at prices that run $8 and under. You can phone 904/255-2431 for current schedules.

**THINGS TO SEE AND DO:** There is, first and foremost, that marvelous **beach,** with all the watersports that come with it—windsurfing, sailing, swimming, etc. Daytona Beach, however, has one very special added attraction, a resident sculptor who delights in creating masterpieces in *sand*. No mere sand-castle artist, **Marc Altamar** can usually be found in Daytona Beach Shores behind the El Caribe motel, putting together marvelous fantasy figures from sand, then applying spray paint to bring them beautifully alive. He also works in more permanent media, such as watercolors, oils, clay, bronze, cement fountains, etc., but takes the greatest pleasure from his rather temporary creations (some of which last an amazingly long time). If you don't find Marc at this spot, you can contact him at P.O. Box 7721, Daytona Beach Shores, FL 32016 (tel. 904/257-5893), to find out just what his schedule is. I urge you to seek him out and watch him as he engages in his unusual form of creative artwork—fascinating!

Say "Daytona" to most people, and you're saying "racing"! And although the **Daytona International Speedway,** 1801 Speedway Blvd., west on U.S. 92 (tel. 904/253-6711), is *sometimes* empty, there are races scheduled all during the year. The Daytona "500" is in February, the Pepsi Firecracker "400" stock-car race is July 4, AMA motorcycle races are early in March, and if you want to know what's doing when you'll be there, write P.O. Box S, Daytona Beach, FL 32015, for a schedule.

There is racing other than the motor kind at Daytona Beach: the greyhounds run at the **Daytona Beach Kennel Club** (west on U.S. 92) from early May to mid-September every night except Sunday, but you can't take the kids along —no minors allowed. Post time is 8 p.m., with 1:15 p.m. races on Monday. Admission is $1; clubhouse, $1.50 (for reservations, call 904/252-6484). And yes, there *is* pari-mutuel betting.

Imagine a Florida sightseeing attraction that's *free!* One of the few in the state is **Sugar Mill Gardens** (follow U.S. 1 to Port Orange, then turn west one mile on Herbert Street; tel. 736-2700, ext. 2462), which, besides the machinery and boiling kettles of the old 1763 sugarmill, offers dinosaur figures in a jungle-like setting. It's open from 9 a.m. to 5 p.m. every day.

Golfers will find 36 holes at **Daytona Beach Golf and Country Club,** 600 Wilder Blvd. (tel. 904/255-4517), open every day, with greens fees of $8.50. There's also the **Par-3 Golf Club and Driving Range** four miles west on U.S. 92, 2500 Volusia Ave. (tel. 904/252-3983), charging $6 for 18 holes, $3 for 9.

You can wager on jai-alai at the **Daytona Beach Jai-Alai Fronton,** just east of I-4 and I-95 on U.S. 92 (P.O. Box 2630, Daytona Beach, FL 32015; tel. 904/255-0222), from February through August, every night except Sunday and Tuesday. Post time is 7:15 p.m. Matinees are Monday and Saturday at noon. Admissions are $1 and up, and sorry, no minors.

# 3. Walt Disney World and Epcot Center

Back in the '60s I drove across Florida's midlands on the way to visit my parents on the west coast. It wasn't a particularly scenic or interesting trip with miles and miles of flatland covered with palmetto and a kind of scrub under-growth, and from time to time outcroppings of palms and pines. Snake country, I thought, and wondered how many of the cattle that seemed to be the major "crop" along the way (I remember my surprise at seeing Florida cowboys) fell victim to snakebite. Winter Haven was there, of course, with the Cypress Gardens and their spectacular water show, and I could have detoured south to Lake Wales and the beautiful Bok Singing Tower—but aside from those bright spots, not much else besides a landscape with an almost desolate kind of beauty.

Well, that drive from Orlando to Tampa is a completely different story today. And the difference is due almost entirely to the late Walt Disney's choice of some 43 square miles on this route for his gigantic Walt Disney World resort area. Besides the Magic Kingdom and Epcot Center, there are hotels, golf courses, riding paths, lakes, campgrounds, and all the conveniences—and luxuries—that tourists expect at a Disney-run resort. The cows are still there, and Kissimmee (it takes some practice, but pronounce it "Kis-*sem*-mee") is a rather important livestock market. But I'm quite sure that some of those cow-boys I saw more than a decade ago (as well as others who would have grown up to that profession) are now happily herding tourists around Disney World or otherwise engaged in seeing that they are housed, fed, and sent away happy, clutching souvenirs of every description. I don't know precisely what Walt Disney World has meant to this area's economy in terms of dollars and cents, but the figure must be astronomical. On just one December day in 1982, over 120,000 people passed through the gates; and since the resort opened in 1971, more than 100 million have been drawn here, among them three U.S. presidents (Nixon, Ford, and Carter). It's staggering, and both Kissimmee and Lake Buena Vista are modern-day boom towns, with nearby Orlando (20 miles east) coming in for its share of the prosperity as well.

As for the Magic Kingdom, that's exactly what it is—magic. And Epcot Center is a sort of magical glimpse into the future. I must confess that I first approached the whole thing with some cynicism. "Bring money" was my first thought, and I rather expected a glorified kind of ripoff. Not so. First of all, not only is everything well managed (*nothing* has been overlooked in planning for such crowds), but my lasting impression is one of a staff enjoying their duties

every bit as much as the paying guests and a delightful kind of "let's all have fun together" attitude. And the cost was another surprise. After your initial ticket purchase, I found that, depending on your sales resistance and willpower, you could drop a bundle in shops and restaurants or have a marvelous time window-shopping and snacking. If there was any "hustle" in this relaxed, happy carnival, I didn't run into it.

Even your entrance to the Magic Kingdom is a little magical—by monorail to the Main Street Depot (you can also get there by ferry), whose arched entryways lead to the six "lands," each with its own theme carried out in architecture, landscaping, shops, music, and "adventures": Main Street U.S.A., Adventureland, Frontierland, Liberty Square, Fantasyland, and Tomorrowland. Another monorail journey takes you to futuristic Epcot Center. You won't want to rush through either once you're there, so don't plan to "do" Walt Disney World in just one day.

Outside the confines of the Magic Kingdom, there's horseback riding; swimming, sailing, motorboating, and waterskiing on clear lakes that have over four miles of sandy beaches; golf, tennis, steamboat excursions, nature hikes, and delightful picnic spots—all linked to the Kingdom by monorail trains, buses, launches, or ferryboats.

At Lake Buena Vista, there's a Shopping Village that's a joy to visit, even if you don't buy a single item. In a lovely setting, there are shops featuring products from all over the world, all sorts of restaurants, lounges with entertainment, and pedal boats and "flote botes."

And while Walt Disney World and Epcot Center are certainly the major attractions in this whole area, they should not eclipse others that are just a little bit away. Cape Canaveral, with NASA's Kennedy Space Center, is an easy day trip; Cypress Gardens at Winter Haven are as spectacular now as they were before Disney's competition arrived; Kissimmee has Gatorland for a glimpse of Florida's native wildlife; and there are several other sightseeing destinations close at hand that make the Walt Disney World area an ideal base.

**WHERE TO STAY:** If there's one thing you'll find plenty of in the area, it's places to stay, and they run the price gamut from luxury to budget. There are resort hotels right on Walt Disney World grounds, as well as a 600-acre campground. Nearby Lake Buena Vista (four miles and about ten minutes away) has high-rise resort hotels, vacation villas, and town houses. These are, without doubt, the choice places to stay and they all provide transportation to and from the Magic Kingdom. But they don't come cheap, and the other end of that large price range is found in motels clustered around Walt Disney World, Kissimmee, and Orlando.

### At Walt Disney World

Advance booking is absolutely necessary for any of the accommodations on the grounds (with as much notice as possible), and you can reserve at any by calling 305/824-8000 (the best time to call is between 5 and 11 p.m.). There's also a reservation service in the City Hall on Main Street U.S.A. in the Magic Kingdom, should you go for a day and decide to stay over (although you take a chance on finding a vacancy). Rates at all Walt Disney World hotels for double rooms (which accommodate up to three children along with two adults) are in the $115 to $175 range, depending on the view. Under-18s stay free in the same room with their parents.

The architecture and setting of **Polynesian Village** will make you start shopping for a grass skirt—it's that "South Seas" in atmosphere and decor. Its 636 rooms are in two-story "longhouses" and there's entertainment and dining in the "Great Ceremonial House." The whole complex is set in tropical gardens with winding pathways right on the Seven Seas Lagoon. The South Seas motif extends to the rooms, which are certainly in the luxury class, some with king-size beds and all colorfully decorated. There are two pools (with lifeguards), a sand beach, and the smaller people will find a playground. There's a home for Fido in the kennel, a sauna, beauty and barber shops, and shopping in several boutiques.

The **Contemporary Resort** borders on the futuristic in design and decor, and its huge lobby has a monorail stop. The rooms are as modern as tomorrow, with extra-large beds and two washbasins. There are two pools, a beach, a playground, a health club and sauna, and Ping-Pong in the recreation room. Pets are also welcome here in the kennel. Lounges provide entertainment and music for dancing; and there are several dining rooms.

The third Disney resort hotel was built with golfers in mind. Strangely named the **Disney Inn,** it is right next to the fairways. It's smaller than the other two, but has entertainment in the lounges and excellent dining rooms. Guest rooms are contemporary in decor and very nicely furnished. You don't *have* to play golf, of course—there's tennis (on lighted courts), and a heated pool.

Campers never had it so good as at **Fort Wilderness Campground,** a 600-acre resort for outdoor people. In total, 828 sites (including some for tents) are located in the wooded area. Those for campers have full hookups, a grill, water, and a disposal system. And for those would-be campers among you, Fort Wilderness offers Fleetwood Trailers that will sleep up to six and are fully equipped. There's a restaurant in Pioneer Hall and the Campfire Snackbar, as well. Two trading posts sell camping supplies, groceries, beer, and film. Full campsites are $28 to $32; Fleetwood Trailers, $105 to $110.

## At Lake Buena Vista

You'll be surrounded by luxury at any one of the resort hotels in Lake Buena Vista, so if you don't get the booking you prefer, rest assured that you won't be disappointed with a substitute. Space doesn't permit a detailed description of rooms, decor, etc., but all rooms are spacious, well appointed, and tastefully decorated; all these hotels have excellent dining facilities; most have entertainment in lounges; and all look askance at pets except for Howard Johnson's, where they're welcome. There is frequent shuttlebus service to and from the Magic Kingdom from Hotel Plaza (where all are located), but there is a small fee each way. (Mail should be addressed to each hotel, c/o Hotel Plaza, Lake Buena Vista, FL 32830.)

The **Americana Dutch Resort Hotel** (tel. 305/828-4444, or toll free 800/624-4109) has double rooms that will accommodate two adults and up to three children for $89 and up. **Howard Johnson's** (tel. 305/828-8888) charges $105 and up, and at the **Hotel Royal Plaza** (tel. 305/828-2828) rates range from $90 up.

**Vistana Resort,** P.O. Box 22051, Lake Buena Vista, FL 32830 (tel. 305/239-3100, or toll free 800/327-9152, 800/432-9197 in Florida), has luxurious two-bedroom/two-bath villas that sleep up to six people at one reasonable price. Many units feature a private Jacuzzi and video-disc player, and there's daily maid service. Two swimming pools and shuttle service to all Walt Disney World attractions. Prices range from $140 to $250, and there are three-bedroom villas available at slightly higher rates.

## Elsewhere in the Area

I don't really know how many motels there are in the Greater Walt Disney World Area, but one of my lasting impressions is of the "mini-cities" made up of nothing but clusters of motels along every major highway. And those highways are important: when you have your confirmed reservation, be *sure* to note the *exact* location of the motel, or you could wind up, as I once did, driving through the maze of highways and Interstates from one member of the chain to another before you reach the right one! So if there's a highway exit number given, mark it in red on your map and look carefully to save yourself a lot of time and aggravation.

There are about 40,000 hotel, motel, and condominium rooms in the Orlando area, and now there's a convenient service that can book you almost anywhere you designate. Write or call the **Orlando Central Reservation Center,** 771 S. Kirkman Rd., Suite 107, Orlando, FL 32811 (tel. toll free 800/322-2220, 800/235-2220 in Florida).

It is seldom that I feel "a motel is a motel is a motel," but I must confess that I saw little to distinguish one from the other here, except in the case of one or two luxury, resort-type motels (such as the **Orlando Hyatt Hotel,** 6375 W. Spacecoast Pkwy., Kissimmee, FL 32741; tel. 305/396-1234), and since their rates are only a little lower than those inside Walt Disney World and at Lake Buena Vista, I'd opt anytime for the latter. For that reason, I'll skip detailed descriptions of the ones below unless there's something really distinctive about a particular one, and you may assume that a Holiday Inn is a Holiday Inn. From my own experience, I'd say that price and location (i.e., convenience to Walt Disney World) should be the guiding factors in making a choice, and none of these listed is more than 30 minutes away. When reserving, be sure to ask about bus transportation to and from Walt Disney World—many motels furnish it for guests. Keep in mind that I-4 runs southwest from Orlando right past Walt Disney World, whose main entrance is on U.S. 192 not far west of its intersection with I-4; the Florida Turnpike is north of the main entrance, but its intersection with I-4 is within convenient driving distance; and an address of "Turnpike Exit 65" will be *east* of Kissimmee, farther away from Walt Disney World than the other two intersections.

In the moderate price range, these are all good, dependable motels with standard accommodations:

The **Holiday Inn East,** 5678 Spacecoast Pkwy., Kissimmee, FL 32741 (tel. 305/396-4488, or toll free 800/523-2309)—on U.S. 192 just east of I-4—has 512 deluxe rooms, the "Only for Kids" movie theater, clubhouse, and restaurant for children, two swimming pools, and a lounge with entertainment and dancing. Double-room rates are seasonal, ranging from $50 up.

**Larson's Lodge—Kissimmee,** 2009 W. Vine St., Kissimmee, FL 32741 (tel. 305/846-2713, or toll free 800/624-5905 and 800/327-9074)—on U.S. 192 seven miles east of I-4—has two pools, a Jacuzzi, and entertainment in the lounge; doubles start at $40.

The **Holiday Inn,** Haines City, FL 33844 (tel. 813/424-2211)—at the junction of I-4 and U.S. 27, about a 15-minute drive to Walt Disney World—has family-type entertainment and soft drinks for the kids in its Circus Lounge. There's also bus transportation (for a small fee) to and from Walt Disney World. Doubles start at $45.

The **Days Lodge–Disney East,** 5820 Spacecoast Pkwy., Kissimmee, FL 32741 (tel. 305/396-7900, or toll free 800/327-9126)—on U.S. 192, three miles east of the Walt Disney World main gate—is an apartment motel with three-room housekeeping apartments, all completely equipped (there's a small utensil deposit), which sleep six comfortably for $55 to $85 double, $6 for each additional person. There are three pools, two restaurants, and a cafeteria (where children under 12 eat free with their parent!).

The **Rodeway Inn–East Gate,** 5245 Spacecoast Pkwy., Kissimmee, FL

32741 (tel. 305/396-7700)—on U.S. 192 one mile east of I-4—has double rooms for $40 and up.

In the *budget* range, the **Colonial Motor Lodge,** 1815 W. Vine St., Kissimmee, FL 32741 (tel. 305/847-6121, or toll free 800/325-4348)—on U.S. 192 east of I-4—has some kitchen units, two pools, and double room rates of $28 to $40 (kitchens cost $54 to $60).

The **Days Inn** at the intersection of I-4 and Fla. 528A, 7335 Sandlake Rd., Kissimmee, FL 32819 (tel. 305/351-1900, or toll free 800/325-2525), has lake fishing from the shore, golf privileges, restaurant, pools, and playgrounds. Double rooms are $35 to $40.

A very conveniently located **Days Inn** is at 7980 Spacecoast Pkwy., Kissimmee, FL 32741 (tel. 305/396-1000, or toll free 800/327-9173), on U.S. 192 five miles west of I-4. Here double room rates are $36 and $48.

## Campgrounds

**Outdoor Resorts, Orlando,** Rte. 5, Box 621, Clermont, FL 32711 (tel. 305/422-7461), is situated on 165 acres, with 980 full-service sites just five miles from Walt Disney World. There's a lake with beach, tennis, mini-golf, a nine-hole (par three) golf course, two pools, and a restaurant. Contact them directly for current rates.

There's an inexpensive campground at **Southport Park,** in a secluded wooded area about 20 miles south of Kissimmee on the shores of Lake Tohopekaliga (south from Kissimmee on Fla. 531, 13 miles to Southport Road, then six miles east). There are full-service sites and some "primitive" ones for those who really like to rough it. There is a store, two comfort stations, a pavilion, picnic shelters, a boat ramp, boat basin, and access channel to the lake. It's a long way from the gloss of the Walt Disney World campground, but then so are the rates: $10 for water, electricity, and sewer hookups; $9.50 for water and electricity only; and $8 for undeveloped sites. For reservations, contact the Park Manager, Southport Park, 2001 Southport Rd., Kissimmee, FL 32741 (tel. 305/933-5822).

## DINING AT WALT DISNEY WORLD:
Go elegant or go casual—you'll find the right place to eat either way at Walt Disney World or Lake Buena Vista. Whether it's pancakes and eggs as you start your exploration of the Magic Kingdom or a champagne brunch you need to get your day off on the right foot, the Disney folks have anticipated your needs and provided for them.

### Casual Dining

To begin with, Main Street U.S.A. can furnish breakfast, lunch, or dinner at the **Town Square Café,** a Victorian-style restaurant with prices in the $4 to $10 range (lunch and dinner), or at the garden-style **Crystal Palace Restaurant** (same price range). Or you can stop anytime for pastries and coffee at the **Main Street Bakery,** for ice cream cones at **Borden's Ice Cream Parlor,** for hamburgers and hot dogs at the **Plaza Pavilion** or **Refreshment Center,** or for snacks and soft drinks at the **Station Break** directly below the railroad station.

Adventureland serves Polynesian entrees (as well as hamburgers and hot sandwiches) at the **Adventureland Veranda,** tropical punch and snacks at the **Veranda Juice Bar** and **Sunshine Tree Terrace,** and hot dogs and beverages at **El Pirata y El Perico.**

**Aunt Polly's** serves sandwiches, snacks, and beverages on a porch overlooking the water on Tom Sawyer Island in Frontierland (and there's also a **Mile Long Bar** and **Pecos Bill's Café** in this "land").

Liberty Square has one of my favorite eating places in Walt Disney World, the **Liberty Tree Tavern,** a colonial-style eatery with lunches and dinners that run from $6 to $12 and that feature Patriot's Pot Roast. For seafood and fried chicken, it's the **Columbia Harbour House,** also in Liberty Square, which has the **Fife and Drum** and **Sleepy Hollow Refreshments** for snacks.

In Fantasyland, **King Stefan's Banquet Hall** (in Cinderella Castle) has beef, chicken, seafood, and salads (in that same moderate price range) at lunch and dinner, and you can snack at **Lancer's Inn, The Round Table, Troubador Tavern,** and **Pinocchio Village Haus.**

Tomorrowland has a great natural-foods specialty shop, the **Lunching Pad,** that serves yogurt, sandwiches, salads, snacks, and juices. Hot dogs, hamburgers, and sandwiches are featured at the **Tomorrowland Terrace** and the **Space Bar.**

At **Epcot Center,** you'll find casual eating at every one of the international pavilions in the World Showcase area around the lagoon. Depending on your ethnic preference at the moment, you can sample the wares at Mexico's Cantina de San Angel, Germany's huge Biergarten, or France's Au Petit Café, all at snack-food prices.

I sampled the wares of several of these and found all to be of high quality and hot dinners and lunches quite tasty, so I don't hesitate to say that it is quite possible to eat every meal in the Magic Kingdom and go away well fed and not much poorer. Especially compared to prices in other resort areas, these are surprisingly low.

The same applies at Walt Disney World Village and Lake Buena Vista, where the **Lite Bite** and **Heidelberger's Deli** have sandwiches and other snacks; **Cap'n Jack's Oyster Bar** has seafood (of course); the **Village Verandah** serves all three meals; and the **Village Restaurant,** although casual, has gourmet dinners and hot sandwiches, seafood, and salads for lunch.

### Dining in Style

For more elegant eating, there are the resort hotels in Walt Disney World and Lake Buena Vista, and just because you've bought an all-day ticket, you aren't precluded from slipping out for lunch or dinner and then returning without an additional fee—just be sure to have your hand stamped as you leave, and you'll be waved right through when you get back. **Arthur's,** at the Buena Vista Palace Hotel (tel. 805/827-2727) and **El Cid,** at the Royal Plaza Hotel (tel. 305/ 827-3055) are both excellent choices, with dinner prices in the upper ranges.

Over in Walt Disney World Village at Lake Buena Vista, the finest gourmet fare comes to table in the **Empress Room** on the Promenade Deck of *The Empress Lilly* Riverboat, a replica of an authentic 1800s sternwheeler anchored in the lagoon. The decor is elegant Louis XV, cuisine and service are very French, and prices run $16 to $38. You must reserve here (tel. 305/828-3900), and coats and ties are required. Also on the Promenade Deck is the **Empress Lounge,** a lovely setting for after-dinner coffee flambé or liqueur.

**AFTER DARK:** There's something going on all over Walt Disney World when the sun goes down.

There's **Captain Cook's Hideaway Lounge** in the **Great Ceremonial House** on the lobby level, open from 6:30 p.m. to 1:30 a.m. (last call for drinks, 1 a.m.).

The **Top of the World,** in the Contemporary Resort Hotel (on the 15th floor), has dinner-dancing shows with big-name entertainment (in season). There's an entertainment charge of $7.50 for adults, $3.75 for children (seating for dinner is at 6 p.m. for the 7:45 p.m. show, 9:15 for the 11 p.m. performance). To reserve, phone 305/824-8000.

Entertainment in a relaxed atmosphere prevails at the Disney Inn's Trophy Room.

In Lake Buena Vista Village, the **Baton Rouge Lounge** on the main deck of the *Empress Lilly* is a Dixieland jazz spot every night; and the **Village Lounge** has some of the top jazz musicians from all over the country every night except Sunday. No cover, no minimum in the Baton Rouge Lounge, $5 minimum at the Village Lounge.

**THINGS TO SEE AND DO IN WALT DISNEY WORLD:** There's a right way and a wrong way to plan a Walt Disney World visit. The *wrong* way is to allow only half a day, with no regard for the scope of the place and the time you'll spend moving around. The following tips from my own experience will, I hope, help you plan to "do" this enchanting world the right way.

First of all, before you leave your motel, *dress comfortably*. You'll be doing a lot of walking, so be sure your shoes are old friends, even if they don't look quite as spiffy as those new ones. And while shorts are certainly acceptable (and you'll see a lot of them), remember the intensity of that Florida sun and protect shoulders and other vulnerable parts of your anatomy (it's a good idea to take along a small bottle of suntan lotion). And whatever you do, don't forget sunglasses—the glare is sometimes brilliant.

Arrival time can be important for a hassle-free visit. Even though the park doesn't open until 9 a.m., the huge parking lot will be open by 7 a.m., trams will be running to the main entrance (ticket windows also open early), and the Main Street U.S.A. stores are open then. Breakfast on Main Street or the Land Pavilion (at Future World) while you're waiting for the attractions and rides to open, and before the crowds descend, is a relaxed way to begin the day. One very important note: Be *sure* you note (write it down, if need be) the name of your parking lot section (they're named for Disney characters, Goofy, Doc, etc.)—it's a *big* lot! And because the heat can turn your car into an oven during the day, leave the windows down just a little—not all the way, because Florida rains come up very suddenly.

Among the things that impressed me most about the meticulous planning that has gone into Walt Disney World were the facilities for handicapped visitors. For example, a special guidebook for the handicapped is available at City Hall in the Magic Kingdom or Earth Station at Epcot Center, and there's a special parking lot for guests in wheelchairs (it's adjacent to the Ticket Center; inquire at the Auto Plaza when you drive in). Wheelchairs can also be rented at the Stroller Shop just inside the entrance (or you can bring your own, of course), and there are ramps for wheelchairs at each street corner in the Main Street U.S.A. section. A first-aid station is located just off Main Street beside the Crystal Palace and in Epcot Center next to the Odyssey Restaurant.

Once inside, it's important not to try to see everything at once and not to walk until you're exhausted. There are plenty of snackbars and refreshment centers handy for a short rest break, and the whole day will be more pleasant if you take advantage of them. Besides, crowd-watching can be a very enjoyable part of your visit, and it's easier to do when you're not mingling.

What will it cost? Well, as we go to press, you can buy a one-day ticket at $24.50 for adults, $19.50 for ages 3 to 12. But that will entitle you to *either* the Magic Kingdom *or* Epcot Center—not to both. Unless you're really pressed for time, a much better deal is the three-day World Passport: $61 for adults, $49 for ages 3 to 12. An even better bargain (in the same age brackets) is the four-day World Passport: $71 and $57. These give you admission to Epcot Center and Magic Kingdom attractions, plus unlimited use of the transportation facilities throughout the system. If you wish to leave the grounds at any time during the day and return later on, be sure to have your hand stamped at the exit gate for reentry on the same day.

There's a complete **Official Guide to Walt Disney World** available at most bookstores, or you can order it by mail: send $6.95 plus $1 for postage and handling to Chatham Books, 60 E. 42nd St., New York, NY 10165. If you need any further details, contact: Walt Disney World Co., Dept. GL-N, P.O. Box 40, Lake Buena Vista, FL 32830 (tel. 305/824-4321).

Now, as they say at Walt Disney World, you're ready for your "Magic Kingdom Adventure" and a futuristic adventure at Epcot Center. You'll step off the monorail at the Walt Disney World Railroad Station, with a floral portrait of Mickey Mouse out front, and walk right onto Main Street U.S.A., a two-block stretch that leads to Cinderella Castle. And if the sight of that 18-story medieval castle doesn't get you in the mood for a day of pure fantasy, then you probably should turn around and go home! You may be surprised too, as I was, to see how the landscaping enhances every part of the park—some of the most beautiful plantings I've encountered in Florida are in the plazas and along the walkways here.

How you plan your day, of course, is a personal thing, but here's some of what you'll find in each "land" in the Magic Kingdom, each radiating from the castle like spokes in a wheel.

**READER'S RECOMMENDATION:** "To avoid the waiting lines, try going counterclockwise around the park. Most people do not think of it, and you reach the attractions after the first rush. It has worked for us every time, even in the crowded Easter season" (S. Higgins, Laurence Harbor, N.J.).

## Main Street U.S.A.

You'll be in turn-of-the-century America here, and along the street is a silent "cinema," penny arcade, and an old-fashioned ice-cream parlor. It is an excellent set-the-mood atmosphere, with horse-drawn trolley and horseless carriages passing by, plus street entertainment and parades of Disney characters from time to time (which is true in every section).

## Adventureland

You'll have to look close to see that those gorillas, elephants, hippos, and Tiki birds are "Audio-Animatronics" creations and not the real thing in this jungle setting. The Swiss Family Island Treehouse is here; there's a Jungle Cruise, a Caribbean Arcade with pirate games, and a Spanish fort, where you sail through mysterious grottoes, plunge down a waterfall, and land in the midst of a pirate raid.

## Frontierland

A Wild West "front street," lined with boardwalks, even has a brass-railed saloon, and there are wooden forts complete with Indian raids, a "Country Bear Jamboree" with a zany troupe of singing bears. And across the river is Tom Sawyer Island with Injun Joe's Cave, the Magnetic Mystery Mine, Big Thunder Mountain Railroad, and old Fort Sam Clemens (you can cross over by log raft or on "explorer canoes").

## Liberty Square

This is Colonial America brought to life, and if you don't see anything else, try not to miss the Hall of Presidents, where animated, life-size figures are so real and the presentation so effective that you truly believe that *is* Abraham Lincoln rising to speak. Not far away is the lively Haunted Mansion, where it's fun to be frightened out of your wits. You can catch the show at the Diamond Horseshoe Revue or take a river cruise on sternwheel steamboats.

## Fantasyland

Don't be so sure this one's only for the kids—grownups, too, love the charm of all those Disney characters wandering around. You'll see Dumbo, Snow White (and her Dwarfs, it goes without saying), and scores of other familiar figures. They all perform in concert at the Mickey Mouse Revue, and you can ride on Peter Pan's Flight, Mr. Toad's Wild Ride, or the Cinderella Golden Carousel. "It's a Small World" features doll-like figures in costumes from all over the world, and "20,000 Leagues Under the Sea" takes you aboard a Jules Verne submarine for a journey under the sea.

## Tomorrowland

If you've ever wanted to blast off on a rocket trip, Space Mountain is the place to do it. "Mission to Mars" is fun too, and the "Carousel of Progress" is a liberal education in the contributions electricity has made to our lives.

## River Country

A separate ticket is required for this re-created "Ol' Swimming Hole" located west of Pioneer Hall in Fort Wilderness. You get there by boat or coach from the Magic Kingdom (pick up tickets at the main entrance); and if you're camping at Fort Wilderness, the narrow-gauge railroad will take you within walking distance. However you get there, bring a bathing suit. There's a 260-foot water-flume slide, rafts you can pole down winding rapids and under waterfalls, and even rope swings out over the water. Your admission ticket covers all charges, except for snacks and box lunches at "Pop's Place" and beach towel rentals at the bathhouse.

**EPCOT CENTER:** You can get from the Magic Kingdom to Epcot (whose full name is "Environmental Prototype Community of Tomorrow") by monorail and from some of the resort hotels by bus. For details on either, call the special information line at 305/824-4500. Drivers will find an Epcot Center exit on I-4 about halfway between those for Rte. 535 and U.S. I-92, and parking costs $1.

At Epcot, you'll encounter "worlds" instead of "lands," and if you find some variance from the descriptions in this book, keep in mind Walt Disney's own words when speaking of the concept back in 1966: "It will be a community of tomorrow that will never be completed." Thus the present Epcot will be constantly changing as new technologies are introduced, old exhibits altered, and every effort made to keep up with our changing world. However, the following will give you some idea of what to expect, and all your surprises are sure to be pleasant ones.

First of all, Epcot Center is nearly twice as large as the Magic Kingdom, so plan on a *lot* of walking. Its shape is something like a huge hourglass, with Future World at the top, World Showcase at the bottom.

## Future World

This is where you'll find the huge "geosphere" which has become Epcot's symbol. Known as **Spaceship Earth,** it holds "time machine" rides which take you through some 40,000 years to show the development of communication. From Egyptian hieroglyphics to the Phoenician alphabet to manuscripts laboriously copied in monasteries to Gutenberg's first printing press, to the most modern means of communication, you'll see realistic scenes presented in great detail until you finally arrive at the top of the geosphere and its vast dome sprinkled with tiny sparkling stars.

Your descent from that lofty perch will land you at **Earth Station,** a sort of official "City Hall" of Epcot Center. This is where you can learn how the whole

ORLANDO
AND VICINITY

complex operates, locate lost children (or other items), make dinner reservations at one of the restaurants on the grounds, and get an immediate answer to almost any query from the World Key Information Service.

**Communicore,** comprised of two glass-walled arcs on either side of a pleasant plaza, is devoted to last-minute technology, and this is perhaps the area that will see the most changes over the years as every new development is incorporated and old methods discarded. Communicore East is the scene of an entertainment revue named the "Astuter Computer Revue," which will educate you on just how all the mechanics of running Epcot are managed through the use of computers. Of special interest, too, is the Energy Exchange sponsored by Exxon, which explores all sources of energy—past, present, and future. In Communicore West, there's the fascinating Futurecom exhibit devoted to information gathering, with some exciting new methods of display.

That asymmetrical, mirrored pyramid is the home of the **Universe of Energy,** where you ride in solar-powered vehicles through scenes depicting the entire spectrum of energy uses, from prehistoric times to the space age. The **World of Motion** (appropriately enough, housed in a wheel-shaped structure) traces man's efforts to move more swiftly, from the invention of the wheel to spaceships. Some of the most spectacular special effects in all of Epcot are found in the **Journey into Imagination** show, presented in a truncated glass pyramid. In addition to the show and endless opportunities to turn your own imagination loose, there's a very good 3-D motion picture which presents the world from a child's point of view. And in a huge, six-acre, skylighted pavilion, **The Land** examines the production of food in all its aspects. There's also a short boat ride passing through three distinct environments: a rain forest, prairie, and desert.

## World Showcase

Arranged along the shore of the World Showcase Lagoon, pavilions of Canada, China, France, Germany, Italy, Japan, Mexico, and the United Kingdom radiate from the central American Adventure. Designed to present the *essence* of each culture, each will leave you with much the same impressions you would bring home from an actual visit to the country. There are shops, restaurants, films, craft exhibits, and entertainment, as well are larger-than-life World Showcase "dolls" in ethnic costumes strolling the walkways. This is a good place to end your Epcot day, and if you should find yourself at one pavilion with a yen to be at one across the lagoon, there are boats to save you the long walk around.

**OTHER ATTRACTIONS IN THE AREA:** Between Orlando and Walt Disney World, at I-4 and the Bee Line Expressway, is **Sea World of Florida,** 7007 Sea World Dr. (tel. 305/351-0021), the world's largest marine-life theme park. It takes four to six hours to see the five major shows, which include performances by Shamu the killer whale, dolphins, seals, sea lions, and otters. There are daily ski shows too, and seal and dolphin feeder pools, where guests get into the act. Exhibits include a 150,000-gallon re-creation of a coral reef. Hundreds of exquisitely plumed birds roam freely through the 135-acre park. You can take a rest at the Fountain Fantasy Theatre, or shop for a pearl-bearing oyster whose prize can be mounted in nearby gift shops. More than a dozen concessions, ranging from snow-cone kiosks to full-service restaurants, serve a variety of foods. Park hours are 9 a.m. to 7 p.m. (later during summer, Christmas, and Easter), year round. Admission is $16 for adults and $13 for children 4 through 12.

About 30 minutes southwest of Orlando, at I-4 and U.S. 27, **Boardwalk and Baseball** (tel. 305/422-0643) features a classic American amusement park. There are thrill rides, live entertainment, and a midway, all connected by a wooden boardwalk. Some 31 rides, including a giant log flume and huge wooden roller coaster, offer fun for just about everybody. *Colorado Riders,* a live western show filled with horses, wagons, and some 40 cast members; *Grand Canyon—The Hidden Secrets,* in the IMAX Theatre; and *Professor Bubble's Magic Fun Factory* are presented daily at the 110-acre park. Also featured are major-league baseball fields that will serve as spring training home to the Kansas City Royals. Baseball exhibitions will be highlights at batting cages and the park's entrance, and a baseball memorabilia exhibit and "Homeplate" gift shop carry out the theme. Hours are 9 a.m. to 8 p.m., 10 p.m., or midnight, depending on the day of the week and the season (call for exact hours). Admission is $17 for adults, $13 for children 46 or more inches tall and seniors aged 55 and over.

**DAY TRIPS FROM WALT DISNEY WORLD:** It will take you about 70 minutes to drive east to the Kennedy Space Center's **Spaceport USA.** Entrances are well marked off U.S. 1, I-95, Fla. 405, Fla. 520, Fla. 50, and Fla. 3. There's no admission charge, no charge for parking, free kennel service, free guided walk-through tours, and they'll even loan you a camera if you left yours at home. There's so much to see that you can spend three or four hours, or the entire day. There's a nominal fee for the IMAX presentation called *The Dream Is Alive,* narrated by Walter Cronkite and shown on a screen 5½ stories high and 70 feet wide. There's also a tour (for a nominal fee) aboard a double-decker bus. The Red Tour goes to **Kennedy Space Center,** with the first bus departing at 9:45 a.m. Stops are made at Flight Crew Training, where a lunar module sits on a simulated moon surface. Also shown in a simulated launch control center is the flight of Apollo 11, the mission that landed man on the moon. From there, you proceed to the Vehicle Assembly Building and on to a viewing site on the Atlantic Ocean that allows you to photograph both space shuttle launch pads 39A and 39B. Next, you stop to view the giant Crawler Transporter, which moves the space shuttle to the launch pad, and next the Saturn V exhibit at the Vehicle Assembly Building. The Blue Tour is of **Cape Canaveral Air Force Station,** east of the Kennedy Space Center. All operations at the Kennedy Space Center and Cape Canaveral Air Force Station can be altered without notice, since this area is, after all, an operating space base. Kennedy Space Center's Spaceport USA opens at 9 a.m. every day except Christmas and certain launch and landing days.

It's less than an hour's drive south to Winter Haven and Florida's **Cypress Gardens,** just off Fla. 540 West (tel. 813/324-2111), an entertaining day for the entire family. The snowy theme of the ice skating revue (a surprise in Florida!), the fast-paced waterski show, and the high-diving and snow-ski acrobatics of Aquacade are presented several times daily. Scenic electric boat rides and guided tours pass thousands of exotic plants and flowers at one of the world's most famous botanical gardens. The Animal Forest, an accredited zoological park, showcases a rare collection of threatened and endangered species from around the world, an educational alligator-handling demonstration, exotic bird revue, and Florida's largest walk-through aviary. Southern Crossroads is a replica of an antebellum town; Kodak's Island in the Sky has an impressive scenic 16-story-high revolving photo platform; and there are kiddie rides and shopping for the grownups. Cypress Gardens is open from 8 a.m. until sunset daily, with extended hours during peak seasons. Admission is $15 for adults, $10 for ages 3 to 11, and for those under 3, it's free.

**Silver Springs** is about 90 minutes away to the northwest, and here you'll encounter the world's largest group of crystal-clear springs, which you can view through glass-bottom boats. There is also a deer park (petting allowed, even encouraged) and on a semitropical island a Reptile Institute (petting not advised). All told, you'll probably need about four hours if you want to take it all in. It's open from 9 a.m. to 5:30 p.m., and one admission covers everything inside, even boat rides (adults pay $9.75; ages 3 through 11, $7).

## 4. Palm Beach

Back during the Civil War, a northern horticulturist named **A. O. Lang** made the decision that noninvolvement in the conflict was his own best personal course of action (pacifist or deserter? he's been called both!) and headed for a region as far removed as possible from the battlefields. He landed in Florida in what is now Palm Beach, and although he had no such intention, profoundly influenced the future direction of the area. You see, he became intensely interested in native plant life and experimenting with new plants, and the natives followed his lead. Otherwise they might never have planted the coconuts that washed ashore when the Spanish barque *Providencia* was shipwrecked offshore in 1878. The palms that grew from those victims of the sea literally transformed a barren ribbon of sand into a tropical setting that led Henry M. Flagler, the railroad magnate, who started the winter migration south to Florida, to build a magnificent hotel, institute civic improvements, and begin the formal landscaping that has characterized Palm Beach ever since. The little resort was first named Palm City but was hurriedly renamed (in time to get the change off by a waiting mail boat) when the U.S. Postal Service advised there was already a Florida city by that name and a new one was necessary. (So who's ever heard of Palm City . . . ?)

The rest is history, of course. Encouraged by Flagler, the wealthy came in droves, making Palm Beach the "Newport of the South"; and they brought with them an opulence that still lingers, although a creeping commercialism can be discerned around the edges. Automobiles, for example, were once banned on many streets but now drive freely, although bicycling on paths closed to motorists is still a favorite way of getting around.

Palm Beach is on the northern end of a 14-mile-long island only three-quarters of a mile wide at its widest point. Across Lake Worth, its western water boundary, lies West Palm Beach, which Flagler envisioned as a center for commercial enterprises that would be banned in Palm Beach itself. It has, however, developed into a resort in its own right, connected to Atlantic beaches by bridges and offering Lake Worth boating and other water sports.

Together, the Palm Beaches have a lot of charm to offer today's traveler, whether in that rarified millionaire class or a middle-income tourist with an itch to vacation in an atmosphere of restrained elegance.

**WHERE TO STAY:** You don't have to be a millionaire to vacation at Palm Beach, but let's face it, money helps. The truly wealthy, of course, stay in those magnificent private "vacation villas" of 20-some and more rooms that line County Road and North Ocean Boulevard. But there have always been hotels for those a shade less rich, and some of them rival the mansions in elegance. Recent years have seen more and more high-rise rental properties, even motels, go up against the Palm Beach horizon, and while "budget" doesn't really apply to most, "reasonable" (at least, by Palm Beach standards) is possible.

### The Oldest, the Most Expensive, and the Best

The hotel scene at Palm Beach has been dominated almost from the start by **The Breakers,** South County Road, Palm Beach, FL 33480 (tel. 305/655-6611, or toll free 800/833-3141). The stately Renaissance-style Breakers has all the grandeur of a palatial Italian villa, and it is a visual beauty both inside and out. Elegance pervades the entrance, the lobby, and other reception rooms and extends to every one of the 568 guest rooms and suites. The lush tropical gardens, swaying palms, manicured lawns and oceanfront location add to the Mediterranean illusion. This is one of those memorable hotels that has hosted royalty, and the well-trained, gracious staff makes every single guest feel he's (or she's) joined that august company. Tennis, anyone? There are 14 courts. Golf? Tee off at one of the two 18-hole golf courses, or try out the putting green. And there's croquet, sailing, windsurfing, bike trails, and an Olympic-size oceanside pool, plus a private beach. As for cuisine, continental dining in the magnificent Florentine Room with its frescoed ceiling is the ultimate! Food, wines, and service vie for top billing, and there's dinner music for dancing. Even if you don't stay in the hotel, treat yourself to at least one six-course dinner—entrees start at $15 and service begins at 6 p.m. (jackets and reservations are a must). The intimate Alcazar Lounge, with a marvelous ocean view, has nightly entertainment. The Breakers has been called a "Palace by the Sea," and it takes that compliment very seriously. During "the season" (December to mid-April), doubles start at an astronomical $245, dropping June 1 through September 30 to much lower rates, with many bargain packages available.

### Newer

The **Palm Beach Ocean Hotel,** 2770 and 2830 S. Ocean Blvd., Palm Beach, FL 33480 (tel. 305/582-5381, or toll free 800/327-9407), occupies more than ten acres of oceanfront property. This is "plush" in the modern vein, and guest rooms are the last word in comfort and eye appeal. Two of the four salt- and freshwater pools are heated, while the younger set has its own kiddie pool and playground. There are tennis courts and shuffleboard. Doubles range from $60 to $110 from late December to late April, and drop from May 1 to December 15.

The **Heart of Palm Beach Motor Hotel,** 160 Royal Palm Way, Palm Beach, FL 33480 (tel. 305/655-5600), is not on the ocean, but the lovely, palm-lined street on which it stands is only minutes away. Rooms are beautifully decorated in contemporary fashion, and the cozy and intimate cocktail lounge overlooks a really smashing pool, as does the excellent restaurant. It is within walking distance of Worth Avenue and the financial district. Double room rates descend from the $120 to $260 range seasonally.

**Howard Johnson's,** 2870 S. County Rd., Palm Beach, FL 33480 (tel. 305/582-2581), is one of the best of this chain that I've visited. Rooms border on plush, with tasteful resort decor, balconies, extra washbasins, and many king-size beds; there's a pool, very nice dining room, and a cocktail lounge. Rates for double rooms range from a high of $45 to $100 down, depending on the season.

**WHERE TO EAT:** Palm Beach prides itself on its fine restaurants, as well it might. They do, after all, cater to a moneyed clientele that knows—and demands—good food and service.

**Providencia,** 251 Royal Palm Way (tel. 305/655-2600), is one of the finest, where you're likely to see Palm Beachers in the know relaxing in the attractive setting of rattan furniture and tropical flowers. The top-notch continental cuisine includes such specialties as grenadin de veau, lobster bisque, steak Diane flambé, and veal Normande. The European chefs know what they're about, as the several *Holiday* Awards displayed here attest. Lunch ($6 to $10) is served from 11:30 a.m. to 2:30 p.m., and dinner ($18 to $35) from 6 to 10 p.m. It's closed on Sunday between Mother's Day and Thanksgiving, jackets are required at dinner, and reservations are suggested.

Palm Beach was the winner when Marcello Capriccio moved his restaurant south from Long Island. **Capriccio's,** 336 Royal Poinciana Plaza just opposite the Poinciana Playhouse (tel. 305/659-5955), is quietly elegant, with vine-covered ironwork, chandeliers, and tables set with linen cloths and crystal glasses in a room decorated in browns, golds, and greens. The menu is continental with a heavy Italian emphasis, and before the move from New York it had received four stars from the *New York Times*'s discriminating Craig Claiborne. Lunch is in the $6 to $11 range (11:30 a.m. to 3 p.m.), dinner from $16 to $25 (6 to 11 p.m.), and there are special pretheater dinners and late suppers when the Playhouse is in production. Best reserve for dinner. Closed Sunday and Saturday for lunch and all day Monday.

**Testa's,** 221 Royal Poinciana Way (tel. 305/832-0992), is one of Palm Beach's oldest restaurants, having been run by the same family for over half a century. Italian specialties (like veal, boned chicken cacciatore, etc.) are superb, as you might expect, and sirloin steak, seafood, and (especially) strawberry pie are just as good. Besides serving delicious food, this place is loaded with charm, whether you eat indoors, on the patio, or at the sidewalk café. Open from 7 a.m. to 1 a.m., Testa's serves all three meals at moderate prices (breakfast, $3 to $8; lunch, $6 to $14; dinner, $6 to $16).

**AFTER DARK:** You'll find Palm Beach's nightlife in the cocktail rooms of major hotels, like the elegant **Colony,** 155 Hammon Ave., and the **Alcazar Lounge** of the Breakers, South County Road.

The **Royal Poinciana Playhouse,** 70 Royal Poinciana Plaza (tel. 305/659-3310), presents first-rate Broadway musicals and dramas, though these are usually scheduled during the January–March "season." There are exceptions, however, so it's worth a call to see if they're in production while you're there.

Check, too, to see what is in production at the **Burt Reynolds Dinner Theater,** 1001 Indianatown Rd., Jupiter (tel. 305/746-5566). Top stars often appear in musicals and drama.

**THINGS TO SEE AND DO:** For detailed sightseeing information, contact the **Palm Beach Chamber of Commerce,** 45 Coconut Row, Palm Beach, FL 33480 (tel. 305/655-3282).

Back in 1901 Henry M. Flagler, the Standard Oil tycoon and pioneer developer of the Florida east coast, built a magnificent marble palace at Palm Beach for his wife. After it was sold by his heirs in 1925, it was a luxury hotel until Flagler's granddaughter became president of a group that bought the mansion, restored the rooms and furnishings, and opened it to the public as the **Henry Morrison Flagler Museum.** From the 110- by 40-foot columned marble entrance hall, with its painted ceilings and gilt Louis XIV furniture, through a succession of period rooms, the museum reflects the lifestyle of the Flaglers when they were residents here, and many of the pieces you see are the original furnishings. In addition, there are special collections of paintings, porcelain, dolls, and family memorabilia. Flagler's private railway car, *The Rambler,* is on the grounds and is included in the tour. The museum is open every day except Monday from 10 a.m. to 5 p.m., with a $3.50 admission for adults, $1.25 for children (under 6, free). It's on Coconut Row (tel. 305/655-2833).

**Lion Country Safari,** P.O. Box 16066, West Palm Beach, FL 33416 (tel. 305/793-1084), 15 miles west of West Palm Beach, provides a closeup look at free-roaming prides of lions, antelopes, giraffes, zebras, and many other exotic animals. It's just off Fla. 80 (from the Florida Turnpike, take exit 36 or 40 and follow the signs; from I-95, take exit 50 west). They don't permit convertibles inside the wildlife preserve (and I, for one, wouldn't really want to explore it with the top down), but there's free parking and you can rent an air-conditioned closed car. And if you bring along a pet, there are very good (and free) accommodations for them while you're visiting the wild animals. Lion Country is open every day of the year from 9:30 a.m. to 4:30 p.m., and there's an $8 charge for everyone over 3 (free for under-3s). That includes the Safari Camp and several rides (like the elephant ride) in the theme park, as well as miniature golf, a reptile park, aviaries, and a petting zoo. For campers, the Lion Country Safari KOA is adjacent to the park.

On **Hutchinson Island** (five miles east of Stuart, on East Ocean Boulevard), over a scenic drive of causeways and bridges, there's a unique leftover from 1876. A colony of six "houses of refuge" was built here for people shipwrecked off the Florida coast, and the one you'll see is the only one remaining. It was first called "Gilbert's Bar Station" after a 19th-century Spanish pirate who made his headquarters in a local inlet, from which he sailed forth to plague coastal shipping before he was caught and hanged in Boston in 1834. The restored **House of Refuge** (tel. 305/255-1961) is now open every day except Monday and holidays from 1 to 5 p.m., with a charge of 75¢ for adults, 50¢ for children. An interesting look at life along the coast a hundred years ago.

*Note:* If Hutchinson Island works its magic on you and a longer stay would suit your holiday mood, one of Florida's leading resorts will turn your stay into something very special indeed. **Indian River Plantation,** 385 N.E. Plantation Rd., Hutchinson Island, Stuart, FL 33494 (tel. 305/225-3700, or toll free 800/327-4873), has secluded beaches and one- or two-bedroom oceanfront hotel suites that give you a front-row seat for those glorious sunrises over the Atlantic. In addition, fully equipped two-bedroom villas are just steps away from championship tennis courts and overlook the golf course and the lake. There are sundecks and heated swimming pools, a marina, boat rentals and sailing nearby, waterskiing instruction, and bicycle rentals for leisurely island exploring. The Inlet Restaurant is an elegant setting for dress-up dining; the Porch Restaurant provides more casual meals. Both adult and children can participate in planned daytime activities, and after dark there's dancing and live entertainment. Rates begin at $130 for suites, $150 for villas. Ask about special tennis or golf packages.

**Pier fishing** (no charge) is available at the **Lake Worth** and **Juno Beach** piers.

There are more than 70 **golf** courses in the immediate area, and among those open to the public are: **North Palm Beach Country Club,** at U.S. 1, North Palm Beach (tel. 305/626-4344), with greens fees at $9 and $18 and carts $8 and $14 each; the **West Palm Beach Country Club,** (Parker Avenue and Forest Hill Boulevard intersection, West Palm Beach (tel. 305/582-2019), where greens fees vary from $10 to $15 over the year, and carts are $12 to $14; **Palm Beach Lakes Golf Club,** 1100 N. Congress Ave., West Palm Beach (tel. 305/683-2700), with greens fees of $13, carts at $15; and the **Forest Hill Golf Club,** 3332 Forest Hill Blvd., West Palm Beach, a quarter-mile west of Congress Avenue (tel. 305/965-2332), with greens fees of $9 to $12, carts at $15.

**Tennis** courts in the area open to the public include: the **Lake Worth Racquet and Swim Club,** 4090 Coconut Rd., Lake Worth, off Lake Worth Road east of Military Trail (tel. 305/967-3900), a private club open to visitors if courts are available. This is the home of the Mario Martinez Top 100 Tennis Academy, and there are 15 courts, an Olympic-size pool, dining room, and lounge. Fees are $10 per hour, with weekly rates available.

There's greyhound racing at the **Palm Beach Kennel Club,** Belvedere and Congress Roads, West Palm Beach (tel. 305/683-2222), from late October through April every night except Wednesday and Sunday at 8 p.m., with 12:30 p.m. matinees on Monday, Thursday, and Saturday. Admission is 50¢, and no minors are admitted.

Jai-alai can be viewed at the **Palm Beach Sports Theater,** 1415 W. 45th St.,

West Palm Beach (tel. 305/844-2444), from early November to early April every night except Sunday and Monday at 7:15 p.m., and there are noon matinees on Wednesday and Saturday. Admissions range from $1 to $5. No one under 18 admitted.

**SHOPPING:** Whether just looking or buying, shopping is almost a recreation in Palm Beach because of the concentration of exclusive boutiques, unique specialty shops, and the sheer beauty of the shopping districts. There are branches of world-famous department stores (Saks Fifth Avenue, for instance), Paris couture clothing shops (Courrèges is one), famous American designer clothes (like Lilly Pulitzer), jewelry shops, novelty shops, and . . . well, the list is endless. You can find most of them in one of these shopping areas:

**Worth Avenue,** a palm-lined, world-famed avenue of shops, galleries, and restaurants, has courtyards and "vias" that give it an old-world flavor.

The **Royal Poinciana Plaza,** on Royal Poinciana Way at Coconut Row, is a relatively new addition to the shopping scene, but one which retains the traditional flavor of Palm Beach architecture. There are over 28 shops, restaurants, free parking areas, and the Poinciana Playhouse.

**Palm Beach Mall** is in the western section, on Palm Beach Lakes Boulevard at I-95 in West Palm Beach, and it's the largest shopping mall in the Palm Beaches, with more than 90 stores, pools, fountains, and scenic bridges.

## 5. Boca Raton

Just 22 miles south of Palm Beach and 45 miles north of Miami, Boca Raton is one of Florida's premier resorts. That this is so is due almost entirely to the efforts of one man back in the '20s. Addison Mizner, maverick architect, flamboyant man-of-the-world, and dreamer extraordinaire, brought to reality a fantasy that made the overblown Florida fantasies of that golden era's free-spending millionaires look almost ordinary.

Having tired of his Palm Beach pioneer role, he set out to turn some 17,500 acres at Boca Raton (nothing more than a sleepy oceanfront hamlet at the time) into a dream city for only the super-wealthy. One writer described Mizner's vision as one of "a happy combination of Venice and Heaven, Florence and Toledo, with a little Greco-Roman glory and grandeur thrown in." What he brought into being in 1926 was the Cloister Inn, an elaborate, pseudo-Spanish-style hostelry furnished with Spanish and Central American antiques and set in lush tropical gardens. The great, near-great, and new-rich-who-*wanted*-to-be-great flocked down to the Cloister in droves, and for one fabulous season Mizner reigned as undisputed king of his self-created kingdom. His timing, however, was more than a little off—it was the very next year that the Florida land boom came to a crashing end. In no time at all the luxurious hotel and its gardens were being reclaimed by native swamp and jungle, and it seemed the high old times of that one shining year were gone forever.

It wasn't until 1930 that the resort reopened as the Boca Raton Club, totally renovated to erase the scars of neglect, and made, if possible, even more exclusive than it had been under Mizner's rule. Once again Boca Raton witnessed private railroad cars and palatial yachts deposit the wealthiest of the wealthy on its doorstep, and the little town's economy revolved around the club. Since then, with the exception of the World War II years, which saw the club's conversion into "the most elegant barracks in history," both club and town have prospered. Now named the Boca Raton Hotel and Club, the hotel preserves Mizner's original fantasy, combining in perfect harmony the opulence of the past with the ultimate in modern-style accommodations (see below). Meanwhile, the town of Boca Raton (natives call it "Ra-*tone,*"; newcomers, "Ra-

*tahn*" has developed as a resort area independent of its most luxurious hotel, as well as the site of Florida Atlantic University and a cultural center of this part of the state.

**WHERE TO STAY:** *The* place to stay—as true these days as in the beginning—is the **Boca Raton Hotel and Club,** Camino Real, Boca Raton, FL 33432 (tel. 305/395-3000, or toll free 800/327-0101). If yours is a romantic nature, book into the Cloister, where much of Addison Mizner's dream lives on in his original style. Today's public rooms, guest rooms, patios, gardens, and both the Cathedral and Patio Royale dining rooms would gladden that eccentric's heart and will quicken your own. Those more attuned to the modern world can opt for the Tower, where deluxe corner rooms and suites overlook Lake Boca Raton. The Top of the Tower dining room serves gourmet continental cuisine along with spectacular views of both lake and ocean. On the resort estate's championship golf course grounds, the Golf Villas have complete kitchens, balconies, and patios, with continuous shuttle service to the hotel and all its facilities. Across the Intracoastal Waterway and right on the Atlantic, the Boca Beach Club is a sophisticated, European-style hotel whose rooms boast such niceties as a well-stocked mini-refrigerator. There's continental dining in the Shell dining room and evening entertainment in the adjoining lounge. As you can see, absolutely nothing in the pampering department has been overlooked, whether your tastes hark back to the hotel's founder's days or are geared to today and tomorrow. There's literally something for everyone. In season, doubles in the Cloister are in the $260 range; in the Tower, $355; Golf Villas apartments, $355; and oceanfront Beach Club rooms, $395. Rates drop from April to December. There's an automatic 17% service charge on all à la carte food orders, and a daily service charge for all other gratuities.

The **Best Western University Inn,** 2700 N. Federal Hwy., Boca Raton, FL 33431 (tel. 305/395-5225, or toll free 800/528-1234), has nicely appointed rooms, a pool, tennis courts, restaurant, and lounge. In-season doubles run $79 (lower other months); those under 12 stay free in the room with their parents, and there are family rates available.

**WHERE TO EAT:** **La Vieille Maison,** 770 E. Palmetto Park Rd. (tel. 305/391-6701, or 421-7370), is the place for elegant dining in a beautifully appointed old house. Choose from several rooms, from balcony to courtyard. It's a French menu featuring veal, lamb, seafoods, and an excellent wine list. Dinner prices average about $40 without wine, and hours are 6:30 to 10 p.m. May through October, and 6 to 10 p.m. November through April. Reservations are a must.

**THINGS TO SEE AND DO:** Beach activities, golf, and tennis are primary vacation offerings, with the **Caldwell Playhouse** (tel. 305/368-7509) and the **Royal Palm Dinner Theatre** (tel. 305/426-2211) offering periodic productions. The **Boca Raton Center for the Arts,** 801 W. Palmetto Park Rd. (tel. 305/392-2500), sponsors demonstrations and workshops as well as interesting art exhibits.

*Chapter XVI*

# GREATER MIAMI AND THE BEACHES

IF, AS O. HENRY WROTE, New York is "Baghdad on the Hudson," then surely Miami and Miami Beach could be called "Baghdad on Biscayne Bay"! Metropolitan Miami is like nothing so much as one large bazaar from which you can pick and choose the wares that suit you best—glittering hotels so elaborate they assume an unreal air rising against Miami Beach's skyline; rows of less pretentious motels for less affluent travelers; magnificent rococo estates built by "up north" millionaires during the '20s; lush tropical plantings everywhere; streets teeming with throngs of sun worshippers tanned a nutty brown and busy doing everything *but* worshipping the sun; lavish nightclubs and intimate lounges; an entire section that is Old Havana transplanted; patches of arty shops and bohemian artists; other islands of stores so exclusive they're almost intimidating; and an assortment of sightseeing attractions so vast they could make it hard for you to get to that glorious beach, the star attraction that started the whole thing. And some 12 million visitors gravitate to this mecca of golden treasures every year.

It hasn't always been so. As with much of the rest of Florida, Henry Flagler probably is largely responsible for Miami's development, since his railroad in the late 1800s (built, it is said, after he received a gift of frost-free oranges from Mrs. Julia Tuttle at a time when citrus fruits were frozen as far south as Palm Beach) made it easy to reach. By 1913 there was a wooden bridge leading from

Miami to Miami Beach, a swampy mangrove strip of land that John Collins had tried unsuccessfully to use for growing coconuts and avocados as money crops. Collins, however, made the first of Miami Beach's spectacular land deals when he sold 1,600 acres—much of it under water—to an Indianapolis industrialist, Carl G. Fisher. Undaunted, Fisher set about dredging up the bay and building a series of small islands, offered a block of oceanfront land to anyone who would put a luxury hotel on it, and built six polo fields as an appeal to wealthy Northerners.

With the 1920s boom came the payoff for Fisher's investment; his holdings were estimated to have a value of over $100 million, and those sun-seeking crowds were pouring in. Across the bay, Miami had been transformed by the railroad from a remote tropical village of weather-beaten shacks into a bustling business center. The future for the metropolitan area wasn't just rosy—it looked positively golden. Then came the 1929 crash, and it hit hard, with fortunes disappearing overnight and land values spiraling downward. But as the national economy began to recover and people once more could turn their attention to leisure-time pursuits, Miami came out of the doldrums and again transformed its natural resources of tropical temperatures and long stretches of beach into money-making assets. By the end of World War II it was solidly on its feet again, and in the years immediately after the war it built more new hotels than any one single area in the world.

In the last few years Miami Beach south of Lincoln Road has seen a resurgence in what had become a rather seedy, run-down section of the town. Thanks to the interest and efforts of a dedicated group of art deco buffs, more and more of the interesting buildings of the late '20s and early '30s are being restored to their original state. Several have been refurbished in the style of that era, and one by one others are being brought back to reflect Miami Beach in its heyday.

While Miami has had more than its share of bad press in recent years with respect to crime and the Cuban refugee flood, most tourists are not touched by either. Normal precautions, of course, are in order (keep valuables locked in hotel safes, etc.), but on the whole the area presents a pleasant, safe atmosphere.

Today's visitors will be welcomed with open arms, and Miami, according to their tastes and income, will be luxurious or gaudy, quiet and restful or lively

**GUIDE TO THE NUMBERED POINTS OF INTEREST ON THE MIAMI AND VICINITY MAP:** 1.—Seminole Okalee Indian Village; 2.—Dania Jai Alai Fronton; 3.—Gulfstream Park Racetrack; 4.—Calder Race Course; 5.—Monastery of St. Bernard; 6.—Biscayne College; 7.—Biscayne Kennel Club; 8.—Barry College; 9.—Hialeah Park Racetrack; 10.—Miami Jai Alai Fronton; 11.—Miami Stadium; 12.—Watson Park; 13.—Miami Municipal Auditorium; 14.—Orange Bowl Stadium; 15.—Dade County Auditorium; 16.—Flagler Kennel Club; 17.—Miami Merchandise Mart; 18.—Tamiami Trail; 19.—Miamarina—Bayfront Park; 20.—Miami Beach Convention Center; 21.—Ocean Front Auditorium; 22.—Marine Stadium; 23.—Planet Ocean; 24.—Seaquarium; 25.—Vizcaya Art Museum; 26.—Museum of Science & Planetarium; 27.—Historical Museum of So. Florida; 28.—"Miracle Mile"; 29.—Little Havana; 30.—Coconut Grove artist district; 31.—City Hall & Marina Dinner Key; 32.—University of Miami; 33.—Bill Baggs State Park—Cape Florida Lighthouse; 34.—Fairchild Tropical Garden; 35.—Parrot Jungle; 36.—Serpentarium; 37.—Monkey Jungle; 38.—Miami Seaquarium; 39.—Miami Wax Museum; 40.—Coral Castle; 41.—Orchid Jungle

and honky-tonk, a sports center for golfing and taking in the races or a splendid showcase for high fashions to be shown off at celebrity-filled watering spots.

# 1. Getting Your Bearings

"Miami" to most of us means the entire metropolitan area—Miami itself, Miami Beach, Coral Gables, Coconut Grove, Key Biscayne, Bal Harbour, Golden Beach—and some people even consider Hollywood, Hallandale, and Fort Lauderdale a part of "Miami" (but *not* the people who live there). Actually, I suppose you could lump most of coastal Dade County (Hollywood, Hallandale, and Fort Lauderdale are over the line in Broward) under the "Greater Miami and the Beaches" label for practical purposes.

**MIAMI:** Biscayne Boulevard (U.S. 1) is Miami's "show" street, with hotels and business buildings lining parts of it (its boast is that you can buy anything from a 55¢ orange drink to a $75,000 yacht along the boulevard); an eight-lane stretch shaded by royal palms (between S.E. 1st Street and N.E. 5th Street); 62-acre **Bayfront Park** (where you can pick up tons of information from the **Greater Miami Chamber of Commerce** in the City Auditorium, or stroll down shaded walkways bordered with brilliant flowering plants, or take in an open-air concert at the bandshell); and an access road leading off to **Dodge Island,** the 300-acre seaport from which cruise ships depart for the Bahamas and West Indies.

Once off Biscayne Boulevard, however, the street system can be confusing, to say the least—you can cover a lot of ground backtracking when you've reached *North*west 8th Street instead of *South*west 8th. The thing to remember is that the street-numbering system begins at **Miami Avenue and Flagler Street** and is divided into quadrants from that point: northeast, northwest, southeast, and southwest. Streets and terraces run east and west, avenues and places north and south. Sounds simple enough, doesn't it? Well, it *is*—until you hit Coral Gables, for just one example, with its Spanish-named streets, or Hialeah, where a nonsystem of streets and avenues is so perplexing your only salvation will be a map and sheer persistence.

As a matter of fact, your very *first* acquisition if you're driving should be a city map, either from the **Greater Miami Convention and Visitors Bureau,** 4770 Biscayne Blvd., Miami, FL 33137 (tel. 305/573-4300), or a news vendor. If you *still* get lost, my best advice is to ask directions (which can get confusing too), or park the car and take a cab. A cheaper way of getting around, of course, is the excellent network of **Metropolitan Transit Authority** buses and rapid transit system (fares are by zone, and there's an "exact fare" policy). Special fare discounts are available for the elderly, handicapped, and students. The Convention and Visitors Bureau can furnish route maps, or you can call the MTA at 305/638-6700 for specific route information.

Since the advent of Castro, Miami has served as a gateway to the U.S. for Cubans who could not, or did not wish to, live under his regime. So many have come here and settled down, in fact, that the entire city has taken on a Latin flavor, with the native Anglo culture gaining an exuberance and *espirito* which adds a decided fillip to any visit.

In an area of small, two-story homes and sometimes sagging shops around S.W. 8th Street and West Flagler Street, the concentration of Cuban culture is so heavy that a **"Little Havana"** has come into being. "Calle Ocho" (which is S.W. 8th Street, U.S. 41, or the Tamiami Trail, depending on which map you're reading) is Little Havana's "Main Street"—and a stroll down any part of its 30-block length is like a trip to Old Havana with a slightly anglicized architecture (although Spanish-style street lamps and window signs that read "English spoken here" tend to overshadow building styles). There are shops of all descriptions, factories where cigars are rolled by hand, over 300 restaurants, and lots of sidewalk coffee counters where the strong, aromatic Cuban coffee is an ideal pick-me-up when you're suffering from street fatigue. (For more about "Little Havana," see "Sightseeing.")

Across the Rickenbacker Causeway lies **Key Biscayne,** but **Virginia Key** comes first as you cross the park-like causeway (there are swimming, boating, and fishing areas all along the sides of the four-lane road). The Seaquarium and Marine Stadium are both on this palm-filled island (see "Sightseeing"), and a bridge connects it to Key Biscayne, a 4½-mile island that holds Crandon Park with its outstanding zoo, elegant private homes and hotels, and Cape Florida State Park at the southern tip (again, see "Sightseeing").

Back on the Miami side of the Rickenbacker Causeway, **Coconut Grove** is a tropical Greenwich Village, with resident and visiting artists, musicians, craftspeople, boutiques with all sorts of artwork for sale, excellent restaurants, and tiny, winding roads and streets with homes of every architectural style set back in wooded plots. The best and most fun way to see Coconut Grove is on a bike, and there are several rental shops where you can get one for an hour, a half day, or an entire day.

**Coral Gables** is a different cup of tea—handsome (sometimes elegant) homes set in landscaped grounds, a wide shopping boulevard (Miracle Mile—see "Shopping"), and a street "system" that will drive you wild. Unless you want to just wander, which isn't a bad idea, arm yourself with a Miami city map. Despite the trouble, though, Coral Gables warrants a look-see, for it's a totally planned community, with a strict building code, no billboards, and a confined business district. All in all, it is probably tropical city living as we all envision it and as we seldom see it.

The Orange Bowl Stadium, in the 1500 block of N.W. 3rd Street, is where the Miami Dolphin football team plays its home games and, of course, where the Orange Bowl Festival culminates three weeks of festivities with that all-important Orange Bowl game on January 1.

**Hialeah** (see "Sports"), with its beautiful race track, is up in the northwest section, and it's a distribution center for many of the city's department stores and appliance manufacturers. Like Coral Gables, it requires a map for any detailed exploration.

**MIAMI BEACH:** Miami Beach is connected to the mainland, three miles west across Biscayne Bay, by five causeways. The oldest, **MacArthur Causeway,** leaves the beach at 5th Street, arriving at Miami's 12th and 13th Streets. You'll see several small, well-cared-for islands to the north as you drive across, with private homes and docks out front (Al Capone lived on one for a while). The Japanese Tea Garden (see "Sightseeing") is on Watson Island near the Miami side, and this is also where the Goodyear blimp and helicopters offer airborne sightseeing tours (see "Tours"). Dade Boulevard, just north of Miami Beach's 17th Street, runs into the **Venetian Causeway** (there's a 25¢ toll), which ends at Miami's 15th Street. That enormous waterfront building you see on the Miami side is the *Miami Herald* building, one of the most modern newspaper plants in the world, and you can arrange a guided tour by telephone (tel. 305/350-2491). At 41st Street (Miami Beach), the **Julia Tuttle Causeway** is one of the most heavily traveled of the five, since the drive over is quick and it connects with expressways at Miami's 36th Street. Then comes the **John F. Kennedy Causeway,** at Miami Beach's 71st Street, but if you use that name, you're likely to get very strange blank looks from the natives—it exits at 79th Street in Miami, and I've never heard it called anything but the **79th Street Causeway** (even addresses of restaurants along its route are listed that way). Farther north, the **Broad Causeway** (96th Street at the beach, 125th Street on the mainland) charges a 15¢ toll.

The long (7½ miles), narrow (one to three miles wide) island that is Miami Beach is considerably easier to get around than its older, larger sister city across the bay. Its main artery is **Collins Avenue,** which runs north and south its entire length, with the Atlantic on one side, Indian Creek on the other. East-west streets are numbered, beginning at the south end of the island. **Lincoln Road** (an eight-block shopping mall sometimes called the Fifth Avenue of the South—see "Shopping") is a major east-west dividing street between 16th and 17th Streets, with the older, less expensive hotels to the south (some of which, dating from the '30s and '40s, are being restored to their original art deco beauty), those fabulous new (and expensive) establishments running all the way north to 87th Street, through exclusive **Surfside** and **Bal Harbour** to **Haulover Park** at 108th Street. Although hotels stand shoulder to shoulder the entire route, the beach is dotted with block-long **parks at 23rd, 46th, 65th, and 71st Streets.** Beyond Haulover Park, which has every sort of resort facility open to the public—beaches, rental boats, inexpensive restaurants, bicycles, tennis courts, etc.—the more moderately priced motels begin at 159th Street and run through the **Sunny Isles** section all the way up to 19th Street, giving way there to the quiet residential community of **Golden Beach.**

The beach, which had suffered from erosion in recent years and has been repaired by the U.S. Army Corps of Engineers, is best, in my opinion, both at the Sunny Isles section to the north of Miami Beach proper and at **South Beach,** on the southern tip of the island, although it really is fine all the way up.

One of your lasting impressions of Miami Beach is bound to be of the lush, vibrant tropical trees and plants that line the streets, fill the parks, and create a garden-like setting for the whole place. Well, those gorgeous, flower-filled vistas weren't plunked there by Mother Nature—remember, this was once nothing more than mud and mangroves. The city nursery spends a fortune each year to raise more than a million plants, renewing the elaborate displays with just-blooming flowers as each species fades.

There are two vacation attractions I've never seen advertised for Miami Beach, yet they both are free, fun, and almost unavoidable. The first is people-watching (which can be fascinating here because of the incredible mix of rich and not-so-rich, knowns and unknowns, and the wide variety of ethnic groups), and the other is lobby-hopping (you can *feel* rich just by walking through those gilded portals, and it doesn't cost a cent to look!). Of course, with all that beach and the wealth of sightseeing to be done in the area, you may have to skip the lobbies, but for a spare hour or two, you can't beat it, especially for the price.

## 2. Where to Stay

The cost of a motel or hotel room in the Greater Miami area will depend on several factors. First of all, the location makes a *big* difference in price. Miami Beach proper runs from Government Cut (an access channel to Miami's port facilities) north to 88th Street south of Lincoln Road (which is between 16th and 17th Streets) rates tend to be less and hotels older. The fabulous and very expensive "Hotel Row" extends from Lincoln Road north all the way through Surfside and Bal Harbour to Haulover Park. North of Haulover Park, from 159th to 195th, Sunny Isles is lined with a more moderately priced "Motel Row." Since that entire stretch is only about 12 miles long, and since the beach itself above and below "Hotel Row" is as good as that of the high-rent district, a visitor looking primarily for sun and surf can save an unbelievable amount just by staying at one end or the other. And even more savings can be effected by the location of the *room*. Often by foregoing an oceanfront room, you can save substantially. And, of course, the quality of the motel or hotel will help determine your cost. Almost all, however, will have a pool, the beach is either right out front or just across the street, and many of the moderately priced motels have extras that compare favorably with expensive places in other resorts.

*When* you go will also have a tremendous bearing on what you pay. The winter months are, as you'd expect, the most expensive, and from December 15 to April 1 "budget" often moves up into the "moderate" range. However, as more and more people discover that Miami Beach is well within their means in the summer, if not the winter, and that year-round attractions are just as appealing in July as in December, the "seasons" are blurring in everything but price, with much the same service, entertainment, and plush-resort atmosphere all year. The prices I've listed with each accommodation indicate the lowest and the highest charged during the year: there are usually several gradations in between. Lowest rates are generally in effect in May and June and from September through mid-December, and July and August rates as a rule run lower than those from December to April. Of course you may not see as many celebrities on the beaches or "big-name" performers in the clubs during these lesser seasons (Miami Beach doesn't really have an *off*-season anymore); but then, that may not be why you're going!

Unless otherwise noted, the hotels and motels listed below are oceanfront.

If the wealth of accommodations available at Miami Beach seems a little overwhelming, the **Miami Beach Resort Hotel Association** can make your booking simpler—and probably save you money as well. They have established a toll-free telephone service (tel. 800/531-3553) to provide reservations at major hotels, or if you wish, find a package booking to cover hotel, rental car, nightclub tickets, and sightseeing arrangements. The package deals (and many are available with discount airline fares) may be booked through travel agents as well as directly through the central reservations number.

**DELUXE:** The **Fontainebleau Hilton,** 4441 Collins Ave., Miami, FL 33140 (tel. 305/538-2000, or toll free for reservations only 800/445-8667), has long been queen of the beach, with her graceful, gleaming white quarter-circle main structure overlooking the newly rebuilt 300-foot-wide white sand beach and the Atlantic on one side, the picturesque Intracoastal Waterway and Collins Avenue on the other. Now, after a $43-million spruce-up and expanded by the acquisition of an adjoining hotel and the installation of a state-of-the-art health spa, she almost seems to preen in the Miami Beach sun. The 1,206 rooms, including 61 suites, are indeed something to preen about—their size, to begin with, and their comfort and luxurious furnishings to finish with. Some have period decor, others contemporary, but all are, simply put, smashing. And then there are the public rooms: a vast lobby edged with live tropical plants, black and white marble columns, and a marble floor partially covered by a bright, tropical green carpet. There are huge standing candelabra, crystal chandeliers, and a baby grand piano over by the circular bar which looks out onto the grounds and the sea beyond. Every service you can imagine is offered to guests, and you can dine whenever and wherever the notion strikes you, from a snack at poolside to elegant continental dishes in the Dining Galleries to early-morning or late-night meals in the garden-style Chez Bon Bon. And there's entertainment aplenty, with the Poodle Lounge keeping late hours alive. On the 18 acres of grounds there's a gigantic half-acre pool complete with an island and five-story-high "magic mountain" which sports four waterfalls. There are lighted tennis courts, golf privileges (with transportation to and from the courses), pool tables, sailing, and windsurfing.

As for prices, well, they're not cheap (doubles start at $125 and suites at $275), but the Fontainebleau offers special packages that are well within the bargain range for this type of accommodation. In 1987, for example, there was a seven-day/six-night Rainbow Extended Stay package that included a day at the spa for the extraordinary price of $399 per person, double occupancy. Also, they follow the Hilton policy of not charging for children who share their parents' quarters. Incidentally, the prices quoted here are for high season and drop other months.

The **Alexander Hotel,** 5225 Collins Ave., Miami Beach, FL 33140 (tel. 305/865-6500, or toll free 800/327-6121), is elegance personified. No mere deluxe rooms here, but spacious one- or two-bedroom suites. The large living rooms flow into a dining area, kitchens come fully equipped with an honor bar, and there are two baths and a private terrace. Furnishings are superb (some suites even come with a piano in the living room), and public spaces set the tone with subdued colors, a sweeping lobby stairway, and antiques or reproductions used effectively. For those times you decide to make use of that marvelous kitchen, there's a pantry service to deliver groceries, and for other meals there are the gourmet French restaurant Dominique's, Dominique's Terrace, and the more casual Top of the Falls. Other facilities include a 600-foot beach, tennis, two lagoon swimming pools, private marina, and golf and sailing close by. The Alexander is truly a "home away from home" in the grand manner. In season, rates start at $180 for one-bedroom ocean-view suites ($350 for oceanfront), $225 and $450 for two-bedrooms. Costs go down other months.

In Miami's Coconut Grove, the **Grand Bay Hotel,** 2669 S. Bayshore Dr., Miami, FL 33133 (tel. 305/858-9600), is another hostelry of unsurpassed elegance. Its distinctive pyramid shape rises to afford panoramic views of Biscayne Bay and the nearby marina, and its luxurious furnishings and appointments begin with an antique-filled lobby decorated in soft pastels. Guest rooms exude an old-world charm, with original antiques, fresh flowers, an honor bar, and even a television in the marble bath. There's an excellent restaurant, a lounge with lots of rich woodwork, and atop it all, a branch of the international nightspot, Regine's. Doubles during high season are in the $200-and-up range.

The **Doral-on-the-Ocean,** 4833 Collins Ave., Miami, FL 33140 (tel. 305/532-3600), is quite a place all by itself, but its guests also enjoy use of the elegant Doral Country Club's facilities over in Miami (five golf courses, 15 tennis courts, lake fishing, etc.). The oceanfront Doral also has tennis, as well as basketball, volleyball, Ping-Pong, a heated pool, and cabañas for beachgoers. Newly renovated guest rooms are quite as luxurious as the stunning baroque decor of its lobby and public rooms, and have refrigerators, extra washbasins in separate dressing rooms, and for the height of luxury, book one of the new penthouse Presidential Suites. And there's a lovely rooftop dining room with a view. Cocktail lounges, of course. Doubles start, seasonally, at $145 to $185, and there are several attractive vacation packages available at lower rates.

The **Doral Hotel and Country Club,** 4400 N.W. 87th St., Miami, FL 33178 (tel. 305/592-2000, or toll free 800/327-6334), has won just about every major hotel award in existence, and with good reason. Although just minutes away from Miami's International Airport, it's set in 2,400 beautifully landscaped acres that hold five 18-hole championship golf courses, 15 tennis courts (clay and hard surface), an Olympic-size pool, a 24-stable equestrian center, a separate Corporate Lodge especially designed for top executives, a world-class Spa Resort, and 650 deluxe guest rooms. Beautifully designed, decorated, and furnished, most guest rooms have private balconies, and some have parlor and/or sitting room combinations. The lovely Garden Terrace Restaurant is done up in soft spring colors and overlooks a golf course so difficult it's been dubbed the "Blue Monster" (such is the quality of Doral's courses that it's the site of the annual Doral Ryder Open PGA Tournament). Guests here have full use of all facilities at its sister hotel, Doral Hotel-on-the-Ocean (see above), and there's complimentary transportation between the two. Doubles begin at $185 for standard rooms, $215 for deluxe rooms, and $235 for luxury rooms. Special Christmas, Winter Golf Classic, and other assorted packages reduce these rates substantially.

### At Bal Harbour

The majestic **Sheraton Bal Harbour,** 9701 Collins Ave., Bal Harbour, FL 33154 (tel. 305/865-7511, or toll free 800/654-5040), sits on ten beautifully landscaped acres along the oceanfront in Bal Harbour Village, an area that is fast becoming one of the liveliest and most interesting in Greater Miami. Beauty, as well as luxury, are the keynote, beginning with its stunning two-story atrium lobby. Many of its 685 rooms have balconies overlooking the ocean, and all are superior in decor, furnishings, and comfort. Amenities include two pools, a health club, boat rentals, a shopping arcade, barber, and a beauty shop. High-season rates for doubles begin at $125, suites at $275 (lower other months), and children under 18 stay free in the same room with their parents.

### At Key Biscayne

Out on Key Biscayne, the **Sonesta Beach Hotel,** 350 Ocean Dr., Key Biscayne, FL 33149 (tel. 305/361-2021), provides that rare combination of a world apart and all that the Miami world holds literally just a short drive away. The gleaming white structure rises above lush tropical grounds, its face to the ocean and a private beach. You'll know you're in a special place from the moment you enter its spacious marble lobby, its walls hung with eye-catching artwork. The 293 guest rooms, recently renovated, also are decorated with original artwork and exquisitely furnished. No detail of comfort and convenience has been overlooked, and what with the excellent (and elegant) Two Dragons restaurant to serve up gourmet Oriental dishes (the Rib Room features continental and American cuisine, there's a nouvelle American gourmet menu in Desires Restaurant & Lounge, and the Snackerrie has beachfront picnic-style food), the Desires Lounge for cocktail hour, a health club for spurts of active ambition (as well as ten Laykold tennis courts), an oceanfront pool for swimming or sunning, and a marvelous "Just Us Kids" program to free time for adult loafing, it's quite possible to settle in and never leave the premises during a perfect vacation. There's even a lively disco on hand in the Desires Lounge after 10 p.m. to fill the evening hours. If you prefer a *real* "home away from home," there are secluded villas available with two to five bedrooms, luxuriously furnished, and each with a private pool. Rates for doubles begin at $175, and villas range from $275 to $550, with many very good winter vacation packages such as the "Free Wheels Deal" that in 1987 ran as low as $270 per person, double occupancy, for three nights and four days, including a rental car.

### A European-Style Charmer

European, or art deco? Well, the lovely little **Hotel Place St. Michel,** 162 Alcazar, Coral Gables, FL 33134 (tel. 305/444-1666), is a delightful combination of both that whisks you back to an era of lighthearted elegance. The canopied entrance and small lobby are faced with original Spanish tile, the front desk is an antique, two-sided English secretary, and the two-story hotel's exterior is topped by a Moorish belltower, complete with red-tiled cupola. Only 30 rooms here, each distinctively furnished with antiques such as armoires with inlaid wood and beveled dressing mirrors. Ceiling fans, lace curtains, and wood parquet floors are featured in all, as are Tiffany glass or art deco table lamps. Whimsical touches come in the form of an upright Singer sewing machine, complete with iron treadle, that serves as a TV stand and other intriguing uses of relics of the past (both American and European). The marvelous little restaurant off the lobby has the look and menu of a Parisian café and has become a popular lunchtime rendezvous for the Coral Gables business community, since the Place St. Michel is centrally located in the downtown area. Rates are surprisingly moderate, in the $70 to $85 range for doubles (including a continental breakfast of juice, coffee, and croissant).

**ART DECO HOTELS:** For a totally different Miami Beach vacation, head down south of Lincoln Road to the Art Deco National Historic District and two hotels that reflect what has come to be called "Tropical Deco." The **Cardozo Hotel,** 1300 Ocean Dr., Miami Beach, FL 33139 (tel. 305/531-1235), and the **Carlyle Hotel** (on the opposite corner—same telephone number) are both on the National Register of Historic Places, and both are owned and operated by a partnership headed by Andrew Capitman, whose mother actually spearheaded the art deco revitalization movement. Just across Ocean Drive from Lummus Park and the sea, they have been restored to the era of their birth with loving care.

The Cardozo, built in 1939, was one of the most fashionable resorts on the beach before World War II. You may recognize it as the setting for the Frank Sinatra film, *Hole in the Head,* although since that filming, Andrew and his crew have stripped away all the wallpapers, quasi-luxurious carpeting, and other trappings that hid its original artistry in layers added over the years. There are 70 rooms, smaller than luxury hotels of today, but charmingly furnished in the style of the '30s and guaranteed to give you delusions of having stepped into one of the movies from that period. The Carlyle Hotel, built in 1941, has the same classic art deco features as its older sister, and its 76 rooms perfectly complement the wrap-around period exterior. Both the Café Cardozo and the Café Carlyle have become gathering spots to Miami Beach residents and the young artists who are beginning to congregate in droves in this area. Double rates range from $95 up, and there are special package deals offered from time to time.

**EXPENSIVE:** The **Golden Nugget Resort Motel,** 18555 Collins Ave., Miami Beach, FL 33160 (tel. 305/932-1445), has an exceptionally nice private beach, three pools (one is just for the small fry), and a children's counselor who heads planned activities. There are efficiencies among the 120 rooms, all of which are brightly decorated, and most rooms face either pool or ocean. There's a very nice dining room, a coffeeshop, and a cocktail lounge. Seasonal rates here range from $57 to $80 for doubles, and efficiencies are an additional $10 a day.

Many of the 162 rooms at the **Chateau-by-the-Sea,** 19115 Collins Ave., Miami Beach, FL 33160 (tel. 305/931-8800), have balconies, and some have private patios. Rooms are about average in size, sporting comfortable, contemporary furnishings, and there are some kitchenettes available. Facilities include an oversize heated swimming pool, a wading pool, a playground, free golf privileges, a recreation room, Ping-Pong, and free in-house movies. For nighttime recreation, the bar has entertainment and dancing year round. Double-room rates run $50 to $85 seasonally (cots and cribs are free).

Patches of green lawn and plantings of flowers and shrubs give the **Radisson Pan American Resort Motel,** 17875 Collins Ave., Miami Beach, FL 33160 (tel. 305/932-1100), a pleasing, manicured look, and inside there's the same well-kept air. Furnishings are modern, with bright resort colors dominating, and rooms (which open to a private terrace or balcony) have refrigerators and two double beds. In addition to the Olympic-size pool, you'll find shuffleboard and a nine-hole putting green. Both the dining room and lounge (which has entertainment at night) have beamed ceilings and lots of light woods around. Double rooms range in season from $110 to $198, lower the rest of the year, and cribs and cots are free.

The air of subdued elegance in the pretty lobby of the **Monaco Luxury Resort Motel,** 17501 Collins Ave., Miami Beach, FL 33160 (tel. 305/932-2100), extends to most of the rooms. Colors are cheerful and bright, furnishings modern, and there's a refrigerator in every room. The private beach is some 200 feet long, and there's a heated pool and a kiddie pool. Depending on location of the room and the season, double rooms range from $40 to $70, efficiencies run an additional $7, and rooms can be arranged to accommodate up to four people.

You can call collect to reserve at the **Suez Resort Motel,** 18215 Collins Ave., Miami Beach, FL 33160 (tel. 305/932-0661). Most of the modern-decor rooms have refrigerators, and there are kitchenettes available. Recreation facilities are on a par with those elsewhere—two pools (and a lifeguard), a wading pool, tennis court, children's playground, shuffleboard, volleyball, and a children's counselor. The oceanfront dining terrace is delightful (but you can eat inside if you prefer) and the cocktail lounge has nightly entertainment. Double rooms run from $60 to $70 seasonally; kitchenettes are an extra $10.

**MODERATE:** From the moment you walk into the light, airy, glass-walled lobby of the **Dunes Motel,** on the ocean at 170th Street (tel. 305/947-7511), decorated in soft yellows, greens, and white, you'll encounter a kind of casual elegance that you'll find also in the beautifully appointed rooms, all of which are efficiency units. This is one of the prettiest of the moderately priced motels, with large, picture-windowed rooms, palm-thatched shade shelters, an Olympic-size pool alongside the smaller one for children, a patio-pool bar, and supervised activities for the younger set. The private beach runs for more than 400 feet out front. It's also within walking distance of shopping and theaters (some restaurants as well, although the one on the premises is excellent). There's entertainment and dancing at night in the cocktail lounge. Double-room rates vary according to location as well as season, and range from $50 to $90.

Near the northern end of "Motel Row," the **Ocean Roc Resort Motel,** 19505 Collins Ave., Miami Beach, FL 33160 (tel. 305/931-7600, or toll free 800/327-0553), used to be a Holiday Inn. It's an unusually well-maintained place right on the ocean, with extra-large rooms (all with refrigerators and two double beds, and nicely furnished) which have private balconies. There's a swimming pool with a separate section for kids, a game room, a dining room with an ocean view, and a bar. The location is quieter and more restful than most, yet still convenient to shopping. Rates are in the $30 to $60 range, with efficiencies an additional $10.

If you prefer to be right in the heart of Miami Beach, in the Lincoln Road area, your best bet for comfort, convenience, and moderate rates is the **Fairfax Hotel,** Collins Avenue at 18th Street, Miami Beach, FL 33139 (tel. 305/538-3837). This is one of Miami Beach's nicest small hotels (only 86 rooms), and an exception to the usual impersonal hotel service. The Fairfax staff is friendly, as well as efficient and helpful. Rooms are unusually large and nicely done up, and there are apartments just right for families. Although not on the ocean, Fairfax guests have the use of a private pool and beach just across the street. This is a good buy for those facts alone, but bonuses come in the form of Abe, David, and Marilyn Sheffman, the family owners-operators of the Fairfax. Seasonally varying rates for doubles range from $25 to $50.

If you're looking for a family-style kosher hotel, you can't do better than the **Tarleton**, 2469 Collins Ave., Miami Beach, FL 33140 (tel. 305/538-5721, or toll free 800/327-3110), run by the third generation of the Jacobs family. This pretty oceanfront hotel has a large, lovely dining room looking out to the ocean that is operated under strict rabbinical supervision, with a resident *mashgiach*. Dietary laws are adhered to, and there's a synagogue right on the premises with daily services. Rooms are comfortable and attractive, and there's a game and card room, and a theater for movies. Rates range from $36 to $48 for oceanfront doubles, $35 to $40 for others.

**CAMPGROUNDS: Holiday Park,** 3140 W. Hallandale Beach Blvd., Hallandale, FL 33009 (tel. 305/981-4414), and **Trinity Towers,** 3300 Pembroke Rd., Hollywood, FL 33021 (tel. 305/962-7400), are just a mile apart, with 168 full-hookup sites each, heated pools, showers, recreation hall, and laundry facilities, all convenient to Metropolitan Miami, dog tracks, race tracks, golf course, jai-alai, etc. Rates start at $12.

## 3. Where to Eat

When visitors to the Greater Miami area aren't sunning themselves on the beaches or traveling from one sightseeing attraction to another, they're eating—sometimes it seems to me there are almost as many places to eat as there are hotel *rooms!* They range from gourmet restaurants to sandwich shops, from French haute cuisine to seafood to steaks to kosher-deli fare. Prices, too, run the gamut from the top of the bank account to the bottom of the budget register. Each section of this metropolitan and beach area has its own "special" places, and I've listed them for you. And since Latin cuisine is a category all its own, you'll find Spanish and Cuban restaurants listed separately.

**MIAMI BEACH: Café Chauveron,** 9561 E. Bay Harbor Dr., Bay Harbor Islands (tel. 305/866-8779), was internationally known even before the restaurant moved from New York to Miami Beach. The Provençal cuisine still rates the prestigious Mobil five-star award, and the lovely waterfront setting makes it an even more exciting dining experience. In fact, there's a cocktail terrace right on the water—for those who arrive by boat! Inside, all is subdued elegance, with oil paintings, peach linen and hand-blown wine glasses on the table, and perhaps the best, most knowledgeable service in these parts (the wine list is truly a fine one, and the staff can guide the inexperienced through its labels). Menu selections include seafood (in the French manner, of course), beef, veal, lamb (which is superb), and game in season, and prices (they're à la carte) start at $19.50. The doors open at 6 p.m. daily and they take orders until 11 p.m., but don't think you can just drop in—reservations are absolutely necessary, and the jacket requirement strictly observed. In my book, this is *the* place for extra-special dining, and even if it scuttles the budget temporarily, one dinner here is worth a week of hamburgers later.

The **Dining Galleries** in the Fontainebleau Hilton Hotel, 4441 Collins Ave. (tel. 305/538-2000), is just about the ultimate in elegance. Luxurious furnishings, rich fabrics, crystal chandeliers, statuary and other works of art, fresh flowers and growing plants in abundance, and a standard of service hard to come by even in the most expensive restaurants. All that, and food which can only be described as gourmet. Veal Romanoff is only one of the continental specialties of this magnificent room, which overlooks the gardens. Breads and pastries are baked in their own kitchen, and there's entertainment nightly. Prices are in the $17 to $25 range for entrees on the à la carte dinner menu, and on Sunday there's a table d'hôte brunch, $22.50 for adults, $11.25 for children. The wine list is excellent, as is the selection of European desserts and coffees, so use these prices as a beginning point. Whatever your final charge, it will be little enough for such elegance.

**The Forge,** 432 Arthur Godfrey Rd. (tel. 305/538-8533), just *may* be the most opulent eatery on the Gold Coast of Florida. Several dining "salons," each unique in its own grandeur, are filled with exquisite antiques, art objects, crystal chandeliers, stained-glass Tiffany-style lamps, and a staggering collection of art nouveau. There is an expensive hush throughout—all noise is absorbed by intricately designed crushed velvet which covers the floors and some of the walls. The Forge's fabulous walk-in wine cellar boasts one of the most extensive collections of classical rare wines in the country, most of which are museum pieces purchased at special auctions. The cellar is also stocked with an enormous selection of French, Italian, American, Spanish, Austrian, and Greek table wines. Cuisine at the Forge is sophisticated American liberally dotted with unusual continental and nouvelle cuisine specialties. À la carte entrees start at $16. Steaks and roast rib of beef are prime aged, and there is a great assortment of international appetizers, entrees, and fabulous desserts. The Lounge at the Forge features live musical entertainment for listening and dancing, and the beat goes on from 9:30 p.m. to 5 a.m., seven days a week. The Forge serves from 6 p.m. to 2 a.m. and reservations are suggested.

**THREE MIAMI BEACH INSTITUTIONS:** Joe's Stone Crab Restaurant, 227 Biscayne St. (tel. 305/673-0365), takes honors in the institution department— it's been here since 1913 and has been collecting one of those coveted *Holiday* Awards every year since 1961. The large, 350-seat place has a simple decor of tile floors, dark pecky-cypress walls, and high ceilings. Stone crabs are, of course, the star of the extensive menu, and they're costly, but the other seafood items are more reasonably priced and perfectly cooked. Prices run all the way from $5 (for fried oysters) to $22. Joe's is open from 5 to 10 p.m. every day; and in spite of its size, you'll have to wait (it can be as long as two hours)—there are no reservations, and no exceptions.

**Gatti Restaurant,** 1427 West Ave. (tel. 305/673-1717), has been operated by the same family for over 60 years, and is the second-oldest restaurant on the Beach. Well loved by residents and visitors who return each season, it's almost a social center as well as a first-class restaurant—come to dinner on opening day at Hialeah, and you'll find the racing crowd gathering here after they've won or lost at the track. Many celebrities have made this a regular eating place, both because of the cuisine and because they too met with a friendly reception, with little fuss or feathers about their presence. As for the food, it's Italian, featuring outstanding pasta, the freshest of seafoods, and classic dishes such as veal parmigiana or chicken tetrazzini. The service is fast and friendly, even when the place gets crowded, as it frequently does. The wine list is good, the pastries are luscious, and entrees on the à la carte menu range from $13 to $25. Hours are 5:30 to 10:30 p.m., except for Monday when it's closed, and I strongly recommend reservations. Closed from Mother's Day to November 1.

There's been a Roney Pub in this area (the first was in Coral Gables) for almost 30 years. With the emphasis on dark woods, beamed ceilings, lots of brass, and good food at prices which send you away stuffed for under $7, there seems to be little danger of its disappearing. The long lines are attracted in part by the low prices, in part by the ample portions (everybody leaves the Roney with a doggy bag—it's a Miami Beach tradition), and in large part by the quality of the food. The large menu offers fresh seafood, chicken, beef, and combination platters, and all entrees include a potato (with a choice of baked, stuffed, or fried) and a large salad, as well as freshly baked bread. All for prices that range from $8 (for which you can get a half of a baked chicken large enough for two) to $11 (only if you have a huge appetite). This is the place to take the family, or just come alone for good eating that won't break the budget. You'll find the **Roney Pub and Restaurant** at 2305 Collins Ave. (tel. 305/532-3353), and never mind reservations—you'll just have to wait in line, although it moves very quickly. Hours are 5 to 11 p.m. The newer **Roney Pub South** is located at 105th Avenue and North Kendall Drive.

**OTHERS:** On the lower level of the Fontainebleau Hilton Hotel, 4441 Collins Ave. (tel. 305/538-2000), the delightful **Chez Bon Bon** stays open from 7 a.m. to 2 a.m.—a cheerful place to begin the day or to end a late evening when hunger pangs attack at bedtime. There's a garden motif to the decor and a casual atmosphere no matter what the hour. Breakfast menus are extensive and range from $1.25 to $6.50; lunch entrees (including a burger selection) are $5.50 to $10; and dinner selections, $7 to $15 (except for burgers, which are the same $5.50 as at lunch). There are good offerings of fresh seafood, beef, chicken and pasta.

La **Rumba Restaurant,** 2008 Collins Ave. (tel. 305/538-8998), is one of Miami Beach's best restaurant buys in the Lincoln Road area. Open seven days a week from 7:30 a.m. to midnight, it serves all three meals at incredibly low prices. This family-run place has been in operation for over 15 years at the same location, and has a devoted local clientele who come for the friendly service as much as for the excellent Cuban cuisine. Specialties include the breakfast specials until 11 a.m. that cost only $2, a dinner special from 3 to 7 p.m. at $4.50, and excellent entrees of paella, chicken with yellow rice, and fish filet in green sauce at prices of $4 to $10. All prices are for complete dinners. A guitar player entertains in the attractive dining room, one wall of which is devoted to a three-dimensional mural of Carnival in Cuba.

Another excellent restaurant in this area is **Gino's Italia Restaurant,** 1906 Collins Ave. (tel. 305/532-6426). It's the province of Sam Gino, who's been here for 15 years and lives upstairs with his family. The decor is one of arched doorways, lots of greenery, fountains, and statuary. There's live music some evenings and an extensive menu of pasta, seafood, and northern Italian specialties. Veal is prepared in no fewer than nine mouthwatering ways, and chicken in five. Hours are 4 to 11 p.m., the price range is $7 to $20, there's a good wine list, and the place is always filled.

There are several good, inexpensive places to eat at Miami Beach. Well-known **Wolfie's,** with two locations, at 195 Lincoln Rd. (tel. 305/538-0326), and 2038 Collins Ave. (tel. 305/538-6626), and **Pumpernik's,** 6700 Collins Ave. (tel. 305/866-0246), have a complete deli menu, with blintzes, corned beef and pastrami, smoked fish, bagels, etc., overstuffed sandwiches, and very good desserts. A complete dinner at any one of these will run no more than $6 and of course, you can put together one of your own for less. They are both open seven days a week.

Among the several outstanding restaurants in the Bal Harbour Shops, on 96th Street at Bal Harbour Boulevard, these are recommended: **Café Ambiance** (tel. 305/861-9700), elegant, with French cuisine and outstanding desserts; **Coco's of Bal Harbour** (tel. 305/864-2626), ultramodern indoor café and lovely outdoor garden; and **Tiberio** (tel. 305/861-6161), gourmet northern Italian dishes in an elegant setting.

**READERS' DINING SELECTIONS:** "We had the most fabulous meal of our entire Miami Beach vacation at **Dominique's,** in the Alexander Hotel 5225 Collins Ave. (tel. 305/865-6500). It was expensive, but the place was so elegant, the service so polished, and the food so superior that we felt we'd found a bargain" (S. Caliri, Englewood, N.J.). . . . "We found a jewel of a restaurant near the airport. The **Thai House,** 715 E. 9th St. (tel. 305/887-0561), serves great food at reasonable prices" (D. Sheffman, Atlanta, Ga.).

**MIAMI:** The main dining room of **The Depot,** 5830 S. Dixie Hwy. (that's U.S. 1 South; tel. 305/665-6261), is a reproduction of a South Florida, turn-of-the-century railroad station, and this whole place will gladden the heart of any confirmed train lover. There's railroad memorabilia all over the place, but the tables themselves are really the star attraction. Each has a glass top through which you view a miniature N-gauge train traveling through a tiny American countryside. Or if you prefer, you can dine in a reproduction of Henry Flagler's private dining car, complete with opulent 1895 furnishings. With so much attention given to decor, it wouldn't be surprising to find the food less than spectacular, but such is *not* the case at The Depot. They've won the *Holiday* Award every year since 1974, and *Institution* magazine's menu design award. Just one example of the care given to food preparation: The prime ribs are roasted in a rock-salt cast to preserve natural juices. Other specialties include lobster Thermidor and veal au chasseur. Entrees start at $17, and cocktails, dinner, and a late supper are served from 5 p.m. until 2 a.m. every day except Monday. Don't come without a reservation.

The **Sorrento,** 3059 S.W. 8th St. (tel. 305/643-3111), has been owned and operated by the same family for over 30 years. The Amanzio family serves a classic Italian menu in a simple, unpretentious setting, with Florentine statues, paintings, and lovely chandeliers. Located in the "Little Havana" section of Miami, it draws a diversified clientele. Specialties include chicken Florentina, veal Valdostana, and crabmeat cannelloni; prices are moderate. It's a friendly, relaxing place, and is open from 11:30 a.m. to 11 p.m. weekdays (except Tuesday, when it's closed), until midnight on Friday and Saturday, and from 2 to 11 p.m. on Sunday.

A delightful lunch spot is in the Design District, 35 N.E. 40th St.—the **Piccadilly Hearth** (tel. 305/576-1818), in a secluded little plaza surrounded by antique shops, interior decorator shops, and a piano garden with a fountain. Inside, it has the dark-wood look of an English pub, and the lunch menu (priced from $4.50) features quiche, salads, sandwiches, and chili con carne, along with seafoods, burgers, and eggs Benedict. The lounge has "jolly hours" from 4:30 to 7 p.m., with reduced prices, and there's dinner, featuring continental cuisine, fresh seafood, and romantic candlelight (much more expensive than lunch, beginning at $12) from 5:30 to 10 p.m. It's open every day except Sunday.

**LATIN:** Miami's "Little Havana" is filled with Cuban- and Spanish-style restaurants, and half the fun is finding your own favorite (see "Sightseeing," below). Latin cuisine shows up too, in several other restaurants around town.

Authentic Spanish dishes are the specialty of the **Madrid,** 2475 S.W. 37th Ave. (tel. 305/446-2250), a longtime Miami favorite. Arroz con pollo, shrimp enchilada, and fried spiced pork are bestsellers, and prices range from $5 to $14, although there are lunch specials as low as $3.50. Incidentally, if you get there during "Happy Hour," 4 to 6 p.m., drinks are only $1.50 and hot Spanish hors d'oeuvres are free. Monday through Thursday, hours are 11 a.m. to 11 p.m.; they're open until midnight on Friday and Saturday.

**Juanito's Centro Vasco,** 2235 S.W. 8th St. (tel. 305/643-9606), has a Spanish-Basque tavern air, and the owner-chef is known for his lobster Thermidor (my personal favorite, though, were the eggs flamenco—delicious!). The very modest prices (dinners start at $4 à la carte, $11.50 for a complete dinner) belie the quality of the food here. It's open every day from noon to 11:30

p.m.—a friendly place for good, inexpensive Latin meals, and there's a Flamenco show each night Wednesday through Sunday.

Just across Palm Avenue from the back entrance and stables of Hialeah Race Track, **El Viajante Segundo,** 2846 Palm Ave. (tel. 305/888-5465), is a family-run Cuban restaurant that is large, bright (almost to the point of gaudiness, with lots of red Formica, veined mirrors, black iron gratings, and fluorescent lights), moderately priced, with some of the best Latin food in the city. Fried plantains, arroz con pollo, paella, black- or white-bean soup, and snapper in green sauce are just a few of the dishes they do really well. Prices start at $7, but what comes to the table at that price is as tasty as anything you'll find at more expensive restaurants. In fact, both food and service are way above what you'd expect for the cost, and among its regular patrons are many Miamians who can well afford to eat in more elegant surroundings. It's open from 11 a.m. to 10:30 p.m. every day.

There are loads more places to try in "Little Havana"—see "Sightseeing," below, for additional suggestions.

# 4. Nightlife

Nightlife in Miami Beach can be almost anything—spectacular shows and revues with elaborately costumed showgirls, "name" entertainers in supperclub acts, jazz ranging from classical to pop, or "sing-along" entertainment in small bars and lounges. Be forewarned, however, that the splashy shows (mostly in the larger hotels) don't come cheap—depending on your thirst and whether or not you have dinner, you can pay as much as $150 for a table for four! If you're there for the show only, although many of the rooms advertise "no cover, no minimum," there is often a "beverage charge" (translation: "cover") which will probably include only one drink—after that, you pay and pay and pay. The smaller establishments usually have no such charge and your tab will be strictly up to you, although they *do* frown on nursing a single drink through an entire evening's entertainment.

Not all the excitement after dark is at the beach. Miami's Cuban nightspots are as lavish as those across the bay (and a good deal cheaper) and there are jazz places that feature the country's best.

The really *big* names come to Miami Beach after Christmas and stay for the "season"; in fact, some of the hotel rooms close down during the summer and fall, so check on this before you plan your evening out. If the star element is what you want for your money, you'd best plan to come in season, but I must add that the Latin shows I've seen in Miami were terrific, without a "headliner" in sight—and the food was superb too.

One final word of caution: The after-dark scene is a fast-changing one, and while these listings represent what's going on *at the time of writing,* be sure to call ahead and also check current newspapers and entertainment guides found at most hotels and motels.

**MIAMI BEACH:** The **Sheraton Bal Harbour,** 9701 Collins Ave. (tel. 305/865-7511), puts on what many believe to be the most lavish, best-produced show in Miami Beach in its Bal Masque Room. This French revue features casts of up to 30 showgirls, Ziegfeld-like sets and costumes, some pretty exciting dancing, and top entertainment stars. Show times are 9 p.m. (dinner served from 7 p.m.) and 11 p.m. (no food). Be sure to reserve—and bring money!

At the **Fontainebleau Hilton,** 4441 Collins Ave. (tel. 305/538-2000), Poodles is the place for a swinging late night.

For dinner and dancing in luxurious settings, try the **Starlight Roof** at the

Doral, 4833 Collins Ave. (tel. 305/532-3600); or **Henri's** at the Konover, 5445 Collins Ave. (tel. 305/854-1500).

The **New Swinger Lounge, Bird Lounge,** and **Persian Room** in the Marco Polo Hotel, 192nd Street and Collins Avenue (tel. 305/932-2233), offer musical entertainment, often featuring top-name entertainers.

**MIAMI:** Miami's most flamboyant nightclubs are both Latin, both run by the same people, and both (for my money) representative of the best buys in this kind of nightlife. The **Flamenco,** at 991 N.E. 79th St. (tel. 305/751-8631), features a Spanish musical group and show orchestra, and entrees that run $8 to $27. At night, the large room (plush with lots of red velvet and Victorian-style white furniture) is the setting for two different shows, both lavish and both so Spanish you'll think you're in sunny Spain. Show times are 9:30 and 11:30 p.m., and jackets are required. The same is true at **Les Violins,** 1751 Biscayne Blvd. (tel. 305/371-8668). The quality of both productions is just tops, and there's a sense of fun that reflects their Cuban ownership. Best of all, if you really want to make a night of it, you pay the modest cover charge just once and can stay through both shows, with perhaps dinner in between. Incidentally, the food is as good as the entertainment, with continental and Spanish cuisine featured (for example, there's pork Havana style and coquille violin) on a menu with more than 30 entrees.

**MUSIC AND DRAMA:** For concert-goers and Broadway show-lovers, Miami periodically provides evening entertainment of the first order. Although not everything listed below will be in production at all times, a phone call to any one of them will let you in on what's current when you're there.

The **Greater Miami Opera,** 1200 Coral Way (tel. 305/854-1643, or 854-7890 for the box office), presents a season of grand opera featuring world-renowned artists from December through April at the **Dade County Auditorium,** 2901 W. Flagler St., Miami; and a special Summer Pops concert series in July on the water at **Miami Marine Stadium,** 3601 Rickenbacker Causeway, Key Biscayne.

The **Theatre of the Performing Arts,** 1700 Washington Ave., Miami Beach (tel. 305/673-8300), brings Broadway shows like the long-running *Grease* to town at various times during the year, with top-caliber stars. The **Miami Beach Symphony** also performs here with outstanding soloists.

Broadway musicals and drama can also be seen at the **Coconut Grove Playhouse,** 3500 Main Hwy. (tel. 305/442-2000), one of the best equipped in the country.

# 5. Sports

Sports facilities in the Miami Beach area are practically unlimited, whether you want to participate or just spectate.

**FISHING:** There's bridge fishing at both the **MacArthur and Rickenbacker Causeways;** the Rickenbacker has over 2,800 feet of catwalks equipped with benches. And there are piers which allow fishing at **Haulover Park,** north of Bal Harbour on A1A (go straight out Collins Avenue from Miami Beach); the **Sunny Isles Pier,** 167th Street and Collins Avenue, and **Pier Park,** Ocean Drive and 1st Street, Miami Beach. For deep-sea fishing, there are charter boats available at most of the area marinas, including the **Bayfront Miamarina** in downtown Miami, the **chamber of commerce docks** at the east end of MacArthur Causeway, **Crandon Park Marina** on Key Biscayne, **Dinner Key Marina** in Coconut Grove, and **Haulover Park,** on A1A north of Bal Harbour. Charges run about $45 per person for a half day.

**GOLF:** The City of Miami **Melreese Municipal Course,** 1802 N.W. 37th Ave., Miami (tel. 305/635-6770), has 18 holes, greens fees of $10 in winter, $8 in summer, and a charge of $14 for carts.

The **Key Biscayne Course** on Crandon Boulevard (tel. 305/361-9129), charges $11 greens fee weekdays, $13 weekends (hours are 8 a.m. to 4 p.m.). From 4 p.m. until dark, fees are reduced. Carts are $14 for 18 holes, $10 for 9 holes.

The **Doral Country Club,** 4400 N.W. 87th Ave., Miami (tel. 305/592-2000), has five courses open to the public after guest reservations have been filled. Greens fees here are $30 to $50; carts, $26.

**Haulover Beach Park,** 10800 Collins Ave. (tel. 305/947-3525), charges $8 per nine holes during the day, $10 at night.

*Your hotel or motel may very well have guest privileges at these or other area courses, so be sure you check before striking off on your own.*

**TENNIS:** **Flamingo Park,** Michigan Avenue at 12th Street, Miami Beach (tel. 305/673-7761), has 17 public courts, 13 of which are lighted for night play. Hours are 9 a.m. to 9 p.m., with a small fee, and lessons can be arranged.

**Haulover Beach Park,** 10800 Collins Ave., north of Bal Harbour (tel. 305/947-3525), has six units of public courts.

**North Shore Park,** 350 73rd St., Miami Beach (tel. 305/673-7754), has 13 public parks, 11 lighted. Lessons are available, and hours are 9 a.m. to 9 p.m.

The four units of public courts at **Calusa Park,** Crandon Boulevard on Key Biscayne (tel. 305/361-2215), are free, and lessons are available.

**HORSE RACING:** **Hialeah Park,** one of the world's most beautiful sites, has been honored and dedicated as a National Historic Place. Located in Hialeah, just north of Miami International Airport on East Fourth Avenue between 21st and 32nd Streets, the park is open year round, but closed to visitors two weeks prior to racing season. Other times, it's open to the public without charge, and horse-lover or not, you shouldn't miss it, if only for its beautiful colony of some 400 flamingos. A few were imported from Cuba in 1932, and thanks to this wildlife sanctuary, they have proliferated to the present number.

The grounds at Hialeah are a masterpiece of landscaping, with lush tropical palms, pines, and oak shading vibrant flowering plants. There are formal gardens, complete with fountains and statuary, and the stunning French Mediterranean clubhouse and grandstand, with ivy-covered walls and sweeping stone staircases. Here, too, is the Shipwreck Aquarium, the cabin of a sunken clipper ship re-created to house coral reef fish; plus an exhibit of English carriages, stagecoaches, a French walking ring, and of course the paddocks and racetrack itself. For a modest charge you can tour by tram, which makes several stops as it circles the grounds. Lunch is available at the sightseeing center snackbar on the clubhouse terrace that overlooks the infield lake (and don't miss the displays of racing silks and memorabilia inside the elegant clubhouse). Hours are 9:30 a.m. to 5 p.m. daily except during the racing season. When the horses are running, admission is $3 to the grandstand, $5 to the clubhouse. (No minors allowed during racing hours). Call 305/885-8000 for current information.

**Calder Broward Race Course,** 210th Street and N.W. 27th Avenue, Miami (tel. 305/625-1311), has summer (from early May), fall, and winter (till mid-January) thoroughbred racing (post time, 1 p.m.). Admission is $1.50 to the grandstand, $3 to the clubhouse. If you want a reserved seat in either location there's an additional $1.50 charge, and you can reserve by phone. The grandstand has a cafeteria and snackbars, and more elegant dining is available in the clubhouse and Turf Club.

**Gulfstream Park Race Track,** U.S. 1, Hallandale, has racing from January through May, with a $2 charge for grandstand admission, $4 for the clubhouse.

Special buses are run to all three tracks by **American Sightseeing** (tel. 305/ 871-2370), **Gray Line** (tel. 305/633-0375), and **MTA** (tel. 305/638-6117).

**GREYHOUND RACING:** Dog racing is a year-round Florida attraction, and you can watch and wager on the greyhounds at **Flagler Dog Track,** N.W. 37th Avenue and 7th Street, Miami; **Biscayne Kennel Club,** I-95 at N.W. 115th Street, Miami; or **Hollywood Greyhound Track,** Pembroke Road, Hollywood. Racing is offered nightly except Sunday, with matinees as scheduled. Check local schedules for which track is open, hours, and other details.

**JAI-ALAI:** If you've never seen a jai-alai game and like your sports fast and furious, you're in for a treat. The game originated with 17th-century Basques and came here from Spain. The *pelota,* a virgin-rubber ball covered with goat-skin, is kept in play by skillful players using a *cesta,* a curved basket of reed, strapped to the wrist. Play is exciting and dangerous, and jai-alai players are re-garded with much respect. The **Jai-Alai Fronton** is at N.W. 36th Street and 36th Avenue, Miami (tel. 305/633-9661). Games start at 7:30 p.m., and the season is from mid-December through mid-September. Oh, yes, there's parimutuel bet-ting.

# 6. Shopping

Miami has some of the best shopping areas on the East Coast, and you'll find specialty shops of every description not far from wherever you stay. Here follows just a sampling of what to expect:

The exclusive, very elegant **Bal Harbour Shops** center, at Collins Avenue and 97th Street, is a 600-foot-long mall liberally sprinkled with over 100 flower-ing orange trees, shrubs, and bushes interspersed with splashing fountains. The 31 stores on the mall include such famous names as Neiman-Marcus and Martha (designer fashions), and prices are as high as the names are famous.

Farther south, there's the **Lincoln Road Mall,** where about 180 shops occu-py eight blocks of an open-air mall beautifully decorated with walkways lined with greenery, flowering plants, and fountains. Also known as the International Market Place, it's great strolling and browsing territory. Or if you want to give your feet a break, there's an electric tram to take you from one end of the mall (which is blocked to traffic) to the other. There are some exclusive shops in the Market Place, but there are also many little specialty boutiques with unusual items for sale at moderate prices.

Over on the mainland, the **163rd Street Shopping Center,** N.E. 163rd Street between 12th and 15th Avenues, is also an open-air mall, with more than 75 stores. Prices range all over the scale from one shop to another.

**"Miracle Mile"** is in Coral Gables, a four-block-long parkway lined with planters, benches, and some 150 beautiful shops and restaurants. More exclu-sive names here, along with generally higher prices.

Even if you're only window shopping, don't miss the experience of shop-ping "à la Latino" along **Calle Ocho,** S.W. 8th Street in Miami. The variety is staggering—delicately carved Spanish guitars, mantillas, bullfight posters, love-ly filigree jewelry, oil paintings, sculptures, clothing (the garment industry here is second only to New York's), Spanish versions of Scrabble (a neat way to pick up the language), and even furniture (only lack of space prevented my bringing home a rocker patterned after those Cuban mothers use to lull their babies to sleep). It's a colorful, lively area, with plenty of little Cuban restaurants and sandwich shops for foot-resting stops. Prices are less expensive here, although you shouldn't expect "native" bargains—this *is* Miami, not the real Havana. (See "Sightseeing," below, for some specific shopping stops in "Little Havana.")

And if all this isn't enough, there are more than 500 shops and department stores in downtown Miami.

## 7. Tours

If you'd like to leave the driving to **American Sightseeing,** 4300 N.W. 14th St., Miami, a half-day bus tour of Miami Beach and Miami costs $16.75 for adults, $8.25 for children. Call 305/871-2370 for reservations for this and many other tours.

For romantic and exciting sightseeing boat tours of the Miami Beaches and downtown, **Nikko Gold Coast Cruises,** Haulover Park Marina Docks, 10800 Collins Ave., Miami Beach (tel. 305/945-5461), offers various cruises at 10 a.m. and 2 p.m.: Millionaires Row and Biscayne Bay ($6.50 for adults, $3 for children); Miami Seaquarium ($8 and $4); Villa Vizcaya ($14 and $7); and Fort Lauderdale ($11.50 and $6).

For a nautical night out, try an evening cruise of the Miami Beach area aboard the **Freedom** from 7 to 10 p.m. at the Haulover Park Marina. The price of $22 includes dinner and dancing. For reservations, call 305/947-6105.

The **Island Queen** covers the Miami Beach waterfront with two-hour cruises leaving at 10:30 a.m., and 1:30 and 3:30 p.m. Tickets are $7.50 for adults and $5.50 for children. For further information, call 305/379-5119. The boat leaves from Bicentennial Park in Miami.

For **walking tours** of historically significant art deco buildings, stop by the office of the **Miami Design Preservation League,** 1300 Ocean Dr. (tel. 305/672-1836 or 672-2014).

If you're interested in a bus tour of **Jewish points of interest in Miami Beach,** contact **Dr. Sam Brown,** Newport "S," Apt. 4086, Deerfield Beach, FL 33441 (tel. 305/421-8431). His day-long bus and walking tours cover such diverse sites as the Cuban Hebrew Circle Congregation and a mikveh, a bathhouse for ritual purification. Dr. Brown also offers a separate cultural and artistic tour of the Miami Beach area including Temple Emanuel, the Bass Museum, Garden Center, the Hebrew Academy, and other attractions.

**Gray Line,** c/o A-1 Bus Lines, 1642 N.W. 21st Terrace, Miami, FL 33142 (tel. 305/325-1000), has bus tours that go as far afield as Walt Disney World and the Florida Keys. Call for times and prices.

## 8. Sightseeing

Miami area sightseeing can be almost anything you want it to be, from strolling down Calle Ocho to visiting an elaborate Renaissance palace, to watching Flipper the dolphin perform. For full details of Miami, go by the **Greater Miami Convention and Visitors Bureau,** 4770 Biscayne Blvd., Miami, FL 33137 (tel. 305/573-4300).

**ART DECO HISTORICAL DISTRICT:** What has been called a "rebirth" has begun at the south end of Miami Beach, with the restoration of many fine buildings constructed during the '30s in the then-fashionable art deco style. Spearheaded by the Miami Beach Design Preservation League (in the Cardozo Hotel, 1300 Ocean Dr.; tel. 305/672-1836 or 672-2014), the move to bring back the colors originally used in these distinctive buildings, as well as the artwork, furnishings, and fixtures of the period, has resulted in a delightfully fresh atmosphere in this area, which had become run-down over the years. There's been an influx of talented young artists, writers, photographers, etc., which lends excitement as well. All this is not to say that you won't encounter plenty of those retirees who have made this part of the Beach their home for years—it's just that there's a new spirit afoot, and you'll miss an important part of what's going on in Miami Beach if you fail to spend some time south of Lincoln Road.

First of all, stop by the office of the Preservation League to pick up their guide of the district—you'll want to loiter a while in the Café Cardozo to soak up some of the atmosphere, since this hotel has undergone one of the best restorations of all. Armed with the guide, you can then set out on foot to see what has been accomplished in a relatively short time. **Washington Avenue** is a key art deco showcase, and one of the most striking buildings is the **Washington Storage Company,** designed as a storage facility for the wealthy who visited Miami Beach only during the season. Then there's the post office with its rotunda sporting a W.P.A. mural depicting Florida historical scenes. Then there's . . . well, space limitations prevent my listing more, but the guide and the friendly staff of the Preservation League (as well as just about anyone you meet along the streets down here) will fill you in. Or better yet, come down for the annual Art Deco Weekend, usually in mid-January.

**READERS' ART DECO SUGGESTION:** "For great atmosphere, go to the **Cardozo Café** or the **Carlyle Grill.** It's like stepping back to the light and tropical days of the 1930s. The Carlyle and the whole art deco district is the best—absolutely the best—vacation spot in Miami Beach!" (C. Andersen and T. King, Dyersburg, Tenn.).

**LITTLE HAVANA:** Miami's Cuban quarter covers a wide area, but Calle Ocho (S.W. 8th Street) spreads out a huge sightseeing feast along a 30-block stretch, with colorful shops, intriguing restaurants, and always the industrious, friendly Cubans and their infectious gaiety. The best way to explore this little bit of Old Havana (and I say this from foot-weary experience) is to ride by car or bus (bus route 5, 28, or 29 will take you there) from 7th Avenue to S.W. 37th Avenue, taking in the scene as you pass by and picking out the areas particularly appealing to you; then make your way back east, parking your car (or getting off the bus) at each one. You'll spot S.W. 37th Avenue by the beautiful Spanish-style Douglas entrance to Coral Gables.

You may want to stop at the **Versailles Plaza,** at S.W. 35th Avenue, to explore the shopping center containing stores like **Carrousel las Piñatas,** specializing in those candy- and toy-filled papier-mâché figures that Latins take great delight in breaking open at children's parties. **Bello Plaza,** at S.W. 25th Avenue is more traditional-Spanish in style, with decorative lampposts and wooden balconies. On the block between S.W. 23rd and S.W. 22nd Avenues, look for the **Madrid Gift Shop,** a veritable treasure trove of Spanish handcrafts, wrought-iron wall lamps, wine bags, woven shawls, even Toledo swords to take home and hang on the wall. Right next door is the narrow **Mini-Gallery,** really just a hallway, hung its whole length with paintings. At S.W. 19th Avenue, the **Libros Españoles** carries only books published in Spain, an interesting place to browse, even if you're not really fluent in the language.

In the block between 18th and 19th Avenues, you'll see sidewalk displays (crates, actually, filled to the brim) of tropical fruits set out by the **Amado Fruit Shop** in front of the Monaco Building. The **Tamiami Shopping Center** is here too, and it and the Monaco Building are filled with specialty shops of all descriptions (there's even a Chinese restaurant in the shopping center). Between 18th and 17th Avenues, you'll find the **Hector and Lily Tobacco Company,** where they still hand-roll the Cuban-style cigars, and the **Miguel Company** in the middle of the block sells handmade guitars that are works of art. Right around the corner, on 17th Avenue, there's a many-hued outdoor garden where the **Pouparina Florists** feature hanging baskets of flowers and plants.

You'll want to see both sides of Calle Ocho between 15th and 16th Avenues. At **Ultra Records,** you can buy the latest Spanish "top ten," or you can catch a flick in Spanish at the **Tower Theater.** At 13th Avenue, you'll come to the **Cuban Memorial Plaza,** with its Bay of Pigs Monument, a place that has deep meaning for the Cubans living here. There's **Fritas Domino** at 12th Avenue (with Cuban hamburgers and skinny french fries served in a bun), **Lisboa Restaurant** a little farther east (another inexpensive Cuban eatery), **La Gran Via Bakery** at 9th Court, and . . . well, it's all territory best explored personally. You're certain to find your own special part of Calle Ocho, and wherever it is, there will be those marvelous little sidewalk coffee counters selling steaming cups of strong Cuban coffee.

You might keep an eye out for these restaurants, as well, just in case your feet give out when you're close to one: **El Meson de la Tortilla,** 1620 S.W. 8th St. (tel. 305/541-6293); **Casa Juancho,** 2436 S.W. 8th St. (tel. 305/642-2452); **Casablanca Cafeteria and Restaurant,** 2300 S.W. 8th St. (tel. 305/642-2751); and **Perezsosa Bakery Co.,** 1444 S.W. 8th St. (tel. 305/858-3939), for great Cuban sweets to eat as you walk or take back to your hotel.

One thing is sure—when you climb back in the car or on the bus, you'll feel you're returning from a foreign country and should have your passport handy!

**KEY BISCAYNE:** Do yourself a favor and plan at least one full day to explore Key Biscayne. Actually, it'll take you some time to get there (across Rickenbacker Causeway), because who could drive past **Virginia Key** without stopping? Not only is the island a joy to drive around, with its palm-fringed beaches; it also holds three not-to-be-missed sightseeing attractions. First of all, there's the **Seaquarium** (tel. 305/361-5703), a 60-acre complex of re-created habitats that make sea mammals, rare birds, and even rare turtles feel right at home. There's the Flipper Show (you remember him, the TV star performing dolphin) —he and his friends do high jumps and other tricks; Salty the sea lion and friends star in "It's Magic" Show where the audience joins right in; the Top Deck Show where a family of dolphins compete in athletic games and even walk on their tails. Lots more here too, and the monorail trip gives you a terrific view of Virginia Key, Key Biscayne, and the whole bay area. The Seaquarium is open every day from 9 a.m. to 5 p.m. (shows are continuous): adults pay $10; ages 6 to 12, $5.

Right across the highway is **Planet Ocean** (tel. 305/361-5786), where you can see Florida's only iceberg! You can also climb inside a submarine on a make-believe "voyage to the bottom of the sea," listen in on radio transmissions between ships at sea, examine more than 100 exhibits that explain the importance of the oceans to this planet, and see films on the history of the planet Earth. Admission is $5.50 for adults, $2.75 for children 6 to 12 (under 6, free); hours are 10 a.m. to 6 p.m., but the box office closes at 4:30 p.m.

Nearby is the $2-million, 6,500-seat **Marine Stadium,** a huge concrete structure which serves as a viewing stand for motorboat racing and for evening concerts with the orchestra playing from a barge moored in front. The concerts have been going on since 1965, with consistent full houses. Private boats can pull up and enjoy the music, and boatowners find it's a good way to beat traffic jams going home. When the weather is good (and that's most of the time), concerts are on Friday or Saturday nights. When nothing is scheduled, you can inspect the stadium itself, at no charge, from 8 a.m. to 5 p.m.

Over the bridge from Virginia Key is Key Biscayne, and **Crandon Park** (tel. 305/361-5421), once a coconut plantation, with beautifully landscaped picnic grounds and play areas and a three-mile palm-lined beach. Lunch or have dinner at the delightful waterfront **Sundays on the Bay Restaurant,** 4000 Crandon Blvd. (tel. 305/361-6777). Incidentally, there's another Sunday's on the Bay at Haulover Beach, 4000 Crandon Blvd. (tel. 305/945-6065).

The center section of Key Biscayne holds its shopping area and luxurious private residences (this is where Richard Nixon had his Florida White House when he was president, in a cul-de-sac with strategically placed guardhouses to keep away the gawkers and the demonstrators). On down at the very southern tip of the Key is lovely **Cape Florida State Park** (you may hear this called the Bill Baggs Park—it's the same thing): 406 acres of trees and plants and wildlife, and a museum complex that features the **Cape Florida Lighthouse,** with the keeper's home and office restored to its 1855 condition. In 1836 Seminole Indians attacked this lighthouse and set fire to its interior, trapping the keeper at the top. That wily character, however, threw a barrel of gunpowder down into the flames, making enough of a bang to be heard by the navy ship *Motto,* which steamed in to his rescue from 12 miles out at sea. If you can make it up the spiral staircase to the top, your huffing and puffing will be rewarded with a really spectacular view of the whole Biscayne Bay area and an Atlantic seascape that's breathtaking. Tours of the lighthouse are at 10:30 a.m. and 1, 2:30, and 3 p.m. It's closed on Tuesday. Admission to the park is $1 for each driver, 50¢ for passengers and pedestrians, and there's another $1 charge for the museum and lighthouse. Hours for the park are 8 a.m. to sunset.

## JAPANESE TEAHOUSE AND GARDEN: On **Watson Island,** just east of U.S. 1 on MacArthur Causeway, the Japanese Teahouse and Garden is a memorial to a Tokyo industrialist's admiration for Miami and Miami Beach. When he visited here some years ago, he was so impressed with the place that he started sending gifts back to the city—first several hundred wild orchids; an eight-ton statue of Hotei, the Japanese god of good fortune; an ancient stone lantern; and finally a ceremonial teahouse which was built in Japan, then taken apart and shipped to Miami. Japanese carpenters came with the pieces to see that they were put back together properly. Like "Little Havana," it's like a visit to another country, and it doesn't cost a cent. To arrange a visit, call the Miami Parks and Recreation Department (tel. 305/579-6916).

## VIZCAYA: In 1914 James Deering, the International Harvester tycoon, began construction on what turned out to be a Renaissance palace to hold artworks he'd been collecting abroad for 20 years or more. He named it the Villa Vizcaya, 3251 S. Miami Ave. (tel. 305/579-2813), just off U.S. 1; you can't miss it, signs are prominently posted for several miles, and it's estimated to have cost Deering some $10 million by the time the 70 rooms and elaborate gardens were completed. Small wonder, for he kept more than 1,000 craftsmen working for five years, and architects were given ample time to plan rooms around some of his treasures. The formal gardens, with seven separate areas, fountains, statuary, and reflecting pools, cover some 10 acres, and there are another 20 acres of unspoiled "jungle." Inside the mansion, there are splendid frescoed ceilings, a tapestry that belonged to Robert Browning when he lived in Italy, and priceless antiques and paintings in every room. Offshore (from the steps leading down to the bay), a stone version of Cleopatra's barge serves as a breakwater. The estate is open every day except Christmas from 9:30 a.m. to 5 p.m. (last tickets sold at 4:30 p.m.), admission is $5 for adults and $3.50 for ages 6 to 11 (under 6, free).

## MUSEUM OF SCIENCE AND SPACE TRANSIT PLANETARIUM: Right across the street from Vizcaya is the Museum of Science and Space Transit Plan-

etarium, 3280 S. Miami Ave. (tel. 305/854-4247), with free parking and picnic tables on the grounds. The museum is completely refurbished in the exciting mode of the Exploratorium in San Francisco, with over 80 hands-on exhibits in the fields of energy, sound, light, chemistry, biology, physics, and optics, as well as fascinating displays of unusual natural history dioramas of the Everglades and coral reefs, including slides and movies. Also included in the $3 and $2.25 admission price is the Animal Exploratorium where you can tickle tarantulas, hug boas, and handle saltwater animals in their small tanks. Hours are 10 a.m. to 6 p.m. Upstairs, the Southern Cross Observatory allows a close look at the heavens on weekend evenings. The Space Transit Planetarium has hourly shows from noon until 8 p.m., with programs in Spanish on Saturday and Sunday at 5:30 p.m. Admission is $4 for adults and $2 for children ages 2 to 12.

**METROZOO:** Miami has an excellent zoo, located on more than 185 acres at 12400 S.W. 152nd St. (tel. 305/251-0400). Housed in cageless, native-style habitats, more than 50 species of animals happily gape at visitors who come to gape at them. Especially notable are the white tigers and the Malayan village. A monorail allows a comfortable, easy-on-the-feet overview, and there's a lakefront restaurant and observation deck. Hours are 10 a.m. to 5:30 p.m., and admission is $4.50 for adults, $2 for ages 2 to 12.

**BASS MUSEUM:** Several impressive paintings from Rubens' studio, sculptures, tapestries, and an extensive collection of old-master paintings are highlights of the Bass Museum, 2100 Collins Ave. (tel. 305/673-7530). There are also excellent concert, film, and lecture series. Hours are 10 a.m. to 5 p.m. Tuesday through Saturday; adults pay $2; students with ID, $1; under 16, free.

**METRO-DADE CULTURAL CENTER:** Opened in 1984, this beautiful four-story complex of Mediterranean-style buildings surrounding a central plaza houses the **Center for the Fine Arts** (tel. 305/372-7666), the **Historical Museum of Southern Florida** (tel. 305/375-1492), and the **Metro-Dade Main Library.** The address is 101 W. Flagler St., and you should plan at least a half a day here.

**PARROT JUNGLE:** The Parrot Jungle, 11000 S.W. 57th Ave., 11 miles southwest of Miami at the junction of Red Road, which is also S.W. 57th Avenue, and Killian Drive, which is S.W. 112th Street (tel. 305/666-7834), is nothing less than paradise for bird lovers. Macaws and rainbow-colored exotic birds fly free; more than 100 flamingos, cranes, and swans cluster around a lake; and chatty mynah birds keep up a steady stream of conversation. For a few cents in a vending machine, you can buy birdseed and perhaps coax one onto your shoulder for a memorable snapshot. There's a 45-minute open-air show in which birds ride tiny bicycles, roller skate, drive a car, and do simple arithmetic tricks. Adults pay $7.50; ages 6 to 12, $3.50.

**MONKEY JUNGLE:** Still farther south, off U.S. 1 at 14805 S.W. 216th St. (tel. 305/235-1611), the monkeys at Monkey Jungle must get a big kick out of running free while the humans are caged! In a re-created Amazon rain forest, you'll see foilage from South America and strange-looking monkeys. King and Mitzi, two charming gorillas, live here, along with some 600 monkeys and apes, and there are shows every hour with monkeys riding toy cars and performing other tricks. It's open from 9:30 a.m. to 5 p.m. every day, and admission is $6 for adults, $3 for ages 5 through 12.

## 9. Fort Lauderdale

Although fiercely loyal residents are quick to tell you that Fort Lauderdale is *not* a part of the Greater Miami Area, it *is* close enough to make an attractive alternate base for a South Florida vacation. Indeed, it offers enough attractions on its own to thumb its nose at Miami, just a short drive south on I-95 or U.S. 1 for day trips. Known as the "Venice of America," one-tenth of its surface is water, with over 300 miles of canals in the Greater Fort Lauderdale Area and 165 miles of navigable inland waterways in the city itself. It is truly a city of boats, with nearly 30,000 registered to residents, and some 10,000 more visiting during winter months. There are 27 miles of beaches, over 75 golf courses, 550 tennis courts, the Dania Jai-Alai, Pompano Beach Harness Raceway and Gulfstream Park Race Track, and the Hollywood Greyhound Track—enough to keep the most energetic vacationer hopping!

**WHERE TO STAY:** With more than 1,000 accommodations offering some 20,000 hotel rooms, you have a wide choice as to location, style, and price range.

Top of the list has to go to **Pier 66 Hotel and Marina,** 2301 S.W. 17th St. Causeway, Fort Lauderdale, FL 33316 (tel. 305/525-6666, or toll free 800/327-3796). This luxury resort set in 22 acres facing the Intracoastal Waterway features unusually large rooms, many with private patios or balconies, and all beautifully furnished. Facilities include a private marina, three pools, tennis, putting green, health club, Jacuzzis, a gourmet restaurant and two more casual eateries, and a revolving rooftop lounge with entertainment, dancing, and spectacular 180° views. Doubles are in the $150 to $210 range in season, lower during the summer.

If you've ever had a secret yen to live on a houseboat, the **Marina Bay Resort,** Marina Bay Drive, Fort Lauderdale, FL 33312 (tel. 305/791-7600, or toll free 800/321-2619), is just the place to do it. Nicely appointed hotel suites and efficiencies actually float on water here in two-story houseboats moored in a bay of the New River. Each houseboat holds either four or six units, and your neighbors are magnificent private yachts in adjacent slips whose owners are likely to be members of the private club run by the Marina Bay (guests automatically become members for the length of their stay). The resort sits in a lush tropical setting "landscaped" with all sorts of interesting and whimsical nautical flotsam and jetsam. There's an oversize pool, sauna, whirlpool, tennis courts, golf ten minutes away, a lounge with live music, a garden pub and cookout area, and the New River Storehouse, a very good restaurant. Seasonal rates for doubles range from $100 to $130, but there are bargain weekend rates year round. For example, in-season weekends are a low $75 per person for three days and two nights, and that rate drops to a mere $67 from April through November.

**Holiday Inn–Oceanside,** 3000 E. Las Olas Blvd., Fort Lauderdale, FL 33316 (tel. 305/463-8421), has a rooftop pool, recreation room, and dancing. Some rooms have private patios or balconies, and all are nicely furnished. Doubles start at $60 in season, dropping other months.

**WHERE TO EAT:** It's a smörgåsbord! Some 3,000 restaurants in the Greater Fort Lauderdale Area serve up every sort of cuisine you can dream up, then add a few you'd never think of.

Be sure to have at least one dinner at the **Mai-Kai,** 3599 N. Federal Hwy. (tel. 305/563-3272), a longtime favorite in this area, which is about as authentically Polynesian as you can get this side of the Pacific. Owner Bob Thornton has run the restaurant complex for more than 30 years with the assistance of his

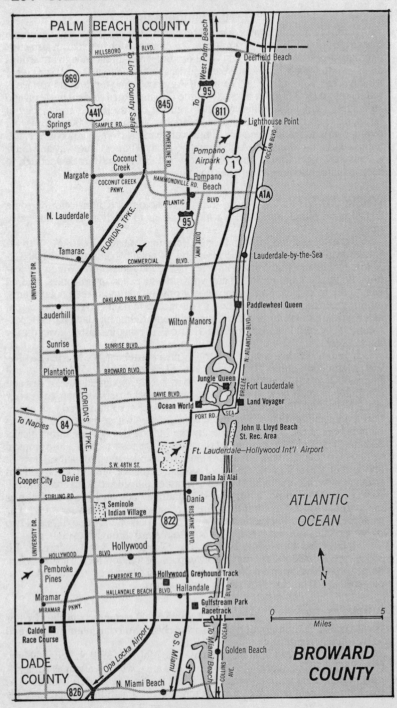

wife, who was born in Tahiti. Under her guidance they have created what is very nearly a native village, with landscaped gardens set about with carvings and artifacts brought from the South Pacific. The extensive menu has been carefully developed to offer such dishes as Peking duck, Chinese steamed trout, and a delicious chicken curry. One of the things that makes the Mai-Kai special, however, is the nightly entertainment—native dancers are brought over regularly to perform authentic dances which illustrate ancient legends and rituals. It's a first-rate show in its own right, but an education in Polynesian lore as well. There are two shows nightly: one for the early dinner (5 to 7:30 p.m., with a price range of $9 to $19), and one for the later seating (at 7 to 10:30 p.m., with prices of $11 to $23). You don't have to dine in the show room—there are lovely, smaller rooms that are quieter and more intimate (and it is only in those rooms that the elaborate specials listed above may be ordered), and if you order from the lighter menu in the Molokai Lounge, there's a second-drink-free policy from 5 to 7 p.m. All in all, the Mai-Kai is a treat not to be missed, and could provide one of the most memorable evenings of your Florida holiday. Best reserve.

If there is any such thing as "casual" sophistication, **Yesterday's,** 3001 E. Oakland Park Blvd. (tel. 305/551-4400), has it. Overlooking the Intracoastal Waterway, the rambling restaurant is a lush mixture of tropical greenery, plush plum-colored velvet, art deco etched glass, and pretty waitresses whose attire includes large, floppy-brimmed hats. In the lower level (eye level with those boats docked alongside), there's a sort of lighthearted elegance, with velvet booths and fan-backed chairs. The Upstairs Porch is much more in the vein of a friendly, casual tavern with lots of brick, wood, and brass, as well as a knockout view of the waterway through casement windows. The Deco Bar is a deep-purple retreat, and the Key West Room is all natural woods and nautical deck chairs. As for the menu, seafood dominates, with specialties like sautéed scallops in champagne sauce, seafood quiches, grouper provençal, and a creamy coquilles St. Jacques. There's also a nice selection of Italian pasta, veal, beef, lamb, chicken, and duck. Lunch prices run $6 to $10; dinner, $10 to $20. Hours are 11:30 a.m. to midnight, and reservations are a good idea at this popular restaurant.

The **Bangkok Room,** 900 E. Atlantic Blvd., Pompano Beach (tel. 305/785-5055), is a small, sparkling jewel of a restaurant. The mirrored wall reflects pretty table settings, soft lighting, and muted colors, making for an intimate, relaxed dining atmosphere. Owner Mike Apipattanamontagg and his pretty wife, Pavina, are very much in evidence, which accounts for the personal attention that makes eating here such a pleasant experience. And the food is superb. Talented chef Uitti Iustanachaipanit rules the kitchen with a delicate hand, producing crispy noodles and puff pastry (which comes wrapped around curried beef) and Thai eggrolls that are incredibly light. Seasonings are a beautiful mixture of spices, and they reached a pinnacle for me in the deep-fried whole red snapper which came to table topped with Thai chili and garlic sauce (it's "spicy fish" on the menu). There are many more delicacies that make this a standout among Fort Lauderdale restaurants, and the price range is a moderate $7 to $16. Lunch hours are 11:30 a.m. to 3 p.m., and dinner is 5 to 10 p.m. Monday through Friday.

A final note about one of those special places visitors usually never find out about. Remember those little neighborhood restaurants and bars where everybody dropped in for good food that didn't break the budget and where friendly chats with the staff were a part of every visit? Well, in Fort Lauderdale, you'll find exactly that sort of place at **Ernie's,** 1843 S. Federal Hwy. (tel. 305/523-8636). It's been a favorite with residents for over 30 years, and the conch chowder, fritters, and salad are famous for miles around. It's a plain place, with a bar on one side and tables scattered around the other side—much the look of a '20s roadhouse—and there's a happy mingling of imbibers at the bar and diners at the tables. Barbecue (it comes on thick slices of Bimini bread, as well as in complete dinners) is also a specialty. Incidentally, that great conch chowder is served with a bottle of sherry so you can season to taste, and it's available to take away in pints and quarts, hot or frozen. Prices run from $1 (for a cup of chowder) to $6.50 for complete dinners. Upstairs there's a patio bar where drinks and food are served beneath colorful striped awnings, but I must confess I never got beyond that convivial downstairs room straight out of my memories!

**THINGS TO SEE AND DO:** For detailed sightseeing information, contact the **Greater Fort Lauderdale Chamber of Commerce,** 208 S.E. Third Ave., Fort Lauderdale, FL 33301 (tel. 305/462-6000).

If you can tear yourself away from all that water, a relaxing way to see the town is via the **Voyager Sightseeing Train.** It leaves from 600 S. Seabreeze Blvd. several times a day for 90-minute narrated tours of old and new Fort Lauderdale. Fares are $5 for adults, $2.50 for ages 3 through 12. Call 305/467-3149 or 463-0401 for exact schedules.

**Paddlewheel Queen Cruises** (tel. 305/564-7659) leave from the dock one block south of Oakland Park Beach Bridge for 2½-hour cruises on the Intracoastal Waterway. There are luncheon and dinner cruises at varying prices; sightseeing cruises are $4.50 for adults, $3.50 for ages 3 through 11.

The **Discovery Center Museum,** 231 S.W. Second Ave. (tel. 305/462-4115), is a "hands-on" art, science, and history museum in the historic old New River Inn. There are some 22 exhibit areas in the three-building complex. It's an interesting visit for all ages, and admission is $2, free for those 3 and under. Hours are noon to 5 p.m. Tuesday through Friday, 10 a.m. to 5 p.m. on Saturday, and noon to 5 p.m. on Sunday.

The **International Swimming Hall of Fame Museum,** 501 Seabreeze Blvd., has an Olympic-size pool open from 10 a.m. to 4 p.m., as well as star-studded exhibits and periodic demonstrations and competitions.

# Chapter XVII

# THE FLORIDA KEYS AND THE EVERGLADES

### 1. From Key Largo to Key West
### 2. Key West
### 3. The Everglades

THE SOUTHERN END OF FLORIDA is exclusively devoted to nature —wild and unspoiled in the Everglades National Park, civilized and exploited to the hilt by mankind along the Keys. Perhaps "exploited" is not the right word, for although all the natural treasures of that string of 45 islands reaching 100 miles out to sea southwest of the continental United States are utilized for sea-oriented occupations or leisure pursuits, a slowed-down, no-hassle outlook so pervades the Keys that commercialism loses its sharp edge and seems more like convenience than exploitation.

At any rate, Mother Nature outdoes herself from Miami south to Key West and due west across the Everglades to where the state's west coast curves north along the Gulf of Mexico.

## 1. From Key Largo to Key West

Before you set out on the Overseas Hwy. (that's U.S. 1, which runs the length of the East Coast from Fort Kent, Maine, to Key West), you should know that almost any kind of vacation amusement you're looking for will be somewhere along that drive. Sportsmen will find all the water sports, of course (there are over 600 varieties of fish in these waters, a living coral reef, and underwater shipwrecks to be explored by divers, and pleasure boats for hire), as well as golf, tennis, and horseback riding. For solitude-seekers, there are secluded fishing camps and quiet motels on the smaller keys (with more than 150 motels and some 5,000 rooms from which to choose, you can find the right one). For livelier sorts, there are lounges with nightly entertainment and 130 restaurants for eating that can border on the exciting. Sightseers will find performing sea mammals, a state park full of natural wonders, and cruise boats (some with glass bottoms to reveal the reef). It is, if you drive straight through, only a 3½-hour drive, but you'll be missing too much if you do it that way—plan at least half a day; or even better, spend the entire day ambling over the 42 bridges that connect the Florida Keys. Incidentally, 37 of those bridges have been widened, making the drive much easier.

It hasn't always been so easy to reach the Keys. Until 1912, in fact, they lay in tropical, mosquito- and roach-infested isolation (a local legend says that before the advent of radio communication, natives could tell a storm was brewing when the roaches got restless). But then Henry M. Flagler ran his Florida East Coast Railroad all the way to Key West, with a ferry train going on to Havana, and the outside world poured in. After a killer hurricane left the railroad in shambles in 1935, the U.S. government took over the right-of-way and opened up the Overseas Hwy. in 1938. The mainland connection, however, failed to disturb the West Indies–island atmosphere of the Keys, an asset that is probably responsible for most of that large influx of visitors.

As you head south on U.S. 1, the easternmost fringes of the Everglades National Park will be on your right, and on both sides of the road are vast vistas of red mangrove, that hardy plant whose twisted roots build up land surfaces and provide a natural shelter for native birds and fish. **Jewish Creek Bridge** is the first of the 42 you'll cross (those huge mounds of branches on top of power poles are osprey nests, added on to each year by the industrious birds). The 18-inch aluminum pipeline on your left is something of an engineering marvel and a true "lifeline," for it carries fresh drinking water from the mainland to Key West—it is above ground (or water) most of the way.

**Key Largo,** where buccaneers once put in to fill their water casks, is the first key (key means a low island or coral reef, by the way), and the 21-mile-long, 3½-mile-wide John Pennekamp Coral Reef State Park is here. The only continental underseas park in the country, it was named for an associate editor of the *Miami Herald* who was largely responsible for preserving both this stretch of coast and the Everglades. Divers have a field day exploring the living coral reef, and less venturesome souls can view it by glass-bottom boat. Key Largo also has a plentiful supply of rental boats and guides for bonefishing, as well as a concentration of air-conditioned, full-service motels and a huge shopping plaza.

You'll notice the milepost markers all along the Overseas Hwy.: they keep you informed of the mileage from each one to Key West. At MP (milepost) 84, only a few minutes from **Islamorada,** is the Theatre of the Sea, where you can pet a shark, shake hands with a porpoise, or just watch them go through their acts. Islamorada means "purple isle" in Spanish, and the name was given this key when a Spanish explorer saw mounds of the violet Janthina sea snails on its shores. The town by that name is the third largest in the Keys, and there are good motels, restaurants, and shops here, as well as a memorial monument to those who perished in the 1935 hurricane. On **Long Key,** between MP 69 and 68, the town of **Layton** was a favorite haunt of Zane Grey, the writer of Old West stories, and one of the town's waterways is named for him. When you reach MP 56 you'll be in the very heart of the Keys, where the towns of **Key Colony Beach, Marathon Shores,** and **Marathon** have a total population of 8,000, the second largest in the islands. At MP 54 there's an interesting stretch of specialty shops, a seafood restaurant, and the Aqua Dome Aquarium (a floating barge with a geodesic dome) on your right, a picturesque, relaxing stopping point. Marathon's municipal airport has scheduled daily flights both south to Key West and north to Miami, Tampa, and Kissimmee (Walt Disney World territory), and charter service to wherever you want to fly. If you plan to spend a few days on the Keys before going on to Key West, Marathon is a good location, since it's midway.

Leaving Marathon, you begin the most famous stretch of the Overseas Hwy., the **Seven Mile Bridge** (which is really two-tenths of a mile shorter than seven miles). It's a spectacular drive, with the green waters of the Atlantic and blue Gulf of Mexico coming together directly under your car! Beyond **Sunshine**

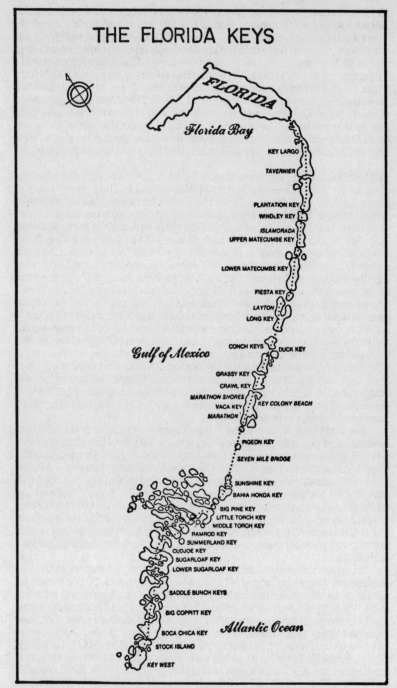

**Key,** the southern exit of the Seven Mile Bridge, there's a state park on **Bahia Honda Key** and a still-standing remnant of Flagler's railroad. Next comes **Big Pine Key,** second in size only to **Key Largo** and the only one on which you'll find Caribbean pines and tiny white-tail key deer (only 38 inches from stem to stern and 26 to 32 inches high), which are so shy they're seldom seen, except in the very early morning or at dusk. Those small islands scattered between MP 16 and 11 are the **Saddlebunch Keys,** many of them unnamed, and a naval air station is on **Boca Chica,** between MP 8 and 6. **Stock Island,** at MP 5, is now a part of the municipality of Key West, and this is where the all-important water desalinization plant converts sea water to fresh. Shrimp boats dock here too, and sometimes luxury yachts as long as 100 feet can be seen moored at the docks. We'll take in all these sights one by one, but first let's find some shelter for the night.

**WHERE TO STAY:** "Accommodations" take on a unique meaning when applied to the **Jules Undersea Lodge,** 51 Shoreland Dr. (P.O. Box 756), Key Largo, FL 33037 (tel. 305/451-2353). The world's first submerged luxury "inner-space" lodging, the 50-foot-long, 20-foot-wide habitat holds two private suites, berth-style beds, a private bath, and a living area with a galley set up for meals (supplied from above—you don't have to cook). Each suite has a 42-inch picture window through which to observe the rich sea life that surrounds the sunken habitat, and after a few hours there it's virtually impossible not to begin to fall into the underwater rhythm of that life, an experience totally different from that of the typical scuba-diver—much like the difference between a "tourist" and a houseguest. It was just this sort of exhilarating experience gained over many years of working with ocean-oriented projects that prompted Gary Gerburg to set about making it possible for mere mortals to move closer to understanding the sea's delicate relationship to man and to think more intelligently about how its resources may be wisely utilized to enrich human life. His two partners in what was a monumental undertaking are Ian Kiblick, who developed, operated, and managed the La Chalupa sealab that is now the Jules Undersea Lodge, and Dr. Neil Monney, former director of ocean engineering at the U.S. Naval Academy—together, this formidable team has over 80 years of ocean research and industry experience.

With that kind of "know-how," it isn't surprising that the developers have covered every possibility to assure safety and comfort as well as lifelong memories. They carefully selected a protected lagoon for safety and for maximum visibility because the bottom is seldom disturbed, and they designed a Mission Control Center topside connected to the submerged habitat and equipped with independent backup systems in case of emergencies. Each guest is given basic scuba-diving instructions before entering the habitat, skills that will enable each to make day or night excursions into the lagoon through the "Moon Pool" exit. The control center is manned around the clock, ever ready to render any needed service, and gourmet meals are passed down to guests for simple microwave preparation.

It's a fascinating experience, and for the moment, a rather expensive one (at $600 per couple per night). That rate comes down to $250 per person for groups of six, the maximum capacity, and rates cover all expenses, including meals, diving gear, and all amenities. Because many people combine a one-night stay beneath the surface of the lagoon with an onshore hotel stay, Jules Undersea Lodge uses the Holiday Inn Key Largo Resort as their booking base (see below), and reservations may be made by calling toll free 800/THE-KEYS.

Movie buffs, as well as would-be underwater explorers, will want to stay at the **Holiday Inn Key Largo Resort,** at MP 100 (P.O. Box 708), Key Largo, FL 33037 (tel. toll free 800/THE-KEYS, ext. 50, or 800/HOLIDAY). This is where you'll find the *African Queen,* the original steamboat from the Humphrey Bogart–Katharine Hepburn movie of the same name. The newly decorated guest rooms run from $72 double occupancy for a standard room to $130 for a "King Harbor View." Accommodations, however, are not the sum total of what this Holiday Inn has to offer: from this base, you can take the glass-bottom boat to view spectacular coral reefs in the John Pennekamp Underwater State Park, take scuba or snorkel tours from the resort docks, go reef fishing, rent boats, play tennis, and visit the exciting new Jules Undersea Lodge (see above).

The **Sheraton Key Largo,** MP 97.5, Key Largo, FL 33037 (tel. 305/852-5553, or toll free 800/325-3535), is one of the Keys' newest luxury resort hotels, with 200 deluxe rooms overlooking Florida Bay. All rooms have king-size beds, mini-bars, and private balconies. One of the nicest features here is the strip of undisturbed wilderness between the hotel and the bay, with a wooden board-walk leading through the natural growth. Christina's gourmet restaurant is first-rate, specializing in local seafoods, and other amenities include a health club and tennis. Doubles range from $115 to $175 in winter months to a low of $85 to $125 in summer.

At MP 82, the **Cheeca Lodge,** P.O. Box 527, Islamorada, FL 33036 (tel. 305/664-4651, or toll free 800/327-2888), is probably best known as a sports-men's spot, with emphasis on the excellent fishing. But for dedicated beach-combers like me, it has an appeal hard to equal. Built by A&P millionaires as an exclusive fishing club, the lodge sits right on the edge of the Atlantic, and is ap-proached through landscaped grounds that serve as a buffer from highway noise —you enter another world when you turn into its gates. The main lodge looks serenely out over the water, with a pretty, glassed-in dining room for superbly prepared meals and guest rooms beautifully furnished and designed for the ulti-mate in comfort. Those on the top floor have balconies. In addition to the lodge, there are "villas," or individual cottages, which may be had with just bedroom and screened porch or with a studio/kitchenette and Bahama beds. There's an executive golf course, four tennis courts, a swimming pool, and a 525-foot fish-ing pier (they'll cook your catch for your dinner) for more active types. For me, it's quite enough to savor the peace and relaxation at the Cheeca, strolling along the water's edge or perhaps keeping an eye on Frank, the resident pelican that presides over the fishing pier. The staff, from manager to bell captain, is both friendly and efficient, creating a sort of small-town atmosphere. Double-occupancy rates for lodge rooms run $170 to $185, depending on whether you have an ocean or pool view (the penthouse goes for $195), and villas facing the ocean are $205; others, $185.

## On Marathon Key

The **Key Colony Beach Motel,** Ocean Drive, Key Colony Beach, FL 33050 (tel. 305/289-0411), is on the northern end of Marathon Key. To reach it, turn off U.S. 1 toward the Atlantic Ocean at MP 53.5, drive to the end of the main road leading through Key Colony Beach, then turn left—the pretty blue-and-white motel is just a short half block down Ocean Drive. The attractive bedrooms, furnished in modern style with cool, clear resort colors, have couches that open to sleep two, a refrigerator, and an oceanfront location or an ocean view. A private white sand ocean beach, a freshwater heated pool, boat and scuba-diving equipment rentals, and an excellent restaurant and lounge (with enter-tainment) are all within easy walking distance. Golf is also available in the area. Winter rates start at $60; summer rates are lower. PBA has daily flights from Marathon to both Miami and Key West, and there is an 8,000-foot runway for private planes.

The small **Lagoon Motel and Marina,** 7200 Aviation Blvd., Marathon, FL

33050 (tel. 305/743-5463), is just off the Overseas Hwy. (headed south, turn right at MP 50). Betty Keller is the personable owner of this very clean, rather quaint motel, which has a solar-heated pool, docks, a fishing dock, and gas and ice in the marina. Rooms are comfortably furnished and air-conditioned, with cable TV. Double rooms range from $35 to $45, seasonally; efficiencies, $40 to $50; and two-bedroom cottages, $56 to $70.

### A Campground

Nine miles south of Marathon (on U.S. 1, of course), the **Sunshine Key Campground** has almost 400 sites with full hookups, LP gas service, flush toilets, a laundry, store, snackbar, recreation hall, shuffleboard, tennis, swimming, boating, and fishing. Rates are $26 and up (with monthly rates available), depending on location. For reservations, write Rte. 1, Box 790, Sunshine Key, FL 33043 (tel. 305/872-2217).

**WHERE TO EAT:** The seafood's great from Key Largo to Key West, and no matter where you stop to eat on the drive down, you're likely to spot a place farther along that you'll be sorry you missed.

But before listing some of the better-known spots, let me tell you about **Herbie's**, 6350 Overseas Hwy., at MP 51 in Marathon (tel. 305/743-6373). It's a real "island" sort of place and has become perhaps my own favorite stopping point on any drive along the Keys.

A low, one-story, green-and-white building set back from the highway, it's easy to bypass, but keep an eye out for the tall sign announcing Herbie's Seafood, and you'll be in for a real treat. It's been here since the '40s (was known for years as Maggie's Chowder House) and serves some of the freshest seafood (they get two fresh deliveries a day) you'll find hereabouts at low, low prices and in an atmosphere that's downright convivial. The conch fritters are without doubt the best on the Keys, and there's a full selection of chowders, fish (on plates or sandwiches), and for non-seafood-lovers, burgers and chili. The raw bar opens at 2 p.m. Prices are in the low range of $1.50 to $3. Best of all, you'll eat with locals in either the screened-in, porch-style bar area, or the outside patio, or in a slightly larger dining area entered by an oldtime screened door. Nightly specials feature homemade Italian dishes, steaks, and *great* seafood for prices of $4 to $9. Hours are 11 a.m. to 10 p.m. Monday through Saturday, and it's closed on Sunday. Don't miss this place!

At the Islamorada Yacht Basin (look for the large mermaid signboard), the **Lorelei Restaurant** (tel. 305/664-4657) is built out on the dock, and its decor is a faithful reproduction of early Keys furnishings, with Bahama fans, turn-of-the-century, hand-blown crystal light fixtures, rustic furniture, and trellis-supported greenery used as partitions between tables. Seafood is the specialty here, and a real treat is the Shrimp Lor-e-lie (sautéed in butter with a touch of garlic, mushrooms, and imported cheese, broiled to utter perfection) at $15. Even if you come for lunch, it's worth a return evening trip here just to watch the spectacular sunset from such a lovely spot. And if you're a dessert lover, the Key lime pie is so good here that one lady offered to trade her yacht for the recipe! Open daily from 11 a.m. to 2:30 p.m. and 5:30 to 10:30 p.m.

With a more rustic dockside atmosphere, the **Castaway** (tel. 305/743-6247) is at the foot of 15th Street in Marathon. You'll have to look for this one—it's at the water's edge in the heart of a little fishing community, and you'll see its name on a highway sign (on your left driving south) that lists six other establishments. Turn left and go to the end of 15th Street, then turn right and you'll see the blue-and-white Castaway dead ahead. It's been famous in the area for over 30 years for shrimp steamed in beer, and since the original owner retired, Georgina Hosek has kept things just as they've always been. You can eat inside in a small, plain room with fishing nets on the walls and red-checked tablecloths, or outside right over the water. The famed specialty comes with french fries and coleslaw; seconds are on the house. There's a whole menu of other seafood dishes, all at moderate prices ($5 to $12), and beer and wine are both available.

A reader wrote in about **Mac's Bar-B-Que,** on Key Largo (tel. 305/451-9954), to say that "it doesn't look like much on the outside, but what food!" Well, it certainly is unpretentious from the outside, and he most certainly is right about the food you'll find inside. Between MP 101 and 102, Mac McGilvary has been dishing up what he calls "Alabama-style" barbecue for the past 24 years, and it has become a favorite of locals, as well as travelers. The tangy, spicy-sweet barbecue comes in the form of pork or beef, ribs, and chicken, and you can have full plates (complete with salad, potato, and garlic bread) or sandwiches. Mac also offers good local seafood and desserts which feature homemade Key lime pie. Prices range from $1.50 to $10, and he's open from 11 a.m. to 9 p.m. every day except Wednesday. Beer and wine.

Up on Islamorada, a fish-eater's paradise stretches for about an eighth of a mile, where some six or more excellent restaurants line U.S. 1: **Marker 88, The Chesapeake, The Plantation Yacht Harbor, Ziggies, The Coral Grill, Sid and Roxie's Green Turtle Inn,** and probably another one or two by the time you read this. All have fairly moderate prices, all serve food so fresh you can taste the sea, and none will be a disappointment. So if this is where you are when it's time to eat, close your eyes and pick one.

**READER'S DINING SELECTION:** "The best moderately priced seafood buffet anywhere is **The Coral Grill,** at Islamorada. It is served 4:30 to 9:30 p.m. weekdays and noon to 9 p.m. on Sunday. Check it out in the upstairs dining room" (M. Ozer, Philadelphia, Penna.).

**THINGS TO SEE AND DO:** For full sightseeing details, contact the **Florida Keys Visitors Bureau,** P.O. Box 1147-FD, Key West, FL 33041 (tel. toll free 800/FLA-KEYS).

Now, let me say that with all that water, the Keys are not true beach country. There is good swimming at state parks and a few campsites where sand has been pumped up to create beaches, but in general the water is shallow, without much surf, and even wading isn't such a good idea because of sharp coral rock underwater. So swimmers should probably stick to the more than 120 pools at motels and recreation areas.

The Keys *are,* however, a fisherman's dream come true, and there's never a charter boat far away for deep-sea fishing or smaller rental boats for close-in waters. Divers, also, will find diving shops all along the Keys, many with scheduled boat trips and instructors with maps of particularly interesting diving sites. Stop in at the railroad caboose **Visitors Center,** MP 82.5, Islamorada.

The **John Pennekamp Coral Reef State Park** is on the east coast (well, *off* the coast, actually, since it's underwater) of Key Largo and has a fantastic, brilliantly colored array of marine and plant life. Facilities include a Visitors Center, picnic sites, swimming and wading areas, fishing, a marina, boat rentals and launching ramps, a snackbar, and nature trails. But the highlight of a stop here has to be either diving (and many visitors try their hand at underwater photography) or viewing the vivid coral from glass-bottom boats. The 2½-hour boat trip costs $10 for adults, $5 for ages 11 and under, and they leave at 9 a.m., noon, and 3 p.m. There are guides to accompany divers (for reservations and rates, call 305/451-1621). The park is open from 8 a.m. to sunset, and there's a 50¢-per-person admission charge, plus $1 for each vehicle operator.

At Islamorada, the **Theater of the Sea** (it's 1½ miles north of town at MP 84) has continuous marine-life performances, with sharks, huge sea turtles, stingrays, jewfish, tarpon, sea lions, and five dolphins. Each 90-minute show costs $8 for adults, $4.75 for ages 5 to 12. Hours are 9:30 a.m. to 4 p.m.

## 2. Key West

Key West has been robbed of its major industry three times so far: a lighthouse and an active U.S. Coast Guard did away with the lucrative "wrecker" trade that made Key West the richest community per capita in the country; a thriving cigar-making population was lured to Tampa after a disastrous fire destroyed many of the Key West cottages and factories; and Greek sponge divers arrived, stayed just long enough to put Key West divers out of business with their newer, faster method of collecting sponges, then moved on to Tarpon Springs, taking the sponge business with them. Yet, hardy, not-to-be-defeated Key Westers have pulled themselves up by the bootstraps once again and today the tourist business is booming so well that it would be no real surprise to see that "richest community" tag someday reappear.

"Individualistic" is the one word that applies to almost every phase of Key West life—it has a positive talent for taking bits and pieces of architecture, culture, business enterprise, and personality from any source that comes along, putting them together, and coming up with something that is uniquely Key West. "Conchs" (it's pronounced "konk" and means a native-born; you're a "freshwater Conch" if you move here and stay for seven years, but you have to be *born* in Key West to drop the "freshwater") have a genealogical background that might be English, Bahamian, Cuban, New England, or U.S. southern—or an interesting combination of several of these. They live and work in buildings that might have been brought over from the Bahamas board by board and reassembled, constructed in the Cuban style by the cigar makers, put together by skilled ship's carpenters, or all three. And what comes out of all this many-ingredient blend is a highly individualistic, survival-oriented Key West personality—realistic yet lighthearted, canny in business dealings yet open-handed with all visitors.

The five-mile-long, three-mile-wide island of Key West was discovered by Spanish explorers in the 16th century and named Cayo Hueso, which means "bone island," corrupted over the years to its present name. Its first owner, a Spanish cavalry officer, sold the island in 1821 to John Simonton, an Alabama merchant. After Commodore David Porter rid the area of pirates (by using shallow-draft barges to chase the blackguards into the shallow key coastal waters), a U.S. naval base was established in 1823, and in 1828 Key West incorporated to become a bona fide town. Spongers and fishermen came from the Bahamas, and by 1850 the sponge industry employed 180 ships and did a $750,000 annual trade. But they used long poles to spear sponges from the boat after spotting them through glass-bottom buckets and refused to adopt the "walk along the bottom" techniques of Greek newcomers, which ultimately brought about their downfall. Salvagers of shipwrecks (which they did nothing to prevent and were accused of encouraging) made fantastic fortunes. There is even one story of a "wrecker" who brought a coffin, complete with corpse, ashore from a wreck, then ransomed it to the grieving family, much to the glee of his fellow Conchs. Then the reefs were marked by lighthouses and that bonanza from the sea disappeared.

Cuban cigar makers, fleeing Spanish rule in their homeland, came over in 1868 and were soon producing as many as 100 million cigars a year. Then fire struck and the Tampa city fathers offered them the world on a silver platter if they'd bring the industry there, which they did. During the Civil War, although there was a substantial Rebel population, the Union managed to hold the port all through the war. Henry Flagler gave the city a new lease on life, the Depression and 1935 hurricane took it away again, and it remained for the freshwater pipeline from the mainland and World War II (which made it a major antisubmarine and training base) to get things going again. Key West now looks to its tourist trade for not only a lasting prosperity this time, but an ever-growing one, and it will go to almost any length to develop it (there was a time when a city administrator ordered all men to wear shorts in order to look "quaint" for the tourists—needless to say, that didn't last long).

**GETTING YOUR BEARINGS:** The best way to get an overall look at all this rich background is to take the **Conch Tour Train** or **Old Town Trolley** (see "Tours") 1½-hour trip around the town, with commentary on more than 60 points of interest and how they figure into Key West's checkered history. After that, walking or bike riding (or a moped, if you prefer) is the best means of transportation; some streets are narrow and winding, and driving can be difficult if you don't know your way around.

There are also first-rate city buses on all the main Key West streets that will get you back and forth. You'll recognize them by the legend "Guagua de Cayo Hueso" on their sides—don't worry about how to say it, everybody in Key West calls them the "Wah-Wah," which is more or less how *guagua* sounds.

You might start at **Mallory Square** (it used to be headquarters for the Mallory Steamship Company), with the now-abandoned naval station on one side and the site of that Havana railroad ferry depot on the other. This is where Key Westers and visitors congregate each day to view what has got to be the most gorgeous sunset in the western hemisphere and to give a healthy cheer when the sun quite suddenly drops below the horizon. It's also a gathering place for all sorts of street musicians and craftspeople, giving it a carnival air at the end of the day. Facing the water is a cluster of small shops, restaurants, and bars; if you decide to begin looking around Key West here, be sure to allow enough time, it's the best loitering area in town! The **Key West Chamber of Commerce** is on the square too, with plenty of maps, brochures, and a friendly staff.

However you get around, you can pretty well find the historical points by following **Pelican Path,** a well-marked, carefully planned route through Old Town (we'll head there ourselves later). Incidentally, a big part of Key West's renewed prosperity is due to the foresight back in 1960 of native son Mitchell Wolfson, who bought up the stately old home in which James J. Audubon was a guest when he made his famous folio of birds in this area, then restored it and opened it to the public as the Audubon House. Never slow to recognize a good thing, other Conchs got together to begin a restoration that literally changed the face of the older part of Key West, which was seedy, to say the least. As a result, you can now wander through such landmarks as the Oldest House (built in 1828), Ernest Hemingway's Key West home (he lived here from 1931 to 1961, loved the town because "people don't stare at me here," and here wrote such classics as *To Have and Have Not, Snows of Kilimanjaro,* and *For Whom the Bell Tolls),* the East and West Martello Forts, and some of the most charming little shops you'll find anywhere in restored old buildings along Duval Street (look for **Pirate's Alley** in a pint-sized cul-de-sac with a fountain—it's special).

The other end of Key West is another story. This is modern Key West, separated from the Old Town, as one native told me, "by about three miles and 150 years." Many of the larger motels are here, and shopping centers are very much like those you'd expect to see almost anywhere.

**WHERE TO STAY:** If you bring the children, chances are you'll prefer to stay on the north end of the key—it's quieter there and motels have more family-geared facilities. If, on the other hand, strolling through Old Town at all hours and participating in the swinging (and sometimes noisy) nightlife is what you have in mind, there are hotels and motels galore clustered at the southern end of town.

### Along the Northern Rim

The **Best Western Key Ambassador,** 1000 S. Roosevelt Blvd., Key West, FL 33040 (tel. 305/296-3500, or toll free 800/528-1234), has been owned by the same family since it opened back in 1952. Since then it has grown into a complex of buildings housing more than 100 guest rooms with classifications of deluxe, moderate, and standard, plus studios. Those studio rooms are equipped with a king-size bed, queen-size sleeping sofa, and a refrigerator, or two double beds and a love seat. Others come with two double beds or with one king-size. All are nicely furnished, and all have private balconies, almost all screened. A nice touch here is the complimentary continental breakfast served in a bright breakfast room on the premises. There's also free coffee in the lobby 24 hours a day, and on Tuesday, Thursday, and Saturday there's an outdoor barbecue for guests. You can have a light lunch out by the heated swimming pool at the Cheekie Hut (which also serves a full breakfast for a small charge), and picnic in facilities right on the grounds. For the health conscious, there's a physical fitness center. The staff, most with long years of service here, are exceptionally friendly and concerned for your comfort and helpful in assisting your sightseeing (also, the Old Town Trolley makes a stop here, a great convenience). Rates are seasonal, ranging from $70 to $160, and senior citizens receive a 10% discount in low season (April 21 to December 20).

The **Inn at the Wharf,** 2400 N. Roosevelt Blvd., Key West, FL 33040 (tel. 305/296-5700, or toll free 800/225-6178), is centrally located between Old Town and the airport at the northern end of the island. Just across the road, The Wharf (from which it takes its name) is currently being developed and will have restaurants, art galleries, unusual shops, and a dolphin show. Rooms are comfortably furnished, and there's a pool, with tennis and golf available nearby. Rates range seasonally from $48 to $65, and there are five-day snorkeling packages in the $169 to $250 range.

The **Holiday Inn–Gulfside,** 1111 N. Roosevelt Blvd., Key West, FL 33040 (tel. 305/294-2571, or toll free 800/HOLIDAY), is an especially handsome member of this chain, in a landscaped setting. There's a large pool, playground, and a private beach on the gulf. Tennis courts are well maintained. The restaurant serves all three meals, and there's a cocktail lounge as well. They will pick up and deliver to the airport if you wish to fly in. Rates are seasonal—beginning at $88 for a double in December and dropping after April.

The **Days Inn Motel,** 3852 N. Roosevelt Blvd., Key West, FL 33040 (tel. 305/294-3742, or toll free 800/325-2525), has 18 suites and 116 rooms, all with modern furnishings and color TV, in a pretty, landscaped setting. There's a pool and children's playground. Transportation is provided to and from the airport. Rates run $70 to $80 for doubles, $90 to $100 for kitchen units in winter, less in summer. There's also a family priced restaurant and 24-hour gasoline service.

### At the Southern Tip of the Island

Back in 1921 the Flagler organization (of railroad fame hereabouts) opened the doors of a grand, 200-room, Spanish Renaissance-style hotel on the triangular property at the foot of Reynolds Street, with more than 1,100 feet of prime beachfront, and named it the Casa Marina. It very quickly became the winter playground of wealthy Northerners like the Astors, actors (including

Gregory Peck), poets Robert Frost and Wallace Stevens, bandleader Guy Lombardo, and a host of other celebrities. With the demise of the railroad after that disastrous hurricane, the hotel fell on lean times, and over the years has seen service as an officers' club for the army during World War II, a training center for the Peace Corps, and a military command post during the missile crisis at nearby Cuba. Then in 1962 its doors closed and the once-elegant hotel quietly went to seed. In 1978 the Marriott chain obtained a franchise for the still-solid building and has poured nearly $10 million into a restoration and renovation that makes **Marriott's Casa Marina Resort,** 1500 Reynolds St., Key West, FL 33040 (tel. 305/296-3535, or toll free 800/626-0777), once more a real showplace.

Determined to keep the building's exterior essentially the same as it was in Flagler's day, Marriott retained the red-tile roof and high arched windows of the lobby. Nor did they destroy the massive wooden staircase that circles up from the lobby to the third floor. That lobby sets the tone for the grandeur of the rest of the hotel, and magnificent wooden columns and beams frame some pretty impressive artifacts and furnishings dating back to the '20s and '30s. The Key West Historical Society has recognized the excellence of the restoration with an award. Landscaping on the grounds is so impressive that it has won two awards. And an interesting note on the restoration is the network of cisterns discovered beneath the building which were used to catch rainwater that fed into them from spouts on the roof. Although water is not a problem now, Marriott has opened up the cisterns and now uses them to store rainwater to be used in landscaping.

All 251 rooms (some in a new wing) are quite large and furnished with wicker and rattan accented by bright tropical colors. There's a free-form, heated, freshwater pool (with a delightful open-air bar and barbecue pavilion), a 20-foot Jacuzzi, a fishing and boating pier, lighted tennis courts, a game room, exercise room, an elegant restaurant (Henry's) with elegant food and service, and the Calabash Lounge, with top-quality show-band entertainment (much patronized by natives as well as by visitors). A final comment: While the Casa Marina *is* elegant, it's anything but pretentious, and you'll find the same relaxed, laid-back atmosphere that prevails in the rest of Key West. Seasonal rates range from $160 to $230 for doubles in winter, considerably less during summer months.

The **Pier House,** 5 Duval St., Key West, FL 33040 (tel. 305/294-9541), is right at the edge of Old Town at the spot where the Gulf of Mexico and the Atlantic come together. It's an ideal place from which to watch that spectacular sunset, and all the luxury rooms (some with patio or balcony) are convenient to the pool and the private gulf beach. Boats, water-sports equipment, bicycles, and mopeds can all be rented. The hotel also has one of the best restaurants in town (see "Where to Eat") as well as the Havana Docks Bar, a perfect place to watch the sun go down. Doubles start at $125 in high season, lower other months.

The **Holiday Inn La Concha Resort Hotel,** 430 Duval St., Key West, FL 33040 (tel. 305/296-2991, or toll free 800/HOLIDAY), began life back in 1926, and as the town's only downtown "high-rise," all of seven stories high. For a long period it reigned as a lively social center, then in the '60s a decline set in that lasted until 1986, when a $20-million restoration brought it back to life in even grander style than in the beginning. The striking new lobby of pink-and-gray granite, with lots of glass and bleached woods, bespeaks the taste and care that have gone into the restoration. There are now 160 rooms, four bars, three restaurants, a pool, and its resurrected seventh-floor bar, The Top, which is a local favorite for sunset watching. Some 87 of the guest rooms are in the hotel's historic wing and have much the same decor as of old: poster beds, lace curtains, lamps with fringed shades, and furnishings from the '20s. A new wing holds 73 rooms done up in contemporary style, and around the pool, sundecks on multi-levels, a gazebo, and a pool bar are focal points for conviviality. The ground-floor Oyster Bar is fast becoming as much a local mecca as the old Mermaid Bar that originally occupied this space. Other amenities include a health club. Rates for doubles range from $150 to $270 in high season, $85 to $185 in low.

The **Reach Resort**, 1435 Simonton St., Key West, FL 33040 (tel. 305/296-5000, or toll free 800/874-4118), is at the foot of Simonton Street at the Atlantic Ocean. The sprawling peach-colored complex is an elegant mix of contemporary architecture and Victorian white gingerbread trim. The 150 terraced guest rooms and suites have Mexican tile floors, luxurious furnishings, and even an automatic coffee pot for a freshly brewed cup when you first wake up. Celebration is the gourmet New American cuisine restaurant with a white-marble and mahogany setting, and the more casual Emma's leans toward tropical fare. There's live entertainment nightly, a health club, and all sorts of beach activities. Doubles are $175 to $250 in high season, $95 to $120 in low.

Over on South Beach (the Atlantic side), the pretty **Santa Maria Motel**, 1401 Simonton St., Key West, FL 33040 (tel. 305/296-5678), has rooms, efficiencies, and suites. Furnishings are modern and comfortable. In addition to the pool, there are beach facilities only a few steps away. The West Indies Lounge is lively, with frequent entertainment, and there's a good restaurant. They'll pick up from the airport. Doubles run $60 and up in winter, but drop other months.

On a quiet residential street, just two blocks from the beach and tennis courts, **El Patio Motel**, 800 Washington St., Key West, FL 33040 (tel. 305/296-6531), is a charming place to stay. Its Spanish-style main building surrounds an inner courtyard with tropical plantings. The swimming pool has a sundeck, and there's another rooftop deck for sunning. All Old Town attractions and restaurants are within easy walking distance. There are standard motel rooms, efficiencies, and two-room apartments, all nicely furnished. Winter rates begin at $70; summer and spring, $36.

For a room directly on the Atlantic, there's just one place to find it—the **South Beach Oceanfront Motel**, 508 South St., Key West, FL 33040 (tel. 305/296-5611). Rooms are attractively furnished, and I found the Olympic-size pool, private fishing pier, and sundeck to be centers of congeniality for guests to chat, share outdoor snacks, and even enjoy impromptu concerts. Rates start at $70 for doubles in summer, $105 in winter (efficiencies, $115).

Three other very nice motels of equal quality and similar (or lower) rates under the same ownership and management are: the **Southeast Ocean Inn**, 1300 Simonton St.; the **Southernmost Motel**, 1319 Duval St.; and the **La Mer Hotel**, 506 South St. For reservations at all, telephone 305/294-6663.

## Budget and Very, Very Good

Although I don't always travel budget, my next stay in Key West will most assuredly be spent at **Key Lime Village**, 727 Truman Ave., Key West, FL 33040 (tel. 305/294-6222). This delightful complex of accommodations sits back from the street amid lush tropical planting and consists of cottages, efficiencies, motel rooms, and (truly budget) rooms in the inn. The two-story, yellow-and-white inn was Key West's first motel located in the heart of Old Town, and if for no other reason, I'd stay there for the friendliness and helpfulness of the staff. However, the rooms themselves are far above average for the price range, and the cottages are self-contained homes away from home, fully equipped, and all are air-conditioned. There's a pool and sundeck, with a shaded lounging area (a small, perfect garden centered by an impressive sculpture) just perfect for afternoon or evening cocktails (no service, you bring your own). In addition, the community room holds TV, music, and games. Rates? Unbelievably low. Cottages are $34 in summer, $56 in winter; efficiencies run $40 in summer, $60 in winter; and rooms with private bath cost $30 to $48, $28 to $38 without bath (you share the one down the hall). There's a rather macabre story centered around a resident in the '40s—if you've a strong stomach, ask Paco about it. All rates are for single or double occupancy.

## Guesthouse Accommodations

Guesthouses are beginning to bloom like tropical plants in Key West, and it's an ideal way to travel, so I'll tell you about some of my own favorites here.

A reader wrote to extol the charms of **Eaton Lodge**, 511 Easton St., Key West, FL 33040 (tel. 305/294-3800), and when I made a visit there, I found her raves were quite in order. This century-old home has paneled walls, a lovely antique-filled parlor, a lush garden with winding pathways that lead to a brick terrace, and Matilda, a resident peahen which often struts near the whirlpool. The handsome furnishings and warm, gracious management are the work of a Scotsman, Sam Maxwell, and a Wisconsin native, Dennison Temple, who lived in England for many years and often returns scouting for antiques. Each guest room is different, but all have ceiling fans. The coachhouse out back has been converted to guest rooms with verandas and studio apartments with patios. Rates during the winter months range from $90 to $180, and are reduced by about one-third in summer. All rates include a continental breakfast, and stays of seven days or more earn discounts of 10%. *P.S.:* The owners will arrange transportation to the airport or yacht club via a marvelous old London taxi.

**Duval House,** 815 Duval St., Key West, FL 33040 (tel. 305/294-1666), is another Victorian residence that has passed the century mark and been lovingly restored to retain all the charm of that era while incorporating modern comfort and convenience. Rooms are individually decorated and furnished with lots of wicker and antiques, with both ceiling fans and air conditioners, and all have private baths. A continental breakfast is served in the tropical garden, and the pool has an adjoining lounge with TV, games, and reading materials. The friendly staff here are quite knowledgeable about Key West dining, nightlife, shopping, etc., and happy to share their expertise with guests. Rates range from $55 to $90 during winter months, $40 to $70 in summer.

The **Eden House,** 1015 Fleming St., Key West, FL 33040 (tel. 305/296-6868), is in a renovated 1924 Conch house close to almost everything in Old Town. It's a relaxing place, with a cool, white lobby complete with Bermuda fans and wicker furniture. Relaxing, yes; dull, decidedly not. There's a sense of subdued liveliness about the place that is very appealing, and it seems to attract interesting guests. The rooms are simply furnished and comfortable, with ceiling fans instead of air conditioning (there's also a pool to cool you off), and you share a guest television in the hall or lobby. Rooms are available with private bath or shower, with a bath shared by adjoining rooms, and with bath and shower down the hall. A nice feature here is Rich's Restaurant, which serves all three meals at moderate prices (and the food is very good). Seasonal rates average $65 for private bath, $55 for adjoining bath, and $50 without bath.

## Campgrounds

**Seaside Resort, Inc.,** an adult resort, is six miles northeast of town on U.S. 1 (MP 10.5), with 199 sites, all with full hookups. There's LP gas service, flush toilets, showers, a laundry, store, recreation hall, shuffleboard, two pools (as well as ocean swimming), boating, fishing, and a marina with pub, and rates start at $20, with weekly rates available. No children, no pets; self-contained RVs only, with two adults per unit. To reserve, write: 55 Boca Chica Rd., Key West, FL 33040 (tel. 305/294-9515).

A turn left at the city limits on U.S. 1 (MP 5), then three blocks south on Stock Island, will bring you to **Boyd's Key West Campground,** Stock Island, Key West, FL 33040 (tel. 305/294-1465), with 100 sites, most of them full hookups. They have LP gas service, flush toilets, a laundry, recreation room, swimming in a tidal pool, boating, and fishing. Leave dogs at home; most other pets allowed. Rates start at $14.

**WHERE TO EAT:** Seafood, Cuban dishes, French menus—they're all in Key West and in astounding numbers. Here are a few of my favorites:

The **Pier House Restaurant,** 1 Duval St. (tel. 305/294-9541), is sheer luxury in both setting and cuisine. The glass-walled waterfront room is delightful, with dining also on the deck over the water. At night, the unusual underwater lighting of the sea, filled with a variety of colorful tropical fish, is nothing short of breathtaking. The gourmet kitchen turns out such delights as Caribbean ceviche, native conch marinated with lime juice and coconut, and truly superb seafood and continental and Caribbean dishes, all complemented by an extensive wine list. Prices average $16 and up. For more casual and less expensive meals, the Harbour-View Café has dining inside or at the water's edge on a large outdoor deck, with a selection that ranges from burgers and sandwiches to fresh native seafoods and local conch specialties. The Pier House Restaurant is open for lunch and dinner daily and serves a Sunday brunch that's an island tradition. Reservations are strongly suggested, no matter when you plan to come. The café opens at 7:30 a.m. daily for a sunny breakfast and serves until 10 p.m. There's live entertainment nightly, with dancing upstairs in the Havana Docks Bar.

**Louie's Backyard,** 700 Waddell (tel. 305/294-1061), is a delight. Set in a large old restored Conch house, it has dining inside, on porches (upstairs and down), and on an outdoor wooden deck. Best of all, the food is some of the best I had in Key West, with such specialties as Cajun ribsteak a nice relief from my usual steady diet of seafood when I'm in the Keys. Appetizers include very good pasta selections, as well as an unusual hot fried-chicken salad. Prices are a bit steep (expect to pay somewhere around $20 for dinner), but exceptionally good value, especially in such a setting and with service that's friendly as well as efficient. Hours are 11:30 a.m. to 2 a.m. (there's music in Billy Webb's Bar until the wee hours).

**Captain Bob's Shrimp Dock,** 2200 N. Roosevelt Blvd. (tel. 305/294-6433) is located about midway through the island, and if there's a larger, or more reasonably priced, menu around, I haven't run into it. The emphasis, of course, is on seafood, and I'm especially fond of both the shrimp steamed in beer and the spiced shrimp. Both come with salad and a choice of french fries or boiled potato and both cost under $10. The Captain's Platter, at $15, is a whopper that holds plenty of fish, clams, scallops, shrimp, and lobster. Incredibly light "honey biscuits" are a house specialty that comes with every meal, and if you pig out on them and want more, an extra order is just 15¢. For non-seafood-lovers, the menu provides steak, pork chops, ham, and chicken, all at low prices. Captain Bob's is open for breakfast from 7 to 11:30 a.m., lunch from 11 a.m. to 5 p.m., and dinner from 5 to 10 p.m. (until 11 p.m. on Friday). No reservations necessary in this large, friendly place.

You may have a bit of trouble finding **Gloria's Garden Café,** 618 Duval St.—it's sort of in the *inside* of the 600 block of Duval. Just go along the walkway beside the Guild Hall Gallery, or come in from Fleming Street by the "Conch Walk" passageway. True to its name, this is a garden setting, and even the covered, indoor space opens to the outside. The menu consists of light dishes such as salads and quiches, sandwiches, as well as local seafoods, a few chicken, beef, and veal selections, and a stir-fried vegetable plate. Prices range from as low as $4 to a high of $15. Hours are 6:30 a.m. (for breakfast) to 10:30 p.m. Monday through Saturday; closed Sunday after the Sunday brunch that is served from 10 a.m. to 3 p.m.

**Danny's Fish Market and Restaurant,** 627 Duval St. (tel. 305/296-3777), is so popular with both locals and visitors that you'd best come at an off hour to avoid standing in line for a table. The moderate-size place has an unpretentious, oldtime café atmosphere, and they serve some of Key West's best conch chowder here, at the amazingly low price of $2. Conch fritters are just as good, and go for a mere $3.75 a dozen. Almost any local seafood is on the menu, and all prices are correspondingly low. In fact, the fish dinner goes for only $6.75 and seconds are just $1! It's open every day from 11 a.m. to 11 p.m., and as I said, best come between normal mealtimes, especially in the winter months.

**Shorty's Diner,** 215 Duval St., has been in the same family for some 40 years, passing from father to son, and is much loved by Key Westers. And rightly so. This is where you can feast on scrumptious lobster, oysters, fish, shrimpburgers, clili, steak, veal, conch fritters and chowder, etc., for well under $5 in the company of locals loitering at the counter over a second cup of coffee, reading the day's newspaper, or simply visiting with neighbors. Shorty's is just what those of us who remember diners remember! It's open from 6:30 a.m. to 3 p.m. weekdays and Saturday, (except Thursday, when it's closed), and on Sunday from 6:30 a.m. to 2 p.m. or, as the sign on the door says, "'til A.J. wants to close."

The **Half Shell Raw Bar** at the foot of Margaret Street (on the waterfront next to the turtle kraals) has a decided dockside air, and the specialty is oysters and clams shucked to order in the open-air raw bar. This *very* informal place also serves stone crabs, conch chowder, conch fritters, and hickory-smoked fish in the dining room, along with cocktails, wine, and beer. Prices are moderate, and this is a "don't miss." Open 11 a.m. to 11 p.m., except on Sunday, when they open at noon.

### Cuban

**El Cacique,** 125 Duval St., dishes up native Cuban dishes at budget prices. You'll find the usual pork, black beans, fried plantains, and Cuban bread, but take my word for it and try the Cuban-mix sandwich that combines ham, pork, salami, cheese, and pickles, and is accompanied by that strong, aromatic Cuban coffee.

**AND THE BARS:** Key West bars have been famous for years, and you'll know why after just one night (or afternoon, for that matter), of bar hopping—they're great, all of them, with a lively informality that turns cocktail hour into a party, whenever it happens to fall.

One of the most popular bars in town is The Top, at La Concha Hotel, where disco reigns long after the sun has set.

You won't want to miss **Sloppy Joe's,** 201 Duval St., "Papa" Hemingway's favorite hangout. Many a day the husky Ernest could be found working away at a corner table in the bar (whose doors open to the sidewalk), his manuscript pages held securely by a beer-mug paperweight to protect them from the breeze from ceiling fans and wafting in from outdoors. It's all there just as it was then, except that now there are Hemingway mementos all over the place, including a sailfish that the writer landed and proudly hung (it was a rare night when that happened, according to all accounts).

Another Hemingway favorite was The Oldest Bar, at 428 Greene St., but don't look for it by that name—it's now **Capt. Tony's Saloon,** a gathering spot for locals and visitors alike, many drawn by the jazz musicians and other entertainers who show up nightly.

Also on Duval Street (no. 224) is the **Bull and Whistle Tavern,** where live entertainment is featured. It's upstairs room is a showcase for paintings by local artists and has a great balcony overlooking Duval Street for people-watching.

**TOURS:** One of two tours should come *first* (even if you're strictly an on-your-own sightseer). The **Conch Tour Train** takes you on a 1½-hour narrated drive over the entire island, pointing out 60 historical sites and giving a vivid history of Key West. Tours leave daily, 9 a.m. to 4 p.m., from depots at 303 Front St. (Mallory Square) and 3850 N. Roosevelt Blvd. (tel. 305/294-5161). Fare is $7 for adults, $3 for ages 3 to 11. No need to reserve, just show up and hop aboard one of the open-air motorized trams. The **Old Town Trolley,** 1910 N. Roosevelt Blvd. (tel. 305/296-6688), is styled after those in San Francisco and also takes in the historical highlights of Key West. In addition, your ticket entitles you to discount coupons to a dozen sightseeing attractions. You can buy your ticket at several leading motels around the island and board at any point, hopping off to use those discount coupons to take in something en route, then reboarding when the next trolley comes along. Fare is $8 for adults, $3 for children.

The glass-bottom boat *Capt. Nemo* departs from the Galleon Marina on two-hour cruises over living coral reef, with an informative narrative about the formations. Call 305/294-8856 for reservations, rates, and schedule.

To visit **Fort Jefferson** on Dry Tortugas, the massive hexagon-shaped fortress which confined the heroic Dr. Mudd (who was imprisoned for setting John Wilkes Booth's leg after the assassination of President Lincoln), for so many years, call the Key West Seaplane Service at 305/294-6978. It's a thrilling flight, during which a magnificent view of the waters and islands surrounding Key West is yours all the way.

**THINGS TO SEE AND DO:** Make your very first stop the **Key West Chamber of Commerce,** 402 Wall St. (tel. 305/294-2587).

Sightseeing by bike or moped is certainly *the* way to go, as I said, and there are several rental places in town. Look for bikes and mopeds at **Moped Hospital,** 601 Truman Ave. (tel. 305/296-3344). There's no license or insurance required with the neat little motorized bikes, and you don't have to wear a helmet.

The **Audubon House,** 205 Whitehead St. at Green, was the first of Key West's historic houses to be restored and opened to the public. It was built by Capt. John H. Geiger, a "wrecker" who entertained John J. Audubon there in 1832 when he was studying birdlife on the Keys. Period furnishings re-create that era. It's open every day from 9 a.m. to noon and 1 to 5 p.m., and admission is $3 for adults, $1 for ages 6 through 12.

The **Hemingway House,** 907 Whitehead St., is a Spanish colonial house of native rock dating from 1851 that Nobel Prize winner Ernest Hemingway bought in 1931 and owned until 1961, one of his most productive writing periods. When he was in residence, there were some 50 cats here, and their descendants (at least, some of them) are still on the grounds. In fact, there is a cat fountain Hemingway constructed from a Spanish olive jar and a plumbing fixture he found at Sloppy Joe's. The house is very nearly the way it was when he lived there, filled with treasures he brought back from Spain, Africa, and Cuba. Admission is $3 for adults, $1 for children, and hours are 9 a.m. to 5 p.m.

On the south side of the island (South Roosevelt Boulevard), the **East Martello Fort** was constructed in 1861 and now holds an art and historical museum, with displays representing the cigar-making, sponging, fishing, and railroad industries. There's a lookout tower, a moat that is now a botanical garden, and a section of the museum is devoted to writers who have lived and worked in Key West. Adults pay $3; children, $1; and hours are 9:30 a.m. to 5 p.m. every day. About three-quarters of a mile away, the **West Martello Fort** is now occupied by the Key West Garden Club, and its tropical plants are on display without charge to the public.

*Kraal* is an Afrikaans word that means enclosure, and down at the foot of Margaret Street, the **Turtle Kraals** are holding pens for some of the largest turtles in captivity, including the hawksbill and loggerhead. There are also sharks, rays, moray eels, and tropical fish here, as well as an old cannery that is now a museum and a tower over 500 feet high for a breathtaking view of the harbor. And nearby are the shrimp-boat docks (which don't charge for strolling!). The Kraals (pronounced like "corrals" said very fast) are open every day from noon to midnight and there's no admission charge. An open-air bar/restaurant offers barbecued chicken, ribs, and lobster.

If fishing is your thing, the place to go is **Garrison Bight,** a sheltered cove about midway up the island's north shore (U.S. 1 runs alongside), where you'll find the city's charter docks and both bay and deep-sea boats for hire, with or without a guide. If you're not fishing yourself, it's fun to come down about 4 p.m. to see the boats return with happy and unhappy tourists aboard, depending on the day's catch.

**Tennis** players will find free courts at **Bayview Park** (close to the geographical center of the island) and near the ocean at **County Beach.** They're all concrete with compo surfacing, and they were very well maintained when I was there.

Of course, the one thing you *must* do at least once during your stay is go down to **Mallory Square at sunset.** It's a ceremony, and people who've lived here for years still observe the ritual. The great cumulus clouds seem to catch fire, then when the fiery red sun drops (very suddenly) into the sea, they quickly burn out to a purple gray. There's a cheer from those in the square and a great feeling of camaraderie among the crowd, which is likely to be composed of every age, at least two or three musical groups, and handicrafters spreading their wares out for inspection on the ground.

The sun*rise* is rather spectacular at Key West too, and the best place to watch it is from the **White Street Pier,** where you'll meet fishermen and dock workers getting out early.

# 3. The Everglades

Third largest of our national parks, the **Everglades National Park** (c/o Superintendent, P.O. Box 279, Homestead, FL 33030; tel. 305/247-6211) measures some 1½ million acres (about the size of Delaware), and it is the largest subtropical wilderness still existing in North America. Half land, half water, the Everglades' highest points are no more than 8 feet above mean sea level, and even the bay bottoms are no more than 16 feet below that level. In short, it's a shallow, swampy, very flat area that is the only sanctuary left for many North American species of birds and animals. This is the only place in the country, for example, where the Cape Sable sparrow and the great white heron are still extant. The manatee (sea cow) and crocodile are protected here, and an occasional Florida panther can still be seen. Alligators, sea turtles, and snakes of every ilk are quite common within the preserve. Vegetation is much like that of Cuba and the West Indies, with six species of palms, ferns, orchids, air plants, and everywhere the mangrove—some as tall as 75 feet in the Shark River forest areas. Much of the parkland is covered with sawgrass, a tough plant with barbed blades and razor-sharp edges that can grow as tall as ten feet.

The road through the park begins at the Visitor Center 12 miles southwest of **Homestead** on Rte. 9336 and runs 38 miles southwest to **Flamingo.** There are exhibits, orientation programs, and detailed maps and other information at the center. A $2-per-car entrance fee is charged, which covers all occupants until noon of the following day.

Inside the park, you'll find clearly marked interpretive trails and raised boardwalks leading out over the swamp. But you won't find food for sale until you reach Flamingo, and that 50-mile drive will take much longer than you expect, so best stock up with picnic provisions or snacks. Another thing: Fire is one of the most dangerous hazards in the Everglades, and smoking is absolutely *out* except in designated areas. And pets must be kept on leash at all times. Also, remember that the creatures you see are *wild:* by no means try to feed them, and keep as much distance as possible between you and the alligators!

Continuing on the main road, you'll come to the **Royal Palm Visitor Center,** where the Anhinga Trail and the Gumbo Limbo Trail lead off into the wilderness. About two miles farther along, there are campgrounds ($5 a day), picnic facilities, and trails at **Long Pine Key.** A little over eight miles on is **Pa-hay-okee Overlook,** where you can park your car and follow an elevated trail to a high platform overlooking the Shark River Basin. From here to Flamingo, there are several other boardwalks into mangrove forests and mahogany groves. At Flamingo, which is on the tip of the mainland at Florida Bay, there's a motel (see "Where to Stay"), restaurant, campgrounds ($4 a day per walk-in site), picnic facilities, service station, marina, sightseeing, and houseboats, fishing boats, canoes, and interpretive programs. Facilities for tents, campers, and motor-coaches cost $5 per day, with no electrical or water hookups. Spaces are limited, so don't plan to stay overnight without checking before you enter the park. Flamingo is the end of the line, and you must retrace the same ground leaving. However, nothing stays the same very long in the Everglades, and you'll see subtle changes on the return trip—different animals appearing, perhaps, or shadings of light in the afternoon that differ from those in the morning.

At **Shark Valley,** about 35 miles from Miami Beach on U.S. 41, the Tamiami Trail (see Chapter XV), there are open-air tram rides on the 15-mile loop road, but no private cars are allowed. It's along this route that you'll see Miccosukee Indians, as much at home in the Everglades as the wild creatures. All along the way are Indian villages, some of which are open to visitors for a small fee. Notice, too, the flood-control stations on the side of the highway and the canals and levees constructed by the South Florida Water Management District to protect some 18 counties from flood and drought. There are airboat ride stations as well, most operated by Seminoles; while they can't take you into the park itself, since airboats are prohibited, a ride through the Everglades areas north of the highway can be quite exciting.

When you reach the Shark Valley entrance turnoff, you'll see the **Miccosukee Indian Village and Restaurant** (P.O. Box 440021, Tamiami Station, Miami, FL 33144), and that's the last chance you'll have to buy food until you emerge from the park, since there is not even a settlement at the end of this trail. The village (tel. 305/223-8380 weekdays, 223-8388 on weekends) contains an authentic Indian family campsite, culture center, and museum, and there are demonstrations of alligator wrestling as well as guided walking tours and airboat rides in the Everglades. Admission to the village is $5 for adults, $3.50 for children under 12, and hours are 9 a.m. to 5:30 p.m.

When you get to **Shark Valley** itself, the 15-mile loop road is closed to private vehicles, but there's an open-air tram on which you're given a two-hour tour, with a 30-minute stop midway at a 40-foot observation tower. Adults pay $2; children, $1. The Shark Valley route, while not nearly so long as the main road to Flamingo, does give you a representative glimpse of the Everglades without consuming an entire day to get it. If you're hooked by this introduction, you can return to Homestead and set out on the longer route.

**WHERE TO STAY:** For dyed-in-the-wool nature lovers and adventurers, a drive through the Everglades or a one-day exploration just isn't enough. Well, way down at the southernmost point on the continental U.S., where Florida's west coast curves eastward to the Keys, the **Flamingo Lodge, Marina & Outpost** vacation resort, Everglades National Park, (P.O. Box 428), Flamingo, FL 33030 (tel. 813/695-3101), is a haven for those hardy souls, as well as for fishermen or families who want to *really* get away from it all without giving up solid comfort. Managed by TW Services, Inc., the Flamingo Lodge has the only overnight accommodations actually inside the park. You can have a room in the motel itself (all rooms have picture windows and modern furnishings) or choose a fully equipped housekeeping cabin or houseboat, or tie up in your own boat (up to 60 feet) at one of the 100 rental slips in the marina.

From here you can take Bay Cruises of Florida Bay and Whitewater Bay, or the Wilderness Tram that travels the Snake Bight Trail for a closeup view of Everglades wildlife (see "Things to Do," below). There are sunset cruises to top off the day. Or you can go it alone by renting a canoe or outboard motorboat and a complete camping outfit for a day or so in the backcountry—there are marked water trails and maps to guide you into the wilderness and back out. If fishing is your game, there's a free boat ramp if you bring your own, as well as charter boats captained by guides who know how to find the tarpon, snook, redfish, sea trout, snapper, and other fish that abound in these waters. But be sure to reserve such equipment at the same time you book at the lodge to avoid disappointment.

As for the lodge itself, it has a lounge, full-service marina, pool, patio area, gift shop, and a very good restaurant with a wide range of entrees and prices, and they'll even cook those fish you had such a good time catching. The Park Service maintains a Visitor Center and Museum close by the gift shop, staffed by professional naturalists. Rates for double-occupancy rooms start at $37 (summer) and $67 (winter).

**THINGS TO DO:** At Flamingo, **boat trips** come in several varieties, the longest of which costs $10 for adults, $5.50 for ages 6 through 12. You can also rent pontoon-type party boats equipped with barbecue grills (write Flamingo Lodge, P.O. Box 428, Everglades National Park, Flamingo, FL 33030).

From the Ranger Station located a half mile south of Everglades City (Fla. 29 south of U.S. 41), **sightseeing boats** through the national park leave at regular intervals from 9 a.m. to 5 p.m. Fares range from $9 to $10.50 for adults (children, half that). For information and reservations, contact Everglades National Park Boat Tours, Inc., P.O. Box 119, Everglades City, FL 33929 (tel. 813/695-2591).

For complete details on any *specific* plan you'd like to make for an Everglades visit, write: Superintendent, Everglades National Park, P.O. Box 279, Homestead, FL 33030 (tel. 305/247-6211).

**A SPECIAL WAY TO SEE THE EVERGLADES:** You can actually make the 'Glades your home for an entire week by joining a **North American Canoe Tour** (contact: David A. Harraden, 65 Black Point Rd., Niantic, CT 06357; tel. 203/739-0791 weekdays). Groups of six to ten meet in Everglades City to launch canoes, beginning a 109-mile journey through backwater bays, a mangrove forest, Alligator Creek, Shark River, and a lot more before the week ends at Flamingo. It's seven days of the most intimate association with nature, and nights are spent at campsites with intriguing names like Camp Lonesome, Canepatch Campsite, and Willy Willy. There are 15 trips each year (planned during the winter and early spring, November to April), and you must be over 16 to participate (under 16, and you'll need parental consent). NACT furnishes all equipment and food, as well as transport between Naples and the Everglades. Contact them at the above address for schedules and reservations.

# Chapter XVIII

# THE GULF COAST OF FLORIDA

## 1. Fort Myers and the Lee Island Coast
## 2. Sarasota
## 3. St. Petersburg–Tampa

THE WEST COAST OF FLORIDA, on the shores of the Gulf of Mexico, is considered by many to be the best of all possible Florida worlds. Beaches more tranquil than those along the East Coast's Atlantic, metropolitan centers that offer entertainment, culture, and convenience without Miami's hurly burly, and the old-world flavor of Tarpon Spring's Greek settlement plus the Cuban accent of Ybor City in Tampa combine to give a gentler air to this part of Florida's vacationland. Those who live here point with pride—and just a hint of smugness—to the fact that Floridians from Miami and other points east vacation regularly at Naples, Venice, and Sarasota.

## 1. Fort Myers and the Lee Island Coast

Strung along the coastline of Lee County is a chain of islands that has earned this area the name "Lee Island Coast." Major tourist destinations falling under that catch-all are Sanibel Island, Captiva Island, Fort Myers Beach, Bonita Beach, Pine Island, Cape Coral, and Lehigh, although there are literally *hundreds* of islands—many very small and uninhabited, named and unnamed—accessible to the vacationer with a boat or those who opt to rent one. Tiny little Cabbage Key (see "Where to Stay") is a prime example, and serves to tempt you to explore these offshore refuges as fully as time will permit.

Approached from the south, **Fort Myers** is your first encounter with this stretch of sun-drenched, beach-bound vacation territory. More than 70 varieties of palms line Fort Myers's streets, making it one of the loveliest towns on the Gulf Coast. Thomas Edison came in 1885, fell in love with the place, and returned every winter for nearly half a century, living and working on a 14-acre riverside estate.

Situated some 15 miles up the broad Caloosahatchee River, Fort Myers is connected to its beaches and offshore islands by two bridges and causeways. On seven-mile-long **Estero Island,** Fort Myers Beach is only three blocks across at its widest point, with the gulf on one side and Estero Bay on the other. Its hotels, motels, restaurants, and shopping centers are set in wooded plots that (except for the busy intersection where San Carlos Boulevard from town joins Estero

Boulevard at the beach) reinforce the tropical island atmosphere. It's a relaxed, family-oriented beach resort, although nighttime entertainment in restaurants and lounges often carries on until quite late.

**Sanibel and Captiva Islands,** across a toll bridge ($1.50 each way) at the end of McGregor Boulevard, are in the path of gulf tides that wash ashore interesting, and sometimes rare, shells. One of my earliest Florida memories is of running through a mosquito-laden thicket from the one paved road on Sanibel to reach the wide sand beach and walk in undisturbed pleasure at the water's edge, watching the shell harvest of each new wave. Today the mosquitos are practically all gone, thanks to an effective pest-control program, paved roads lead all over the island, and resort communities and private residences have appeared in such numbers that those beaches are seldom, if ever, deserted. Crowded they're *not,* however, and "shelling" is still a delight, drawing Sunday wave-watchers from nearby towns.

Incidentally, those tiny, many-colored clams you'll see burrowing into the sand here and on almost all Gulf Coast beaches are coquinas, sometimes called "butterflies" because that's what they look like when the shell opens up to form two "wings." People hereabout make a delicious coquina chowder, but it requires a *lot* of time and effort. Chances are you'll pick up at least one or two with the clam still alive inside, and be warned—there'll be an ungodly stench if you leave them around for long. You can clean them one of two basic ways: boil them rapidly for about five minutes and pick out the insides with a fork, or freeze the shell and the little critter's remains will slip out easily when it's defrosted. If there's still an odor, soak the shells overnight in alcohol.

Sanibel is also the site of the **"Ding" Darling Wildlife Refuge,** a five-mile, unspoiled mangrove swamp and uplands area that takes about half an hour to drive through, unless you loiter (and I'll bet you do!) to observe the native and migratory birds that have found a sanctuary here.

Fishermen most often go after tarpon in the waters off Fort Myers, and there are plenty of charter boats with experienced guides. Pier fishing is fun too, though, and Fort Myers Beach has a free 600-foot public pier out into the gulf for fishing or just watching.

**WHERE TO STAY:** Fort Myers Beach, Sanibel, and Captiva Islands are ideal vacation headquarters, all just a short drive away from sightseeing attractions, with the sparkling waters of the Gulf of Mexico right out front for a dip before and/or after you stint behind the wheel. If you *really* want to get away from it all, head for Cabbage Key.

*Note:* If you're coming from Florida's east coast or the Keys, you'll pass through **Naples** en route to the Lee Island Coast, and you may want to stop in that pretty town for overnight pampering at the **Ritz-Carlton, Naples,** 280 Vanderbilt Beach Rd., Naples, FL 33963 (tel. 813/598-3300, or toll free 800/241-3333). It's a 14-story, Mediterranean-style resort whose courtyard opens to the sea and three miles of beach. There's a pool, tennis courts, golf course, fitness center, gourmet restaurant, and entertainment with dancing. As for guest rooms, they are the epitome of elegance executed in a distinctly tropical decor. Winter rates for doubles range as high as $200 to $300, while summer rates drop as low as $98 to $200. As with all Ritz-Carlton hotels, however, even the highest rates offer maximum value for dollar.

### Fort Myers Beach (Estero Island)

The **Holiday Inn,** 6890 Estero Blvd., Fort Myers Beach, FL 33931 (tel. 813/463-5711, or toll free 800/HOLIDAY), is at the southern end of the main drag, but close enough to the center of things to be convenient. Its 103 luxuriously furnished rooms, efficiencies, and apartments all have pool or gulf views (some have both), and there are tennis courts and shuffleboard. The Sunset Dining Room, overlooking the pool with the gulf beyond, serves all three meals at moderate prices, with a pretty good wine list. There's entertainment and dancing most nights in the lounge. It's a restful place, with beautifully landscaped grounds and a 540-foot white-sand private beach. From December 15 to May 2 doubles start at $102 (gulf-front apartments at $120), and then drop. Children under 12 stay free in the same room with their parents.

The 22 guest rooms at **Mariner's Boathouse,** 7630 Estero Blvd., Fort Myers Beach, FL 33931 (tel. 813/463-8787), are called "cabins." And one look will tell you why—they're all decorated with a nautical theme that does indeed give you the feeling of being aboard a well-appointed private yacht in your own cabin. All have two bedrooms and accommodate up to six people, with queen-size beds and built-in bunks and two baths. Kitchens—oops, galleys!—are fully furnished, right down to microwave ovens and dishwashers, and glass doors open out to screened-in porches (no, *decks*). The Boathouse game room provides billiards, Ping-Pong, and video games, and there are a pool and a spa. Daily rates range from $125 (per *unit*) in season down to $85 other months (two-night minimum stay), and there are very attractive weekly rates available.

The **Best Western Beach Resort,** 684 Estero Blvd., Fort Myers Beach, FL 33931 (tel. 813/463-6000, or toll free 800/528-1234), has a wide range of accommodations, from efficiencies to motel rooms to suites. All have private balconies. Doubles for guest rooms are $92 to $98 in season, and lower the rest of the year.

One of the oldest, most atmospheric hotels on the beach is the **Pelican,** 3040 Estero Blvd., Fort Myers Beach, FL 33931 (tel. 813/463-6139). It began as a honeymoon hideaway aboard a beached two-story houseboat in the early 1900s, when "Ma" Turner cooked for her guests by kerosene lamps in the galley. It grew, as all good things do, and served as an officers' barracks for Page Field personnel during World War II. Garrett and Esther Reasoner took over from "Ma" in the '50s, and their children carry on the place today. Its age doesn't show once you step inside the plain wooden buildings that make up the small complex. All rooms, efficiencies, and cottages are completely modern, and each is tastefully decorated, with a very homey air. Most of the hotel rooms don't have private baths, only a lavatory each, but there are centrally located showers and baths. Buz and Ann Reasoner have created a real "home away from home" for vacationers in this old hotel, and even the two meals a day (at the Pelican Restaurant, about which more below) under their Modified American Plan rates have that special, cared-for flavor. Those rates are mandatory from November 1 to May 1, when bookings are taken by the week only, starting at weekly rates of $280 to $315 for a cottage duplex, $350 for a cottage efficiency, $455 for a two-bedroom cottage, with a $15-per-person surcharge for the MAP. European Plan (no meals included) daily rates, May to October, start at $45 and $55. Don't expect to get in, though, unless you reserve months in advance—they have scores of regulars who book from year to year.

## Sanibel Island

The **Sonesta Sanibel Harbour Resort, Spa & Tennis Club,** 5610 McGregor Blvd., Fort Myers, FL 33908 (tel. 813/466-4000, or toll free 800/223-2721), is actually located at the foot of the Causeway on the Fort Myers side, but is just a short drive away from Sanibel Island itself. For the tennis-oriented, this is *the* place to stay—it's the home of the Jimmy Connors U.S. Tennis Center, with a world-class spa that includes an aerobic and weight room, exercise swimming pool, jogging trail, sauna and steambaths, racquetball courts, whirlpools, massage rooms, hot and cold splash tubs, loofa bath, herbal wrap, game room, and . . . well, the list is a long one! Qualified instructors and physical fitness experts are on hand to assist in individual fitness programs. The Tennis Center holds a stadium, clubhouse, pro shop, and lighted tennis courts, where tournaments, clinics, and exhibitions are year-round events. Guest rooms are the latest word in luxury, with some 105 extra-large vacation apartments, and there is an equally elegant restaurant and lounge. Rates for double-occupancy packages range from $165 for three days and two nights to $798 for seven days and six nights.

On Sanibel Island itself, **Sanibel Island Hilton Inn,** 937 Gulf Dr., Sanibel Island, FL 33957 (tel. 813/472-3181, or toll free 800/237-1491), represents luxury in a distinctively "island" manner. The self-contained resort inn is a sprawling complex of two-story, tropical-style buildings with deluxe hotel rooms and kitchenette units as well as smashing one- and two-bedroom grand deluxe suites with full kitchens and extra-large living and dining room areas, all spread along a superb private beachfront. All rooms have balconies and refrigerators, and facilities include one of Sanibel's best restaurants (see "Where to Eat"), a pool, putting green, rental bicycles, sailboats, and nearby golf privileges. Rates for singles or doubles are in the $160 to $275 range in season, lower other months, and there are several very attractive, money-saving packages available in most seasons.

The two-story **Casa Ybel Resort,** 2255 W. Gulf Dr., Sanibel Island, FL 33957 (tel. 813/472-3145), has 114 fully equipped kitchen units, some with one bedroom, others with two, and very attractive gulf-front villas. There's a pool, wading pool, tennis, sailing, and whirlpool, as well as the lovely Thistle Lodge restaurants. Winter rates are $185 for one-bedroom units, $200 for two; all rates are lower other months.

**Sanibel Cottages,** 2341 W. Gulf Dr., Sanibel Island, FL 33957 (tel. 813/472-1868), has a distinctly Victorian charm, with romantic two-bedroom villas rimmed with white-railinged porches and fitted inside with furnishings that reflect the tropical setting (including ceiling fans and a whirlpool tub in the master bath). Kitchens are fully equipped, and the gourmet Thistle Lodge (see "Where to Eat") is right next door for those times you'd rather not cook. Amenities include a whirlpool spa, pool, boat rentals, tennis, and nearby golf privileges. Seasonal rates (based on up to four people) range from $140 to $250 daily, with weekly rates available.

The **Sundial Beach & Tennis Resort,** 1246 Middle Gulf Dr., Sanibel Island, FL 33957 (tel. 813/472-4151, or toll free 800/237-4184), has 13 tennis courts and five swimming pools. If golf's your thing, there are privileges at a course not far away. Morgan's Market is the restaurant that specializes in just-caught seafood and adds choice, aged beef to the menu, all served in a room with a spectacular view of the gulf. As for accommodations, all are suites (efficiency, deluxe, or two-bedroom) with private terrace or balcony and fully equipped kitchen. Double-occupancy rates range from $90 to $250, depending on location.

The **Castaways,** 6460 Sanibel Captiva Rd., Sanibel Island, FL 33957 (tel. 813/472-1252), is located on the gulf and the bay, and has air-conditioned cottages with kitchens (some studios). There's a pool, restaurant, boat dock, and fishing pier. Winter rates run from $60 to $160 lower other months.

### Captiva Island

If it's peaceful seclusion you want, with recreational facilities that are endless, **South Seas Plantation Resort and Yacht Harbor,** Captiva Island, FL 33924 (tel. toll free 800/237-3102), has just what you're looking for. Scattered within this 330-acre enclave that once was a key lime and coconut plantation at the end of the island are some 600 rental accommodations, all in the luxury class. They range from deluxe hotel rooms in Harbourside Village to one- and two-bedroom Tennis, Bayside, and Beach Villas, two-bedroom Marina Villas and Beach Cottages, two- and three-bedroom Land's End Village Condominium Villas, three-bedroom Gulf Cottages, and two-, three-, and four-bedroom beachfront homes. A true smörgåsbord of possibilities! As for amenities, there's a par-36, 9-hole golf course, with 18 additional holes available at the Dunes Country Club on neighboring Sanibel Island; 22 tennis courts; 17 swimming pools; a beautiful yacht harbor; windsurfing; jet skis; rental powerboats; charter fishing; and two miles of private beach. And after all that activity (unless you opt for beach-bumming), you certainly won't go hungry, not with the likes of Chadwicks Restaurant in its tropical island setting, or the elegant King's Crown Dining Room. Cap'n Al's Pub overlooking the Yacht Harbor is a popular haven for imbibing or casual meals. Seasonal rates for that wide choice of accommodations start at $145 for one or two persons in a hotel room, $160 to $175 for a one-bedroom villa (single or double), and $320 for one or two people at Land's End Village.

**'Tween Waters Inn,** Gulf Drive, Captiva Island, FL 33924 (tel. 813/472-5161), provides one of the most "islander" environments you could wish for. Set astraddle a narrow neck of land between the gulf and the bay, parts of the inn date back to the early years of this century, and the additions that have come since are all in complete harmony with the original blue-gray, white-trimmed tropical-style buildings. There are motel-style guest rooms in two- and three-story wings, efficiencies, and attractive individual cottages scattered about the shaded grounds. Many have private balconies or patios. Besides 1,000 feet of private beach, amenities here include a charming Florida/Victorian restaurant whose Friday-night seafood buffet, prime rib specialty on Saturday, and Sunday brunch draw scores of locals; the Crow's Nest Lounge, where there's entertainment and dancing in season; a pool complex featuring an Olympic-size pool, a wading pool, and a decked lounging area complete with poolside bar; tennis courts; a game room; a marina with supply store and guides for fishing and/or sailing; boat, canoe, and bicycle rentals; lawn games; and picnic tables with outdoor grills. This is also a departure point for island cruises to Cabbage Key, where a two-hour stop allows time for lunch and exploring (see "Things to See and Do"). In-season rates for doubles start at $115, efficiencies at $125, and cottages at $140. Rates are lower the rest of the year, and there are very good package deals available from early May to mid-December.

## Cabbage Key—A Very Special Place

**Cabbage Key Inn,** P.O. Box 489, Bokeelia, FL 33922 (tel. 813/283-2278), is *indeed* a very special place, and admittedly it will not appeal to every vacationer. But such is its romantic appeal that it caught the imagination and fancy of novelist Mary Roberts Rinehart when her son and his wife purchased the island for only $2,500 and set about building a winter estate. The intrigued writer was much involved in planning the residence and its surrounding grounds, and it may have been her influence that perched the main building atop an ancient Caloosa Indian shell mound some 38 feet high, giving it one of the highest elevations in this part of the state. All that was back in the 1920s and early 1930s.

By the time Phyllis and Rob Wells (educators from North Carolina afflicted with a persistent need to live near the water) arrived on the scene in 1976, the island was again for sale, the main residence having been converted into a small (six rooms) inn in 1942. They've made a few changes, all of which would no doubt have delighted the Rineharts—the main floor of the residence is now a marvelous restaurant, a solar-energy system has been installed, and an old concrete foundation now holds a new, vastly increased-capacity water-storage tower (around which an observation deck affords breathtaking views). Still, the six working fireplaces, five porches, and grounds "landscaped" to nature's original design blend into a harmonious setting guaranteed to soothe the most savage beast and calm the most jangled nerves. Which is not to say that Cabbage Key is dull—far from it! Its location directly across from Marker 60 on the Intracoastal Waterway and the lively but low-key hospitality of the attractive hosts draw boaters who make this a regular stop each trip (sometimes with such notables as singers Neil Diamond and Jimmy Buffet, actor E. G. Marshall, or newsman Roger Mudd in tow), make this a popular lunch stop on island cruises from Captiva Island, and serves as a focal point for weekend gatherings of locals from the mainland. All of which makes for a relaxed conviviality you're free to join or just observe, as the spirit moves you.

In addition to the six rooms in the inn, there's a lovely cottage on the grounds that sleeps six, and 1988 rates are an astonishingly low $45 per person. How to get there if you're not boating? Just call Rob and he'll arrange for Terry Forgie, dockmaster extraordinaire, to pick you up from a Pine Island marina in the Cabbage Key skiff. (Terry is also the owner of a jewel-like sailboat, sometimes available to guests for charter.)

As I said in the beginning, Cabbage Key is not designed to appeal to all comers. But if you long to take body and soul to where they can fine-tune back to the sights and sounds and delights of the natural world in the company of kindred spirits, Cabbage Key is definitely for *you!*

**WHERE TO EAT:** Again, the beaches have a lot to offer; you can eat well and never venture to the mainland. Some landbound exceptions, however, are included in this listing.

### Fort Myers Beach (Estero Island)

The **Pelican Restaurant,** 3040 Estero Blvd. (tel. 813/463-6139), which began life in "Ma" Turner's galley, has gone on to be one of the best around, and people drive relatively long distances to eat here. Crossing an outside wooden plank deck, you step first into the Pegleg Lounge, a cozy place sporting an old wooden sign with the legend: "Sailors Rest, Miss Sally Small, Prop. Miss Small Can Accommodate up to 14 Sailors Per Night." By all means tarry long enough to see the model of an 1879 tea clipper that hangs over the bar and the kegs and baskets and other dockside memorabilia piled around the walls. Once you are inside the rather small dining room, with its walls of windows to the gulf, manager Phil Reasoner will see to it that you understand the reason the place is so popular. If you order one of the many seafood entrees, you can be sure it will be fresh—the Reasoner family has its own boats which supply the restaurant. As for beef specialties, they also have their own butcher to assure good cuts from prime meats. And everything is cooked to order. Prices are moderate: the native seafood platter, for instance, is $11.75; boiled native stone crab claws, the same. You really should eat here at least once—and make it early in your visit, so you will have time to come back. Open 5 to 10 p.m. for dinner (year round).

A Fort Myers Beach friend sent me to **Charley Brown's,** 6225 Estero Blvd. (tel. 813/463-6660), saying, "This place is a real treat." Well, I found she hadn't exaggerated in the least—it *is* a treat. In a waterfront setting (the enclosed-porch/dining room named Snoopy's overlooks the water), Charley Brown's serves excellent seafood, steak, and other beef dishes (like kebabs and prime ribs), amid lots of greenery. Service is as outstanding as the food, and there's an assortment of special drinks from the bar (try their house special, the Dirty Mouse). Prices on the semi à la carte menu range from $9 to $17, with children's plates in the $3 to $4 range. Hours are 5 to 10 p.m.

## Sanibel/Captiva

For truly elegant dining, the **Brass Elephant,** in the Hilton Inn, 937 E. Gulf Dr., Sanibel Island (tel. 813/472-3181), reflects the island's warm, tropical ambience. It's a marvelous blend of rattan and antique furnishings, lots of brass, and burnished natural woods. Seafood, as you'd expect, is a highlight here, but the sophisticated menu also includes such delicacies as rack of lamb persillade, medallions of veal in sauce espagnole and fettuccine Alfredo. Prices are in the upper ranges, with dinner running from $15 to $22 (a special children's menu runs about $7.50). All three meals are served, with hours of 7 a.m. to 11 p.m. (from 10 a.m. on Sunday, when there's a smashing champagne brunch). Best reserve.

**Chadwick's,** at South Seas Plantation, Captiva Island (tel. 813/472-5111), is a beautiful restaurant with an airy, tropical decor. There's a continental menu that capitalizes on the fresh seafood available here, plus beef and chicken dishes. The atmosphere is romantic, the service is polished and friendly, and the food is outstanding. Add "fun" to that list of superlatives if you come along for one of their special events: Tuesday for the Polynesian Paradise buffet, Friday for the Seafood Delight buffet, and Sunday for a terrific champagne brunch. Lunches focus on lighter fare, like salads, quiches, and sandwiches. All three meals are served, and hours are 7:30 a.m. to 2 p.m. and 6 p.m. to midnight, with music every night from 8:30 p.m. on. Lunches run $5 to $9, and dinners, $10 to $20. Reservations are a must at night.

**Thistle Lodge,** at Casa Ybel Resort, 2255 W. Gulf Dr., Sanibel Island (tel. 472-9200), is a lovely restaurant serving New Orleans cuisine. Do try their "blackened grouper." Hours are 11 a.m. to 2 p.m. and 6 to 10 p.m. every day except Sunday, when a sumptuous brunch is set out from 10 a.m. to 2 p.m. Prices are moderate, with lunches in the $5 to $11 range, and dinners from $12 to $22. Book ahead at night.

Join the people who live down here for almost any meal at the **'Tween Waters Inn,** Sanibel-Captiva Road, Captiva Island (tel. 813/472-5161; for details, see "Where to Stay").

The **Café Orleans,** 1473 Periwinkle Way, Sanibel Island (tel. 813/472-5700), is the perfect place for breakfast, lunch, or dinner. Marty (it's a "she") and John Vroman-Vrolyk are island-lovers from way back and came here from Puerto Rico. Their breakfasts have become famous and they have a wide offering of early-a.m. dishes. I found, in fact, the best eggs Benedict this side of New York in this small island restaurant (they're called Kay's Delight on the menu and come topped with a special piquant sauce far better than the usual bland hollandaise). Besides the omelets, french toast, waffles, etc., there's a long list of sandwiches, homemade soups and chowder, and an extensive wine list. Breakfast is 7 a.m. to 2 p.m. and lunch from 11 a.m. to 2 p.m. year round; dinner is from 6 to 9:30 p.m. in season only; and prices are in the budget-to-moderate range. Closed Monday.

## Fort Myers and Vicinity

Located in two of Fort Myer's old Victorian homes, connected by a beautiful garden courtyard and country kitchen, **The Veranda,** Second and Broadway (tel. 813/332-2065), is a treat to visit—and the food's good too. Furnishings are authentic antebellum antiques, and there's a huge old wooden bar, porches, and that courtyard for al fresco dining. The menu features seafood specialties like blackened redfish, veal dishes, and special desserts at prices a little above moderate (starting at $12). There's entertainment every night in the lovely lounge, which opens at 11 a.m. The restaurant serves lunch from 11:30 a.m. to 2:30 p.m. ($4.50 to $9) and dinner from 5:30 to 11 p.m. Closed Sunday.

Smitty's has been a Florida west coast institution for almost 25 years (you'll find one at Venice and Port Charlotte as well as in Fort Myers). In Fort Myers, **Smitty's,** 2240 W. 1st St. (tel. 813/334-4415), specializes (as do all three) in custom-aged western beef and superb fresh, hand-breaded seafood. All breads and pastries are home-baked, and desserts like Key lime pie and brandy Alexander cream pie are scrumptious. Dress is casual in Dollison's Lounge, where you can sip in comfort to enjoy live entertainment—a little more "dressy casual" in the Beef Room. Hours are 11 a.m. to 10:30 p.m. (on Sunday from noon to 9:30 p.m.) and prices run $8 to $16.

**NIGHTLIFE:** It's mostly in the lounges of motels or restaurants—this is not nightclub territory.

For dancing, there's the **Celebrity Lounge** in the Sheraton, 8900 S. Tamiami Trail (tel. 813/936-4300), or the **Sunset Room,** Holiday Inn at Fort Myers Beach (see "Where to Stay").

Entertainment goes on nightly in the **Celebrity Lounge** (see above); the **Likeke Lounge** of the Holiday Inn at Fort Myers Beach; the **Pago Pago Lounge** of the Holiday Inn in town, 2066 W. 1st St. (tel. 813/334-2123); and **The Veranda** (see "Where to Eat").

On Sanibel Island, **Thistle Lodge** at Casa Ybel Resort, 2255 W. Gulf Dr. (tel. 813/472-9200), and **Morgan's Market Lounge,** at the Sundial Beach & Tennis Resort, 1246 Middle Gulf Dr. (tel. 813/472-4151), have evening entertainment. On Captiva, it's the **Crow's Nest** at 'Tween Waters Inn, Sanibel-Captiva Road (tel. 813/472-5161), and **Chadwick's,** at South Seas Plantation (tel. 813/472-5111).

**THINGS TO SEE AND DO:** Beach things top the list at Fort Myers and its islands—swimming (and the beaches are safe, with few strong tides to worry about), fishing from pier, surf, or boat, shelling (especially on Sanibel and Captiva Islands), or just plain toasting on the palm-fringed sands.

The **Shell Factory,** four miles north on U.S. 41, has an eye-popping display of shells from all over the world in a large building that houses a museum of rare shells, shellcraft and art supplies, aquarium displays, glass blower, candlemaker, gourmet department, a gift shop, and a snackbar. A lot of the shells are on sale, and there's no admission charge. Open from 8 a.m. to 7 p.m.

The **Thomas A. Edison Home,** 2350 McGregor Blvd., was prefabricated in Maine and shipped down by schooner. The inventer spent his winters here for almost 50 years, and his furnishings are still here, as is his laboratory, still intact (and some of his early lightbulbs have been burning 12 hours a day ever since he made them!). The guided tour includes the lab and workshops, the house, a museum of Edison's inventions, and the 14-acre botanical gardens filled with tropical trees and plants. Hours are 9 a.m. to 4 p.m. except Sunday, when they are 12:30 to 4 p.m. Admission is $4 for adults, $1 for ages 6 through 12.

At the **City Yacht Basin,** foot of Lee Street, you can board the **Jungle Cruise** for a three-hour narrated ride either up the Caloosahatchee right to the edge of the Everglades or through the Intracoastal Waterway. Both are informative, fascinating looks at Florida wildlife. Fares and departure times change seasonally, so call 813/334-7474 for schedules and reservations.

Spend a few delightful hours on the water, with a stop on Cabbage Key (see "Where to Stay") with **Island Cruises,** 'Tween Waters Inn Marina, Sanibel-Captiva Road, Captiva Islands (tel. 813/472-5161, 472-5462 after 6 p.m.). The **Island Queen II** carries only 38 passengers, and you'll cruise through Pine Island Sound on the sheltered Intracoastal Waterway, stopping for lunch or dinner at

Cabbage Key Inn. Prices are $20 for adults, half that for children under 12. Cruises are 10 a.m. to 3 p.m. and 5:30 to 10:30 p.m.

If you've ever suspected a seagoing spirit lurking deep within your soul, you can liberate it by booking with **Adventure Sailing Escape.** This is a marvelous program that sets you aboard your own yacht, instructs you in skippering, then takes you along in a flotilla where expert help is always right at hand if you run afoul of any watery emergencies. They tell me that the most inexperienced novice will soon be handling the sleek sailing vessels skillfully and some first-timers even find the confidence to "free sail" away from the flotilla from time to time. Dockage each night is at or near gourmet dining establishments, so no need to worry about galley duties. The Escape includes seven days (six nights) aboard a Commodore 26-foot sloop, meals, dockage fees, fuel and ice, guest privileges at resorts along the way, and round-trip transfers from the Fort Myers airport. For complete details, rates, and reservations, contact: Adventure Sailing Escape, 'Tween Waters Inn Marina, Sanibel-Captiva Road, Captiva Island, FL 33942 (tel. 813/472-5161). So, ahoy, all you repressed sailors out there, time to break sail!

For a one-on-one or small-group water exploration, **Capt. Bob Sabatino** is an ideal guide. He'll take you fishing, on a sightseeing cruise, shelling on isolated beaches, or just about whatever you specify. Contact him at P.O. Box 29, Captiva Island, FL 33924 (tel. 813/472-1451), for rates and reservations.

Nature lovers will want to visit **Corkscrew Swamp Sanctuary,** on Fla. 846, exit 17 off I-75 (tel. 813/657-3771), between Fort Myers and Naples, where a two-mile-long boardwalk winds through lush tropical growth, cypress trees, and aquatic plants. Storks, alligators, and other animals live here in abundance. It's open daily from 9 a.m. to 5 p.m., and admission is $4 for adults, $2 for students, free for those under 6.

**READER'S SUGGESTION:** "In a spate of ecological consciousness, Sanibel environmentalists are urging shell harvesters to leave live shells on the beach. It seems that even the mollusks are endangered by civilization, with the prettiest species being collected so fast that they have no chance for propagation" (S. Reifler, Clinton Cove, N.Y.).

## 2. Sarasota

There have been "tourists" in Sarasota from as far back as the early 1700s, when Cuban fishermen set up camp along the gulf shores here and established a brisk trade with local Indians. Indians of one tribe or another (there were several) had known about the sunny climate and bountiful waters for longer than that —20,000 years longer, recent archeological finds reveal. The Spanish (tourists of a sort themselves) had been through in the 1500s (Hernando de Soto landed on Longboat Key in 1539), and pirates sailed in and out of the bays and bayous for years; José Gaspar Gasparilla, one of the most notorious, made his headquarters in nearby Charlotte Harbor. Tourism really took off, however, during the land-boom years of the early 1920s, faltered, then ceased when the boom became a fizzle. But John Ringling, when he moved his circus's winter headquarters down in 1927, brought economic salvation in the form of a huge construction and maintenance payroll. Not content with investing in a multi-million-dollar estate for his private residence, Ringling also interested himself in all sorts of civic improvements, building the Ringling Causeway and putting hundreds of thousands of dollars into local colleges and artistic institutions. His legacy to the city and the state was enormous, for he left an immense personal fortune, that impressive home, and a priceless art collection housed in its own magnificent museum, all of which play their part in drawing today's tourists—many of whom, like Ringling, find the climate (both weatherwise and culturally) so agreeable they stay on to become Sarasota's most enthusiastic residents.

The natural blessings that make Sarasota so appealing to natives, tourists, and tourists-turned-residents are many. The city, from its gracefully curving waterfronts, looks across Sarasota Bay to long, narrow islands, or keys, and beyond to the blue waters of the Gulf of Mexico. Brilliantly colored bougainvillea, hibiscus, azaleas, and flame vines blaze in the shade of assorted palms and pines, and more color is reflected in bay and gulf waters when the sun rises and sets in startling splendor. In such a setting, the arts—in many forms—have bloomed too, to such a degree that Sarasota has become the virtual "culture capital" of Florida. Artists, writers, artisans, actors, and circus performers (artists of another stripe) make this their permanent home and seem to flourish. True, this is resort country, yet its attractions don't wane with the seasons, and all year long sun and sand must complete with concerts and theater and galleries and museums for the tourists' time and attention.

The city's physical beauty is evident in almost every quarter (except perhaps on the shopping-center-and-service-station-bordered stretches of the Tamiami Trail north and south of town). Downtown Sarasota creates a lasting first impression with beautifully landscaped Bayfront Drive and **Island Park,** a small island man-made from bay bottom sand and filled with native plantings that provide a serene setting for boats of all description docked at Marina Jack.

Bayfront Drive takes the visitor across Ringling Causeway, past **Bird Key** (once the home of Henry Ringling North and now an exclusive residential community and yacht club) and onto **St. Armands Key.** Ringling's influence is once more felt on this pretty, circular island, for it was he who first laid out the tropically landscaped park at its center, and the statues it now holds come from his private collection. Around the park, on a circular drive, shops, restaurants, art galleries, and boutiques have gabled windows, striped awnings, and wrought-iron grillwork that impart a European air. Due west from St. Armands Circle is **Lido Key,** with its string of resort hotels, half-mile-long public beach (which, in true Florida style, also has a swimming pool), and imaginative children's playground. A turn north at St. Armands Circle takes you to **Longboat Key,** via a humpback bridge to Lido Shores, site of some striking (and expensive) waterfront homes, then across a concrete-and-steel bridge to the Longboat Key Golf and Country Club. It stands on land that Ringling once thought would hold an ultra-luxury hotel, the Ritz, which would bring even more wealth into the Sarasota area. This was one dream, however, that failed, and construction was halted just 60 days before the scheduled completion date.

Just south of Lido Keys lies **Siesta Key,** a beach community more casual than Lido or Longboat, with vacation resorts and private homes nudging each other in groves of peppertrees, mangrove, palms, and pines. This key, with unspoiled, virtually wild northern and southern edges, has attracted scores of artists and writers, drawn by its charm and the seclusion they're able to find here. Siesta Key Public Beach stretches along the gulf shore, with grills and picnic tables, a large children's playground, and all-weather tennis courts. Turtle Beach, on the southern tip, is narrow, but has an "untouched by human hands" kind of beauty. Human hands have, however, added grills and both open and sheltered picnic tables, but in a manner that has enhanced, not spoiled, nature's creation.

Away from the water, there are those Ringling museums, a 28-acre Civic Center with an auditorium, recreation club, art association, library, community house, 40 shuffleboard courts, seven lighted tennis courts, and 15 bowling alleys. And downtown, historic **Mira Mar Plaza** is a one-block-long shopping mall (on Palm Avenue) of graceful arches, wrought-iron balconies, and lovely little gardens.

**WHERE TO STAY:** It goes without saying that accommodations right on the gulf will cost you more. What *should* be said, however, is that Sarasota has many very desirable motels with lower rates than those on the beachfront which are really *more* convenient to sightseeing attractions. So it becomes a question of priorities. In any case, the drive to a gulf beach from any of these motels on the Tamiami Trail (that's U.S. 41) will be no more than 10 or 15 minutes.

Not on the beach, but definitely the most elegant place in town, is the **Hyatt Sarasota,** 1000 Boulevard of the Arts (tel. 813/366-9000, or toll free 800/228-9000), just across from Van Wezel Performing Arts Hall. It soars 12 floors above Sarasota Bay and is a tower of modernity, with soft shades of browns, beige, blues, and muted reds setting off high glass lobby windows, with wood used lavishly in combination with aluminum to create a striking effect the minute you walk inside the door. Its 297 rooms are decorated in contemporary furnishings of the luxury sort, with oversize beds. Peppercorn's Restaurant, with colorful tablecloths and fresh plants on the table, looks out over the water and serves outstanding meals from breakfast through dinner which draw a big local following. The Horse and Chaise Lounge has entertainment and dancing in an elegant setting. The Boathouse, built on stilts over the lagoon, is a casual, friendly place to eat or drink (or both) at watered-down prices, and may be reached by boat (as well as by foot over the wooden walkway from the hotel lobby). There are tennis courts a short distance away, and golfers have guest privileges at some 16 local courses. Other extras include a heated pool, plus sail and power charter boats. And if you arrive in Sarasota aboard your own boat, the Hyatt Sarasota has a private marina which will accommodate it. Double-room rates start at $95, year round. Children up to the age of 18 stay free with their parents.

Over on Lido Beach, the **Coquina on the Beach,** 1008 Ben Franklin Dr., Sarasota, FL 33577 (tel. 813/388-2141), has large, airy rooms with tropical furnishings, completely equipped kitchenettes, private balconies or patios, and a heated pool with hydrotherapy jets. This is a small (less than 50 units), very friendly motel directly on the gulf (their private beach has thatched shade shelters), with recreation facilities that include sailboats, shuffleboard, picnic tables, and an outdoor grill. Rates are $95 and up during the winter season (February 1 through April 30), lower other months.

There are eight units for the handicapped at the **Silver Beach Resort,** 4131 Gulf of Mexico Dr., Longboat Key, FL 33548 (tel. 813/383-2434), five miles north of the Longboat Key Bridge on Fla. 789. Rooms are exceptionally nice, some with oversize beds. It's directly on the gulf and has a heated pool, shuffleboard, Ping-Pong, picnic tables, a putting green, and grills (there's a restaurant across the street). There is also limo and taxi service to the airport. During the February to April season, double rooms are $65 (kitchen units, $72 to $96), with lower rates from April through January.

A modestly priced motel at Lido Beach, the **Surf View Motel,** 1121 Ben Franklin Dr., Sarasota, FL 33577 (tel. 813/388-1818 or 388-1649), is across the street from the gulf, and has rather small, but cozy, rooms, nicely furnished with modern appointments, as well as some beachfront units. There's a warm, friendly atmosphere here, plus personalized service, a heated pool, shuffleboard, and beach privileges. Both one- and two-room efficiencies are available (some with two baths) at rates that start at $35 (one room) during the summer season and $57 from February through April.

The **Best Western Royal Palms Motel,** 1701 N. Tamiami Trail, Sarasota, FL 33580 (tel. 813/365-1342), is a motel with budget rates, large, comfortable rooms and efficiency units, a heated swimming pool, shuffleboard, a restaurant next door, and free coffee in rooms. During the winter season, doubles start at $48; in summer, $35. Efficiencies are $4 more. Children under 12 stay free and cribs are furnished without charge.

## Campgrounds

From the junction of I-75 and Hwy. 780 (Fruitville Road), go one mile east on Hwy. 780 to the **Camperland Sun N Fun RV Resort,** which has over 1,050 spaces in a semi-wooded, grassy suburban park. Most are full hookups; there are LP gas, flush toilets, showers, laundry, restaurant, recreation hall, recreation room, swimming pool, boating (no motors), lake fishing, mini-golf, planned group activities, 18 shuffleboard courts, horseshoes, volleyball, and local tours. Adults only; open all year. For full details, rates, and reservations, write them at 7125 Fruitville Rd., Sarasota, FL 33582 (tel. 813/371-2505).

The **Sarasota Lakes RV Resort,** 1674 University Parkway, Sarasota, FL 33580 (tel. 813/355-8585), has 420 sites, all with full hookups. You can reach them from exit 40 on I-75. All roads are paved, including sites, with concrete patios and picnic tables and individual yard lights. There are LP gas, flush toilets, a laundry, recreation hall, shuffleboard, swimming pool, and tennis courts. Rates start at $16.50 for two, depending on the season.

**WHERE TO EAT:** Sarasota's good eating places are spread all over the place, from St. Armands Key to downtown to the Tamiami Trail (both north and south). For convenience, I'll group my favorites by location.

## Around the Circle on St. Armands Key

For the past five years, Titus Letschert, a native of Holland, and Norbert Goldner, who hails from Berlin, have turned out such consistently good food at **Café L'Europe,** 431 Harding Circle (tel. 813/388-4415), that they've collected the *Holiday* Award for excellence for several years running. The cuisine (under the direction of chef August Mrozowski) is continental, with such specialties as roast duckling with black cherries and cognac sauce and veal Cordon Bleu, and so is the decor. The café is completely charming, with its four dining rooms accented by pink brick, arches, antique Italian tile, and lots of greenery. Lunch is served from 11 a.m. to 3 p.m., dinner from 5:30 to 10 p.m. (on Sunday from 6 to 10 p.m.), and if the crowds I encountered are usual, as I understand they are, reservations are a good idea. Entrees run $15 to $22 at dinner, less at lunch.

The **Columbia Restaurant,** St. Armands Circle (tel. 813/388-3987), is the Sarasota branch of its famous Tampa (Ybor City) parent. This was one of the first fine restaurants on St. Armands and has been voted one of Florida's top restaurants by *Florida Trend Magazine* for several years. The decor is classical Spanish, as is the cuisine. Paella is the dish most asked for here, but my own favorite is the black-bean soup—I could make a meal of it, and did once. In the Patio lounge, a cool oasis of Florida deco colors, green plants, and cozy seat groupings, there's dancing to a lively Latin group. The Columbia opens for lunch at 11 a.m., serves dinner until 11 p.m. (on Sunday from 1 to 11 p.m.), and the lounge stays open until 2 a.m. every day. Prices are in the $9 to $20 range for dinner, $6 to $10 for lunch, with a children's menu for less.

## Downtown Sarasota

I've been going to **Marina Jack's,** Marina Plaza, Island Park, right on the city's waterfront (tel. 813/365-4232), almost as long as I've been going to Sarasota, and I've suffered through at least one change of ownership, with differing levels of competence in the kitchen. But the setting for this place is so gorgeous that I'd munch on a hot dog happily just to sit and view the comings and goings in the boat basin or to see a boat pull up and dock right outside so its crew can come in to eat. The present owners (since 1979) have things shipshape once more. The food is good, the view even better than I remembered, and the guitar music downstairs in the cozy Deep Six Lounge a perfect way to end the evening. Do treat yourself to a hour or two here—daytime, at sunset, or after dark when the lights on the water are dreamy. There's a large menu, mostly seafood, and prices for complete dinners start at $8. I had the seafood platter, and it was delicious. Open daily from noon to 3 p.m. and 5 to 10 p.m. There are also marvelous lunch and dinner cruises that cost a mere $4 above menu prices. Call for days and hours.

At the Forest Lakes Golf Club, two blocks north of Webber, **The Rainforest,** 2401 S. Beneva Rd. (tel. 813/924-1221), is a relaxed place with lots of greenery and good food at moderate prices. Meals of beef (with prime ribs as specialty), seafood, veal, chicken, and duck run $10 to $14. There's also a very good Sunday brunch (11:30 a.m. to 2:30 p.m.) for $6. There's dancing in the lounge nightly except Monday from 8:30 to 1:30 a.m. Dinner hours are 5 to 9 p.m., lunch from 11:30 a.m. to 2:30 p.m., seven days a week, and dress is casual to dressy.

The **Old Heidelberg Castle,** 3rd Street and Washington Boulevard (tel. 813/366-3515), is another Sarasota institution. It's a fun place, specializing in German food (American dishes and seafood, also), a continuous show, and dancing to a Bavarian band, and you'll see all age groups out on the floor. The atmosphere is that of a Munich beer hall, with menu specialties like wienerschnitzel, sauerbraten, and fresh pig's knuckles. Complete dinner prices start at $9.25. Lunch is served from 11 a.m. to 2:30 p.m., dinner from 4:30 p.m. until everybody goes home (on Sunday, it's 4:30 to 11 p.m.). Happy Hour is 4 to 6 p.m. with low, low prices for drinks.

**NIGHTLIFE:** Entertainment and dancing in the various restaurants and lounges around Sarasota make up most of the after-dark activity. Besides **Old Heidelberg, Marina Jack's,** and **Columbia,** all mentioned under "Where to Eat," there's country music at **Shannon's Way Pub,** 3904 Tamiami Trail; jazz and soft rock at **Playground South,** 1927 Ringling Blvd.; and the **Moonraker Lounge** of the Holiday Inn North, 8221 N. Tamiami Trail. On Longboat Key, listening and dancing music is in the **Shipwreck Lounge** of the Holiday Inn, 4949 Gulf of Mexico Dr., and the **Tree House Lounge** of the Longboat Key Hilton, 4711 Gulf of Mexico Dr.

**THINGS TO SEE AND DO:** Many of Sarasota's sightseeing attractions are strung along North Tamiami Trail (U.S. 41), from about 27th Street all the way to the airport. The Civic Recreation Center, which includes Van Wezel Performing Arts Hall, is just off the Trail, on the bayfront, between 6th and 4th Avenue. Bayfront Drive (still part of that Tamiami Trail) runs along the water's edge and past the city marina, headquarters for many charter fishing boats.

### Theater

The **Asolo** (pronounced *"Ah*-slow") **State Theater Company of Florida** stages a repertory of seven plays from mid-February through Labor Day in the Asolo Theater in the **Ringling Museums** (tel. 813/355-5137). The theater itself is a treat (see "Sightseeing"), and performances are usually of top quality—in fact, several of our leading Broadway stars have done a repertory stint here before going on to fame. Call for schedules and ticket prices.

The enthusiastic (and very good!) **Players of Sarasota** have a year-round schedule of drama, comedy, and musicals, staged in their own 500-seat theater on 9th Street between Coconut and North Tamiami Trail (tel. 813/365-2494).

The concert season at **Van Wezel Performing Arts Hall,** 777 N. Tamiami Trail (tel. 813/953-3366), runs from September through June (with occasional mid-summer specials) and includes concerts, ballet, plays, films, and lectures. Call them to see what's scheduled and what prices are when you're in town.

The **Sarasota Opera Association** presents opera in a beautifully restored Mediterranean Revival theater called the **Sarasota Theater of the Arts,** at 61 N. Pineapple (tel. 813/953-7030). Performances run during February and March.

## Sightseeing

Even if you're a confirmed beach bum and sightseeing isn't on your agenda, *do* plan to take time out for the **Ringling Museums** (tel. 813/351-1600). They have to be seen to be believed, and you'll get far more than your $6 worth! The mansion (named Ca' d'Zan, which means House of John in Venetian dialect) was built by that master showman, John Ringling, for his Mable in 1925. He spent more than $1,500,000 and patterened it after the Doge's Palace on the Grand Canal in Venice. By the time he died in 1936, he'd amassed a priceless art collection, built a magnificent museum to house it on his estate overlooking the gulf, and arranged to leave estate, mansion, museum, and his personal fortune to the State of Florida. The elaborately furnished home is just as he lived in it, complete with a $50,000 Aeolian pipe organ and gold bathroom fixtures. The museum holds one of the largest Rubens collections in this country, along with art of the 17th, 18th, 19th, and 20th centuries (the classical marble building, with columns, arches, and courtyard, is worth seeing for itself alone). The state has added a **Museum of the Circus,** a treasurehouse of circus memorabilia from ancient times to Ringling Bros. days, and the **Asolo Theater,** an original 1798 Italian theater that was taken, piece by piece, from the castle of Catherine Cornaro at Asolo near Venice, Italy, and reassembled in a building of its own next to the Museum of Art. Now, is *that* a bargain at just $6? Ages 6 to 12 pay $2.50. Hours are 9 a.m. to 7 p.m. Monday through Friday, until 5 p.m. on Saturday, and Sunday hours are 11 a.m. to 6 p.m. And children under 6 are admitted free with an adult.

Nostalgia buffs will delight in **Bellm's Cars & Music of Yesterday,** 5500 N. Tamiami Trail, with its 170 antique, classic, and racing cars, and 1,400 antique music boxes and turn-of-the-century arcade. They've all been expertly restored to working order and their original splendor, and it's a real treat to hear hurdy-gurdies, calliopes, and nickelodeons tinkling away. There are hourly guided tours from 8:30 a.m. to 6 p.m. Monday through Saturday, on Sunday from 9:30 a.m. Adults pay $4.50; ages 6 through 16, $2.

There are two outstanding gardens open to the public in Sarasota. **The Jungle Gardens,** 3701 Bayshore Rd.—that's two miles north of the city center on U.S. 41, then two blocks west on Myrtle Street—has formal gardens also, but the real feature is the 16-acre wild jungle laced with winding trails through more than 5,200 varieties of palms, tropical plants, and flowering shrubs—an ecologist's delight! The wildlife includes monkeys, alligators, leopards, flamingos, waterfowl, emus, parrots, and macaws. And there's a "Jungle Bird Circus" with performing birds as well as a reptile show featuring alligators and snakes. The gardens are open from 9 a.m. to 5 p.m. every day, with admission charges of $5 for adults, $3 for ages 6 to 16, free for those 5 and under.

The **Marie Selby Botanical Gardens,** 811 S. Palm Ave., at the corner of U.S. 41 at downtown Sarasota bayfront, is the world's only botanical garden devoted to epiphytic "air" plant research and display. It has a world-renowned Orchid Identification Center and the International Bromeliad Identification

Center, and houses one of the world's best orchid collections, as well as Florida's finest display of hibiscus. A tropical display house features exotic tropical blooms in a rain-forest setting, and there's a museum devoted to botany and the arts. There's a trellis walk, waterfall, and winding paths through tropical plantings around the 16-acre peninsula. The gardens, as well as the plant, book, and gift shops, are open every day except Christmas from 10 a.m. to 5 p.m. Admission is $4, free to under-12s when accompanied by an adult.

### A Day in the Country

Seventeen miles east of Sarasota on Fla. 72, the **Myakka River State Park** is an outstanding wildlife area, with more than 238 identified bird species, deer, raccoon, otter, bobcats, and large rookeries. There's a bird walk along the lake, or you can rent a bike, or take a guided boat tour or the train tour (in season). There is picnicking at three designated areas, a refreshment concession, interpretive center, canoe rentals, campsites, and cabins with daily rates. If you want to do more than just look around, call 813/924-1027 between 8 a.m. and 5 p.m. for specific information, current rates, and reservations for any of the available facilities. Or write: Myakka River State Park, 13207 Fla. 72, Sarasota, FL 34241.

### Sports

Golfers can try their skill at the **Meadows Golf Club,** 3101 Longmeadow (tel. 813/371-1100), 2½ miles east of U.S. 301. Play is challenging on the Francis Duane–designed 18-hole course, and the scenery is picturesque. There are shady, tree-lined fairways at the **Foxfire** course, 7200 Proctor Rd. (tel. 813/921-7757), one mile east of I-75.

There are public **tennis courts** at **10th Street and U.S. 41; Gillespie Park,** 8th Street and Gillespie; **17th Street and Tuttle Avenue; Bee Ridge Park** on Wilkinson Road; on **Siesta Beach;** and at the **Newtown Community Center** at Myrtle Avenue and U.S. 301.

## 3. St. Petersburg–Tampa

Tampa Bay, where it bites into the mainland of Florida's west coast, creates a long, wide peninsula on the gulf side that is dominated by St. Petersburg and a smaller, narrow one jutting out into the bay itself that holds Tampa and, at its very tip, MacDill Air Force Base. Together they comprise what is commonly called Tampa–St. Pete by natives, or the Greater Tampa Bay Area by the more scholarly. By whatever name, this is a section rich in history, blessed by a subtropical climate, and so "healthy" that the American Medical Association pronounced it an excellent place for preventive-medicine living.

That AMA pronouncement almost did St. Petersburg in—after, of course, promoting a tremendous boom when hundreds of retiring couples chose this as their "last resort." So welcomed were the aging immigrants at first that rows of green benches were put up all along Central Avenue to provide convenient resting places, and curbs had ramps for wheelchairs or cane-carrying citizens. The population swelled with elderly residents, and one day the city fathers woke up to the fact that their senior-citizen image was beginning to hurt the town's long-range growth. A vigorous attack was launched to publicize the youthfulness of the majority of its residents (as well as the activeness of its elders) and the green benches disappeared. Pushing its "Sunshine City" label, St. Petersburg lured new industry and upgraded resort facilities along the string of offshore islands called the **Holiday Isles** (that's St. Petersburg Beach, Treasure Island, Madeira Beach, Redington Beach, Indian Rocks Beach, and Belleair Beach), with the result that young, old, and middle-aged mingle happily here today.

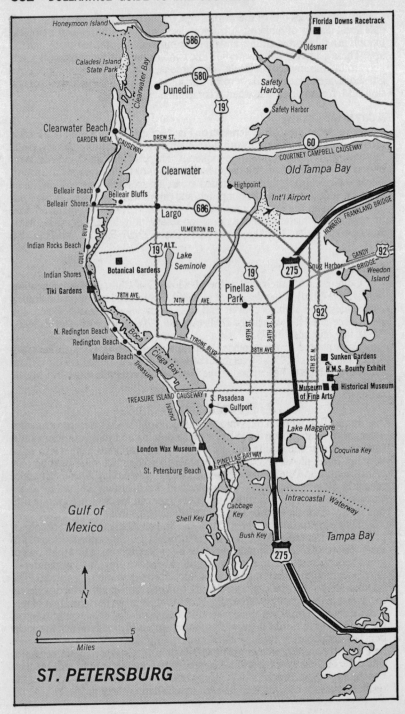

Honeymoon Island

Florida Downs Racetrack

586

Oldsmar

Caladesi Island
State Park

580

Safety
Harbor

Dunedin

19

Safety Harbor

Clearwater Beach

GARDEN MEM. CAUSEWAY

DREW ST.

60

COURTNEY CAMPBELL CAUSEWAY

Old Tampa Bay

Clearwater

Highpoint

Int'l Airport

Belleair Beach

Belleair Bluffs

686

Belleair Shores

Largo

ULMERTON RD.

Indian Rocks Beach

ALT.
19

Lake
Seminole

Indian Shores

Botanical Gardens

19

275

Snug Harbor

92

GANDY BRIDGE

Weedon
Island

Tiki Gardens

78TH AVE.

74TH AVE.

Pinellas
Park

N. Redington Beach

Boca

Redington Beach

TYRONE BLVD.

Madeira Beach

49TH ST.

34TH ST. N.

88TH AVE.

92

4TH ST. N.

Sunken Gardens

H.M.S. Bounty Exhibit

Museum
of Fine Arts

Historical Museum

TREASURE ISLAND CAUSEWAY

S. Pasadena

Gulfport

Lake Maggiore

London Wax Museum

PINELLAS BAYWAY

St. Petersburg Beach

Coquina Key

Gulf of
Mexico

Shell Key

Cabbage
Key

Intracoastal Waterway

Bush Key

Tampa Bay

275

N

0        5

Miles

**ST. PETERSBURG**

The beaches are connected to the mainland by the free St. Petersburg Beach Causeway, and Pinellas Bayway which charges a 30¢ toll. Gulf Boulevard runs the length of the Holiday Isles. Getting around St. Petersburg itself is fairly easy if you remember that all avenues, terraces, and places run east and west, streets and ways run north and south, and Central Avenue is the north-south dividing line. There is a very good bus system for the city and suburbs, and the **St. Petersburg City Transit Company** gives route info if you call 813/893-RIDE. The island communities are served by **Gulf Beach Transit** (tel. 813/896-2655).

Across the bay, Tampa has never had any problem with an image of senility; it's been a busy commercial center almost from the start when the U.S. Army early on established a fort here to protect the strategic harbor. Long before U.S. settlers arrived, however, the bay had attracted the Spanish, who were hounded by out native Indians, and pirates who found it a convenient hiding place. One of those, José Gaspar Gasparilla, prompts a modern-day festival that rivals New Orlean's Mardi Gras for sheer energy and color; a pirate galleon, the *José Gasparilla,* complete with costumed crew and captain, sails up Tampa Bay in early February to end five days of celebration to "capture" Tampa and parade through the streets on fantastic floats.

Occupied by federal troops during the Civil War and the object of a Confederate blockade, Tampa nevertheless flourished, and when both Henry B. Plant's railroad and the Cuban cigarmaking industry from Key West arrived simultaneously in the 1880s, it boomed. Even the Spanish-American War proved profitable for Tampa, when it was made a primary outfitting and embarkation port for U.S. troops.

Today MacDill Air Force Base continues the military emphasis that's always been so important in Tampa: **Ybor** (pronounced "*Ee*-bo") **City** is a self-contained town of Cuban cigarmakers that preserves the color and gaiety of their homeland; and although vacation pursuits are important, industries like the Anheuser-Busch Brewery provide an enduring commercial prosperity.

Driving in Tampa is simplified by the fact that Florida Avenue divides east from west, John F. Kennedy Boulevard and Frank Adamo Drive divide north and south, numbered avenues run east and west, and numbered streets run north and south. If you want to park the car and depend on public transportation (and it's pretty good), **Tampa City Bus Lines** will provide route and fare information if you call 813/251-1078.

**WHERE TO STAY:** St. Petersburg Beach is the perfect vacation headquarters in this area. Two causeways lead to the mainland and sightseeing in St. Pete and Tampa, while a lovely beach drive goes north through the other Holiday Isles, then across to a coastal mainland highway on up to Clearwater and Tarpon Springs. If you're in the mood for it, Walt Disney World is just two hours east on I-4 and Weeki Wachee's water show about an hour north on U.S. 19.

Looking for all the world like a huge, pastel-pink strawberry sundae sculpted in the shape of a Moorish castle and set in a dish of sugar-white sand, the **Don CeSar Beach Resort Hotel,** 3400 Gulf Beach Blvd., St. Petersburg Beach, FL 33706 (tel. 813/360-1881), is clearly the most elegant place to stay on the beach. Built back during the '20s boom years, it lay vacant after the boom subsided, served as a rest and rehabilitation center during World War II, did a stint as a government office building, was vacated and threatened with demolition, was rescued and restored by local citizens, and in 1975—perhaps its proudest moment—earned a place on the National Register of Historic Places! Today the hotel has spacious rooms and suites with sumptuous furnishings (all with water views and some with private balconies), a heated pool, whirlpool, playground for the kids (and a "Kids Ltd." activities program), parasailing, jet skis, aquabikes, and lighted tennis courts. The high-ceilinged, elegant (there's just no other word for polished marble and tile floors, marble columns, and crystal chandeliers) lobby and public rooms set the tone for the three restaurants and even the breakfast rooms. After dark, there's dancing and entertainment, and the old-fashioned ice-cream parlor puts the whipped cream on the sundae, so to speak. Double-room rates range from $95 to $150, depending on season and location. Certainly above the moderate level, but not at all out of line for this kind of old-style beach luxury.

The **Sandpiper Beach Resort,** 6000 Gulf Blvd., (P.O. Box 66307), St. Petersburg Beach, FL 33736 (tel. 813/360-5551, or toll free 800/237-0707), offers a variety of luxury accommodations. There are hotel rooms with wet bar, fridge, and coffeemaker, and one-, two-, and three-bedroom suites. Executive suites on the Concierge Level enjoy many extras, plus the personal services of the concierge. Facilities at this deluxe resort include both a beachfront and an enclosed pool, fully equipped exercise room, beachfront dining at Piper's Patio Café, and gourmet meals in the Brown Derby Restaurant and Lounge. This resort and its sister, **TradeWinds Beach Resort Hotel,** 5500 Gulf Blvd., (P.O. Box 66307), St. Petersburg Beach, FL 33736 (tel. 813/360-7002, or toll free 800/237-0707), are unique in their concern for preserving the natural environment of this fragile beachfront. In fact, they have been awarded the prestigious Phoenix Award for "ongoing involvement in environmental and cultural preservation programs"— reason enough, in my book, for choosing these elegant hostelries for a vacation with folks who take care not to exploit and deplete Florida's coastal natural resources! In-season rates at both are in the $126 to $150 range for doubles; one-bedroom suites, $138 to $200. Lower rates other times of the year, and there's no charge for children under 12 sharing with their parents. Both hotels also have attractive packages available.

Directly on the gulf, with its own stretch of private beach, the **Holiday Inn,** 5300 Gulf Blvd., St. Petersburg Beach, FL 33706 (tel. 813/360-6911, or toll free 800/HOLIDAY), has exceptionally well-decorated rooms with oversize beds and resort-style furnishings, with poolside efficiencies and king-size "leisure rooms" also available. The pool is freshwater and heated, and both food and beverages are available poolside. Up in the rooftop restaurant, the view of the gulf and Boca Ciega Bay makes dining (or cocktails in the Galleon Lounge) a spectacular sort of thing. The kids will stay busy in the game room when they tire of the beach, and there are sail and paddleboat rentals. Double rooms start at $90 in winter, then drop.

Farther north, the **Bilmar Beach Resort,** 10650 Gulf Blvd., Treasure Island, FL 33706 (tel. 813/360-5531, or toll free 800/826-9724), has 175 units in eight-, four-, and three-story buildings strung directly along the gulf. Some have private patios, others have balconies, and all have refrigerators. All are spacious and nicely decorated in beach colors. There are two pools, miniature golf, and tennis courts. There's also a lovely dining room and entertainment in one of the two lounges. Double rooms cost $80 and up in winter, considerably less in summer.

Set on 200 feet of beachfront, the **Buccaneer Resort Motel,** 10800 Gulf Blvd., Treasure Island, FL 33706 (tel. 813/367-1908), has rooms that are spacious, stylishly decorated, and open onto a covered ground-floor veranda or the second-floor balcony veranda. Besides the beautiful pool, there's a hot tub, shuffleboard, a card room, and tables and umbrellas on the beach lounging area. Nearby, you'll find tennis, golf, and charter fishing. Rates for doubles are $39 and up in winter, lower in summer.

You can opt for the usual double room or a villa apartment (accommodates up to four) or a beachfront apartment (holds up to six) at **The Alden,** 5900 Gulf

Blvd., St. Petersburg Beach, FL 33706 (tel. 813/360-7081, or toll free, 800/237-2530). Most of the rooms and apartments have either private balconies or patios, affording real privacy. Recreation facilities include two heated pools, lighted tennis courts, game room, cookout facilities, two Jacuzzi spas, sundeck, and of course that gulf beach. Furnishings in all facilities are modern, with lots of tasteful colors used in decorating. The rates are $65 in winter for double rooms, $83 and up for the fully equipped villa apartments.

Not directly on the gulf, but convenient to it, is the **Tarpon Springs Days Inn,** at 816 U.S. 19 in Lake Tarpon (P.O. Box 786, Tarpon Springs, FL 33589; tel. 813/934-0859, or toll free 800/325-2525), with double rooms and suites at $38 to $52 (weekly rates also available).

There's an all-suite **Guest Quarters Hotel** (see Chapter I) at 555 N.W. Westshore Blvd., Tampa, FL 33609 (tel. 813/875-1555, or toll free 800/424-2900), with rates of $115 to $165. Highly recommended.

**WHERE TO EAT:** Good restaurants, in all price ranges, are strung up and down the Holiday Isles and as far up as Clearwater and Tarpon Springs. St. Petersburg and Tampa, of course, have their share, but my theory is that most of your time will be spent nearer the shore, so we'll head there first.

## St. Petersburg Beach and Holiday Isles

On the Treasure Island Causeway at Gulf Boulevard, **Gigi's** (tel. 813/360-6905) is one of a South Florida chain. In a setting of red carpets, wood-paneled walls with lots of arches, and stone fountains, Gigi's serves good Italian dinners (and if the large menu skipped anything, *I* didn't spot it) and pizza. Wine is available by the glass, carafe, or bottle. Lunch is relaxed, and at dinner the ambience is enhanced by candlelight. Prices are moderate. It opens at 11 a.m., closes at 11 p.m. daily, and there's take-out and delivery service.

Farther north on the beach, at Redington Shores (one mile north of the bath club), the **Red Cavalier,** 17855 Gulf Blvd., (tel. 813/393-8741), begins its swashbuckling theme right in the entrance, where there's a mini-gallery of paintings portraying cavaliers through the ages. Inside the informal, comfortable dining room—with its wall of windows and high, peaked ceiling—there's a menu featuring Danish lobster tails, top sirloin, prime ribs, and fresh seafood, all at moderate prices (beginning at $6.75). The Bonfire Lounge, in an Old English setting, has a Happy Hour from 4 to 6 p.m. and entertainment every night except Sunday and Monday. Doors open every day at 11 a.m. (1 p.m. on Sunday) and close at 10 p.m.

Indian Rocks Beach is home to the famous Tiki Gardens (see "Sightseeing") and **Trader Frank's Restaurant and Lounge,** 19601 Gulf Blvd., Indian Shores (tel. 813/595-2567). Here Jo and Frank Byars have created a little corner of Polynesia, and the cuisine carries out that theme with specialties like hula tail shrimp at dinner, with even lunchtime hot dogs and hamburgers dressed up with a little pineapple and Polynesian "Kikiki" labels. It's a fun, informal place for lunch or dinner, or cocktails in the Wiki-wiki Lounge (try a Tiki Typhoon or Hawaiian Sunset, just for kicks), all served by sarong-clad waitresses, at prices much more moderate than the somewhat touristy surroundings would lead you to expect (starting at $7.50 for dinner, $3.75 for lunch). If the Tiki Gardens are on your sightseeing agenda, then Trader Frank's should be on it for lunch or dinner. Hours are 11:30 a.m. to 10 p.m. seven days a week.

## In Clearwater

Just a hop, skip, and a jump north of the Holiday Isles, Clearwater has a restaurant that has become famed throughout the state since it started in a modest manner back in 1957. The **Kapok Tree Restaurant,** 923 McMullen Booth Rd. (tel. 813/726-0504), takes its name from the gigantic tree that came from India as a seedling and now is the focal point of the restaurant. Like the tree, that small restaurant has grown into a huge, rambling establishment, with a garden-palace-theater sort of environment that brings to mind the Tivoli outside Rome or the other one in Copenhagen—or a combination of the two! The Terrace Room, Grand Ballroom, and Tropicana Room are among eight spectacular dining spaces. The gardens, full of plants and fountains and sculpture, are a special treat. The menu is almost as large as the restaurant, and prices are just above budget: (dinners begin at $8 and run to $17). Corn fritters come with complete dinners of chicken, shrimp and other seafood, and steak and other beef dishes. The Kapok Tree is more like an experience than a restaurant. Call to check hours and reserve.

### Tarpon Springs

A day at Tarpon Springs wouldn't be complete without Greek food. In fact, lunch at the Plaka Restaurant followed by an afternoon of browsing, a sponge-boat trip, or the Spongeorama show (see "Sightseeing") and then dinner at Louis Pappas's elegant restaurant is a day a traveler's dreams are made of!

The **Plaka,** 769 Dodecanese Blvd., (tel. 813/934-4752), is a marvelous little Greek restaurant that seats 76 in the vine-trellised dining room. Ted and Goldie Varas call their gyro (that's ground beef with herbs and spices wrapped in pita bread with onions, tomatoes, and tsadziki sauce) the "Greeks' answer to McDonald's," and it sells for $3. The special Greek salad is all it should be, with lettuce, tomatoes, onions, green pepper, feta cheese, beets, cucumbers, Greek olives, Greek peppers, and anchovies, accompanied by bread and butter—for $2.50. A glass of retsina, the wine of Greece, at $1, makes it a lunch to remember. The Plaka used to be a Greek pastry shop, and the delicacies are still made for Ted and Goldie by a local pastry shop from recipes brought over years ago. They, and all other items on the menu, can be bought to take out.

**Louis Pappas' Restaurant,** 10 W. Dodecanese Blvd., at the corner of Alt. U.S. 19 and Anclote River (tel. 813/937-5101), is a completely different kind of Greek restaurant. On the Anclote riverfront right where you turn to go down to the sponge docks, it is as much museum as restaurant, although the food is first-rate. Doric, Ionic, and Corinthian designs are worked into the architecture and decor, with Greek lamps dangling over tables, statues scattered about, a life-size, three-dimensional mural of the *Death of Hector,* and green plants adding a touch of garden atmosphere. It's a large place, and even has docking facilities for those who come by water. The menu, which features Greek salad, has seafood, of course, kalamarakia (that's squid), moussaka, and prime ribs and steak. Dinners start at $8, and you get a lot of Greek elegance as well as good food for the moderate prices. Hours are 11:30 a.m. to 11 p.m. daily.

### St. Petersburg

Just across the Sunken Gardens (see "Sightseeing"), **Bradford's Coach House,** 1900 4th St. North (tel. 813/822-7982), creates a restful Olde English setting with old brick and stained glass. It's been here since 1934 and is dearly beloved by the natives (much more so than the newer branch at 132 2nd St. North, which has a "restaurant modern" atmosphere). The menu features prime ribs, choice steaks, frogs' legs, and seafood, all at moderate prices (beginning at $3.50 for lunch, $7 for dinner). There are five separate rooms, including a lounge with entertainment in the evening. It's a good idea to reserve at this popular spot.

## Tampa

*The* restaurant in Tampa is the **Columbia,** in Ybor City at 22nd Street and 7th Avenue (tel. 813/248-4961). Covering an entire city block and seating more than 1,500 people, the Columbia was called "the finest Spanish restaurant in the world" by the Spanish government some years ago. The restaurant started back in 1905 and has grown to include 11 dining rooms. The interior can only be called splendid, with lots of decorated tile, arches, iron grillwork, paintings, and porticoes. José Greco–type waiters seem to have been created to match the setting. Specialties are, of course, Spanish, with paella and black-bean soup leading the list. Dinner can run anywhere from $9 to $21, and you'll dine while watching flamenco dancers. Open from 11 a.m. until midnight every day of the year, and in spite of its size, you'd best reserve.

Another Tampa restaurant much loved by locals is **Bern's Steak House,** 1208 S. Howard Ave. (tel. 813/251-2421). In a setting of antique furnishings, gilt-framed paintings, and statuary, the specialty here is aged beef, but equally notable are the vegetables, fresh from the owner's farm. Seafood is the freshest, since fish and lobster come straight from three tanks in the kitchen. Desserts are a specialty. There's also an excellent wine cellar. Prices are in the $16-and-up range, hours are 5 to 11 p.m., and reservations are definitely in order.

**NIGHTLIFE:** Typical of the after-dark activity in this area are: the revolving **Bali Hi Lounge** at the top of the St. Petersburg Beach Hilton Inn, 5250 Gulf Blvd. (tel. 813/360-1811), where entertainment and dancing go on until 2 a.m. every day except Monday, and the 11th-floor location showcases spectacular sunsets; and the **Kon-Tiki Supper Club** in the Hawaiian Inn, 6200 Gulf Blvd., St. Petersburg Beach (tel. 813/367-1902). These are only examples—almost all major hotels and motels and many leading restaurants and lounges feature some form of entertainment in the evening. Check local newspapers or *Guide* for current goings-on.

**THINGS TO SEE AND DO:** The biggest attraction along this stretch of the Gulf Coast is the **beach** and related sports. However, if you can take just so much sun and sand and water, there's plenty to keep you otherwise occupied.

## Tours

**Gray Line** buses, c/o Gulf Coast Gray Line, P.O. Box 145, St. Petersburg, FL 33731 (tel. 813/822-3577), tour St. Pete and the surrounding territory, with varying departures and prices.

Over on St. Petersburg Beach, the *Capt. Anderson* sails from the pier behind Dolphin Village Shopping Center, 4901 Gulf Blvd. (tel. 813/360-2619), every Tuesday, Wednesday, Friday, and Saturday on dinner-dance cruises. The cruise lasts from 7 to 10 p.m., and the $17.50 (adult) and $15.50 (children) fare includes dinner and entertainment. There are daytime sightseeing cruises Tuesday through Saturday from 2 to 4 p.m., and these cost $4.50 for adults, $2.50 for children.

## Theater

Check after September 1987 for what's doing at the **Tampa Bay Performing Arts Center.** Plans are for a 300-seat Studio Theatre and a 2,400-seat Festival Hall, both of which will undoubtedly stage outstanding productions.

## Fishing

All sorts of fish lurk in these waters, and catches of 40 to 50 are not unusual when a particular species is in season. Among those that lure the boats out again and again are pompano, whiting, sheepshead, trout, kingfish, drum, flounder, mackerel, and redfish—that's not a complete list, by any means. If pulling them in is what makes you happy, check with your hotel for the names of charter boats currently operating in the area—they change much too rapidly for me to give you reliable information.

## Golf

Golfers won't have to look far for courses—they're all over the place. A few of the many that are open for public play are: the **Clearwater Golf Park,** 1875 Airport Dr., in Clearwater (tel. 813/447-5272); the **Glen Oaks,** in Clearwater at 1345 Court St. (tel. 813/446-7275); and the **Pasadena Golf Club** at 1600 Royal Palm Ave. South in St. Petersburg (tel. 813/341-3641). Greens fees and cart costs vary, and reservations should be made as far in advance as possible.

## Tennis

The **St. Petersburg Tennis Center,** 650 18th Ave. South (tel. 813/894-4378), has a clubhouse and 19 courts open to the public. On Treasure Island, the **Paradise Island Tennis Club,** 10315 Paradise Blvd. (tel. 813/360-6062), has 21 courts, six lighted, and the clubhouse is open to the public. In Clearwater, the **Bayfront Municipal Courts** are at 3 Pierce St., with nine courts and metered lights—no reservations.

## Sailing

You'll find sailing instructions, sailboat rides on Tampa Bay, charter sailboats, and sightseeing cruises at the **Municipal Marina, 300 2nd Ave. SE,** St. Pete.

## Sightseeing

The **St. Petersburg Chamber of Commerce** may be contacted at 100 2nd Ave. North (P.O. Box 1371), St. Petersburg, FL 33731 (tel. 813/821-4069); the **Greater Tampa Chamber of Commerce** is at 801 E. Kennedy Blvd. (P.O. Box 420), Tampa, FL 33601 (tel. 813/228-7777).

If you stay at St. Petersburg Beach, you can't miss the **London Wax Museum** at 5505 Gulf Blvd. (across the street from the gulf side). And you really *shouldn't* miss it—as my grandmother used to say, "it's a curiosity." Every single one of the more than 100 life-size wax figures was created by Louis Tussaud in London (the very best in this field). Historical figures are here, there's a chamber of horrors that will give you the creeps (and a thrill!), and the kids will love such storybook characters as Sleeping Beauty, Little Miss Muffet, and Red Ridinghood. There's an ice-cream parlor and video game room as well. Admission is $4 for adults, $2 for ages 4 through 12; it opens at 9 a.m. with varying closing times (usually between 5 and 7 p.m.) every day except Sunday, when it opens at noon.

North of St. Petersburg Beach, at Indian Shores, the **Tiki Gardens,** 19601 Gulf Blvd., are landscaped with tropical plants, birds, temples, and statuary, creating a South Seas environment that's enchanting. Ten shops offer imports and there's a Polynesian restaurant, Trader Frank's (see "Where to Eat," above). Garden tours ($2 for adults, $1 for ages 3 through 12) run from 9:30 a.m. to 10:30 p.m.

If you've ever heard of St. Petersburg's famous "Million Dollar Pier," don't look for it now. It stood for some 40 years at the foot of Second Avenue NE, jutting out into Tampa Bay, but in recent years it's been replaced by a **Mu-**

**nicipal Pier** that holds a sort of upside-down pyramid. The five-level complex houses 19 ethnic-oriented shops, restaurants, a cocktail lounge (fun place to watch the sailboats below), and an observation deck (great at sunset!). The view of the bay and the harbor with its hundreds of yachts is fantastic and the shops are fun.

Docked at the pier is **H.M.S.** *Bounty,* the authentic replica of the famous ship that Metro-Goldwyn-Mayer had made in Nova Scotia (from the original blueprints on file in the British Museum) for their epic *Mutiny on the Bounty.* Even the setting seems authentic, for the Vinoy Basin at the pier has been turned into a bit of Tahiti to surround the ship. On board, the recorded voices of Charles Laughton as Captain Bligh and Clark Gable in his role of Fletcher Christian brings the true-life drama into focus as you roam the decks. This little bit of history come alive is open from 9 a.m. to 10 p.m. every day, and admission is $4 for adults, $2.25 for ages 4 through 12.

One of Florida's most beautiful tropical gardens is at St. Petersburg. The **Sunken Gardens,** 1825 4th St. North, are open every day from 9 a.m. until 5:30 p.m., and it's not inconceivable that you could spend an entire day wandering through the pathways past the more than 7,000 varieties of native Florida trees and exotic plants that have been transplanted here from all over the world. And wildlife is here too, in the walk-through aviary with its hundreds of colorful birds, monkeys, and even African pgymy goats. There's also an impressive *King of Kings* biblical presentation. Well worth the $5 admission ($3.50 for ages 6 through 12).

Maybe it's not strictly a sightseeing attraction, but if you come to St. Petersburg from any route other than U.S. 19 South and miss the **Sunshine Skyway,** it's worth a trip out to see the series of bridges and causeways that stretch some 15 miles across lower Tampa Bay to the Bradenton side. Cross the four-mile-long main Skyway Bridge (it stands about 15 stories above the water) for a 50¢ toll, or stop short of it in one of the recreation areas, where there are facilities for fishing, picnicking, and swimming.

In Tampa, don't miss **Ybor City,** the famous Latin section founded in 1886 by Vicente Martinez Ybor after Tampa's Board of Trade made the cigarmakers of Key West an offer they couldn't refuse to move their industry north to this area. The two-mile-square area, bounded by Nebraska Avenue, 22nd Street, Columbus Drive, and East Broadway, is a self-contained Cuban "city," loaded with cigar factories and Latin charm that spills out from stores and restaurants. Building façades with ornate grillwork and old brick walls, garden patios, sidewalk cafés, and art displays—but most of all, the infectious gaiety of the people who inhabit this place—combine to create an atmosphere so authentic the complex has been recorded in the National Register of Historic Places. Lots of little Cuban eateries and the famous Columbia Restaurant (see "Where to Eat") are here.

Another "don't miss" in Tampa is **Busch Gardens, The Dark Continent,** 3000 Busch Blvd. (tel. 813/988-5171), Tampa, on Fla. 580, 2½ miles east of its junction with I-75 (you'll see the Busch Boulevard exit). This 300-acre park with its turn-of-the-century African theme has one of the largest collection of mammals, reptiles, and birds in North America, including a 60-acre veldt, the Serengeti Plain, where more than 400 head of big game roam free. You can view it from steam train, monorail, or skyride. Also, Moroccan shopping bazaar and trained animal shows; *African Queen* boat cruise, Python thrill ride, Swinging Vines, Monstrous Mamba, log flume, and games area; Anheuser-Busch brewery tour; bird gardens with trained bird shows; white tiger exhibit; food facilities; and travel park for overnight camping. Timbuktu is patterned after the mystical city of the 16th century with more rides, dolphin show, and 1,200-seat

Festhaus restaurant. Open daily from 9:30 a.m. to 6 p.m. with extended summer hours. One admission includes all, $17.50. Children 2 and under, free. Parking is $2 per vehicle.

One block east of Busch Gardens is **Adventure Island,** a 26-acre water park with 300-foot body flumes, wave pool, main pool, kiddie pools, 40-foot speed slide into a pool, picnic areas, and food facilities. Admission and parking are separate from the Busch Gardens: $10.50 for ages 3 and up.

## Tarpon Springs

I'm always a little afraid to go back to Tarpon Springs (about 30 miles north of St. Petersburg on Alternate U.S. 19) for fear the colorful old Greek settlement will have changed. Well, to be honest, it *has* changed since I first discovered it back in the early '60s, but the changes haven't spoiled its charm, and the crowds of tourists all seem to take on the relaxed, hospitable personality of hardy Greek sponge divers who built the community on the Anclote River and its bayous. They came here after a dismal attempt to establish themselves among the sponge divers of Key West (they were "invited" to leave by the Key Westers and after a period of what amounted to war, they moved here—a happy choice, as it turned out). The **Tarpon Springs Chamber of Commerce** is at 124 E. Lemon St., Tarpon Springs, FL 33589 (tel. 813/937-6109).

Strolling Dodecanese Boulevard along the sea wall, watching the sponge boats (decorated with Greek symbols), browsing through the curio shops, stopping for lunch (see "Where to Eat") in a friendly Greek restaurant, attending the sponge auctions in the courtyard of the **Sponge Exhibit** (Tuesday and Friday mornings), taking in the **Spongeorama Exhibit Center,** 510 Dodecanese Blvd. (tel. 813/937-4111), and roaming through the re-created Greek village within its confines (it's open from 10 a.m. to 5 p.m. and costs $1 for adults, 50¢ for ages 4 through 11), or just walking from the sound of one Greek record to another and playing Zorba in my mind—all make this a magical place for me, and it gets better every time I go back. Of course, there are other things to see here too— like the magnificent Byzantine-style **St. Nicholas Greek Orthodox Cathedral** at 36 N. Pinellas Ave. There's no fee to visit the church, but you must be "properly attired."

I've never managed to be at Tarpon Springs for the **Festival of Epiphany** on January 6 when the priest blesses the waters, young boys dive for a golden cross, everybody joins in the parade through town wearing traditional Greek costumes, and the whole town joins in a night of revelry, with banquets, native dancing, and high spirits. Someday, I promise myself, I'll make that event. In the meantime, Tarpon Springs is the highlight of every visit I make to this part of Florida's Gulf Coast, and it's bound to be a delight to any tourist.

**READER'S HOTEL SUGGESTION—TARPON SPRINGS:** "Innisbrook Resort, P.O. Box 1088, Tarpon Springs, FL 34286 (tel. 813/937-3124), is all you could ask for if you're looking for a complete sports resort in a semitropical climate. There are marvelous golf courses, tennis courts, racquetball courts, no fewer than six swimming pools, and three clubhouses with excellent restaurants. Accommodations are in really luxurious condominiums. They're less than a half hour from the Tampa airport, and they'll arrange to meet your plane. Our best recommendations" (Mrs. S. Debnam, Virginia Beach, Va.).

## Weeki Wachee Spring

About 60 miles north of St. Petersburg on U.S. 19 (at its intersection with Fla. 50), is a "mermaid show" that makes the drive worthwhile. Weeki Wachee Spring, Brooksville, FL 34298 (tel. 904/596-2062), is actually the source of a river that runs 12 miles to the Gulf of Mexico, producing more than 168 million gallons of water a day, and so deep that they've measured only as far as 150 feet down and don't know how much farther it is to the bottom, although they've probed another 400 feet with lights. Well, around this natural wonder, there's a million-dollar auditorium where up to 400 people can watch underwater ballet, comedy, and acrobatics through 19 *very thick* plate-glass windows. When the show is over, you can go on the Wilderness River Cruise down the Weeki Wachee River, where an Indian trading post, Seminole Indian animal traps, and lots of wild animals can be seen on shore. The whole thing costs $8 ($5 for ages 3 through 11), and—you should pardon the pun—it's one whale of a show! Hours are 9 a.m. to 6 p.m.

# Chapter XIX

# ALONG THE GULF FROM FLORIDA TO NEW ORLEANS

### 1. Florida's Panhandle (Panama City)
### 2. Mobile, Alabama
### 3. Mississippi's Gulf Coast (Pascagoula and Biloxi)

THE QUICKEST WAY TO DRIVE to New Orleans from Florida's west coast is north from St. Petersburg via U.S. 19 to where it intersects with I-10 just beyond Capps, then follow **I-10** all the way across. That's if you're in a hurry. Be warned, however, that you'll miss some of Florida's most glorious beaches, a great deal of worthwhile sightseeing, and you won't even get a *glimpse* of the gulf.

A far more interesting and scenic alternative is that offered by **U.S. 98,** which branches off U.S. 19 at Perry, to Panama City (through Apalachicola and Port St. Joe), then on through Pensacola to Mobile, Alabama. A short stretch of I-10 from Mobile leads west to U.S. 90, which follows the Mississippi Gulf Coast through Pascagoula, Biloxi, Gulfport, and Bay St. Louis to New Orleans. As I said, this route is *not* the one to follow if you're in a hurry—but there are few more delightful drives than this in the entire Southeast, especially if you allow overnight (or longer) stops along the way. My heartiest recommendations go to stops in Panama City and Mobile or Pascagoula (they're so close to each other you'll probably want to choose one or the other, not all). Biloxi is another popular resort that offers an attractive alternative to Pascagoula. In this chapter, then, you'll find accommodations, restaurants, and sightseeing tips for each of these waystops—and I *hope* you won't opt for that quick I-10 drive!

## 1. Florida's Panhandle (Panama City)

Where Florida's Gulf Coast curves under the top of the state, the 108-mile stretch of pure white sand beach, with an offshore formation that makes for good surf, has been dubbed the "Miracle Strip." More than a dozen resort areas bloom between Panama City and Pensacola, Florida's last outpost before the Alabama Border. Although temperatures here range as much as ten degrees lower than those farther south in the state, beaches are pretty well populated year round, and they have become a mecca for students from neighboring Alabama and Georgia during school holidays. Indeed, many residents from those states weekend along this coast regularly. It's a summer "season" in these parts, and like the St. Augustine area, bargain rates are charged in the winter.

Along the coast, history has seen five national flags fly triumphantly, although some for a remarkably short period. Pensacola, for instance, changed hands some 17 times before it settled down as a permanent part of the U.S.! Inland, around Tallahassee, the terrain changes to rolling hills, great oaks hung with Spanish moss, and crystal-clear lakes, with pre–Civil War mansions lending an Old South air.

For the tourist, the beaches unquestionably hold the greatest attraction. To "do" those, as well as such area sights as Tallahassee's beautiful gardens, Pensacola and its U.S. Naval Air Station, we'll base at Panama City. From here, Tallahassee and Pensacola are each two hours away.

**YOUR PANAMA CITY BASE:** Situated on St. Andrew Bay, just off the Gulf of Mexico, Panama City began life in 1765 as a sleepy little fishing village (the Spanish were there in the 1500s but soon moved on). Today its deep-water harbor and $7-million marina, at the foot of Harrison Avenue, make it an important industrial center as well as a thriving resort city. A little to the west, directly on the gulf, Panama City Beach's *only* business is pleasure—and vacationers find it in full measure along a near-perfect strand of white sand. Accommodations are plentiful and less expensive, generally, than those in South Florida. Southeast of the city, at the end of Fla. 392, St. Andrew State Recreation Area is a 1,063-acre point of land dividing St. Andrew Bay from the gulf. Wide beaches and high dunes make it an attractive area for protected swimming, picnicking, fishing, and boating.

**WHERE TO STAY:** At the beach—that's the logical place for vacationers to stay, and that's where you'll find the following accommodations, either directly on the gulf or not far away.

The **Sandpiper-Beacon Motel,** 17403 West U.S. 98, Panama City, FL 32407 (tel. 904/234-2154), is a family-oriented motel right on the gulf, with a wide variety of accommodations: rooms with refrigerators, most with complete kitchens, and two- and three-room combinations. Furnishings are modern and colorfully decorated. In addition to two outdoor heated pools, there's one indoors, and there are sailboat rentals available. The dining room, open for all three meals, is moderately priced (another convenience for families). Doubles here range from a low of $35 in winter to $55 in the summer.

The smaller **Sea Aqua,** 17643 West U.S. 98, Panama City, FL 32407 (tel. 904/234-2163), also has kitchens and nice, well-furnished rooms on the gulf. No restaurant, but there's one just a block away. Double rooms are $56 to $64 in summer, lower in the fall and winter.

Private patios and balconies are features of most rooms at the **Fiesta,** 13623 West U.S. 98, Panama City, FL 32407 (tel. 904/235-1000), and their units with kitchens will accommodate up to six people (they're large efficiencies, not apartments). Decor is bright, with a slight "south of the border" accent, and there's a pool as well as the gulf out front. The nearest restaurant is a quarter mile away—well within walking distance. Rates during the summer run $55 and up for doubles, $70 and up for kitchen units; both are much lower other months.

Set on 1,500 acres about halfway between Panama City and Pensacola, the **Bluewater Bay Resort,** P.O. Box 247, Niceville, FL 32578 (tel. 904/897-2186, or toll free 800/874-2128), is a short drive from the gulf and attractions of Northwest Florida's "Miracle Strip" along U.S. 98, yet secluded enough to offer peace and tranquility not found elsewhere. Nestled between Choctawhatchee Bay and Eglin reserve lands near Fort Walton Beach on grounds that have won environmental awards for their careful development, the resort has a full-service marina, a swim and tennis club, private beach island, and a championship golf course. Accommodations come in the form of lovely studio, two-, or three-bedroom condominium apartments in Marina Cove Villas that provide hotel services, or beautiful stucco, cypress, and cedar villas. All are completely furnished, and luxury touches include fireplaces, skylights and clerestory windows, screened lanais, wood deck patios and balconies, and wet bars. Choose from Gleneagles Green Villas or the plush Villas of St. Andrews, both alongside the golf course; the Royal Oak Villas bordering the swim and tennis club; or the Bay Villas at the water's edge. The casually elegant Seasons restaurant serves such gourmet specialties as pork Florentine, lamb poivrade, and snapper presto, as well as seafood delivered fresh by local fishermen. For more informal dining, there's the Greenhouse, in the golf clubhouse overlooking a lagoon. I can't imagine a more beautiful place to vacation, whether you're looking for all-day action or all-day loafing! Weekly rentals March through October run $500 to $950, and from $400 to $600 November through February. Doubles at Marina Cove have daily rates that range from $85 to $125, depending on the season.

**WHERE TO EAT:** Right on the waterfront in Panama City, the popular, chef-owned **Capt. Anderson's Restaurant,** 5551 N. Lagoon Dr. (tel. 904/234-2225), is a relaxed, pleasant dining spot with reasonable prices. In a glass-walled dining room with nautical decor, the menu features gulf seafood, as you'd expect, plus charcoal-broiled steaks, which are excellent—as are the rolls and breads, all baked right there. Background music makes it even nicer. Prices are in the $9 to $20 range. It's open from 4 to 10 p.m. every day except Sunday.

Out at the Treasure Island Marina, the **Treasure Ship,** 3605 Thomas Dr. (tel. 904/234-8881), is a magnificent replica of a 1690 Spanish galleon, built on the shores of the Grand Lagoon. Modeled after the *Golden Hind,* Sir Francis Drake's flagship, the Treasure Ship towers 135 feet above the ground, and a variety of restaurants, lounges, and bars occupy its four levels. The truly lavish "Top of the Ship" is a gourmet dining room, with superb food and a very good wine list. Reservations are an absolute must here, and prices on the á la carte menu range from $9 to $22. On Level 3, the "Captain's Quarters" has dancing and live entertainment, with an outside Captain's Walk for enjoying the sunset or stargazing. Another, moderately priced Main Dining Room is walled with glass to give a splendid panoramic view of the lagoon. Informality reigns both at the Main Deck Bar (on Level 3) and the Wharf Galley (Level 1), where drinks and light foods are served. More evening entertainment is in The Brig (Level 1). There's also a game room and gift shops aboard as well, making this a unique family center. The ship opens for light snacks and sightseeing at 10:30 a.m.; dinner is served from 4 to 10:30 p.m. Some areas close during winter months, so you may wish to call ahead.

### In Pensacola

The chef-owned **Driftwood,** 27 W. Garden St. (tel. 904/433-4559), carries out the beachcomber motif in decor and cuisine. Its seafood specialties come mostly from local waters, and everything comes to table piping hot and deliciously prepared (including the steaks that are also featured on their menu). Prices run $5 to $10 at lunch, $10 to $32 at dinner. Hours are 11 a.m. to 3 p.m. and 5 to 10 p.m. (dinner only on Saturday, closed Sunday).

There's both a dining room and a separate oyster bar at the **Oyster Bar,** 709 N. Navy Blvd. (tel. 904/455-3925), where the local seafood is excellent. Informality and moderate prices are the keynotes here. I especially liked the place at lunch—it was busy but friendly and efficient. It's open every day except Tuesday from 11 a.m. to midnight, with lunches in the under-$7 range, dinners from $6 to $12.

In the Seville Square area, an absolute "don't miss" is **Seville Quarter.** A local businessman, Robert Snow, began putting together a dining and entertainment complex in a block of historic old buildings at 130 E. Government St. some years ago. Enlisting the aid of master construction supervisor Robert Pugh, he has restored interiors into **Rosie O'Grady's Good Time Emporium,** a Gay '90s spot that features Dixieland jazz; **Lili Marlene's,** with a World War I aviator's pub atmosphere and entertainment; the **Palace Oyster Bar,** featuring seafood, Italian dishes, and one of the grandest bars I've seen in years; **Coppersmith's Restaurant,** a fine turn-of-the-century dining room; **End o' Alley Bar,** tucked away in a gaslit, Victorian courtyard complete with fountain; and **Phineas Phogg's Balloon Works,** where disco and boogie rule supreme. The place is an unforgettable experience, and I found it hard to tear myself away for the sightseeing on my list. Hours of food service and entertainment vary at the other spots, so call 904/433-7436 for current goings-on. The Quarter is open seven days a week, and after 7 p.m. there's a $4 admission charge to the complex.

There is also a **Morrison's** here, in the Town & Country Mall on Fla. 29, which serves from 11 a.m. to 8 p.m. with the usual good food dished up by this chain. They have a fried fish amandine (not usually found in cafeterias) that I found delicious.

**THINGS TO SEE AND DO:** Around Panama City, water-related activities dominate the scene. There are the beaches, of course, and the Intracoastal Waterway draws boaters (you'll spot numerous public boat ramps). Fishing seems to be the main preoccupation with both visitors and residents, and just a few of the fishing piers open to the public are those at **St. Andrew State Recreation Area,** the **County Pier** on U.S. 98 West, and **Hathaway Bridge,** also on U.S. 98 West. There is very good bass, bream, and perch fishing at the **Dead Lakes State Recreation Area,** 30 miles east on Fla. 22, then north on Fla. 71.

From early May through mid-September, you can bet the dogs at the **Ebro Dog Track** (about 15 miles north of Panama City on Fla. 79). No minors, of course, and admission is $2. Races start at 8 p.m. every night except Sunday.

Golfers can play at the **Signal Hill Golf Club,** West Thomas Drive and Fla. 392 (tel. 904/234-5051), or the **Colony Golf Club,** 112 Fairway Blvd., just off U.S. 30A (tel. 904/234-6586).

At **Anderson's Pier,** Thomas Drive at Grand Lagoon (tel. 904/234-3435), you can charter deep-sea fishing boats, reserve for the boat trip out to **Shell Island** ($4.50 for adults, $2.25 for children), or join sightseeing and dinner cruises. Call for days and hours, which vary. Deep-sea fishing charters are also available.

The **Panama City Chamber of Commerce** is at 12017 W. U.S. 98 (P.O. Box 9473), Panama City Beach, FL 32407 (tel. 904/234-6575).

### In Tallahassee

Contact the **Tallahassee Convention and Visitors Bureau,** 100 N. Duval St. (P.O. Box 1639), Tallahassee, FL 32302 (tel. 904/224-8116).

When the first legislature convened in Tallahassee, it met in a log cabin. That was 1824, and since then, Tallahassee has built an impressive capitol building around the 1845 structure that replaced that log cabin and has grown and prospered on the business of government.

The 22-story **State Capitol** building, on Monroe Street and Apalachee Parkway, sits atop Tallahassee's highest hill, towering above the city. Tours are conducted free of charge from 8:30 a.m. to 4:30 p.m. weekdays, 9 a.m. to 4:30 p.m. on weekends except for major holidays. The Old Capitol, on South Monroe Street, is a classically simple building with columned porticos and a massive dome. Adjacent to the Old and New Capitols is the **Museum of Florida History,** open to the public at no charge.

Five miles northeast of the center of the city, on U.S. 319 (a quarter mile north of I-10), the **Maclay State Gardens,** 3540 Thomasville Rd. (tel. 904/893-4232), cover 308 acres which were once part of a private estate. The gardens cover 28 acres, with one of the South's finest collections of azaleas and camellias, and there is a picnic area on the lakeshore. The Maclay House, with some rooms restored, is open January through April. The gardens open at 9 a.m. and close at 5 p.m., and entrance fees to the park are $1 for each vehicle driver, 50¢ for each passenger; for the garden, it's $2 for adults, $1 for ages 6 to 12.

### In Pensacola

Contact the **Visitor Information Center,** 1401 E. Gregory, Pensacola, FL 32501 (tel. 904/343-4321, or toll free 800/874-1234), for more detailed information on the Pensacola area.

This important seaport that means "navy" to many an ex-enlisted man and officer, changed its national allegiance a total of 17 times; and the town itself moved once, over to Santa Rosa Island, as Spanish, French, English, Confederate, and Union governments fought over it. Since 1914, however, when the U.S. Navy located its **Naval Air Station** here because of the abundance of clear flying days, there has been no question of its nationality.

You can tour the air station on your own in your car, and sentries have free guide maps at the entry gates (it's southwest of town, and you won't have any trouble finding it—just follow the crowd). Don't miss the **Naval Aviation Museum's** fascinating exhibits that trace naval aviation history. Hours are 9 a.m. to 5 p.m. daily except major holidays, and admission is free. For advance information, contact: Naval Aviation Museum, U.S. Naval Air Station, Pensacola, FL 32508 (tel. 904/452-3604).

Be sure to go by **Park Square** and **Plaza Ferdinand** in the historic district. Within walking distance, you'll find interesting specialty shops in renovated historic buildings at **Palafox Place.** Nearby, the **Palafox Pier** area features seafood festivals, outdoor entertainment, markets and fairs.

In the city, go by the **Pensacola Historical Museum,** 405 S. Adams St. at Zaragoza Street (in the 1832 Old Christ Church), as well as the shops in **Seville Square,** at East Government and South Alcaniz Streets. There are interesting old homes and churches and even an oldtime sawmill, all open free to the public, in this park that commemorates the Spanish-English period of Pensacola's history. And don't forget to stop by Seville Quarter (see "Where to Eat"). The museum is open every day except Sunday.

## 2. Mobile, Alabama

Alabama's only seaport, Mobile sits near the head of Mobile Bay on the west side of the Mobile River. Approaching from the Florida coast, you'll get a close look at the docks that are the lifeblood of the busy port, but don't for one moment be misled into thinking that you're approaching an industrial center and nothing else. The Old South is alive and well in this gracious city, even in the center of town, where proud old homes trimmed with iron-grillwork balconies line streets fanning out from Bienville Square.

Mobile, like the southern belle she is, over the years has flitted from one national admirer to the other, with the flags of France, England, Spain, the

United States, and the Confederacy fluttering overhead at one time or another during her long history, which began in 1702. It wasn't until federal troops occupied the city on April 12, 1865, and firmly implanted the Stars and Stripes that Mobile settled down to a life of constancy in her national identity.

Today, besides shipping, there's one of the largest drydock and shipbuilding centers on the gulf located here. In addition, industry encompasses chemicals, steel, petroleum refining, food processing, and pulp and paper production. All of which makes Mobile a fascinating mixture of old and new—and during Mardi Gras (the two weeks preceding Lent), her French heritage takes over, with mystic society parades each evening that rival those of New Orleans.

**WHERE TO STAY:** The city itself offers much sightseeing, along with accommodations that afford both comfort and convenience. However, there is a nearby spot—Point Clear—which combines a resort atmosphere with sightseeing just a short drive away.

### In Mobile

The **Malaga Inn,** 359 Church St., Mobile, AL 36602 (tel. 205/438-4701), is a small, utterly charming hotel consisting of restored 1862 twin town houses, with a garden courtyard and fountain. Many of the original furnishings are in evidence in public rooms. Guest rooms are nicely furnished, many with oversize beds. There's a pool and an excellent restaurant (see "Where to Eat"). You really can't do better if the graciousness for which the South is noted is what you're after. Double rates run $45 to $52, and all rates increase slightly during Mardi Gras.

The **Best Western Admiral Semmes,** 250 Government Blvd., Mobile, AL 36633 (tel. toll free 800/432-4441), is a large, attractive motor hotel conveniently located to downtown. Rooms are spacious and decorated in above-average motel decor. There's a pool, restaurant, and lounge. Doubles run $45 to $50, and children under 18 stay free with their parents.

More moderately priced accommodations (though of very high quality) are to be found at the **Red Carpet Inn,** 3651 Government Blvd., Mobile, AL 36609 (tel. 205/666-7750), where doubles begin at $20.

### In Point Clear

Halfway down Mobile Bay, 23 miles east of Mobile on U.S. 98, Point Clear has been a resort area for Southerners since shortly after the Civil War. The **Marriott's Grand Hotel,** Point Clear, AL 36564 (tel. 205/928-9201), carries on today, and the key word here is luxury. From the warm, awe-inspiring lobby that rises two stories high and centered by a huge fireplace, filled with brass, porcelain, and antiques, and paneled and beamed by cypress, to the cypress-paneled rooms and cottages, quiet elegance holds sway. The dining room makes each meal an experience, especially if you get there early enough to sit next to the glass-walled end that overlooks the bay. As for facilities, there's a little bit of everything: a 27-hole championship course, deep-sea fishing, sailing, water-skiing, a pool and a beach area, bowling on the green, shuffleboard, skeet and trap shooting, a recreation hall, dancing and entertainment in the Bird Cage cocktail lounge, and if you have a favorite activity I've left out, it's probably there too. There's free bus service to the Mobile airport, and the hotel will arrange sightseeing tours. The Grand Hotel operates on the Modified American Plan (breakfast and full-course dinner included in rates), and offers rooms in the main building, the Bay House, and cottage units for two to eight persons. Rates, *per person,* for double occupancy range from $95 to $125. They offer a wide variety of golf and family package plans. No pets.

**WHERE TO EAT:** At Point Clear dining is pretty well restricted to the Grand Hotel listed above (however, that's no handicap, since it's well above average). In Mobile, you'll find restaurants galore—here are my favorites:

The **Malaga Inn,** 359 Church St. (tel. 205/433-5858), features gracious dining in a Spanish setting. There's background music, and jacket and tie are a must in the evening. Specialties here include escalopes de veau au parmesane, lump crabmeat pestalozi, and steak peperonata, as well as other continental dishes, all exceptionally well prepared and served. The dining room is open for all three meals (7 a.m. to 10:30 p.m.), with breakfast running $2.45 to $6; lunch, $3 to $9; and dinner, $8 to $30. Closed Sunday and holidays.

**Wintzell's Oyster House,** 605 Dauphin St. (tel. 205/433-1004), prides itself on serving oysters "fried, stewed & nude," but other seafood dishes come to table just as tasty as the bivalves. This is a casual, friendly place for lunch or dinner, and very popular with locals. Hours are 11 a.m. to 9 p.m., and prices run $3 to $14, with children's plates at $3.

**THINGS TO SEE AND DO:** The **Tourist Information Center** is at 451 Government St., Mobile, AL 36602 (tel. 205/433-6951).

For a look at a classic "Old South" mansion, visit **Oakleigh,** 350 Oakleigh Pl. at Savannah Street. It was built by slaves between 1833 and 1838, and bricks for the first floor were handmade right on the premises. The Historic Mobile Preservation Society has restored the house to its pre-1850 period, complete with authentic furnishings. There are interesting displays of period portraits, silver, china, jewelry, and Mardi Gras memorabilia. Oakleigh is open from 10 a.m. to 4 p.m. Monday through Saturday, 2 to 4 p.m. on Sunday; and admission is $3.50 for adults, $1 ages 6 through 18. Closed major holidays.

The **Richards–DAR House,** 256 N. Joachim St. (tel. 205/438-7320), is a restored Italianate town house built around 1860. It holds period furniture and has a lovely curved, suspended staircase and elaborate ironwork. It's open from 10 a.m. to 4 p.m. Tuesday to Saturday, and 1 to 4 p.m. on Sunday; closed major holidays. Admission is $2 for adults, 50¢ for children under 12.

There's a free **Fine Arts Museum of the South** (tel. 205/343-2667) on Museum Drive on the south shore of the lake in Langan Park featuring antiques, crafts, paintings, and prints. Hours are 10 a.m. to 5 p.m. Tuesday through Sunday, except holidays.

About one mile east of Mobile via Bankhead and George C. Wallace Tunnels on Battleship Parkway (U.S. 90), the battleship **U.S.S. *Alabama*** is moored as a memorial to World War II servicemen from Alabama. Tours, from 8 a.m. to sunset, cost $5 for adults, $2.50 for ages 6 to 11. Also in the memorial park are the submarine U.S.S. *Drum* and World War II aircraft.

One of Mobile's most spectacular showplaces is about 20 miles southwest (via U.S. 90 or I-10 and Bellingrath Road) near Theodore. On more than 800 acres, the gardens were developed with the help of French, English, and American landscape architects, and in addition to the 70 varieties of native trees, there are 250,000 azalea plants (200 varieties), gardenias, camellias, roses, water lilies, dogwood, and hydrangeas. The **Bellingrath home** holds collections of Dresden and Meissen porcelain, china, crystal, and Oriental rugs, and is furnished with antiques. Plan plenty of time for your visit so you can enjoy the many wooded walks through the gardens. Hours are 7 a.m. to dusk; admission is $5 for adults, $2.50 for ages 6 through 11 for the gardens, $5 more for the home, which is open to limited numbers at one time from 8 a.m. to 5 p.m. No matter what time of the year you come, you can be sure something will be blooming at Bellingrath. If you're passing by and want to stop, there's a restaurant at the entrance, as well as kennels for pets of owners who want to tour the gardens.

## 3. Mississippi's Gulf Coast (Pascagoula and Biloxi)

The 65-mile Mississippi Gulf Coast is a traveler's paradise. Along with the world's longest man-made beach (hurricanes have devastated the beaches time and again, but constant maintenance keeps them intact most of the time), you'll find the coast drive edged by modern hotels, one lovely old home in Pascagoula that's become an inn, countless fine restaurants, and gracious homes. The history of the region is rich in Spanish and French domination, and Mardi Gras is a big event all along the coast. As for scenery, it is breathtakingly lovely (between, that is, the commercial clusters dotted along the way). This is a short drive, but it's one you'll want to make leisurely, and for that reason I'm including accommodations and restaurants in two of the most popular stopping points, as well as sightseeing tips at each. The only problem you're likely to encounter is deciding *where* to reserve, for there are hundreds of first-rate hotels and motels along the coast. But *do* reserve ahead if you can, for during the summer season it is quite possible to find almost every room booked, especially on weekends when residents of Mississippi and its neighboring states head for the gulf.

**PASCAGOULA:** This shipbuilding center dates back to 1718, and its colorful history even further back. Long before the advent of white men in Mississippi, the peaceful Pascagoula Indian tribe lived here, and when a young warrior fell in love with a princess from the fierce Biloxi tribe and spirited her away, the Biloxis went on the warpath. Finding themselves outnumbered and outfought, the Pascagoulas (so the legend goes) walked into the river holding hands and chanting a song of death until the last voice was hushed by the dark waters. Only a romantic legend? Perhaps. Still, there is, to this day, an unexplained singing sound plainly heard in late summer and autumn months in the stillness of Pascagoula evenings, and it seems to come from the river—scientists have never come up with a satisfactory reason for the singing!

### Where to Stay

Nearly as romantic as the legend of the Singing River is **Longfellow House,** 3401 Beach Blvd., Pascagoula, MS 39567 (tel. 601/762-1122). Once named "Bellvue," the main house was built in 1850 by slave traders from New Orleans. Since then, it has been a girl's school (run by a headmaster who turned out to be something of a rascal), fallen into the hands of wealthy Northerners who had a penchant for drink, become the property of a sea captain, and finally the happy home of a plantation owner and banker and his family. Somewhere along the way, Henry Wadsworth Longfellow was supposed to have stayed here, and some say he wrote "The Building of the Ship" during his visit.

Today the house itself is used only for the dining room (a lovely, sunny room looking out over wooded grounds), the popular lounge (which has entertainment and is always filled with locals as well as guests), offices of the inn, and private parties in the upstairs rooms. Guest rooms are in one- and two-story cottages scattered along pleasant walkways through vast lawns and planted gardens. Rooms are much larger than in most luxury hotels, and nicely furnished, either opening onto or overlooking the landscaped grounds. There's a pool, golf, tennis, racquetball, shuffleboard, sailing or boating, and charter-fishing trips can be arranged. For all the feeling of elegance and pampering by the friendly staff, rates run only $45 and up for doubles, $65 to $100 for one- and two-bedroom suites.

In a more modern vein, the **La Font Inn,** on U.S. 90 East, Pascagoula, MS 39567 (tel. 601/762-7111), is a large, pleasant two-story motel just off the highway, with spacious rooms overlooking the pool, steambaths in some rooms, and oversize beds in many. A lifeguard is on duty at the pool in summer, and there's a playground and wading pool for the young folk. The dining room is reasonably priced and very popular with natives. Doubles here start at $55.

## Where to Eat

At the **La Font**, U.S. 90 East (tel. 601/762-7111), Sunday dinner is an event, with a fixed-price menu ($7.50 for adults, $6.75 for children), with a changing menu that might well be baked ham with wine sauce, fresh crabmeat Newburg, veal scaloppine, or roast leg of lamb. Vegetables are really fresh and nicely prepared, and the price includes five courses. Dinner prices run $7 to $22. Breakfast hours are 6 to 10 a.m.; lunch, from 11 a.m. to 2 p.m.; and dinner, from 6 to 10 p.m.

Although not in Pascagoula, you should know about **Trilby's** restaurant, on U.S. 90 in Ocean Springs (tel. 601/875-4426). Some 19 miles west of Pascagoula on U.S. 90, the historic little town of Ocean Springs, Mississippi, was the first permanent European settlement in the Mississippi Valley and has in recent years become quite an arts-and-crafts center. The resort itself is worth a stop, but a meal at Trilby's makes it virtually a "must." In the more than 45 years of its operation, it has become a tradition along this part of the Gulf Coast. The low, unpretentious building holds a warm, gracious interior, where works of local artists are displayed along with a collection of antique clocks from around the world. Seafood is outstanding here (do try the oyster pie if the bivalves are in season), but there's also an excellent selection of beef, lamb, and chicken entrees. Entree prices are in the $10 to $15 range, and hours are 11:30 a.m. to 2 p.m. and 6 to 10 p.m. Tuesday through Saturday, and 11:30 a.m. to 2 p.m. on Sunday; closed Monday.

## Things to See and Do

First of all, if you want to become a true believer in that old Indian legend, try to go down to the **Pascagoula River** (two blocks west of the courthouse) on a hot summer evening just about twilight. You'll hear it faintly at first, then experience the odd sensation of hearing the humming sound swell in volume and seem to come closer to where you stand. The strangest thing of all is that although you *know* it's very near—almost underfoot—you are totally unable to pinpoint exactly where it comes from. It seems to come from any point to which you direct your attention. Go; then I *dare* you to pay any heed to scientists who say it *may* be sand scraping the hard slate bottom of the river!

Five blocks north of U.S. 90 or eight miles south of I-10, the **Old Spanish Fort**, 4602 Fort St., was built in 1718 by the French, later captured by the Spanish. Said to be the oldest fortified structure in the Mississippi Valley, its walls are of massive pine timbers held together with a mixture of oyster shells, mud, and moss. It's open from 10 a.m. to 4 p.m. daily (except Thursday and major holidays), and admission is $2 for adults, $1 for children.

Two interesting sightseeing destinations are inside the old **L & N Railroad Station** at Magnolia and Railroad Streets. Mississippi crafts are on display at the **Senior Craft Shop,** 612 Downtown Plaza (one block away), where needlework, quilts, jewelry, toys, and ceramics made by senior citizens of Pascagoula and vicinity are featured. Original paintings, pottery, and prints by area artists are in the **Old Gallery** (in the station). There's no charge to visit either—the gallery is open from 11 a.m. to 3 p.m. Monday through Friday; the Craft Shop, from 10 a.m. to 4:30 p.m. Tuesday through Saturday. Both are closed on holidays.

**BILOXI:** This is one of the prettiest towns along the gulf, with Spanish moss trailing from tall trees and magnolias, camellias, roses, and crape myrtle lining its streets. On a peninsula, with 25 miles of coastline, Biloxi first became a resort about the mid-19th century, when inland cotton planters discovered the pleasures of the shore. The only industry that intrudes is the seafood industry, and hundreds of shrimp boats operate out of the town. In early June there's a Shrimp Festival that culminates in the beautiful Blessing of the Fleet ceremony. Ship Island, 12 miles across Mississippi Sound, was the landing place for seagoing vessels (the sound itself is shallow) in the early days of settlement and was the first glimpse of their new home for some 80 "casket girls" sent over by the French government to marry the settlers (everything they owned was packed in small, wicker "caskets," hence the name).

## Where to Stay

The **Royal d'Iberville,** 3420 W. Beach Blvd., Biloxi MS 39531 (tel. 601/388-6610), has large rooms, many with balconies, and extra basins in separate dressing rooms. There's a split-level swimming pool, lighted tennis, and golf privileges at nearby courses. The dining room is above average, and the lounge has dancing and entertainment. Doubles are $65 to $75.

More moderate in price, and quite nice, is the **Beach Manor Motel,** 325 E. Beach Blvd., Biloxi, MS 39530 (tel. 601/436-4361). There's a sundeck overlooking the gulf, and a lounge that sometimes has live entertainment and dancing. There are kitchenettes as well as nicely appointed rooms. Doubles are $36 and up on weekdays, $38 and up on weekends and holidays, and kitchenettes run $7 more.

## Where to Eat

In a converted house and slave quarters built in 1737, **Mary Mahoney's Old French House,** 138 Rue Magnolia (tel. 601/374-0163), oozes charm, with fireplaces, antiques, a patio for cocktails, and courtyard dining. Of course, you can't eat charm, and at this place the food measures up to its surroundings. Try the lobster George or the red snapper. Semi à la carte prices range from $6 to $10 at lunch, $11 to $20 at dinner. Hours are 11 a.m. to 10:30 p.m. every day except Sunday and Christmas. It's a good idea to reserve.

**White Pillars,** 100 Rodenburg Ave. at West Beach Boulevard (tel. 601/432-8741), is in a restored southern mansion set back from U.S. 90. Gourmet cuisine stars here, with specialties such as eggplant Josephine and trout en papillotte. In addition to the main dining rooms, there's enclosed patio dining, and entertainment and dancing. Hours are 5 to 11 p.m., and it closes on Monday and Christmas. This is another place reservations are in order. Prices are in the $12.50 to $19.50 range.

For more casual dining at family-oriented prices, you can't do better than the **Sea 'n Sirloin,** 3455 W. Beach Blvd. (tel. 601/388-6387). It's a big place right on the water, with wide windows to let you enjoy the view as well as the food. The à la carte menu has shrimp boiled in the shell, oysters on the half shell, fried crab claws, and a host of other seafoods at moderate prices, with $19 the top price (for the sea 'n sirloin special—sea being lobster stuffed with crabmeat). But perhaps the best buy on the gulf is the buffet served six days a week here. The price is just $6 on weekdays, $7 on Sunday, and $8 on holidays. This is definitely a place to bring the family! Hours are 11 a.m. to 10 p.m., seven days a week.

## Things to See and Do

Contact the **Biloxi Chamber of Commerce,** 1036 Fred Haise Blvd. (P.O. Drawer CC), Biloxi, MS 39533 (tel. 601/374-2717).

If you're a Civil War buff, you'll want to visit **Beauvoir,** the home of Jefferson Davis for the last 12 years of his life. Some years after his release from a federal prison, the former Confederate president came south and, among other things, wrote *The Rise and Fall of the Confederate Government.* After his death, Beauvoir was used as a home for Confederate veterans, and in 1941 turned into a Confederate shrine. On the 56-acre grounds are the home, the little white pavilion Davis used as his library and study, a guest cottage, two museums, and the Confederate cemetery. It's five miles west of Biloxi on U.S. 90 (West Beach Boulevard), and open daily except Christmas from 9 a.m. to 5 p.m. Admission is $4 for adults, $3 for over-65s and military personnel, $2 for ages 6 to 16, and free for under 6.

Not far from Beauvoir is the **Biloxi Lighthouse,** built in 1848 (on West Beach Boulevard—U.S. 90—at the foot of Porter Avenue). During "that" war, when federal forces were approaching, the intrepid lady lighthouse keeper climbed to the top, removed the lens, and buried it. Still, when Lincoln was assassinated, the citizens of the town painted the entire structure black. It's white now, and automated (but for some 62 years, the light was faithfully tended by a mother-and-daughter team).

# Chapter XX

# INTRODUCTION TO NEW ORLEANS

## 1. By Way of Background
## 2. Traveling to New Orleans
## 3. Traveling Within New Orleans

AMONG AMERICAN CITIES, New Orleans reigns supreme in my affections. I say that without reservation (although with a slight apology to New York City) and with the knowledge that many thousands share my love for this lively, lovely old city. From her beginnings, she has had room for all comers and a gracious welcome for those just passing through. You could love her for that alone, but there's much, much more to beguile you in the Crescent City.

There's all that history, of course, and when you walk the narrow streets and see old, old buildings trimmed with fancy ironwork—not set aside as museums, but as functional today as when they were built (even though the functions have changed)—it almost seems that long skirts and frock coats should be passing rather than blue jeans and sweatshirts. It doesn't take much imagination to picture Gen. Andrew Jackson deep in conference with privateer Jean Lafitte over a table at the Old Absinthe House. Or to see with the mind's eye calico-clad black women swaying through the streets hawking sweet pralines as they balance on their heads huge wooden bowls filled with the sugary treats. Then, just around a corner, there's the brassy sound of jazz or the low moan of the blues spilling out into the streets and you know it's the 20th century and this city is anything *but* lost in its past.

There's a vitality about New Orleans that keeps her eternally young, never mind the accumulation of years. She draws the young like a magnet while holding the old close to her heart. I'll not soon forget the night in Preservation Hall when a very young Swedish clarinet player sat in with men who've been playing jazz since it began, and all were comfortable and happy in the music they made together. I guess you could say there's no generation gap in New Orleans. You see that around Jackson Square too, where artists of all ages sit at their easels painting and sketching with varying degrees of expertise, at ease with life and each other. Or at the Café du Monde across from the square near the old French Market, where New Orleanians and visitors alike congregate for strong, hot café au lait and beignets (that's pronounced "baan-yaas" and they're a cross between a doughnut and a cruller, liberally sprinkled with powdered sugar—absolutely delicious!) at all hours of the day and night, young and old rubbing elbows happily.

And if New York is a "melting pot," New Orleans is more a "melding pot," for there's a soft blending of race, color, nationality, and accent—everything and everyone seem to come together here in terms of interests that unite rather than spawn conflict. The explanation, of course, lies in the city's long history of widely differing groups who met headlong in combat, only eventually to join hands in mutual enterprise.

# 1. By Way of Background

Founded in 1718 by Sieur de Bienville, the strategically located settlement was named for the then Regent of France, Duc d'Orleans. Around the Place d'Armes (now Jackson Square) streets were laid out and rude huts built in what we know as the French Quarter, or Vieux Carré (it means Old Square and its pronounced "vew-ka-*ray*"). Government buildings and a church were added, and one of the most successful promotion campaigns in history drew shiploads of settlers from Europe, Africa, and the Caribbean—merchants, royalty, exiles, criminals, slaves—all expecting to find a paradise on earth. Whatever their reactions when they arrived to find swampy land, mosquitoes, and the rawness of frontier life, they stayed on to implant the niceties of European culture adapted to New World circumstances. Ursuline nuns came in 1727 and were soon importing "casket girls" (poor, but "nice" French girls who brought their belongings in casket-line trunks) to wed settlers and provide "respectability"—or so the nuns hoped, although one could, and still can, find "respectability" defined in many different terms in New Orleans!

As the little colony grew and prospered, it reflected much of the gaiety and fashion of the French court as practiced by aristocrats who arrived in ever-increasing numbers. Descendants of this privileged class were the original "Créoles," although with time the name has come to mean well-to-do French-speaking natives of mixed French and Spanish ancestry. It also offered refuge to Acadians from Nova Scotia, most of whom soon moved out to become farmers and trappers (ancestors of present-day "Cajuns," who still speak French in their own peculiar style), and was a welcomed shore leave for seafarers who added their own dash of spice to the color and growing sophistication of the city.

In 1762 New Orleanians woke up to find that their king, Louis XV, had given Louisiana, along with its residents, to his cousin, Charles III of Spain, beginning a period of hostility and revolution on the part of Frenchmen who bitterly resented the new rule. It wasn't long, however, before Spanish and French were intermarrying and the city took on yet another hue. After two disastrous fires in 1788 and 1794 which left most of New Orleans in ashes, a proud new town began to emerge, much of it erected in the Spanish style of brick and plaster buildings with many arches, courtyards, balconies, and, of course, attached slave quarters. Tile markers at every corner still list the old Spanish street names.

By this time New Orleans was a prize much desired by the English and Americans, and the French government also wanted it back. Governor Carondelet surrounded the city with five forts connected by a strong city wall (which, significantly, had cannons pointing both inside and out!), but in 1800 it was quietly given back to France, which held control until 1803, when Napoleon sold all of Louisiana to the United States for $15 million, a move all natives viewed with horror, since all Americans were considered barbarians. Americans, when they found no welcome in the warm-blooded Vieux Carré, set to work building their own New Orleans "uptown" north of Canal Street. Splendid homes began to appear in what is now the Garden District and their commercial section took on a boom-town air. Since "downtowners" desperately needed some of that up-town Yankee money, and since the newcomers found themselves drawn to the vitality and warmth of downtown, and because everyone joined in a constant battle against hurricanes, yellow fever epidemics, and floods, a spirit of unity gradually developed between the two sections. And when Andrew Jackson called for volunteers from every segment of New Orleans citizenry to protect the city from British attack in 1814, some 5,000 responded. With cannon and ammunition supplied by the privateer Jean Lafitte, they soundly defeated 8,500 seasoned British troops, saving the city and the Mississippi for the U.S., and emerging with a confidence that was largely responsible for the most prosperous and glamorous era yet known in the delta city.

Increasingly wealthy cotton and sugarcane planters built mansions upriver and maintained luxurious town houses in New Orleans, making frequent visits to attend festivals, parades, opera, theater, banquets, and spectacular balls (some, the "Quadroon Balls," were held soley to introduce beautiful mulatto girls to the gentry as possible mistresses), or to patronize opulent gambling halls and resplendent "bawdy houses." Hard-working Irish and German immigrants poured in, along with Italians, all of whom added bits of culture and tradition to the already-exciting milieu. For a time New Orleans was the richest city in the country, and its citizens enjoyed a truly exotic existence.

The Civil War ended all that and the town went through a bitter period of Reconstruction from the time federal troops marched in during 1862 until they finally left in 1877. Since then, although some of its flamboyance is gone, New Orleans has clung to its unique heritage, learned about drainage and epidemic control, given birth to American jazz, and most of all, retained an enthusiasm for fun in almost every form that is simply not equaled any other place. Today's visitor will find the French Quarter still marked by its original "downtown" settlers' architecture and lifestyle, "uptown" still vibrating with Yankee business enterprise, and the combination one of the friendliest, heartwarming cities in the world. Incidentally, natives pronounce it "New *Orl*-yons"!

**NEW ORLEANS CLIMATE:** Light-weight clothing is all you'll need in New Orleans most seasons, for the average mean temperature is 70°, and I have found that a medium-weight raincoat will usually provide enough warmth any time; although during winter months, you might want to carry along a somewhat heavier coat, since it can get down to the high 50s. With a total annual rainfall of 63 inches, the city can be damp and it's a good idea to have an umbrella and that raincoat handy.

**TELEPHONE AREA CODE:** When telephoning to New Orleans, the area code for all sections of the city is 504.

## 2. Traveling to New Orleans

New Orleans is a "gateway" city, and as such has entry transportation of almost every kind available.

**BY AIR:** There are no fewer than 18 airlines serving New Orleans from within the United States and from South America: American, Atlanta Air, Aviateca, Continental, Delta, Eastern, LACSA, Midway, New York Air, Ozark Air, Pan American, Piedmont, Royale, Southwest, Taca International, Trans Star, Trans World Airlines, and USAir.

**BY TRAIN:** Amtrak has runs to New Orleans from both coasts and Chicago, and several tour packages that make New Orleans a bargain as well as a joy.

**BY BUS:** Greyhound and Continental Trailways serve New Orleans, as do Southeastern Stages, Texas Bus Lines, Gulf Transport, Arrow Coach, and ABC Coach.

**BY CAR:** From Picayune, Mississippi, you can travel I-59 to New Orleans; from Baton Rouge, U.S. 61; and from Biloxi, Mississippi, or the west coast of Florida, I-10.

## 3. Traveling Within New Orleans

The first thing that must be said about traveling around New Orleans is not to do anything or go anywhere until you've stopped by the **Visitor Information Center** at 529 St. Ann St. (tel. 504/566-5031), in the French Quarter. Operated by the Greater New Orleans Tourist and Convention Commission, and the Louisiana Tourist Development Commission, the center is a veritable fount of information: they have excellent maps for walking or driving tours, booklets on restaurants, accommodations, tours, special attractions, and just about anything you could want to know. The staff is multilingual, as befits this city of so many accents, and as friendly as any you're likely to meet.

**GETTING YOUR BEARINGS:** The layout of New Orleans is fairly simple, and getting around is not at all difficult. The historic **French Quarter** (Vieux Carré), where the city began, lies in a 13-block-long area between Canal Street and Esplanade Avenue. Directions are apt to be given by New Orleanians as "riverside" or "lakeside" (referring, of course, to "toward the Mississippi River" or toward "Lake Pontchartrain"), and in that context, North Rampart Street is the "lakeside" boundary, the Mississippi the "riverside." "North" or "South" on street names simply refers to north or south of Canal Street, although most streets change their names when they cross Canal. As for building numbers, they start at 100 on both sides of Canal, and at 400 in the Quarter at the river (that's because four blocks, already numbered, of the original settlement were lost to the river before the levee was built). Jackson Square is at the very heart of the Quarter, facing Decatur Street "riverside" and Chartres Street "lakeside," bounded on one side by St. Ann Street, by St. Peter Street on the other. Across Decatur Street from the square is pretty little Washington Artillery Park, with its splashing fountain, back of which the elevated Moon Walk (named for Mayor "Moon" Landrieu), complete with benches and hanging lanterns, runs along the riverfront.

The business district is directly above Canal Street from the French Quarter, and toward the lake. The lovely **Garden District** is bounded roughly by St. Charles Avenue, Magazine Street, and Jackson and Louisiana Avenues. Farther along St. Charles Avenue, you'll find Loyola and Tulane Universities, and Audubon Park. "Fat City" can be reached via Veterans Hwy. to Causeway Boulevard—its other boundaries are West Esplanade and Division Street. Lake Pontchartrain lies out Canal Street to West End Boulevard or Pontchartrain Avenue.

**BY CAR:** Thrifty, National, Hertz, Avis, Budget, Econo-Car, and Dollar Rent-A-Car car rentals are available both within and near the airport. The driving tour detailed on the Visitor Center map can't be beat if you plan to spend much time behind the wheel. The very helpful brochure, "Park Smart," is a guide to off-street parking lots and garages in the French Quarter and the central business district and is distributed free at many hotels and all tourist offices, or you can call 504/587-1830. On-street parking is metered at 25¢ per 20 minutes. In the French Quarter, all streets are one way, and during daylight hours on weekdays, Royal and Bourbon Streets are closed off as pedestrian malls between the 300 and 700 blocks.

**BY BUS:** From that same Visitor Information Center, you can pick up a copy of

"Visitour," a map and guide which shows all bus routes, clearly marked with bus numbers. All bus fares are 60¢ except expresses, which are 65¢.

A very special bus ride if your feet really aren't up to a walking tour of the French Quarter is the **Vieux Carré Minibus.** This quaint little transit line leaves Canal and Bourbon Streets from 6 to 9:30 a.m. and 4 to 6 p.m. on weekdays; or you can board at Bourbon and Iberville from 9:30 a.m. to 4 p.m. and 6 p.m. to 12:30 a.m. weekdays, and all day on Saturday, Sunday, and holidays. It'll cost you just 60¢ to see all of the French Quarter in comfort, although I personally recommend the hoof-it route.

**A TOUR BY TROLLEY:** No matter how else you see New Orleans, reserve at least an hour and a half to ride the famous old **St. Charles streetcar** (which, incidentally, has been named a National Historic Landmark). The trolleys run 24 hours a day, at frequent intervals, and the fare is 60¢. For the most complete look at "uptown" along the historic old avenue, board at Canal and Carondelet Streets (just across Canal Street from Bourbon Street), sit back, and look for landmarks in this part of town. Lafayette Square is at the 500 block of St. Charles, and just across from it, the 1840s Gallier Hall, which was the seat of the city's ruling fathers for 100 years.

At Lee Circle, a little farther on, you'll see a huge statue of the general (Robert E., that is), and from here on, it's fun to watch the homes that line the street as they change from Greek Revival architecture to Victorian to early 1900s. From Jackson Avenue on, the houses are surrounded by gardens, not the other way around as in the Quarter, giving rise to the "Garden District" name of this area of huge mansions built before the Civil War. Loyola and Tulane Universities are located at the 6000 block, across from Audubon Park with its huge old live oaks, zoo, lagoons, children's amusement park, tennis courts, and a municipal golf course. The park extends all the way to the levee at the Mississippi and is a worthwhile stop if you have the time—you can always catch the next trolley for the remainder of the ride up St. Charles.

The ride back to your beginning point will cost another 60¢, and I like to change sides on the return trip to see all the things I missed going out. This is without a doubt the best $1.20 buy in New Orleans.

**BY HORSE AND CARRIAGE:** Who could resist the authentic old horse-drawn carriages that pick up passengers at Jackson Square? Drawn by horses suitably adorned with flower-and-ribbon-trimmed straw hats, the carriages cover 2¼ miles of the French Quarter, with drivers giving a nonstop monologue on the historic buildings along the way. They operate from 9 a.m. to midnight in good weather, and the cost is either $6 or $7 (I paid $7, but was quoted the lower price by another driver, so it might pay to shop a little), with those under 12 paying half fare.

**BY FERRY:** One of New Orleans's nicest treats is absolutely free. It's the 25-minute ferry ride across the Mississippi from the foot of Canal Street, and it's a joy, whether you go by day for a view of the busy harbor or at night when the lights of the city reflect in the mighty river. It takes 25 minutes for each crossing, so be sure to allow about an hour for the round trip. It carries car and foot passengers, in case you want to do some West Bank driving between trips.

**BY FOOT:** Within the French Quarter and the Garden District there simply is no better way to get around than by foot, and the Visitor Information Center, 529 St. Ann St. (tel. 504/566-5031), has a very good walking-tour map. Distances are not difficult to manage, and only by ambling can you really see the charm of both places. In the Quarter, glimpses of lovely patios and courtyards come one after another as you stroll the narrow sidewalks, and you can stop to listen to live jazz pouring from the open doorways of several saloons that have nonstop music most of the day. In the Garden District, walking permits you to drink in the beauty of formal gardens that surround the mansions. See the listing below for two excellent guided walking tours.

**TOURS:** Friends of the Cabildo (tel. 504/523-3939) is a nonprofit, volunteer group that sponsors a two-hour guided walking tour of the French Quarter, leaving from the Presbytere, 751 Chartres St., at 9:30 a.m. and 1:30 p.m. Tuesday through Saturday except holidays. You'll be asked for a $5 donation ($2.50 for ages 13 to 20, and free for those 12 and under), and no reservations are necessary; just show up, donations in hand.

Some of the most delightful walking tours are conducted by the **Jean Lafitte National Historical Park Folklife and Visitor Center,** 916-918 N. Peters St. (in back of the French Market, along Dutch Alley). Among the 1½-hour tours offered are "History of New Orleans," "City of the Dead," and a "Tour du Jour," which remains a mystery until you arrive to find out which historical subject they'll be exploring that day. There's another, 2½-hour "Faubourg Promenade," which combines walking with streetcar rides, and you must reserve for that one. There's no charge, and you can call 504/589-2636 for exact schedules—the center is open and tours conducted every day except Christmas, New Year's, and Mardi Gras.

**Gray Line Tours,** 1793 Julia St. (tel. 504/525-0138), has City Tours ($16), a combination Paddle and Wheel Tour ($23), a Plantation Tour ($29.50, includes all entry fees), and an After Dark Tour ($32) that includes two nightclubs, drinks, gratuities, and cover charges. They'll call for and deliver you to selected hotels.

If the horse-drawn carriages represent romance on land, they are matched on the river by several oldtime steamboats that leave from the foot of Canal Street for **river cruises.** For complete details, contact the **New Orleans Steamboat Co.,** 2340 International Trade Mart, New Orleans, LA 70130 (tel. 504/586-8777).

The elegant paddlewheeler, *Créole Queen,* is docked at the Poydras Street Wharf right next to the Hilton Hotel. There are daily river, plantation, and battlefield cruises departing at 10 a.m. and 2 p.m. One promenade deck is covered, and there are very nice inner lounges with air conditioning. Cocktail and snackbar service are available on all cruises. The fare is $11 per person, and you can book by calling 504/529-4567 or 524-0814. Nightly jazz and dinner cruises are $28 per person.

The gracious *Natchez* (tel. 504/586-8777 or 524-9787) leaves from the Toulouse Street Wharf for 2½-hour "up and down the Mississippi" cruises. Facilities include both snackbars and dining rooms, as well as cocktail lounges. Adults pay $10.50; children 6 to 12, $5.50; and those under 6 travel free.

The delightful *Cotton Blossom* zoo cruises leave the Canal Street dock daily, and you can purchase either round-trip or one-way tickets (perhaps returning by the St. Charles streetcar), both of which include admission to the zoo. Adults pay $10.50 round trip; ages 3 through 15, $5.50. You'll find food and beverage services aboard. Call 504/586-8777 for schedules and reservations.

There's a daily bayou cruise aboard the *Bayou Jean Lafitte,* departing the Toulouse Street Wharf at 11 a.m. and returning at 4 p.m. Tickets are $14.50 for adults, and $7.50 for ages 6 to 12. Call 504/586-8777 for reservations.

*Chapter XXI*

# NEW ORLEANS HOTELS AND RESTAURANTS

## 1. Hotels, Motels, and Guesthouses
## 2. Restaurants

TRUE TO HER HERITAGE of hospitality to the traveler, New Orleans today is lavish in her offering of accommodations and cuisine. No matter what the budget, taste, or style, the Queen City is certain to have at least one establishment that fits the bill exactly.

### 1. Hotels, Motels, and Guesthouses

In the years that had elapsed since my last visit to New Orleans before researching the first edition of this book, hotels and motels had sprung up all over the place, and I almost dreaded going back—I couldn't bear the thought of the French Quarter being defaced with high-rise, modern monstrosities, no matter how luxurious inside or how much easier they made a stay in the city. I needn't have worried: everything within the Quarter has been kept to the same style as the historic old buildings lining the streets, and it is sometimes difficult to tell if a "new" hotel has been built from scratch or simply placed inside the shell of one of the gracious old buildings. The older hotels are still there, even more comfortable and elegant than I remembered, and the motor hotels do away with that ever-present problem, parking. As for the guesthouses, they are a different breed in New Orleans, for instead of the slightly frayed rooms that usually go with the name, many of those here are furnished with antiques and presided over by people who love the city and want their guests to do the same, making them "hosts" in the true sense of the word.

**Bed & Breakfast, Inc.,** 1360 Moss St., New Orleans, LA 70152 (tel. 504/525-4640, or toll free 800/220-9711), is run by personable Hazell Boyce, who can help you find lodgings in luxurious 19th-century mansions or in modern residences. Expect to pay anywhere from $35 to $75, double occupancy, but Hazell takes a special delight in ferreting out the most inexpensive digs for students.

In short, accommodations in New Orleans, no matter what the price range, are likely to give the visitor more than just a place to lay a weary head.

Before listing recommendations in the various sections, I should warn you that even with the thousands of new rental rooms in New Orleans, there are times when there isn't a bed to be had. If you're planning to come to the city during a holiday or at Mardi Gras time (it begins soon after Christmas, when the Carnival season opens and lasts until "Fat Tuesday," the last day before Lent), it isn't an exaggeration to say you should reserve as far in advance as possible, and in the case of Mardi Gras, as much as a year ahead! There is always the chance, of course, that you'll run across a cancellation and be able to book at the last minute, but that chance is remote, to say the least. A good time to visit if you want to miss crowds and hard-to-find lodging, is in the month immediately following Mardi Gras or in the fall months, when the weather is mild enough to be comfortable and the streets are not nearly so thronged as at other times.

As I've stated throughout this book, the prices quoted are as of the time of writing and subject to change. Another thing you should know is that *all* prices go up for holidays and Mardi Gras.

**IN THE FRENCH QUARTER:** For my money, the *only* place to stay in New Orleans is in the Quarter—it is the very heart and soul of the city, pumping life and vitality into its own confines and beyond. There's a concentration of accommodations that should make it possible (except, of course, during Mardi Gras) for you to find the type of hotel that suits you in the price range you want if you book far enough in advance.

### Hotels

The French Quarter's largest, and one of its oldest, hotels has been family operated by three generations of Monteleones. Covering almost the entire 200 block of Royal Street, the 600-room **Monteleone Hotel,** 214 Royal St., New Orleans, LA 70140 (tel. 504/523-3341), seems to keep growing and expanding over the years without losing a trace of the charm that has been a trademark since its beginning. Rooms cover the whole decor spectrum, from luxurious, antique-filled suites to more modern, very comfortable family rooms. The trellis-trimmed, green-and-white Le Café restaurant is a favorite among native New Orleanians, and the Carousel Bar, which slowly revolves under its red-and-white striped canopy, also draws the locals. Up on top, the fabulous Sky Terrace has to be seen to be believed: there's a heated swimming pool, a putting green, the 9-to-5 Bar and the exquisitely elegant Sky-lite Lounge, really a rooftop club that features top-notch live entertainment, such as the famous "Dukes of Dixieland." This is, for my money, the "Grand Old Lady" of New Orleans hotels and well worth the more-than-modest prices. Rates begin at $95 and range to $150 for double occupancy.

Much newer, and very elegant, is the **Omni Royal Orleans,** 621 St. Louis St., New Orleans, LA 70140 (tel. 504/529-5333, or toll free 800/THE-OMNI), considered by many as "the" place to stay. The rooms and public rooms here reflect the same old-world style as does the outside, with its New Orleans grili-work. Guest rooms, too, are sumptuously furnished, with many extra touches, like a "good-night mint" and beds turned down at night. You can dine informally in the Café Royale's garden setting or go gourmet in the classic Rib Room (see "Restaurants"). The Touche Lounge is a sidewalk café by day, a cozy gathering place at night. In the Esplanade Lounge, there's soft music after 8 p.m. Doubles here are in the $115 to $180 range, with frequent special rates that run lower.

Yet another luxury hotel in the Quarter is the **Royal Sonesta,** 300 Bourbon St., New Orleans, LA 70140 (tel. 504/586-0300), also adorned with those lacy New Orleans balconies. It's large, with some 500 rooms, including split-levels overlooking the outdoor pool or patio. Begue's, its premier restaurant, offers a daily buffet of New Orleans favorites and at night elegant French and Créole cuisine. The Green House Garden Café overlooks the patio and fountain, with lighter dining featuring salads, seafood and Créole specialties. Best of all, it's right smack in the middle of Bourbon Street action. Doubles start at $105, with very attractive packages available.

Still in the luxury class, but quite different in style, is the small, European-style **Maison de Ville**, 727 Rue Toulouse, New Orleans, LA 70130 (tel. 504/561-5858, or toll free 800/634-1600), built in 1742. In addition to gem-like rooms, all furnished with antiques, there are cottages available, one of which was John Audubon's residence when he was painting *Birds of America* in the 1820s. The very personal service here includes a breakfast of fresh orange juice, croissants, steaming chicory coffee, which you may have in your room, or on the patio, or in the parlor, and complimentary sherry and port served in the afternoon and evening. Morning and evening newspapers are delivered to your room and that almost-vanished shoe-polishing service is available—just leave them outside your door at night and notify the desk. The intimate Parisian-style Bistro restaurant offers dining inside or out in the pretty courtyard. Double-occupancy rooms begin at $110, suites at $185, and cottages at $275.

The **Westin Canal Place**, 100 Rue Iberville, New Orleans, LA 70130 (tel. 504/566-7006, or toll free 800/223-5672), has one of the most convenient locations in town—right at the river on the Canal Street edge of the French Quarter. Its window-walled 11th-floor lobby is a masterpiece of Carrara marble, fine paintings, and antiques, a lovely setting for afternoon tea. A handsome English-style pub and Le Jardin restaurant (see "French Quarter Dining") are just steps away. All rooms have marble foyers and baths, as well as refrigerators. Sweeping river views are part of the extras here. There's a garage for parking ($10), concierge service, a heated pool with poolside beverage service, a putting green, 18-hole golf privileges, and a special elevator descending directly to Canal Place shops, barbershop, and beauty salon. Rates start at $145 for doubles.

You couldn't ask for a better location than the **Bourbon Orleans**, 717 Orleans St., New Orleans, LA 70116 (tel. 504/523-2222, or toll free 800/521-5338) —it's on the corner of Bourbon and Orleans, right in the heart of the French Quarter. Nor could you ask for a more beautiful or gracious hostelry. Its public rooms include the historic New Orleans Ballroom, which opened in 1817 and became the center of the city's social whirl. The Bourbon Orleans continues that tradition of elegance, and its guest rooms are a rare blend of antique (Queen Anne and Chippendale) and traditional furnishings, and some bedrooms feature two-poster canopied beds. Unusually attractive are the split-level suites, all of which come equipped with marble-top wet bar and well-stocked mini-bar. Prices range from $115 to $140 for doubles, and the town-house suites run $160 to $255. Highly recommended.

The sophisticated elegance of the **St. Louis**, 730 Rue Bienville, New Orleans, LA 70130 (tel. 504/581-7300), makes this a very special place, with a decided European flavor. The courtyard with its huge marble fountain, antiques, and gilt-framed oil paintings are indicative of the luxury you'll find in the guest rooms. Some rooms have private balconies overlooking the courtyard. Doubles run $130 to $160, with suites starting at $195. Children under 12 stay free with their parents.

The lovely **Place d'Armes Hotel**, 625 St. Ann St., New Orleans, LA 70116 (tel. 504/524-4531), has one of the most magnificent courtyards in the Quarter, surrounded by its 78 lovely rooms. Furnishings are in a traditional style, most with fabric wall coverings. A complimentary continental breakfast is served to all guests. The location just off Jackson Square makes sightseeing a breeze. Bedrooms start at $65, double occupancy.

## Motels

Right in the heart of everything is the **de la Poste Motor Hotel,** 316 Chartres St., New Orleans, LA 70130 (tel. 504/581-1200). The 100 rooms are all spacious and comfortable, and most either overlook the Grande Patio and pool or face onto one of the more interesting French Quarter streets. The courtyard, incidentally, has a magnificent staircase leading up to a second-level outdoor patio. Parking is free, there's a babysitting service, and children under 12 pay nothing when occupying the same room as their parents. Double-occupancy rooms begin at a stiff $97, but location, accommodations, and service all qualify as deluxe.

The **Landmark Bourbon,** 541 Bourbon St., New Orleans, LA 70130 (tel. 504/524-7611), sits on the site of the 1859 French opera house, the first one built in the U.S., which burned to the ground in 1919. It's hard to tell, however, that the present building hasn't been here for just that many years, so well have the planners integrated its design into New Orleans traditional architecture. All rooms have a Deep South decor and oversize double beds, and some have balconies overlooking Bourbon Street. The Reunion Café serves sumptuous Créole dishes, and the Cabaret has live entertainment. Prices here hinge on whether or not your room faces Bourbon Street and has a balcony. Doubles without same begin at $95; those with are higher.

A restored row mansion and a macaroni factory have been combined to create **Le Richelieu Motor Hotel,** 1234 Chartres St., New Orleans, LA 70116 (tel. 504/529-2492). The folks here are proudest of their VIP suite, which has three bedrooms, a super kitchen, and even a steamroom—and goes for $300 a night! But the "ordinary" guest rooms I saw were all exceptionally nice and *much* less expensive (doubles begin at $75). The large courtyard holds a pool, where you lunch poolside. Most rooms have balconies and all overlook either the French Quarter or the pool and courtyard. There's free parking on their private lot.

There are no fewer than *five* patios—each one a real jewel—at the family-owned **Hotel Provincial,** 1024 Chartres St., New Orleans, LA 70116 (tel. 504/581-4995, or toll free 800/535-7922). The 1830s building has kept its high-ceilinged rooms, and each one is decorated in a distinct style with imported French and authentic Créole antiques. My favorite holds a huge carved mahogany double bed with a high overhanging canopy topped with a carved tiara. Gaslights on the patios and the overall feeling of graciousness make this one a real delight, a tranquil refuge from the rigors of sightseeing or nighttime revelry. Rates run $70 and up for a double-occupancy room, and there's free on-site parking.

The **Château Motor Hotel,** 1001 Chartres St., New Orleans, LA 70116 (tel. 504/524-9636), is one of the best buys in town, both in terms of comfort and just plain charm. Its flagstone-paved courtyard is bordered by an awning-covered café, where breakfast or lunch may be taken in the out-of-doors and the classic statuary and fountains add a continental touch. There are some four-poster beds as well as bed-living room combinations, and the morning newspaper is delivered free daily. Parking is free. Doubles here begin at $58, with a 10% discount for senior citizens.

## A Luxury Guesthouse

**Grenoble House,** 329 Daphine St., New Orleans, LA 70112 (tel. 504/522-1331), is a French Quarter town house centered around a courtyard that holds a heated pool with a whirlpool spa and a barbecue pit. The 17 suites are beautifully furnished with a mix of fine antiques and the best of modern fittings; all have fully equipped kitchens, and each one is different. All have king- or queen-size beds, there's a sofa bed in each living room, and a continental breakfast is included in the rate. A nice "extra" here is the concierge service—they'll book theater tickets, restaurants, sightseeing tours, and even arrange a gourmet dinner brought to your suite or a private cocktail party in the patio if you want to entertain friends. Rates begin at $125 for a one-bedroom suite with queen-size bed; a one-bedroom with a king-size bed goes for $160; and two-bedroom suites start at $225.

## Other Guesthouses

I met Mrs. Junius Underwood, proprietor of the **French Quarter Maisonnettes,** 1130 Chartres St., New Orleans, LA 70116 (tel. 504/524-9918), over morning coffee—hers, not mine. When I apologized for the intrusion, she quickly assured me, "I haven't had a hot cup of coffee in years, but I don't mind, I'd much rather chat with my guests." This gracious lady presides over an 1825 mansion that you enter through a wide carriage drive paved with flagstones leading to the plant-filled courtyard with its three-tiered fountain. Most rooms open onto the courtyard and each is comfortably furnished and has its own private bath. The location is a sightseer's dream: across the street is the historic Beauregard House, next door is the original Ursuline Convent built in 1734 and said to be the oldest building in the Mississippi Valley, and just a few blocks away is the old French Market, so handy for coffee and beignets to begin or end the day. Best of all, there's Mrs. Underwood, whose thoughtfulness toward guests extends to furnishing a privately printed brochure containing tips on dining, sightseeing, shopping, and almost anything else to make your visit more entertaining and comfortable, all gleaned from her intimate, longtime association with New Orleans. And there's Jesse, who has worked here for years and whose pleasant personality and always-cheerful assistance adds immeasurably to your stay. Rates run $40 and up, and there is parking for a slight fee.

Two of the French Quarter's most gracious hosts, Jim Weirich and Don Heil, welcome guests in their lovely old home at **623 Ursulines St.,** New Orleans, LA 70116 (tel. 504/529-5489). Centered around a courtyard that holds blooming orchids, azaleas, crape myrtle trees, and magnolias, are four suites in old slave quarters. All are thoroughly modern and have a bedroom, living room, and private bath. There are three suites of comparable size in the main house. An added bonus is its convenient location, just footsteps away from all major sightseeing in the Quarter. Rates begin at $46 for double occupancy, and there's garage parking for an additional charge.

Down on the *quiet* end of Bourbon Street, the **Lafitte Guest House,** 1003 Bourbon St., New Orleans, LA 70116 (tel. 504/581-2678, or toll free 800/331-7971 outside Louisiana), is in a residential neighborhood, yet close enough to the action for easy walking. The four-story brick building, adorned with balconies on the upper floors, was built in 1849, and the restoration has retained marble fireplaces and 20-foot-high ceilings. Furnishings are a mix of antiques and upholstered furniture. A telephone in each room and a continental breakfast are included in rates, which run $65 to $95 single, $75 to $105 double. Parking is free.

The **Hotel Villa Convento,** 616 Ursulines St., New Orleans, LA 70116 (tel. 504/522-1793), is really a small inn that is run much like a guesthouse by the Campo family. The 24 rooms in the restored Créole town house are nicely furnished and have full baths, TVs, and telephones. Some face onto the patio, others have balconies, and there's a small, cheery breakfast room just off the lobby where orange juice, coffee, and croissants make up the continental breakfast. The central courtyard features a three-tiered fountain and tropical plants. Doubles here begin at $45, with suites running $90 and the unusually attractive loft rooms for families (a king-size bed and two twins) at $65.

**OUTSIDE THE QUARTER:** Convenience based on special interests may well lead you to prefer accommodations outside the Quarter, and there is a wide variety from which to choose.

## Hotels

The **Pontchartrain Hotel,** 2031 St. Charles Ave., New Orleans, LA 70140 (tel. 504/524-0581), is as elegant as its Garden District location. Rooms are beautifully furnished, many with service bars; service is so polished you'll feel pampered (for example, your bed is turned down at night and nightclothes laid out); and the gourmet cuisine of the Caribbean Room is internationally known. Everything in this 50-year-old New Orleans institution is in the continental tradition, and "deluxe" is the only word that fits. Prices, too, fall into that category, with double rooms beginning at $105.

The luxurious **Fairmont Hotel,** University Place, New Orleans, LA 70140 (tel. 504/529-7111), is just one block from the French Quarter. The famous Sazerac Restaurant is sheer elegance; some of the best shows in town are featured in the Blue Room; and the Sazerac Bar is open mornings as well as evenings. Rooms are plush, with elegant modern furnishings. Prices are, of course, also in the luxury range, with a $150 beginning rate for double occupancy.

Over on the riverfront (in an area some are now calling the "River Quarter"), the **New Orleans Hilton Riverside and Towers,** Poydras Street at the Mississippi River, New Orleans, LA 70140 (tel. 504/561-0500, or toll free 800/HILTONS), radiates such New Orleans character that it's hard to believe it hasn't been here forever, in spite of its appearance. This *is* a modern, high-rise hotel all right, but inside the public rooms are warm with shades of tea roses and emerald green and lots of mahogany paneling. And the food and entertainment reflect the Crescent City perfectly, as do the hospitals and efficient staff. That consummate New Orleanian, Pete Fountain, entertains in his own club here, and the excitement of the Riverwalk development is just outside. Guest rooms are unusually spacious, many with river views (others overlooking the cityscape). Doubles are in the $121 to $160 range, and the luxurious suites start at $375.

The **Windsor Court Hotel,** 300 Gravier St., New Orleans, LA 70140 (tel. 504/523-6000 or toll free 800/262-2662), is a pretty, all-suite hotel filled with original works of art and antiques, and all rooms are beautifully furnished, including refrigerator, wet bar, oversize beds, and balconies. There's valet parking ($8), concierge service, indoor tennis, and 18-hole golf privileges; a health club and a heated pool with poolside service; and free in-room movies. British afternoon tea is served in the lobby. Rates are in the $145 to $195 range for doubles.

The **Holiday Inn Crowne Plaza,** 300 Poydras, New Orleans, LA 70130 (tel. 504/525-9444, or toll free 800/522-6963), has 450 units, suites, a concierge floor, valet parking ($7), and a restaurant and lounge with entertainment. It's an attractive hotel that includes among its many amenities a heated pool with poolside beverage service, exercise room, cable TV, and free in-room movies. Suites and the 22 rooms on the luxury-level Concierge Floor come with a complimentary continental breakfast and refreshments, refrigerators, and a private cocktail lounge, all at higher rates than the standard $113 to $123 for doubles.

## Motels

The **Quality Inn Midtown,** 3900 Tulane Ave., New Orleans, LA 70119 (tel. 504/486-5541, or toll free 800/228-5151), is just minutes away from the Quarter, and rooms are nicely decorated, above average in size for this price range. There's a gourmet restaurant, a lounge with live entertainment, and free off-the-street parking. Doubles begin at $50.

The **Holiday Inn–East Highrise,** 6324 Chef Menteur Hwy., New Orleans, LA 70126 (tel. 504/241-2900, or toll free 800/465-4329), is northeast of the city at the junction of U.S. 90 and I-10. Rooms are typical of this chain (that is, they're attractive and comfortable), and there's a pool, dining room, and entertainment in the lounge except on Sunday. Doubles are in the $52 to $60 range. In the other direction, the **Holiday Inn–Gretna,** 100 West Bank Expressway (tel. 504/366-2361, or toll free 800/238-8000), offers attractive rooms just across the river from the city. There's a pool, dining room, and a lounge. Doubles run $45 to $52.

## A Guesthouse

Right at the edge of Audubon Park, the **Park View Guest House,** 7004 St. Charles Ave., New Orleans, LA 70118 (tel. 504/861-7564), is an old Victorian hotel—it's on the National Register of Historic Landmarks—with comfortable rooms at bargain prices. There's a large lounge (with a lovely stained-glass window) and dining room where a complimentary continental breakfast is served. Most rooms have private baths, and those that don't only share with one other room. Double rooms cost $55 to $65 per day. This location is especially convenient if you plan to visit Tulane, Loyola, or Dominican Universities.

## A Campground

**KOA New Orleans West,** 219 S. Starrett Rd., River Ridge, LA 70123 (tel. 504/467-1792), has large, shaded sites for both tents and trailers, a pool, store, laundromat, and tour arrangements. To reach it, take I-10 to Williams Boulevard, then south 2½ miles to Jefferson Hwy. and left three-quarters of a mile. Rates are $21.

# 2. Restaurants

Just as her people are a mixture of many cultures, New Orleans's cuisine reflects a rich blending of much of the world's cooking. As a well-known New Orleans cook once wrote, the food is "grandchild to France, descendant to Spain, cousin to Italy, and also is full-fledged southern." That just about says it, except that she might have added the West Indies and American Indians to that gastronomic ancestry.

The "haute cuisine" and provincial French recipes brought to the New World by early settlers fast acquired the flavorings of native herbs and filé (ground sassafras leaves) used by local Indians, the Spanish saffron and peppers that arrived a little later, West Indian vegetables, spices, and sugarcane, and African influences that survived the slave-boat voyages and made their way into white kitchens as black women took over much of the cooking. Out of all this came a distinctive Créole cuisine found only in New Orleans. Italian touches came later, adding another dimension to the city's tables, and dishes from the American South were retained virtually intact.

Along with their love of the exciting combinations—and they are endless—that resulted from this "stew" (or perhaps "gumbo" is a better word) of international cooking, the people of New Orleans have inherited an appreciation for fine service in elegant surroundings and have acquired a sense of fun that permits gourmet dishes to appear in the plainest of settings and the plainest meal of boiled crayfish or red beans and rice to come to table in the fanciest of eateries. And no matter where a meal begins, it's likely to end down in the French Market over café au lait and hot beignets.

If you're in the mood for that perfect service and posh setting, you'll find it at your elbow. Or if taste and budget call for simpler dining, that too is never far away. "Downtown" in the French Quarter or "uptown" in the newer part of town, good eating is an integral part of any visit to New Orleans.

**FRENCH QUARTER DINING:** The city's best—certainly the most famous—restaurants are right here. Read on.

### The Top Restaurants

When I put together the first edition of this book, I made the sad decision to omit any mention of **Arnaud's,** 813 Bienville St. (tel. 504/523-5433). The kitchen had deteriorated into nothing short of a mess, and although I had loved the place over the years, it simply could not be recommended at that time. Well, since then there's been a dramatic change, and I have found myself sharing the excitement of New Orleans friends at what has happened at Arnaud's—under the new direction of Archie Casbarian, not only has the interior been restored to its former grandeur, but the *food* is again worthy of the praise it once knew. The restaurant was built in 1918 by a Count Arnaud, and Mr. Casbarian has retained the original menu specialties, along with exciting new dishes created by Christian Gille, a Frenchman with outstanding credentials. Try shrimp Arnaud, oysters Bienville, crabmeat imperial, trout meunière, or pompano en croûte, at prices that range from $10 to $23 on the à la carte menu, and any or all of them are *certain* to reach your table in a state of pure perfection. This has been a favorite place to eat, especially during Carnival season, with locals for years, and now it is reclaiming their devotion. Especially popular is the jazz brunch on Sunday from 10 a.m. to 2:30 p.m. and the Richelieu Bar anytime. Hours are 11:30 a.m. to 2:30 p.m. for lunch, 6 to 10 p.m. for dinner. Don't leave without seeing the stunning display of Mardi Gras costumes upstairs.

Who hasn't heard of **Antoine's,** 713 St. Louis St. (tel. 504/581-4422), and dreamed of at least one meal in this legendary restaurant that has been run by the same family for more than 145 years? Just entering the ironwork-adorned building sets the tone, and once inside you're in a world of white tile floors, slowly turning antique ceiling fans, 14 separate rooms that run the gamut from plainness to grandeur—and tuxedo-garbed waiters. As for the food, choose from such classics as oysters Rockefeller, pompano en papillote, chicken Rochambeau, or filet de boeuf Robespierre en casserole; or settle for something simpler from a menu that lists more than 150 selections. To accompany your choice, you have at your disposal one of the richest wine cellars in America. Be sure to bone up on your French before you come, for there's not a word of English on the à la carte menu. Prices are à la carte, and complete dinners run upward of $20 per person. Lunch hours are noon to 2 p.m., dinner from 5:30 to 9:30 p.m. It closes Sunday.

**Brennan's,** 417 Royal St. (tel. 504/525-9711), is a longtime favorite with residents and visitors alike. There's just no way to describe their beautiful patio —you have to see it to believe it. "Breakfast at Brennan's" has become internationally famous, and you can breakfast here even in the evening. Only, if that's what you have in mind, don't plan another meal that day—you'll want to be able to do justice to the sumptuous dishes listed on a menu that tempts you with items like eggs Hussarde (poached eggs atop Holland rusks, Canadian bacon, and marchand de vin sauce, topped with hollandaise sauce and accompanied by grilled tomato) or pompano Pontchartrain amandine (sautéed in butter with grilled almonds, lump crabmeat, and lemon butter sauce). Even their omelets are spectacular. You see, this is not your typical bacon-and-eggs breakfast, but breakfast in the old tradition of antebellum days in the Quarter, and if you really want to do it right, order one of their complete breakfast suggestions. Typical is the selection that starts with egg Sardou (poached egg atop creamed spinach and artichoke bottoms, served with hollandaise sauce), followed by quail in burgundy sauce (served over wild and white rice), and topped off by crêpes Fitzgerald (served with a sauce of crushed strawberries flamed in maraschino), Brennan's hot French bread, and hot chicory coffee. Brennan's is open every day from 8 a.m. to 2:30 p.m. and 6 to 11 p.m. with breakfast and lunch prices of $15 to $25; dinner will run $20 to $34.

The **Rib Room,** 621 St. Louis St. (tel. 504/529-7045), in the Royal Orleans Hotel, has long been a favorite of New Orleanians. It's an attractive room with lots of brick and wood, high ceilings, and arched windows. The back wall is dominated by open rôtisserie ovens. Specialties here are (what else!) beef. Roasts are exceptional, as are prime ribs, filets, sirloins, brochettes, tournedos, and steak au poivre. The extensive menu also lists veal, lamb, duckling, and seafood, all excellent. At lunch, salads and a variety of egg dishes are also offered. Lunch hours are 11:30 a.m. to 3 p.m., with prices ranging from $8 to $16; dinner is served from 6 to 11 p.m., at prices of $18 to $30. Do treat yourself to at least one dinner here.

## Also Good

One of the loveliest of French Quarter restaurants is the **Court of Two Sisters,** 613 Royal St. (tel. 504/522-7261), where you can dine outside in a courtyard filled with flowers, fountains, and low-hanging willows or in the Créole Patio Room. Créole and French cuisine are the specialties here, and if you fall in love with their original-recipe lemon-lime sauces, they'll sell you some to take home. You'll know you've found a friendly establishment from the very first, for a sign just inside the door lists their hours as: "Jazz Buffet 9 a.m.–3 p.m., Dinner 5:30–11 p.m. Browsing 3:30–5 p.m. Have a nice day!" You can accept the invitation to browse and enjoy a cocktail in the courtyard while you're about it. Reservations are necessary for dinner, which features such delicacies as shrimp Toulouse, crabmeat Rector, and sirloin tips à la Créole. Prices at dinner for a complete meal start at $23, and à la carte prices run $15 to $20. Other meals are lower. In their **Ye Olde Court Tavern,** 614 Rue Bourbon, you'll find drinks and New Orleans "po-boy" sandwiches.

Don't worry about reservations at **Galatoire's,** 209 Bourbon St. (tel. 504/525-2021)—they don't accept them. So, unless you take a tip from the natives and go to lunch before noon or dinner before 6 p.m., you'll stand in line outside along with everyone else. It's worth a wait to eat in this family-run restaurant that serves possibly the best fish dishes in town. Try the trout Marguèry (with shrimp in a lovely white sauce). Prices are in the $8-and-up range on the à la carte menu. It's open from 11:30 a.m. to 9 p.m. Tuesday through Saturday, noon to 9 p.m. on Sunday; closed Monday.

Elegance in an eclectic mode is the keynote at **Café Anglais,** 221 Royal St. (tel. 504/529-2603). Decor gracefully mixes antiques, oil paintings, and avant-garde works of art to create a relaxed, yet exciting ambience. Silver carving wagons roll out roasts, and there's a caviar and champagne bar; yet the primary emphasis is on the freshest of local ingredients and New Orleans specialties such as barbecued shrimp and broiled redfish (a change from the blackened variety). Hours are 11:30 a.m. to 2:30 p.m. Monday through Friday and 6 to 10 p.m. Monday through Thursday, until 11 p.m. on Friday and Saturday. Dinner will run about $25 to $30. It's a good idea to reserve.

Moran's **Riverside Restaurant,** 44 Market Place (tel. 504/529-1583), is surely one of the most *romantic* places to eat in the French Quarter—it sits atop the Bazaar Building of the renovated French Market complex and affords sweeping views of both the market and the river. The dining room is done in low-key elegance, with a window wall facing out to the river and soft lighting. The cooking is French-Italian (with homemade pasta), and specialties include seafood, chicken, lamb, veal, and steak. I especially like the lemon-butter sauce on shrimp scampi "Don Josey," but almost any dish is likely to have you raving. Outstanding on the dessert list is their amaretto parfait. Prices range from $14 to $24 on the à la carte menu, and hours are 6 to 11 p.m., with reservations absolutely necessary most nights.

Just across from the French Market, the **Café Sbisa,** 1011 Decatur St. (tel. 504/561-8354), is much favored by the artistic crowd in New Orleans, with some of her best writers and painters showing up regularly. It's easy to see why, when you enter the casually elegant café with its ceiling fans, potted greenery, and endless mirrors. The atmosphere is relaxed, and the food is exceptional, with seafood specialties like smoked fish, swordfish, mussels, salmon, clams, and a very good bouillabaisse. Lamb, duckling, and steaks are also good. Prices run $13 to $24, and hours are 6 to 11 p.m. Monday through Thursday, till midnight on Friday and Saturday. Sunday features a champagne brunch from 11 a.m. to 3 p.m. and dinner from 6 to 10 p.m.

## Very Reasonable and Very Good

One of the delights of exploring New Orleans's French Quarter is discovering the many small, inexpensive places to eat, some just as exciting as the better-known restaurants. What you'll find here is sort of a thumbnail sketch of some of my own favorites. But do explore on your own and let me know about your special "finds."

One of the French Quarter's most charming casual eateries is **La Madeleine,** 547 St. Ann St., at Chartres Street (tel. 504/568-9950). One of a chain of French bakeries, La Madeleine's centerpiece is a brick, wood-burning oven that turns out a wide variety of breads, croissants, and brioches. A glass case up front holds marvelous pastries to take out or eat in the cafeteria section, where quiches, salads, soups, sandwiches, and other light entrees are available. Delightful for a continental breakfast or light lunch. Eat well for $5 to $10. Hours are 7 a.m. to 8 p.m. Monday through Thursday, to 9 p.m. Friday through Sunday.

**Molly's,** 732 Toulouse St., is an Irish bar and restaurant I discovered during a rainy day in the heart of the Quarter when I ducked in for an Irish coffee and stayed to enjoy a dozen fried oysters, french fries, and salad for just $6.75, and I never had better anywhere else in the city. That says a lot for the kitchen here, especially since there is a very wide variety of offerings on the menu. It's open 24 hours a day and is a great place to watch all sorts of New Orleans types, as well as tourists who find it as I did. Breakfast is served at any hour, which makes it a special favorite of night owls who have a taste for bacon and eggs after a night on the town. For a special treat, order Irish coffee—the best I've had outside the Emerald Isle.

Jim Monaghan, original owner of Molly's (he's since sold it), is now a leading citizen of Decatur Street, with three very good eating establishments, and boundless enthusiasm for the restoration of what had become a very seedy part of the Quarter. **Molly's at the Market,** 1107 Decatur St. (tel. 504/525-5169), serves breakfast all day, and the extensive lunch and dinner menus offer American, Italian, and Irish dishes for under $6. So fond am I of Molly's that I find myself heading in that direction almost anytime hunger pangs strike.

The **Original Melius Bar,** 622 Conti St. (tel. 504/581-2723), is an attractive, rather large place with lots of exposed brick, dark wood, and overhead fans. It's a great lunch favorite of lawyers, bankers, and, surprisingly, waiters from some of the more elegant restaurants in the neighborhood. A sample price here is $3.50 for red beans and rice. Lunch is from 11 a.m. to 3:30 p.m. but it stays open until 2 or 3 a.m. for drinks. On Wednesday there's draft beer for 25¢ a glass after 8 p.m., and Wednesday through Saturday there's dancing in the back room.

Over on Jackson Square, the **Café Pontalba,** corner of Rue Chartres and Rue St. Peter, is an old-fashioned, tiled-floor, high-ceilinged café with doors that are left open to the street. It's generally full, but the busy atmosphere is part of the charm, and the menu is both extensive—from burgers to seafood to Créole—and moderate to cheap. This is also a good foot-resting, elbow-bending stop, and if there's a drink they don't serve—alcoholic or otherwise—I can't think of it.

The **Napoleon House,** 500 Chartres St. (tel. 504/524-9752), is at the corner of Chartres and St. Louis Streets, and is so named because at the time of the "Little Corporal's" death there was actually a plot ahatching in this 1797 National Landmark house to snatch him from his island exile and bring him back to New Orleans. The third floor was added expressly for the purpose of providing a home for him after the rescue. It wears its history well and with dignity; there is a limited menu of po-boys, Italian muffuletta sandwiches, and pastries ($2 to $3.50); and the jukebox plays only classical music! This is Dick Cavett's favorite New Orleans haunt, as well as a very popular spot with residents. Hours are 11 a.m. to 1 or 2 a.m.

A real favorite with locals, the **Port of Call,** 838 Esplanade Ave. (tel. 504/523-0120), is a cozy, pub-ish sort of place (lots of wood) with probably the best hamburgers and steaks in town. Pizza is also on the menu, as well as a dish I *really* liked, mushrooms in wine. Prices can run anywhere from $4 to $16, depending on your culinary mood (hamburger or steak), and because it's always packed at regular lunch and dinner hours, I like to drop in during off-hours (or sometime after 7 p.m., when neighborhood residents get together at the bar to relax). Hours are noon to 1 a.m., with food service until around midnight.

The **Coffee Pot,** 714 St. Peter St. (tel. 504/523-8215), has been known for its breakfasts (which are served all day) since the 1940s. And what a breakfast you can put together from the large menu! Omelets come with just about everything you can think of—oysters or shrimp, chicken livers, red beans, ham and cheese, and there's even a "soul food" creation. Eggs Benedict, eggs Créole, pancakes (strawberry, pecan, and sliced apple are just a few of the varieties), biscuits, and fresh fruit juices are all here. In addition, there are lunch or dinner dishes such as country steak, a Gulf Coast seafood platter, red beans and rice with smoked sausage, and a dozen others for prices of $3.50 to $9, and a large selection of po-boys. Desserts are homemade and delicious (try Cousin Pearl's bread pudding or a fruit cobbler). Hours are 8:30 a.m. to 10:30 p.m.

On the corner of Royal and St. Ann Streets, the **Père Antoine Restaurant** (tel. 504/581-4478) is an attractive tile-floored place with a huge mirror in back and flowers out front. Cajun cookery is the specialty here, with Cajun redfish (cooked in a rich tomato sauce, a nice change from "blackened"), shrimp, or crayfish étoufée, featured. The seafood platter (with catfish, shrimp, scallops, crab, and Cajun popcorn—that's deep-fried seasoned shrimp) is a real bargain at $13. For lighter meals, there are soups and salads, sandwiches and burgers, omelets, and New Orleans favorites like red beans and rice, jambalaya, and chicken Créole. Prices range from as low as $3.50 up to $13, and hours are 9 a.m. to midnight daily.

**Captain Al's Seafood & Oyster Bar,** 635 Bourbon St. (tel. 504/524-3817), adjoins the Maison Bourbon, home of some of the street's best jazz, and is open from 11 a.m. to 2 a.m. daily. The very moderately priced menu ($4.50 to $11) offers—in addition, of course, to oysters—traditional New Orleans dishes like red beans and rice, shrimp étouffée, barbecued shrimp, and Cajun jambalaya. There's also a wide range of specialty drinks, as well as some 16 brands of beer. Eat inside or in the small courtyard out back—in either, you'll dine to the sound of jazz.

**Nugents,** 811 Conti St. (tel. 504/523-8619), is a small bar and restaurant with an interesting and somewhat quaint dining room in the rear. The menu features fried oysters and trout, burgers, red beans and rice, fettuccine, omelets, and a variety of sandwiches, with the highest price on the menu $5.50, most in the $3.50 to $5 range. Hours are 8:30 a.m. to 4 p.m., and they serve breakfast all day. The bar is open until 3 a.m.

### The Jackson Brewery

The old landmark Jackson Brewery, at the edge of Jackson Square on Decatur Street, has come to new life. While it no longer brews Jax Beer, it now houses an eclectic collection of shops and restaurants. The third level is devoted to a fascinating array of food stalls serving everything from boiled crayfish to barbecued shrimp, gumbo, oysters, pastries, and at least a dozen other New Orleans foods. Joe Cahn has moved his famous **New Orleans School of Cooking** (tel. 504/525-2665) to this location and will teach you how to cook jambalaya, bread pudding, and pralines (among other things), then serve a full meal that's included in the price of the demonstration. On the second level, look for the **Brewhouse Café & Bar,** a 19th-century-style eatery that offers indoor and outdoor dining (a great place for breakfast, which is served from 7:30 a.m.). On the fourth level, you'll find **Visko's** (tel. 504/522-2082), one of New Orleans's long-established seafood restaurants.

The **Louisiana Grocery & Feed Company,** in the Jackson Brewery (tel. 504/942-7527), is an offshoot of famed chef Paul Prudhomme's K-Paul's, and as you'd expect, Cajun cooking is the order of the day. Jambalaya, shrimp loaf, and chicken-and-andouille (smoked sausage) gumbo are just a sample of the goodies that come at prices that range from $3 to $7. Hours are 10 a.m. to 10 p.m., and there's take-out service as well as free delivery in the French Quarter and central business district.

### In the French Market

You'll find the **Café du Monde,** across from Jackson Square, absolutely habit forming! More than once, I found myself headed back across the Quarter to sit at one of the little round tables for a spell of people-watching and a steaming cup of café au lait (strong chicory coffee laced with hot milk) and the indescribably good beignets. Except for milk, that's all they serve, but a $1.40 order (for three of the doughnuts and coffee) is filling enough to serve for breakfast or a light lunch. New Orleanians have been coming here for years—it's open around the clock—and visitors flock back again and again. Besides your fellow customers, there's all of Jackson Square, with the horse carriages lined up across from the café, spread out before you, as well as shoppers headed for the French Market a little farther along Decatur Street.

### For Your Sweet Tooth

There's been an **Angelo Brocato's Original Italian Ice Cream Parlor** in New Orleans since 1905, and except for a brief interruption, Brocato's has been in the French Quarter. This is the family on whom the city's most demanding hostesses have for three generations depended to cater those occasions for friends and special guests when sweets must reach the heights of sheer perfection. Happily, you'll now find them back in new quarters at 537 St. Ann St. (tel. 504/486-1465), serving their fabulous ice cream, Italian ices, cannolis, and a whole feast of other pastries from 9 a.m. to 8 p.m. Monday through Friday, until 7 p.m. on Saturday and Sunday.

When that craving for something sweet hits you, you can also head for **Croissant d'Or,** 617 Ursulines St. (tel. 504/524-4663). It's an old-fashioned, light, and cheerful place with tile floors, ceiling fans, and a bakery case across one side that will send you into fits of indecision—the array of gorgeous goodies is staggering. Maurice Delechelle is the master baker here, and his kitchen turns out galettes bretonnes (butter cookies), pain au chocolat (chocolate bread), cygne swan (an eclair in the shape of a swan filled with whipped cream), croissants, brioches, and all sort of Danish pastries. Prices start at 55¢ and hours are 8 a.m. to 5:30 p.m. seven days a week.

When you're in the Jackson Square area, look for tiny **La Marquise** at 625 Chartres St., also run by Mr. Delechelle, with the same mouthwatering offerings and a small outdoor courtyard for diners.

**OTHER LOCALES:** Moving out of the French Quarter, you'll find you can eat surprisingly well elsewhere in this city:

### Award Winning

Since it opened in 1948, the **Caribbean Room** in the elegant Pontchartrain Hotel, 2031 St. Charles Ave. (tel. 504/524-0581), has won a list of culinary awards as long as your arm, and it really epitomizes New Orleans cuisine at its finest. The decor, like that of the rest of the hotel, is refined (almost understated) luxury. As for service—well, impeccable and solicitous come to mind. Their French and Créole kitchen turns out specialties like shrimp saki and backfin crabmeat with a lovely creamy, rather tart house dressing (actually, it's a combination of two, mustard and French) that have made fans of Arthur Rubinstein, Gerald Ford, Mary Martin, and a host of other celebrities. Dinner prices, while high ($15 to $25 for entrees), are certainly not exorbitant for such attention to detail in both food and service, and luncheon is quite reasonable. Reservations are advisable for both lunch (noon to 2 p.m.) and dinner (6 to 9 p.m.).

### Very Good

The unusual, rather grand blue-and-white building at the corner of Washington Avenue and Coliseum Street was built as a restaurant in 1880 by Emile Commander, and **Commander's Palace** (tel. 504/899-8221) has been a favorite of New Orleanians ever since. The patio, fountains, lush tropical plants, and soft colors are a perfect backdrop for Créole specialties. If you're a jazz buff, don't miss their famous Jazz Brunch (on Saturday and Sunday from 11 a.m. to 2 p.m.), where Dixieland is played by jazz greats. Brunch prices begin at $13, dinner at $23, and both menus are table d'hôte. Weekday lunches are à la carte from $8.50.

You'll find the **Bon Ton Café,** 401 Magazine St. (tel. 504/524-3386), absolutely jammed at lunch with New Orleans business people, and at dinner you'll be seated *only* if you have reservations. Such popularity is certainly well deserved, and Al Pierce, its owner, is well qualified to have earned it. He grew up on the banks of Bayou Lafourche, learned Cajun cooking from his mother, came to New Orleans in 1936, bought the Bon Ton in 1953, and since then has been serving up seafood gumbo, crayfish bisque, jambalaya, crayfish omelet, and other Cajun dishes in a manner that would make his mother proud. This is a small, utterly charming place, and one not to be missed if you want to sample true Cajun cooking (it's more subtle than Créole, and makes use of shallots, parsley, bell peppers, and garlic). Hours are 11 a.m. to 2 p.m. and 5 to 9:30 p.m. Monday to Friday. Prices run $6.50 to $13 at lunch, $14 to $18 at dinner.

A little bit of Paris has settled into New Orleans quite nicely at the **Restaurant de la Tour Eiffel,** 2040 St. Charles Ave. (tel. 504/524-2555). In its English translation, that's the Eiffel Tower Restaurant, and that is what it *actually* is— this is the very structure that once served Parisian patrons at the 562-foot level of Paris's Eiffel Tower. Owners Daniel Bonnot and John Onorio bought the dismantled restaurant and reassembled it here in New Orleans, a rather fitting thing to do, considering New Orlean's French connection. Now perched a mere 25 feet above ground, the restaurant is a study in decor of the '30s, and the menu is that of a French bistro with strong New Orleans overtones. Trout meunière, coq au vin, sole stuffed with crabmeat mousse, and rack of lamb are among entree offerings, and desserts are especially good. You are, in fact, quite welcome to drop in for coffee and dessert at the end of a New Orleans evening. Prices are in the $9 to $14 range for entrees, and daily hours are 11:30 a.m. to 2:30 p.m. and 6:30 to 11 p.m., with bar and dessert service even later.

### Good—And Easy on the Budget

Just across from City Park, within sight of the famous "dueling oaks," the **Tavern on the Park,** 900 City Park Ave. (tel. 504/486-3333), is a delightful recreation of art deco eateries of the Prohibition era. The historic building is a marvelous setting for the restaurant's steak and seafood specialties, with broiled cold-water lobster, fresh trout, and superb steaks high on the list of local favorites. Hours are 11:30 a.m. to 10 p.m. Sunday through Thursday, until 11 p.m. on Friday and Saturday.

**Flagon's Wine Bar & Bistro,** 3222 Magazine St. (tel. 504/899-6471), is a pleasant, lighthearted spot for a simple glass of wine, a light repast of sandwiches and/or desserts, or a full meal of such delicacies as redfish in parchment or duck breast in cabernet sauce. Pastas are delicious (try the pasta with crabmeat, dill, and fried buster crab). There are more than 40 fine wines available by the glass, with as many as 350 good vintages to buy by the bottle. Prices are moderate, the ambience is great, and hours are 11:30 a.m. to 2:30 p.m. and 6 to 11 p.m., seven days a week.

**Riverbend Restaurant,** 734 S. Carrollton Ave. (tel. 504/861-7551), is an attractive uptown neighborhood restaurant adjacent to the main Riverbend shopping area (it's right at Stop 44 for the St. Charles streetcar). There's a large menu of steaks, seafood, salads, pastas (fettuccine with shrimp is my personal favorite —really terrific), sandwiches, and breakfast offerings of omelets, pancakes, and egg combinations. Any one of their excellent continental coffees (Café Royale with brandy; Italian with Frangelica; Jamaican with Tía Maria; Mexican with Kahlúa; Spanish with Kahlúa and rum; or Irish with whisky) is a great way to end your meal. Prices are very low, with the highest item on the à la carte menu running only $11. Back of the main dining room, with an entrance on Maple Street, the Bar at the Bend is a friendly and very popular "dropping in" spot for locals as well as others who have come to shop at Riverbend. This is, in fact, the ideal place for lunch or dinner to begin or round off a shopping foray. Hours are 7 a.m. to 11 p.m. daily (to 1 a.m. on Friday and Saturday).

There's been a lounge run by the same family in the old brick building that now houses **Ernst's Café,** 600 S. Peters St. (tel. 504/525-8544), since 1902. Its brick walls, high ceilings, and heavy timbered bar make it an interesting and attractive setting for excellent sandwiches, sausage and eggs, red beans and rice, and po-boys at prices that won't top $10. If the weather is fine, eat outside on the long balcony that gives a good view of the river. Hours are 8 a.m. to 2:30 p.m. Monday through Saturday.

**Lido Gardens,** 4415 Airline Hwy., Metaire (tel. 504/834-8233), is the kind of local restaurant you're likely to have a New Orleans friend tell you about. It's been a favorite with residents for years, and on *my* first visit, it became an instant personal favorite. In a low, roadside building, Lido Gardens is a friendly, relaxing restaurant serving some of the best Italian cooking hereabout. There are red-checked tablecloths, a wishing well (hung with wine bottles) in the center of the room, and various members of the Mongiat family waiting to make you feel at home. The pasta dishes are superb (my Italian friend insists the lasagne is the best he's ever eaten away from home), and veal dishes come in a number of traditional recipes, including piccata, milanese, scaloppine, parmigiana, saltimbocca, and the marvelous involtini (prosciutto and cheese rolled in veal and simmered with butter, wine, and rosemary). Prices run $7 to $12. They're open every day except Sunday: lunch from 11 a.m. to 2 p.m. (no lunch on Saturday), dinner from 5 to 9 p.m. Monday to Thursday, until 10 p.m. on Friday and Saturday.

The **Camellia Grill,** 626 Carrollton Ave. (tel. 504/866-9573), is another locally popular restaurant, serving omelets, sandwiches, salads, and desserts at moderate prices. It's on the trolley line near the Riverbend Shopping Center, and prices are in the $2 to $4 bracket.

## Out of Town

About 30 minutes' drive on U.S. 90 west of the city, past Avondale, there's a plain plywood building with a shell front painted white that holds one of the area's best restaurants. **Mosca's** (P.O. Box 52403, New Orleans, LA 70152; tel. 504/436-9942) was started in 1946 by Lisa and Provino Mosca, and since their death, son Johnny and daughter Mary have carried on their unique style of cooking that combines elements of Italian and local Créole cuisine. If an evening in the countryside appeals to you, by all means make the drive and try dishes you'll find nowhere else. I can especially recommend the Italian crab salad (they use vinegar to flavor the crab and pickle the vegetables—delicious!) at $7 for an appetizer portion. And Mosca's Italian oysters are a treat, even at $17. Other specialties are quail with wild rice and roasted potato, squab and Cornish hen, also with wild rice and potato, and chicken cacciatore (you get the whole chicken) at prices of $13 to $20. Everything is prepared to order, and a wait of 40 minutes is sometimes necessary. As you can see, prices aren't cheap, and they accept no checks or credit cards, but for a real dining experience, Mosca's can't be beat. Since hours sometimes vary, best call ahead.

*Chapter XXII*

# NEW ORLEANS: THINGS TO SEE AND DO

### 1. Seeing the Sights
### 2. Nightlife
### 3. Festivals
### 4. The Sporting Life
### 5. Shopping

AN ENTIRE BOOK could be written on things to see and do in New Orleans—it's a city that cannot be seen or fully enjoyed hurriedly. And no matter how carefully you plan your time, you're certain to get back home and realize you've missed at least one thing you should have seen or done. People who live here will tell you that the only thing to do is move and settle in to a lifetime of learning the city, and there are many tales of people who've come here "on a lark," as one man put it, and stayed on for years. But since that isn't possible for you and me, I'll do my best to give you a list, and you'll surely have your own by the time you've been in New Orleans a day or so.

I'd like to point out again, however, that *no one* should set out to see the city without first stopping by the **Tourist Commission** at 529 St. Ann St. (tel. 504/566-5031). Both the walking- and driving-tour maps they provide are circular tours, easy to follow, and so informative they are mini-courses in New Orleans history and culture. Two days—one for walking, the other for driving—set aside for these tours at the beginning of your stay will give you the best introduction to this grand old city.

In the meantime, here are my personal suggestions:

## 1. Seeing the Sights

**AROUND THE FRENCH QUARTER:** Because of the wealth of sightseeing in this small area, I've divided my list into categories that I hope will be helpful to you in deciding just what you'd like to see first. Since there are so many of them and they are so lovely, let's start with—

**KEY TO THE NUMBERED REFERENCES ON THE FRENCH QUARTER MAP:**
1.—Old Bank of Louisiana; 2.—Old Bank of the U.S.; 3.—Old La. State Bank; 4.—N.O. Court Building; 5.—Casa Faurie; 6.—The Hermann House; 7.—Maison Seignouret; 8.—Merieult House; 9.—Casa de Comercio; 10.—Court of Two Lions; 11.—LeMonnier House; 12.—Maison de Fléchier; 13.—Maison LeMonnier; 14.—Spanish Arsenal; 15.—LaBranche House; 16.—St. Anthony's Garden; 17.—Salle d'Orléans; 18.—Père Antoine's Alley; 19.—The Presbytère; 20.—St. Louis Cathedral; 21.—The Cabildo; 22.—Pirates Alley; 23.—Pontalba Buildings; 24.—1850 House; 25.—Court of the Two Sisters; 26.—Old Ursulines Convent; 27.—Beauregard House; 28.—Soniat House; 29.—Clay House; 30.—LaLaurie House; 31.—Thierry House; 32.—The Gallier House; 33.—Lafitte's Blacksmith Shop; 34.—cornstalk fence; 35.—Miltenberger Houses; 36.—"Madame John's Legacy."

## Historic Homes

The classic New Orleans home is built around an open courtyard or patio, frequently centered with at least one fountain. Besides being a feast to the eye, these restful oases provided a gathering place for families and served as natural air-conditioning systems in the steamy summers.

**On Royal Street:** No. 631 is the second-oldest building on this street and was the residence for a time of the famous singer Adelina Patti, who gave the 1777 house its name of **Patti's Court.** The house at **no. 640** was built in 1811 and was the city's first "skyscraper." The most notable occupant, however, was Antoine Alciatoire, who took up residence in 1860 and operated a boarding house whose food became so famous that it led to his opening a restaurant, the same one his family still runs today, Antoine's. The **LaBranche Home,** at no. 700, has some of the loveliest lace ironwork in the city (stand across the street for the best view). Nos. 900, 906, and 910 are the **Miltenberger Mansions,** built by a wealthy widow in 1838 for her three sons, and are splendid indeed.

The **Gallier House** at no. 1132 was the home of the talented architect responsible for many of the fine old homes in the French Quarter. It is open to the public and you can see it restored to its original 1860 state for a fee of $3 for adults, $1 for children 5 to 11, and no charge for those under 5. Hours are 10 a.m. to 4:30 p.m., with the last tour at 3:45 p.m.

Go by to see **no. 1140** in broad daylight, otherwise you may hear ghostly moans or the savage hissing of a whip or catch a glimpse of a small black child walking on the balcony! The story behind this haunted house, built in 1831, is a New Orleans horror tale: The very beautiful and socially prominent Delphine LaLaurie lived here and entertained lavishly, until a night in 1834 when fire broke out and neighbors crashed through a locked door to find seven starving slaves chained in painful positions, unable to move. After rescuing the prisoners, the citizens turned on Madame LaLaurie and her family, but they dashed away in a carriage and fled to Europe, never to return until her body was returned several years later and, even then, she had to be buried in secrecy.

The Italian villa at **no. 1315** was built by John Gauche in 1856, who had the cast-iron balconies imported from Germany.

**On Bourbon Street:** No. 624 is the **Fortin House,** built in 1834 by a young doctor for his bride. Walk back into the patio and you can see how neighbors often built connecting doorways between their courtyards. The very small, cottage-like building at **no. 941,** now an interesting bar, is said to be where the Lafitte brothers operated Lafitte's Blacksmith Shop as a front for a prosperous slave trade. Notice the brick-between-posts construction—this is one of the few buildings of the type that survives.

**On Chartres Street:** No. 617, the **Bosque Home,** is a Spanish-style home built in 1795. In the rear of the carriageway are three separate patios opening one into the other. The **Beauregard House** at no. 1113 is a "raised" Créole cottage with Doric columns and twin stairways with wrought-iron railings. After the Civil War, Confederate Gen. P. G. T. Beauregard lived here in a rented room while looking for work. Novelist Frances Parkinson Keyes bought it in 1944 and restored it as her winter residence. It's open to the public for a fee of $3 for adults,

**DOWNTOWN NEW ORLEANS**
(Orientation and Transportation)

$2 for senior citizens and students, and $1 for children over 13. Hours are 10 a.m. to 3 p.m. (last tour begins at 2 p.m.) Monday through Saturday.

**On St. Peter Street and St. Ann on either side of Jackson Square:** The **Pontalba Apartments,** 16 rowhouses on each street, were built in 1850 and 1851 by Micaela Almonaster Pontalba in an effort to stop residents from moving out of the Quarter. Said to be the first apartment buildings in the U.S., they hold fascinating shops on the first floor and luxury apartments on the upper. (See "Parks and Amusement Areas" for more about Jackson Square.)

**On Dauphine Street:** No. 430, the **Pierre Cottage,** is another example of the brick-between-posts construction of the 1700s. Bricks for the building were made in the courtyard and shells from Lake Pontchartrain were used in the mortar. The **Audubon House,** a small cottage at no. 511, was the home of the famous naturalist, John Audubon, and his family when he did much of his work here.

**On Dumaine Street:** At no. 632, you'll find what some historians believe to be the oldest building in the Mississippi Valley, although records found in the last few years reveal that it was actually *rebuilt* in 1788, using some materials salvaged from the fire of that year. Named **"Madame John's Legacy,"** after a short story by George Washington Cable referred to it by that title in 1874, the house is now operated as a museum, and two rooms are restored as typical 1830 New Orleans rooms. The rest of the rooms have exhibits of furnishings, textiles, and decorative arts from that period. I especially liked the woven things from the Acadian region. Open daily except Monday and holidays from 10 a.m. to 6 p.m.; admission is $3 for adults, $1 for students, free for ages under 12.

## Other Interesting Buildings

**On Royal Street:** No. 334, once the old Bank of Louisiana, was built in 1827. At no. 339, the 1800 **Bank of the United States** was one of the four banks that stood on each corner of this intersection, making it the financial hub of the city. No. 417 was once the Casa Faurie, originally built (in 1801) for the grandfather of Edgar Degas, the French painter. It saw much entertainment on a grand scale when it was a private residence, and the tradition is carried on today at **Brennan's,** its present occupant.

**On Bourbon Street:** The **Old Absinthe House,** at no. 238, was built in 1806 by two Spaniards and is still owned by their descendants. When prohibition officers closed the place during the '20s, the marble bar and absinthe drip fountains were rescued and wound up in the **Old Absinthe Bar,** at 400 Bourbon St.

**On Chartres Street:** The **Napoleon House,** at no. 500, was planned as Napoleon's refuge after an ill-fated rescue plot. Jean Lafitte's brother (under the alias Dominique You) had been hired to captain a trim racing boat and spirit the Little Corporal away. Alas, Napoleon died three days before the boat was to sail from New Orleans; there are some in town who will tell you that his death was not a natural one, but that he was murdered when his captors learned the not-too-well-kept secret. Stop in here for a few minutes of classical music and refreshment and you'll almost be transported back to those exciting days by the atmosphere.

The **Cabildo,** at no. 701, has had a long and varied history. The original was built in 1769 by the Spanish, burned in 1788, was replaced, then burned again in

1794, and the present building, completed in 1795, incorporates the remains of its two predecessors. It has housed both French and American government offices, been the scene of the signing of the Louisiana Purchase, and hosted both Pierre Lafitte (as a criminal in jail) and Lafayette (as a visiting celebrity whose royal treatment contrasted vividly to that of Lafitte). The state museum it now holds reflects all this and much more of the city's history (Napoleon's death mask is here). Admission is $2 for adults, $1 for children 12 and over, free under that; and it's open Tuesday through Sunday from 9 a.m. to 5 p.m. (See "Tours" for the excellent walking tour that originates here.)

You can't miss the **St. Louis Cathedral,** at no. 721—it dominates the Jackson Square area and is one of the most famous churches in the U.S. A really magnificent building, it was first constructed in 1724, burned in that 1788 holocaust, and was rebuilt in 1794. "Uptown" Americans used to say that God spoke only in French here! There are free guided tours from 9 a.m. to 5 p.m. Monday through Saturday, 1 to 5 p.m. on Sunday.

**Pirate's Alley,** which runs between the Cabildo and the cathedral, was supposedly used by buccaneers even before the alley was cut and officially named Ruelle d'Orléans, Sud. On the other side of the cathedral, **Père Antoine's Alley** was named for a priest much loved for his good works. In **St. Anthony's Garden** behind the cathedral, many a duel was fought by hot-blooded Créole gentlemen over the "honor" of beautiful mulatto women at the Quadroon Balls.

The **Presbytere,** at no. 713, was meant to be the rectory for the cathedral and is a twin architecturally to the Cabildo. It served instead as a courthouse until 1911, when it was taken over by the **Louisiana State Museum.** If you pay the small admission fee (same as for the Cabildo), you'll see not only some very fine formal art, but very lively folk and native art as well.

On the site of the Old Ursuline Convent, the **Archbishop Antoine Blanc Memorial** (tel. 504/561-0008) is located at no. 1112 and includes the oldest building in the city, erected in 1752. For its first 74 years it was the convent of the Ursuline nuns, then the residence of the archbishops for the next 74 years. Currently it is the home of the Archdiocesan Archives, and part of the premises are open to the public on Wednesday afternoons only, with a small admission fee.

At no. 1116, the **Ancient Chapel** of the archbishops was erected in 1845. It served as the house of worship for French, Spanish, Irish, German, and Italian immigrants, and is now Our Lady of Victory Chapel and the National Shrine of St. Lazarus, open for daily mass.

**On Orleans Street:** No. 717 was the site of those famous (or infamous!) Quadroon Balls, begun in 1838, at which ambitious mothers would trot out their loveliest mulatto daughters in the hope they'd be chosen by a "gentleman" as his mistress and set up in one of the small cottages over on Rampart Street. When a "free man of color," Thomy Lafon, bought the building in 1873 for the Negro Sisters of the Holy Family, the ballroom became a chapel for their orphanage. Today it's a luxury hotel.

**On St. Peter Street:** The best time to go to **Preservation Hall** (no. 726) is at night, when the place is filled with some of the best jazz in the Quarter, but a daytime stop will give you an intriguing look through the big, ornate iron gate at a lush, tropical courtyard in the back. **Pat O'Brien's** now occupies what was known as the Maison de Flechier (no. 718) when it was built for a well-known planter in 1790. **Le Petit Théâter,** the oldest nonprofessional theater in the country, has been at no. 616 since 1922, but the Spanish-style building has had such widely diverse tenants as cafés, bars, and the first bishop of New Orleans.

382 DOLLARWISE GUIDE TO THE SOUTHEAST

**On Decatur Street:** The **U.S. Customs House** (no. 100) was begun in 1847 on the site of old Fort St. Louis, but it wasn't completed until 1913.

Stretching down Decatur Street (nos. 800, 900, 1000), on the river side, is the **Old French Market,** which has been a marketplace since Choctaw Indians traveled to the riverbank here to peddle their wares. The Spanish erected a market building, but when it was destroyed by a hurricane in 1812, it was replaced the very next year by the Butchers' Hall (that's the building closest to Jackson Square), and two more were added in 1822 and 1872. Still growing, the Market was given a fourth building as recently as 1975. There's much restoration going on to spruce the place up, but what you'll most likely want to do here is just wander through the market stalls piled high with fresh fruits and vegetables that make you hungry just to see them and stop by the praline shops for a nibble of candy you can see being made. This is one of my favorite places in the city, and I warn you, be sure to allow plenty of time—you won't want to leave.

If you've ever harbored a secret desire to see that **Streetcar Named Desire** immortalized in the Tennessee Williams play, you'll find it behind the **Old U.S. Mint** at no. 1300 (just behind the French Market), restored to its original 1906 style and housing the **Jazz Museum and Carnival Museum.** The mint was constructed on the site of Fort St. Charles and operated until 1910. On Saturday and Sunday, a public **flea market** is held in its shadow—great fun.

**BEYOND THE QUARTER:** The "American" sections of New Orleans are pretty spread out, but you can see them easily using public buses or, in the case of the Garden District, the St. Charles trolley.

### The Garden District

The Garden District is so called because of the lavish formal gardens that were the pride of wealthy planters who built the lovely "town" mansions you'll see along St. Charles Avenue and the numbered streets that cross it. A ramble through the pleasant streets will be a highlight of your trip if you try to imagine the interiors of these large homes with their colonnaded "galeries" and ironwork balconies. If you could peep inside (and you can at certain times of the year—see "Festivals," below), you'd be treated to a decor of ornate moldings, mahogany banisters, and mantels of rosewood or Italian marble, winding staircases, crystal chandeliers, and priceless antiques—the "uptown" Americans were determined to equal, if not outdo, those snooty French aristocrats in the Quarter, and they certainly came close!

But before you get to the residential section, be sure to stop by **Gallier Hall,** 524 St. Charles Ave., completed in 1850 as the city hall of the American section. It was designed by Gallier (who, significantly, was the architect of so many memorable Quarter homes), and it is here that Mardi Gras comes to a climax each year with the crowning of the Carnival King and Queen.

Also, take time to go by **Lee Circle,** which stands in the middle of St. Charles Avenue a little above Gallier Hall. Planned as the Place du Tivoli in 1806, it was a cultural center and had a children's merry-go-round in the middle until 1884, when the general's statue was erected (Yankees please note—he's facing north!).

The **residential section** of the district begins just after Felicity, and on **1st Street,** look especially for nos. 1134 (Confederate President Jefferson Davis visited here often and died while a guest in 1889), 1236, and 1239. No. 1427 2nd St. was built in 1845 and was moved to its present location from a nearby plantation. On 3rd Street, notice (you really can't help noticing!) nos. 1331, 1415, and 1417; and on 4th Street, nos. 1241 and 1448. On 7th Street, nos. 1221 and 1215 were twins when they were built as wedding gifts for two sisters, but as you can see, they've taken on individual personalities with modifications over the years. George W. Cable lived at 1313 8th St., and entertained such famous writers as Mark Twain and Joel Chandler Harris (he wrote the Uncle Remus stories) in the house that was built off the ground to prevent flood damage and (so he thought) yellow fever.

**St. Charles Avenue** itself makes interesting touring, and the trolley ride is a comfortable way to go (see "Tours"). Look for the **St. Charles Christ Church Cathedral** (no. 2919). This is the fourth structure since 1805, and even it has suffered the loss of its tall steeple in a 1915 hurricane.

The home at no. 2926 has a gallery for every room, and the 12-inch space between inner and outer walls made for comfortable temperatures year round. The exclusive **Orleans Club** (a private social and cultural women's club) now occupies 5005 St. Charles, but it was originally built in 1868 by a Colonel Lewis as a wedding gift for his daughter. A World War II hero is honored by the gift to the city by his family of the **Milton Latter Memorial Library** at 5100 St. Charles.

The largest Catholic university in the South, **Loyola**, is at 6363 St. Charles, and close by, at no. 6823, is **Tulane**, with its medical school that dates back to 1834. There's another campus downtown, but this is where it all began. Another school going back to the 1800s is **St. Mary's Dominican College** (it's across the avenue from the other two), a girls' school in an ornate white wooden building with outside balconies running the length of each floor.

**Audubon Park** has an entrance on St. Charles also (see "Parks and Amusement Areas," below).

### Carrollton

In 1812 a tiny settlement sprang up around Gen. William Carrollton's camp at the very end of St. Charles Avenue, and it grew into a thriving town with a resort hotel and a railroad depot (for the streetcar line). The levee to control the Mighty Mississippi displaced both hotel and depot, but the area continued to grow. The school you'll see at 719 South Carrollton was the Carrollton Courthouse from 1855 to 1874, but the best reason for going out there today is to see **Riverbend,** a really charming section of homes that has been transformed into a shopping area. To reach it, turn right off Carrollton Avenue at Burthe, then left on Dublin.

### Bayou St. John and Lake Pontchartrain

When Bienville chose New Orlean's location, it was partly because Bayou St. John and Lake Pontchartrain provided a sort of back door that made for easy defense. To retrace what began as an Indian route long before there were Frenchmen here, start near the Old Mint in the French Quarter and walk (or drive) down Esplanade Avenue, one of the quietest and prettiest in the Vieux Carré, to Rampart Street. Turn left and you'll be following the line of the wall (or ramparts) that connected three forts on this northern border of the original city. There is no trace of either wall or forts today, but you will come to **Congo Square** (now known as Beauregard Square), a quiet park that began as an Indian camp, but was given over by the city fathers as a gathering place for slaves on Sunday afternoons to sing and dance and "let off steam" so that, hopefully, the secret voodoo ceremonies would be reduced, or at least be brought out in the open. Unfortunately, not only did the meetings continue among slaves and even attract prominent French residents, but Congo Square became the scene of wild, sensual dancing accompanied by beating drums, fights precipitated by heightened emotions, and a source of fascination for as many as 2,000 spectators who would congregate to watch the dancing until a 9 o'clock cannon boomed curfew for all slaves.

Just behind the square, you'll see the **Municipal Auditorium** and **Theatre of the Performing Arts,** where the unique New Orleans "art" of Mardi Gras balls is practiced.

At Bienville, turn right again onto **Basin Street** (you remember that street, of course, as the birthplace of jazz), which used to be the main drag of Storyville, a red-light district that held so many houses of ill-repute that a "Blue Book" was actually compiled advertising the charms of over 700 prostitutes and the "sporting palaces" that flourished along with fancy saloons! It operated as a wide-open den of iniquity from 1897, when Alderman Sidney Story attempted to clean up the French Quarter by moving sin outside its boundaries, until 1917, when the U.S. Navy complained about the bad effect of so much vice in such proximity to our wartime servicemen. (Actually, it was the secretary of the navy who requested that the district be closed down—not a single complaint was recorded as coming from the troops.)

In the 400 block of Basin Street, you'll find the first of New Orleans's "Cities of the Dead," inhabited by above-ground tombs: **St. Louis Cemetery** #1 (#2 is behind a housing project on St. Louis, and #3 is farther out Esplanade). The city's low, just-above-sea-level location made burial in above-ground vaults a necessity. Often the outer walls of cemeteries would be made up of rows of attached vaults stacked one above the other, while vaults inside the walls formed "streets," giving the appearance of a miniature city. If you feel in need of a little help from that Queen of Voodoo, Marie Laveau, look for her grave. Faithful believers have marked it with crosses, and some say that even now a "gris gris" (which is pronounced "gree gree" and might be anything from a string around a bone to a doll stuck with pins) left overnight there and then placed on the doorstep of the person you want to influence will absorb the power of this "free" mulatto woman who—for a small fee, of course—worked miracles for New Orleanians, black and white, rich and poor, for nearly 70 years. *One note of warning:* It's best to visit this cemetery with a companion since there have been occasional muggings among the tombstones.

Turn right on Toulouse, then left on Rampart. On your right you'll see the **Quadroon Quarters,** the small cottages maintained by Créole gentlemen for their mistresses and the children they fathered. Looking at them gives rise to a wonder that these were such prized positions among mulattos—until you remember that along with "mistress" went the title "free"!

At Esplanade, turn left and go about 20 blocks (you'll need a car for this expedition) to Moss, then turn left and follow the banks of **Bayou St. John,** which formed a lake-to-river link by means of an old Indian trail that led from bayou to the Mississippi. On this side of the bayou there are several old plantation homes built in the 1780s and early 1800s, the most notable of which is the **Pitot House,** 1440 Moss St., home of Mayor James Pitot, which is open to the public only Wednesday through Saturday from 10 a.m. to 3 p.m. ($3 for adults, $1.50 for children; groups may arrange visits at other times by calling 504/482-0312). It is a typical West Indian plantation house, with wide galleries on three sides and large columns supporting the second floor—interesting to see from the outside if you should happen to drive out on, say, a Monday.

You'll have to return to Esplanade to cross the bridge and take the first left turn onto Wisner Boulevard, which runs along the other side of the bayou. The entrance to **City Park,** with its famous old dueling oaks and the **Museum of Art** (see "Parks and Amusement Areas" and "Museums," below) is on Esplanade before you make the turn. Stay on Wisner (past some very grand modern homes) until you reach Robert E. Lee Boulevard, turn right to Elysian Fields Avenue, and then turn left. The **University of New Orleans** will be on your left.

Now turn left onto Lakeshore Drive. **Lake Pontchartrain** is some 40 miles long and the 23¾-mile bridge that goes across is the longest in the world. You'll pass the **Mardi Gras fountain,** with plaques of Mardi Gras krewes around its base, and come to the **Coast Guard Lighthouse** at West End, a tiny park in the midst of marinas, an old fishing village, **Bucktown,** and the **Southern Yacht Club,** the second oldest in the country. It's easy to spend time in this charming spot, and if you can time your trip out for late afternoon, you'll see the Mardi Gras fountain beautifully lighted in Mardi Gras colors of purple, green, and gold after dark on the drive back.

## Other Points of Interest

The site of the Battle of New Orleans is now **Chalmette National Historical Park,** on St. Bernard Hwy. To get there, take Rampart Street and stay to the left as it becomes St. Claude, which will, in turn, become St. Bernard Hwy. It was out here in a cane field that Gen. Andrew Jackson pulled together a ragtag army made up of Créoles, "free men of color," Indians, and Americans (Kentucky and Tennessee soldiers, mostly) with a few Germans and Acadians, to man the rampart he'd put up from the river to a nearby swamp. With cannon, flints, and gunpowder supplied by Jean Lafitte (and also a goodly number of his priva-teers), they repulsed a massive British head-on attack on January 8, 1815, with over 2,000 enemy casualties (285 killed), with only a few casualties themselves. The British retreated, but remained in camp for ten days before they went back to their ships and sailed away. The irony is, of course, that the Peace of Ghent treaty ending the war had been signed (although not ratified) a full two weeks before the bloody encounter!

To sports fans, New Orleans means the **Superdome.** It's at the 1500 block of Poydras Street, not far from the French Quarter. The largest building of its kind in the world, looking for all the world like a grounded saucer, it seats some 72,000 people. Tours are conducted daily from 9 a.m. to 4 p.m. Call 504/587-3810 for information.

The **Rivergate Exhibition Center,** at 4 Canal St., is another modern giant of a building, although it isn't nearly as huge as the Superdome. Its next-door neighbor, the **International Trade Mart** at 2 Canal St., is even closer to the river and has an observation deck that you can reach by inside or (for the more stout-hearted) outdoor elevators. The trip up on the outside costs $2.50 for adults, $1.50 for children under 12. The view up there is spectacular—the busy harbor traffic, the French Quarter, the rest of the city stretching beyond, all are breath-takingly beautiful from 31 stories up. And two flights farther up, you can watch it unfold in comfort from the **Top of the Mart** revolving cocktail lounge (see "Nightlife").

**"Fat City"** is a collection of discos, restaurants, lounges, and shops that developed in an affluent section of modern apartment buildings. It is bounded roughly by Veterans Hwy., Causeway Boulevard, West Esplanade, and Divi-sion Street, and draws many locals when French Quarter nightlife palls.

## PARKS AND AMUSEMENT AREAS: Down in the French Quarter, lovely **Jackson Square** serves as a focal point for artists and craftsmen who set up shop outside the iron railings. But it wasn't always like that. Back in 1721 the square was a dusty drill field (the French called it Place d' Armes, and it was Plaza de Armas to the Spanish). It was the Baroness Micaela Pontalba, the same one who built the apartments on each side, who transformed it by putting up the fence, planting it like a garden, and installing benches so it could be enjoyed as a park. That was in 1851, and the present name was bestowed in 1856, when the impressive Andrew Jackson statue was added. That statue, incidentally, is by

Clark Mills and was the first equestrian sculpture to be made with more than one hoof unsupported.

**Audubon Park,** with an entrance on St. Charles Avenue across from Tulane University and another on Magazine Street, is one of the prettiest spots in New Orleans. The oaks here turn walkways into covered alleys, and there are winding lagoons, fountains, and statuary, as well as a very nice zoo. As far as I'm concerned, this park (once part of plantation) is complete enough with the trees and paths and a general atmosphere of peace and quiet. But if you're looking for recreation facilities, they're here too. There's an 18-hole golf course, picnic facilities, tennis courts, a swimming pool, horseback riding, and bike rentals. For full details, call 504/861-2537.

**City Park,** at the end of Esplanade and the beginning of the City Park Avenue, was also once part of a plantation. Look for the **New Orleans Museum of Art**—just to the left you'll see those ancient old oaks under which men of honor settled their disputes in the late 1700s and early 1800s (remember all those old movies with the dueling scenes at dawn?). **Children's Storyland,** Victory Drive across from the tennis courts, is an enchanted place for youngsters, with Mother Goose characters in papier-mâché. This park is really beautifully landscaped, and has *four* golf courses, boating lagoons, tennis courts, horseback riding, a miniature train, and an amusement area with carnival rides for children.

## MUSEUMS: Many of the museums in historic homes and buildings have already been described, but here are some more that you won't want to miss.

The **Historic New Orleans Collection–Museum/Research Center,** 355 Royal St. (tel. 504/523-4662), is housed in four buildings that consist of a museum, gift shop, and comprehensive research center for state and local history. The Williams Gallery, free to the public, presents changing exhibitions that focus on Louisiana history and culture. Guilded tours are available of both the founders' elegant residence and the Louisiana history galleries. The residence of Gen. and Mrs. L. Kemper Williams is a charming, eclectrically furnished home that reflects the gracious mid-20th-century lifestyle of its owners. A tour of the history galleries, located in the 1792 Merieult House, brings to life some 200 years of the past through original maps, paintings, photographs, documents, and rare books. Tour hours are 10 a.m. and 3:15 p.m. Tuesday through Saturday, and admission is $2 for each tour. No children under 12 are permitted in the Williams residence, but there is a "touch tour" for the blind. Hours for the research center and gallery (both free) are 10 a.m. to 4:45 p.m. Tuesday through Saturday.

The **New Orleans Museum of Art** is on LeLong Avenue in City Park, and is housed in a building that is itself a work of art. The neoclassic, columned main building is a beauty, inside and out. The Delgado Great Hall on the first floor leads to a branched staircase at the back that rises to a mezzanine overlooking the hall. Beautiful! And the art inside does justice to its housing.

The museum's permanent collection includes works from the Kress Collection of Italian Paintings, and galleries of contemporary, Oriental, and African art, and portrait miniature paintings. In addition to its permanent collection, the museum often schedules major international exhibitions. General admission charges are $1.50 for children (3 to 17) and senior citizens (over 65), $3 for adults (18 to 64); museum members are admitted free at all times. The museum is open from 10 a.m. to 5 p.m. Tuesday through Sunday; closed Monday and all legal holidays. Additional information about special exhibition hours and fees may be obtained by calling the Public Relations Office (tel. 504/488-2631).

The **Confederate Museum,** at 929 Camp St., was established in 1889, close enough to the end of the Civil War for many donations to be in better condition than is sometimes true of museum items. You'll find battle flags, weapons, personal effects of Confederate President Jefferson Davis, part of Robert E. Lee's silver camp service, and many portraits of Confederate military and civilian personalities. A series of detailed pictures traces Louisiana's history from secession through Reconstruction. There's a $2 charge for adults, $1 for students, 50¢ for children under 12. Open Monday through Saturday from 10 a.m. to 4 p.m.

If you *really* want to see what went on down in Louisiana from the discovery of the lower Mississippi River by LaSalle in 1699 until the beginning of this century, there's no better place to do it than the **Musée Conti** at 917 Conti St. (tel. 504/525-2605). The 31 tableaux, with 144 life-size wax figures, are historically accurate and beautiful to see. There's also a just-for-fun Haunted Dungeon, with 23 figures (like Dracula, Frankenstein, and the Wolf Man) in ten settings. Admission is $5 for grownups, $3 for ages 13 to 17, $2.50 for ages 5 to 12, free for under-5s with adults. Open daily at 10 a.m. except Christmas and Mardi Gras Day.

# 2. Nightlife

**JAZZ:** The joyous, soul-lifting music form that is jazz grew out of the anger, fear, love, joy, pride, and back-breaking toil that filled the emotional lives of blacks in New Orleans from the days of slavery up to the advent of "Storyville."

When the restricted area around Basin Street opened up highly competitive bordellos, saloons, and nightclubs, black musicians moved their vibrant, expressive music inside from street corners to provide entertainment for paying customers, and it wasn't too long before it began showing up in the white man's world of college campuses, riverboats, "respectable" nightclubs, and restaurants. New Orleans–born masters of the art, such as Louis Armstrong and "Jelly Roll" Morton, left Storyville and moved upriver to St. Louis and Memphis, and eventually carried their music to Chicago, New York, and the West Coast. Others—"Papa" Celestin, Bunk Johnson, and Sweet Emma Barrett, to name just a few—stayed on in New Orleans, keeping the free-spirited music alive at the scene of its birth.

Today jazz permeates the French Quarter, with black and white, newcomers and oldtimers joining together to keep it filling the air at all hours of the night and day. As for those oldtime jazz funerals, you can still occasionally see one, the jazzman being escorted to his final resting place by a band playing sorrowful dirges, followed by "second liners" (shuffling, hand-clapping mourners). It's on the return trip, after the departed has been "freed," that the mood turns lively and the mourners really get into the "liberate" swing of things.

## Strictly Jazz

Jazz in its purest form is found at **Preservation Hall,** 726 St. Peter St., unaccompanied by such refinements as air conditioning, drinks, or even (unless you get there *very* early) a place to sit down. The shabby old building offers only hot, foot-tapping, body-swaying music, played by whatever top professionals happen to be in town on a particular night. And nobody seems to mind the absence of those other refinements—the place is not only packed, its windows are filled with faces of people who stand on the sidewalk for hours just to listen! After one night, I was hooked.

Part of the fun is never knowing who will be there—the place holds a special spot of affection in the hearts of jazzmen, and some of the greatest drop in to play when they're in town. Another part is knowing that no matter who's sitting in, they'll all be good and they'll have as good, if not better, a time as their enthusiastic audience. The whole atmosphere is one of an informal jazz session, and even the younger generation—there are lots of fascinated children every night I go—joins in the spirit of things. Admission is an unbelievably low $2, and if you want to sit on one of the much-sought-after pillows right up front or the couple of rows of straightbacked chairs just behind them, get there at least 45 minutes before doors open at 8 p.m. Otherwise you stand. The music goes on until 12:30 a.m., with long sets being interrupted by ten-minute breaks and the crowds continually changing as parents take children home at bedtime and sidewalk listeners move in to take their places. They also have a marvelous collection of jazz records on sale, some of them hard-to-find oldies.

Pete Fountain, the clarinetist, has moved out of the French Quarter (but not far away) to the **New Orleans Hilton** at Poydras Street and the Mississippi River. The somewhat plush interior—gold chairs and banquettes, red-velvet bar chairs, white iron-lace-railinged gallery—sets the mood of the popular night-spot. Pete performs on Tuesday, Wednesday, Thursday, Friday, and Saturday. The club, named simply **Pete Fountain's** (tel. 504/523-4374 or 523-3105), is closed Sunday and Monday. Call for current show times, rates, and reservations.

**Maison Bourbon,** 641 Bourbon St., also opens its doors to the sidewalk and employs three bands every day to play from 11 a.m. to 2 a.m. Owners John Keifer and Albert St. Germaine have added a plus for jazz lovers by recording the sessions so that you can spin at home the music you heard live. Incidentally, right next door, Capt. Al's Seafood House features fresh seafood at moderate prices, and the longest oyster bar in New Orleans.

Down by the river, **Tipitina's,** 501 Napoleon Ave. (tel. 504/899-9114), is an old bar with a stage at one end that seems to draw jazz, blues, and reggae musicians like a magnet. It's anything *but* elegant, but you're likely to hear the best music in town here, especially late at night. There's a dance floor too, so if you're so inclined you can move with the music. Depending on who's on stage, there's no charge or up to an $8 cover charge. Open seven days a week, as is their Créole restaurant (5 to 10 p.m.), and Sunday through Wednesday the music starts as early as 9:30 p.m.

In the French Market area, **Storyville Jazz Hall,** 1104 Decatur St. (tel. 504/525-8199), offers traditional New Orleans jazz every night at 8 p.m., and contemporary music beginning at 12:30 a.m. There's dancing, food service, and an admission charge of $2. Incidentally, children are welcome if they come with adults.

**Lulu White's Mahogany Hall,** 309 Bourbon St. (tel. 504/525-5595), has the decor of a famous old bordello and occupies a site that has housed a jazz club perhaps longer than any other in New Orleans. There's jazz, Tuesday through Saturday from 9 p.m. to 2 a.m., with no cover charge. This is where you'll find the famous Dukes of Dixieland when they're in town.

## Other Nightspots

It's not jazz that will set your feet tapping at **Ryan's 500 Pub,** 441 Bourbon St. (tel. 504/525-7269), but the lively tones of Irish jigs, reels, and ballads. Michael Ryan, who came to New Orleans to run a pub at the 1984 World Fair, stayed on to open one of Bourbon Street's better establishments. The interior is a nice mix of signposts and other memorabilia from Ireland and ceiling fans with fluted light globes that are pure New Orleans. Four Irish lads known as the Celtic Folk sing traditional Irish songs and play the rousing tunes that quite often bring patrons to their feet for a bit of a dance. Danny Doyle, as fine an Irish voice as you'd ever want to hear, alternates with the group, and the music goes on from noon until closing. Guinness stout is on tap and comes in the "proper" Irish pint glass, there's Harp lager from Ireland, and they serve a terrific Irish coffee. A smaller bar in the rear is called the Irish Harp and opens to St. Louis Street. There's also a gift shop with an excellent selection of Irish crafts, woolens, tweeds, records, books, and jewelry.

You might walk right past the small **Fritzel's European Bar and Cuisine,** 733 Bourbon St. (tel. 504/561-0432), but that would be a big mistake, for since 1974 this 1836 building has attracted some of the city's best musicians who perform on the tiny stage in the back. There are frequent jam sessions here in the wee hours when musicians end their stints elsewhere and gather to play for just themselves. Richard Payne, bassist with Lou Sino's jazz band at Maison Bourbon, put me on to it—such is its fame among musicians that he had learned about it from a friend in the Vienna Symphony! The bar stocks a variety of German liqueurs, as well as imported beers, and there's a menu of German sandwiches (knackwurst, bratwurst, etc., on Black Forest bread), hamburgers, po-boys, and red beans and rice, all at budget prices. But go along late at night if you want to catch "musicians' music."

**Pat O'Brien's,** at 718 St. Peter St. (tel. 504/525-4823), has been famous for as long as I can remember for its gigantic rum-based Hurricane drinks, served in 29-ounce hurricane-lamp-style glasses. But it's equally well known for the good entertainment offered in one of the most beautiful patios in New Orleans and the lounge that features at least four entertainers nightly. There's a neighborhood air about the place and the sing-alongs will quickly make you feel at home with everybody else there. There are three bars here; the main bar is open from 10 a.m. to 4 a.m., the patio bar from 11 a.m. to 4 a.m., and the lounge from 2 p.m. to 4 a.m. (to 5 a.m. on Friday and Saturday). There's no minimum, no cover.

**Chris Owens Club,** at the corner of Bourbon and St. Louis Streets (tel. 504/523-6400), features who else but Chris Owens, a very talented singer and dancer, in a one-woman show of jazz, popular, and blues music. Between shows, there's dancing on an elevated dance floor and electrifying light and sound everywhere. There's no cover, but the $12 admission covers the show and one drink. Showtime is 10 p.m. and midnight Monday through Saturday. Reservations are a good idea. The club is closed Sunday.

If it's supper club entertainment you're in the mood for, some of the biggest names in show business (for example, Ella Fitzgerald, Joel Grey, and Tina Turner) are booked into the **Fairmont Hotel's Blue Room** University Place (tel. 504/529-4744). Performance times are 9 and 11 p.m., and the price of the show alone varies from $15 to $20. Dinner and drinks are extra, but not required. Call for reservations.

The revolving lounge at the top of the International Trade Mart at 2 Canal St., appropriately called the **Top of the Mart** (tel. 504/522-9795), offers musical entertainment nightly. The ever-changing view is part of the fun—you move three feet per minute and make the full circle in 90 minutes. It's open from 10 a.m. to 1 a.m. Monday through Friday, 11 a.m. to 2 a.m. on Saturday, and 4 p.m. to midnight on Sunday.

For disco, try **Rainforest** in the New Orleans Hilton Hotel, 2 Poydras St. and the Mississippi River (tel. 504/561-0500). Drinks are reasonable here, and the decor is sensational, with lots of flashing lights, smoky mirrors, and even—believe it or not—a periodic rainstorm, complete with thunder. Dress is casual, and sometimes very colorful, depending on the crowd. A fun place to go if you like this kind of thing.

## On the Sexy Side

Two of the famous female-impersonator clubs in New Orleans are the **Gunga Den,** 325 Bourbon St., which presents a "Powder Puff Review," and the

**Silver Frolics,** 427 Bourbon St., with the "Me o My" show. If it's strip shows you want, you'll find them right along this part of Bourbon Street.

## Theater and Cabaret

The **Saenger Theatre,** 143 N. Rampart St. (tel. 504/525-1052), is a marvelous old theater of Renaissance Florence decor, elegant with glittering chandeliers, statuary, and a ceiling twinkling with stars and studded with drifting clouds. It's theater in the grand style, and top Broadway shows perform on a regular basis.

The **Municipal Auditorium,** 1201 St. Peter St. (tel. 504/522-0592), is in the Cultural Center and is host to a variety of entertainments, including the circus, ballet, concerts, and most of the Mardi Gras balls.

The oldest nonprofessional theater troupe in the country, **Le Petit Théâtre,** 616 St. Peter St. (tel. 504/522-2081), periodically puts on plays that rival the professionals in excellence. Check when you're in New Orleans to see if they're in production.

The **University of New Orleans Department of Drama and Communications** offers first-rate productions in theater, many by modern American playwrights such as Tennessee Williams and Horton Foote. The season also includes original award-winning films and video productions. Ticket prices are $5 or less (senior citizens pay $3). Call 504/268-6317 for information on current productions.

The **UNO ImaginAction Theáter** performs especially for children, and its short plays and improvisations encourage participation by the young audience. Tickets are $2, and you can get exact show dates by calling 504/286-6317.

# 3. Festivals

**MARDI GRAS:** This is the festival of festivals in New Orleans! It has been celebrated along the banks of the Mississippi since Bienville arrived in 1699, and many residents prepare for it all year long, designing costumes and floats and planning the elaborate balls. To get the most out of any Mardi Gras visit, arm yourself (I urge this strongly) with the handy **New Orleans Mardi Gras Guide** published by Arthur Hardy, P.O. Box 8058, New Orleans, LA 70182. It costs $2.95, postpaid, and is invaluable. If you don't write ahead, look for it on newsstands.

The Carnival season actually opens shortly after Christmas, as "mistick krewes" begin to hold their more than 60 masquerade balls. Festivities pick up momentum as Shrove Tuesday (Mardi Gras means literally "Fat Tuesday"), the last day before Lent, approaches. Street parades start about 12 days before Mardi Gras Day, and they are a sight to behold, with satin-covered horses, the beat of drums in the streets, masked crowds shouting the traditional "Throw me something, mister," the mad scrambling for beads and "doubloons" as those on the floats respond to the cries, the colorful, noisy blending of music and nonsense and just plain fun. On Lundi Gras ("Fat Monday"), King Rex arrives by boat at the foot of Canal Street to set off a night of outdoor entertainment and dancing at Spanish Plaza. When the big day finally arrives, the Mistick Krewe of Comus—the first carnival organization and the one that introduced street parades—holds its glittering parade, along with the krewes of Rex and Zulu, and everything comes to a happy climax at the grandest of all the balls, reigned over by the King and Queen of Carnival. Then it's all over until the next year, and New Orleanians repair to their homes to begin planning for bigger and better things when Mardi Gras comes around again.

Literally thousands of outsiders pour into New Orleans for what is really the city's "family party," and they are warmly welcomed by its citizens. But rooms can be scarce as hens' teeth and prices increase a bit. Still, it is a *very* special occasion and everyone should participate at least once before departing this earth. When your turn comes, be sure to plan as far ahead as you can (a year in advance isn't too long) and leave your inhibitions at home—there's no place for them in the revelry of Mardi Gras!

**THE NEW ORLEANS JAZZ AND HERITAGE FESTIVAL:** For two weekends (and a full week between) in late April or early May of each year, jazz, folk, gospel, Cajun, and popular music take over the city. There are concerts indoors and out, parades, and Louisiana foods and crafts are on sale. It's another carnival, and it draws internationally known musicians to join those already on the scene for the season of fun, food, and good music. For dates and specific information, contact the New Orleans Jazz and Heritage Festival, 1205 N. Rampart St., New Orleans, LA 70116 (tel. 504/522-4786).

**SPRING FIESTA:** Since 1947 the Spring Fiesta has opened on the first Friday after Easter and continued for 19 days of touring plantations, Vieux Carré and Garden District homes, and other showplaces in the area. Many are open only during this period, and visitors are conducted on the two- to three-hour city tours by costumed hostesses. Plantation tours take a full day. There's a beautiful "Patios by Candlelight" tour, a "Night in Old New Orleans" parade, an art show, a festival of flowers, and a historical pageant. For tour information and reservations (which are a must), contact the Spring Fiesta Association, 826 St. Ann St., New Orleans, LA 70116 (tel. 504/581-1367).

**THE FOOD FESTIVAL:** Once a year, in early July, New Orleanians celebrate their love of good eating with a smashing food festival. Just about every chef in the city participates by preparing an array of specialties that you just have to see to appreciate its scope! Some are literally works of art, others picture-pretty dishes of humble, everyday foods. And best of all, you can sample most of them, portions costing anywhere from 25¢ to $1. Festivities include spaghetti-eating contests, special river cruises, musical performances, and lots more. To top it all off, there's a final grand gourmet dinner party. You can get details by writing the New Orleans Food Festival at P.O. Box 2410, New Orleans, LA 70116 (tel. 504/522-7273).

## 4. The Sporting Life

**FOOTBALL:** That palatial **Superdome** is the scene of all home games for the New Orleans Saints football team. Call 504/587-3810 for ticket information.

**HORSE RACING:** The "Sport of Kings" has always been a favorite of New Orleanians, and there's racing at the **Fair Grounds**, 1751 Gentilly Blvd. (tel. 504/944-5515), from November to late March. It's the third-oldest track in the U.S., and admission to the grandstand will cost you $1; to the clubhouse (and you should call for reservations), $4.

**TENNIS:** There are public tennis courts at both **City Park** and **Audubon Park**, and hourly rates are low. They're usually pretty crowded during summer months, so it's a good idea to call Audubon at 504/861-2537 and City Park at 504/482-2230 to check on availability before making the trip.

**GOLF:** Both parks also have public golf courses, and to reserve starting times and check on the reasonable greens fees, call 504/482-4888 for City Park courses, 504/861-9511 for Audubon.

## 5. Shopping

Like everything else in New Orleans, shopping is fun. And you can find almost anything your heart desires—if you can't find the article, you can find someone to make it for you! The place is loaded with craftsmen and artisans in almost every conceivable material: cast iron, wood, leather, fabric, brass, plastic, and precious metals. You can even have one of those marvelous oldtime overhead fans shipped back home. The following listing of shops is far from complete, but if you don't see something here that particularly interests you, be assured that you'll find it when you get there. Be sure to pick up the handy "Shopping Guide" published by the Tourist Office.

Hours for most shops are 10 a.m. to 5 p.m. every day except Sunday. Many, however, are open later on Saturday night and on Sunday afternoon, especially in the French Quarter, where souvenir shops are likely to be open until 11 p.m. every day of the week.

**MAJOR SHOPPING CENTERS:** At the foot of Canal Street, where it reaches the Mississippi River, a stunning new shopping center, **Canal Place**, 333 Canal St., holds branches of some of this country's most elegant shops. The three-tiered mall has polished marble floors, a landscaped atrium, fountains, and pools. Stores in this sophisticated setting include Bally of Switzerland, Charles Jourdan, Christian Aujard, Guy LaRoche, Godiva Chocolatier, Gucci, Ricarde Fine Jewelry, Saks Fifth Avenue, Laura Ashley, and Tabbi.

**The French Market,** Decatur Street: Shops in the Market begin on Decatur Street across from Jackson Square, and include candy, cookware, fashions, crafts, toys, New Orleans memorabilia, and candles.

**The Marketplace,** 1015 Decatur St., is just across from the French Market. This attractive arcade is housed in an old warehouse and holds small shops lining a brick road. Among items on sale are brass and copper, quilts, soaps, baskets, music boxes, blended coffees and teas, and clocks. From time to time there are craft demonstrations, street musicians, or some other form of entertainment.

Just across from Jackson Square, the **Jackson Brewery,** at St. Peter and Decatur Streets, an old brewery building has been transformed into a joyful jumble of shops, cafés, delicatessens, restaurants, and entertainment. The 60 shops within its walls include fashions, gourmet and Cajun-Créole foodstuffs, toys, hats, crafts, pipes, posters, and souvenirs. The Brewery is open from 10 a.m. to 10 p.m., seven days, although most shops close at 5:30 or 6 p.m.

**Magazine Street,** a major uptown thoroughfare, runs from Canal Street to Audubon Park, with some six miles of more than 120 shops, some in 19th-century brick storefronts, others in quaint, cottage-like buildings. Among the offerings are antiques, art galleries, boutiques, crafts, and dolls.

The **Riverbend** district is in the Carrollton area. To reach it, ride the St. Charles streetcar to Stop 44, then walk down Maple Street one block to Dublin Park, site of an old public market once lined with open stalls. Nowadays, renovated shops inhabit the old general store, a produce warehouse made of bargeboard, and the town surveyor's raised-cottage home. Among the outstanding shops are Mignon Faget Ltd., New Orleans's nationally known high-fashion jewelry designer; Yvonne LaFleur, whose romantic fashions have appeared on television and movie screens; and the Cache Pot, a concentration of unusual quality gifts. The Riverbend Restaurant (see Chapter XXI) is an attractive and convenient place for lunch and dinner after shopping.

The newest shopping development, **Riverwalk,** is an exciting covered mall right along the river from Poydras Street to the Convention Center. Among the many specialty shops at this location, you'll find Sharper Image, Abercrombie & Fitch, and Banana Republic. Several eateries and periodic free entertainment.

**ANTIQUES:** Boyer-Antiques—Dolls & Buttons, 241 Chartres and 404 Chartres, has the usual assortment of antiques, plus an enchanting collection of old dolls and doll furniture. Open from 9:30 a.m. to 5 p.m. Monday to Saturday.

You'll find all sorts of miniature soldiers and military antiques at **Le Petit Soldier Shop, Inc.,** 528 Royal St., as well as antique helmets, swords, books, and prints. Open from 10 a.m. to 5 p.m. Monday through Saturday.

Antique weapons, jewelry, and rare coins are the specialties at **James H. Cohen,** 437 Royal, who advertise that they "buy, sell, and horse trade."

**St. Charles Antiques Ltd.,** 2125 St. Charles Ave. (tel. 504/524-0243), is set in a turn-of-the-century mansion and filled with marvelous antiques, with heavy emphasis on the English and Oriental.

**ART GALLERIES:** At **Nahan Galleries,** 540 Royal St., (tel. 504/524-8696), they specialize in important, signed graphics by Chagall, Miró, and Calder (among others), and are worldwide representatives for important international artists such as Max Papart, Paolo Boni, etc. Open from 9:30 a.m. to 5:30 p.m. seven days a week.

The best selections of limited-edition graphics and jazz posters are found at **Bergen Galleries** at 730 Royal and in Jackson Brewery. Open from 10 a.m. to 7 p.m. daily.

**BRASS AND COPPER:** You won't believe the sheer number of items at the **Brass Menagerie,** 524 St. Louis St.! They have everything from chandeliers and lanterns to bathroom faucets to brass locks to antique doorknobs to bathroom fixtures to whatever else you can name. They specialize in antique, period, and contemporary fine, solid-brass hardware. They're open from 9 a.m. to 5:30 p.m. Monday through Friday, and 10 a.m. to 5 p.m. on Saturday.

**CAMERAS AND FILM:** One of the city's most complete camera shops is the **K&B Camera Center,** 227 Dauphine St. (tel. 504/524-2266), with a wide selection of cameras and other electronics, as well as film and other camera supplies. Fast film developing is also featured. Hours are 8 a.m. to 6 p.m. Monday through Friday, to 2 p.m. on Saturday.

**CANDIES AND PRALINES:** Once you taste New Orleans pralines, you'll want to take some home. And if your bags are already filled, most shops will mail them for you. One of my favorites among the many praline shops is **Aunt Sally's,** in the French Market at 810 Decatur. You can watch skilled workers fashioning the goodies, so you know they're fresh when you get them. The shop also carries souvenirs and imported gifts, and they'll ship anything you buy. Open from 8 a.m. to 6 p.m. every day.

**Laura's Praline Shoppe,** 115 Royal, has been in business since 1913 and makes all kinds of candies, pralines, and jellies as well as hand-dipped chocolates. Also, all Créole condiments. Open from 8 a.m. to 10 p.m. daily.

**CLOTHING:** Meyer the Hatter, 120 St. Charles St. (tel. 504/525-1048), has been topping New Orleans males for over 90 years, and carries such leading names as Dobbs, Stetson, and Borsalino. Open from 9:30 a.m. to 5:30 p.m. Monday through Saturday.

**Yvonne LeFleur / New Orleans,** 8131 Hampson St. (tel. 504/866-9666), out in the Riverbend shopping section, is the fantasy kingdom ruled by talented designer Yvonne LeFleur. Her romantic creations have been seen in many films and will set any female dreaming. Prices are surprisingly moderate, and there's a lovely perfume that also bears her name. Hours are 9:45 a.m. to 6 p.m. Monday through Saturday, until 8 p.m. on Wednesday and Thursday.

**DEPARTMENT STORES:** The **Maison Blanche** department store at 901 Canal is world famous for quality and luxury goods. This is good browsing country, and it is open from 9 a.m. to 6 p.m. Monday through Saturday, staying open until 7 p.m. on Thursday. There are also branches in Metairie, Plaza Lake Forest Shopping Center in New Orleans East, the Clearview Shopping Center, and the Westside Shopping Center in Gretna.

**D. H. Holmes Company Ltd.,** 819 Canal, is another longtime New Orleans favorite. Incidentally, its restaurant and cafeteria have very good food at very reasonable prices.

**Saks Fifth Avenue** has a branch at Canal Place, at the foot of Canal Street.

**FANS:** Because I'm an incurable romantic, I can't think of a better cooling system (no, not even air conditioning!) than those slow-turning ceiling fans you see all over the South. So it was a real treat to see the marvelous old restored specimens at the **White Pillars Emporium,** 8312 Oak St. in the Carrollton section.

**FOODS:** If you want to try your hand at making those scrumptious beignets, you can buy the mix at the **Café du Monde**'s retail store, 813 Decatur St., and to make it complete, do get a tin of their famous coffee. They also do a thriving mail-order business all over the U.S. Open from 9:30 a.m. to 6 p.m. seven days a week.

**IMPORTS:** **Faraway Places Imports,** 110 Carondelet St. (tel. 504/524-4722), has yielded up several treasures at near-bargain prices for me, and I think you'll find their stock of imported ladies' Indian clothing, jewelry, brass, artware, and leather bags a delightful shopping bazaar.

**PIPES:** Because I'm a pipe smoker (no letters, please—women have been smoking pipes for centuries!), I was intrigued by Mr. Edwin C. Jansen's **Ye Olde Pipe Shoppe,** 306 Chartres St. (tel. 504/522-1484). The shop was established in 1868 by Mr. Jansen's grandfather, August, and in addition to the present, third-generation owner's briar pipes that he handmakes, there is a great collection of antique pipes put together by his father and grandfather.

Date_____

FROMMER BOOKS
PRENTICE HALL PRESS
ONE GULF + WESTERN PLAZA
NEW YORK, NY 10023

Friends:

Please send me the books checked below:

## FROMMER'S $-A-DAY GUIDES™

*(In-depth guides to sightseeing and low-cost tourist accommodations and facilities.)*

| | | | |
|---|---|---|---|
| ☐ Europe on $25 a Day .............. $12.95 | ☐ New Zealand on $25 a Day ......... $10.95 |
| ☐ Australia on $25 a Day ............. $10.95 | ☐ New York on $45 a Day............. $9.95 |
| ☐ Eastern Europe on $25 a Day ........ $10.95 | ☐ Scandinavia on $50 a Day........... $10.95 |
| ☐ England on $35 a Day.............. $10.95 | ☐ Scotland and Wales on $35 a Day..... $10.95 |
| ☐ Greece on $25 a Day................ $10.95 | ☐ South America on $30 a Day ........ $10.95 |
| ☐ Hawaii on $50 a Day................ $10.95 | ☐ Spain and Morocco (plus the Canary |
| ☐ India on $15 & $25 a Day ........... $9.95 |    Is.) on $40 a Day .................. $10.95 |
| ☐ Ireland on $30 a Day................ $10.95 | ☐ Turkey on $25 a Day ................ $10.95 |
| ☐ Israel on $30 & $35 a Day .......... $10.95 | ☐ Washington, D.C., on $40 a Day ..... $10.95 |
| ☐ Mexico on $20 a Day ............... $10.95 | |

## FROMMER'S DOLLARWISE GUIDES™

*(Guides to sightseeing and tourist accommodations and facilities from budget to deluxe, with emphasis on the medium-priced.)*

| | | | |
|---|---|---|---|
| ☐ Alaska ........................... $12.95 | ☐ Cruises (incl. Alaska, Carib, Mex, |
| ☐ Austria & Hungary ................. $11.95 |    Hawaii, Panama, Canada, & US) ..... $12.95 |
| ☐ Belgium, Holland, Luxembourg ...... $11.95 | ☐ California & Las Vegas .............. $11.95 |
| ☐ Egypt............................ $11.95 | ☐ Florida............................ $10.95 |
| ☐ England & Scotland ................ $11.95 | ☐ Mid-Atlantic States ................. $12.95 |
| ☐ France........................... $11.95 | ☐ New England ...................... $11.95 |
| ☐ Germany.......................... $11.95 | ☐ New York State .................... $11.95 |
| ☐ Italy............................. $11.95 | ☐ Northwest ........................ $11.95 |
| ☐ Japan & Hong Kong ................ $12.95 | ☐ Skiing in Europe ................... $12.95 |
| ☐ Portugal (incl. Madeira & the Azores) . $11.95 | ☐ Skiing USA—East ................... $10.95 |
| ☐ South Pacific...................... $12.95 | ☐ Skiing USA—West ................... $10.95 |
| ☐ Switzerland & Liechtenstein ......... $11.95 | ☐ Southeast & New Orleans............. $11.95 |
| ☐ Bermuda & The Bahamas........... $10.95 | ☐ Southwest......................... $11.95 |
| ☐ Canada .......................... $12.95 | ☐ Texas............................. $11.95 |
| ☐ Caribbean ........................ $12.95 | |

**TURN PAGE FOR ADDITIONAL BOOKS AND ORDER FORM.**

## THE ARTHUR FROMMER GUIDES™

(Pocket-size guides to sightseeing and tourist accommodations and facilities in all price ranges.)

| | | | | |
|---|---|---|---|---|
| ☐ Amsterdam/Holland | $5.95 | ☐ Mexico City/Acapulco | $5.95 |
| ☐ Athens | $5.95 | ☐ Minneapolis/St. Paul | $5.95 |
| ☐ Atlantic City/Cape May | $5.95 | ☐ Montreal/Quebec City | $5.95 |
| ☐ Boston | $5.95 | ☐ New Orleans | $5.95 |
| ☐ Cancún/Cozumel/Yucatán | $5.95 | ☐ New York | $5.95 |
| ☐ Dublin/Ireland | $5.95 | ☐ Orlando/Disney World/EPCOT | $5.95 |
| ☐ Hawaii | $5.95 | ☐ Paris | $5.95 |
| ☐ Las Vegas | $5.95 | ☐ Philadelphia | $5.95 |
| ☐ Lisbon/Madrid/Costa del Sol | $5.95 | ☐ Rome | $5.95 |
| ☐ London | $5.95 | ☐ San Francisco | $5.95 |
| ☐ Los Angeles | $5.95 | ☐ Washington, D.C. | $5.95 |

## FROMMER'S TOURING GUIDES™

(Color illustrated guides that include walking tours, cultural & historic sites, and other vital travel information.)

| | | | | |
|---|---|---|---|---|
| ☐ Egypt | $8.95 | ☐ Paris | $8.95 |
| ☐ Florence | $8.95 | ☐ Venice | $8.95 |
| ☐ London | $8.95 | | |

## SPECIAL EDITIONS

| | | | | |
|---|---|---|---|---|
| ☐ A Shopper's Guide to the Best Buys in England, Scotland, & Wales | $10.95 | ☐ Marilyn Wood's Wonderful Weekends (NY, Conn, Mass, RI, Vt, NH, NJ, Del, Pa) | $11.95 |
| ☐ A Shopper's Guide to the Caribbean | $10.95 | ☐ Motorist's Phrase Book (Fr/Ger/Sp) | $4.95 |
| ☐ Bed & Breakfast—N. America | $8.95 | ☐ Swap and Go (Home Exchanging) | $10.95 |
| ☐ Fast 'n' Easy Phrase Book (Fr/Ger/Ital/Sp in *one* vol.) | $6.95 | ☐ The Candy Apple (NY for Kids) | $11.95 |
| ☐ Honeymoons Guide (US, Canada, Mexico, & Carib) | $12.95 | ☐ Travel Diary and Record Book | $5.95 |
| ☐ How to Beat the High Cost of Travel | $4.95 | ☐ Where to Stay USA (Lodging from $3 to $30 a night) | $9.95 |

## ORDER NOW!

In U.S. include $1.50 shipping UPS for 1st book; 50¢ ea. add'l book. Outside U.S. $2 and 50¢, respectively.

Enclosed is my check or money order for $_____

NAME _____

ADDRESS _____

CITY _____ STATE _____ ZIP _____

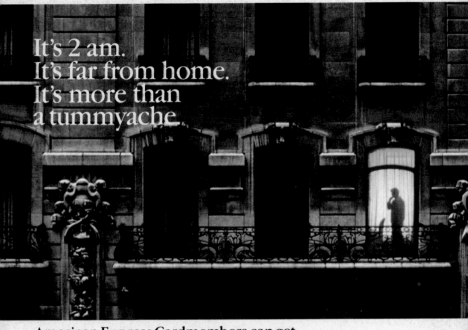

It's 2 am.
It's far from home.
It's more than
a tummyache.

## American Express Cardmembers can get emergency medical and legal referrals, worldwide. Simply by calling Global Assist.℠

What if it really is more than a tummyache? What if your back goes out? What if you get into a legal fix?

Call Global Assist – a new emergency referral service for the exclusive use of American Express Cardmembers. Just call. Toll-free. 24 hours a day. Every day. Virtually anywhere in the world.

Your call helps find a doctor, lawyer, dentist, optician, chiropractor, nurse, pharmacist, or an interpreter.

All this costs nothing, except for the medical and legal bills you would normally expect to pay.

Global Assist. One more reason to have the American Express® Card. Or, to get one.

For an application, call 1-800-THE-CARD.

Don't leave home without it®

# If you lose cash on vacation, don't count on a Boy Scout finding it.

Honestly.

How many people can you trust to give back hundreds of dollars in cash? Not too many.

That's why it's so important to help protect your vacation with American Express® Travelers Cheques.

If they're lost, you can get them back from over 100,000 refund locations throughout the world. Or you can hope a Boy Scout finds it.

## Protect your vacation.

AMERICAN EXPRESS **Travelers Cheques**